Index to Poetry
by
Black American Women

RECENT TITLES IN
BIBLIOGRAPHIES AND INDEXES IN AFRO-AMERICAN
AND AFRICAN STUDIES

Black Immigration and Ethnicity in the United States:
An Annotated Bibliography
Center for Afroamerican and African Studies, The University of Michigan

Blacks in the American Armed Forces, 1776-1983: A Bibliography
Lenwood G. Davis and George Hill, compilers

Education of the Black Adult in the United States: An Annotated Bibliography
Leo McGee and Harvey G. Neufeldt, compilers

A Guide to the Archives of Hampton Institute
Fritz J. Malval, compiler

A Bibliographical Guide to Black Studies Programs in the United States:
An Annotated Bibliography
Lenwood G. Davis and George Hill, compilers

Wole Soyinka: A Bibliography of Primary and Secondary Sources
James Gibbs, Ketu H. Katrak, and Henry Louis Gates, Jr., compilers

Afro-American Demography and Urban Issues: A Bibliography
R. A. Obudho and Jeannine B. Scott, compilers

Afro-American Reference: An Annotated Bibliography of Selected Resources
Nathaniel Davis, compiler and editor

The Afro-American Short Story: A Comprehensive, Annotated Index
with Selected Commentaries
Preston M. Yancy, compiler

Black Labor in America, 1865-1983: A Selected Annotated Bibliography
Joseph Wilson, compiler and editor

Martin Luther King, Jr.: An Annotated Bibliography
Sherman E. Pyatt, compiler

Blacks in the Humanities, 1750-1984: A Selected Annotated Bibliography
Donald Franklin Joyce, compiler

The Black Family in the United States: A Revised, Updated,
Selectively Annotated Bibliography
Lenwood G. Davis, compiler

Black American Families, 1965-1984: A Classified, Selectively
Annotated Bibliography
Walter R. Allen, editor

Index to Poetry by Black American Women

Compiled by

Dorothy Hilton Chapman

Bibliographies and Indexes in Afro-American and African Studies, Number 15

GREENWOOD PRESS
New York • Westport, Connecticut • London

LIBRARY OF CONGRESS CATALOGING-IN-PUBLICATION DATA

Chapman, Dorothy Hilton, 1934-
Index to poetry by Black American women.

(Bibliographies and indexes in Afro-American and African studies, ISSN 0742-6925 ; no. 15)
Bibliography: p.
1. American poetry—Afro-American authors—Indexes. 2. American poetry—Women authors—Indexes. 3. Afro-American women in literature—Indexes. 4. Women and literature—United States—Indexes. I. Title. II. Series.
Z1229.N39C45 1986 016.811'008'09287 86-14936
[PS153.N5]
ISBN 0-313-25152-5 (lib. bdg. : alk. paper)

Library of Congress Catalog Card Number: 86-14936
ISBN: 0-313-25152-5
ISSN: 0742-6925

First published in 1986

Greenwood Press, Inc.
88 Post Road West, Westport, Connecticut 06881

Printed in the United States of America

The paper used in this book complies with the Permanent Paper Standard issued by the National Information Standards Organization (Z39.48-1984).

10 9 8 7 6 5 4 3 2 1

To my granchildren Jermaine Jay, Dessalyn Geneva, and Dawn Nicole Murray

CONTENTS

Foreword by Louis Edna Gibson West ix

Preface xiii

Key to Abbreviations for Books Indexed xv

TITLE AND FIRST LINE INDEX 1

AUTHOR INDEX 265

SUBJECT INDEX 334

FOREWORD

The Black American women poets for more than two centuries have entertained, inspired, and influenced their followers. Through their creative genius and eloquent expressions, they give a very sensitive and intimate view of the Black experience in America. In style, content, and tone, their poetry reflects the social, political, and economic climates of their generations, the eighteenth and nineteenth centuries, the Harlem Renaissance Period (roughly 1917-1935, peaking in the 1920s), and the Black movement beginning in the 1960s.

The road to public recognition for these American Black women poets has been long and hard. Their poetry for many years was not taken seriously and was considered by some to be of little literary significance. Consequently, only a select few found their way into the established mass media, though many were gifted poets and prolific writers. In the earlier years, they relied almost exclusively on the Black press and other obscure publications as major outlets for their poetry. A few white magazines such as the Atlantic Monthly, Poetry, and Harper's Bazaar published some of their work, but most of the mainstream publishers refused to publish poets known to be of color. Nevertheless, a small number of Black women poets somehow managed to get their poems published by well-known publishers, and some were given critical attention; regrettably, though, most of their poetry was never read or appreciated by the general public.

Despite this historical neglect and the general lack of opportunity for public recognition, a few Black American women poets not only influenced Black literary thought and Black intellectual and cultural life, but also had a major impact on general American culture. In so doing, several of these Black women attained national and internatnational acclaim. Phillis Wheatley (1753-1784) was the first so-called "Negro" to achieve such distinction. Because of her quick intellect, creative genius, and facility with words, an appreciation of her work spread at home and abroad. Her first volume, Poems on Various Subjects, Religious and Moral, was published in 1773 while she was in London, and she thereby became the first Negro American to publish a volume. The second Negro woman to achieve national acclaim for her poetry was Frances E. W. Harper (1825-1911) during the early nineteenth century. Harper may be regarded as one of the early feminists as she used her poetry to champion the rights of all women, black and white alike, and to protest against the evils of slavery.

A succession of gifted Black women poets followed Harper. However, it was five decades later, during the Harlem Remaissance, before another Negro woman, Georgia Douglas Johnson (1886-1966), received national recognition for her poetry and other literary endeavors. Like Frances Harper, Johnson used her creative work to exploit the themes of color and racism in Negro life in America. Her poetry is laced with the newfound racial pride that surfaced at this time, immediately following World War I. This new attitude was embraced by the Black community and encouraged and nurtured by such national organizations as the NAACP (National Association for the Advancement of Colored People) and the National Urban League, and also by Black intellectuals such as W.E.B. DuBois and Booker T. Washington. Johnson's creative work, along with that of her sister poets and other literary contemporaries during the Harlem Renaissance period, had a major influence upon American and other Western cultures.

After more than one hundred seventy years and a long list of talented poets of color in America, a fourth woman poet, Gwendolyn Brooks (1917-), became the first so-called "Afro-American" to receive the Pultizer Prize (1950), for her second volume, Annie Allen, published in 1949. Brooks also chosen Poet Laureate of Illinois in 1969, and in 1973 was named Consultant on Literature to to the Library of Congress. Brooks may be considered a transitional poet, bridging the Harlem Renaissance and the Black Movement. She, like her sister poets before her, used her poetry to describe the Black experience. Moreover, as she became involved in the Black Movement. Brooks used her poetry to inspire and free the Black community of its preconditioned images. By her own admission, Brooks went through an identity crisis during the '40s and '50s--from a period of rejection of her Blackness to acceptance in the late '60s. Her poem "We Real Cool" reflects this change. Another trait of Brooks, her love for people, is also reflected in her poetry. According to George Kent, her biographer, she expressed this love in her poem "Sundays of Satin-Legs Smith." In this poem she presents a zoot-suited street figure from the '40s, not as a colorful figure but "as an artist who is putting his life together in a certain kind of way, as someone responding to an instinct for beauty that is often garnished or misguided but is still profoundly human."[1] For more than four decades, by the sheer mastery of her craft, Gwendolyn Brooks has remained one of the most celebrated Black American poets. Her life is illuminated by outstanding achievements.

By about 1954, nearly three decades after the peak of the Harlem Renaissance, America and its Black society were in the midst of another "great awakening," as a surge in social, educational and political reforms arose from the Civil Rights Movement. In the wake of this came the National Feminist Movement (Black and white) and the Black Movement of the '60s and '70s. The Black American women poets, especially the young poets of today, are committed to these causes and are deeply involved in them. Because of their committment and participation in the national movements, increased attention is given them by the print and electronic media and various public forums. There is also an increase in public recognition and a growing awareness and appreciation of their creative work by both blacks and whites. In addition, the poetry of these young Black women is sought after by the mass media and is popular on many of the college and university campuses. Although this change in public attitude is welcome and the opportunity for Black women poets to have their work published by some of the leading publishers is a major accomplishment, the Black press, especially Broad-

side Press of Detroit, remains the primary market for their poetry.

The Black American women poets of the '60s and '70s are generally referred to in Black literary and intellectual circles as the "New Black" poets. They broke with the traditional Black verse in style, content and tone. Their poetry is often angry, bitter and politicalized and, more often than not, written in street language of the urban ghetto and steeped in racial pride. In this regard, they discarded the word "Negro" and used the word "Black" to describe themselves and their people. Two themes, "Black is Beautiful" and "Black Power," emerged to symbolize racial pride and were embraced by such organizations as the Southern Christian Leadership Conference (SCLC) and Operation PUSH. They exploited to the fullest by the New Black powts. Typical of this new breed of Black American women poets are Nikki Giovanni, Maya Angelou, and Sonia Sanchez. The creative works of these talented women and others like them make a strong statement on racial pride and Black life in America. Their uniquely crafted poetry not only has a powerful influence on the "Black" image but a strong impact on American culture. They have introduced an unusual poetic style that has changed, perhaps for some time to come, traditional Black verse. Their creative genius, uninhibited style, forceful tone, colorful language, and musical quality, coupled with intense racial pride has influenced older poets, including Gwendolyn Brooks, who so aptly described them as "sassier" and "inclined to take things into their own hands to bring about change."[2] Certainly, they may be considered voices on the cutting edge of the Civil Rights Movement.

Recently, Alice Walker (1944-), also a gifted Black woman poet, attained national recognition for a hit screen production of her book The Color Purple (1982), which received eleven Academy Award nominations during the 1986 season. Amid this growing national interest in the Black American women poets, the literary status now accorded their creative work demands a higher quality of objective criticism, and for this, the work must be accessible. Consequently, the Index to Poetry By Black American Women is an excellent reference tool for an area that needs much work. It should be welcomed by the serious scholar, the student, and the casual reader interested in Black poetry.

The Index to Poetry by Black American Women expands and updates the original list of Black women poets included in the Index to Black Poetry, which was published in 1974 by G. K. Hall and Company. Comprehensive in coverage, it begins with Lucy Terry (1746) and continues to the present. The volume is divided into three major indexes, Title and First Line, Author and Subject.

The Title and First Line Index presents a retrospective portrayal of the poetic expressions on the Black experience in America, as seen through the eyes of Black women poets as they wrestle with life, their Black identity and womanhood. The most poignant examples of this struggle are revealed in the Title and First Line Index through their use of words and skillfully crafted phrases, whether in early Negro dialect or colloquial language of the Black community. Examples include the first line, "O' de wurl' ain't flat," from Lucy Ariel Williams', "North Boun'," Maya Angelou's "My guilt is 'slavery's chains,' too long" from "Guilt" in Just Give Me a Cool Drink of Water 'Fore I Diiie, and Fareedah Alash's (Ruby C. Saunders) first line "Hush your mouth," from Hush, Honey. From these titles and first lines, one can feel or sense the poet's style and tone. A study of this section of the Index to Poetry by Black American Women indicates that these poets follow only the dictates of their own creative "clock"; essentially this is true of

of all the New Black women poets.

The Author Index is unique in that it brings together for the first time the most complete listing to date of Black American women poets and their poems in one volume. It also gives proper attention to those Black American women poets who may otherwise have been neglected or overlooked.

Some eleven hundred themes included in the Subject Index offer an excellent historical view of Black life in America as experienced by the Black women poets. As in the Index to Black Poetry (1974), the most recurring themes are "death," "love," "men," "women," and "religion." However, a closer examination of the Subject Index shows that the Black American women poets exhibit a wide range of interests including family and human relationships as expressed in such themes as "mother," "father," "girls," "boys," and "lost love." Several of the poets such as Wheatley, Brooks, Giovanni, Angelou and Sanchez are fascinated with "Africa." Themes like "slavery," "discrimination," "racism," and "poverty," are popular. Many of the Black women wrote of their Black heroes, such as Malcolm X and Martin Luther King, Jr.

Although many of these poets use their poetry in an attempt to change the image and status of Blacks in America, they are not all-consumed by racism; neither are they always angry or at odds with American society. There are lighter moments in their poetry, moments of reflection and self questioning, as evidenced in themes such as "children," "flowers," "dreams," and prayer." There are also moments when the poets are at peace with themselves- accepting their "Blackness." At such times their poetry overflows with racial pride.

The Index to Poetry by Black American Women codifies more than two hundred years of poetry by Black women of America in one comprehensive and easy to use volume. It is a much needed reference and should prove helpful to the scholar, student, and others interested in Black poetry.

Notes

1. "Gwen Brooks Loves People." Biography, Chicago Defender, 6 June 1979, p.5.
2. Ann Waldron, "Books; Gwendolyn Brooks on Poetry and Black Identity," Zest. Houston Chronicle. 17 February 1975, p.22.

Louis Edna Gibson West
Business Library
Texas Southern University
Houston, Texas

PREFACE

This is the first of a two-volume index of Black American poetry. The second volume, on Black American men poets, is forthcoming. Here, one hundred twenty books by individual women poets are indexed, as are eighty-three anthologies of Black American poetry. Some of the books were selected from The Negro in the United States: A Selected Bibliography by Dorothy Porter (Library of Congress, Washington D.C., 1970) and North American Poets: A Bibliograhpical Checklist of Their Writings. 1760-1944 by Dorothy Porter (Hattiesburg, Miss.: Book Farm, 1945). The poetry section of the Heartman Collection of the Texas Southern University Library (Houston, Texas) provided a wealth of sources and works. For a full list of books indexed refer to the Key to Abbreviations for Books Indexed that follows.

In all, over four thousand poems by over four hundred female poets are included, the most prolific of the poets being Maya Angelou, Gwendolyn Brooks, Lucille Clifton, Nikki Giovanni, Georgia Douglas Johnson, and Audre Lorde. In addition, some one hundred eighty-five anonymous poems are included, among them several traditional folk songs, spirituals, and gospel tunes. No attempt was made to identify the anonymous poems as being by male or female poets. They are included in this vol-

ume on female poets simply because it is shorter.

The volume is organized in three major sections: the Title and First Line Index, the Author Index, and the Subject Inex. Arrangement is alphabetical throughout. The Title and First Line Index indicates for each entry, the author and the abbreviations for the book or books in which the poem is to be found with the page number. For titles, all the main words are capitalized, following conventional rules; for first lines, only the initial word and proper nouns are capitalized. Where the title and first line are the same, only the title is given, followed by two asterisks. The Author Index lists the titles alphabetically under each author. The Subject Index indicates general key word descriptions for the poems, and each subject is followed by a list of authors and titles.

I should like to extend by thanks to Ms. Rebecca Richard for her encouragement, Mrs. Mattie Grant for her patience in securing books through interlibrary loan, and the students at Texas Southern University for indicating by their interest the need for such an index.

KEY TO ABBREVIATIONS FOR BOOKS INDEXED

AfAA — Afro-Arts Anthology. Newark. New Jersey: Jihard Productions (1969). 47p.

AfAAu — Afro-American Authors. William Adams. Boston: Houghton Mifflin Co. (1972). 165p.

AfAV — Afro-American Voices. Ralph Kendricks. New York: Oxford Book Co. (1970). 349p.

AfAWA — Afro-American Writing: An Anthology of Prose and Poetry. Richard A. Long, ed. New York: New York University Press (1972). 2 vols. 794p.

ALC — Autumn Love Cycle. Georgia Douglas Johnson. Freeport, New York: Books For Libraries Press (1971). 79p.

ALTRGR — All the Renegades Ghosts Rise. Thulani Davis. Washington, D.C.: Anemone Press (1978). 62p.

AmLNA — American Literature by Negro Authors. Herman Dreer, ed. New York: Rhe Macmillan Co. (1950). 334p.

AmNP — American Negro Poetry. Arna Bontemps, ed. New York: Hill & Wang Co. (1963). 197p.

AnA — Annie Allen. Gwendolyn Brooks. New York: Harper (c1949). 60p.

ANP — Anthology of Negro Poetry by Negroes, An. New Jersey: Works Progress Administration (n.d.). 140p.

AnSIR — And Still I Rise. Maya Angelou. New York: Random House (1978). 54p.

AOS — Anatomy of Soul. Jean "Phoenix" Collins, ed. Houston, Texas: Texas Southern University Press Club (1972). 28p.

AVAN — Anthology of Verse by American Negroes. Newman Ivey White, ed. Durham, North Carolina: Moore Publishing Co. (c.1968). 250p.

BANP — Book of American Negro Poetry, The. James Weldon Johnson, ed. New York: Harcourt, Brace & World (c1922, 1950, 1958,1971). 300p.

BCF — 'Bout Cullud Folkes. Lucy Mae Turner. New York: Henry Harrison. (c1938). 64p.

Bec — Beckonings. Gwendolyn Brooks. Detroit: Broadside Press (1975) 16p.

BeEa — Bean Eaters, The. Gwendolyn Brooks. New York: Harper & Bros.

BeYM — Between You and Me. Marva Tatum Smith. Lufkin, Texas: Myriad Publishing Co. (1978). 32p.

BFBTBJ — Black Feeling Black Talk Black Judgment. Nikki Giovanni. New

	York: William Morrow (1970). 98p.
BiGa	Big Gate, The. Elma Stuckey. Chicago: Precedent Publishing Inc. (1976). 95p.
BlALP	Black American Literature Poetry. Darwin Turner, ed. Columbus, Ohio: Charles E. Merrill Co. (1969). 132p.
BlEx	Black Experience, The. Francis E. Kearnes, ed. New York: Viking Press (1970). 650p.
BlFi	Black Fire. Imamu Amiri Baraka (LeRoi Jones) New York: William Morrow (1968). 670p.
BlGBG	Black Girl Black Girl. Leatrice Emeruwa. Beachwood, Ohio: Sharaqua Publishing Co. (1976). 28p.
BlIA	Black Literature in America. Houston Baker, Jr. ed. New York: McGraw-Hill Book Co. (1971). 110p.
BlIMT	Black Bird in My Tree, A. Jennifer Blackman Lawson. Palo Alto, Ca.: Zikawuna Communications Co. (1979) 56p.
BlLi	Blackamerican Literature, 1760-Present. Ruth Miller. Beverly Hills, Ca.: Glenco Press (1971). 536p.
BlP	Black Poets, The. Dudley Randall, ed. New York: Bantam Books (1971). 353p.
BlPo	Black Poetry. Dudley Randall, ed. Detroit: Broadside Press (1969). 48p.
BlSi	Black Sister: Poetry by Black American Women, 1746-1980. Erlene Stetson. Bloomington, Indiana: Indiana University Press (1981). 312p.
BlSp	Black Spirits: A Festival of New Black Poets in America. Woodie King, ed. New York: Random House (c1972) 252p.
BluB	Blues Book for Blue Back Magical Women, A. Sonia Sanchez. Detroit: Broadside Press (1974). 62p.
BlUn	Black Unicorn, The. Audre Lorde. New York: W. W. Horton (1978). 122p.
BlVo	Black Voices. Abraham Chapman, ed. New York: New American Library (1968). 718p.
BlW	Black Wisdom. Frenchy Jolene Hodges. Detroit: Broadside Press (c1971). 30p.
BlWOA	Black Writers of America. Richard Barksdale, ed. New York: Macmillan Co. (1972). 917p.
BOL	Black Out Loud. Arnold Adoff, ed. New York: Macmillan (1969). 86p.
BrA	Broadside Annual, The. Jill Witherspoon Boyer. Detroit: Broadside Press (1972). 22p.
BrBV	Bronze: A Book of Verse. Georgia Douglas Johnson. Boston: B. J. Brimmer Co. (1922). 101p.
BrT	Broadside Treasury, A. Gwendolyn Brooks, ed. Detroit: Broadside Press (c1971). 188p.
BTB	Beyond the Blues. Rosey E. Pool, ed. Lympne, Kent: Hand and Flower Press (c1962) 188p.
BTh	Brown Thrush, The: The Anthology of Verse by Negro Students at Talladega College. Lillian W. Voorhees and Robert W. O'Brien, eds. Bryn Athyn, Penna.: Lawson-Roberts Publishing Co. (c1932). 67p.
CaD	Caroling Dusk. Countee Cullen, ed. New York: Harper (1927). 237p.
CaEADW	Cat Eyes and Dead Wood. Melba Joyce Boyd. Highland Park, Michigan: Fallen Angel Press (1978). 43p.
CaPWY	Can I Poet with You? Mae Jackson. Detroit: Broadside Press (1969) 20p.

CaTR Cables to Rage. Audre Lorde. London: Paul Breman (1970) 28p.

ChG Christmas Gif'. Charlemae H. Rollins, ed. Chicago: Follett Pub. Co. (1963). 119p.

ChOM Child of Myself. Patricia Parker. San Lorenzo, C.,: Shameless Hussy Press (1972). Unpaged.

ChOSa Chants of Saints. Michael S. Harper, ed. Urbana: University of Illinois Press (1979) 436p.

ChPON Chosen Poems, Old and New. Audre Lorde. New York: Norton (1982) 115p.

ClAB Clearing and Beyond, The. May Miller. Washington: The Charioteer Press (1974). 49p.

CNAW Calvalcade, Negro American Writing from 1760 to the Present. Arthur P. Davis, ed. Boston: Houghton Mifflin Co. (c1971). 905p.

CoAAAW Confirmation: An Anthology of American Women. Amiri Baraka, ED. New York: Quill Press (1983). 418p.

COAG Coagulations: New and Selected Poems. Jayne Cortez. New York: Thunder's Mouth Press (1984). 112p.

COAL Coal. Audre Lorde. New York: W. W. Norton & Co. Inc. (c1968, 1970, 1976) 70p.

CoCRD Cotton Candy on a Rainy Day. Nikki Giovanni. New York: William Morrow & Co. (1978). 93p.

DaGe Daughter's Geography, A. Ntozake Shange. New York: St. Martin's Press (1983). 77p.

DaS Dark Symphony. James Emanuel, ed. New York: The Free Press (1968). 604p.

DaTAOP Dark Testament and Other Poems. Pauli Murray. Norwalk, CT, Silvermine (1970). 106p.

DeDF Dear Dark Faces: Portraits of a People. Helen E, Simcox, ed. Detroit: Lotus Press (1980) 104p.

DeRi Deep Rivers, a Portfolio: 20 Contemporary Black American Poets. Naomi Long Madgett, ed. Detroit: Lotus Press (1974). 20p.

DOBB Dices or Black Bones: Black Voices of the Seventies. Adam David Miller, ed. Boston: Houghton Mifflin Co. (1970). 142p.

DoOAT Down of a Thistle. Margaret Danner. Waukesha, Wisconsin: Country Beautiful (1976). 144p.

DrF Dream Farmer. Jill Witherspoon Boyer. Detroit: Broadside Press (1975). 24p.

DuSAE Dunbar Speaker and Entertainer. Alice Dunbar-Nelson. Napierville, Illinois: Nichols & Co. (1920). 288p.

EaNAW Early Negro American Writers. Benjamin Brawley, ed. New York: Dover Publications, Inc. (1970). 305p.

EBAP Early Black American Poets. William H. Robinson, ed. Dubuque, Iowa: W. C. Brown Co. (c1969) 275p.

EBAT Ebony and Topaz: a Collectanea. Charles S. Johnson, ed. New York: Opportunity, National Urban League (1927). 164p.

EbR Ebony Rhythm: An Anthology of Contemporary Negro Verse. Beatrice M. Murphy, ed. New York: Exposition Press (c1948). 162p.

EcFTH Echoes from the Hills. Bessie Woodson Yancey. Washington, D. C.: The Associated Publishers, Inc. (1939). 62p.

EgT Ego-Tripping and Other Poems for Young People. Nikki Giovanni. New York: Lawrence Hill (1973). 37p.

EmDH Empress of the Death House, The. Toi Derricotte. Detroit: Lotus Press (1978). 51p.

ExAE	Exits and Entrances. Naomi Long Madgett. Detroit: Lotus Press (1978). 69p.
FaP	Family Pictures. Gwendolyn Brooks. Detroit: Broadside Press (1970). 23p.
FBPA	Forerunners: Black Poets in America. Woodie King, ed. Wash-INGTON, D.C.: Howard University Press (1975). 127p.
FeAV	Festivals and Funerals. Jayne Cortez. New York: The Author (1971). 44p.
FiCi	First Cities, The. Audre Lorde. New York: The Poets Press (1968). Unpaged.
FMP	For My People. Margaret Walker. New Haven: Yale University Press (1942). 58p.
FoAAM	Forty Acres and a Mule. E. Sharon Gomillion: Diana Press (1973). 27p.
FoM	For Malcolm: Poems on the Life and the Death of Malcolm X. Dudley Randall and Margaret G. Burroughs, eds. Detroit: Broadside Press (c1969). 126p.
FrLWP	From a Land Where Other People Live. Audre Lorde. Detroit: Broadside Press (1973). 46p.
GaBW	Galaxy of Black Writing, A. B. Baird Shuman, ed. Durham, North Carolina: Moore Publishing Co. (1970). 441p.
GANIV	Great American Negroes in Verse, 1723-1965. Eloise Crosby Culver, ed. Washington, D.C.: Associated Publishing, Inc. (c1966). 80p.
GLOWC	Glowchild and Other Poems. Ruby Dee, ed. New York: The Third Press (1972). 111p.
GoNAE	Good News About the Earth. Lucille Clifton. New York: Random House (1972). 16p.
GoS	Golden Slippers: An Anthology of Negro Poetry for Young Readers. Arna Bontemps, ed. New York: Harper & Bros. (c1941). 220p.
HeAEG	Heart As Ever Green, The. Carolyn M. Rodgers. Garden City, New York: Anchor Press (1970). 32p.
HeD	Heralding Dawn: An Anthology of Verse. John Mason Brewer, ed. Dallas, Texas: Superior Typesetting Co. (c1936). 45p.
HeTMWL	Hello to Me With Love, Poems of Self-Dicovery. C. Tillery Banks. New York: William Morrow & Co. (1980). Unpaged.
HoC	Homecoming. Sonia Sanchez. Detroit: Broadside Press (1969). 32p.
HoFTD	Hold Fast to Dreams. Arna Bontemps, ed. Chicago: Follett Publishing Co. (1969). 192p.
HoIGO	How I Got Ovah. Carolyn M. Rodgers. Garden City, New York: Anchor Press/Doubleday (1975). 79p.
HWOP	Heart of a Woman and Other Poems, The. Georgia Douglas Johnson. Boston: The Cornhill Co. (1918). 62p.
IABW	I Am a Black Woman. Mari Evans. New York: William Morrow & Co. (c1938, 1964, 1967, 1968, 1969, 1970). 95p.
IADB	I Am the Darker Brother: An Anthology of Modern Poems by Negro Americans. Arnold Adoff, ed. New York: Macmillan (c1968). 128p.
IATWMB	I Am That We May Be. Damali (Denise Burnett). Chicago: Third World Press (1974). 21p.
IfWCF	If Words Could Set Us Free. Gertrude Blackwell Bailey. Hicksville, New York: Exposition Press (1974). 59p.
ImIB	Images in Black. Johari Amini. Chicago: Third World Press (1969). 13p.

ImOAAF — Impressions of African Art Forms. Margaret Danner. Detroit: Broadside Press (1960). Unpaged.

InDM — Inside the Devil's Mouth. Pamela Cobb. Detroit: Lotus Press (n.d.). 44p.

IrLa — Iron Lace. Margaret Danner. Millbrook, New York: Kriya Press (c1968). Unpaged.

ITBLA — Introduction to Black Literature in America. Lindsay Patterson, Comp. & ed. New York: Publishers Comp. Inc. (1968). 302p.

ITM — In the Mecca. Gwendolyn Brooks. New York: Harper & Row (c1968). 54p.

ItND — It's a New Day. Sonia Sanchez. Detroit: Broadside Press (1971). 29p.

ITSA — I, Too Sing America. Barbara Standford, ed. New York: Hayden Book Co. (1971). 308p.

IvBAW — I've Been a Woman: New and Selected Poems. Sonia Sanchez. Sausalito, Ca.: The Black Scholar Press (1978). 101p.

JGM — Just Give Me a Cool Drink of Water 'Fore I Diiie. Maya Angelou. New York: Random House (c1971). 48p.

JuB — Judith's Blues. Judy Dothard Simmons. Detroit: Broadside Press (1973). 22p.

JuBa — Jump Bad. Gwendolyn Brooks. Detroit: Broadside Press (1971). 188p.

KAL — Kaleidoscope: Poems by American Negro Poets. Robert E. Hayden, Comp. New York: Harcourt, Brace & World (c1967). 231p.

LetGSW — Let's Go Somewhere. Johari Amini. Chicago: Third World Press (1970). 31p.

LiS — Life Styles. Marion Nicholas. Detroit: Broadside Press (1971). 22p.

LoP — Love Poems. Sonia Sanchez. New York: Third Press (1973). 101p.

LoSBM — Love Song to Black Men. Linda Brown Bragg. Detroit: Broadside Press (1974). 32p.

LUP — Lincoln University Poets. Waring Cuney. Langston Hughes, and Bruce Mc Wright, eds. New York: First Editions Press (c1954). 133p.

MaDBL — Mad Dog Black Lady. Wanda Coleman. Santa Barbara, Ca.: Black Sparrow Press (1979). 133p.

MBP — Magic of Black Poetry, The. Raoul Abdul, ed. New York: Dodd, Mead & Co. (c1972) 318p.

MELVA — Melva. Melva Eloise Tatum. Lufkin, Texas: Myriad Publishing Co. (n.d.). Unpaged

MiFe — Mixed Feelings. Olean Bess. St. Albans, New York: The Author (1972). 196p.

MoCAP — Modern and Contemporary Afro-American Poetry. Boston: Allyn and Bacon (1972). 193p.

MoGl — Morning Glories. Josephine D. (Henderson) Heard. Atlanta: Franklin Printing & Pub. Co. (1902). 142p.

MoIB — Movement in Black: The Collected Poetry of Patricia Parker, 1961-1978. Patricia Parker. Trumansburg, New York: The Crossing Press (1978). 157p.

MoOP — Mouth on Paper. Jayne Cortez. New York: Bola Press (1977). 63p.

MoSu — Moonrise Sunset. Eleanor Thomas-Grumback. Madison, Wisconsin: FAS Publishing Co. (1979). 24p.

MuDLSG — Mules Done Long Since Gone. Colleen McElroy. Seattle, Wash-

ington: Harrison-Madrona Center (1972). 36p.

MyFe — Mystic Female, The. Pinkie Gordon Lane. Van Buren, Ark.: Bailey Press (1978). 52p.

MyH — My House. Nikki Giovanni. New York: William Morrow & Co. (1972). 69p.

MyNIB — My Name Is Black: An Anthology of Black Poets. Amanda Ambrose, ed. New York: Scholastic Book Service (1973). 160p.

NaABE — Naked Against the Belly of the Earth. Joanne Jimason. Washington, D.C.: The Common Ground Press (1977). 37p.

NaEd — Nappy Edges. Ntozake Shange. New York: St. Martin Press (1978). 148p.

NaPr — Natural Process. Ted Wilentz, ed. New York: Hill and Wang (1970). 181p.

NBP — New Black Poetry, The. Clarence Majors, Comp. New York: International Publishers (c1969). 156p.

NeBV — New Black Voices. Abraham Chapman, ed. New York: New American Library (1972). 606p.

NeCa — Negro Caravan, The. Sterling A. Brown, ed. New York: Arno Press (1969). 1082p.

NegVo — Negro Voices. Beatrice M. Murphy, ed. New York: H. Harrison (c1938). 173p.

NeHS — New York Head Shop and Museum. Audre Lorde. Detroit: Broadside Press)1974). 56p.

NeJCL — Nethula Journal of Contemporary Literature. Washington: Nethula Publishing (1974). 35p.

NeNRe — New Negro Renaissance, The. Arthur Paul Davis, ed. New York: Holt, Rhinehart & Winston (1975). 538p.

NiBPo — Nine Black Poets. R. Baird Shuman, ed. Durham North Carolina: Moore Publishing Co. (1968). 236p.

NIGHT — Nightstar, 1973-78. Mari Evans. Los Angeles: Center for Afro-American Studies, University of California (1981). 78p.

NNPUSA — New Negro Poets U.S.A. Langston Hughes, ed. Bloomington: Indiana University Press (c1964). 127p.

OcJo — October Journey. Margaret Walker. Detroit: Broadside Press (1973). 38p.

OhPWFW — Oh Pray My Wings Are Gonna Fit Me Well. Maya Angelou. New York: Random House (1975). 67p.

OnATM — One and the Many. Naomi Long Madgett. Hicksville, New York: Exposition Press (1956). 94p.

ONC — Once. Alice Walker. New York: Harcourt, Brace & World (c1968). 81p.

OnOW — On Our Way. Lee Bennett Hopkins, ed. New York: Alfred A. Knopf (1974). 63p.

OrW — Ordinary Woman, An. Lucille Clifton. New York: Random House (1974). 94p.

PAL — Pomes and Letters. Phillis Wheatley. New York: C. F. Heartman (c1915). Mnemosyne Reprint (c1969). 111p.

PaNP — Passion: New Poems, 1977-1980. June Jordan. Boston: Beacon Press (1980). 100p.

PBFH — Poems. Frances E. W. Harper. Philadelphia: The Author (1900). 90p.

PBK — Poems by Kali. Kali Grosvenor. New York: Doubleday. (1970). 62p.

PePo — Peacock Poems, The. Sherley Williams. Middletown, Ct.: Wesleyan University Press (1978). 87p.

PFND — Prophets for a New Day. Margaret Walker. Detroit: Broadside

Press (1970). 32p.

PhN Phantom Nightinggale Juvenilia. Naomi Long Madgett. Detroit: Lotus Press (1981). 132p.

PiLAF Pink Ladies in the Afternoon. Naomi Long Madgett. Detroit: Lotus Press (1972). 63p.

PoBA Poetry of Black America, The. Arnold Adoff, ed. New York: Harper & Row Publishers (1973). 552p.

PoBBl Poems by Blacks. Fort Smith, Arkansas: South and West, Inc. (n.d.). v.2, 61p.

PoCo Poem Counterpoint. Margaret Danner. Detroit: Broadside Press (1969). 23p.

PoFAP Poetic Facts and Philosophy. Al Ethelred Blackeley, ed. New York: Al Ethelred Blakeley & Co. Pub. (1936). 23p.

PoN Poetry of the Negro, 1746-1949. Langston Hughes and Arna Bontemps, eds. Garden City, New York: Doubleday (1949). 429p.

PoNe Poetry of the Negro, 1746-1970. Langston Hughes and Arna Bontemps, eds. Garden City, New York: Doubleday (1970). 645p.

PPW Poems. Phillis Wheatley. Julian D. Mason, Jr., ed. Chapel Hill: University of North Carolina Press (1966). 113p.

Rec Re: Creation. Nikki Giovanni. Detroit: Broadside Press (1970). 48p.

ReFNA Readings from Negro Authors. Otella Cromwell, ed. New York: Harcourt Brace and Co. (1931). 388p.

ReHL Respect Honesty Love to All Sisters. The Poets of Sudan, Inc. n.p.: Sudan Arts Southwest, Inc. (n.d.). Unpaged.

RePOP Revolutionary Petunias and Other Poems. Alice Walker. New York: Harcourt Brace and Jovanovich, Inc. (1973). 70p.

Resur Resurrections. Gloria Oden. Homestead, Florida: Olivant Press (1978). 147p.

RIOT Riot. Gwendolyn Brooks. Detroit: Broadside Press (1969). 22p.

RoATW Rock Against the Wind. Lindsay Patterson, ed. New York: Dodd, Mead & Co. (1973). 172p.

RoCO Rocks Cry Out, The. Beatrice M. Murphy. Detroit: Broadside Press (1969). 24p.

Scar Scarification. Jayne Cortez. New York: Bola Press (1973, 1978), 63p.

SCh Some Changes. June Jordan. New York: E. P. Dutton & Co. (1971). 86p.

ScWh Screaming Whisper, A. Vanessa Howard. New York: Holt, Rinehart, Winston (1972). 59p.

SiAS Sixes and Sevens. Paul Breman, ed. London: Paul Breman (1962). 96p.

SiSH Singing Sadness Happy. Lyn. Detroit: Broadside Press (1972). 32p.

SoBB Songs of a Black Bird. Carolyn M. Rodgers. Chicago: Third World Press (1969). 39p.

SOC Songs of Creation. Marion Cuthbert. New York: Woman's Press National Board of the Womens' Christian Association (c1949). 46p.

SoITM Sometimes I Think of Maryland. Jodi Braxton. New York: Sunbury Press (1977). 51p.

SoOM Soon One Morning. Herbert Hill, ed. New York: Alfred A. Knopf (1963). 617p.

SoS Soulscript, Afro American Poetry. June Jordan, ed. Garden City, New York: Doubleday (c1970). 146p.

SoTPN Songs to a Phantom Nightingale. Naomi Long Madgett. New

York: Fortuny's Publishers, Inc. (1941). 30p.

SPGB — Selected Poems. Gwendolyn Brooks. New York: Harper & Row (1963). 127p.

StBS — Star by Star. Naomi Long Madgett. Detroit: Lotus Press (1970). 63p.

StIB — Street in Bronzeville, A. Gwendolyn Brooks. New York: Harper & Brothers Pub. Co. (1945). 57p.

Suga — Sugarfields. Barbara Mahone. Detroit: Broadside Press (1970). 32p.

TGWL — To Gwen with Love. Patricia L. Brown, ed. Chicago: Johnson Pub. Co. (1971). 149p.

ThHSD — Three Hundred and Sixty Degrees Coming at You. Sonia Sanchez, ed. N.p., 5X Publishing Co. (1971). 190p.

ThTDID — Things That I Do in the Dark. June Jordan. New York: Random House (1977). 203p.

ThWRNW — Those Who Ride the Night Winds. Nikki Giovanni. New York: William Morrow & Co. (1983). 62p.

TiTBi — Tie that Binds, The. Gloria Oden. Homestead, Florida: Olivant Press (1980). 37p.

TNV — Today's Negro Voices. Beatrice M. Murphy, ed. New York: Julian Messner (1970). 141p.

TTW — Tree Tall Women. Harryette Mullen. Galveston, Texas: Energy Faith Communication, Inc. (1981). 66p.

TwW — Two-Headed Women. Lucille Clifton. Amherst: University of Massachusetts (1980). 60p.

TYBP — 3000 Years of Black Poetry. Alan Lomax, ed. New York: Dodd, Mead (1970). 261p.

UNBP — Understanding the New Black Poetry. Stephen Henderson, ed. New York: William Morrow & Co. (1973). 394p.

VaT — Vacation Time: Poems for Children. Nikki Giovanni. New York: William Morrow & Co. (1980). 59p.

VoDLM — Voo Doo/Love Magic. Angela Jackson. Chicago: Third World Press (1974). 23p.

VoFHR — Voices from the Harlem Renaissance. Nathan Huggins, ed. New York: Oxford University Press (1975). 438p.

WABP — We a BaddDDD People. Sonia Sanchez. Detroit: Broadside Press (c1970). 72p.

WeDNNM — We Don't Need No Music. Pearl Cleage Lomax. Detroit: Broadside Press (1972). 16p.

WGC — Walk God's Chillun. Lucile D. Goodlett. Dallas, Texas: The Kaleidograph Press (c1933). 74p.

WhIAM — Where Is All the Music. Mari Evans. London: Paul Breman (1968). 24p.

WhOL — When One Loves. Nola Richardson. Millbrae, Ca.: Celestial Arts (1974). 96p.

WhSIT — What Shall I Tell My Children Who Are Black? Margaret Burroughs. Chicago: M.A.A.H. Press (1968). 32p.

WiRYPS — Will the Real You Please Stamd Up? June Vanleer Williams. Bryn Mawr, Pennsylvania: Torrance Pub. Co. (1983). 85p.

WITM — Woman in the Moon. S. Diane Bogus. Stanford, CT.: Soap Box Co. (1977). 70p.

WiTh — Wind Thoughts. Pinkie Gordon Lane. Fort Smith, Arkansas: South and West, Inc. (1972). 59p.

WLOV — We Lift Our Voices and Other Poems. Mae V. Cowdery. Philadelphia: Alpress (1936). 68p.

WoATM — Women and the Men, The. Nikki Giovanni. New York: William

Morrow & Co. (1978). 58p.

WoOGB World of Gwendolyn Brooks, The. Gwendolyn Brooks. New York: Harper & Row (1971). 426p.

WoTa Woman Talk. Sandra Royster. Chicago: Third World Press (1974). 23p.

YoBBI You Better Believe It. Paul Breman, ed. Middlesex, England: Penguin Books (1973). 552p.

ABOUT THE COMPILER

DOROTHY HILTON CHAPMAN, Heartman Librarian at Texas Southern University in Houston, is the author of *Index to Black Poetry*.

TITLE AND FIRST LINE INDEX

Aardvark. Julia Fields. BOL p. 33; NiBPo p.75
Abandoned. Vanessa Howard. ScWh p.45
Abandoned Baby. June Jordan. SCh p.12; ThTDID p.156
Abbie, Jerry. When Ossie spoke a man began to cry. Sharon Bourke. UNBP p.374
Abbreviation. Lyn. SiSH p.25
Abe Lincoln freed the nigger. Anonymous. BlWOA p.313
Abe Lincoln was a poor man's son. Eloise Culver. GANIV p.33
Abortions will not let you forget. Gwendolyn Brooks. AfAWA p.579 BlP p.165; BlSi p.100; BlWOA p.715; MoCAP p.79; SoOM p.557; SPGB p.3; StIB p.3; WoOGB p.5
About Atlanta. Ntozake Shange. DaGe p.45
About Communication. Johari Amini. ImIB p.11
About Enrique's Drawing. June Jordan. ThTDID p.188
About Flowers. Wanda Coleman. MaDBL p.123
About Long Distances on Saturday. June Jordan. ThTDID p.70
About Man. Johari Amini. ImIB p.10
About Our Silences. S. Diane Bogus. WITM p.17
About Religion. Audre Lorde. BlUn p.105
About the Birds and the Be's. S. Diane Bogus. WITM p.15
About the Reunion. June Jordan. ThTDID p.65
Abraham Lincoln, Great Emancipator, 1809-1865. Eloise Culver. GANIV p.33
Abraham Lincoln shit he never walked nowhere to read a book. June Jordan. SCh p. 75; ThTDID p.114
Accept Me. Eleanor Thomas-Grumbach. MoSu p.4
Accept me for the person that I Am. Eleanor Thomas-Grumbach. MoSu p.4
Acceptance Speech. Jayne Cortez. COAG p,84
Accident. Maya Angelou. JGM p. 15
Accident Edgecome General Hospital May 16, 1968, Julia Fields. GaBW p.310; NiBPo p.71
Accidental far into the longer light, or smoking clouds. June Jordan. SCh p.38; ThTDID p.49
Accordingly. May Miller. ClAB p.40
Accounts Payable. Wanda Coleman. MaDBL p.93
Achievement. Naomi Long Madgett. PhN p.18
ACLU Mountain states Regional Office came across a welfare application, The. Pinkie Gordon Lane. BlSi p.230
Acquaintance. Jennifer Blackman Lawson. BlIMT p.43
Acquittal. Thulani Davis. AlTRGR p.58

Across the dark and quiet sky when sunbeams have to go to bed. Nikki Giovanni. VaT p.47
Across the flesh and feeling of Soledad. Jayne Cortez. BlSi p.151; Scar p.29
Across the yawning chasm men call race. Katharine Beverly. NegVo p.14
Adam and Eve. Lucille Clifton. GoNAE p.30
Adieu. Constantia E. Riley EbR p.126
Adieu, New England's smiling meads. Phillis Wheatley. AmLNA p.22; BlWOA p.42; PAL p.48; PPW p.57
Admiration. Josephine D. (Henderson) Heard. MoGl p.36
Admonitions. Lucille Clifton. BlP p.251; DOBB p.55
Adulthood. Nikki Giovanni. AfAWA p.772; BFBTBJ p.68; MoCAP p.169; NaPr p.23
Adulthood II. Nikki Giovanni. CoCRD p.54
Advance of Education. The. Josephine D. (Henderson) Heard. MoGl p.24
Advent. Naomi Long Madgett. PhN p.45
Advice. Gwendolyn B. Bennett. BlSi p.75; CaD p.156
Advice. Ntozake Shange. NaEd p. 129
Advice to the Girls. Frances E. W. Harper. AfAV p.83; RoATW p.92
Advice to the Lovelorn. Mae V. Cowdery. WLOV p.31
Advice to Young Ladies. Ann Plato. ANP p.11
Affirmation. Harryette Mullen. TTW p.61
Aflounder the uncompssed darkness of doubt in search of the path to the goal. Georgia Douglas Johnson. BrBv p.79
Africa. Lucille Clifton. GoNAE p.15
Africa. Maya Angelou. OhPWFW p.28
Africa. Nikki Giovanni. WoATM p.44
Africa. Nola Richardson. WhOL p.47
Africa Drifting Through me Sings. Margaret Danner. DoOAT p.116 IrLa p.29
Africa: I turn to meet this vast land of bitter-sweet. Margaret Danner. DoOAT p. 116; ImOAAF p.1; IrLa p. 29
Africa is a young man bathing. Nikki Giovanni. MyH p.49
Africa take my hands from the newspaper shack. Jayne Cortez. FeAF p.38
Africa I. Nikki Giovanni. MyH p.47
Africa II. Nikki Giovanni. MyH p.49
African America. Gertrude Blackwell Bailey. IfWCF p.12
African Beauty Rose. Kattie M. Cumbo. NiBPo p.44
African Images. Alice Walker. ONC p.3
African Madness. Eleanora E. Tate. BrA p.16
African Night Suite. Jayne Cortez. FeAF p.38
After. Maya Angelou. JGM p.17
After. Naomi Long Madgett. BTB p.147
After. Nola Richardson. WHOL p.55;OnATM p.13; Phn p.116
After a first book. Audre Lorde. CaTR p.9
After a Visit to the Home of Ex-Slaves. Bessie Woodson Yancey. EcFTH p.28
After All is Said and Done. June Jordan. ThTDID p.69
After all--mine is the joy. Georgia Douglas Johnson. ReFNA p.26
After all, silly goose, your laying days are over. Naomi Long Madgett. OnATM p.50
After church on Sunday I learned to love the gospel music. Audre Lorde. BlUn p.105
After dinner we take to the streets. June Jordan. ThTDID p.184
After Eli Whitney's gin brought to generations' end battered flesh and broken bones. Maya Angelou. OhPWFW p.54

After Enrique's Drawing. June Jordan. ThTDID p.188
After 5 kids she closed the shop. Toi Derricotte. EmDH p.45
After His Flight. Wanda Coleman. MaDBL p.130
After Hours. Naomi Long Madgett. PhN p.94
After Kent State. Lucille Clifton. GoNAE p.1; MoCAP. p. 142
After Mother was Buried.** Gloria Oden. RESUR p.107
After Parting. Naomi Long Madgett. OnATM p.48
After sickness and a begging from her bed. June Jordan. ThTDID p.26
After Such Knowledge what Forgiveness. Carolyn M. Rodgers. HeAEG p.48
After the all been done and I one old creature carried on. Lucille Clifton. TwW p.40
After the baths and bowel work, he was dead. Gwendolyn Brooks AnA p. 8; WoOGB p.72
After the Fifth Day. Sonia Sanchez. LoP. p.23
After the good fairy. Quandra Prettyman. BOL p.18
After the illness and fever had fled, and you lay as cold as stone on your bed. Naomi Evans Vaughn. EbR p.150
After the Quarrel. Pinkie Gordon Lane. DeRi p.9; WiTh p.24
After the Rain.** Harryette Mullen. TTW p.25
After the Rain. Joanne Jimason. NaABE p.36
After the Rain. Vanessa Howard. ScWh p.5
After the war when rationing was over was a plenty names. Lucille Clifton. TWW p.18
After you been with some body. Sherley Williams. PePo p.47
After You Change Me. Nola Richardson. WhOL p.73
Afterglow. Georgia Douglas Johnson. ALC p.70
Afterglow, The. Naomi Long Madgett. SoTpn p.22
Afterimages. Audre Lorde. ChPON p.102
Afterlove. Audre Lorde. COAL p. 43
Afternoon Off. Lucia M. Pitts. EbR p.121
Afterthought, An. Pinkie Gordon Lane. WiTh p.58
Afterwards. Jennifer Blackman Lawson. BlIMT p.53
Again. Naomi Long Madgett. OnATM p.28
Again it is the vigrant May. Georgia Douglas Madgett. ALC p.39
Again we meet—a flashing glance. Georgia Douglas Johnson. HWAOP p.60
Against the day of sorrow lay by some trifling thing. Georgia Douglas Johnson. AmNP p.21; HoFTD p.20
Age. Kattie M. Cumbo. GaBW p. 286; NiBPo p.45
Age. Nikki Giovanni. CoCRD p. 44
Aged one and wise, were you twenty-two again. Pauli Murray. DaTAOP p.50
Ageless I am; timespent. Amanda Ambrose. MyNIB p.151
Aging yellow men with wavy hair who were never called "Black." Carolyn M. Rodgers. HoIGO p.32
Agnew rushes into the waiting room. Vanessa Howard. ScWh
Agony and the Bone, The. Delores Kendrick. TGWL p.60
Agrionia. Sonia Sanchez. LoP p.26
Ah can't be no revolutionareeeeee eeee. Nia nSabe. ThHSD p. 81
Ah, children dear, the hour draws near. Ann Plato. ANP p.12
Ah haaaa/beware beware my dear of rabid dogs. Ntozake Shange. NaEd p.110
Ah, how poets sing and die. Anne Spencer. BANP p.218; CaD p.50; KAL p.37
Ah! How the wind raves this bitter night. Lauretta Holman Gooden. HeD p.15
Ah, I know what happiness is...!

Blanche Taylor Dickinson. ANP p.130; CaD p.107; RoATW p. 148
Ah, little road all whirry in the breeze. Helene Johnson. AmNP p.101; BANP p.280; BlSi p.80; CaD p.221; GoS p. 176; PoN p.154; PoNe p.266; ReFNA p.50
Ah Look, Here Comes the Forsythia. Carolyn M. Rodgers. HeAEG p. 4
Ah! Love! I shall not seek to penetrate. Georgia Douglas Johnson. ALC p.49
Ah me--would there were some place to hide. Lycurgus J. Alee. NegVo p.9
Ah, Momma. June Jordan. ThTDID p.37
Ah puts no confidence in March. Bessie Woodson Yancey. EcFTH p.62
Ah, such a child she was. Naomi Long Madgett. PhN p. 73
Ah, you are cruel. Anne Spencer. CaD p.47
Ahab's gaily clad fisherfriends, questing under the blue skies. Sarah Webster Fabio. DOBB p.27; PoBA p.205; UNBP p.241
Ah'm bowed down but God's gwine raise me. Lucy Mae Turner. BCF p.46
Ain it a shame. Mari Evans. NIGHT p.58
Ain't been on Market Street for nothing. Margaret Walker. BlSi p.98; FBPA p.107; NeBV p.203; PFND p.7; UNBP p.161
Ain't got no wedding ring. Leatrice Emeruwa. BlGBG p. 27
Ain't got time for a bite to eat. Mari Evans. IABW p.55
Ain't I a Woman? Sojourner Truth. BlSi p.24
Ain't No Blues Song. Jennifer Blackman Lawson. BlIMT p. 55
Ain't nobody better's my Daddy. Maya Angelou. OhPWFW p.65
Ain't That Bad? Maya Angelou. AnSIR p.43
Ain't the Only Place. Alice Lovelace. HoDo p.31
Alabama. Julia Fields. PoBA p. 319; PoNe p.420
Alabama Centennial. Naomi Long Madgett. BlALP p.111; BlP p.197; StBS p.60
Alabama Memories. Harryette Mullen. TTW p.2
Alabama Poem. Nikki Giovanni. ReC p.33; WoATM p.54
Alafia. Odara (Barbara Jones) BlFi p.356
Alarm Clock, The. Mari Evans. BOL p.6; DaS p.509; IABW p.59; ITSA p.249; WhIAM p.18
Alarm clock sure sound loud this mornin'. Mari Evans. BOL p.6; DaS p.509; IABW p.59; ITSA p.249; WhIAM p.18
Alaska. Margaret Danner. DoOAT p.35
Alberta, Alberta. Jayne Cortez. MoOP p.29
Album: Photo 2. Naomi Long Madgett. DeRi p.5; ExAE p.13
Alcoholic, diabetic, epileptic, scum. June Vanleer Williams. WiRYPS p.9
Aliens. Georgia Douglas Johnson. BrBV p.37
Aliens, The Pamela Cobb. DeRi p.8; InDM p.14
All, The. S. Diane Bogus. WITM p.39
All-conquering death by the resistless pow'r. Phillis Wheatley. PAL p.47; PPW p.55
All day long the sun's been shining. Bessie Woodson Yancey. EcFTH p.9
All day she heard the mad stampede of feet. Helene Johnson. VoFHR p.35
All day the world's mad mocking strife. Georgia Douglas Johnson. BrBV p. 28
All Day We've Longed for Night. Sarah Webster Fabio. BlSi p.141; DOBB

p,28
All deep there stirs the throb of spring. Georgia Douglas Johnson. HWAOP p.54
All filmy down she drifts in filmy stuffs and all. Gwendolyn Brooks. BeEa p.45; WoOGB p.343
All God's Chillin Got Shoes. Anonymous. BlEx p.5
All hail! fair vistas break upon the view. Georgia Douglas Johnson. BrBV p.93
All Hallows Eve. Audre Lorde. NeHS p.40
All Hung Up. Kattie M. Cumbo. NiBPo p.46
"All I can say is I'm glad my mother let me out." Margaret Danner. DoOAT p.16
All I Gotta Do. Nikki Giovanni. ReC p.25; WoATM p.6
All I know is his name. Ntozake Shange. NaEd p.133
All I wanted was your love. Mari Evans. BlP p.184; IABW p.20; PoBA p.191; RoATW p.140; UNBP p.251; WhIAM p.22
All Lives, All Dances and All is Loud. Anonymous. MBP p.11
All night long the bright hooves fall. May Miller. ClAB p.14
All night my bed was rocky. Naomi Long Madgett. ExAE p.36
All of them are six. June Jordan. SCh p.49; ThTDID p.101
All of these real people-are real. Patricia Parker. MoIB p.101
All our words are framed on the walls. Colleen McElroy. MuDLSG p. 3
All praise be to Allah only the mistakes. Mari Evans. BlVo p.480; IABW p.82
All Praises Due to Alah. Mae Jackson. CaPWY p.13
All problems being as personal as they are have to be largely of our own making. Nikki Giovanni. CoCRD p.26
All Right Mama! June Vanleer Williams. WiRYPS p.19
All that I can see of you are your swift strong hands resting lightly on the porch railing. Countess W. Twitty. EbR p.148
All that I ran from I held in my hands. Quandra Prettyman. PoBA p.260
All that night I prayed for eyes to see again. Alice Walker. ONC p.39
All the best minds come into wisdom early. Lucille Clifton. GoNAE p.21
All the bldgs fell thru. Ntozake Shange. DaGe p.61
All the Clocks. Carolyn Rodgers. BlSp p.184
All the clocks are off or have stopped in the Black Ghetto. Carolyn Rodgers. BlSp p.184
All the pretty baubles spread are not the answer to my need. Georgia Douglas Johnson. ALC p.31; ANP p. 87; ReFNA p.26
All the Renegade Ghosts Rise. ** Thulani Davis. AlTRGR p.43
All the World Moved.** June Jordan. NBP p.89; PoBA p. 303; Sch p.24; ThTDID p.13
Allyou violated ones with gentle hearts. Margaret Walker. BlP p.157; BlPo p.24; FoM p.32; PFND p.18; PoBA p.150; UNBP p.165
Alla Tha's All Right, But. June Jordan. PaNP p.52
Allah is the most high. Anonymous. MBP p.61
Alloted a four-by-four square. Yvette Johnson. TNV p.57
Alone. Maya Angelou. OhPWFW p. 18
Alone. Nikki Giovanni. BrT p. 65; EgT p.20; ReC p.10; WoATM p.37
Alone I tiptoe through the stars. Naomi Long Madgett. BlP p.195; OnATM p.40; StBS p.52
Alone mingus in the best lives of which some touch. Mari Evans. WhIAM p.16
Alone, not blue, just alone! Kattie M. Cumbo. NiBPo p.56
Alone! yes, evermore alone-- isolate each his way. Georgia Douglas Johnson, AVAN p.208

HWAOP p.29
Aloofness. Pauli Murray. DaTAOP p.83
Alphaomegadeltasigmakappazeta sssssss (sing-song fashion) Carolyn M. Rodgers. SoBB p. 27
Already I am no longer looked at with lechery or love. Gwendolyn Brooks. BeEa p.39; SPGB p.94; WoOGB p.337
Although he has not seen Pepita, Loam Norton considers Belsen and Dachau. Gwendolyn Brooks. BlPo p.22
Although he Returned to the Parsonage for Lunch Father Spent Tuesdays and Thursdays Visiting. ** Gloria Oden. TiTBi p.7
Although I work and sweat and gleam so shiny bright. Iola Brister. EbR p.14
Always. Naomi Long Madgett. OnATM p.35
Always at dusk, the same tearless experience. Angelina Weld Grimke. CaD p.37
Always in the middle of our bloodiest battles. Audre Lorde. ChPON p.47; FrLWP p. 29
Always there are children. Nikki Giovanni. WoATM p.58
Am gonna take me seriously. Sonia Sanchez. BrT p.140; WABP p.48
Am I Not a Human Being. E. Sharon Gomillion. FoAAM p.9
Am I to be cursed forever with becoming somebody else on the way to myself: Audre Lorde. ChPON p.40; FrLWP p.27
Amamil is white, The. Kali Grosvenor. PBK p.44
Ambassador. Bessie Woodson Yancey. EcFTH p.27
Amber-child of love colour of honey. Mitchelene Morgan. ThHSD p.17
Ambition. Josephine D. (Henderson) Heard. MoGl p.120
Ambrosia. Julia Fields. GaBW p. 301
Amen Sister. Colleen McElroy. MuDLSG p.8
Amen sister fans the heat toward the Lord. Colleen McElroy. MuDLSG p.8
America. Maya Angelou. OhPWFW p.29
America/an overdeveloped animosity stamping out the dreams. Vanessa Howard. ScWh p.3
America land of free/dom. Sonia Sanchez. HoC p.18
America Negra. Anita Scott Coleman. EbR p.48
America 1973. Jayne Cortez, Scar p.21
America the men & women in the early stages of your youth. Carolyn M. Rodgers. HeAEG p.67
American Beauty Rose. Kattie M. Cumbo. NiBPo p.44
American Cancer Society or There is More Than One Way to Skin a Coon, The. Audre Lorde. ChPON p.68; NaPr p. 71; NeHS p.7
American Coach of Aesthetics, An. Margaret Danner. ImOAAF p.13
Amid the surging throng one face I sought. Josephine D. (Henderson) Heard. MoGl p.99
Amoeba is lucky it's so small, An. Nikki Giovanni. ThWRNW p.45
Among everybody's acquaintances is always that one reflective. Julia Fields. BlLi p.530
Among farms and forests a family labors for sustenance and meaning. Pamela Cobb. InDM p.23
Amos is a shepherd of suffering sheep. Margaret Walker. PFND p,25
Amos - 1963. Margaret Walker. PFND p.25
Amour. Georgia Douglas Johnson. ALC p.46
AMSAC. Margaret Danner. ImOAAF p.7
An u got a re vo lu tion goin'. Sonia Sanchez. WABP p.68
Analysis. June Vanleer Williams

WiRYPS p.9
Anatomy. Harryette Mullen. TTW p.48
Anatomy of Frustration. Kattie M. Cumbo. GaBW p.287
Ancestor on the Auction Block. Vera Bell. YoBBI p.104
And Always. Jayne Cortez. Scar p.41
And always having to speak in spaces. Jayne Cortez. Scar p.41
And always there are the children. Nikki Giovanni. WoATM p.58
An Another Look at You. Jayne Cortez. Scar p.20
And Another Thing. Nikki Giovanni MyH p.62
And await the Answers. Alice Walker. RePOP p.34
& Bearers. Carolyn M. Rodgers. HeAEG p.29
And Beauty's All Around. Julia Fields. NiBPo p.72
And besides, you were my father and I loved you fiercely. Pinkie Gordon Lane. WiTh p. 11
...and bless Uncle Jim, amen. Frenchy J. Hodges. BlW p.18
And Death went Down. Josie Berry. NegVo p.13
And did I think the fall unbeautiful when I was young? Naomi Long Madgett. OnATM p. 11
And Don't Think I Won't be Waiting. Audre Lorde. ChPON p.89; NeHS p.32
And every now and then I think about the river. Nikki Giovanni. BFBTBJ p.13
And every thing that if any thing begins again. Sonia Sanchez. WABP p.39
And fall Shall Sit in Judgment. Audre Lorde. NNPUSA p.20
And finally the air settles down to a comfortable moist calm. Pinkie Gordon Lane. MyFe p. 14
And From Your Mouth. ** Jayne Cortez. Scar p.59
And God saw the light. Mae Jackson. CaPWY p.17
And He Carves These "Dudes". Margaret Danner. DoOAT p.93
And his Fingers Peeled. Alice Walker. RePOP p.56
And how will future history classify you. Beatrice M. Murphy. RoCo p.10
& i a beginner in yr/love say no. Sonia Sanchez. BlP p.238; NaPr p.129; RoATW p.55; WABP p.38
And I entered into young womanhood. Sonia Sanchez. BluB p.30
And I moved and went and sat next to a white man. Carolyn M. Rodgers. HoIGO p. 21
And I say to you enjoy this time. Barbara Malone. Suga p.22
And I used to play around a lot. Wanda Coleman. MaDBL p.30
And I, Woman cloaked in blues sit knitting prison days. Irma McClaurin. BlSi p.197
And if the sun comes how shall we greet him? Gwendolyn Brooks. AnA p.50; SPGB p. 62; WoOGB p.114
And in the first place the flowing of the river. June Jordan. PaNP p.73
And in the Hourly Making. Alice Walker. RePOP p.35
And in the quiet of our moist blackness. Pearl Cleage Lomax. WeDNNM p.7
And it Shall Come to Pass. Josephine D. (Henderson) Heard. MoGl p.123
And it will be ours. Sonia Sanchez. ItND p.28
And it's familiar this fact of flame. Jayne Cortez. COAG p.48; MoOP p.54
And Liz got mad. Ruth Duckett Gibbs. GLOWC p.20
And now a moment of feeling my limbs. Pinkie Gordon Lane. MyFe p.43
And now as one who closes up the house and goes uncaring where. Georgia Douglas Johnson. ALC p.21
And now the ripped air slowly, slowly mends. Pinkie Gordon Lane. DeRi p.9; WiTh p.24

And now to overcome what? Jayne Cortez. COAG p.84
And one night in my tennis shoe smell I was no longer influenced by invisible crimes. Jayne Cortez. FeAF p.43
And our tree grew as trees do (up) Paulette Jones. TGWL p.58
And several strengths from drowsiness campaigned. Gwendolyn Brooks. BlP p.170; ITM p.49; PoBA p.163; WoOGB p.421;
And She Bleeds. Ntozake Shange. NaEd p.123
And she shall be the friend of youth for age. Angelina Weld Grimke. ANP p.87; ReFNA p.24
And since each day is a long shadow stretching the evening. Pinkie Gordon Lane. WiTh p.43
And So it is With Love. Mae V. Cowdery. WLOV p.39
And so they came. Lillie Kate Walker Benitez. UNBP p.313
And so we Talk. Countess W. Twitty. EbR p.147
And some days I would like to embrace my weary brown neighbors on this narrow filthy street. Pearl Cleage Lomax. WeDNNM p.14
And some where distantly there is an answer. Angela Jackson. VoDLM p.19
And Sometimes I Sit. Nikki Giovanni. ReC p.47; WoATM p.18
And still the days went by. Naomi Long Madgett. PhN p. 74
And/Still/We/Live/On...Vanessa Howard. ScWh p.1
And still we wear our uniforms. Gwendolyn Brooks. AmLNA p. 90; SPGB p.28; StIB p.57; WoOGB p.59
And suddenly I felt at one with the waves. Margaret Danner. DoOAT p.26
And the blue dusk folded us into our narrow room. Naomi Long Madgett. ExAE p.62
And the Hotel Room Held Only Him. ** Mari Evans. IABW p.37; WhIAM p.17
And the Joy. Sonia Sanchez. IvBAW p.81
And the night I undressed myself. Pearl Cleage Lomax. WeDDNM p.12
...And the Old Women Gathered. ** Mari Evans. BlLi p.434; BlSi p.146; DaS p.510; DeDF p.47; KAL p.175; NNPUSA p.79; PoBA p.187
And the people live till they have white hair. Gwendolyn Brooks. SPGB p.61
And the small fry little folk slant-eye devil gooks. June Jordan. ThTDID p.147
And the sun exploded in my soul. Katherine L. Cuestas. EbR p.76
And the trumpet sounds. Sonia Sanchez. BluB p.52
And Then. Johari Amini. ImIB p.13
And they were mostly all blk. Sonia Sanchez. WABP p.34
& Then. Ntozake Shange. NaEd p.45
And Then She Said. Alexis De Veaux. CoAAAW p.98
And there is no finality. Pinkie Gordon Lane. WiTh p.57
And there like a huge scaly rat in a mesh. Margaret Danner. DoOAT p.106
And they shall rise and cast their mantles by. Georgia Douglas Johnson. BrBV p.15
And this silly wire (which some consider essential, connected us and we came together) Nikki Giovanni. BFBTBJ p.12
And though I heard the eagle's cry. Jennifer Blackman Lawson. BlIMT p.9
And Through the Caribbean Sea. Margaret Danner. AfAWA p. 638; BlP p.152; DoDAT p. 117; PoCo p.15
And to Lake Michigan's lions that guard Chicago's art. Margaret Danner. DoOAT p. 21
And to Their Friends. Margaret Danner. DoOAT p.23
And to this man who turned

the other cheek. Margaret Danner. DeDF p.95; DoOAT p. 98; IrLa p.18; PoCo p.51; UNBP p.231
And we came that sun day etheridge & i to that quiet/looooking/ street. Sonia Sanchez. TGWL p.86; WABP p.58
Ane We Shall Eat to Live. Jeanette Adams. ThHSD p.32
And we will lace the jungle on and step out. Lucille Clifton. GoNAE p.19
And What About the Children. Audre Lorde. CaTR p.17; ChPON p. 15; COAL p.46; NaPr p.68; PoBA p.24
And what do I have to make me smile. Frenchy J. Hodges. BlW p.7
And what of the old bearded man collecting bottles. Sonia Sanchez. LoP p.38
And what sane (Western) reason is there. Margaret Danner. DoOAT p.95
And when I come to see you again, I will bring my gifts. Mae V. Cowdery. WLOV p.43
And when I first went back to church I was not there. Carolyn M. Rodgers. HeAEG p. 35
And when I was all alone facing my adolescence. Nikki Giovanni. MoCAP p.172
And When she Died We Cried. Carolyn M. Rodgers. HeAEG p. 36
And When she Thought of Him. Alice Walker. RePOP p.54
And when she was lonely...she would go into the room. Nikki Giovanni. ThWRNW p.57
And When the Fire Won't go Out. S. Diane Bogus. WITM p.25
And When the Revolution Came. Carolyn M. Rodgers. HoIGO p. 65
And when this modern onyema of touch. Margaret Danner. DoOAT p.91
And when you have forgotten the bright bedclothes on a Wednesday and a Saturday. Gwendolyn Brooks. BlP p.168
SoOM p.559; StIB p.18; WoOGB p.20
And While we are Waiting. Carolyn M. Rodgers. JuBa p. 127
And Who Are You? June Jordan. SCh p.21; ThTDID p.98
And who shall separate the dust which later we shall be. Georgia Douglas Johnson. AmNP p.20; ITBLA p.155; PoBA p.22; TYBP p.209
And wilt thou come no more. Josephine D. (Henderson) Heard. MoGl p.114
And yet there were times when sun turned to willows. Pinkie Gordon Lane. PoBBl p.12; WiTh p.48
And you begin to grow, but no one notices. Barbara Anne Baxter. TNV p.16
And you have wrapped a web about the darkest dreams. Pinkie Gordon Lane. WiTh p.24
And you wake up and you roll over and see me. Pearl Cleage Lomax. WeDNNM p.5
And you white girl shall I call you sister now? Carolyn M. Rodgers. HoIGO p.49
Andre. Gwendolyn Brooks. MyNIB p.66
Angela. Damali (Denise Burnett) IATWMB p.15
Angela Davis. Alice S. Cobb. BlSi p.147
Angela Davis tall, fair, and Wiry-haired, black people prayed and hoped for you. Alice S. Cobb. BlSi p.147
Angels. Lucille Clifton. TwW p.31
Angels craving for a lark rubbed the stars to make a spark. Gwendolyn Bennett. HeD p.2
Angie Saves Her Man. Lucile D. Goodlett. WGC p.64
Angrily I looked at the squirming mass thrust upon the muddy ground. Jeanette Adams. ThHSD p.32
Anguish. Pauli Murray. DaTAOP p.88
Animal runs, it passes, it dies

and it is the great cold, The Anonymous. TYBP p.3
Animal squats in the corner beside thespians. Judy Dothard Simmons. JuB p.21
Anna Speaks of the Childhood of Mary her Daughter. Lucille Clifton. TwW p.35
Anniad, The. Gwendolyn Brooks. AnA p.19; BlSi p.102; SPGB p.38; WoOGB p.83
Annie Allen. Gwendolyn Brooks. SPGB p.31; WoOGB p.61
Anniversary. Audre Lorde. ChPON p.4; COAL p.68
Anniversary. Beatrice M. Murphy. NegVo p.113
Anniversary. Jill Witherspoon Boyer. DrF p.12
Anonymous Verse from a Puerto Rican Christmas Card. Anonymous. ChG p.81
Anonymous water can slide under the ground. Lucille Clifton. TwW p.55
Anonymous Witness. Naomi Long Madgett. ExAE p.57
Another Day. Isabella Maria Brown. PoNe p.342
Another Drink—Feet tilted on the grass. Julia Fields. GaBW p.301
Another Man Don Gon. Anonymous. BlWOA p.459
Another of the clowns is dead. Sonia Sanchez. LoP p.31
Another Time, Another Place. Kattie M. Cumbo. NiBPo p.47
Another youthful advocate of truth and right has gone. Ada. BlSi p.21
Answer, The. Judy Dothard Simmons. JuB p.10; UNBP p. 465
Answer, The. Phillis Wheatley. PPW p.84
Answer, to the Rebus by the Author of These Poems, An. Phillis Wheatley. PAL p.93; PPW p.60
Answer to yo/question of am I not yo/woman even if u went on shit again. Sonia Sanchez. BlP p.238; NaPr p.129; RoATW p.55; WABP p.38
An't M'lissy's Tater Pies. Bessie Woodson Yancey. EcFTH p.40
Antigone and Oedipus. Henrietta Cordelia Ray. BlSi p.40; EBAP p.141
Anunt jemina dead. Kali Grosvenor. PBK p.33
Anxiety. Ruby Berkley Goodwin. NegVo p.61
Any Woman's Blues. Sherley Williams. PePo p.11
Any Woman's Blues. Sherley Williams. PePo p.25
Apollo's wrath, to man the dreadful spring. Phillis Wheatley. EaNAW p.44; PAL p.94; PPW p.97
Apologia. Mari Evans. IABW p. 47
Apology. Sonia Sanchez. LoP p. 34
Apology To an Old Man Who Only Wanted to Chat. Jennifer Blackman Lawson. BlIMT p.18
Apology to my Little Daughter for Apparent Neglect. Margaret T. G. Burroughs. WhSIT p.10
Apology (To the Panthers) Lucille Clifton. GoNAE p. 6
Apparation of my early markings. Thulani Davis. AlTRGR p.57
Appeal to my Countrywomen, An. Frances Ellen Watkins Harper. BlSi p.31; PBFH p. 72
Appearances. Jayne Cortez. Scar p.17
Appendix to the Anniad. Gwendolyn Brooks. AnA p.30; BlSi p.111; SPGB p.50; WoOGB p.94
Apple trees are blooming out, The. Lucy Mae Turner. BCP p.64
Apple Trees By the River. Lucy Mae Turner. BCP p.64
Apples. Ariel Williams Holloway. BTh p.30
Apples spotted and scarred on the outside. Ariel Williams Holloway. BTh p.30
Apprehension. Pinkie Gordon Lane. WiTh p.56

April in Your Eyes. Naomi Long Madgett. PhN p.46
April is On The Way. Alice Dunbar Nelson. EbAT p.52; ReFNA p. 32
April Longing. Mary Wilkerson Cleaves. EbR p.46
Arabs ain't got no/thing, The. Sonia Sanchez. IvBAW p.72
Archangels have the power to shift. Margaret Danner. DoOAT p.129
Archibald McLeish is a name for baseball bats. Carole Gregory Clemmons. NiBPo p.86
Are these millions of white velvety petalled bell. Margaret Danner. PoCo p.22
Are you French? Eleanor Weaver. NegVo p.162
Are you out there trying to cop a bag. E. Sharon Gomillion. FoAAM p.27
Aretha. Mae Jackson. CaPWY p.7
Aretha churchless wo manned a Columbus ship. S. Diane Bogus. WITM p.43
Aretha come bring your piano. Mae Jackson. CaPWY p.7
Aria. Carole Gregory Clemmons. NiBPo p.84
Arise, my soul, on wings enraptur'd, rise. Phillis Wheatley. EBAP p.101
Armageddon. Georgia Douglas Johnson. ALC p.32
Armor. Georgia Douglas Johnson. ALC p.57; RoATW p.136
Arrival. Naomi Long Madgett. PiLAF p.30
Arrive in the afternoon, the late light slanting. Gwendolyn Brooks. MoCAP p.83; SPGB p. 90; WoOGB p.333
Arrive: the ladies from the Ladies' Betterment League arrive in the afternoon. Gwendolyn Brooks. BeEa p.35; MoCAP p.83; WoOGB p.333
Art in the Court of the Blue Fag (1) Wanda Coleman. MaDBL p.81
Art in the Court of the Blue Fag (2) Wanda Coleman. MaDBL p.83
Art in the Court of the Blue Fag (3) Wanda Coleman. MaDBL p.84
Art in the Court of the Blue Fag (4) Wanda Coleman MaDBL p.89
Art in the Court of the Blue Fag (5) Wanda Coleman MaDBL p.95
Art in the Court of the Blue Fag (6) Wanda Coleman MaDBL p.101
Art of Charles White is like making love in the early evening, The. Nikki Giovanni. ThWRNW p.28
Art thou the child who led me from all things. Naomi Long Madgett. PhN p.118
Artful Pose. Maya Angelou. OhPWFW p.35
Artic Tern in a Museum. Effie Lee Newsome. PoN p.56; PoNe p.71
Artisan. Audre Lorde. BlUn p.87
Artist looked up from his painting and saw in his doorway there a tiny maid with pecan-colored skin and a mass of black tangled hair. Constance Nichols. EbR p.110
Artists' and Models' Ball, The. Gwendolyn Brooks. BeEa p.67; BlVo p.461; WoOGB p.365
As a Basic. Linda Porter. OnOW p.7
As a Businessman. Margaret Danner DoOAT p.92
As a child I was constantly reminded of the size of my eyes. Elouise Loftin. PoBA p.514
As a goldfish sees the world. L. Doretha Lowery. BTh p.63
As a Masai warrior with his burning spear. Lethonia Gee. BlFi p.222; RoATW p. 24
As a young Black man from Augusta, Georgia it was very hard. Olean Bess. MiFe p.11
As Critic. Margaret Danner. TGWL p.29
As elusive sleep descends I dream of Christmas. June Vanleer Williams. WiRYPS p. 85
As evening's cloak upon our moral

heads descends. Constance E. Berkley. PoBBL p.43
As for the hopes that others fondle. Margaret Danner. DoOAT p.136
As I am, I should be able to balance water jugs on my head. Carolyn M. Rodgers. JuBa p.116
As I Grow Up Again. Audre Lorde. ChPON p.44; DeRi p.17; FrLWP p.17
As (i) lay the patient on the operative table i remove his horn-rimed glasses. Alicia Loy Johnson. NiBPo p.155
As I look into each different face, I am exalted. Margaret Danner. DoOAT p.114; IrLa p.11
As I sat down, the old lady waitress asked "Is someone joining you dear?" S. Diane Bogus. WITH p.8
As I walk alone, the world seems a vacuum. Eleanor Thomas-Grumbach. MoSu p.24
As I was going to town. Lula Lowe Weeden. CaD p.22
As long as you can walk in higher places. Eleanor Weaver. NegVo p.161
As my eyes stroke these kittens. Margaret Danner. DoOAT p.38
As my heart burned I discovered memory. Audre Lorde. NeHS p.25
As o'er thy loved one now in grief ye bendeth. Josephine D. (Henderson) Heard. MoGl p.83
As Other Women Give Birth to Children.** Gloria Oden. RESUR p.29
As polished as the dull satin dress. Margaret Danner. DoOAT p.45
As possible as yeast. Lucille Clifton. OrW p.59
As-Salaam-Alaikum my Black Princess the morning awaits u. Sonia Sanchez. BlSp p.118 ItND p.7
As Seen by Disciplines. Gwendolyn Brooks. ITM p.44; PoBA p. 159; WoOGB p.416
As Simple as That. Nola Richardson. WhOL p.67
As soon as the first delicious chortle smashed the air, I became a wiser, smarter, and more intuitive person. Margaret T. G. Burroughs. WhSIT p.29
As spring came in I recalled that other year. May Miller. ClAB p.39
As suddenly as love the evening burns a low red. June Jordan. ThTDID p.78
As the pine day's green lengthens into blue space. Linda Brown Bragg. LoSBM p.23
As the steel is tried and tested. Bessie Woodson Yancey. EcFTH p.20
As the word came to prophets of old. Margaret Walker. BlP p.160
As the word was given to prophets of old. Margaret Walker. BrT p.150; PFND p.22
As things be/come, let's destroy. Nikki Giovanni. BFBTBJ p.39; BOL p.9; EgT p.22; PoBA p. 450
As we all probably realize on some level, people are basically selfish. Nikki Giovanni. BFBTBJ p.87
As we fight we learn nothing human is all nice. Lyn. SiSH p.12
"...As when emotion too far exceeds its cause" Elizabeth Bishop. Gloria Oden. KAL p.183; MoCAP p.96; RoATW p.143
As You Entered my Life.** Patricia Parker. MoIB p.131
As you search over this year with eyes your heart has sharpened. Audre Lorde. BlUn p.46
Asante Sana, Te Te. Thadious M. Davis. BlSi p.280
Ash at the end of our street peels like papyrus, The. Rita Brady Keifer. NeJCL p.8
(Aside, An) Carolyn M. Rodgers. SOBB p.19

Ask the March skies how constant is your joy. Naomi Long Madgett. OnATM p.32
Aspect of Love, Alive in the Ice and Fire, An. Gwendolyn Brooks. AfAWA p.585; BlP p. 179; RIOT p. 21
Assassin dealt America a shattering blow to her solar plexus. Beatrice M. Murphy. RoCo p. 10
Assassination. Patricia Parker. DOBB p.110
Assets, Bessie Woodson Yancey. EcFTH p.21
Assets. Jayne Cortez. Scar p. 53
Association. Naomi Long Madgett. PhN p.27
Associations: years of being ashamed. Wanda Coleman. MaDBL p.121
Assurance. Josephine D. (Henderson) Heard. MoGl p.21
Astrologer Predicts at Mary's Birth, The. Lucille Clifton. TwW p.34
Astronaut of Inner Space, The. Harryette Mullen. TTW p.43
Asylum. Regina Williams. CoAAAW p.378
At April. Angelina Weld Grimke. BlSi p.61
At day I see the pretty flowers. Naomi Long Madgett. PhN p. 14
At each turn I hear. Sonia Sanchez. LoP p.9
At fifteen pain called me. Carolyn M. Rodgers. HeAEG p.7
At first I thought you were talking about... Audre Lorde. BlUn p.29
At home I must be humble, meek, surrendering the other cheek. Georgia Douglas Johnson. EbR p.94
At Home in Africa. Margaret Danner. DoOAT p.112
At Home in Dakar. Margaret Danner. BlSi p.133; FBPA p.50
At last, at last the sage of Anacostia is at rest. Josephine D (Henderson) Heard. MoGl p.125
At last we killed the Roaches. Lucille Clifton. OrW p.81
At least it helps me to think about my son. June Jordan. ThTDID p.12
At least one poem for you, George. Pinkie Gordon Lane. WiTh p.27
At morn when gentle breezes play. Josephine D. (Henderson) Heard. MoGl p.109
At night the trees catch stars in their branches and hold them. Harryette Mullen. TTW p.21
At Sea. Vera Guerard. TNV p. 46
At the Art Exhibit, Luis Suarez, cuban accented. Carole Gregory Clemmons. NiBPo p.88
At the Carnival. Anne Spencer. BANP p.215; BlSi p.68; CaD p.53; CNAW p.271; KAL p.35; KAL p.271; NeCa p.352; NeNRe p.81; PoN p.52; PoNe p.62
At the Center of Me. Sonia Sanchez. IvBAW p.71
At the ceremony of Emobo I feel your embrace. Kattie M. Cumbo. BlSi p.137
At the Ebony Circle. Helen G. Quigless. TNV p.94
At the hairdresser's. Gwendolyn Brooks. StIB p.35;
At the Lincoln Monument in Washington, August 28, 1963. Margaret Walker. PFND p.16
At the lip of a big black vagina. Wanda Coleman. MaDBL p.13
At the Top. Wanda Coleman. MaDBL p.16
At the top of your tie the dressy maroon number with me. June Jordan. ThTDID p. 20
At Times One Can Know. Thulani Davis. AlTRGR p.62
Athwart the sky the great sun sails. Georgia Douglas Johnson. HWOP p.21
Atonement. Naomi Long Madgett. PhN p.20

Atrocities. Nikki Giovanni. MyH p.54
Attar. Georgia Douglas Johnson. ALC p.28
Attend my lays, ye ever honour'd nine. Phillis Wheatley. ANP p.10; BlWOA p.42; CNAW p.12; EaNAW p.40; ReFNA p.5
August. Akua Lezli Hope. CoAAAW p.142
August The 12th. Lucille Clifton. TwW p.10
August 'twas the twenty-fifth seventeen hundred forty-six. Lucy Terry. BlP p.37; BlSi p.12; EBAP p.4; ITBLA p.27; PoN p.3; PoNe p.3
August 28, 1967, Marci dear, we have talked some about this thing. Johari Amini. LetGSW p.14
Aunt Agnes Hatcher Tells. Lucille Clifton. TwW p.18
Aunt Dolly. Carolyn M. Rodgers. CoAAAW p.313
Aunt Jamima Dead. Kali Grosvenor. BlSp p.106
Aunt Jessie. Wanda Coleman. MaDBL p.116
Aura. Harryette Mullen. TTW p. 40
Autobiography. Pamela Cobb. InDM p.42
Autumn. Georgia Douglas Johnson. ALC p.6
Autumn. Sonia Sanchez. IvBAW p.68
Autumn a bonfire of leaves. Sonia Sanchez. IvBAW p.68
Autumn Morning. Patricia Parker. ChOM p.30; MoIB p.151
Autumn Night. Naomi Long Madgett. PhN p.33
Autumn Poems. Nikki Giovanni. ReC p.13; WoATM p.32
Autumnal. Naomi Long Madgett. PhN p.34
Awake my soul...awake! Mae V. Cowdery. WLOV p.60
Awaken a flower/petal turn from the bulb. Fayola Kamaria Ama. CoAAAW p.48
Awakening. Naomi Long Madgett. PhN p.77
Awakening. Pinkie Gordon Lane. WiTh p.44
Awakening rumor of the necessity for your death. Audre Lorde. BlUn p.66
Away from earth and it's cares set free. Josephine D. (Henderson) Heard. MoGl p. 40
Away From you These Sheets are Mummy Tapes. Sonia Sanchez. IvBAW p.70
Awning of funeral home along Harlem's broad avenues, yawn, The. Adrienne Ingrum. CoAAAW p.158
Awriiiight mm yeah caught the black boy talkin. Judy Dothard Simmons. UNBP p.364
Axis. Pamela Cobb. InDM p.28
Azure skies and pink pools are for the young. Pinkie Gordon Lane. WiTh p.28

- B -

Babies are crying, The. Katherine Dunham. GaBW p.297
Babies I have not been able to have, The. Toi Derricotte. EmDH p.14
Babies of Biafra, The. Katherine Dunham. GaBW p. 297
Baby baby tell me what did I do wrong? Mari Evans. NIGHT p.12
Baby Hair. Constance Nichols. EbR p.110
Baby Mine. Negro Work Song, USA. MyNIB p.44
Baby You are Sweet. Sonia Sanchez. IvBAW p.69
Back Again. Pinkie Gordon Lane. WiTh p.44
Back Home in Benin City. Jayne Cortez. Scar p.28
Back in those days white folks made public provisions for us. Jennifer Blackman Lawson. BlIMT p.27
Back Into the Garden. Sarah Webster Fabio. BlSi p.139; DOBB p.31
Backdoor Blues. Anonymous. BlWOA p.887
Backslidin'. Bessie Woodson

Yancey. EcFTH p.44
Backstage. Jill Witherspoon Boyer DrF p.11
Backward Look, A. Pinkie Gordon Lane. WiTh p.55
Backwater Blues. Anonymous. AfAWA p.303
Bad Johnny. Sandra Royster. WoTa p.22
Bad Man Ballad. Anonymous. AfAWA p.298
Bad-Man Stagolee. Margaret Means. FMP p.35
Bad Penny. Naomi Long Madgett. OnATM p.51
Bahamas-I. Kattie M. Cumbo. NiBPo p.48
Bahamas-II. Kattie M. Cumbo. NiBPo p.48
Baker's boy delivers loaves, The. Effie Lee Newsome. CaD p.58; GoS p.26
Baker's Boy, The. Effie Lee Newsome. CaD p.58; GoS p.26
Balances. Nikki Giovanni. BFBTBJ p.90; MoCAP p.171
Ballad.. Sonia Sanchez. LoP p.41
Ballad for Ashes. Audre Lorde. BlUn p.65
Ballad for Sterling Street, The. Sonia Sanchez. BrT p.146; WABP p.66
Ballad for the Brother. Freedah Allah. RoATW p.109
Ballad From Childhood. Audre Lorde. ChPON p.73; NeHS p.41
Ballad of Chocolate Mabbie. Gwendolyn Brooks. SPGB p.7; StIB p.12; WoOGB p.14
Ballad of Late Annie, The. Gwendolyn Brooks. AnA p.10
Ballad of Pearl May Lee. Gwendolyn Brooks. StIB p.42; WoOGB p.44
Ballad of Rudolph Reed, The. Gwendolyn Brooks. BeEa p.62; SoS p.46; SPGB p.110; WoOGB p.360
Ballad of the Brown Girl. Alice Walker. ONC p.72
Ballad of the Free, The. Margaret Walker. PFND p.10; UNBP p. 166
Ballad of the Hoppy-Toad. Margaret Walker. BlSi p.99; FBPA p.107; NeBV p.303; PFND p.29; UNBP p.161
Ballad of the Light-Eyed Little Girl, The. Gwendolyn Brooks. AnA p.41; SPGB p. 56; WoOGB p.105
Ballade Des Belles Milatraisses. Rosalie Jonas. BlSi p.55
Ballet, like a chosen sprig, must be grafted. Margaret Danner. DoOAT p.54; IrLa p.24
Ballit of de Boll Weevil, De. Anonymous. ITBLA p.121
Baptism. Alice Walker. RePOP p.23
Bare Uncovered Bulb, A. Yvette Johnson. TNV p.56
Barred. Naomi Evans Vaughn. EbR p.150
Barren. Audre Lorde. NeHS p.23
Bars Fight, August 28, 1746. Lucy Terry. BlP p.37; BlSi p.12; EBAP p.4; ITBLA p. 27; PoN p.3; PoNe p.3
Bathroom is a Meeting Place, The. Carolyn M. Rodgers. HeAEG p.44
Baton Rouge. Pinkie Gordon Lane. WiTh p.19
Baton Rouge #2. Pinkie Gordon Lane. MyFe p.24
Bats. Effie Lee Newsome. GoS p.193
Battle, The. Gwendolyn Brooks. StIB p.37; WoOGB p.39
Battles have not halted, The. Margaret Danner. DoOAT p.96
Bazaar. Audre Lorde. BlUn p.107
Be a Good Sport. ** Bessie Woodson Yancey. EcFTH p.26
Be Cool Brother. E. Sharon Gomillion. FoAAM p.26
Be cool you say. E. Sharon Gomillion. FoAAM p.26
Be Daedalus. Nanina Alba. PoBA p.169; PoNe p.329
Be Daedalus: make wings. Nanina Alba. PoBA p.169; PoNe p. 329
Be Like This Porcupine Fish. Margaret Danner. DoOAT p.75
Be me a Pharaoh. Maya Angelou. OhPWFW p.31
Be Michael. Margaret Danner. DoOAT p.130
Be Nobody's Darling. Alice Walker.

RePOP p.31
Be who you are and will be. Audre Lorde. ChPON p.42; FrLWP p.7
Be quiet awful woman. Lucille Clifton. OrW p.57
Be silent and listen. Pamela Cobb. InDM p.38
Beach With Okra & Greens/on their Honeymoon/Banda Abao, Curacao. Ntozake Shange. DaGe p.74
Beaches: Why I Don't Care for Them. Wanda Coleman. MaDBL p.121
Beachscape. Barbara Mahone. Suga p.22
Beads around my neck. Alice Walker. ONC p.3
Beale Street (Of the Mind) Reaffirmed. Margaret Danner. DoOAT p.95
Bean Eaters, The. Gwendolyn Brooks. BeEa p.16; BlEx p. BlSi p.101; ITBLA p.217; KAL p.159; MoCAP p.81; PoBA p.154; SoS p.23; SPGB p.72; TYBP p.245; WoOGB p. 314
Bear the Rhythm of Your Name. Sonia Sanchez. IvBAW p.79
Beatitude, A. S. Diane Bogus. WITM p.50
Be A Trice does the dinner. Mari Evans. IABW p.58
Be A Trice has the dinner done. IABW p.58
Beaufort, fair Beaufort thou art a favored spot. Josephine D. (Henderson) Heard. MoGl p.35
Beautiful, Black and Beloved. Margaret T. G. Burroughs. GLOWC p.49; WhSIT p.19
Beautiful Black Me. Loretta Rodgers. RoATW p.78; ThHSD p.82
Beautiful Black Men. Nikki Giovanni. BFBTBJ p.71; BlP p.320; BrT p.57; EgT p.25
Beautiful night, I walk into you. Kattie M. Cumbo. NiBPo p.55
Beautiful? You Are the Most. Margaret Danner. DoOAT p.132; IrLa p.5; PoCo p.9
Beautiful you rise upon the horizon of heaven. Anonymous. MBP p.3; TYBP p.21
Beauty lodged just fleetingly today within my grasp. Ethylynne E. Holmes. NegVo p.75
Beauty of Black, The. Margaret T. G. Burroughs. WhSIT p.18
Beauty Shoppe. Gwendolyn Brooks. AnA p.53; WoOGB p.117
Because. Nikki Giovanni. CoCRD p.47
Because. Sonia Sanchez. AfAA p.3; LoP p.14
Because a burning sword notches both of my doorposts. Audre Lorde. BlUn p.25
Because beer tingles like tear drippings. Melba Joyce Boyd. BlSi p.285; CaEADW p.34
Because he cared for plants he earned the name "Green Thumb." Eloise Culver. GANIV p.45
Because I am not just I alone. Naomi Long Madgett. AmLNA p. 86; OnATM p.52
Because I Can. Naomi Long Madgett. PhN p.53; SoTPN p.20
Because I know deep in my own heart. Pauli Murray. BlSi p.93
Because I love you, have created out of you, I want to own you. S. Diane Bogus. WITM p.31
Because I starve in my hunger. Coston Vale. NegVo p.159
Because no man would taste you. Lucille Clifton. TwW p.13
Because of Beauty. Sharon Scott. TGWL p.89
Because of its spines the thistle has been misrepresented. Margaret Danner. DoOAT p.14
Because of you I have lost my night to heaven. Countess W. Twitty. EbR p.147
Because they passed it on to U. Angela Jackson. VoDLM p.15
Because we failed for a child who died from an overdose of heroin. Angela Jackson. VoDLM p.15
Bedbug. Anonymous. GoS p.15; MBP p.41; UNBP p.88
Bedtime Story. Nayo. NeBV p.382; YoBBI p.437

Beep Beep Poem, The. Nikki Giovanni. CoCRD p.68
Beer Drops. Melba Joyce Boyd. BlSi p.285; CaEADW p.34
Bees, The. Audre Lorde. NeHS p. 45
Before/And After. Johari Amini. JuBa p.167; LetGSW p.27
Before Autumn Leaves Turn Gold. Dorothy Lee Louise Shaed. NegVo p.138
Before I Started to School.** Gloria Oden. RESUR p.115
Before I travel to you. Sonia Sanchez. IvBAW p.75
Before the depression my father bought a used green chandler. Naomi Long Madgett. DeRi p. 5; ExAE p.13
Before the Feast of Shushan. Anne Spencer. BANP p.213; BlSi p.69; CNAW p.264; NeCa p.353; NeNRe p.82
Before the fireplace Grandma Bernice stuffed our plump, yellow palms. Melba Joyce Boyd. CaEADW p.4
Before very long. E. Sharon Gomillion. FoAAM p.27
Beginning for New Beginnings, A. Angela Jackson. VoDLM p.19
Beginnings and End. Naomi Long Madgett. StBS p.15
Behind the Curtain. June Vanleer Williams. WiRYPS p.43
Behold nothing surpasses books. Anonymous. MBP p.1
Behold the Bridge. Corinne Lytle. NegVo p.103
Behold! the living thrilling lines. Georgia Douglas Johnson. HWOP p.46
Being and Nothingness. Nikki Giovanni. CoCRD p.89
Being continually dissatisfied with one's work is not necessarily growth. Thulani Davis. AlTRGR p.60
Being Property Once Myself. Lucille Clifton. GoNAE p.1
Being woman, I write this poem. Pinkie Gordon Lane. WiTh p. 41
Being you, you cut your poetry from wood. Gwendolyn Brooks. BeEa p.68; BTB p.51; DaSp p.501; PoBA p.154; WoOGB p. 366
Believe it love. June Jordan. ThTDID p.59
Believe me--when I say that love like yours, at this belated hour. Georgia Douglas Johnson. ALC p.6
Believe not that all lovely things shall last. Naomi Long Madgett. OnATM p.15
Bell jangles...jars loud. Leatrice Emeruwa. BlGBB p.25
Belle Island. Margaret Danner. PoCo p.22
Belligerent and beautiful as a trapped ibis. Audre Lorde BlUn p.68
Bells, bells, bells, let the bells ring. Sonia Sanchez. BluB p.24
Beloved, in what other lives or lands have I known your lips. Maya Angelou. AnSIR p.13
Beloved where I have been if you loved me. June Jordan. ThTDID p.52
Below de Line. Bessie Woodson Yancey. EcFTH p.46
Bend to Spring. June Vanleer Williams. WiRYPS p.62
Bending waist deep blackfingered smiling sure good mornin madam this is C.T.R. Reed. Mari Evans. NIGHT p.24
Beneath the black elm's verdant shade. Josephine D. (Henderson) Heard. MoGl p.99
Beneath the burden of overjoy tremble, o wires, from east to west! Frances E. W. Harper. EaNAW p.297
Beneath the carving drag of wood the land moves slowly. Audre Lorde. ChPON p.6; COAL p.10; FiCi p.17; SiAS p.41
Beneath the green a flame of scarlet leaps. Naomi Long Madgett. OnATM p.16
Benediction. Georgia Douglas Johnson. BrBV p.50; GoS p. 187
Benison Given, A. Maya Angelou. AnSIR p.27
Benjamin Banneker (Astronomist,

Surveyor, Inventor, 1731-1806, Maryland) Eloise Curver. GANIV p.;3
Bereft. Josephine D. (Henderson) Heard. MoGl p.79
Beserk on Hollywood Boulevard. Wanda Coleman. MaDBL p.80
Beside my man I lay. Judith Bracey. ThHSD p.57
Bessie of Bronzeville visits Mary and Norman at a Beach-House in New Buffalo. Gwendolyn Brooks. BeEa p.59; WoOGB p. 59
Bessie on my wall: the thick triangular nose wedged in the deep brown face nostrils. Sherley Williams. ChOSa p.117
Best for Me, The. Nola Richardson. WhOL p.71
Best Friends. Patricia Parker. MoIB p.103
Best Loved of Africa. Margaret Danner. DoOAT p.73; IrLa p. 22; PoBA p.137
Bête Noire. Harryette Mullen. TTW p.23
Beth. Margaret Danner. DoOAT p. 109
Between a Dancer & a Poet. Ntozake Shange. NaEd p.108
Between Me and Anyone Who Can Understand. Sharon Scott. JuBa p.174
Between Ourselves. Audre Lorde. BlUn p.112
Between rising and now is the non-communication of our labors for daily bread. S. Diane Bogus. WITM p.10
Between sky and sea I stood. May Miller. ClAB p.25
Between 3 and 4 o'clock in the morning she wakes to see the brightest star. Jodi Braxton. SoITM p.31
Between trains it rains. Linda Brown Bragg. LoSBM p.7
Beulah. Elma Stuckey. BiGa p.51
Beverly Hills, Chicago. Gwendolyn Brooks. AnA p.48; SPGB p.61; WoOGB p.112
Beware of body's fire. Pauli Murray. DaTAOP p.76
Beware of the man who listens much and talks little. Josephine D. (Henderson) Heard. MoGl p.103
Beyond Sisters. Wanda Coleman. MaDBL p.33
Beyond What. Alice Walker. RePOP p.69
Beyond Words. Pinkie Gordon Lane. WiTh p.47
Bicentennial Poem #21,000,000. Audre Lorde. BlUn p.90
Bidding, The. Jennifer Blackman Lawson. BlIMT p.22
Big Beautiful bronze man. Jayne Cortez. Scar p.31
Big Bessie Throws Her Son Into the Street. Gwendolyn Brooks. SPGB p.127
Big black lady who has forgotten who she is. Pamela Cobb. InDM p.36
Big Fat Mama. Anonymous. BlWOA p.888
Big Fine Woman From Ruleville. Jayne Cortez. CoAAAW p.94
Big Gate, The. Elma Stuckey. BiGa p.10
Big John Henry. Margaret Walker. FMP p.49
Big Mama. Jennifer Blackman Lawson. BlIMT p.3
Big Maybelle. Paulette Childress White. DeDF p.99; DeRi p.1
Big old houses have passed away. Jodi Braxton. SoITM p.6
Big Slim Gunter lose 'e job. Lucile D. Goodlett. WGC p.43
Big snake swaller up de lil' un. Bessie Woodson Yancey. EcFTH p.59
Bill exists. Ronda Davis. JuBa p.62
Biography. Naomi Long Madgett. OnATM p.25
Bird Catcher, The. Anonymous. TYBP p.28
Bird delicious to the taste, A. Phillis Wheatley. PAL p.92
Bird flies free it is also bound, A. Ann Wallace. GLOWC p.106
Bird is Singing, A. ** Lucy Mae Turner. NegVo p.157
Birds flew south earlier this year, The. Nikki Giovanni. WoATM p.33
Birds of Paradise. Nzadi Zimele-

Keita. CoAAAW p.396
Birmingham. See Poems: Birmingham 1962-1964. Julia Fields
Birmingham. Margaret Walker. PFND p.14; PoBA p.149
Birmingham. Nancy L. Arnez. RoCo p.21
Birth. Linda Thomas. GLOWC p.30
Birth in a Narrow Room. Gwendolyn Brooks. AnA p.3; BlSi p.102; PoN p.191; PoNe p. 335; WoOGB p.67
Birth of Jesus, The. Josephine D. (Henderson) Heard. MoGl p.58
Birth of Memory, The. Lucy Mae Turner. BCF p.29
Birth of the Poet, The. Quandra Prettyman. BOL p.18
Birth of Time, The. Josephine D. (Henderson) Heard. MoGl p.49
Birthday Memorial to Seventh Street, A. Audre Lorde. ChPON p.80; NeHS p.10
Bishop James a Shorter. Josephine D. (Henderson) Heard. MoGl p.77
Bitch! I want to scream. Patricia Parker. MoIB p.125
Bitches Brew. Joanne Jimason. NaABE p.20
Bitter Black Bitterness. Nikki Giovanni. BFBTBJ p.18; BOL p.9
Bitter Lemon. Leatrice Emeruwa. BlGBG p.4
Bitter tears are stone, The. Audre Lorde. ChPON p.4; COAL p.68
Bitter wind was blowing as I left the city. Amma Khalil. HoDo p.81
Black. Barbara Jean Knight. PoBBl p.19
Black: a Chant for Children. Naomi Long Madgett. PiLLAF p.62
Black--Bearded Poet. Gwendolyn Mitchell. NeNP p.52
Black Boy. Ophelia Robinson. AmLNA p.52
Black Can be Beautiful. Mary Bohanon. GaBW p.256
Black child...so small tiny segment of wondrous color. Constance E. Berkley. GLOWC p.43
Black Children. Carole Gregory Clemmons. TGWL p.20
Black Decision at Sundown. Linda Brown Bragg. LoSBM p.23
Black Disabled Veteran, The. Damali (Denise Burnett) IATWMB p.14
Black Draftee from Dixie, The. Carrie Williams Clifford. BlSi p.82
Black Dust. Wanda Coleman. MaDBL p.106
Black Elm, The. Josephine D. (Henderson) Heard. MoGl p.99
Black Eurydice. Carole Gregory Clemmons. NiBPo p.86
Black Expressions. Johari Amini. LetGSW p.15
Black eye laced in pancake. Wanda Coleman. MaDBL p.84
Black Faces. Anita Scott Coleman. EbR p.51
Black faces lifted to the Heavens ...searching. Thelma Parker Cox. TNV p.28
Black Finger, The. Angelina Weld Grimke. AmNP p.17; NeNRe p.366; PoBA p.15; PoN p.49
Black folks have got to be superhuman. Linda Brown Bragg. LoSBM p.6
Black Future. Kattie M. Cumbo. GaBW p.288
Black Genesis. Mae Jackson. CaPWY p.17
Black Girl, Black Girl. Leatrice Emeruwa. BlGBG p.28
Black girl, black girl, why are you crying. Leatrice Emeruwa. BlGBG p.28
Black girl going into the woman her mother desired, A. Audre Lorde. ChPON p.55; FrLWP p.29
Black Goddess. Katie M. Cumbo. NiBPo p.49
Black Haiku. Frenchy J. Hodges. BlW p.22
Black hands felled the forests. Bessie Woodson Yancey. EcFTH p.23
Black Heart as Ever Green. Carolyn M. Rodgers. HeAEG p. 53

Black Is. Kali Grosvenor. PBK p. 104
Black Is... Sandra E. Stevens. GaBW p.401
Black is a basic. Linda Porter. OnOW p.7
Black is beautiful color. Sandra E. Stevens. GaBW p.401
Black is Black. Kali Grosvenor. PBK p.15
Black is Not the Man. Gertrude Blackwell Bailey. IfWCF p.10
Black is; slavery was; I am. Gloria Oden. BlSi p.123
Black is something to laugh about. Kali Grosvenor. BlSp p.104
Black is the color of my little brother's mind. Barbara Mahone. Suga p.18
Black Jam for Dr. Negro. Mari Evans. AfAWA p.683; BlP p. 183; BlVo p.481; BlWOA p. 818; DaS p.512; IABW p.77; PoBA p.188; UNBP p.250; WhIAM p.19
Black Joy. Ayo Sharpe. HoDo p. 90
Black Judgments. Nikki Giovanni. BrT p.60; BFBTBJ p.98; TNV p.33
Black Licorice. Carolyn M. Rodgers. HeAEG p.5
Black Lotus/A Prayer. Alicia Loy Johnson. NBP p.74
Black love can be a tragedy in America. Aishah Sayyida Mali Toure. RoATW p.169
Black Magic. Sonia Sanchez. BlP p.233; BrT p.137; HoC p.12; IvBAW p.7; RoATW p.30
Black Mail. Alice Walker. RePOP p.38
Black Man! Carolyn M. Rodgers. SOBB p.15
Black Man From Atlanta. ** Virginia Williams. GaBW p. 425
Black man has been identified with the United States since its very beginning. Gertrude Blackwell Bailey. IWCSF p.58
Black Man's Feast. Sarah Webster Fabio. PoBA p.203; PoNe p.393
Black Mayflower. Dorothy Randall. ThHSD p.38
Black Memorial Day. Frenchy J. Hodges. BlW p.25
Black men bleeding to death inside themselves. Audre Lorde. BlUn p.40
Black men were safe when tomtoms slumbered. Pauli Murray. DaTAOP p.18
Black Mother Woman. Audre Lorde. ChPON p.52; DeDF p.19; FrLWP p,16
Black Music Man. Lethonia Gee. BlFi p.222; RoATW p.24
Black Night in Haiti, Palais National, Port-Au-Prince, A Ntozake Shange. DaGe p.33
Black Ode. Maya Angelou. JGM p.37
Black on the Back of Black. Margaret Danner. DoOAT p. 96
Black people in America must establish a talking-drum. D. T. Ogilvie. YoBBI p.515
Black Poet to Saint Exupery, A. Carole Gregory Clemmons. GaBW p.269
Black Poetry Day, A. Alicia Loy Johnson. BOL p.13; GaBW p.341; NiBPo p.149
Black Power. Nikki Giovanni. BFBTBJ p.37; BrT p.53
Black Power in the Making. Olean Bess. MiFe p.2
Black Power Language. Margaret Danner. DoOAT p.82
Black Pride. Margaret Burroughs. BlSi p.118
Black pride, black pride, we remember well. Margaret Burroughs. BlSi p.118
Black Prince, The. Alice Walker. ONC p.69
Black Prince, A. Olean Bess. MiFe p.1
Black prince upon my bed. Nola Richardson. WhOL p.47
Black Queen Blues. Mari Evans. NIGHT p.13
Black Recruit. Georgia Douglas Johnson. EbR p.94
Black revolution is passing you bye. Nikki Giovanni. BFBTBJ p.24; BlBi p.533; BrT p.50

Black Sampson, The. Josephine D. (Henderson) Heard. MoGl p.71
Black Separation. Nikki Giovanni. BFBTBJ p.15
Black Sheba. Jodi Braxton. SoITM p.3
Black Sister. Kattie M. Cumbo. BlSi p.135; NiBPo p.66
Black skin against bright green. Kattie M. Cumbo. BlSi p.135; NiBPo p.66
Black Soldier. Mary Wilkerson Cleaves. EbR p.45
Black some think black is ugly. Kali Grosvenor. PBK p.26
Black Students. Julia Fields. NBP p.49
Black sugar-cane lady Papa Doc wa'nt your daddy. Amina Baraka. CoAAAW p.71
Black Sun. Johari Amini. ImIB p. 6
Black Taffy. Peggy Susberry Kenner. JuBa p.100
Black this, black that, black the other thing. June Vanleer Williams. WiRYPS p.38
Black Thoughts. D. T. Ogilvie. YoBBI p.515
Black Unicorn, The. Audre Lorde. BlUn p.3
Black unicorn is greedy, The. Audre Lorde. BlUn p.3
Black we are we disappear to dance. Vanessa Howard. ScWh p.23
Black Wedding Song, A. Gwendolyn Brooks. Bec p.10
Black Wisdom. Frenchy J. Hodges. BlW p.21
Black Woman. Anonymous. BlWOA p.889
Black Woman. Eleanor Thomas-Grumbach. MoSu p.15
Black Woman. Georgia Douglas Johnson. BlALP p.43; BrBV p.43; DeDF p.22; NeNRe p. 25
Black Woman. Naomi Long Madgett. BlSi p.130; FBPA p.95; PiLAF p.54; PoBA p.183
Black Woman. E. Sharon Gomillion. FoAAM p.18
Black woman black woman black woman of mine. E. Sharon Gomillion. FoAAM p.18
Black woman in a blond wig. Virginia Williams. GaBW p. 427
Black woman! let yr man (ev'ry black man be yr here) Carolyn M. Rodgers. SoBB p.18
Black woman lost in hot cat eyes. Colleen McElroy. MuDLSG p.13
Black Woman Never Faints, A. ** Harryette Mullen. TTW p.17
Black Woman Throws a Tantrum. Nayo. NeBV p.383
Black Woman's Hole. Wanda Coleman. MaDBL p.21
Black would-be-poet told me a story, The. Wanda Coleman. MaDBL p.67
Black Writer, A. Johari Amini. ImIB p.12
Black You Are. Gertrude Blackwell Bailey. IfWCF p.53
Blackbird, The. Linda B. Graham. GaBW p.313
Blackman Blackman...get off that corner where you stand. Gertrude Blackwell Bailey. IfWCF p.52
Blackman has Done His Part, The. Gertrude Blackwell Bailey. IfWCF P.58
Blackness Is...Linda Brown. GLOWC p.45
Blackness is a title. Bwendolyn Brooks. CoAAAW p.82
Blackness is more than nappy hair. Linda Brown. GLOWC p.45
Blackstone Rangers, The. Gwendolyn Brooks. BlALP p.104; PoBA p.159; WoOGB p.416
Blackstudies. Audre Lorde. ChPON p.94; NeHS p.52
Blacktop black top black top top black black top. Marion Nicholes. LiS p.16
Blackwoman Portrait, A. Jennifer Blackman Lawson. BlIMT p.2
Blackwoman to Blackman: I. Jennifer Blackman Lawson. BlIMT p.50
Blackwoman to Blackman: II, Jennifer Blackman Lawson. BlIMT p.51
Blame me not for pleasing castle dreams. Ruth E. J. Sarver. EbR p.128

Blanked, blocked, blind who know nothing of our sight, The. S. Diane Bogus. WITM p.69
Blasting loudspeakers amplifying screeching noises of on-stage glamor. June Vanleer Williams. WiRYPS p.43
Bleeker Street. Jayne Cortez. Scar p.50
Blending comes to mind, A. May Miller. ClAB p.17
Blessing Without Company. Anonymous. BlP p.17
Blind. Gertrude Blackwell Bailey. IfWCF p.47
Blind are We Who Cannot Tell the Bitter from the Sweet. Vanessa Howard. ScWh p.41
Blind as I may be, I will never forget what God has done for me. Gertrude Blackwell Bailey. IfWCF p.47
Blind Betty. Wanda Coleman. MaDBL p.30
Blind, Cripple and Crazy. S. Diane Bogus. WITM p.69
Blind Street. Georgiana Oliver. NegVo p.118
Blistering, the long black Jockey's ear deafens. Sarah Webster Fabio. BrT p.171
Blizzard. Lyn. SiSH p.31
Blk/chart (to be sed everyday, slowly) Sonia Sanchez. WABP p.33
Blk/people are we CIA agents. Sonia Sanchez. WABP p.19
Blk/Rhetoric. Sonia Sanchez. IvBAW p.18; MoCAP p.137; NaPr p.128
Blk/Woman/Speaks, A. Sonia Sanchez. LoP p.68
Blk/woooomen chant. Sonia Sanchez. WABP p.45
Blood brothers and sisters, know me. Margaret T. G. Burroughs. WhSIT p.15
Blood caked hair and eyes. Lyn. SiSH p.5
Blood flows and mingles. Nancy C. Arnez. RoCo p.19
Blood is Thicker than Water, But... Frances Garcia. ThHSD p.63
Blood stagnant from want of motion. Pamela Cobb. InDM p. 12.
Blood stains. Union Street in Mississippi. June Jordan. ThTDID p.117
Blood Suckers. Jayne Cortez. COAG p.59
Blood will not serve. Julia Fields. NiBPo p.68
Bloodbirth. Audre Lorde. CaTR p.8; NaPr p.70
Bloodlines. Carolyn M. Rodgers. HeAEG p.17
Bloomdino feathers of barbwire cries. Jayne Cortez. FeAF p.12
Blossoms line the hillsides. Bessie Woodson Yancey. EcFTH p.10
Blow Hot Soul Sister. Patricia Parker. ChOM p.10; MoIB p. 49
Blow our country a life color you the children of jazz. Sonia Sanchez. ItND p.9
Blue. Carolyn M. Rodgers. HeAEG p.19
Blue/Black Poems. Alicia Loy Johnson. GaBW p.338
Blue/Black Poems (Or call them by Their Rightful Names) Alicia Loy Johnson. NiBPo p.146
Blue is my favorite color. LaVerne Davis. GLOWC p.39
Blue is this night of stars. Pauli Murray. BlSi p.92
Blue poems black poems beautiful blue/black poems come back. Alicia Loy Johnson. GaBW p. 338; NiBPo p.146
Blue Ribbons for the Baby Girl. June Jordan. CoAAAW p.181
Blue sleep and night blue sky. Harryette Mullen. TTW p.57
Blues, A. Jayne Cortez. FeAF p.30
Blues. Leatrice Emeruwa. BlBGB p.15
Blues. Quandra Prettyman. BOL p.60
Blues. Sonia Sanchez. BlFi p. 254; IvBAW p.36; LoP p.30
Blues ain't culture. Sonia Sanchez. MoCAP p.135; NeBV p. 337; WABP p.54
Blues calling my name, The.

Gayl Jones. ChOSa p.376
Blues Come From Texas, The. Anonymous. BlWOA p.647
Blues in B^b. Mari Evans. NIGHT p.12
Blues (in Two Parts) Val Ferdinand. NeBV p.374
Blues is Something to Think About. Sherley Williams. PePo p.37
Blues lady with the blacked face. Jayne Cortez. BlSi p.160; MoOP p.28
Blues Poem, A. Leatrice Emeruwa. BlGBG p.12
Blues Today, The. Mae Jackson. BOL p.63; Capwy p.9; PoBA p.496
Blustering to breathe while ram-like thrusts batter at my lungs. S. Diane Bogus. WITM p.63
Boats in Winter. Julia Fields. NiBPo p.69
Bocas: a Daughter's Geography. Ntozake Shange. DaGe p.21
Bodies are lamps and their life is the light. Mae V. Cowdery. WlOV p.16
Bodies broken on the Trail of Tears, The. Lucille Clifton. GoNAE p.12
Bold Nat Turner by the blood of God rose up preaching on Virginia's sod. Margaret Walker. PFND p.10; UNBP p. 166
Bole Tally. May Miller. ClAB p.32
Bondage. Georgia Douglas Johnson. BrBV p.77
Boneman. Margaret Danner. DoOAT p.92
Boneman and My Senufo Masque, The. Margaret Danner. DoOAT p.91
Booker T. Washington, pioneer in Industrial Education. 1865-1915. Eloise Culver. GANIV p.43
Boots are Being Polished. ** Patricia Parker. MoIB p.74
Bordentown School. Naomi Long Madgett. PhN p.16
Born down in Georgia, die in Tennessee. Frency J. Hodges. BlW p.17
Born of the sperm of the Father. Linda Thomas. GLOWC p.30
Boss Communication. Mari Evans. NIGHT p.9
Bottle tops, broken glass sidewalk chips, dirty halls all the things my mind recalls. Mara Moja Tu Kali. ThHSD p.59
Bottled: New York. Helene Johnson. BlSi p.78; CaD p.221; GoS p.126; NeNRe p.213; PoBA p.104
Bought and Paid For. Mary Bohanon. GaBW p.257
'Bout Cullud Folkses. Lucy Mae Turner. BCF p.7
'Bout de Moon. Lucile D. Goodlett. WCG p.23
Bowery Street. Jayne Cortez. COAG p.14; Scar p.55
Boxes. Nikki Giovanni. CoCRD p.34
Boy, The. Naomi Long Madgett. PiLAF p.27
Boy Breaking Glass. Gwendolyn Brooks. WoOGB p.408
Boy Died in my Alley, The. Gwendolyn Brooks. Bec p.5
Boys. Elma Stuckey. BiGa p.2
Boys, Black. Gwendolyn Brooks. Bec p.15
Boys I don't promise you nothing Lucille Clifton. BlP p.251; DOBB p.55
Bran Bread. Linda Brown Bragg. LoSBM p.5
Bread, cast on the water, will return... Nell Chapman. EbR p.29
Bread on the Water. Nell Chapman. EbR p.29
Break, Break My Heart for Love is Done. Georgia Douglas Johnson. ALC p.53
Breaking dead leaves 'neath my feet, The. Georgia Douglas Johnson. HWOP p.6
Breaklight. Lucille Clifton. OrW p.85
Breakthrough. Carolyn M. Rodgers. BlP p.263; HoIGO p.35; SoBB p.31
Breast Examination. Wanda Coleman. MaDBL p.131

Breath of life imbued those few dim days, The. Jessie Redmond Fauset. CaD p.70
Breath on my neck with wind of Indian summer. Melba Joyce Boyd. CaCADW p.21
Breathless today I run along the shore. Naomi Long Madgett. OnATM p.28
Bricks. Jayne Cortez. Scar p.38
Bride of Love--A Child. Mitchelene Morgan. ThHSD p.17
Bridge of Friendship and Understanding, The. Margaret Danner. DoOAT p.17
Bridge Party of Gaps in Teeth Ain't New. Marion Nichols. LiS p.21
Bridge Through my Window. Audre Lorde. ChPON p.17; COAL p.32; FiCi p.7
Brief Synoposis, A. Carolyn M. Rodgers. HeAEG p.7
Bright pattern on a dark bed. May Miller. ClAB p.22
Bright sun flower yellow tiger was at my bedroom door, A. Nikki Giovanni. MyH p.56
Bright uncanny music was beating through the room. Audre Lorde. ChPON p.67; NeHS p. 28
Bring back the life of Claude Reece, Jr. Jayne Cortez. COAG p.31
Bring me some music that you like make it heavy. Jodi Braxton. SoITM p.46
Bring out the glasses of crystal. Mae Jackson. CoAAAW p.168
Brisk walk on a half-cold September day, A. Pinkie Gordon Lane. PoBBl p.18; WiTh p.48
Britannia's isles proclaim that freedom is their theme. Ann Plato. BlSi p.45
Broadway Uptown. Carolyn M. Rodgers. HeAEG p.40
Broken promises & shattered dream. Eleanor Thomas-Grumbach. MoSu p.17
Bronze Queen. Gertrude Parthenia McBrown. EbR p.104
Bronzed Knights, The. Eleanor Thomas-Grumbach. MoSu p.14
Bronzeville Breakthrough. Sarah Webster Fabio. TGWL p.37
Bronzeville Man With a Belt in the Back. Gwendolyn Brooks. BeEa p.48; IADB p.16; ITBLA p.217; PoBA p.157; SPGB p.100; WoOGB p.346
Bronzeville Mother loiters in Mississippi, Meanwhile, A Mississippi Mother Burns Bacon, A. Gwendolyn Brooks. BeEa p.19; BLIA p.331; SPGB p.75; WoOGB p.317
Bronzeville Woman in a Red Hat. Gwendolyn Brooks. BeEa p.53; SPGB p.103; WoOGB p.35
Brooding. Jayne Cortez. COAG p.26; MoOP p.8
Brooks start with cloud condensation. Nikki Giovanni. ReC p.12; TGWL p.48
Brother. Jean. AOS p.25
Brother. Johari Amini. JuBa p.166; LetGSM p.17
Brother Alvin. Audre Lorde. BlUn p.54
Brother-as-Salaam--Alaikum sister-Owa--Alaikum--Salaam. Sonia Sanchez. LoP p.72
Brother Baptis' on Woman Suffrage. Rosalie Jonas. BlSi p.56
Brother, Brother, I Dearly Love Thee But... Bobbretta M. Elliston. PoBBl p.20
Brother brother liabilities are wasted. Johari Amini. JuBa p.166; LetGSM p.17
Brother Freedom. Margaret T. G. Burroughs. FoM p.22
Brother I Don't Want to Hear About How my Real Enemy is the System. Patricia Parker. ChOM p.2; MoIB p. 46
Brother of the Hour. Marion Nicholes. LiS p.15
Brother... the Twilight. Mari Evans. BlSp p.72; IABW p. 90
Brother... the twilight of your lions. Mari Evans. BlSp p.72; IABW p.90
Brother to the firefly lights

the night. Effie Lee Newsome. AmNP p.19; CaD p.55; NeNRe p.217; PoBA p.21; PoN p.55; PoNe p.70
Brother stands on the corner with hate in his heart for no one in particular society in general, A. Jean. AOS p.25
Brotherhood. Georgia Douglas Johnson. BrBV p.17
Brothers and sisters you may dream dreams. Frenchy J. Hodges. BlW p.20
Brothers at the Bar. Naomi Long Madgett. NeBV p.297; PiLAF p.57
Brothers brothers everywhere. Johari Amini. BlP p.230
Brothers Sent to the Nam.** Anonymous. ThHSD p.26
Brown as the Field.** Gloria Oden. RESUR p.75
Brown Child's Prayer, A. Nancy L. Arnez. ReCO p.20
Brown girl chanting to drums on Sunday. Pauli Murray. DaTAOP p.40
Brown leaf catching too much sun. Naomi Long Madgett. PhN p.40
Brown Menace or Poem to the Survival of Roaches, The. Audre Lorde. ChPON p.92; NeHS p.48
Brown Silky Eyes Flashing Stories at Me. ** C. Tillery Banks. HeTMWL p.18
Brudder, keep your lamp trimmin' and a-burnin'. Anonymous. BlWOA p.240
Brushes and paints are all I have. Gwendolyn B. Bennett. CaD p. 155
Bud, The. W. Blanche Nivens. BTh p.60
"Build me a house," said the master. Frances E. W. Harper PBFH p.25
"Build me a nation," said the Lord. Frances E. W. Harper. PBFH p.75
Building, The. Frances E. W. Harper. PBFH p.25
Building in salt is no better than building in sand. Naomi Long Madgett. PiLAF p.63
Bull, The. Carole Gregory Clemmons. NiBPo p.87
Bully of the Brazos. Zelma Smith. HoDo p.97
Bump d'Bump. Maya Angelou. AnSIR p.47
Burdens of All, The. Frances E. W. Harper. PBFH p.90
Burglars stole my love story, The. Thulani Davis. AlTRGR p.30
Burial. Alice Walker. RePOP p. 12
Burial of Sarah. Frances E. W. Harper. PBFH p.61
Buried birds are usually dead. Toi Derricotte. EmDH p.50
Buried Deep. Edythe Mae Gordon. NegVo p.66
Burning Sharp. Alice Walker. RePOP p.39
Bury me in a free land. Frances E. W. Harper. ANP p.17; AVAN p.42; BlP p.40; BlWOA p.225; CNAW p.103; EBAP p.36; NeCa p.296
Burying Ground. Elma Stuckey. BiGa p.6
Bus driver say move back! Mari Evans. IABW p.24
Bus stop waits are not for obviously Blacks. Johari Amini. ImIB p.8; UNBP p.354
Bus Trip--Rest Stop--1950. June Vanleer Williams. WiRYPS p.33
Bus Window. June Jordan. SCh p.63
Bus window show himself a wholesale florist. June Jordan. SCh p.63
But beyond the anxiety. June Jordan. ThTDID p.72
But can see better there, and laughing there pity the giants wallowing on the plain. Gwendolyn Brooks. AnA p.14; KAL p.157; PoNe p.336; WoOGB p.78
But dog...that ain't him. Johari Amini. LetGSM p.25
But even were it true that dead men go. Margaret Danner. DoOAT p.62
But ever stand through the ages of humanity's ebb and flow.

Nannie M. Travis. EbR p.143
But I had called the office. Nikki Giovanni. BFBTBJ p.14
But I Say. Jill Witherspoon Boyer. DeDF p.101; DrF p.7
But I shall sit without mouring. Pinkie Gordon Lane. WiTh p. 59
But if I tell you my heart swings wider. June Jordan. ThTDID p.77
But, if restricted kittens of kittens of African descent grow into fierce cats. Margaret Danner. DoOAT p.139
But in the crowding darkness not a word did they say. Gwendolyn Brooks. AmNP p.140; PoBA p.154; PoN p.190; StIB p.1; WoOGB p.3
But in the saying let not despair cast its shadow. Pinkie Gordon Lane. TGWL p.66; WiTh p.40
But my life is not portable now. Audre Lorde. BlUn p.116
But often now the youthful eye cuts down the own daily veiling. Gwendolyn Brooks. SPGB p.27; StIB p.54; WoOGB p.56
But She Was Known to Be. Alice Walker. RePOP p.55
But the night is far beyond shadows. Pinkie Gordon Lane. WiTh p.37
But the whole thing is a miracle-see? Nikki Giovanni. BFBTBJ p.37; BrT p.53; EgT p.27
But what can you teach my daughter. Audre Lorde. BlUn p.98
Butterflies fan fragile, filmy wings. Naomi Long Madgett. DeDF p.54
Butterfly. Ethlynne E. Holmes. NegVo p.75
Butterfly, The. Nikki Giovanni. MyH p.18
Buy me an airplane. Marva Tatum Smith. BeYM p.6
By all things planetary, sweet I swear. Gwendolyn Brooks. AnA p.55; CNAW p.525; SoOM p.565; WoOGB p.119
By Glistening, Dancing Seas. Lethonia Gee. BlFi p.221
By now the stimulation of the sixties seems asleep. Margaret Danner. DoOAT p.126
By Their Fruits. Margaret Danner. DoOAT p.109
Byron, I know your wild tempestuous ways! Naomi Long Madgett. OnATM p.29; PhN p.110
Byways and bygone and long nights long. Maya Angelou. AnSIR p.42

- C -

C. C. Rider. Carolyn M.Rodgers. HoIGO p.17; NaPr p.115
C. T. At the Five Spot. Thulani Davis. AlTRGR p.53
Cables to Rage or I've Been Talking on This Street Corner A Hell of a Long Time. Audre Lorde. ChPON p.70; NeHS p.15
Cage Alive With Vibrations, The. Mari Evans. NIGHT p.48
Caged Mongoose, The. Constance Hollar. PoN p.322
Cain. Lucille Clifton. GoNAE p.32
Cala Vendor's Cry. Anonymous. ITBLA p.125
Calculated passion. S. Diane Bogus. WITM p.19
Caledonia. Colleen J. McElroy. BlSi p.288
California Prodigal. Maya Angelou. AnSIR p.19
Ca'line's Prayer. Lucille Clifton. MoCAP p.141
Call for Black Unity, A. Kattie M. Cumbo. GaBW p.289
Call Her Back. Jodi Braxton. SoITM p.5
Call her Betts. Margaret Danner. DoOAT p.109
Call it neither love nor spring madness. Pauli Murray. AmNP p.106; DaTAOP p.74; PoBA p.108; PoN p.159; PoNe p.279; RoATW p.14
Call it our craziness even. Lucille Clifton. OrW p.21
Call Letters: Mrs. V. B. Maya Angelou. AnSIR p.52

Call me your deepest urge toward survival. Audre Lorde. ChPON p.92; NeHS p.48
Call the Night. Jayne Cortez. Scar p.27
Call to Prayer. Anonymous. TYBP p.43
Call Unto Me. Alvies Carter. AOS p.24
Callie Ford. Gwendolyn Brooks. BeEa p.61; WoOGB p.359
Calling black people. Anonymous. AfAA p.1
Calling Dreams. Georgia Douglas Johnson. BrBV p.23
Calling it Quits. June Jordan. PaNP p.74
Calling Me. Bessie Woodson Yancey. EcFTH p.3
Calling of Names, The. Maya Angelou. JGM p.43
Calling of the Disciples, The. Lucille Clifton. GoNAE p.40
Calling on all Silent Minorities. June Jordan. ThTDID p.71
Calling you from my kitchen. June Jordan. PaNP p.85
Calm, The. Damali (Denise Burnett) IATWMB p.21
Calming Kali. Lucille Clifton. OrW p.57
Calmness Hits the Careless Streets. Howard. ScWh p.37
Calvary Way. May Miller. BTB p. 151
Came a stranger late among us. Josephine D. (Henderson) Heard. MoGl p.81
Came up the stairs and talked to me for a few minutes. Wanda Coleman. MaDBL p.69
Cameo No. I. June Jordan. SCh p.75; ThTDID p.114
Cameo No. II. June Jordan. SCh p.76; ThTDID p.115
Camouflage. Naomi Evans Vaughn. NegVo p.160
Can I have a word wid you. Ntozake Shange. NaEd p.38
Can I Poet with you roi? Mae Jackson. BOL p.16; CaPWY p.18; PoBA p.487
Can it be true, that we can meet. Josephine D. (Henderson) Heard. MoGl p.23
Can She Go With You? Dolores Abramson. ThHSD p.35
Can she walk with you. Dolores Abramson. ThHSD p.35
Can this consderation cover you from every angle? Margaret Danner. DoOAT p.80
Can we call back the wisdom death breath of griottes almost whisper dies on the cross? Jodi Braxton. SoITM p.5
Can you catch a snowflake on your tongue. Linda Brown Bragg. LoSBM p.30
Can you defy and mock? June Vanleer Williams. WiRYPS p. 83
Can you dig it brother. Marion Nicholes. LiS p.15
Cancers. Nikki Giovanni. ThWRNW p.53
Cancers are a serious condition. Nikki Giovanni. ThWRNW p.53
Candle. May Miller. ClAB p.16
Cannibal Hymn, The. Anonymous. TYBP p.24
Cannonball. Elma Stuckey. BiGa p.80
Canossa. Naomi Long Madgett. PhN p.41; SoTPN p.30
Canst teach the heart purity when it has learned deceit? Josephine D. (Henderson) Heard. MoGl p.102
Cape Coast Castle Revisited. JoAnn Hall-Evans. BlSi p. 191
Capitalism. Mae Jackson. CaPWY p.12
Captive Artist, The. Margaret Danner. DoOAT p.89
c/o Ambust c/o Mike. Sherley Williams. PePo p.26
Carefully the leaves of autumn sprinkle down. Mary Angelou. JGM p.7
Carelessly. Vanessa Howard. ScWh p.47
Carelessly wet raid falls upon the pillow of the undesired. Vanessa Howard. ScWh p.47
Caressing Caresses. Vanessa Howard. ScWh p.34
Caressing caresses I awake to the touch. Vanessa Howard. ScWh p.34

Caressing the calm of the seatide I sit on the ocean rock. Joanne Jimason. NaABE p.15
Caribbean, The. Stephanie Ormsby. PoN p.399
Carl died last night. Carolyn M. Rodgers. NaPr p.115
Carla. Jennifer Blackman Lawson. BlIMT p.15
Carlyle died last night. Carolyn M. Rodgers. HoIGO p.17
Carolina Kingston. Jayne Cortez. MoOP p.52
Carolyn singer of sass and blues, has come again. Angela Jackson. HoIGO p.1
Carousel, The. Gloria Oden. AmNP p.159; DeRi p.4; KAL p.181; PoBA p.185
Carried her unprotesting out of the door. Gwendolyn Brooks. AnA p.45; BlP p.167; CNAW p. 520; SPGB p.58; WoOGB p.109
Carried me miles and miles offshore. Pinkie Gordon Lane. WiTh p.52
Carries an old sweater a woolworth bobbie-soxer wig. Ntozake Shange. NeEd p.79
Cars on avenue swim in wine-w;ne. Wanda Coleman. MaDBL p.49
Cars Screech, Sirens Roar with Discontentment. Vanessa Howard. ScWh p.9
Carve/n. Angela Jackson. VoDLM p.15
Carver, The. Lucille Clifton. OrW p.89
Case in Point. June Jordan. PaNP p.13
Casey Jones. Anonymous. BlWOA p.463
Cat Eyes. Melba Joyce Boyd. CaEADW p.20
Catalogue could have told you if you peeped, The. Johari Amini. LetGSM p.15
Catastrophe. Naomi Long Madgett. ExAE p.28
Catch a Snow Flake. Linda Brown Bragg. LoSBM p.30
Catch of Shy Fish, A. Gwendolyn Brooks. SPGB p.124
Categories. Nikki Giovanni. MyH p.29
Cause nobody deals with Aretha--a mother with four children. Nikki Giovanni. BlP p.327; BrT p.61; PoBA p.454; Rec p.17; WoATM p.15
Cause We are Carving. Sonia Sanchez. IvBAW p.79
Caw, caw, caw...have you ever been in love? Carolyn M. Rodgers. JuBa p.126
Celebration, A. Johari Amini. LetGSM p.28
Celestial choir! enthroned in realms of light! Phillis Wheatley. AfAV p.28; AmLNA p.24; BlLi p.11; BlWOA p. 43; DuSAE p.253; EaNAW p.52; KAL p.5; NeCa p.285; PoN p.6; PoNe p.7; PPW p. 83
Celestial muse! for sweetness fam'd inspire. Phillis Wheatley. PPW p.83
Celestial muse! sublimest of the nine. Phillis Wheatley. EBAP p.108; PPW p.84
Celibacy. Georgia Douglas Johnson. ALC p.61
Celine--Celine. Thulani Davis. AlTRGR p.10
Celine--Celine/whom I like to call. Thulani Davis. AlTRGR p.10
Cellblock Blues. Mari Evans. NIGHT p.45
Cemeteries are places for departed souls. Gwendolyn B. Bennett. CaD p.159; PoN p.110; PoNe p.208
Centripetal Forces. Pamela Cobb. InDM p.22
Ceremony. Johari Amini. BlSi 192
Ceremony. Kattie M. Cumbo. BlSi p.137
Certain boarding schools I've seen, I'd love to go there, too, A. Naomi Long Madgett. PhN p.16
Certain man had seven sons, A. Lucille Clifton. TwW p.11
Certain Peace, A. Nikki Giovanni. MyH p.21
Chain. Audre Lorde. BlSi p.199; BlUn p.22
Chained. Ruth Brownlee Johnson. EbR p.97

Chained Still. S. Diane Bogus. WITM p.24
Chained to iron I am not free. Vanessa Howard. ScWh p.14
Chains are different now, The. Patricia Parker. MoIB p.79
Chains that bind my thinking, The. Alice S. Cobb. BlSi p.146
Chairman of many committees at club meetings she's a must. Mary Carter Smith. PoNe p.388
Chakara. Marion Nicholes. LiS p. 18
Challenge. Lucia Mae Pitts. NegVo p.128
Chalmette. Alice Dunbar Nelson. DuSAE p.251
Chancing into the glance of a pressured into stranger. Margaret Danner. DoOAT p.100
Change. Bessie A. Cobb. NegVo p.35
Change of Season. Audre Lorde. ChPON p.40; FrLWP p.27
Change the channel, honey. Fareedah Allah. RoATW p.109
Change Us. Sonia Sanchez. WABP p.68
Chant for Young/Brothas & Sistuhs, A. Sonia Sanchez. BlP p.240. WABP p.43
Charcoals and blues poured from you. Anasa Jordan. CoAAAW p.177
Charged with wisdom in the interest of justice. Mari Evans. NIGHT p.42
Charles Sumner. Charlotte Forten Grimke. DuSAE p.258
Charles White. Nikki Giovanni. ThWRNW p.28
Charlie's Rhyme. Anonymous. MyNIB p.38
Chatty Charlene, The. Marva Tatum Smith. BeYM p.12
Check out Sidney Poitier as Noble Savage. June Jordan. PaNP p.22
Check the Traps. Melba Joyce Boyd. CaEADW p.19
Chic Freedom's Reflection. Alice Walker. ONC p.37
Chicago Art Scene, 1967 Just as Our African Ancestors Did. Margaret Danner. IrLa p.4
Chicago Defender Sends a Man to Little Rock, The. Gwendolyn Brooks. AfAWA p. 581; AmNP p.142; BeEa p. 32; BlEx p.546; BlVo p. 466; BlWOA p.718; BTB p. 52; CNAW p.521; ITSA p. 242; MoCAP p.82; PoBA p. 155; SPGB p.87; WoOGB p. 330
Chicago in San Francisco & You. Ntozake Shange. NaEd p.142
Chicago Picasso, The. Gwendolyn Brooks. BlP p.169; ITM p.40; WoOGB p.412
Chicago sharks...hung along the lake. Delores Kendrick. TGWL p.60
Chicken-Licken. Maya Angelou. OhPWFW p.43
Chicken, she chided early, should not wait under the cranberries in after-sermon state. Gwendolyn Brooks. AnA p.7; SPGB p.33; WoOGB p.71
Chicken Dead in Old Seas. Maya Angelou. OhPWFW p.57
Child, in the August of your life you come barefoot to me. Carolyn M. Rodgers. HeAEG p.39
Child in the Night. May Miller. DeDF p.96
Child of Another Crime. Blossom Powe. MyNIB p.72
Child Shall Lead, A. Audre Lorde. ChPON p.13; COAL p.42; FiCi p.21
Child steppped into the sunshine today, A. Nancy L. Arnez. RoCO p.20
Childhood. Johari Amini. JuBa p.165; LetGSW p.13
Childhood. Margaret Walker. AfAWA p.522; BOL p.73; FMP p.53; MoCAP p.77; PoBA p.138
Childhood. Thulani Davis. AlTRGR p.23
Childhood/in the Grass. Barbara Mahone. Suga p.20
Childhood remembrances are always a drag. Nikki Giovanni. ABBTBJ p.58; BlP p.48; BlSi p.233; EbT p.16; ITSA p.208;

MoCAP p.169; NaPr p.22; NBP p.53; OnOW p.49; PoBA p.451; SoS p.22; YoBBI p.475
Children. Jennifer Blackman Lawson. BlIMT p.14
Children. Pinkie Gordon Lane. WiTh p.26
Children...any softness would grieve to call them mouths. Carolyn M. Rodgers. HeAEG p.29
Children of courage, we greet you! Pauli Murray. DaTAOP p.41
Children of Lumumba. Stella Ngatho. PoBBl p.57
Children of the Poor, The. Gwendolyn Brooks. AnA p.35; BlVo p.463; BlWOA p.717; DaS p.500; ITSA p.201; SPGB p.52; WoOGB p.99
Children of Their Sin (An Exorcise) A. Carolyn M. Rodgers. HoIGO p.21
Children they move, The. Angela Lewis. PoBA p.513
Children Today - Tomorrow - Men! Georgia Douglas Johnson. GoS p.51
Children we have not borne bedevil us by becoming themselves. Audre Lorde. ChPON p.79; NeHS p. 3
Chile, I don't know what's got into some of these cullid young'uns today. Leatrice Emeruwa. BlGBG p.9
Chill wind sweeps the high places, A. Audre Lorde ChPON p.94; NeHS p.52
Chilled into a serenity. Blanche Taylor Dickinson. CaD p.110
Chillun uv de dus', dat's a wide road leadin' down to de city. Lucile D. Goodlett. WGC p.37
Chocolate. Jayne Cortez. MoOP p.56
Choices. Nikki Giovanni. CoCRD p.68
Chopin Deciphered. Julia Fields. NiBPo p.73
Chorus. Audre Lorde. BlUn p.44
Chorus. Josephine D. (Henderson) Heard. MoGl p.136
Christian, Hindu Little Jew what does brother mean to you? Eloise Culver. GANIV p.80
Christmas Eve in France. Jessie Redmond Fauset. BaNP p.206
Christmas Lullaby for a New-Born Child. Yvonne Gregory AmNP p.153
Christmas Morning I. Carol Freeman. BlFi p.329; MBP p. 75; PoBA p.397; PoNe p.453; TYBP p.255
Christmas morning I got up before the others and ran. Carol Freeman. BlFi p.329; MBP p. 75; PoBA p.397; PoNe p. 453; TYBP p.255
Christmas Soires and the Missing Object of African Art, The. Margaret Danner. ImOAAF p. 8
Chronicle. S. Diane Bogus. WITM p.65
Chrysis. Leighla Lewis. NegVo p.96
Chuck Will's Widow Song. Anonmous. BlP p.19
Church, as some say, (and I do agree) is built in the hearts of men, The. Marva Tatum Smith. BeYM p.11
Church Folks. Bernice Love Wiggins. HeD p.42
Church Lets Out. Jeannette V. Miller. NegVo p.104
Church Service Began at Eleven on Sunday. ** Gloria Oden. TiTBi p.24
Cicatrix. Thulani Davis. AlTRGR p.57
Cinderella. Fareedah Allah. BlSi p.167
Circle of Arms. Harryette Mullen. TTW p.64
Circled by a Horsefly. Helen G. Quigless. TNV p.96
Circles. Kali Grosvenor. BlSp p.105
Cirles, lines, unpainted spaces full of mayhem. Kattie M. Cumbo. NiBPo p.63
Circus. Naomi Long Madgett. PiLAF p.52
Citizen, The. Vilma Howard. NNPUSA p.58
Citizens of the World. Margaret

Danner. DoOAT p.113
City, The. Naomi Long Madgett. PhN p.91; SoTPN p.26
City By the Sea. Josephine D. (Henderson) Heard. MoGl p.66
City Limits. Carolyn M. Rodgers. HeAEG p.42
City Nights. Naomi Long Madgett. ExAE p.29
City of tense and stricken faces. Margaret Walker. BrT p.151; FBPA p.110; PFND p.12
City Park. Claudia E. Jemmott. GaBW p.352
City Songs. Sonia Sanchez. ItND p.13
City Thought. Naomi Long Madgett. AmLNA p.87; OnATM p.17
Civil Service. Constance Nichols. EbR p.109
Civil War was over, The. Eloise Culver. GANIV p.42
Civilizations die hard. Naomi Long Madgett. ExAE p.31
Classified Ad. Tomi Carolyn Tinsley. EbR p.142
Classy Lady. Jennifer Blackman Lawson. BlIMT p.8
Classy lady if I ever saw one. Jennifer Blackman Lawson. BlIMT p.8
Cledie Taylor's brown bird. Margaret Danner. DoOAT p.67
Clever mother mother divine cleverness. Alicia Loy Johnson. TGWL p.55
(Click) sing a funeral ditty. Carolyn M. Rodgers. SoBB p.25
Climbing. Gertrude Blackwell Bailey. IfWCF p.30
Clock. Naomi Long Madgett. PiLAF p.41
Clock on Hancock Street. June Jordan. SCh p.70; ThTDID p. 19
Clogged and soft and sloppy eyes. Gwendolyn Brooks. AnA p.6; SPGB p.33; WoOGB p.70
Close the door when you go. Naomi Long Madgett. PhN p.82
Close those pretty azure eyes, baby girl. Naomi Long Madgett. OnATM p.23
Clouds are not angry, The. Kattie M. Cumbo. NiBPo p.61
Clouds fill the sky. Kattie M.
Clubwoman. Mary Carter Smith. PoNe p.388
Clutter-Up People. Alice Walker. RePOP p.58
Cluttered Letters. Nola Richardson. WhOL p.79
C'mon Now. Ann Wallace. GLOWC p.94
Cmon yall on a safari, into our plantation/jungle/minds. Sonia Sanchez. ItND p.21
Coal. Audre Lorde. BlSi p.198; BTB p.141; ChPON p.10; COAL p.6; FiCi p.4; MoCAP p.121; NeBV p.291; PoBA p.244; SoS p.95; UNBP p.284; YOBBI p.313
Coffee. Wanda Coleman. MaDBL p. 109
Coffee Hour. Pinkie Gordon Lane. WiTh p.52
Cold and shiny long and hard. Rashidah Ismaili. CoAAAW p. 162
Cold beyond metaphor's commenting he, lay all instincts frozen. Julia Fields. NiBPo p.78
Cold death, I hate you! Royal Hughes. NegVo p.82
Cold? no I'm not cold. Wanda Coleman. MaDBL p.35
Cold places beneath sheet. Wanda Coleman. MaDBL p.58
Collage. Wanda Coleman. MaDBL p. 106
Collage for Romare Bearden. Jayne Cortez. PeAF p.22
Collateral Adjective, The. Sherley Williams. PePOP p.42
Collect for Poplarville. Pauli Murray. DaTAOP p.38
Collection. Elma Stuckey. BiGa p.75
College Teacher. Pinkie Gordon Lane. WiTh p.24
Colmes Didn't Discover This World. Kali Grosvenor. PBK p.36
Colonized Mind. Barbara Marshall. TNV p.68
Color Trouble. Pauli Murray. DaTAOP p.30
Colorado prairie weary windswept homestead. Mari Evans. NIGHT p.17
Colorist, The. Anita Scott Coleman. EbR p.50

Colors. Ruth Duckett Gibbs. CLOWC p.38
Colors. Sharon Porter. MyNIB p. 160
Colors for Mama. Barbara Mahone. PoBA p.473; Suga p.15
Colors of animals. Ruth Duckett Gibbs. GLOWC p.38
Colors of the Spirit. Thulani Davis. AlTRGR p.59
Colossal the head of the dead. June Jordan. ThTDID p.193
Coltrane/Poem, A. Sonia Sanchez. UNBP p.274; WABP p.69
Come along, Charon, the night's growing older. Naomi Long Madgett. PhN p.72; SoTPN p. 21
Come, and Be My Baby. Maya Angelou. OhPWFW p.16
"Come away, away from the eucalyptus tree." Carole Gregory Clemmons. NiBPo p.86
Come, brothers all! Georgia Douglas Johnson. BrBV p.17
Come... have do with dillying. Mari Evans. NNPUSA p.77
Come heah, Liza, and set right down. Maurine L. Jeffrey. HeD p.24
Come Home From the Movies. Lucille Clifton. OrW p.23
Come in sweet grief you foxy bastard. Ridhiana. NBP p.111
Come into Black geography. Sonia Sanchez. BluB p.21; IvBAW p. 53
Come let's walk where the lilacs grow. Gertrude Parthenia McBrown. EbR p.104
Come my love into this cave. Sonia Sanchez. LoP p.97
Come now, don't be afraid. Carolyn M. Rodgers. HoIGO p. 79
Come on Home. Sharon Scott. JuBa p.175
Come reluctant night. Sonia Sanchez. LoP p.93
Come ride with my birth, earth mother. Sonia Sanchez. BluB p.23; IvBAW p.55
Come right in this house, Will Johnson! Clara Ann Thompson. AVAN p.133; BlSi p.42
Come Sunday. Mari Evans. NIGHT p.9
Come to guard us, come to bless us. Henrietta Cordelia Ray. AVAN p.153
Come, "Will," let's be good friends again. Josephine D. (Henderson) Heard. MoGl p. 23
Coming in and out of cities. Audre Lorde. BlUn p.36
Coming of Kali, The. Lucille Clifton. OrW p.47
Coming together it is easier to work after our bodies meet. Audre Lorde. BlUn p.81
Commanded to cage, the nightingale sits. Carole Gregory Clemmons. NiBPo p.84
Commencement. Edna Mae Weiss. BTh p.53
Comments. Peggy Susberry Kenner. JuBa p.98
Commitment. Jayne Cortez. MoOP p.44
Common Dust. Georgia Douglas Johnson. AmNP p.20; ITBLA p.155; PoBA p.22; TYBP p. 209
Common Poem, A. Carolyn M. Rodgers. HoIGO p.76
Common Sense. Gertrude Blackwell Bailey. IfWCF p.25
Communication. Lyn. SiSH p.10
Communication. Maya Angelou. OhPWFW p.20
Communication. Nikki Giovanni. EgT p.35; WoATM p.29
Communication. Pinkie Gordon Lane. WiTh p.51
Communication II. Maya Angelou. OhPWFW p.21
Communion in a Small Room. Sherley Williams. PePo p.84
Compassion. Mary Nell Nash. PoBBl p.30
Compensation, The. Ruth E. J. Sarver. EbR p.128
Complete Fulfillment. Mary Bohanon. GaBW p.257
Complexity is like your leg, The. June Jordan. ThTDID p.65
Complicity. Jayne Cortez. COAG p.86
Complot. Pamela Cobb. InDM p.15
Composition in Four Parts. Jennifer Blackman Lawson. BlIMT

p.28
Compulsory Chapel. Alice Walker. ONC p.47
Comradery. Bessie Woodson Yancey. EcFTH p.22
Comtemplate. Colleen McElroy. MuDLSG p.34
Conceit, A. Maya Angelou. OhPWFW p.23
Conceptuality. Mari Evans. NIGHT p.3
Concern for Our Total Environment. S. Diane Bogus. WITM p.66
Concerning One Responsible Negro With Too Much Power. Nikki Giovanni. BFBTBJ p.52; BlP p.323
Concert. Helen G. Quigless. NBP p.102
Conclusion. Audre Lorde. FrLWP p.32
Conclusion. Audre Lorde. ChPON p.47
Concord. Georgia Douglas Johnson. BrBV p.38
Confession. Lucille Clifton. TwW p.58
Confession of a Sinner. Naomi Long Madgett. PhN p.28
Conflict. Mari Evans. IABW p. 19; WhIAM p.10
Conflict. Pauli Murray. DaTAOP p.70
Confusion desuetude and gloom, the traveling of sound. Georgia Douglas Johnson. ALC p.56
Congenital. Katherine Jackson Hunter. BTh p.63; EbAT p. 135
Congenital. Naomi Long Madgett. PiLAF p.35
Coniagui Women. Audre Lorde. BlUn p.8
Coniagui women wear their flesh like war, The. Audre Lorde. BlUn p.8
Conies had Their Hidin-Place, The. Frances E. W. Harper. PBFH p.30
Conjugation. Carole Gregory Clemmons. NiBPo p.88
Conjuh Bag. Lucile D. Goodlett. WGC p.49
Conquest. Georgia Douglas Johnson. AmNP p.24; HoFTD p.102
Conquest. Naomi Long Madgett. ExAE p.51
Conquest. Pauli Murray. DaTAOP p.98
Consciousness. S. Diane Bogus. WITM p.57
Conscription--1940. Pauli Murray. DaTAOP p.64
Consecration. Lois Augusta Cuglar. EbAT p.114
Consider me a memory--a dream that passed away. Georgia Douglas Johnson. ALC p.67
Consider the eternal cat. Naomi Long Madgett. StBS p.14
Consolation. Josephine D. (Henderson) Heard. MoGl p. 115
Consulation. Jayne Cortez. COAG p.11; Scar p.44
Consulting Oracles. Thulani Davis. AlTRGR p.14
Consumed (For Brother LeRoi) Kattie M. Cumbo. NiBPo p.51
Contact Contract. Jodi Braxton. SoITM p.38
Contact Lenses. Audre Lorde. BlUn p.94
Contagion. S. Diane Bogus. WITM p.38
Contemplatin. Jeanette Adams. ThHSD p.66
Contemplation. Georgia Douglas Johnson. HWOP p.5
Contemplation of Suicide: The Temptation of Timothy, The. Gwendolyn Brooks. BeEa p.57; WoOGB p.355
Contemporary/Psalm. Carolyn M. Rodgers. HeAEG p.10
Contentment. Bessie Woodson Yancey. EcFTH p.14
Contentment. Judith Bracey. ThHSD p.57
Contradictory Values. June Vanleer Williams. WiRYPS p.84
Contrast. Mae V. Cowdery. WLOV p.65
Convent Hall. Naomi Long Madgett. PhN p.114
Convergence. Carolyn M. Rodgers. HeAEG p.24
Conversation. Nikki Giovanni. MyH p.11
Conversation With My Grandson, Waiting to be Conceived.

Lucille Clifton. TwW p.32
Conversations in Crisis. Audre Lorde. ChPON p.12; COAL p.33
Conversion. Jodi Braxton. SoITM p.48
Conversion. Pearl Cleage Lomax. WeDNNM p.6
Convert, The. Margaret Danner. BlP p.149; BrT p.40; ImOAAF p.4
Cook's Job Available. June Vanleer Williams. WiRYPS p.65
Cool Breeze. Mae Jackson. CaPWY p.13
Cool breeze blowing. Mae Jackson. CaPWY p.13
Coon Song. Lucile D. Goodlett. WGC p.28
Cop-Out. Patricia Parker. MoIB p.101
Coping. Audre Lorde. BlUn p.45
Coping - I Just Can't Cope. Eleanor Thomas-Grumbach. MoSu p.3
Copyright. S. Diane Bogus. WITM p.31
Cordelia Brown. Anonymous. MBP p.57
Cords. Ruth Brownlee Johnson. EbR p.96
Core of the conversations we never had lies in the distance, A. Audre Lorde. ChPON p.109
Cornelia Hands Around the Shoulders. ** Gloria Oden. RESUR p.17
Corner Coffee Klatch Begins.** Vanessa Howard. ScWh p.48
Cornered and trapped, the bludgeoned and crushed, The. Pauli Murray. DaTAOP p.39; PoBA p.110
Coronach. Johari Amini. ImIB p.1
Cosmic Attack on Poets, The. Carole Gregory Clemmons. NiBPo p.84
Cosmopolite. Georgia Douglas Johnson. BrBV p.58
Cotton Cat, The. Effie Lee Newsome. GoS p.99
Cotton Candy on a Rainy Day. Nikki Giovanni. CoCRD p.21
Cotton Pickin'. Lucile D. Goodlett. WGC p.20
Cotton rows criss cross the world. Maya Angelou. AnSIR p.38
Cotton swaying to and fro. Delores Clinton. EbR p.47
Could I? Nola Richardson. WhOL p.25
Could You Get the Door? Thulani Davis. AlTRGR p.18
Could You Tell Me a Faleshood? Josephine D. (Henderson) Heard. MoGl p.133
Counsel. Pauli Murray. DaTAOP p.76
Count. May Miller. ClAB p.38
Counteraction. Mae Jackson. CaPWY p.12
Country Boy. Harryette Mullen. TTW p.41
Country Lover. Maya Angelou. AnSIR p.4
Country might have been a pioneer land, The. Sonia Sanchez. BOL p.42
Couple, The. Maya Angelou. OhPWFW p.39
Couplet. Virginia Houston. NegVo p.76
Courier. Georgia Douglas Johnson. NeNRe p.379
Cousin Mary. Wanda Coleman. MaDBL p.114
Coventry. Mari Evans. BlVo p. 478
Cover Me With Your Nakedness.** Gloria Oden. RESUR p.135
Covers. Nikki Giovanni. VaT p. 57
Cows graze, horses graze. They eat, eat, eat. Gwendolyn Brooks. Bec p.41
Cozy fire, an open hearth, in spring, the clean sweet smell of earth, A. Bessie Woodson Yancey. EcFTH p.14
Crab Man. Anonymous. ITBLA p. 125
Cracked chessmen lying on a torn checker board. Nancy L. Arnez. RoCO p.22
Cracked Saucer. Elma Stuckey. BiGa p.66
Cracker is not to be played with, The. Sonia Sanchez. WABP p. 50
Craving of Samuel Rouse for clearance to create, The. Margaret Danner. AmNP p.157; BlP p.154; DoOAT p.103;

UNBP p.229; YoBBI p.103
Crawl Into Bed. ** Quandra Prettyman. BOL p.74
Crazy Blues. Anonymous. BlWOA p.888
Crazy Woman, The. Gwendolyn Brooks. BeEa p.46; HoFTD p. 136; MBP p.28; SPGB p.99 WoOGB p.344
Creation, The. Claire Turner. NegVo p.156
Creation of Man, The. Anonymous. MBP p.7
Creature to pet and spoil, A. Anonymous. AfAV p.12
Credo. Georgia Douglas Johnson. BlALP p.44; BrBV p.53; PoBA p.23; PoBA p.44
Creed. Anne Spencer. CaD p.51
Crescendo. Dorothy F. Blackwell. EbR p.6
Cricket and the Star, The. Effie Lee Newsome. GoS p.75
Crimson Rose, A. Thelma L. Clement. BTh p.54
Crimson rose at twilight sighed, A. Thelma T. Clement. BTh p.54
Crisp and curly hair has he. Ophelia Robinson. AmLNA p.52
Crispus Attucks, Revolutionary War Hero about 1723-1770 Massachusetts. Eloise Culver. GANIV p.11
Critic, The. Marva Tatum Smith. BeYM p.12
Critical look? I ain't takin' no critical look. Ridhiana. GLOWC p.55
Crocuses, The. Frances E. W. Harper. BlSi p.33; PHFH p.4
Crooked Woman/Okra Meets Greens in Strange Circumstances. Ntozake Shange. DaGe p.57
Croon the deep brown. Mari Evans. WhIAM p.13
Cross, The. Georgia Douglas Johnson. BrBV p.28
Cross. Naomi Long Madgett. PhN p.65
Cross is ready, The. Wanda Coleman. MaDBL p.101
Cross oceans into my heart. Ntozake Shange. NaEd p.133
Crowd was very still but tense, The. Eloise Culver. GANIV p. 73
Crucifixion. Anonymous. AfAWA p.107
Crucifixion. Spiritual. BlP p. 29
Crusade. S. Diane Bogus. WITM p.5
Crutches. Nikki Giovanni. CoCRD p.32
Crying against the money of dead bodies. Jayne Cortez. FeAF p.34
Crystal Shreds. Dorothy Vena Johnson. NegVo p.85
Cultural Awareness. Nikki Giovanni. BFBTBJ p.87
Cultural Cathedrals. Margaret Danner. DoOAT p.23
Cultural Isolation. Pamela Cobb. InDM p.44
Culturally Deprived. Naomi Long Madgett. PiLAF p.59
Curiosity. Lucy Mae Turner. BCF p.49
Curiosity am a painful disease. Lucy Mae Turner. BCF p.49
Curling them around; hold their bodies in obscene embrace. Lucille Clifton. OrW p.75
Current Events. June Jordan. PaNP p.7
Curtain. Georgia Douglas Johnson. ALC p.69
Curtains of twilight are drawn in the west, The. Georgia Douglas Johnson. HWOP p.41
Curved back now from the notes. Carole Gregory Clemmons. GaBW p.270
Curving Stonesteps in the Sun. Mari Evans. NIGHT p.46
Cut your fingernails on Monday, you cut them for news. Jodi Braxton. SoITM p.13
Cutting Greens. Lucille Clifton. OrW p.75
Cuz he's Black & poor he's disappeared. Ntozake Shange. DaGe p.45
Cuz it says nigger. Sonia Sanchez. WABP p.57
Cyclops in the Ocean, The. Nikki Giovanni. ThWRNW p.38
Cynic. Tomi Carolyn Tinsley. EbR p.141

- D -

Dad. Bessie Woodson Yancey. EcFTH p.32
Daddy sits in his brown leather chair. Melba Joyce Boyd. BlSi p.281; CaEADW p.3
Daddy 12/02 - 5/69. Lucille Clifton. GoNAE p.27
Daddy's in the hospital. Nola Richardson. WhOL p.11
Daffodils. Judy Dothard Simmons. JuB p.19
Dahomey. Audre Lorde. BlUn p.10
Dahomey smiles through the space in your baby street Haitian nigga teeth. Jodi Braxton. SoITM p.40
Daily Fantasy. Countess W. Twitty. EbR p.148
Damit Blackman what are you going to do. Kattie M. Cumbo. BlSi p.135; NiBPo p.47
Dance, The. Colleen McElroy. MuDLSG p.28
Dance. Lula Lowe Weeden. CaD p. 229
Dance Committee, (Concerning Jean-Leon Destine), The. Nikki Giovanni. BFBTBJ p.43
Dance of the Abakweta. Margaret Danner. AfAWA p.634; ImOAAF p.3; IrLa p.26; MoCAP p.88; NNPUSA p.30; PoNe p.163
Dance She Does, The. Harryette Mullen. TTW p.59
Dance with me. Nikki Giovanni. ThWRNW p.52
Dancer, The. Brenda Connor-Bey. CoAAAW p.76
Dancer, The. Julia Fields. GaBW p.302
Dancers, The. Nilaja. ThHSD p. 60
Dancin' the funky chicken. Maya Angelou. AnSIR p.43
Dancing below the eye of your navel. Joanne Jimason. NaABE p.35
Dandelion Stares, The. Lula Lowe Weeden. CaD p.229
Danger follows like a lurking shadow. Pinkie Gordon Lane. WiTh p.53
Daniel. Lucille Clifton. GoNAE p.35
Danny Takes the Bus. Naomi Faust. DeDF p.102
Dare to Struggle Dare to Win. Lyn. SiSH p.16
Dark an' stormy may come de wedder. Anonymous. BlP p. 16
Dark, black robe one day at night. Ronda Davis. JuBa p.58
Dark Blood. Margaret Walker. FMP p.15
Dark children running in the streets joy screaming about a kite. Carolyn M. Rodgers. HoIGO p.19
Dark Hands. Nannie M. Travis. EbR p.142
Dark hands, grown strong battling with oppression. Nammie M. Travis. EbR p.142
Dark is the face of Harriet. Margaret Walker. ITSA p.45; OcJo p.14; PoN p.181; PoNe p.320
Dark life is moist with hidden waters. Helen Aurelia Johnson. NegVo p.87
Dark night and pale moonlight. Dorothy F. Blackwell. EbR p.6
Dark People. Kattie M. Cumbo. BOL p.46; NiBPo p.52
Dark people line the sidewalks of the street after dark. Kattie M. Cumbo. BOL p.46; NiBPo p.52
Dark phases of womanhood of never havin been a girl. Ntozake Shange. BlSi p.270
Dark Phases. Ntozake Shange. BlSi p.270
Dark so Dark. Vanessa Howard. ScWh p.32
Dark so dark little light little sense of reality. Vanessa Howard. ScWh p.32
Dark stairs me walking up them. Wanda Coleman. MaDBL p.79
Dark stranger my heart searches him out "Papal," A. Alice Walker. ONC p.17
Dark Testament. Pauli Murray. AmNP p.107; BlSi p.84;

DaTAOP p.12; MyNIB p.79
Darkened bedroom, the double bed, the whispers of the city night, The. Sherley Williams. BlSi p.260; PePo p.30
Darkness and a Blueslady. Joanne Jimason. NaEBE p.27
Darlene Blackburn. Marion Nicholes. LiS p.12
Darlene Blackburn burns the torchlike movement of her body. Marion Nicholes. LiS p.13
Darling, Don't Be. Judy Dothard Simmons. JuB p.17
"Darlin", he said, "I never meant to hurt you." Josephine D. (Henderson) Heard. MoGl p.68
Darn Near Dark. Naomi Long Madgett. PhN p.64
Darwin Evolved or Tripping Ain't Natural. Jean Collins. AOS p.6
Date, The. Gwendolyn Brooks. StIB p.34; WoOGB p.36
Daufuskie. Mari Evans. NIGHT p.25
Daufuskie (Four Movements) Mari Evans. BlSi p.142
Daufuskie: Jake. Mari Evans. NIGHT p.27
Daufuskie: Janis. Mari Evans. NIGHT p.29
Daufuskie: The People Gather. Mari Evans. NIGHT p.28
Dave Garroway's Mr. J. Muggs often thumps. Margaret Danner. ImOAAF p.11
David. Carole Gregory Clemmons. GaBW p.270; NiBPo p.81
David, marble dressed, Florentine jeweled, stood created. Carole Gregory Clemmons. GaBW p.270; NiBPo p.81
Dawn. Angelina Weld Grimke. ReFNA p.24
Dawn. Georgia Douglas Johnson. HWOP p.7
Dawn came at six today. Alice Walker. ONC p.49
Dawn Cities. Mae V. Cowdery. WLOV p.7
Dawn of Love, The. Henrietta Cordelia Ray. BlSi p.39; EBAP p.142
Dawn's Carol. Henrietta Ray. ANP p.129; AVAN p.152
Day after conference, The. Josephine D. (Henderson) Heard. MoGl p.33
Day after day I sit and write, and thus the moments spend. Ann Plato. ANP p.11
Day breaks without tanks. Audre Lorde. BlUn p.100
Day brings the heat of success. Wanda Coleman. NaDBL p.132
Day by day the treads of white multiply. Georgia Douglas Johnson. ALC p.15
Day drunk with the nectar of newness, A. Maya Angelou. OhPWFW p.22
Day fades into night. Vanessa Howard. ScWh p.36
Day feels put together hastily like a gift for grateful beggars, The. Audre Lorde. ChPON p.45; FrLWP p.19
Day hangs heavy loose and grey, The. Maya Angelou. OhPWFW p.13
Day I Lef' My Home, The. Negro Work Song, USA. MyNIB p.41
Day now draweth to its close, The. Josephine D. (Henderson) Heard. MoGl p.91
Day of peace, a day of peace, A. Alicia Loy Johnson. NiBPo p.159
Day of sunny face and temper, A. Gwendolyn Brooks. SPGB p. 127
Day They Eulogized Mahalia, The. ** Audre Lorde. ChPON p.50; FrLWP p.9
Daylight Saving Time. Elma Stuckey. BiGa p.84
Days After. Helen G. Quigless. FoM p.65
Days have kept on coming, The. Lucille Clifton. GoNAE p.27
Days lie dark between our jeweled meetings, The. Georgia Douglas Johnson. ALC p.11
Days of my Mindlessness, The. Mari Evans. NIGHT p.37
De Facto Toilets. Jennifer Blackman Lawson. BlIMT p.27
Deacon Morgan. Naomi Long Mad-

gett. BlSi p.127; ExAE p.15
Dead Days. Georgia Douglas Johnson. ALC p.50
Dead days of rapture and despair I would you hours exhume. Georgia Douglas Johnson. ALC p.50
Dead End Kids. Vanessa Howard. ScWh p.18
Dead Fires. Jessie Redmond Fauset. ANP p.89; BANP p.207; PoN p.66; PoNe p.68; VoFHR p.313
Dead Leaves. Georgia Douglas Johnson. HWOP p.6
Dead 'Oman's Eyes. Lucile Goodlett. WGC p.53
Dead shall rise again, The. Lucille Clifton. GoNAE p.41
Dead Wood. Melba Joyce Boyd. CaEADW p.33
Deadlines For Miracles. Beatrice M. Murphy. RoCO p.14
Dear Are the Names That Charmed Me in My Youth. ** Margaret Walker. OcJo p.31
Dear Daddy. Ava Sanders. ThHSD p.43
Dear daddy, I was much too young. Ava Sanders. ThHSD p.43
Dear Dorothy: In Loving Memoriam. Leatrice Emeruwa. BlGBG p.3
Dear Dorothy, you are gone and we behind cry. Leatrice Emeruwa. BlGBG p.3
Dear Edith. Jennifer Blackman Lawson. BlIMT p.40
Dear friend, since you have chosen to associate my humble thoughts with England's Poet Laureate. Josephine D. (Henderson. MoGl p.51
Dear God, when you send your angels out to do their chores tonight, bid on of them to dust well my star of hope. Myrtle Campbell Gorham. EbR p.71
Dear heart, will e'er there come a time? Josephine D. (henderson) Heard. MoGl p.115
Dear human beings: for forty long years. Myra Estelle Morris. NegVo p.106
Dear human beings: Sunday I heard a lecture. Myra Estelle Morris. NegVo p.108
Dear human beings: yesterday I heard a tale. Myra Estelle Morris. NegVo p.108
Dear Jonno there are pigeons who nest on the Staten Island Ferry. Audre Lorde. ChPON p.87; NeHS p.18
Dear letters, fond letters, must I with you part? Josephine D. (Henderson) Heard. MoGl p.52
Dear Little Boy. Wanda Coleman. MaDBL p.99
Dear Lord, I oft am bowed in grief. Josephine D. (Henderson) Heard. MoGl p.115
Dear master, I am gone. Mae Jackson. CaPWY p.17
Dear Pots, how much love did you (who hate the hatred that he hated back at haters) feel. Margaret Danner. DoOAT p.71; FoM p.6; IrLa p.7
Dear Samson, I put your hair in a jar. Carole Gregory Clemmons. BlSi p.185
Dear Sirs: I have been enjoying the law and order of our community. June Jordan. PaNP p.28
Dear Toni, Instead of a Letter of Congratulations Upon Your Book and Your Daughter Whom You Say You are Raising to be a Correct Little Sister. Audre Lorde. ChPON p.56; FrLWP p.40
Dear, when we sit in that high, placid room. Jessie Redmond Fauset. BlSi p.63; CaD p.66
Death. Gertrude Blackwell Bailey. IfWCF p.26
Death as a Lotus Flower. Anonymous. TYBP p.27
Death comes to all of us. Gertrude Blackwell Bailey. IfWCF p.26
Death cums to us. Johari Amini. LetGSW p.20
Death Dance for a Poet. Audre Lorde. BlUn p.73
Death in Autumn. Julia Fields. NiBPo p.78
Death is a five o'clock door forever changing time. Sonia Sanchez. CoAAAW p.327

IvBAW p.99
Death... lies over this house. Pinkie Gordon Lane. PoBBl p.7 WiTh p.13
Death of a Friend. Pauli Murray. DaTAOP p.69; PoBA p.110
Death of the Old Sea King. Frances E. W. Harper. EBAP p.29; PBFH p.35
Death Prosecuting. Linda Curry. SoS p.7
Death prosecuting life born freedom. Linda Curry. SoS p.7
Death Rites II. Anonymous. TYBP p.3
Debra: An Africanese Name Reading on the Sound of Debra. Ronda Davis. BlSp p.56
Debra U are like de-bra. Ronda Davis. BlSp p.56
December. Josephine D. (Henderson) Heard. MoGl p.61
December 15, 1811 a black well butchered slave named George took leave of old Kentucky. June Jordan. BlP p.245; SCh p.54; ThTDID p.104
December of my Spring, The. Nikki Giovanni. WoATM p.11
Deception. Josephine D. (Henderson) Heard. MoGl p.69
Decisions. Gertrude Blackwell Bailey. IfWCF p.39
Decisions are an anchor. Gertrude Blackwell Bailey. IfWCF p.39
Declaration. Lucia Mae Pitts. NegVo p.128
Decor. Wanda Coleman. MaDBL p.22
Decoration Day. Josephine D. (Henderson) Heard. MoGl p.38
Decry, as you must this frenzied world. Pauli Murray. DaTAOP p.58
Dedication. Naomi Long Madgett. PiLAF p.12
Dedication. Pinkie Gordon Lane. WiTh p.41
Dedication for Joyce Carol Thomas, A. Jennifer Blackman Lawson. BlIMT p.9
Dedication Poem. Frances E. W. Harper. PBFH p.9
Dee Dee said she wouldn't shout in church. Carolyn M. Rodgers. HeAEG p.38
Deep. Naomi Long Madgett. PiLAF p.31
Deep along the reaches of me I remember how you looked that first time. Johari Amini. CoAAW p.50
Deep, deep is the root. Kattie M. Cumbo. NiBPo p.44
Deep, deep to coral reef floors. Kattie M. Cumbo. NiBPo p.48
Deep in this grave her bones remain. Ann Plato. BlSi p.46; EBAP p.115
Deep perfidious, and the hero's fate, The. Phillis Wheatley. PAL p.53; PPW p.97
Deep River. Anonymous. BLIA p. 42; BlLi p.113
Deep River. Spiritual. BlP p. 26
Deep River, my home is over Jordan. Spiritual. BlP p. 26
Deep Song. Gayl Jones. ChOSa p.376
Defeat. Countess W. Twitty. EbR p.146
Defeat is not to lose not to despair. Dorothy Vena Johnson. EbR p.92
Define Revolution. Lyn. SiSH p.12
Definition. Marion Nicholes. LiS p.14
Definition. Nikki Giovanni. CoAAAW p.121
Definition for Blk/Children. Sonia Sanchez. HoC p.19; PoBA p.288
Del, del into my dreams your contagion seeps. S. Diane Bogus. WITM p.38
Delirium. Thulani Davis. AlTRGR p.47
Delirium No. 4. Thulani Davis. AlTRGR p.48
Delta. Margaret Walker. FMP p. 20
Deluge. Georgia Douglas Johnson. HWOP p.57
Delusion. Georgia Douglas Johnson. ALC p.20; RoATW p.116
Delusion. June Vanleer Williams. WiRYPS p.30
Dem Black Executives. E. Sharon

Gomillion. FoAAM p.14
Democratic order such things in twenty years I understand, The. Alice Walker. ONC p.43
Demon, demon, you have dumped me. Lucille Clifton. OrW p.55
Demon: Possessed. June Vanleer Williams. WiRYPS p.15
Demonstrators, The. Beatrice M. Murphy. RoCO p.10
Denial. Mae V. Cowdery. WLOV p.53
Denying the essence of us, saying that I am not she. S. Diane Bogus. WITM p.32
Departure of Summer. Naomi Long Madgett. SoTPH p.29
Departure. Ylessa Dubonee. EbR p.60
Depression. Sonia Sanchez. LoP p.76
Dere was a rapid dismissal today. Ava Sanders. ThHSD p.5
Dere wouldn't a been no village. Lucy Mae Turner. BCF p.15
Dere's No Hidin' Place Down Here. Spiritual. BlP p.25
Desert and a weary way I trod, A. Josephine D. (Henderson) Heard. MoGl p.111
Desert Island. Sandra Royster. WoTa p.16
Deserted Cabin, The. Lucy Mae Turner. BCF p.32
Deserted Wife, The. Josephine D. (Henderson) Heard. MoGl p.85
Deshackled. Nola Richardson. WhOL p.31
Desire. Constance Nichols. EbR p.110
Desire. Georgia Douglas Johnson. BrBV p.24
Desire. Thelma T. Clement. BTh p.23
Desire 1. Thulani Davis. AlTRGR p.3
Despair. Georgia Douglas Johnson. HWOP p.41
Despair. Pinkie Gordon Lane. PoBBl p.13; WiTh p.46
Destiny. Georgia Douglas Johnson. ALC p.40
Destiny. Naomi Long Madgett. StBS p.24
Detached, The. Maya Angelou. JGM p.13
Detroit City. Jill Witherspoon Boyer. DrF p.21
Detroit Michigan. Margaret Danner. DoOAT p.20
Detroit Renaissance. Melba Joyce Boyd. CaEADW p.25
Detroit Summers. Jill Witherspoon Boyer. DrF p.23
Deuce of Cups, The. Wanda Coleman. MaDBL p.67
Devastation. Georgia Douglas Johnson. HWOP p.53
Devil Will Have You, The. Jodi Braxton. SoITM p.13
Dew is on the grasses, dear, The. Georgia Douglas Johnson. BANP p.182; GoS p.77; HWOP p.24; PoN p.57; PoNe p.74
Dialogue. Patricia Parker. ChOM p.14; MoIB p.51
Dialogue. Rashidah Ismaili. CoAAAW p.164
Dialogue With Lije. Linda Cousins. ThHSD p.47
Dialysis Machine Called the Artificial Kidney, The. Pinkie Gordon Lane. WiTh p. 41
Did poetry choose you. Delores Kendrick. TGWL p.61
Did ya ever cry. Sonia Sanchez. IvBAW p.37; LoP p.35
Did you ebber dream of flyin'. Lucy Mae Turner. BCF p.48
Did you ever watch the brilliance of a setting sun. Helen F. Clarke. EbR p.40
Did You Feed My Cow? Anonymous. GoS p.13; UNBP p.87
Did you hear? Alice Walker. RePOP p.47
Did you hear. May Miller. ClAB p.8
Did your poems write like nightmares. Toi Derricotte. EmDH p.47
Didn't My Lord Deliver Daniel.** Anonymous. AfAV p.118; BlEx p.7
Didn't speak their language at all. Sandra Royster. BrA p.14; RoATW p.75; WoTa p.19
Didn't you ever wonder what

make him play like that. Judy Dothard Simmons. JuB p. 11
Die is cast, and we must part, The. Josephine D. (Henderson) Heard. MoGl p.19
Difference, The. Marva Tatum Smith. BeYM p.8
Difference between poetry and rhetoric is being ready to kill, The. Audre Lorde. BlUn p.108
Differences. Valerie Tarver. TNV p.127
Different Points of View. June Vanleer Williams. WiRYPS p. 10
Dig, nigga... any where. Johari Amini. ImIB p.7
Digging. Audre Lorde. BlUn p.55
Dilemma when there's a dilemma. Frenchy J. Hodges. BlW p.21
Dim are your eyes no. Bessie Woodson Yancey. EcFTH p.28
Dink's Blues. Anonymous. BlWOA p.461
Dinner for Three. Pauli Murray. DaTAOP p.77
Dipped Deeply into the Full Ocean. Margaret Danner. DoOAT p.78
Dirge. Naomi Long Madgett. PhN p.60
Dirty, Damp, Dingy Rain. June Vanleer Williams. WiRYPS p. 37
Dis Hammer. Anonymous. BlWOA p.464
Dis sun are hot. Anonymous. BlP p.9
Dis worl mos done. Anonymous. BlWOA p.240
Disappointment. Arlena Howard Benton. BTh p.61
Discard the fear and what was she? Maya Angelou. OhPWFW p.39
Discards. Naomi Long Madgett. ExAE p.63
Disclaimer. Beatrice M. Murphy. RoCO p.11
Disciplinarian, The. Bessie Woodson Yancey. EcFTH p.60
Discord. Nancy L. Arnez. RoCO p.22
Discordant notes detract from all music. Athelstan R. Lalande. NegVo p.90
Dicovering. Sharon Scott. JuBa p.172
Disgrace. Anonymous. MBP p.27
Disguised in my mouth as a swampland. Jayne Cortez. BlSi p.157; COAG p.28; MoOP p.46
Disgusting isn't it, dealing out the damns. Gwendolyn Brooks. StIB p.7; WoOGB p.9
Disillusion. Lillian Brown. BTh p.63; EbAT p.151
Disillusionment. Bessie Woodson Yancey. EcFTH p.33
Dispute Over Suicide, A. Anon-mous. TYBP p.26
Distant time passed, A. Patricia Parker. ChOM p.12; MoIB p.54
Disturbed by consciousness God created creation. Gayl Jones. BlSi p.210; SoS p.15
Dives and Laz'us. Anonymous. TYBP p.197
Divide. Georgia Douglas Johnson. ALC p.58
Divine Afflatus. Jessie Redmond Fauset. EbAT p.27
Divorcee, The. Naomi Long Madgett. OnATM p.41
Divorcee. Toi Derricotte. EmDH p.24
Do, Lawd. Anonymous. BlWOA p. 240
Do Not be Afraid of No. Gwendolyn Brooks. BlWOA p.717; SPGB p.36; WoOGB p.76
Do not call me evil. Jennifer Blackman Lawson. BlIMT p.51
"Do not cheer, men are dying," said Capt. Phillips in the Spanish American War.** Frances E. W. Harper. PBFH p.88
Do not hold my few years against me. Alice Walker. ONC p.61; RoATW p.87
Do Not Pass me By. Naomi Long Madgett. OnATM p.29
Do not seek the garden. Clara H. Haywood. NegVo p.69
Do not speak to me of martyrdom. Sonia Sanchez. BlP p.37; BrT p.25; FoM p.38; HoC p.

p.15; IvBAW p.10; MoCAP p. 134
Do Subways Race.** Kali Grosvenor. PBK p.56
Do Tell Faith/the Divine Natural. Carolyn M. Rodgers. HeAEG p. 34
Do We Be There Waiting. Mari Evans. NIGHT p.61
Do y'all remember when you was in grammar school. Carolyn M. Rodgers. JuBa p.109
Do you blame me that I loved Him? Frances E. W. Harper. BlSi p.26; CNAW p.104; EBAP p. 27; PBFH p.12; RoATW p.58
Do You Know Jesus, His Only Son, Our Lord? Jodi Braxton. SoITM p.30
Do you know your color? Sharon Porter. MyNIB p.160
Do you love your fellow-man? Bessie Woodson Yancey. EcFTH p.24
Do you see this grain of sand. Frances E. W. Harper. PBFH p.3
Do You Think. ** Jayne Cortez. COAG p.12; Scar p.57
Do You Think? ** Josephine D. (Henderson) Heard. MoGl p.55
Do you think I guess in asmuch as so so. Audre Lorde. BlUn p. 29
Doctor asked me if I had sexual fantasies. Wanda Coleman. MaDBL p.70
Dr. Carter G. Woodson Father of Negro History, 1875-1950 Virginia. Eloise Culver. GANIV p.55
Dr. Charles R. Drew Father of the Blood Bank, Washington, D.C., 1905-1950. Eloise Culver. GANIV p.67
Dr. Daniel Hale Williams, Pioneer in Heart Surgery, 1858-1931, Pennsylvania. Eloise Culver. GANIV p.41
Dr. George Washington Carver, Botanist, 1864-1943, Missouri. Eloise Culver. GANIV p.45
Dr. Mary M. Bethune, Founder of Bethune-Cookman College, 1875-1955, South Carolina. Eloise Culver. GANIV p.52
Doctor Say Marse Mind is Sound. Elma Stuckey. BiGa p.34
Doctor Spider. Wanda Coleman. MaDBL p.90
Dr. W. E. B. DuBois, Dean of Historians, 1868-1963, Massachusetts. Eloise Culver. GANIV p.47
Does he think of me in the merry throng. Josephine D. (Henderson) Heard. MoGl p. 17
Does man love art? man visits art, but squirms. Gwendolyn Brooks. BlP p.169; ITM p. 40; WoOGB p.412
Dog Catcher, The. Lucy Mae Turner. BCF p.42
Dog catcher's a mean old man, The. Lucy Turner. BCF p.42
Dog Suicide. Wanda Coleman. MaDBL p.27
Doing. Josephine D. (Henderson) Heard. MoGl p.128
Doing. Marva Tatum Smith. BeYM p.19
Doing Battle with the Wolf. Wanda Coleman. MaDBL p.17
Doing something, do it well. Josephine D. (Henderson) Heard. MoGL p.128
Doll is sitting in a box. Toi Derricotte. EmDH p.30
Doll Poem. Toi Derricotte. EmDH p.30
Dolls who bleat out excuses for their plastic. Jill Witherspoon Boyer. DrF p.22
Domestics. Kattie M. Cumbo. BlSi p.135; NiBPo p.47
Don Wid Driber's Dribin'. Anonymous. BlWOA p.312
Don't ask me where I've been. Wanda Coleman. MaDBL p.65
Don't be discouraged when things don't go your way. Gertrude Blackwell Bailey. EfWCF p. 44
Don't Come Sunday. Nola Richardson. WhOL p.76
Don't Die in January. June Vanleer Williams. WiRYPS p.36
Don't give up your dreams for idle lust. Bessie Woodson Yancey. EcFTH p.16
Don't Go. Sonia Sanchez. IvBAW

p.68
Don't go if you go I won't hear me. Sonia Sanchez. IvBAW p.68
Don't Honey Me (A Love Song to Black Men. Linda Brown Bragg. LoSBM p.24
Don't knock at my door. Georgia Douglas Johnson. BlALP p.43 BrBV p.43; DeDF p.22; NeNRe p.25
Don't let them die out. Sonia Sanchez. PoBA p.290; WABP p.67
Don't look now I'm fading away. Nikki giovanni. CoCRD p.21
Don't make that kind of book no more. Wanda Coleman. MaDBL p.68
Don't make waves. Audre Lorde. BlUn p.95
Don't play me no righteous bros. Sonia Sanchez. HoC p.26; UNBP p.272
Don't speak to me about the mutilation of things. Jayne Cortez. Scar p.17
Don't Tell me You Don't Understand. Vanessa Howard. ScWh p.6
Don't Touch Me Now! ** C. Tillery Banks. HeTMWL p.34
Don't touch the wounds. Nola Richardson. WhOL p.21
Don't Wanna Be. Sonia Sanchez. BlSp p.191
Don't wanna be no pimp. Sonia Sanchez. BlSp p.190; ItND p.15
Door Opens, A. ** C. Tillery Banks. HeTMWL p.38
Doorway That We Hide Behind, The. Dee Dee McNeil. BrA p.19; RoATW p.131
Dope pushers dope pushers git outa our parks. Sonia Sanchez. ItND p.13
Doretha wore the short blue lace last night. June Jordan. SCh p.7; ThTDID p.47
Dose of life is fatal in itself, The. Elma Stuckey. BiGa p. 91
Dotty broke the clock. Nola Richardson. WhOl p.8
Double Dealing. Nola Richardson. WhOL p.75
Double Standard, A. Frances E. W. Harper. BlSi p.26; CNAW p.104; EBAP p.27; PBFH p. 12; PoN p.210; RoATW p.58
Double Take at Relais de L'espadon. Thadious M. Davis. BlSi p.277
Douglas, DuBois, Garvey, King, and Malcolm X, five Black men whose leadership we cherish. Margaret Walker. CoAAAW p.363
Doves are in the eaves, The. Naomi Long Madgett. BTB p. 147; OnATM p.14; PhN p.116; StBS p.18
Down at the hall at midnight sometimes. Lula Lowe Weeden. CaD p.229
Down between 2 monuments the cameras are practically balloons. June Jordan. SCh p.50; ThTDID p.110
Down by the river with winter coming on. Jill Witherspoon Boyer. DrF p.23
Down, down, down, into the nebulous, The abstract. Nancy L. Arnez. RoCO p.23
Down in de bottom wid de coon dawd Shin. Lucile D. Goodlett. WGC p.28
Down in de lane dat's a-leadin' to de rivah. Lucile D. Goodlett. WGC p.27
Down in the dell, a rose-gleam fell. Henrietta Cordelia Ray. BlSi p.37; EBAP p.143
Down in the Lonesome Garden. Anonymous. BlP p.8
Down of a Thistle, A. Margaret Danner. DoOAT p.12
Down on East Pratt Street in Baltimore where the bar on the corner. June Jordan. PaNP p.92
Down the unspun swerve of trackless weeds I travel unaware. Naomi Long Madgett. BlVo p. 476; MoCAP p.92; StBs p.19
Down there a poor woman. Anonymous. TYBP p.47
Down wall street the students marched for peace. Audre Lorde. ChPON p.85; NeHS

p.14
Downtown Vaudeville. Gwendolyn Brooks. AnA p.9; WoOGB p. 73
Dozens, The. Audre Lorde. CaTR p.18; ChPON p.23; COAL p. 45
Dragonfly, The. Nikki Giovanni. VaT p.31
Dragonfly sat on my nose, A. Nikki Giovanni. VaT p.31
Dream. The. Gladys Marie Parker. EbR p.112
Dream, A. Josephine D. (Henderson) Heard. MoGl p.118
Dream. Sonia Sanchez. LoP p.6
Dream Boats. Naomi Long Madgett. PhN p.59
Dream Farmer. Jill Witherspoon Boyer. DrF p.14
Dream I slept with moved catlike to a country well, A. Carole Gregory Clemmons. NiBPo p.88
Dream Like Daniel's. S. Diane Bogus. WITM p.46
Dream Love. Ruth E. J. Sarver. EbR p.128
Dream Market. Cora Ball Moten. NegVo p.111
Dream of Revenge, A. Lauretta Hilman Gooden. HeD p.15
Dream Sequence, Part 9. Naomi Long Madgett. BlP p.195
Dream/Songs from the Moon of Beulah Land. Audre Lorde. BlUn p.75
Dream World. Evelyn Watson. AmLNA p.78
Dreams. Bessie Woodson Yancey. EcFTH p.16
Dreams. Naomi Long Madgett. OnATM p.14
Dreams. Nikki Giovanni. BFBTBJ p.74; EgT p.29; PoBA p.454
Dreams Are So Pale. Katharine Beverly. EbR p.4
Dreams Bite.** Audre Lorde. CaTR p.27; ChPON p.22; COAL p.39
Dreams Common Sense and Stuff. Frenchy J. Hodges. BlW p.16
Dreams have a way of tossing and turning themselves. Nikki Giovanni. MyH p.28
Dreams of the Dreamer, The.** Georgia Douglas Johnson. CaD p.80; HWOP p.2
Drink deep of love's concoction. Josephine D. (Henderson) Heard. MoGl p.102
Drink in the night with me. Naomi Long Madgett. PhN p. 54
Drink to that Gospel Clown Who Rang a Thousand Bills. Sonia Sanchez. LoP p.31
Driver. Elma Stuckey. BiGa p.8
Drivers are dead now, The. Pauli Murray. DaTAOP p.24
Drivin Wheel. Sherley Williams. PePo p.30
Driving Along Interstate 94. Naomi Long Madgett. ExAE p.65
Driving Through New England by Broken Barns and Pastures. ** Lucille Clifton. GoNAE p.10
Driving Wheele. Sherley Williams. BlSi p.260
Drone. Wanda Coleman. MaDBL p.91
Drop-Out. Gertrude Blackwell Bailey. IfWCF p.17
Drug addict I refuse to be, A. Gertrude Blackwell Bailey. IfWCF p.48
Drum, The. Nikki Giovanni. ThWRNW p.30
Drum Major of the Freedom Parade, The. Margaret T. G. Burroughs. WhSIT p.30
Drumdrum drum, humbly we come, A. Gwendolyn Brooks. BlPo p.24; BlWOA p.721; CNAW p.524; ITM p.42; PoBA p.161; PoNe p.338; WoOGB p.414
Drummer King. Barbara Mahone. Suga p.32
Drums, drums, drums. Masses of Black women dancing. Nilaja. ThHSD p.61
Drums Everywhere Drums.** Jayne Cortez. MoOP p.34
Drums...pa-rum...the rat-tat-tat... of drums, The. Nikki Giovanni. ThWRNW p.30
Dry Bones. Anonymous. BlLi p. 125
Dry brown couging beneath their feet, The. Gwendolyn Brooks.

AnA p.48; SPGB p.61; WoOGB p.112
Dry mouths thrist for something wet. Jennifer Blackman Lawson. BlIMT p.53
Drying Spit Blues. Jayne Cortez. MoOP p.16
Dryness is upon the house my father loved and tended, A. Gwendolyn Brooks. SPGB p.69; WoOGB p.309
Duck fats rot in the roasting pan, The. Gwendolyn Brooks. AnA p.11; SPGB p.35; WoOGB p.75
Dudu Ni Dudu. D. T. Ogilvie. YoBBI p.515
Duke. Elma Stuckey. BiGa p.44
Dunbar. Anne Spencer. AmLNA p. 47; BANP p.218; CaD p.50; KAL p.37
During the season of cut organs we shot forward like teeth spokes from runaways. Jayne Cortez. FeAF p.3; PoBA p.345
Dusk. Angelina Weld Grimke. CaD p.46
Dusk. Mae V. Cowdery. EbAT p.26 WLOV p.23
Dusk. Naomi Long Madgett. PhN p.15
Dusk comes quietly in, The. Elma Stuckey. BiGa p.89
Dusk is the dreaded hour. Pauli Murray. DaTAOP p.84
Dusk is the end of a bygone day. Naomi Long Madgett. PhN p.15
Dusk Thoughts. Countess W. Twitty. EbR p.148
Dusks, no dawns, and silver linings have all been melted into half-dollars. Julianne Perry. PoBA p.516
Dusky Harlem here in the Middle west. Naomi Long Madgett. PhN p.88
Dust. Beatris Overby. NegVo p. 119
Dust in de sunshine an' lint on de air. Lucile D. Goodlett. WGC p.20
Dust of ancient pages had never touched his face, The. Maya Angelou. OhPWFW p.21
Dust of broken dreams is in my eyes. Beatris Overby. NegVo p.118
Dying Bondman, The. Frances E. W. Harper. CNAW p.102; ITBLA p.93; PBFH p.117
Dying Slave's Request, The. Josephine D. (Henderson) Heard. MoGl p.124
Dykes of the world are united. Nikki Giovanni. BFBTBJ p.45

- E -

Each body has its art. Gwendolyn Brooks. SPGB p.23; StIB p.47; WoOGB p.49
Each little footstep I hear in the street. Naomi Long Madgett. PhN p.23
Each Night. Mae V. Cowdery. WLOV p.38
Each nite without you and I give birth to myself. Sonia Sanchez. LoP p.95
Each One, Pull One. Alice Walker. CoAAAW p.356
Each Sunday. Nikki Giovanni. WoATM p.9
Each Sunday the people of this town would go to church. Patricia Parker. MoIB p.56
Eagle now has stirred the nest, The. Edna Mae Weiss. EbR p.53
Eagle Rock. Alice Walker. RePOP p.20
Eagles. Nikki Giovanni. ThWRNW p.32
Eagles are a majestic species. Nikki Giovanni. ThWRNW p.32
Early April he began to sniff it. Judy Dothard Simmons. CoAAAW p.332
Early in the Mornin.** Mari Evans. CoAAAW p.108; IABW p.6
Early Losses; a Requiem. Alice Walker. BlSi p.223
Early mist bring back the dawn. Jodi Braxton. SoITM p.48
Early News Report. Naomi Long Madgett. PiLAF p.14
Early one morning Bessie, sweeet, Bessie turned to Billie, Bird & Otis. Carolyn M. Rodgers. JuBa p.115

Early words flit through my mind's bare branches. Naomi Long Madgett. ExAE p.50
Earth. Lucille Clifton. GoNAE p.17
Earth Bosom. Mary Bohanon. GaBW p.258
Earth Bound. Carolyn M. Rodgers. HeAEG p.11
Earth Changes & We Move With It, The. Pamela Cobb. InDM p.39
Earth Eyes Breathing Me.** Sonia Sanchez. IvBAW p.82
Earth is a beautiful place, The. Gwendolyn Brooks. BlP p.176; RIOT p.11
Earth is Not the World, Nor All Its Beauty. Carolyn M. Rodgers. HeAEG p.3
Earth is Not the World, Nor All Its Beauty, Poem II. Carolyn M. Rodgers. HeAEG p.4
Earth Mother. Pamela Cobb. InDM p.16
Earth Mother (Low Singing Is Heard) Sonia Sanchez. BlUn p.24
Earth turns like a rainbow. Pinkie Gordon Lane. BlSi p. 229; MyFe p.37
Earthlings, earthlings why don't you leave us alone. Olean Bess. MiFe p.6
Earthquake of 1886, The. Josephine D. (Henderson) Heard. MoGl p.26
Ease a mask from out of space. Nancy L. Arnez. RoCO p.23
East and West of New Haven/the Heart, as Evergreen. Carolyn M. Rodgers. HeAEG p.70
East of New Haven. Carolyn M. Rodgers. HeAEG p.68
Easter. Inez M. Thurman. NegVo p.149
Easter baskets, matching egg cups of the flesh. Harryette Mullen. TTW p.48
Easter Colors. Harryette Mullen. TTW p.13
Easter Morn. Josephine D. (Henderson) Heard. MoGl p.65
Easter Sunday. Lucille Clifton. GoNAE p.44
Easy Rider. Anonymous. BlWOA p.648
Easy rider, see what you done done, Lawd, Lawd. Anonymous. BlWOA p.648
Ebb with the flow of this soft movement. Mari Evans. BlSi p.142; NIGHT p.25
Ebben tide ib floating past, The. Anonymous. BlWOA p.236
Ebony. Lucy Mae Turner. BCF p.38
Echo. Audre Lorde. FiCi p.16
Echo. Dorothy F. Blackwell. EbR p.5
Echoes. Naomi Long Madgett. ExAE p.53
Echoes. Angels. hosannas. consecrations of mercy. Carolyn M. Rodgers. CoAAAW p.312
Eclipse. Georgia Douglas Johnson. BrBV p.79
Eclipsing my salvation, while usurping my possible damnation. E. Diane Bogus. WITM p.57
Ecology. June Jordan. ThTDID p.195
Ecology Home-Style. Lyn. SiSH p.29
Ecstasy. Georgia Douglas Johnson. ALC p.43
Eddie hung a light globe with the best electric tape. June Jordan. ThTDID p.62
Edge of This Cleaver, The. Lucille Clifton. GoNAE p.23
Eelie got de blue-gum. Lucile D. Goodlett. WGC p.53
Ef ah could, ah sholy would. Anonymous. BlWOA p.465
Ef I had wings like Noah's dove. Anonymous. BlWOA p.461
E'er yet the morning heav'd its orient head. Phillis Wheatley. PPW p.64
Egg Boiler, The. Gwendolyn Brooks. BeEa p.68; BTB p.51; DaS p.501; PoBA p.154; WoOGB p.366
Egg in Each Basket, An. Elma Stuckey. BiGa p.71
Ego. Ntozake Shange. NaEd p. 138
Ego-Tripping. Nikki Giovanni. EgT p.3; Rec p.37; WoATM

p.22
1863, my great grandmother--cut eleven years. Judy Dothard Simmons. JuB p.6
Either heard or taught as girl. Audre Lorde. ChPON p.78; NeHS p.36
El becomes a subway in my lifetime, The. Barbara Mahone. Suga p.19
El Hajj Malik Shabazz. Mari Evans. NIGHT p.70
El Hajj Malik Shabazz/who went through the changes. Mari Evans. NIGHT p.70
El Malojo. Harryette Mullen. TTW p.50
Elaine. Naomi Long Madgett. PhN p.113
Elaine with the late sun on your face. Naomi Long Madgett. PhN p.113
Elderidge. Lucille Clifton. GoNAE p.23
Elegance in the Extreme. Ntozake Shange. NaEd p.131
Elegiac Poem, on the Death of That Celebrated Divine, and Eminent Servant of Jesus Christ, the Late Reverend and Pious George Whitfield. Phillis Wheatley. PPW p.66
Elegy. Margaret Walker. PFND p.31
Elegy. Maya Angelou. OhPWFW p.62
Elegy in a Rainbow. Gwendolyn Brooks. Bec p.9
Elegy: Marion. Pinkie Gordon Lane. WiTh p.12
Elegy Sacred to the Memory of Dr. Samuel Cooper (1784), An. Phillis Wheatley. PAL p.78; PPW p.90
Elegy, To Miss Mary Moorhead, on the Death of her Fatner, The Rev. Mr. John Moorhead, An. Phillis Wheatley. EbAT p.77; PPW p.79
Elegy Written to America. Frenchy J. Hodges. BlW p.17
Elephant. Anonymous. TYBP p.11
Elephant II. Anonymous. TYBP p.3
Elephant Hunter, take your bow! Anonymous. TYBP p.3
Elephant, who brings death. Anonymous. TYBP p.11
Elevation. George Douglas Johnson. HWOP p.8
Elevator Man Adheres to Form, The. Margaret Danner. BTB p.86; CNAW p.764; DoOAT p.68; IrLa p.16; MoCAP p.87; PoBA p.137; PoNe p.161
Elevens. Leatrice Emeruwa. BlGBG p.9
Elijah McCoy, Inventor of the Lubricating Cup, 1843-1929, Michigan. Eloise Culver. GANIV p.40
Eliza. Naomi Long Madgett. PiLAF p.53
Eliza Harris. Frances E. W. Harper. AfAV p.82; NeCa p.294
Ella Mae. Jennifer Blackman Lawson. BlIMT p.5
Emancipation of George-Hector. Mari Evans. AmNP p.165; BlVo p.480; BTB p.105; IABW p.54; MBP p.40; MyNIB p.110
Emancipation Proclamation. Elma Stuckey. BiGa p.62
Emblems. Georgia Douglas Johnson. HWOP p.13
Emmett's mother is a pretty-faced thing. Gwendolyn Brooks. BeEa p.26; PoBA p.155; SPGB p.81; WoOGB p.324
Emotional Con Meets a Virginal Ideal, The. Wanda Coleman. MaDBL p.65
Emotional intangible ethereal-ities difficult to dissect. Johari Amini. ImIB p.11
Emotions of the Blacks. Doris E. Shaw. GaBW p.400
Empress Brand Trim: Ruby Reminisces, The. Sherley Williams. BlSi p.253
Empress of the Death House, The. Toi Derricotte. EmDH p.41
Empty carousel in a deserted park, An. Gloria Oden. AmNP p.159; DeRi p.4; KAL p.181; MoCAP p.95; PoBA p.181
Empty-eyed building reflect

nothing of abandoned life. Regina Williams. CoAAAW p.381
Empty of Seed. Pauli Murray. DaTAOP p.84
Empty Woman, The. Gwendolyn Brooks. SPGB p.119
En bahia women wrap cloth like sun flowers found their heads. Ntozake Shange, NaEd p.127
En Passant. June Jordan. PaNP p.70
Enchantment. Georgia Holloway Jones. EbR p.98
Encounter. Naomi Long Madgett. StBS p.17
End of a line is movement, The. Sherley Williams. CoAAAW p. 392
End of Summer. Naomi Long Madgett. OnATM p.16
End of the Day, The. Gwendolyn Brooks. StIB p.33; WoOGB p.35
Endangered Species, The. Margaret Danner. DoOAT p.59
Ending. Alice Walker. RePOP p. 43
Endless fog winds down a gray eternity, The. Naomi Long Madgett. StBS p.28
Endowed. Margaret Danner. DoOAT p.14
Enemy, The. Alice Walker. ONC p.46
Enemy of Man, The. Alicia Loy Johnson. NiBPo p.155
Enigma. Jessie Redmond Fauset. PoN p.65; PoNe p.66; RoATW p.118
Enough. Ester Louise. CoAAAW p. 198
Enslaved. Elma Stuckey. BiGa p. 63
Envoys. Georgia Douglas Johnson. ALC p.41
Epigram. Iola M. Brister. EbR p.13
Epileptic. Pinkie Gordon Lane. WiTh p.9
Episode. June Vanleer Williams. WiRYPS p.55
Epitaph, An. Josephine D. (Henderson) Heard. MoGl p.84
Epitaph. Naomi Long Madgett. OnATM p.38
Epitaph for a Bigot. Dorothy Vena Johnson. EbR p.91 PoN p.120; PoNe p.226
Epitaph for my Father. Margaret Walker. OcJo p.19
Equal Opportunity. Judy Dothard Simmons. CoAAAW p. 331
Equinox. Audre Lorde. ChPON p.39; FrLWP p.11
Ere yet the morn its lovely blushes spred. Phillis Wheatley. PAL p.34; PPW p.7
Escape. Georgia Douglas Johnson. PoBA p.22
Escape. Mari Evans. IABW p.42
Escape from life to life I pull out fragile faces. Kathy Elaine Anderson. NeJCL p.27
Escape # 1. Naomi Long Madgett. PhN p.19
Escape # 2. Naomi Long Madgett. PhN p.68
Esther, As Lead. Carolyn M. Rodgers. HoIGO p.27
Estimable Mable. Gwendolyn Brooks. FaP p.20; FBPA p. 28
Estrangement. Georgia Douglas Johnson. ALC p.66
Etc. etc. etc. Dorothy C. Parrish. TNV p.87
Eternal spirit of dead dried autumn leaves. Alicia Loy Johnson. NBP p.74
Eternity. Josephine D. (Henderson) Heard. MoGl p.40
Eternity borders life. S. Diane Bogus. WITM p.60
Ethiopia. Frances E. W. Harper. EaNAW p.293
Etta Moten's Attic. Margaret Danner. BrT p.39; DoOAT p.53; MoCAP p.90
Euclid Street. Damali (Denise Burnett) IaTWMB p.18
Eulogy. Audre Lorde. BlUn p. 110
Eulogy for all our Murdered Children. Mari Evans. NIGHT p.39
Eulogy for Alvin Frost. Audre Lorde. BlUn p.40
Eulogy for Philosophers. Julia Fields. NiBPo p.77
Eulogy on the Death of Trees.

Pinkie Gordon Lane. PoBBl p. 17; WiTh p.18
Evahbody's Got Troubles.** Lucy Mae Turner. BCF p.31
Evahwhuh I whuh I look dis mawnin. Anonymous. BlWOA p.464
Eve. Lucy Mae Turner. BCF p.26
Eve of the garden magnificant mother. Lucy Mae Turner. BCF p.26
Even. Audre Lorde. NeHS p.30
Even after thirty years he still detested worms. Naomi Long Madgett. PiLAF p.22
Even Among Thieves. Beatrice M. Murphy. RoCO p.12
Even as the earth thirsts for rain. Mae V. Cowdery. WLOV p.39
Even sunlight dares and trembles through my bars. Maya Angelou. OhPWFW p.49
Even Though. Nola Richardson. WhOL p.81
Even tonight and I need to take a walk and clear my head. June Jordan. PaNP p.86
Even When the Moon Don't Shine. Melba Joyce Boyd. CaEADW p.2
Evening News, The. Audre Lorde. ChPON p.101
Eventide. Georgia Douglas Johnson. HWOP p.22
Ever been kidnapped by a poet. Nikki Giovanni. BlP p.326; BrT p.66; EgT p.1; Rec p. 23; WoATM p.29
Ever notice how it's only the ugly honkies who hate. Nikki Giovanni. BFBTBJ p.81
Ever since I realized there waz someone callt a colored girl. Ntozake Shange. BlSi p.272
Ever Want to Crawl. Nikki Giovanni. Rec p.48; WoATM p.24
Every Monday Father Took the Train to New York City.** Gloria Oden. TiTBi p.4
Every morning he sweeps the porch. Pearl Cleage Lomax. WeNNM p. 15
Every night I dream about ole marse selling my child. Elma Stuckey. BiGa p.27
Every 3 minutes a woman is beaten. Ntozake Shange. NaEd p.114
Every time the earth moves...its me. Nikki Giovanni. ThWRNW p.33
Every year the elephants must come down from the mountains. Pamela Cobb. InDM p.27
Everybody But Me. Margaret Burroughs. BlSi p.121; FBPA p.45
Everybody knows how much I admire beautiful women. Margaret Danner. DoOAT p.57
Everybody Talkin' 'Bout Heaven. Anonymous. AmLNA p.6
Everybody's looking for big mama. Naomi Long Madgett. ExAE p.35
Everyday/now somebody is gettin it on. Ntozake Shange. NaEd p.121
Everyone wants to know how it was in the old days. Audre Lorde. BlUn p.93
Everything changes the old songs click like light bulbs going off. Lucille Clifton. GoNAE p.11
Everything is Wonderful. Jayne Cortez. COAG p.103
Everytime it Rains. Nikki Giovanni. EgT p.21
Everytime you leave me. Nola Richardson. WhOL p.14
Everywhere everywhere there are people. Kali Grosvenor. PBK p.17
Evicted. Beatrice M. Murphy. TNV p.140
Evidently Looking at the Moon Requires a Clean Place to Stand. June Jordan. PaNP p.54
Evil is no black thing. Sarah Webster Fabio. DoBB p.27; PoBA p.205; UNBP p.241
Evolution. Pamela Cobb. InDM p.18
Evolution. Thelma Parker Cox. TNV p.28
Exactly a Question a Minute She Ask. Edna Shaw. NegVo p. 140
Excerpts From a Verse Diary of Somebody Trying to Get Into Gear. June Jordan. ThTDID p.193
Excite my breasts and patrol my

vagrant heart. Jayne Cortez. COAG p.15; Scar p.39
Excuse. Alice Walker. ONC p.75
Exercise in Quits, November 15, 1969. June Jordan. SCh p. 71; ThTDID p.131
Exercises on Themes From Life. Alice Walker. ONC p.79
Exhaust the Little Moment. Gwendolyn Brooks. WoOGB p.115
Existence to me, has always been trying to survive. E. Sharon Gomillion. FoAAM p.6
Exits and Entrances. Naomi Long Madgett. BlSi p.128; ExAE p.47
Exitus. Laura E. Smith. NegVo p.143
Exodus (To My Husbands, Lovers) Patricia Parker. ChOM p.8; MoIB p.37
Expect Nothing. Alice Walker. RePOP p.30
Expect nothing, live frugally on surprise. Alice Walker. RePOP p.30
Expendables, The. Mari Evans. NIGHT p.40
Expenditures Economic Love Song l. Jayne Cortez. COAG p.104
Expiriese Girl Wanted. Ntozake Shange. NaEd p.70
Explanation Always Follows, An. June Jordan. PaNP p.26
Explanations. Lucille Clifton. TwW p.55
Explaining to me that my mind is the obvious assassin. Lucille Clifton. TwW p.56
Explorer, The. Gwendolyn Brooks. BeEa p.13; WoOGB p.311
Exultation. Mae V. Cowdery. WLOV p.26
Eye follows, The. Maya Angelou. AnSIR p.19
Eye of this storm is not quiet, The. Irma McClaurin. BlSi p.196
Eye that pierces with wide precision, The. Helen H. King. TGWL p.63
Eyeballs staring unhinged from sockets. Pinkie Gordon Lane. PoBBl p.11; WiTh p.36
Eyes Gentled at the Corners So. Mari Evans. IABW p.85
Eyes in the Back of Her Head. Harryette Mullen. TTW p.4
Eyes of my Regret. Angelina Weld Grimke. CaD p.37

- F -

F.B.I. came by my house three weeks ago, The. Nikki Giovanni. MyH p.59
Face/As It Must Be/Of Love, The. Toi Derricotte. EmDH p.23
Face in the window...is not the face in the mirror, The. Nikki Giovanni. ThWRNW p.22
Face of Poverty. Lucy Smith. NNPUSA p.45; PoNe p.267
Face on the Sunwarmed Granite. Mari Evans. NIGHT p.43
Faces. Maya Angelou. JGM p.32
Faces and more remember. Maya Angelou. JGM p.32
Faces surround me that have no smell or color no time. Audre Lorde. BlSi p.199; BlUn p.22
Facial. Gwendolyn Brooks. AnA p. 53
Fact is that I don't hate any body any more, The. Carolyn M. Rodgers. HoIGO p.53
Fad. Leatrice Emeruwa. BlGBG p.13
Faded Flowers. Josephine D. (Henderson) Heard. MoGl p.122
"Failure, failure, your face you should hide," June Vanleer Williams. WiRYPS p.9
Faint lose faith when in the tomb their all is laid, The. Georgia Douglas Johnson. BrBV p.63
Faint Violets. Melba Joyce Boyd. CaEADW p.27
Fair morn unbars her gates of gold. Henrietta Cordelia Ray. ANP p.129; AVAN p.152
Faith. Georgia Douglas Johnson. BrBV p.63
Faith. Leona Lyons. NegVo p.99
Fakery. June Vanleer Williams. WiRYPS p.67
Fall-Time. Bessie Woodson Yancey. EcFTH p.54
Fallen, The. Audre Lorde.

ChPON p.67; NeHS p.28
Falling. Claudia E. Jemmott. GaBW p.353
Fame. Josephine D. (Henderson) Heard. MoGl p.24
Fame on All Fours. Ntozake Shanke. NaEd p.82
Familiarize Your Self With Strength. Sonia Sanchez. IvBAW p.74
Family: Growing Up. Jennifer Blackman Lawson. BlIMT p.33
Family had been ill for some time, The. Ntozake Shange. NaEd p.90
Family Member (You Must Be Putting Me On) A. June Vanleer Williams. WiRYPS p.72
Family Of. Alice Walker. CoAAAW p.354
Family or Freedom. Elma Stuckey, BiGa p.52
Family Portrait. Colleen McElroy. MuDLSG p.3
Family Portrait. Naomi Long Madgett. ExAE p.11
Family Resemblance, A. Audre Lorde. ChPON p.18; COAL p.14; FiCi p.3
Family Tree, A. Patricia Parker. ChOMP p.15; DOBB p.111; MoIB p.55
Fanfare, Coda and Finale. Margaret Walker. CoAAW p.372
Fantasia. Naomi Long Madgett. ExAE p.20
Fantasy. Gwendolyn B. Bennett. BlSi p.72; CaD p.158
Fantasy and Coversation. Audre Lorde. CaTR p.26; ChPON p. 24; COAL p.48; NaPr p.66
Fantasy of a Fool. Naomi Long Madgett. PhN p.50
Far From Africa: Four Poems. Margaret Danner. BlWOA p. 816; MoCAP p.88; PoBA p. 134
Far from the seried ranks you sway. Georgia Douglas Johnson. BrBV p.96
Far off heavy crackers Vietnam the New Year. Leatrice Emeruwa. BlGBG p.16
Farewell. Mae V. Cowdery. WLOV p.29
Farewell, March, I shall not miss you when you go. Naomi Long Madgett. PhN p. 43
Farewell to Allen University. Josephine D (Henderson) Heard. MoGl p.18
Farewell to America To Mrs. S.W. Phillis Wheatley. AmLNA p. 22; BlWOA p.42; PAl p.49; PPW p.57
Fascinations. Nikki Giovanni. CoCRD p.60
Fashion-Plate, The. Marva Tatum Smith. BeYM p.11
Fashioned not in the image of the graceful ones. Jennifer Blackman Lawson. BlIMT p.2
Fat boy is a cop. Carolyn M. Rodgers. AfAWA p.777
Father and Daughter. Sonia Sanchez. IvBAW p.29; LoP p.7
Father and Daughter. Sonia Sanchez. LoP p.8
Father holds daughter high above the ground. Jeanette Adams. RoATW p.72
Father I am not equal to the faith required. Lucille Clifton. TWW p.58
Father, I wait for you in oceans. Maya Angelou. OhPWFW p.57
Father (Part I) Harryette Mullen. TTW p.18
Father holds daughters high above the ground. Jeanette Adams. ThHSD p.34
Father, I dreamed of you last night. Norma Lopez Garcia. NeJCL p.28
Father Son and Holy Ghost. Audre Lorde. BTB p.140; ChPON p.9; COAL p.4; FiCi p.13; MoCAP p.121; PoBA p.248; SiAS p.47; UNBP p.285
Father The Year Has Fallen. Audre Lorde. ChPON p.10; COAL p.30; FiCi p.18; PoBA p.246; SiAS p.48
Fattening Frogs for Snakes. Anonymous. UNBP p.90
Faux-Semblant. Johari Amini. ImIB p.4
Fear can drain and grip man's guts. June Vanleer Williams. WiRYPS p.71

Fear Not. Mary Bohanon. GaBW p. 258
Fear to Freedom. Marva Tatum Smith. BeYM p.17
Feast. Mae V. Cowdery. WLOV p. 62
Feathers. Jayne Cortez. COAG p. 15; Scar p.39
February. Patrice M. Wilson. NeJCL p.22
February is the cruelest month. Patrice M. Wilson. NeJCL p. 22
February 13, 1980. Lucille Clifton. TwW p.15
Feeding, The. Toi Derricotte. EmDH p.42
Feeding the Pastor. Elma Stuckey. BiGa p.76
Feel so blakk like stronger than me. Tyki Brown. ThHSD p.71
Feel free like my daddy. Lucille Clifton. GoNAE p.24; PoBA p.308
Feeling no pain he said and continued to smile. Carolyn M. Rodgers. HeAEG p.27
Feet know how to be Negro. Eleanora E. Tate. BrA p.16
Feminism. Carolyn M. Rodgers. HeAEG p.47
Fences. Naomi Long Madgett. ExAE p.66
Festivals & Funerals. Jayne Cortez. FeAF p.9
Fetch out de big pot and fry out de strippin's. Lucile Goodlet. WGC p.24
Few can walk in his class. Eloise Culver. GANIV p.65
Few there were who came to mourn him. June Vanleer Williams. WiRYPS p.36
Few Years After Father Died, A. ** Gloria Oden. RESUR p.59
Few years back and they told me Black means a hole, A. June Jordan. PaNP p.37
Fibrous Ruin. June Jordan. SCh p.11; ThTDID p.159
Fibrous ruin of the skin not year. June Jordan. SCh p.11; ThTDID p.159
Fiction. Georgia Douglas Johnson. ALC p.49
Fiction/Non-Fiction (Okra's Intellect Addresses Greens' Mind) Ntozake Shange. DaGe p.65
Fiddle in de Win'. Lucile D. Goodlett. WGC p.41
Fifteenth Amendment. Frances E. W. Harper. EaNAW p.297
Fifth Michael, The. Margaret Danner. DoOAT p.129
Fifth Street, Exit, Richmond. Naomi Long Madgett. ExAE p.24
Fight, fight... I have no fight within. Kattie M. Cumbo. NiBPo p.64
Fight was at its hottest, The. Josephine D. (Henderson) Heard. MoGl p.76
Fighting, bleeding, falling, dying--dying for the movement. Pauli Murray. DaTAOP p.52
Final Indignity, The. Lyn SiSH p.5
Final Solution, The. Sonia Sanchez. HoC p.18
Finale. June Vanleer Williams. WiRYPS p.85
Finality. Georgia Douglas Johnson. ALC p.47
Finally in silence where bodies lying down. Pamela Cobb. InDM p.21
Finding myself still fascinated by the falls and rapids. Nikki Giovanni. CoCRD p.60
Finding of a Nest the Coming to a Roost, The. Sherley Williams. PePo p.58
Finger Burst His Head.** June Jordan. ThTDID p.160
Fingers flaming inter-clenched blood to blood. Mari Evans. IABW p.87
Fingertips and Quiet Moments. Melba Joyce Boyd. CaEADW p.21
Finis. Georgia Douglas Johnson. ALC p.22
Finis. Pinkie Gordon Lane. WiTh p.17
Finis. Pinkie Gordon Lane. WiTh p.56
Fire darkens the wood turns black, The. Anonymous. TYBP p.5

Fire in me burns, A. Thelma T. Clement. BTh p.23
Fire-Tears-and the torture-chamber. Georgia Douglas Johnson. ALC p.28
Firefly is heedless wandering about, The. Anonymous. DuSAE p.23
Firing Burst His Head. June Jordan. SCh p.42; ThTDID p.160
Firespitters. Jayne Cortez. COAG p.51
Firespitters spitting across the desert. Jayne Cortez. COAG p.51
1st, The. Lucille Clifton. DOBB p.51
First aspect is love, The. Carolyn M. Rodgers. HoIGO p.70; SoBB p.38
First bright day has broken, The. Audre Lorde. BlUn p.38
First Date. Leatrice Emeruwa. BlGBG p.5
First day I shot dope was on a Sunday, The. Sonia Sanchez. BlP p.237; BlSi p.246; IvBAW p.23; NaPr p.126; WABP p.35
First Flakes That Fell on Mother's. Grave, The. Josephine D. (Henderson) Heard. MoGl p.120
First Flight, Then Fiddle. Gwendolyn Brooks. PlPo p.22; PoNe p.337
First Lady. Edna L. Harrison. EbR p.79
First, love came timidly and full of fear. Naomi Long Madgett. OnATM p.36
First Meeting Japanese Style. Barbara Mahone. Suga p.29
First sign was your hair. Carole Gregory Clemmons. PoBA p.489
First, suicide notes should be (not long) but written. Alice Walker. ONC p.74
First they said I was too light. June Jordan. PaNP p.78
First thing you do is to forget that I'm Black, The. Patricia Parker. MoIB p. 68
First time I was sweet sixteen. Nayo. NeBV p.384
First upward he looked. Mary Bohanon. GaBW p.258
First warmth is in her smile, The. Edna L. Harrison. EbR p.79
Firstly inclined to take what is told. Gwendolyn Brooks. SPGB p.26; StIB p.53; WoOGB p.55
Fish does...hip, The. Anonymous. MBP p.11
"Fishers of Men." Frances E. W. Harper. PBFH p.82
Fishin'. Lucile D. Goodlett. WGC p.29
Fishy Poem. Nikke Giovanni. MyH p.9
Fisk is a negroid institution. Sharon Scott. JuBa p.179
Five. Ntozake Shange. NaEd p. 93
Five Black Men... Margaret Walker. CoAAAW p.363
Five hours he spent charting your life-scopes. Leatrice Emeruwa. BlGBG p.13
Five Men Against the Theme. "My Name is Red Hot. Yo Name Ain Doodley Squat." Gwendolyn Brooks. Bec p.6
5 shirts 2 blouses 3 pair of jeans and the iron's on hot for cotton. June Jordan. CoAAAW p.180
5 Winks. Carolyn M. Rodgers. SoBB p.38; UNBP p.344
Fivetenfifteentwenty twenty five thirty thirty fiveforty. Sonia Sanchez. BluB p.26; IvBAW p.57
Flags. Gwendolyn Brooks. AmNP p.141; PoN p.190
Flame. Jayne Cortez. COAG p. 48
Flame-flower, day-torch, mauna loa. Anne Spencer. AmLNA p.47; AmNP p.18; BlWOA p. 627; CaD p.52; CNAW p.272; ITBLA p.155; NeCa p.354; PoN p.53; PoNe p.64
Flames. Mari Evans. BlLi p.434; IABW p.79; WhIAM p.20
Flames had swept the walls. May Miller. ClAB p.23
Flames were loud, The. Julia

Fields. GsNE p.310; NiBPo p. 71
Flamingo. Margaret Danner. DoOAT p.67
Flash or lightning does not satisfy thirst, A. Anonymous. TYBP p.59
Flatted faces rim my vacuum. Mari Evans. NIGHT p.6
Flesh has a way of reaching out. Pinkie Gordon Lane. WiTh p.47
Flesh to flesh with you, we two, so starved. S. Diane Bogus. WITM p.19
Flight. Coston Vale. NegVo p. 159
Flight. Elma Stuckey. BiGa p. 89
Flight. Pinkie Gordon Lane. MyFe p.31
Fling down the night's imperious delay. Naomi Long Madgett. StBS p.26
Fling off de back step. Lucile D. Goodlett. WGC p.41
Flo Show. Sherley Williams. PePo p.29
Floating Thru the Galaxy. Eleanor Thomas-Grumbach. MoSu p.13
Flood Song. Helen F. Chappell. NegVo p.28
Floorwax Mother. Harryette Mullen. TTW p.22
Flop, The. Anonymous. AOS p.8
Flow of hot sake the sweet scent of incense, A. Barbara Mahone. Suga p.29
Flower spoke to me, A. Mary Bohanon. GaBW p.257
Flowers. Gertrude Blackwell Bailey. IfWCF p.34
Flowers. Julia Fields. GaBW p. 303
Flowers for hours remain inert. Nikki Giovanni. VaT p.33
Flutter of a thin linen curtain that is teased, The. S. Diane Bogus. WITM p.58
Flyin'. Lucy Mae Turner. BCF p.48
Flying saucer landed in my living room, A. Nikki Giovanni. CoCRD p.72
Flying-Song. Ntozake Shange. NaEd p.139
Flying Underground. Nikki Giovanni. ThWRNW p.33
Fog Report. Audre Lorde. BlUn p.70
Folded in silent veils of sleep, you calmly rest. Georgia Douglas Johnson. BrBV p.100
Folding of the Feathers the Counting of the Birds, The. Sherley Williams. PePo p.62
Folk. Carolyn M. Rodgers. CoAAAW p.314
Folksong. From the Lillies of the Field. MyNIB p.50
Folks dey talks about de weathah. Bessie Woodson Yancey. EcFTH p.45
Folks just keep complainin.' June Vanleer Williams. WiRYPS p.28
Folks think I talking to myself. Elma Stuckey. BiGa p.25
Follow the Drinkin'-Gourd. Anonymous. AfAV p.120
Follow the train full of bodies. Alice Walker. RePOP p.48
Fondle me caress and cradle me. Mari Evans. BlP p.187; IABW p.32; WhIAM p.11
Food for Thought. Carolyn M. Rodgers. HoIGO p.57
Food for Thought. Val Ferdinand. NeBV p.378
Food Poisoning. Marion Nicholes. LiS p.17
Fool, The. Marva Tatum Smith. BeYM p.21
Foolish, incessant, inconsequential chatter. Naomi Long Madgett. PhN p.104
Footnote to a Part of Life That is Now History. Pamela Cobb. InDM p.19
Footsteps. Georgia Douglas Johnson. ALC p.4
Footsteps. Gertrude Blackwell Bailey. IfWCF p.9
For a Child. Naomi Long Madgett. BTB p.148; CNAW p.772; StBS p.57
For a Discontented Soul. Dorothy Lee Louise Shaed. NegVo p.139
For a Future's Treasury. Pinkie Gordon Lane. WiTh p.47

For a Lady of Pleasure Now Retired Nikki Giovanni. BrT p.67; Rec p.30; WoATM p.19
For a New Mother. Mae V. Cowdery. WLOV p.46
For a Poet I Know. Nikki Giovanni BFBTBJ p.91
For a Young Friend Seeking "Identity". May Miller. ClAB p.31
For All My Dead & Loved Ones. Ntozake Shange. NaEd p.98
For An Intellectual Audience. Nikki Giovanni. BFBTBJ p.35
For Andy Goodman, Michael Schwerner--and James Chaney. Margaret Walker. BlP p.158; BrT p.152; PFND p.18
For Assata. Audre Lorde. BlUn p.28
For Beautiful Mary Brown: Chicago Rent Strike Leader. June Jordan. SCh p.49; ThTDID p.101
For Beauty. Margaret Danner. IrLa p.24
For Bill. Pinkie Gordon Lane. WiTh p.31
For Both of Us at Fisk. Snaron Scott. JuBa p.180
For Brother you know who are you. Marion Nicholes. LiS p.19
For C. G. Because David Came in Hot and Crying From the News. June Jordan. ThTDID p.181
For Christopher. June Jordan. SCh p.39; ThTDID p.11
For Clarice It Is Terrible Because With This He Takes Away All the Popular Songs and the Moonlights and Still Night Hushes and the Movies With Star-Eyed Girls and Simpering Males. Gwendolyn Brooks. BeEa p.50; WoOGB p.348
For Dave: 1976. June Jordan. ThTDID p.83
For De Lawd. Lucille Clifton. DOBB p.53; PoBA p.306
For death, for dying there can be no philosophy. Julia Fields. NiBPo p.77
For Dr. Coffin Who Loves. Carole Gregory Clemmons. NiBPo p.89
For Donna. Patricia Parker. ChOM p.13; MoIB p.31
For E. S. Diane Bogus. WITM p. 26
For Each of You. Audre Lorde. ChPON p.42; FrLWP p.7
For Eric Toller. Margaret T. G. Burroughs. WhSIT p.29
For Ethelbert. June Jordan. ThTDID p.78
For ever and ever and ever, beyond time and space, never, never, never will peace know my face. Lucia M. Pitts. EbR p.120
For Every (One) Barbara Mahone. Suga p.31
For every timid dream that nestles briefly in my palm. Naomi Long Madgett. OnATM p.11
For gardens I have never seen and birds and winds and water. Mae V. Cowdery. WLOV p.22
For Gwen. Maxine Hall Elliston. TGWL p.33
For Gwen. Sharon Scott. TGWL p.89
(For Gwen Brooks) Sonia Sanchez. IvBAW p.68
For Gwen--1969; Margaret Walker. OcJo p.34; TGWL p.95
For Gwendolyn Brooks. Helen H. King. TGWL p.63
For Gwendolyn Brooks. Nikki Giovanni. Bec p.12; TGWL p.48
For Gwendolyn Brooks. Pinkie Gordon Lane. WiTh p.39
For Gwendolyn Brooks--A Whole & Beautiful Spirit. Johari Amini. LetGSM p.11; TGWL p.12
For H.M.G. Virginia Houston. NegVo p.76
For H. W. Fuller. Carolyn M. Rodgers. BlP p.262; HoIGO p.38; SoBB p.30
For Harold Logan. Nikki Giovanni. Rec p.8
For Her. Lucille Clifton. CoAAAW p.87
For Her Her Hiding Place in Whiteness. Lucille Clifton. GoNAE p.25
For his fingers can carve. Mar-

garet Danner. DoOAT p.93
For His Own. Lyn. SiSH p.20
For I am rightful fellow of their band. Gwendolyn Brooks. AfAWA p.578; BlWOA p.717; KAL p.156; PoN p.191; SPGB p.25; StIB p.51; WoOGB p. 53
For Janet Gaillard. Thulani Davis. AlTRGR p.49
For Jim Easter Eve. Anne Spencer. AmNP p.17; PoN p.54; PoNe p.65
For Li'l Bit. June Jordan. PaNP p.71
For Lillie. Carolyn M. Rodgers. HeAEG p.30
For Love. Colleen McElroy. MuDLSG p.30
For Love of Our Brothers. Barbara Mahone. Suga p.26
For Mack C. Parker. Pauli Murray. DaTAOP p.39; PoBA p. 110
For Malcolm. Joyce Whitsitt Lawrence. BrT p.33; FoM p. 20
For Malcolm. Margaret Walker. PoBA p.150
For Malcolm X. Julia Fields. FoM p.33; YoBBI p.398
For Malcolm X. Margaret Walker. BlP p.157; BlPo p.20; FoM p.32; PFND p.18; UNBP p.165
For Malcolm X. Nanina Alba. FoM p.39; PoBA p.169
For Mama. Jill Witherspoon Boyer. DrF p.24
For "Mamie". Fayola Kamaria Ama. CoAAAW p.48
For Marian. Ntozake Shange. NaEd p.112
For Marty. S. Diane Bogus. WITH p.52
For Mary McLeod Bethune. Margaret Walker. OcJo p.32; PoN p.188; PoNe p.326; YoBBI p.155
For Michael Angelo Thompson. June Jordan. ThTDID p.121
For Michael on His Third Birthday. Patricia Parker. ChOM p.12; MoIB p.54
For Moments. Melva Eloise Tatum. MELVA p.18
For Moments in Laughter. Melva Eloise Tatum. MELVA p.18
For Momma. Melba Joyce Boyd. CaEADW p.7
For Mrs. Lightfoot. Margaret Danner. DoOAT p.135
For Muffin. Margaret Danner. DoOAT p.111; IrLa p.1
For My Brother. June Jordan. ThTDID p.64
For My Children. Vanessa Howard. ScWh p.20
For My Friends at the Boys Training School. Jill Witherspoon Boyer. DrF p.18
For My Grandfater Lowell Paxter Mitchell. Harryette Mullen. TTW p.14
For My Grandpa. Vanessa Howard. ScWh p.44
For My Jamaican Sister a Little Bit Lost on the Island of Manhattan. June Jordan. ThTDID p.16
For My Mother. June Jordan. SCh p.3; ThTDID p.25
For my mother I would write a list. June Jordan. SCh p. 3; ThTDID p.25
For my own part I've not lived enough. Nancy L. Arnez. RoCO p.24
For My People.** Margaret Walker. AfAV p.344; AmNP p.128; BlALP p.98; BLIA p.216; BlEx p.498; BlVo p.495; BlWOA p.636; CNAW p.527; DaS p.495; FMP p.13; IADB p.107; ITBLA p.219; KAL p.138; MoCAP p.73; NeCa p.409; NeNRe p.383. PoBA p.144; PoN p.186; PoNe p. 314; YoBBI p.153
For My Singing Sister. Audre Lorde. ChPON p.90; NeHS p.33
For My Sister Molly Who in the Fifties. Alice Walker. RePOP p.16
For myriad lonely autums flesh has yearned. Margaret Danner. DoOAT p.51
For Nina Simone. Kali Grosvenor. PBK p.44
For Nina Simone Wherever You Are. Linda Curry. OnOW p.25

For O.-Two Hung Up. Carolyn M. Rodgers. BlSp p.182; RoATW p.103
For one bright moment heavenly goddess shines. Phillis Wheatley. PPW p.86
For One So Brief and Lovely Day. ** Naomi Long Madgett. OnATM p.15
For Our Fathers. Carolyn M. Rodgers. HoIGO p.58
For Our Lady. Sonia Sanchez. NaPr p.125; WABP p.41
For our life is a matter of faith. Regina Williams. CoAAAW p. 379
For Pan. Pauli Murray. DaTAOP p.86
For Paul Laurence Dunbar. Margaret Walker. OcJo p.33
For Real. Jayne Cortez. PoBA p.344
For Ronald King Our Brother. Sherley Williams. PePo p.76
For Sapphire, My Sister. Alice H. Jones. RoATW p.61; YoBBI p.435
For Sapphires. Carolyn M. Rodgers. HoIGO p.42
(For Sarah Fabio) Sonia Sanchez. IvBAW p.80
For Saundra. Nikki Giovanni. BFBTBJ p.88; BlP p.321; BlWOA p.823; BrT p.57; NaPr p.28; TNV p.34; TYBP p.256
For Sistuhs Wearing Straight Hair. Carolyn Rodgers. SoBB p.14
For Some Black Men. Carolyn M. Rodgers. HoIGO p.46
For Some Poets. Mae Jackson. BOL p.16; CaPWY p.18; PoBA p.497
For Somebody to Start Singing. June Jordan. SCh p.19; ThTDID p.107
For Stokely Carmichel. Kali Grosvenor. PBK p.45
For the Bird Who Flew Against your Window one Morning and Broke His Natural Neck. Lucille Clifton. GoNAE p.18
For the Blind. Lucille Clifton. TwW p.42
For the Brave New Students in Soweto. Jayne Cortez. COAG p.44
For the Brave Young Students in Soweto. Jayne Cortez. CoAAAW p.95; MoOP p.61
For the Candle Light. Angelina Weld Grimke. BlSi p.63; CaD p.45; PoN p.47; PoNe p.55
For the Count. Mae Jackson. CoAAAW p.168
For the first time I be thinkin like I be dealin. Barbara Mahone. PoBA p.473; Suga p.23
For the King and Queen of Summer. Audre Lorde. COAL p.47
For the Lame. Lucille Clifton. TwW p.44
For the Lips of One Grown Weary. Helen F. Chappell. NegVo p.28
For the Mad. Lucille Clifton. TwW p.42
For the Masai Warriors. Nikki Giovanni. EgT p.7
For the Mute. Lucille Clifton. TwW p.44
For the Others. Carolyn M. Rodgers. HeAEG p.62
For the Poet. Adrienne Rich. June Jordan. ThTDID p.194
For the Poets. Jayne Cortez. COAG p.23; MoOP p.6
For the Straight Folks Who Don't Mind Gays.** Patricia Parker. MoIB p.111
For the White Person Who Wants to Know How to be my Friend. Patricia Parker. MoIB p.68
For the woman African in ancestry. Carole Gregory Clemmons. BlSi p.188
For There's No End to the Suffering a Female Will Bear For Beauty. Margaret Danner. DoOAT p.54
For Theresa. Nikki Giovanni. BFBTBJ p.97; MoCAP p.172
For this I love you most. Pauli Murray. DaTAOP p.90
For those of us who live at the shoreline. Audre Lorde. BlUn p.31
For three hours (too short for me) I sat in your home.

Nikki Giovanni. BFBTBJ p.6
For Two Jameses. Nikki Giovanni. Rec p.11
For Unborn Malcolms. Sonia Sanchez. HoC p.28
For Us. Esther Louise. CoAAAW p.201
For Us, Who Dare Not Dare. Maya Angelou. OhPWFW p.31
For us who sometimes fly in Dreams. Esther Louise. CoAAAW p.201
For W.E.B. DuBois. Elma Stuckey. BiGa p.88
For weeks I have been wanting to write this poem. June Jordan. ThTDID p.193
For what is truth? Carolyn M. Rodgers. HeAEG p.61
For what-sa-name. Leatrice Emeruwa. BlGBG p.21
For William Edward Burghardt DuBois on His Eightieth Birthday. Bette Darcie Latimer. PoBA p.199; PoN p.208
For Willyce. Patricia Parker. MoIB p.102
For Women. Carolyn M. Rodgers. HoIGO p.72
For women perspective is more easily maintained. Audre Lorde. ChPON p.78; NeHS p.44
For You. Jean. AOS p.4
For You. Pinkie Gordon Lane. PoBBl p.18; WiTh p.48
Forbidden Things. Alice Walker. RePOP p.64
Forced Retirement. Nikki Giovanni. CoCRD p.26
Foredoom. Georgia Douglas Johnson. HWOP p.19
Foregather. Georgia Douglas Johnson. AmLNA p.73
Forest dwindling narrow and irregular. June Jordan. PeNP p.54
Forest Green. Thulani Davis. AlTRGR p.29
Foresworn, irate, I built a castle. Virginia Houston. NegVo p.76
Forever and forevermore across the heights. Georgia Douglas Johnson. BrBV p.81
Forever Vagrant and Unowned. Mari Evans. NIGHT p.7
Foreward. Angela Jackson. HoIGO p.lx
Forfeiture. June Vanleer Williams. WiRYPS p.82
Forget me not. Ann Plato. EBAP p.116
Forgetfulness. Josephine D. (Henderson) Heard. MoGl p.68
Forgive and forget. Marva Tatum Smith. BeYM p.15
Forgive me if I laugh. Sonia Sanchez. LoP p.41
Forgiving My Father. Lucille Clifton. TwW p.16
Formula. Carolyn J. Ogletree. TNV p.78
Formula. Sonia Sanchez. LoP p.53
Forsaken. Josephine D. (Henderson) Heard. MoGl p.119
47th & Vincennes/Chicago. Carolyn M. Rodgers. HoIGO p.19
40,000 gallons of oil gushing into the ocean. June Jordan. PaNP p.1
47,000 Windows. June Jordan. SCh p.66; ThTDID p.88
Forward Ethiopia! ** Bessie Woodson Yancey. EcFTH p.30
Found Poem. June Jordan. PaNP p.30
4 Ever. Alexis Yancey. AOS p.2
Four great walls have hemmed me in. Blanche Taylor Dickinson. CaD p.110
Four Poems--After the Japanese. Mae V. Cowdery. WLOV p.12
Four string bass plays into the heart of the rain forest, A. Colleen McElroy. MuDLSG p.33
Four Walls. Blanche Taylor Dickinson. CaD p.110
Four walls, four empty, blank and cloistral walls. Naomi Long Madgett. PhN p.114
Fox Fish. Lucile D. Goodlett. WGC p.52
Fragile fabric of our dream, The. Georgia Douglas Johnson. HWOP p.27
Fragile, tiny, just a sprite.

Georgia Douglas Johnson. HWOP p.23
Fragment. Jessie Redmond Fauset. CaD p.70
Fragment Reflection I. Linyatta. JuBa p.77
Fragments From a Parable (of the 1950's) June Jordan. ThTDID p.196
Fragments: Mouse Trap. Nikki Grimes. CoAAAW p.120
Frail children of sorrow, dethroned by a hue. Georgia Douglas Johnson. BrBV p.56; CaD p.75
Frail, warm dream lay shattered like a glass, The. Naomi Long Madgett. OnATM p.37
Frank Albert & Viola Benzena Owens. Ntozake Shange. BlSi p.273; NaEd p.61
Frankie Baker. Anonymous. BlWOA p.462
Frankie Baker was a good gal. Anonymous. BlWOA p.462
Franklin on U.S. History. S. Diane Bogus. WITM p.43
Frankly, I am lonely today. Judy Dothard Simmons. JuB p.15
Frederick Douglass, Freedom Seeker, 1817-1895, Maryland. Eloise Culver. GANIV p.30
Free as a Bird. Ann Wallace. GLOWC p.106
Free at last. Anonymous. BlEx p.8; MyNIB p.42
Free at last, Free at last. Spiritual. BlEx p.8; BlP p. 31
Free earth hungered for free men. Pauli Murray. DaTAOP p.14
Free Flight. June Jordan. PaNP p.55
Free Yourself. C. Tillery Banks. HeTMWL p.68
Freed Slave Song. Anonymous. MyNIB p.42
Freed Slave Song. Fannie Berry. MyNIB p.48
Freedom. Anonymous. BlWOA p.313
Freedom. E. Marie Newsome. RoATW p.150
Freedom/A State of Mind. Eleanor Thomas-Grumbach. MoSu p.19
Freedom at Last. Olean Bess. MiFe p.17
Freedom is a dream. Pauli Murray. BlSi p.84; DaTAOP p. 12
Freedom Song For the Black Woman, A. Carole Gregory Clemmons. BlSi p.188
French Doors: A Vignette. Alexis De Veaux. CoAAAW p. 99
French poodle has a home, he belongs to France. Gertrude Blackwell Bailey. IfWCF p.13
Fresh and fair the morn awaketh. Josephine D. (Henderson) Heard. MoGl p.54
Friday, Father Set Aside for Attention to the Church. ** Gloria Oden. TiTBi p.16
Friday ladies of the Pay Envelope, The. Mari Evans. IABW p.49
Friday the 13th Candlelight March. Adrienne Ingrum. CoAAAW p.158
Friend. Gwendolyn Brooks. Bec p.14
Friend, A. Olean Bess. MiFe p. 3
Friend of mine who raised six daughters, A. June Jordan. PaNP p.13
Friends Come. Lucille Clifton. TwW p.56
Friends terror entered me in white gloves. Jayne Cortez. Scar p.40
Friendship. Athelstan R. Lalande. NegVo p.90
Friendship. Josephine D. (Henderson) Heard. MoGl p.101
Frog burrow the mud. Nikki Giovanni. CoCRD p.81
From a Bus. Joyce Whitsitt Lawrence. NBP p.130
From a group of poems thinking about Anne Sexton on the anniversary of her death. Toi Derricotte. EmDH p.47
From a Logical Point of View. Nikki Giovanni. BFBTBJ p.71
From a Vision. Lyn. SiSH p.30
From a Tenement Window. Naomi Long Madgett. PhN p.104
From a Train. Naomi Long Madgett. PhN p.117

From America: A Poem in Process. June Jordan. PaNP p.96
From an Uprooted Condition. June Jordan. ThTDID p.13
From blue-grey mist and river haze the day is born. Mae V. Cowdery. WLOV p.7
From Cavities of Bones Spun.** Patricia Parker. ChOM p.1; DOBB p.108; MoIB p.45
From cavities of bones spun from caverns of air. Patricia Parker. BlSi p.238; ChOM p.1
From dark abodes to fair ethereal light. Phillis Wheatley. ITBLA p.28; PAL p.88; PPW p.10
From Deep Within. Patrica Parker. ChOM p.33; MoIB p.39
From Detroit in American to Africa's Zanzibar from A as Alaska to Z. Margaret Danner. DoOAT p.17
From each valiant rock and tree, West Virginia. Bessie Woodson Yancey. EcFTH p.3
From Esse to Handy to Hayes. Margaret Danner. DoOAT p. 108
From fair Jamaica's fertile smiles. Ada. BlSi p.20
From Generation to Generation. Naomi Long Madgett. PiLAF p.16
From ignorance and darkness, stupidity, and fears. Margaret Walker. OcJo p.35
From Inside an Empty Purse. Audre Lorde. BlUn p.99
From Inside the Continum. June Jordan. ThTDID p.97
From Montgomery to Memphis, he marches. Margaret Walker. PFND p.25
From my personal album two photos. Nanina Alba. FoM p.39
From Okra to Greens/a Different Love Poem/We Need a Change. Ntozake Shange. DaGe p.59
From Okra to Greens: A Personal Invitation (Reconciliation in Casablanca) Ntozake Shange. DaGe p.70
From our love's conception a growing baby in life's gestation period. S. Diane Bogus. WITM p.18
From right on: wite America. Sonia Sanchez. MoCAP p.135
From Rome's palaces and villas gaily issued forth a throng. Frances E. W. Harper. PBFH 66
From Seven Days Prayer. Naomi Long Madgett. PhN p.120
From slender buildings, square blocks of light pace New York City. Carole Gregory Clemmons. NiBPo p.83
From snow and ice, I woke to find sunny skies. Kattie M. Cumbo. NiBPo p.62
From Space to Time. Carolyn M. Rodgers. HeAEG p.23
From the Cavities of Bones. Patricia Parker. BlSi p.238; DOBB p.108
From the Children of the Poor. Gwendolyn Brooks. MoCAP p. 80
From the first it had been like a ballad. Gwendolyn Brooks. BeEa p.19; BLIA p.331; SPGB p.75; WoOGB p.317
From the Greenhouse. Audre Lorde. BlUn p.101
From the House of Yemanja. Audre Lorde. BlUn p.6
From "The Iconography of Childhood." Sherley Williams. CoAAAW p.383
From the Infinite Bottom to the Infinite Top. Marva Tatum Smith. BeYM p.29
From the long ago lifting of the Geometrically pure pyramids. Margaret Danner. DoOAT p.23
From the porch looking beyond fields yellow and deep. Pinkie Gordon Lane. PoBBl p.9; WiTh p.22
From the scope of the love of God as mind. Margaret Danner. DoOAT p.109
From the Shelter. Naomi Long Madgett. PhN p.40
From the Talking Back of Miss Valentine Jones. June Jordan. ThTDID p.147
From the Talking Back of Miss Valentine Jones: Poem # One.

June Jordan. ThTDID p.39
From white lightnin to bowed heads in red. Jayne Cortez. FeAF p.22
From Who Look at Me. June Jordan. MyNIB p.93
From worshipping I now rise. Georgia Douglas Johnson. ALC p.54
Fros' is on de Punkin, De. Bessie Woodson Yancey. EcFTH p.59
Frost has kissed the flowers, The. Edna Gullins. NegVo p.66
Frost on de bahn-shed an' ice in de moat. Lucile D. Goodlett. WGC p.21
Fruit of Love. Marion Nicholes. LiS p.16
Frustration. Eleanor C. Hunter. NegVo p.83
Frustration, a Heritage. Thelma Parker Cox. TNV p.29
Fry that fro. Bobbretta M. Elliston. PoBBl p.2
Fucked, fulfilled, screwed, satiated, cohabitated, consummated, call it what you will. June Vanleer Williams. WiRYPS p.67
Fugit Amor. Virginia Houston, NegVo p.77
Fulfillment. Helene Johnson. CaD p.219; PoN p.151; PoNe p.262; RoATW p.162
Full Moon: Chason. Jodi Braxton. SoITM p.42
Fuller Brush Day. Patricia Parker. ChOM p.4; MoIB p.32
Funeral, The. Gwendolyn Brooks. StIB p.8; WoOGB p.10
Funeral of Martin Luther King, Jr. Nikki Giovanni. BFBTBJ p.56; BlP p.323; BOL p.30; BrT p.54; EgT p.22; TNV p.37
Funeral Parade, The. Toi Derricotte. DeDF p.42; EmDH p.44
Funeral Poem on the Death of C.E. an Infant of Twelve Months. Phillis Wheatley. PPW p.31
Funereal. Naomi Long Madgett. PhN p.81
Funky blues keen toed shoes. Maya Angelou. AnSIR p.4
Funky Football. Fareedah Allah. BlSi p.170
Funny, That I Live. Nola Richardson. WhOL p.17
Fur Muh' Dear. Carolyn M. Rodgers. HoIGO p.1
Fusion. Georgia Douglas Johnson. BrBV p.60
Future. Gertrude Blackwell Bailey. IfWCF p.30
Future. Sonia Sanchez. BluB p.51
Future depends on the young, The. Gertrude Blackwell Bailey. IfWCF p.30
Future Promise. Audre Lorde. BlUn p.115

- G -

Gabble Gourmet. S. Diane Bogus. WITM p.53
Gadgetry and hip new things don't come cheap. Jill Witherspoon Boyer. DrF p.17
Gambler. Elma Stuckey. BiGa p.78
Games of Games, The. Nikki Giovanni. BrT p.65; Rec p.27
Gamut, The. Maya Angelou. JGM p.4
Gandhi Malcolm X Jesus Christ the deaths of all the love prophets. Pamela Cobb. InDM p.26
Gang Girls. Gwendolyn Brooks. ITM p.47; PoBA p.160; WoOGB p.419
Gang girls are sweet exoitics. Gwendolyn Brooks. ITM p.47; PoBA p.160; WoOGB p.419
Gangan. D. T. Ogilvie. YoBBI p.515
Garbageman: the Man With the Orderly Mind. Gwendolyn Brooks. SPGB p.124
Garden, The. Patrice Wilson. NeJCL p.9
Garden Ghosts. Clara H. Haywood. NegVo p.69
Garden of Shushan! After Eden, all terrace, pool, and flower recollect thee. Anne Spencer. BANP p.213;

BlSi p.69; CNAW p.269; NeCa p.353; NeNRe p.82
Garnishing the Aviary. Margaret Danner. AmNP p.153; BlP p.149; BlPo p.20; DoOAT p. 47; IrLa p.14; MoCAP p.88; NNPUSA p.29; PoBA p.134; UNBP p.229
Garvey. Anonymous. BlWOA p.646
Garvey, Garvey, is a Big Man. Anonymous. BlWOA p.646
Gary Tyler Poems, The. Carolyn M. Rodgers. HeAEG p.57
Gathering of Artists. Alicia Johnson. TGWL p.52
Gave proof through the night that our flag was still there. June Jordan. ThTDID p.139
Gay Bar. Wanda Coleman. MaDBL p.100
Gay Chaps at the Bar. Gwendolyn Brooks. SPGB p.22; StIB p. 46; WoOGB p.48
Gay little girl-of-the-diving-tank I desire a name for you. Anne Spencer. BANP p.215; BlSi p.68; CaD p.53; CNAW p.271; KAL p.35; NeCa p. 252; NeNRe p.81; PoN p.52; PoNe p.62
Gee, I'm so disgusted. Rosa Brooks. AmLNA p.91
Gem-like stars, The. Henrietta Cordelia Ray. EBAP p.144
Gemini. Audre Lorde. ChPON p. 7; COAL p.31; FiCi p.10
Gene. Jennifer Blackman Lawson. BlIMT p.54
Gen'el Jackson. Anonymous. BlWOA p.231
Gen'el Jackson, mighty man. Anonymous. BlWOA p.237
General Robert Smalls. Josephine D. (Henderson) Heard. MoGl p.35
Generation. Audre Lorde. ChPON p.16; COAL p.13; FiCi p.15; NeBV p.288
Generation Gap, The. Fareedah Allah. BlSi p.174
Generation II. Audre Lorde. ChPON p.55; FrLWP p.29
Generations. Judy Dothard Simmons. JuB p.6
Generations. Julia Fields. GaBW p.311; NiBPo p.74
Genevieve what are you seeing in my mirror this morning. Audre Lorde. ChPON p.5; COAL p.66; FiCi p.1
Geni in the Jar, The. Nikki Giovanni. EgT p.31; Rec p.24; WoATM p.14; YoBBI p.478
Genocide doesn't only mean bombs. Audre Lorde. ChPON p.85; NeHS p.46
Genocide Is. E. Sharon Gomillion. FoAAM p.17
Gente. Patricia Parker. MoIB p.135
Gentle man images move. Jennifer Blackman Lawson. BlIMT p.38
George-Hector...is spoiled. Mari Evans. AmNP p.165; BlVo p.480; BTB p.105; IABW p.54; MBP p.40; MyNIB p.110
Gertrude. Gwendolyn Brooks. OnOW p.23
Get Involved. Bernadette Simmons. ThHSD p.36
Get it & Feel Good. Ntozake Shange. NaEd p.50
Get you out my system. C. Tillery Banks. HeTMWL p.42
"Get yourself together" is the tune the ol train hums. Barbara Mahone. Suga p.19
Gethsemane. Georgia Douglas Johnson. HWOP p.20
Gettin Down to Get Over. June Jordan. ThTDID p.27
Getting Up. Patricia Jones. HoDo p.77
Ghetto. Yvette Johnson. TNV p.55
Ghetto Daybreak. June Vanleer Williams. WiRYPS p.37
Ghetto Love Song-Migration. Carole Gregory Clemmons. NBP p.56
Ghetto Moment. Wanda Coleman. MaDBL p.118
Ghetto Song. Pinkie Gordon Lane. WiTh p.37
Ghetto's the talk this year. Nancy L. Arnez. RoCO p.17
Ghost. Audre Lorde. BlUn p.85
Ghost at the Quincy Club, The. Gwendolyn Brooks. BeEa p.45;

WoOGB p.343
Ghostly moon cast chill shadows, A. Naomi Long Madgett. ExAE p.28
Ghosts of Our Parting, The. S. Diane Bogus. WITM p.23
GI Gratitude. June Vanleer Williams. WiRYPS p.69
Giant is furious tonight, The. Naomi Long Madgett. SoTNP p.12
Gift. Alice Walker. RePOP p.57
Gift. Carol Freeman. MBP p.75; PoNe p.435
Gift from Kenya. May Miller. BlSi p.112; ClAB p.29; CNAW p.359
Gift He Gave Unknowing, The. Alice Walker. RePOP p.53
Gifts of America. Vanessa Howard. ScWh p.4
Gilead. Georgia Douglas Johnson. HWOP p.38
Gimme an upsweep, Minnie. Gwendolyn Brooks. StIB p.35; WoOGB p.37
Gimme Dat Ol'-Time Religion. ** Anonymous. AfAV p.119
Giraffe. Anonymous. MBP p.39
Girl Held Without Bail. Margaret Walker. BlP p.156; PFND p. 8; PoBA p.148
Girl, I could have stood it if he'd just said we evil and hankty. Sherley Williams. PePo p.58
Girl in my sister's house wears nightmare hidden in her eyes, A. Audre Lorde. BlUn p.110
Girl With the Ebony Eyes, The. Eleanor Thomas-Grumbach. MoSu p.17
Girl Who Died #1. Alice Walker. RePOP p.42
Girl Who Died #2/for D.P. Alice Walker. RePOP p.45
Git it on, heaven. Judy Dothard Simmons. JuB p.20
Git on Board, Little Chillen.** Spiritual. BlP p.27
Git the word out now. Sonia Sanchez. HoC p.28
Give Him a Chance. Bessie Woodson Yancey. EcFTH p.24
Give Me a Chair. Anonymous. TYBP p.49
Give me a happy heart and suasive tongue. Josephine D. (Henderson) Heard. MoGl p.59
Give me again the flaming torch of truth. Margaret Walker. OcJo p.26
Give me fire and I will sing you morning. Audre Lorde. FiCi p.22
Give Me Jesus. Spiritual. BlP p.28
Give me my freedom lest I die. Mari Evans. FoM p.4
Give me not the life of leisure. Bessie Woodson Yancey. EcFTH p.18
Give me some star beer and a bottle of gin. Jayne Cortez. FeAF p.30
Give Me the Red on the Black of the Bullet. Jayne Cortez. COAG p.31; MoOP p.10
Give me this night oh God. Naomi Long Madgett. PhN p.28
Give me your hand. Maya Angelou. OhPWFW p.23
Give us a world as black as pitch. Edna White Hill. NegVo p.72
Give us flowers while we live. Gertrude Blackwell Bailey. IfWCF ½/34
Given the days of my mindlessness. Mari Evans. NIGHT p.37
Glamour. Georgia Douglas Johnson. HWOP p.59
Glass covers windows to keep the cold away. Nikki Giovanni. VaT p.57
Glimpse. Pearl Cleage Lomax. PoBA p.503
Glimpses. Nola Richardson. WhOL p.8
Glimpses of Africa. Naomi Long Madgett. PiLAF p.50
Glimpses of light shine sharply in the night. Alicia Loy Johnson. NiBPo p.159
Glistening morning grass silver sid-exposed, The. Mari Evans. NIGHT p.5
Gloam Tide. Georgia Douglas Johnson. HWOP p.55
Glory. Ariel Holloway. BTh p.16

Glory in the landscape. Bessie Woodson Yancey. EcFTH p.11
Glowchild. Constance E. Berkley. GLOWC p.43
Gnarled and knotty iron-wrought hands fashioned for the spade and ploy. Anita Scott Coleman. EbR p.50
"Go down death," the master gave the word. Josie Craig Berry. NegVo p.13
Go Down Moses! ** Anonymous. AfAV p.114; AfAWA p.103; BlEx p.7; BLIA p.41; MBP p.79
Go Down, Moses! Spiritual. BlP p.23
Go Down, Ol' Hannah.** Anonymous. BlWOA p.458
Go Down, Old Hannah. Anonymous. TYBP p.200
Go Forth, My Son. Georgia Douglas Johnson. GoS p.187
Go forth, my son, winged by my heart's desire. Georgia Douglas Johnson. BrBV p.50
Go On. Ann Wallace. GLOWC p.56
Go tell it on the Mountain.** Anonymous. ChG p.39; ITBLA p.97; MBP p.69
Go 'way from dat window, "my honey, my love! Anonymous. BlP p.8
Go' Way From My Window.** Anonymous. MBP p.51
Go where you will. Alice Walker. RePOP p.65
Go Work in my Vineyard.** Frances E. W. Harper. PBFH p.31
Goal. Mae V. Cowdery. WLOV p. 18
Goat Child. Patricia Parker. ChOM p.17; MoIB p.19
Goat left this child me still trying to butt my way in or out. Patricia Parker. ChOM p.20
God (a Folk Sermon) Anonymous. MBP p.1
God Bless Our Native Land. ** Frances E. W. Harper. PBFH p.23
God Called an Angel.** Jo Nell Rice. ThHSD p.42
God declares no independence. Lucille Clifton. OrW p.33
God deliver'd Daniel from the lion's den. Anonymous. BlEx p.7
God fashioned you an autumn birch standing stately on a hill. Gertrude Parthenia McBrown. EbR p.104
God Gave Me a Son. Portia Bird Daniel. NegVo p.43
God gave you a little girl. Olean Bess. MiFe p.10
God grant you wider vision clearer skies my son. Georgia Douglas Johnson. BrBV p.48
God is an Indian. Anita Scott Coleman. EbR p.50
God is Kind. ** Mae V. Cowdery. WLOV p.15
God is Near Thee. Josephine D. (Henderson) Heard. MoGl p. 133
God made this world a garden. Eloise Culver. GANIV p.77
God must have scanned the Heavens, said, "It needs just one more light. Eloise Culver. GANIV p.48
God of my father discovered at midnight. Audre Lorde. ChPON p.91; NeHS p.39
God of War, The. Anonymous. AfAV p.12
God Send Easter. Lucille Clifton. GoNAE p.19
God they fear you. Carolyn M. Rodgers. BlP p.261
God Waits for the Wandering World. Lucille Clifton. TwW p.46
God washes clean the souls and hearts of you. Alice Dunbar-Nelson. DuSAE p.240
God Works in a Mysterious Way. Gwendolyn Brooks. SPGB p. 27; StIB p.54; WoOGB p.56
God's Christmas Tree. Eve Lynn. ChG p.98
God's Extermination or Society's Souvernirs. S. Diane Bogus. WITM p.59
God's eyes smiled when he made the moon. Claire Turner. NegVo p.156
God's Gonna Set Dis World on Fire. ** Anonymous. ITBLA p.97

God's Gwine to Take all my troubles Away. Lucy Mae Turner. BCF p.46
God's Mood. Lucille Clifton. OrW p.15
God's Promise. Marva Tatum Smith. BeYM p.2
Goes way back to the days/my father a young man. Wanda Coleman. MaDBL p.114
Goes Without Saying. Thulani Davis. AlTRGR p.38
Goin Down the Road. Anonymous. BlWOA p.461
Going Cold Turkey on Your Ass. C. Tillery Banks. HeTMWL p. 42
Going East. Frances E. W. Harper. PBFH p.63
Going Home. Jennifer Blackman Lawson. BlIMT p.20
Going Home. Joanne Jimason. HoDo p.27
Going Home. Patricia Jones. HoDo p.74
Going to Africa. Linda Brown Bragg. LoSBM p.31
Going to bed is the only affection I know. Thulani Davis. AlTRGR p.33
Going to church, riding smooth past burned out shells. Pearl Cleage Lomax. WeDNNM p.6
Gold is the Shade Esperanto. Margaret Danner. AfAWA p. 637; DoOAT p.39; IrLa p.12
Gold of her promise has never been minded, The. Maya Angelou. OhPWFW p.6
Gold will not buy this voyage. Colleen McElroy. BlSi p.290
Golden wheel pivoted to the core of consciousness. May Miller. ClAB p.13
Goliath of Gath. Phillis Wheatley. BlALP p.11; PAL p.101; PPW p.13
Gone. Josephine D. (Henderson) Heard. MoGl p.99
Gone. Mary Bohanon. GaBW p.259
Gonna give a baby a home. Nancy L. Arnez. RoCO p.17
Gonna knock off early Saturday night. Elma Stuckey. BiGa p.60
Gonna Shout. Anonymous. BlWOA p.237
Gonna shout trouble away. Anonymous. BlWOA
Good Assassination Should be Quiet. Mari Evans. BlSp p. 70; IBAW p.84
Good-Bye. Georgia Douglas Johnson. ALC p.12; AmLNA p.74; RoATW p.96
Good Bye. Josephine D. (Henderson) Heard. MoGl p.127
Good-bye dear day or sunshine. Georgia Douglas Johnson. ALC p.27
Good Friday. Lucille Clifton. GoNAE p.43
Good Friday's Garbage. Edith Brandon Humphrey. HoDo p.35
Good God, A. Mary Bohanon. GaBW p.260
Good Masters. Elma Stuckey. BiGa p.22
Good Mirrors are not Cheap. Audre Lorde. ChPON p.43; FrLWP p.15
Good Mornin' Blues. ** Anonymous. BLIA p.47; ITBLA p.124
Good mornin' sister Anderson. Bernice Love Wiggins. HeD p.42
Good Morning, Captain. ** Anonymous. ITBLA p.121
Good News. Naomi Long Madgett. ExAE p.49
Good Night. Nikki Giovanni. VaT p.59
Good Saint Benedict. ** Anonymous. MBP p.58
Good Times. Lucille Clifton. BlP p.250; DOBB p.52; MoCAP p.140; OnOW p.53; PoBA p.306
Goodbye Can be a Hello. C. Tillery Banks. HeTMWL p.39
Goodbye David Tamunoemi West. Margaret Danner. BlP p.153; IrLa p.9; PoCo p.20
Goodbye, goodbye, if I nevah see you any mo. Anonymous. BlWOA p.234
Goodnight mommy goodnight dad I kiss them as I go. Nikki Giovanni. VaT p.59
Gospel Train, The.** Anonymous. GoS p.62

Gospel Truth, The. Jackie Earley. BlSp p.62; RoATW p.31
Gossamer. Georgia Douglas Johnson. HWOP p.3
Got me a man, now; he's big and Black and strong. Jennifer Blackman Lawson. BlIMT p.55
Got up this morning feeling good & Black. Jackie Earley. BlSp p.65; MBP p.93; SoS p. 127
Graceful Fountain, rising high. Lucy Mae Turner. BCF p.59
Gracious Saviour Let me Make, Neither Error nor Mistake. Josephine D. (Henderson) Heard. MoGl p.35
Grain of Sand, A. Frances E. W. Harper. PBFH p.3
Grand Army Plaza. June Jordan. PaNP p.90
Grand old man of letters, A. Eloise Culver. GANIV p.47
Gra'ma. Colleen McElroy. MuDLSG p.2
Gra'ma was a little bit of a thing. Colleen McElroy. MuDLSG p.2
Gramma Wynn. Melba Joyce Boyd. CaEADW p.6
Gramma Wynn crumbled in a steel hospital bed. Melba Joyce Boyd. CaEADW p.6
Grand Circus Park. Naomi Long Madgett. PiLAF p.15
Grandly isolate as the God of day. Georgia Douglas Johnson. BrBV p.92
Grandma sleeps with my sick Grandpa. Alice Walker. ONC p.70
Grandma's Hands. Melba Joyce Boyd. CaEADW p.4
Grandmothers. Barbara Mahone. Suga p.14
Grandmothers are secrets revealed. Barbara Mahone. Suga p.14
Grandson is a Hoticeberg, A. Margaret Danner. BlSi p.131; FBPA p.51
Grandson is not the wine-sprouting cherub, A. Margaret Danner. BlSi p.131; FBPA p.51
Grass Fingers. Angelina Weld Grimke. BlWOA p.627; CaD p.38; NeNRe p.85; ReFNA p.24
Grass Man. Maami Verano. RoATW p.153; ThHSD p.64
Grass Roots. Mara Moja Tu Kali. ThHSD p.59
Grasshopper World, The. ** Frenchy J. Hodges. BlW p.9
Gray-flowing doubt has momentarily dimmed the destined star. Mary Bohanon. GaBW p.261
Graystone Crest Logan Station, Philadelphia, Pa. Josephine D. (Henderson) Heard. MoGl p.104
Great amazon of God behold your bread. Margaret Walker. OcJo p.32; PoN p.188; PoNe p.326; YoBBI p.155
Great Black masses like amorphus blobs. Kattie M. Cumbo. GaBW p.289
Great Cities Crumble. Gertrude Blackwell Bailey. IfWCF p. 24
Geeat Civil Rights Law (A.D. 1964), The. Mari Evans. IABW p.66
Great Laws, The. Marion Cuthbert. SOC p25
Great Pax Whitie, The. Nikki Giovanni. BFBTBJ p.60
Great singer Nina Simone fills your heart with soul. Linda Curry. OnOW p.25
Great teacher set the last bag of grain under the shed roof. Marion Cuthbert. SOC p.25
Great Truths. Marion Cuthbert. SOC p.37
Greater Friendship Baptist Church, The. Carole Gregory Clemmons. BlSi p. 190
Greek Crazeology. Carolyn M. Rodgers. SoBB p.27
Green Apples. Linda Brown Bragg. LoSBM p.28
Green Arbor, A. Linda Brown Bragg. LoSBM p.12
Green arbor that I once knew, A. Linda Brown Bragg. LoSBM p. 12
Green lawn a picket fence flowers. Alice Walker.

BlSi p.213; ONC p.23; PoBA p.474
Green Leaf. May Miller. ClAB p. 3
Green of Jesus is breaking the ground, The. Lucille Clifton. GoNAE p.45
Green Valley. Dorothy Vena Johnson. PoN p.120; PoNe p.226
Greeness. Angelina Weld Grimke. ANP p.86; CaD p.36
Greeness grows in this ghetto. Damali (Denise Burnett) IATWMB p.18
Greens and fat back pickled pig tails. Marion Nicholes. LiS p.17
Grey clouds floated past my window. Patricia Parker. MoIB p.72
Grey temples, tailored suit contact blue eyes. Colleen McElroy. MuDLSG p.14
Grey trees, grey skies, and not a star. Angelina Weld Grimke. ReFNA p.24
Greyday. Maya Angelou. OhPWFW p.13
Grief Unexplained. June Vanleer Williams. WiRYPS p.77
Griefs of Joy. Pinkie Gordon Lane. MyFe p.45; WiTh p.54
Grim monarch! see, deprived of vital breath. Phillis Wheatley. PAL p.38; PPW p.12; PPW p.71
Grin, you monkey, you! Naomi Long Madgett. OnATM p.59
Grinding Vibrato. Jayne Cortez. BlSi p.160; MoOP p.26
Grits and Rice Grains. Mari Evans. IABW p.48
Groping -- -- --into the future. Georgiana Oliver. NegVo p.118
Group. Patricia Parker. MoIB p.136
Group Therapy. Carolyn M. Rodgers. HeAEG p.44
"Grow in Hope and Grace." Barbara Anne Baker. TNV p.15
Guardianship. Georgia Douglas Johnson. BrBV p.47
Guess I'll go on down to the newsstand. Elma Stuckey. BiGa p.87
Guest, The. Beatrice M. Murphy. NegVo p.115
Guilty. Ruby Berkley Goodwin. EbR p.68
Gulls. Pinkie Gordon Lane. PoBBl p.8; WiTh p.15
Guns and knives aren't enough. Helen G. Quigless. TNV p. 96
Gus. Nikki Giovanni. CoCRD p. 62
Gus, the Lineman. ** Margaret Walker. FMP p.45
G'wan man, now quit yo' foolin.' Bessie Woodson Yancey. EcFTH p.55
Gwen Brooks, A Pyramid. Val Gray Ward. TGWL p.99
Gwendolyn Brooks was usually as quiet as the flow of water that her name evokes. Margaret Danner. TGWL p.29

- H -

Habits. Nikki Giovanni. CoCRD p.57
Had I loved you less, you were mine now. Clara Haywood. NegVo p.70
Hag hand scratch sky. Toi Derricotte. EmDH p.39
Hah! What a joke life is. Nola Richardson. WhOL p.13
Haiku. Sonia Sanchez. IvBAW p. 33
Haiku. Sonia Sanchez. IvBAW p. 34
Haiku. Sonia Sanchez. IvBAW p. 37
Haiku. Sonia Sanchez. IvBAW p. 38
Haiku. Sonia Sanchez. IvBAW p. 42
Haiku. Sonia Sanchez. IvBAW p. 47
Haiku. Sonia Sanchez. IvBAW p. 49
Haiku. Sonia Sanchez. LoP p.9
Haiku. Sonia Sanchez. LoP p.19
Haiku. Sonia Sanchez. LoP p.25
Haiku. Sonia Sanchez. LoP p.28
Haiku. Sonia Sanchez. LoP p.35
Haiku. Sonia Sanchez. LoP p.39
Haiku. Sonia Sanchez. LoP p.45

Haiku. Sonia Sanchez. LoP p.50
Haiku. Sonia Sanchez. LoP p.52
Haiku. Sonia Sanchez. LoP p.54
Haiku. Sonia Sanchez. LoP p.61
Haiku. Sonia Sanchez. LoP p.62
Haiku. Sonia Sanchez. LoP p.69
Haiku. Sonia Sanchez. LoP p.71
Haiku. Sonia Sanchez. LoP p.83
Haiku. Sonia Sanchez. LoP p.85
Haiku. Sonia Sanchez. LoP p.87
Haiku. Sonia Sanchez. LoP p.89
Haiku. Sonia Sanchez. LoP p.93
Haiku. Sonia Sanchez. LoP p.97
Haiku. Sonia Sanchez. LoP p.99
Haiku (Written from Pekin) Sonia Sanchez. LoP p.71
Hail, happy day! when, smiling like the morn. Phillis Wheatley. EaNAW p.39; NeCa p.284; PAL p.73; ReFNA p.6
Hail, happy saint! on thine immortal throne. Phillis Wheatley. BlWOA p.40; EaNAW p.37; EBAP p.100; PAL p.36; PPW p.9
Hail happy saint on thy immortal throne! Phillis Wheatley. PPW p.66
Hail happy saint, on thy immortal throne! Phillis Wheatley. CNAW p.11; EBAP p.100; PAL p.36; PPW p.69
Hail, wanderer, but late returned from Africa's arid sand. Josephine D. (Henderson) Heard. MoGl p.100
Hain't no use to weep. Anonymous. BlP p.8
Haiti. Amina Baraka. CoAAAW p.71
Half the night we spend waiting for stars to come out. Harryette Mullen. TTW p.;9
Halfway between the rain and Washington as we stopped. Audre Lorde. ChPON p.84; Ne HS p.19
Hallet's Peak. Pinkie Gordon Lane. WiTh p.20
Hallelujah. Elma Stuckey. BiGa p.26
Hallelujah, the radio minister cried. Carolyn M. Rodgers. HeAEG p.34
Hamcocks and collard greens on white folks tables. E. Sharon Gomillion. FoAAM p.8
Hampton, Virginia. Nikki Giovanni. WoATM p.33
Hand in hand, we were going to conquer the world and save our souls--remember. Naomi Long Madgett. PhN p.77
Hands. Anita Scott Coleman. EbR p.50
Hands. Beatris Overby. NegVo p.119
Hands & Holding. Ntozake Shange. NaEd p.43
Hands & holding tongues & clits go well together. Ntozake Shange. NaEd p.43
Hands: For Mother's Day. Nikki Giovanni. ThWRNW p.16
Hands of beauty enthralling and rare. Beatris Overby. NegVo p.119
Hands of the future are red, The. Mari Evans. NIGHT p.77
Hanged man broken by fire. Audre Lorde. FiCi p.2
Hanging Fire. Audre Lorde. BlUn p.96
Hanging on the wall, an iron face watches me. Irma McClaurin. BlSi p.195
Happens you will rise, lift from grounded in a spin. Lucille Clifton. TwW p.44
Happiness. Ethlynne E. Holmes. NegVo p.75
Happiness... a wisp. Mari Evans. NIGHT p.7
Happiness is a cruse of sweet-scented oil. Ethlynne E. Holmes. NegVo p.75
Happy Fairies. Gertrude Parthenia McBrown. ReFNA p.53
Happy Heart, A. Josephine D. (Henderson) Heard. MoGl p.59
Happy moments tell me, pray. Josephine D. (Henderson) Heard. MoGl p.49
Hard bitter deep full to the apex. Doris Ann Shaw. GaBW p.400
Hard Freeze, The. Barbara Mahone. Suga p.11
Hard Love Rock. Audre Lorde. ChPON p.21; COAL p.29
Hard Love Rock # II. Audre Lorde. ChPON p.76; NeHS p.24

Hard to be Free. Melva Eloise Tatum. MELVA p.16
Harlem Hopscotch. Maya Angelou. JGM p.48
Harlem Riot, 1943. Pauli Murray. DaTAOP p.35; PoBA p.109
Harlem/Soweto. Safiya Henderson. CoAAAW p.134
Harmony. Bessie Woodson Yancey. EcFTH p.13
Harriet. Audre Lorde. BlSi p. 202; BlUn p.202
Harriet. Lucille Clifton. OrW p.19
Harriet there was always somebody calling us crazy. Audre Lorde. BlSi p.202
Harriet Tubman. Margaret Walker. ITSA p.45; OcJo p.14; PoN p.181; PoNe p.320
Harriet Tubman, Freedom Fighter About 1823-1913, Maryland. Eloise Culver. GANIv p.23
Harry. Audre Lorde. BlUn p.21
Harvest. Nikki Giovanni. ThWRNW p.39
Has an office in Beverly Hills. Wanda Coleman. MaDBL p.90
Has your finger ever been clutched by the hand of a little one? Margaret Danner. DoOAT p.105
Hate. Pauli Murray. DaTAOP p.56
Hate and love, hate and love, circles still remain. Roslyn Greer. TNV p.44
Hatred. Beatrice M. Murphy. NegVo p.114
Hatred. Gwendolyn B. Bennett. AmNP p.73; BANP p.246 BlSi p.73; CaD p.160; PoBA p.82; RoATW p.113; VoFHR p.356
Hattie Scott. Gwendolyn Brooks. StIB p.38; WoOGB p.35
Haunted. Mae V. Cowdery. WLOV p.54
Haunted by poems beginning with I. Audre Lorde. ChPON p. 58; FrLWP p.43
Have I eclipsed the waves? Margaret Danner. DoOAT p. 24
Have you ever been down south. Jennifer Blackman Lawson. BlIMT p.35
Have you ever been hexed by the magic in colors? Margaret Danner. ImOK p.7
Have you ever seen the moon. Lula Lowe Weeden. CaD p.228; MyNIB p.84
Have you ever tried to catch a tear. Patricia Parker. ChOM p.27; MoIB p.38
Have You Ever Tried to Hide? ** Patricia Parker. MoIB p.47
Have you heard the bugle echo as it sounded loud and far? Josephine D. (Henderson) Heard. MoGl p.92
Have you noticed how black is for utility. Marion Nicholes. LiS p.20
Have You Seen It? Lula Lowe Weeden. CaD p.228; MyNIB p.84
Have you seen the rain dripping. Dorothy Vena Johnson. NegVo p.85
Having Had You. Mae V. Cowdery. WLOV p.27
Having had you once and lost you. Mae V. Cowdery. WLOV p.27
Having reached my boiling point. Yvette Johnson. TNV p.55
Having reached perfection as you have. Alice Walker. RePOP p.41
Having tried to use the witch cord that erases the stretch of thirty-three blocks. Carolyn M. Rodgers. AfAWA p.780; HoIGO p.11; NaPr p.121; SoBB p.12; YoBBI p.483
Hawg Killin'. Lucile D. Goodlet. WGC p.21
!!!He!!! E. Marie Newsome. RoATW p.130
He a whale on a Searock. Joanne Jimason. NaABE p.15
He Ain't My Idol. E. Sharon Gomillion. FoAAM p.22
He always had pretty legs. Nikki Giovanni. CoCRD p.62
He bad O he bad. Maya Angelou. OhPWFW p.40
He bowed and scraped and loved ole marse. Elma Stuckey. BiGa p.32

He calls me from his house. June Jordan. ThTDID p.70
He calls to tell me something. Wanda Coleman. MaDBL p.60
He came in looking for mama. Wanda Coleman. MaDBL p.15
He came in slivern armor trimmed with black. Gwendolyn B. Bennett. AmNP p.71; CaD p. 160; ITBLA p.218; PoBA p. 82; PoN p.109; PoNe p.206
He claims he is a white man. Claire Turner. NegVo p.156
He Climbs Inside. Joanne Jimason. NaABE p.14
He Comes. Nola Richardson. WhOL p.87
He comes and goes with quiet step and injured mein. Josephine D. (Henderson) Heard. MoGl p.95
He comes Not To-Night. Josephine D. (Henderson) Heard. MoGl p.30
He comes.....to visit. Nola Richardson. WhOL p.87
He could release the swelling in his ribs. Pinkie Gordon Lane. WiTh p.31
He decided to woo her. Carolyn M. Rodgers. HeAEG p.24
He did not! June Jordan. PaNP p.7
He did not know that loving beauty is loving God. Isabelle McClellan Taylor. EbR p.134
He Didn't Give Up He Was Taken. Thulani Davis. AlTRGR p.17
He died from a bullet wound in the back. June Jordan. Scar p.56
He does not know he is the song that she is singing. Carolyn M. Rodgers. HoIGO p.72
He fell down each step of the subway stairs. Claudia E. Jemmott. GaBW p.353
He gave his son in this world of strife. Dorothy Vena Johnson. NegVo p.85
He got drunk. Mary Bohanon. GaBW p.263
He grew up being curious. Gwendolyn Brooks. AnA p.vi; WoOGB p.63
He had a dream exploded down his throat. Mari Evans. BlSp p.70; IABW p.84
He "had not where to lay his head." Frances E. W. Harper. PBFH p.30
He had a girl who has flaxen hair. Nikki Giovanni. BFBTBJ p.4
He Hath Need of Rest. Josephine D. (Henderson) Heard. MoGl p.75
He is as salt to her. Lucille Clifton. OrW p.11
He is firm and strong. Anonymous. TYBP p.11
He is not dead. Kattie M. Cumbo. GaBW p.288
He is patient, he is not angry. Anonymous. AfAV p.12
He is Shaka the unshakable. Anonymous. TYBP p.16
He is very busy with his looking. Gwendolyn Brooks. FaP p.14
He keeps falling to pieces right before my eyes. Wanda Coleman. MaDBL p.88
He kept imploring me to wait. Naomi Long Madgett. PhN p.66
He kills on the right and destroys on the left. Anonymous. AfAV p.12
He knew why he was there. Jill Witherspoon Boyer. DrF p. 16
He knows Gethsemane. May Miller. DeDF p.97
He Lay in the Alley. Vanessa Howard. ScWh p.49
He lifted up his pleading eyes and scanned each cruel face. Frances E. W. Harper. PBFH p.49
He lived so recklessly that his mamma told him. Elma Stuckey. BiGa p.78
He made it. Margaret Danner. DoOat p.84; IrLa p.6
He Never Said a Mumbling Word. BlLi p.114
He offered me his smile. Anita Anderson. PoBBl p.51
He ordered a beer. June Jordan. ThTDID p.55

He Paid Me Seven (Parody) Anonymous. BlP p.5
He pray, he sing, he shout and cry. Elma Stuckey. BiGa p. 43
He prayed for patience. Clara Ann Thompson. AVAN p.133; BlSi p.42
He Reads My Body Like a Poem.** Harryette Mullen. TTW p.47
He Said Come. Alice Walker. RePOP p.50
He said hanging out with her wax just like hangin out witta man. Ntozake Shange. NaEd p.13
He said he was my friend. Josephine D. (Henderson) Heard. MoGl p.107
He Said She Said She Said He Said. Jymi Jones. AfAV p. 347
He said that she said that her brother was light skin, Jymi Jones. AfAV p.347
He sits at the bar in the Alhambra. Naomi Long Madgett. FBPA p.93; PiLAF p.55; PoBA p.182
He spoke of how he could not love. Mae Jackson. CaPWY p.12
He stood a tall silhouette of love. Vanessa Howard. ScWh p.29
He stood before my heart's closed door. Frances E. W. Harper. PBFH p.58
He stood before the sons of Heth. Frances E. W. Harper. PBFH p.61
He swore that he would not be whipped. Elma Stuckey. BiGa p.40
He That Cometh to Me I Will in Nowise Cast Out. Josephine D. (Henderson) Heard. MoGl p.135
He thinks the confusion is in him and it is. Carolyn M. Rodgers. HoIGO p.28
He, through the eyes of the first marauder saw her. Audre Lorde. ChPON p.5; COAL p.70; FiCi p.11; SiAS p.42
He undresses quick as shucking. Harryette Mullen. TTW p.41
He wanted her to be with him. Brenda Connor-Bey. CoAAAW p.80
He wanted to make love to me. E. Marie Newsome. RoATW p. 130
He was a baaad mothuhfuhya. Mari Evans. NIGHT p.46
He was a lover that's what they said. Jill Witherspoon Boyer. DrF p.11
He was a prose poem. Gwendolyn Brooks. PoBA p.159
He was born in Alabama. Gwendolyn Brooks. BlWOA p.716; CNAW p.516; PoN p.189; SPGB p.10; StIB p.21; WoOGB p.23
He was born when the cotton fields first began to bloom in Mississippi & Georgia. Carolyn M. Rodgers. HeAEG p.57
He was caught in a penitentiary of tears. Jayne Cortez. Scar p.46
He was just a little gangster with a high voice. Nikki Giovanni. Rec p.8
He Was Sad.** Mae Jackson. CaPWY p.20
He was shot, you see shot, you see. Patricia. FoM p.32
He was still here the friend. June Jordan. ThTDID p.181
He was still Uncle Jack to me. Sherley Williams. BlSi p. 253
He was tall and proud and handsome. Iola M. Brister. NegVo p.17
He Was Twenty When He Died.** Gloria Oden. RESUR p.21
He wears a fro real nappy and wide. Leatrice Emeruwa. BlGBG p.15
He went to being called a colored man after answering to "hey nigger." Maya Angelou. JGM p.43
He who saved Ankoma oh nature. Anonymous. TYBP p.14
He will wear new bones again. Lucille Clifton. OrW p.17
He would fly away his dream

would carry him. Carolyn M. Rodgers. HoIGO p.43
Head bent, walking through snow I see you Seboulisa. Audre Lorde. BlUn p.12
Headlines never say good morning any more. Naomi Long Madgett. ExAE p.49
Healer of the New Day. Marion Nicholes. LiS p.22
Healing power is not found in Sterling White. Marion Nicholes. LiS p.22
Healing Stream. Gertrude Blackwell Bailey. IfWCF p.28
Hear in this beamless alley, gray with rain. Naomi Long Madgett. PhN p.90
Hear me, heed me, my beautiful Black and beloved. Margaret T. G. Burroughs. GLOWC p.49; WhSIT p.19
Hear Our Silence. Johari Amini. LetGSM p.24
Hear the prayer from a Plaquemine Jail. Margaret Walker. PFND p.27
Hear the Rhythm of Your Name.** Sonia Sanchez. IvBAW p.79
Hear their viol-voices ringing. Georgia Douglas Johnson. BrBV p.27
Hear ye! Hear ye! Starting July 4th is bring in yr/gun/down/ to yr/nearest/po/lice station. Sonia Sanchez. WABP p. 28
Hear you that shriek? Frances E. W. Harper. AfAWA p.97; AVAN p.41; BlWOA p.225; EBAP p.31
Heart-Blossom. Naomi Long Madgett. OnATM p.36
Heart-Hungry. Josephine D. (Henderson) Heard. MoGl p.43
Heart of a Woman, The.** Georgia Douglas Johnson. AmLNA p. 74; ANP p.86; BANP p.181; BlSi p.58; CaD p.81; HWOP p.1; NeCa p.339; NeNRe p. 76; PoN p.57; PoNe p.73; ReFNA p.26
Heat surrounds your body like an odor. Harryette Mullen. TTW p.40
Heat you left with me last night still smolders, The. Nikki Giovann. Rec p.13; WoATM p.32
Heaven. Naomi Long Madgett. PhN p.24
Heaven Hates With Cosmic Ire. Pauli Murray. DaTAOP p.56
Heaven, ready for reunion. Elma Stuckey. BiGa p.93
Hegira, The. Georgia Douglas Johnson. BrBV p.33
Hegira. Mari Evans. IABW p.31
Hello are u the suicide man? Sonia Sanchez. WABP p.12
Hello, I'm sorry I can't talk to you. June Jordan. PaNP p.83
Hello, Woman! ** Jennifer Blackman Lawson. BlIMT p.6
Helmet of dilated orbs dilated orbs, A. Jayne Cortez. MoOP p.29
Help me to make my heart's a citadel. Ruby Berkley Goodwin. EbR p.67
Help me to forget that flowers die. Naomi Long Madgett. PhN p.35; SoTP p.11
Henry O. Tanner, Painter, 1859-1937, Pennsylvania. Eloise Culver. GANIV p.49
Henry Wadsworth Longfellow, 1807-1882, Maine. Eloise Culver. GANIV p.34
Her arms semaphore fat triangles. Maya Angelou. AnSIR p.26
Her Blood, Driftin Through me Sings. Margaret Danner. ImOAAF p.1
Her counsel was accepted the times are grave. Maya Angelou. AnSIR p.24
Her Cruising Car. Nikki Giovanni. ThWRNW p.34
Her dreams came true & passed all dreams do. Ntozake Shange. NaEd p.93
Her ethic sodden spawn of occidentalism. Johari Amini. ImIB p.5
Her eyes were fire and blood and wild roses. Pinkie Gordon Lane. MyFe p.46
Her face is a meditative frown. Nora Blakely. TGWL p.14
Her face made from a smooth

sheet of chocolate. Harryette Mullen. TTW p.60
Her first man cut the sod and builded with it her first house. Mari Evans. NIGHT p.21
Her friends all call her "Skeeter." Eloise Culver. GANIV p.75
Her grandmother called her from the playground. Nikki Giovanni. MyH p.5
Her life was dwarfed and wed to blight. Georgia Douglas Johnson. HWOP p.39
Her Love Poem. Lucille Clifton. OrW p.55
Her lungs emptied out fear. Wanda Coleman. MaDBL p.122
Her people's done left her. Jennifer Blackman Lawson. BlIMT p.17
Her silence makes hushed vibrations within my wonderment. S. Diane Bogus. WITM p.3
Her Story. Naomi Long Madgett. BlVo p.476; OnATM p.55; PoBA p.183; StBS p.62
Herald Square. Jayne Cortez. Scar p.52
Here and now. Catherine Cater. AmNP p.148; PoN p.102; PoNe p.340
Here are the facts. Gwendolyn Brooks. StIB p.22; WoOGB p.24
Here...Hold My Hand. ** Mari Evans. IABW p.25; RoATW p. 89; WhIAM p.7
Here I Am. ** Jayne Cortez. FeAF p.36
Here I am in Mississippi. Linda Brown Bragg. LoSBM p.22
Here I sit like a bird. Safiya Henderson. CoAAAW p.131
Here in a Chicago museum. Margaret Danner. BrT p.39; ImOAAF p.2
Here in my lateness in nerves of my sweetness. Jayne Cortez. Scar p.28
Here in the wombed room. Maya Angelou. JGM p.5
Here is my card. Jayne Cortez. Scar p.14
Here is where it was dry. Lucille Clifton. GoNAE p.17
Here lies the street of the three balls. Helen Johnson Collins. PoN p.193; PoNe p.346
Here on the edge of uncertainty wondering about my identity. Eleanor Thomas-Grumbach. MoSu p.15
Here rolls another pearl. Margaret Danner. DoOAT p.59
Here we have watched ten thousand seasons come and go. Alice Walker. RePOP p.25
Here where the pirate chieftains sailed. Stephanie Ormsby. PoN p.309
Here where the world is quiet and the grasses wave banners in the breeze. Naomi Long Madgett. OnATM p.13
Here y'all come. Leatrice Emeruwa. BlGBG p.20
Here you are, lady. Patricia Parker. ChOM p.4; MoIB p. 33
Here's a bowl of batter for your spoon to stir. Harryette Mullen. TTW p.39
Here's to Adhering. Maya Angelou. OhPWFW p.5
Heritage. Dolores Clinton. EbR p.47
Heritage. Gwendolyn B. Bennett. AmNP p.73; BANP p.245; BlSi p.77
Heritage. Gwendolyn Brooks. PoBA p.81
Heritage. Harryette Mullen. TTW p.3
Heritage. Mae V. Cowdery. WLOV p.64
Heritage. Naomi E. Buford. EbR p.16
Heritage. Naomi Long Madgett. PhN p.56
Hermit's Sacrifice, The. Frances E. W. Harper. PBFH p.66
He's a man on the roof. June Jordan. SCh p.19; ThTDID p.107
He's bettin on it this yellow mellow bit. Gwendolyn Brooks. AnA p.53
He's Coming Home at Last. Emily Jane Green. EbR p.73

He's gonna chop his way into heaven. Elma Stuckey. BiGa p.1
He's the last train in the station. Wanda Coleman. MaDBL p.63
He's there,sits very still barely breathing. Wanda Coleman. MaDBL p.118
Hesitant door chain back forth, The. Mari Evans. IABW p.26; PoBA p.191
Hesitation. Linda Brown Bragg. LoSBM p.10
"Hey, Baby: You Married?" June Jordan. PaNP p.20
Hey chocolate they say in your high blooded fingers. Jayne Cortez. MiOP p.56
Hey c'mon come out. June Jordan. ThTDID p.71
Hey little Black one. Nilata. ThHSD p.61
Hey, little yellow bus. Joyce Whitsitt Lawrence. NBP p.130
Hey mama, wha's revolution? Nayo. NeBV p.382; YoBBI p.437
Hey music and me only white. Lucille Clifton. CoAAAW p.86
Hey, sisters git yr/blk/asses out of that re/volution. Sonia Sanchez. HoC p.31
Hey There. Sonia Sanchez. LoP p.66
Heyyy mama... whuts to it sistuhh...? Mari Evans. NIGHT p.13
Hezekiah. Elma Stuckey. BiGa p. 29
Hi there, my name is George Washington Carver. June Jordan. PaNP p.44
Hidden in a forest of question. Audre Lorde. BlUn p.73
High above this desert I am becoming absorbed. Audre Lorde. BlUn p.16
High Noon. Naomi Long Madgett. PhN p.57
High on the Hog. Julia Fields. MoCAP p.154
High shayiff tol de depity--hanh! Anonymous. BlWOA p.458
High Tide. Countess W. Twitty. EbR p.146
High/yellow/black/girl walken like the sun u be. Sonia Sanchez. BlSp p.190; ItND p.8
Highway is full of big cars, The. Maya Angelou. OhPWFW p.16
Hijo de Las Americas. Ntozake Shange. DaGe p.49
Hill, The. Ruby Stevens. NeVo p.146
Hills, The. Frenchy J. Hodges. BlW p.8
Hills are calling, The. Frenchy J. Hodges. BlW p.8
Hilltop was our haven, The. Lucia Mae Pitts. NegVo p. 129
His Answer. Clara Ann Thompson. AVAN p.133; BlSi p.42
His artificaial feet calumped in holy rhythm. Naomi Long Madgett. BlSi p.127; ExAE p.15
His body he arched when he play. Sherley Williams. PeP. p. 77
His Body is an Eloquence. Pinkie Gordon Lance. TGWL p.66; WiTh p.40
His brother after dinner once a year would play the piano. June Jordan. SCh p.13; SoS p.28; ThTDID p.14
His desires, growning from timid heights. Sarah Webster Fabio. PoBA p.203; PoNe p. 393
His Excellency General Washington. Phillis Wheatley. AfAV p.28; AmLNA p.24; DuSAE p.253; EaNAW p.52; EBAP p.108; KAL p.5; NeCa p.285; PAL p.51; PoN p.6; Pone p.7; PPW p.89
His Eye Into the Room. Wanda Coleman. MaDBL p.50
His eyes, they are shiny: his face it is clear. S. Diane Bogus. WITM p.49
His Hands. Damali (Denise Burnett) IATWMB p.18
His Hands. Elma Stuckey. BiGa p.68
His hands are oddly gnarled for one so young. Damali

(Denise Barnett) IATWMB p.18
His headstone said FREE AT LAST, FREE AT LAST. Nikki Giovanni. BFBTBJ p.56; BlP p.323; BOL p.30; BrT p.54; EgT p. 22; TNV p.37
His mouth liquid this glitter night beneath stars. Wanda Coleman. MaDBL p.98
His old Flame, Lady, Venice. Wanda Coleman. MaDBL p.46
His only slave freed and gone. Elma Stuckey. BiGa p.63
His soul curdled standing milk. Maya Angelou. OhPWFW p.52
His tongue pursues me through a wake-sleep. Wanda Coleman. MaDBL p.43
His Voice Used to Sing. Sonia Sanchez. IvBAW p.69
Historical Footnote to Consider Only When All Else Fails (for Barbara Crosby) Nikki Giovanni. BFBTBJ p.16
Historical Poem, A. Carolyn M. Rodgers. HeAEB p.59
History. May Miller. ClAB p.10
History bless me with my children's growing rebellion. Audre Lorde. ChPON p.55; FrLWP p. 30
History has made this time for you. Sonia Sanchez. ItND p.10
Hit man has oily fingers, The. Wanda Coleman. MaDBL p.11
Hit wuz somewhere back in fawth. Bessie Woodson Yancey. EcFTH p.52
Hitch hiking through life I Lost the way. Jean Collins. AOS p.6
Ho! Cra-ab Man! Anonymous. ITBLIA p.125
Hold my rooster, hold my hen. Anonymous. GoS p.16; TYBP p.198
Holes in my arms gone gangrene. Jayne Cortez. PoBA p.344
Holy Day. Thelma Lamar. PoBBl p.41
Holy haloes ring me round. Maya Angelou. OhPWFW p.33
Holy Night. Lucille Clifton. TwW p.38
Homage. Naomi Long Madgett. StBS p.14
Homage to Black Madonnas. Margaret T. G. Burroughs. WhSIT p.24
Homage to my Hair. Lucille Clifton. TwW p.5
Homage to my Hips. Lucille Clifton. TwW p.6
Home. Margaret Danner. DoOAT p.51
Home oh home the soul of your variety. Lucille Clifton. GoNAE p.15
Home: Sea to Sea. Jodi Braxton. SoITM p.40
Home Sweet Home. Frances E. W. Harper. PBFH p.26
Homecoming. Mari Evans. WhIAM p.16
Homecoming. Sonia Sanchez. HoC p.9; IvBAW p.3; PoBA p.286
Homecoming-Mass. General Hospital. Lyn. SiSH p.6
Homicide 1973. Jayne Cortez. Scar p.56
Homing Braves. Georgia Douglas Johnson. BrBV p.69
Homophobia racism self-definition revolutionary struggle. June Jordan. ThTDID p.84
Homosexuality (an invention of soul as played to perfection by the pope) Nikki Giovanni. Rec p.38
Honey dripping rain through the spruce. June Jordan. PaNP p.74
Honey people murder mercy U.S.A. June Jordan. PoBA p.305; SCh p.15; SoS p.115; ThTDID p.108
Honey, pepper, leaf-green limes. Agnes Maxwell-Hall. MBP p. 43; PoN p.310; TYBP p.117
"Honey Suckle was the Saddest Odor of All, I Think." Thadious M. Davis. BlSi p. 279
Honey, whin de dusk creep long de piney hill. Lucile D. Goodlett. WGC p.52
Honkies always talking 'bout Black Folks. Nikki Giovanni. BFBTBJ p.21
Hoo-Dooism. Jodi Braxton. SoITM p.15

Hooked on his mother's kisses, he nightly sinks into euphoria. Naomi Long Madgett. PiLAF p.27
Hope. Georgia Douglas Johnson. BrBV p.56; CaD p.75
Hope. Josephine D. (Henderson) Heard. MoGl p.21
Hope is a crushed stalk. Pauli Murray. DaTAOP p.22; MyNIB p.79
Hope Thou in God. Josephine D. (Henderson) Heard. MoGl p.46
Hope! thou vain, delusive, maiden. Josephine D. (Henderson) Heard. MoGl p.21
Horizons. Eleanor Thomas-Grumbach. MoSu p.20
Horizontal rather than vertical this city spreads herself out. Pinkie Gordon Lane. WiTh p.19
Horns protruded from the holes of a skelton. Jayne Cortez. FeAF p.37; NeBV p.236
Horses Graze. Gwendolyn Brooks. Bec p.11
Hosea. Margaret Walker. PFND p.27
Hospital/Poem. Sonia Sanchez. BlP p.236; PoBA p.289; WABP p.29
Hour draws its own design, The. Pinkie Gordon Lane. MyFe p.13
Hour is big with sooth and sign, The. Georgia Douglas Johnson. BrBV p.67
House catch on fire. Anonymous. BLIA p.48; BlWOA p.648; ITBLA p.124
House Cleaning. Nikki Giovanni. BrT p.61
House Nigger. Elma Stuckey. BiGa p.9
House of Desire, The. Sherley Williams. BlSi p.255; PePo p.50
House was dirty, The. Eleanor Thomas-Grumbach. MoSu p.5
Housecleaning. Nikki Giovanni. RoATW p.117
Houses. Nikki Giovanni. VaT p. 35
Houses with peeling skins of gray paint. Harryette Mullen, TTW p.2
How brittle is the thread of life. Josephine D. (Henderson) Heard. MoGl p.109
How Can I Find the Words. Marva Tatum Smith. BeYM p.31
How Can I Forget? ** Alice Robinson. BTh p.46
How Can I Love...** Audre Lorde. SiAS p.44
How can the red rose wilt. Mary Bohanon. GaBW p.263
How can we be unified. Ann Wallace. GLOWC p.104
How Can You Comfort Me? Sonia Sanchez. IvBAW p.79
How Come Dat? Lucy Mae Turner. BCF p.26
How could I know how long that night would be? Naomi Long Madgett. PhN p.61
How Death Came. Anonymous. TYBP p.5
How deftly does the gardener blend this rose and that. Georgia Douglas Johnson. BrBV p.60
How did it happen that we quarreled? Jessie Fauset. CaD p.65
How did You Feel Mary. May Miller. BTB p.151
How do poets write so many poems. Nikki Giovanni. CoCRD p.39
How do we come to be here next to each other in the night. June Jordan. ThTDID p.70
How do you get from here to there. Marva Tatum Smith. BeYM p.2
How do you spell change like frayed slogan underwear. Audre Lorde. ChPON p.73; NeBV p.289; NeHS p.1
How Do You Write a Poem? Nikki Giovanni. Rec p.46; WoATM p.38
How Far Away is Not Soon. Mari Evans. NIGHT p.44
How gauche (I thought at first) to streak her loneliness. Leatrice Emeruwa. BlGBG p.21
How He Is Coming Then. Lucille Clifton. TwW p.37
How horrible it is to reach out. Mary Bohanon. GaBW p.

260
How I can lie to you. Maya Angelou. JGM p.21
How I Got Ovah. Carolyn M. Rodgers. HoIGO p.5
How I Got Ovah II/It is Deep II. Carolyn M. Rodgers. HoIGO p. 77
How I love thy rugged hills, West Virginia! Bessie Woodson Yancey. EcFTH p.2
How is the word made flesh made steel. Audre Lorde. ChPON p.69; NeHS p.9
How little I know you. Naomi Long Madgett. PiLAF p.34
How long baby, how long. Anonymous. BLIA p.48; ITBLA p. 124
How Long Blues. Anonymous. BLIA p.48; BlWOA p.888; ITBLA p.124
How long, how long, has that evening train bin gone? Anonymous. BlWOA p.888
How Long to Live. June Vanleer Williams. WiRYPS p.11
How many death songs will we write? Mari Evans. IABW p. 85
How many of u niggers watched ted kennedy on tv yesterday. Sonia Sanchez. WABP p.24
How Many Silent Centuries Sleep in My Sultry Veins? ** Margaret Walker. PFND p.15
How many ways must I tell you I love you. Nola Richardson. WhOL p.40
How many years since 1619 have I been singing spirituals? Margaret Walker. FMP p.26
How much living have you done? Georgia Douglas Johnson. AmNP p.22
How much love can I pour into you I said. Audre Lorde. BlUn p.75
How My Heart Sinks. Georgia Douglas Johnson. ALC p.14
How near is God to me? Josephine D. (Henderson) Heard. MoGl p.133
How near we are to paradise. Naomi Long Madgett. StBS p. 24
How often must we butt to head. Maya Angelou. OhPWFW p.64
How Old Did You Say? June Vanleer Williams. WiRYPS p.54
How quiet and how still to-day old Bethel's corners 'round. Josephine D. (Henderson) Heard. MoGl p.33
How sad it must be to love so many women. Sonia Sanchez. BlP p.236; BrT p.139; IvBAW p.17; WABP p.14
How say that by law we may torture and chase. Frances E. W. Harper. BlSi p.32
How Shall I Face the Dawn? Naomi Long Madgett. OnATM p.47
How shall your name go down in history. Josephine D. (Henderson) Heard. MoGl p.28
How soft and bright at break of day. Lucy Mae urner. BCF p.45
How soon will you be fun for me. Margaret Danner. DoOAT p. 138
How the days went while you were blooming within me. Audre Lorde. ChPON p.13; COAL p.21; FiCi p.6; PoBA p.246
How the young attempt and are broken differs from age to age. Audre Lorde. ChPON p.15; COAL p.13; FiCi p. 15; NeBV p.288
How to weave your web of medicinal flesh into words. Jayne Cortez. CoAAAW p.94
How Will You Call Me, Brother. Mari Evans. BlSi p.144; NIGHT p.65
However Brief Their Acquaintance With My Father.** Gloria Oden. TiTBi p.1
However the image enters its force remains within my eyes. Audre Lorde. ChPON p.102
Hu! Hu! some fo'ks won't take muffin. Lucy Mae Turner. BCF p.11
Huddled there on the sidewalk is heartbreak. Beatrice M. Murphy. TNV p.140
Hum of the Dialysis Machine,

The. Pinkie Gordon Lane. WiTh p.42
Humbled Rocks. Paulette Childress White. DeDF p.98
Humility. Anita Scott Coleman. EbR p.51
Hunchback girl: she thinks of heaven. Gwendolyn Brooks. ITBLA p.217; KAL p.151; SPGB p.5; StIB p.9; WoOGB p.1
Hunger. Anonymous. TYBP p.156
Hunger makes a person climb up the ceiling. Anonymous. TYBP p.156
Hunters are back from beating the winter's face. Audre Lorde. BlSi p.204; CaTR p. 19; ChPON p.14; COAL p.9; NaPr p.67
Hurt u worried abt a little hurting. Sonia Sanchez. BlFi p.255; HoC p.22; PoBA p.290
Hush By the Hands of Sleep. Angelina Weld Grimke. NeCa p.341
Hush Chillun. Lucile D. Goodlett. WGC p.51
Hush, Honey. Fareedah Allah. BlSi p.164
Hush Now. Dorothy C. Parrish. TNV p.88
Hush now baby, not a peep. Dorothy C. Parrish. TNV p. 88
Hush! yo' mouth it is time to be quiet. Fareedah Allah. BlSi p.164
Hushed by the Hands of Sleep ** Angelina Weld Grimke. CaD p.36
Hushed waves of muttering lap the cathedral stone. May Miller. ClAB p.15
Husks. Georgia Douglas Johnson. BrBV p.81
Husks of dead loves tangle your feet. Dorothy Lee Louis Shaed. NegVo p.139
Hyena. Anonymous. TYBP p.9
Hymn. Alice Walker. ONC p.41
HYmn to Humanity, An. (To S.P.G. Esq.) Phillis Wheatley. PAL p.62; PPW p.45
Hymn to the Evening, An. Phillis Wheatley. AmLNA p.26; ANP p.10; CNAW p.13; EaNAW p.41; PAL p.62; PPW p.26; ReFNA p.5
Hymn to the Morning, A. Phillis Wheatley. ANP p.10
Hymn to the Morning, An. Phillis Wheatley. CNAW p.12
Hymn to the Sun, The. Anonymous. TYBP p.21
Hypocrcisy. Josephine D. (Henderson) Heard. MoGl p. 113

- I -

I. Beverly Thomas. BrA p.16
I. Eleanor Thomas-Grumbach. MoSu p.23
I ain't never left this town. Sherley Williams. PePo p. 46
I ain't no wagon, ain't no dray. Anonymous. GoS p.17
I Almost Remember. Maya Angelou. OhPWFW p.47
I always hated Bigger Thomas. Ntozake Shange. NaEd p. 118
I always hated mama telling me to "stand up straight!" Jill Witherspoon Boyer. DrF p.24
I always like summer best. Nikki Giovanni. BFBTBJ p. 65; BlP p.BlP p.322; BlSi p.237; BOL p.58; BrT p.55; EgT p.15; NaPr p.21; OnOW p.45; PoBA p.480
I always like house cleaning. Nikki Giovanni. Rec p.16; RoATW p.117; WoATM p.24
I always think of a coffin's quiet. Audre Lorde. NaPr p.72
I always think that when I see you. Gwendolyn Brooks. PaP p.20; FBPA p.28
I always wanted to be a bridesmaid. Nikki Giovannni. MyH p.13
I Am. Damali (Denise Burnett) IATWMB p.9

I Am. Dolores Abramson. RoATW p. 83; ThHSD p.36
I am a Black woman. Margaret Walker. CoAAAW p.361
I Am A Black Woman.** Mari Evans. BLIA p.349; CoAAAW p.105
I am a boy. Helen Morgan Brooks. PoNe p.277
I Am A Child of America. ** Patricia Parker. MoIB p.63
I am a child of the valley. Margaret Walker. FMP p.20
I am a clerk. Wanda Coleman. MaDBL p.91
I am a dying girl. Sonia Sanchez. LoP p.26
I am a leaf falling from your tree. Nikki Giovanni. Rec p. 13
I Am a Mad Dog.** Joanne Jimason. NaEBE p.22
"I am a man," Patricia Parker. ChOM p.25
I am a mountain stream, Ho! Ho! Bessie Woodson Yancey. EcFTH p.6
I am a Negro. Bessie Woodson Yancey. EcFTH p.27
I am a slave born Black. Anonymous. MBP p.54
I Am a Spiritual Alcoholic. Anonymous. BTB p.42
I am a teller of tales. Nikki Giovanni. WoATM p.44
I am a trader in dreams. Cora Ball Moten. NegVo p.111
I am a wisp of energy. Mari Evans. NIGHT p.3
I am a woman. Georgia Douglas Johnson. ALC p.25
I am a woman controlled. May Miller. DeDF p.33
I am afraid to laugh! Lucy Ariel Williams Holloway. BTh p.17
I am always lonely for things I've never had. Nikki Giovanni. BFBTBJ p.11
"I am Antar!" he chants. Anonymous. MBP p.66
I am anxious for answers. Akua Lezli Hope. CoAAAW p.142
I Am Black. Kali Grosvenor. PBK p.15
I am Black but still if I die let God take my soul. Kali Grosvenor. PBK p.16
I am bleed mouth nod from an oath in sorrow. Jayne Cortez. COAG p.16; Scar p.12
I am cold sometimes. Pinkie Gordon Lane. WiTh p.56
I am declaring war on my refrigerator, Margaret Porter. CoAAAW p.264
I am deep/bl/soil. Sonia Sanchez. LoP p.68
I am drunk with beauty. Mae V. Cowdery. WLOV p.6 2
I am essence of Rose solitude. Jayne Cortez. COAG p.36; MoOP p.40
I am ever picking it from my body. Wanda Coleman. MaDBL p.126
I am fourteen and my skin has betrayed me. Audre Lorde. BlUn p.96
I am Frightened that the Flame of Hate/Will Burn Me. Vanessa Howard. ScWh p.16
I am getting my masters degree this year. Beverly Thomas. BrA p.16
I am going blind. Lucille Clifton. TwW p.54
I am going to rise en masse. Mari Evans. AfAWA p.684; BlLi p.435; BOL p.50; CNAW p.765; OABW p.70; IABW p.70; NeBV p.245; PoBA p.188; UNBP p.247
I am here in my usual place. Sonia Sanchez. IvBAW p.31; LoP p.11
I am Here to Announce. ** Ronda Davis. BlSp p.48
I am High on the Man Called Crazy. Lucille Clifton. GoNAE p.16
I am in a box. Nikki Giovanni. CoCRD p.34
I am in the mean. Abbey Lincoln. CoAAAW p.189
I am Indian. Anita Scott Coleman. EbR p.48
I am jolly. Toi Derricotte. EmDH p.49
I am kneading my bread Winnie Mandela. Audre Lorde. ChPON p.101
I am lonely. Carolyn M. Rodgers. BlSi p.176; HoIGO

p.47
I am looking for something I know I cannot find. Naomi Long Madgett. PhN p.117
I Am Man.** Tomi Carolyn Tinsley. EbR p.140
I Am New York City.** Jayne Cortez. COAG p.9; Scar p.7
I am not coming to this man's house again. Anonymous. MBP p.56
I Am Not Done Yet. Lucille Clifton. OrW p.59
I Am Not Lazy. Mari Evans. WhIAM p.21
I Am Not My Sister's Keeper: I Am My Sister. Regina Williams. CoAAAW p.381
I am now in the innocence of one. Sonia Sanchez. IvBAW p.42; LoP p.45
I am old and need to remember. Nikki Giovanni. WoATM p.46
I Am On Top. ** Sonia Sanchez. IvBAW p.87
I am rarely vindictive. June Jordan. ThTDID p.67
I am reminded, by the tan man who wings the elevator of rococo art. Margaret Danner. BTB p.86; CNAW p.764; DoOAT p.68; IrLa p.16; MoCAP p. 87; PoBA p.137; PoNe p.161
I am Running Into a New Year. Lucille Clifton. OrW p.45
I am serious about being serious. Mae Jackson. CaPWY p.6
I Am Settling Down. Sonia Sanchez. IvBAW p.70
I Am She. ** Nikki Giovanni. ThWRNW p.56
I am shuddering in my heart, for soon it will be spring. Naomi Long Madgett. PhN p.45
I am so glad to be moving. Audre Lorde. ChPON p.61; FrLWP p.22
I am so sorry to say this but our poor are not as poor as yours. June Jordan. ThTDID p.181
I am so tired, waiting for my heart to break. Virginia Houston. NegVo p.77
I am soft woman. Julia Fields. BiLi p.532; RoATW p.57
I am sorry, beloved. Virginia Houston. NegVo p.77
I am standing on a mountain-top. Naomi Long Madgett. PhN p.25
I am supposed to say it doesn't matter. Audre Lorde. ChPON p.89; NeHS p.32
I am the darker sister. Frances Garcia. ThHSD p.62
I am the downtrodden. Judy Dothard Simmons. CoAAAW p. 330
I am the highway. Pauli Murray. DaTAOP p.62
I am the mother of nightmares. Harryette Mullen. TTW p.29
I am the new sister. Marion Nicholes. LiS p.14
I am the pure lotus. Anonymous TYBP p.27
I am the token Negro. Nikki Giovanni. BFBTBJ p.43
I am the Uncle Tom at whom you scoff and sneer. Beatrice M. Murphy. RoCO p.7
I Am the Weaver.** Abbey Lincoln. CoAAAW p.185
I am the writer who cannot write. Naomi Long Madgett. OnATM p.30
I am tired of it! Helen F. Chappell. NegVo p.28
I am tired so tiiiiiired. Carolyn M. Rodgers. BlSp p.178
I Am Too Much Loved.** Clara H. Haywood. NegVo p.70
I Am Too Past Youth. Johari Amini. LetGSM p.25
I am trying to drain my mind of all secretions. Sonia Sanchez. IvBAW p.35; LoP p.29
I am 25 years old. Nikki Giovanni. BFBTBJ p.95; BlBI p.534; BlP p.319; BOL p.22; BrT p.58; NaPr p.297; NeBV p.250; PoBA p.453; TNV p.35; YoBBI p.476
I Am Untrue Yet I. June Jordan. ThTDID p.156
I am waiting. Alicia Loy Johnson. BOL p.13; GaBW p.341; NiBPo p.149
I Am Waiting.** Vanessa Howard. MyNIB p.155
I am warm. Johari Amini. BlSi p.195; CoAAAW p.51
I am weary, O God. Pauli Murray. DaTAOP p.54

I am weary of passion. Mae V. Cowdery. WLOV p.55
I am weaving a song of waters. Gwendolyn B. Bennett. BlSi p.73
I am writing at the request of Larry Neal, Ed Spriggs and Harold Foster. Odara (Barbara Jones) BlFi p.356
I and He. Marion Cuthbert. SOC p.9
I and I. Jayne Cortez. COAG p.97
I ask no more than you're willing to give. Esther Louise. CoAAAW p.198
I Be Growin Still. Nia nSabe. ThHSD p.71
I became a woman during the old prayers. Lucille Clifton. GoNAE p.6
I been there. Elma Stuckey. BiGa p.21
I beg my bones to be good. Lucille Clifton. OrW p.61
I began with everything. Lucille Clifton. TwW p.12
I believe in the ultimate justice of fate. Georgia Douglas Johnson. BlALP p.44; BrBV p.53; PoBA p.23
I bless the black skin of the woman. Lucille Clifton. GoNAE p.33
I bow to the power of lace. Margaret Danner. DoOAT p.42
I break the hoe. Elma Stuckey. BiGa p.31
I breathe the lyric of my love. Georgia Douglas Johnson. HWOP p.48
I called you through the silent night. Georgia Douglas Johnson. HWop p.30
I came to the crowd seeking friends. Nikki Giovanni. BFBTBJ p.5
I came to their white terror first. Audre Lorde. ChPON p.72; NeHS p.37
I can be alone by myself. Nikki Giovanni. EgT p.20; Rec p. p.10; WoATM p.37
I Can Be Somebody.** Judith Bracey. ThHSD p.57
I can keep my house neat and tidy again. Naomi Long Madgett. PiLAF p.26
I Can Luv Blkman.** Linda Cousins. RoATW p.27; ThHSD p.33
I Can No Longer Sing. ** Mari Evans. IABW p.23; WhIAM p. 4
I can remember the deep shadows' gloom. Naomi Long Madgett. SoTPN p.22
I can remember when I was a little young girl. Jessie Redmond Fauset. ANP p.89; AVAN p. 194; BANP p.207
I can remember wind-swept streets of cities on cold and blustery nights. Margaret Walker. AfAWA p.521; FMP p. 56
I can see your daughter walking down streets of love in revelation. Audre Lorde. ChPON p.56; FrLWP p.40
I can tell you about them. Carolyn M. Rodgers. HoIGO p.5
I cannot fight a memory. Countess W. Twitty. EbR p.146
I cannot leave you gold. Margaret Danner. DoOAT p.76
I cannot recall you gentle yet. Audre Lorde. ChPON p.52; DeDF p.19; FrLWP p.16
I Cannot Sleep. Naomi Long Madgett. OnATM p.13
I cannot swear with any certainty that I will always feel as I do now. Naomi Long Magett. OnATM p.33
I can't do what you can do. Marva Tatum Smith. BeYM p.26
I can't erase the scars. Nola Richardson. WhOL p.53
I can't quite remember how many questions or journalists. Ntozake Shange. NaEd p.17
I can't sleep at night. Anonymous. BlWOA p.888
I can't unlock my eyes because my body will come through. Gwendolyn Brooks. BeEa p.65; WoOGB p.363
I Celebrate the Sons of Malcolm. ** June Jordan. DeRi p.15; SCh p.78; ThTDID p.113
I closed my eyes. Nola Richard-

son. WhOL p.93
I closed my shutters fast last night. Georgia Douglas Johnson. ALC p.3; NeCa p.340; PoN p.59; PoNe p.79
I come each day at nine and leave at five. Sonia Sanchez. LoP p.32
I come from the womb of Africa. Amini Baraka. CoAAAW p.70
I come with the young sun strong in my limbs. Pauli Murray. DaTAOP p.93
I could forgive you if you say you hate us. Beatrice M. Murphy. RoCO p.12
I could grit my teeth and bear up. S. Diane Bogus. WITM p.30
I could have you love me. Thulani Davis. AlTRGR p.39
I could love you Black man. Sonia Sanchez. LoP p.62
I Could Not Know. Lois Royal Hughes. EbR p.90
I could sleep with a man. Ntozake Shange. DaGe p.18
I couldn't tell fact from fiction. Maya Angelou. OhPWFW p.17
I count not him my friend. Josephine D. (Henderson) Heard. MoGl p.101
I crawl to his door. Nikki Grimes. CoAAAW p.120
I cry out, but no one hears. Kattie M. Cumbo. NiBPo p.54
I curse the summer sun. Pauli Murray. DaTAOP p.32
I did not fall from the sky. Audre Lorde. BlUn p.14
I did not know my place. Ruby Berkley Goodwin. EbR p.68
I did not know when I had climbed the hill. Pauli Murray. DaTAOP p.86
I didn't know Bobby Hutton. Sonia Sanchez. HoC p.30
"I Die For All Mysterious Things." Audre Lorde. FiCi p.2
I die. I pass from every lovely thing. Julia Fields. GaBW p.309; NiBPo p.70
I do not ask for love, ah! no. Georgia Douglas Johnson. CaD p.77
I do not know ehen my lessons began. Patricia Parker. MoIB p.136
I do not like the leaden skies. Josephine D. (Henderson) Heard. MoGl p.108
I do not scorn your gay approach. Naomi Long Madgett. SoTPN p.17
I Do Not Sleep Nights Through.** Gloria Oden. RESUR p.31
I don' know no proper words fo t' say up heah. Lucile D. Goodlett. WGC p.33
I Done Got So Thirsty That My Mouth Waters at the Thought of Rain. Patricia Jones. BlSi p.249
I don't know about anything. Sharon Scott. JuBa p.174
I don't know if I am with life. Tyki Brown. ThHSD p.75
I don't know why but I cannot tell a lie. June Jordan. ThTDID p.141
I Don't Pretend to Understand. C. Tillery Banks. HeTMWL p.8
I don't try now to push the days into corners. Pinkie Gordon Lane. WiTh p.58
I don't want a drought to feed on itself. Jayne Cortez. COAG p.102
I don't want to be a doo-wah, hey baby, what's happening sister. E. Sharon Gomillion. FoAAM p.12
I don't want to cry anymore. C. Tillery Banks. HeTMWL p.48
I don't want to touch your little sentiments. Judy Dothard Simmons. JuB p.10; UMBP p.365
I don't want you to think that I don't know the pain. Nikki Giovanni. Rec p.44
I Don't Worry Too Much.** Marva Tatum Smith. BeYM p. 15
I Dream Alone Again.** Ruby Berkley Goodwin. NegVo p. 61
I dream of a place. Audre Lorde. BlUn p.82
I dream of serenity. Kattie M. Cumbo. BlSi p.137

I dreamed myself in a house of yr paintings. Ntozake Shange. DaGe p.65
I dreamed of you last night. Nikki Giovanni. CoCRD p.70
I dreampt of you, sweetheart, last night. Josephine D. (Henderson) Heard. MoGl p.118
I dressed all up for freedom. Nancy L. Arnez. RoCo P.21
I drew a line between the past and present. Naomi Long Madgett. PhN p.79
I drip blood on my way to and from work. Wanda Coleman. MaDBL p.17
I emptied your wastebasket the other day. Naomi Long Madgett. ExAE p.63
I enter your house and the rhythm begins. C. Tillery Banks. HeTMWL p.16
I entreated..."O beloved death." Mae C. Cowdery. WLOV p.18
I exist on the island. Sandra Royster. WoTa p.16
I fear my power impotent. Georgia Douglas Johnson. ALC p.17
I feel a little jumpy around you. Harryette Mullen. TTW p.26
I feel alive, again. Kattie M. Cumbo. GaBW p.287
I feel so new. Elaine Taylor. HoDo p.102
I feel unsafe in the presence of meat eaters. Ntozake Shange. NaEd p.73
I felt today within me life. Marion Nicholes. LiS p.16
I fight for life. Pinkie Gordon Lane. WiTh p.44
I Find No Evil or Three Imanges & Trust. S. Diane Bogus. WITM p.18
I find the world viewed as a whole. Doretta Lowery. BTh p.63
I find you behind the warm/cool darkness of eyes closed. Nora Davis. GLOWC p.10
I follow the curve. Wanda Coleman. MaDBL p.24
I follow the green man. Margaret Danner. DoOAT p.21
I follow the prophet through a world of older people. Jodi Braxton. SoITM p.20
I Followed a Path. Patricia Parker. BlSi p.239; DOBB p.109
I Forgot to Remember. Jayne Cortez. FeAF p.43
I from my window looked at early dawning. Josephine D. (Henderson) Heard. MoGl p. 79
I gather up each sound you left behind. Sonia Sanchez. IvBAW p.30; LoP p.10
I get inspired in the middle of the night. Ntozake Shange. NaEd p.142
I get my degree the spring of '52. Fareedah Allah. BlSi p.175
I get scared sometimes. Wanda Coleman. MaDBL p.23
I give it to you Michael. Sherley Williams. PePo p.84
I go through my rooms like a witch watchman. Lucille Clifton. OrW p.83
I goin' to pizen you. Jodi Braxton. SoITM p.14
I got a dog. Jayne Cortez. Scar p.50
I Got a Home in Dat Rock.** Anonymous. ITBLA p.98
I Got a Home in Dat Rock.** Spiritual. BlP p.25
I got a man fine as he wants to be. Leatrice Emeruwa. BlGBG p.15
I got a shoe, you got a shoe. Anonymous. AmLNA p.6
I got a sore throat. Jayne Cortez. Scar p.53
I got a sweet Black gal. Anonymous. BlWOA p.647
I Got the Blues. Anonymous. TYBP p.203
I guess I'm just plain tired. June Vanleer Williams. WiRYPS p.29
I Guess This is What I Want From You.** Sonia Sanchez. IvBAW p.80
I had a dream a varied dream. Frances E. W. Harper. PBFH p.82
I had a dream last night. Gwendolyn Brooks. MyNIB p.

p.66
I had a dream once. Carolyn M. Rodgers. HeAEG p.71
I had a friend. Damali (Denise Burnett) IMTWMB p.12
I had a liddle rooster. Anonymous. AmLNA p.8
I had a rendezvous with love. Lola Royal Hughes. EbR p.89
I had become callous like most numbed by statistics. Della Burt. BlSi p.163
I Had Five Nose Rings. Ntozake Shange. NaEd p.58
I had forgotten so much in the south. Naomi Long Madgett. OnATM p.53
I had known winters for so long. Mae V. Cowdery. WLOV p.45
I had no thought of violets of late. Alice Dunbar-Nelson. ANP p.84; BANP p.164; BlSi p.65; CaD p.72; PoBA p.12; PoN p.41; PoNe p.46; ReFNA p.32
I had sensed such a soaring new year. Margaret Danner. DoOAT p.19
I had thought of putting an altar here in the house. Isabella Maria Brown. NNPUSA p.61; PoNe p.341
I had to kick the law into their teeth in order to save him. Gwendolyn Brooks. KAL p.152; SPGB p.19; StIB p.30
I had two braids and a rubber ball. Linda Brown Bragg. BTB p.54; LoSBM p.26
I hang on the edge of this universe. Nikki Giovanni. ThWRNW p.46
I hardly remember my mother's face now. Naomi Long Madgett. ExAE p.41
I Hate. Joanne Jimason. NeABE p.12
I Hate Goodbyes. Nola Richardson. WhOL p.93
I hate this maggot of a faggot. Joanne Jimason. NaEBE p.12
I hate to lose something. Maya Angelou. JGM p.8
I Have. Patricia Parker. MoIB p.128
I have a bank account with God. Bessie Woodson Yancey. EcFTH p.17
I have a black look that I like. Colleeen McElroy. MuDLSG p.25
I have a child whose feet are blind. Audre Lorde. ChPON p.13; COAL p.42; FiCi p.21
I have a daughter. Ntozake Shange. DaGe p.21
I Have a Dream.** Patricia Parker. MoIB p.83
I have a dream, my vision is long. Frenchy J. Hodges. BlW p.16
I Have a Friend.** Anne Spencer. CaD p.47
I have a friend who said good food makes him grin. Damali (Denise Burnett) IATWMB p.12
I have a lover who has a lover. Patricia Parker. MoIB p.114
I have a secret to tell you. Carolyn M. Rodgers. HeAEG p.5
I Have a Solitary Lover.** Patricia Parker. MoIB p.121
I have a thirst for happiness. Gertrude Blackwell Bailey. IfWCF p,40
I have all my mother's habits. Nikki Giovanni. BlSi p.236; WoATM p.25
I have always wisht it waznt so hot. Ntozake Shange. NaEd p.106
I have arrived. Mari Evans. AfAWA p.682; BLIA p.348; BlVo p.479; IABW p.68; IADB p.92; ITSA p.248; MyNIB p.100
I have awakened from the unknowing to the knowing. Bette Darcie Latimer. PoBA p.199; PoN p.298; PoNe p.392
I have been a way so long. Sonia Sanchez. HoC p.9; IvBAW p.3; PoBA p.286
I have been all my lovers. Thulani Davis. AlTRGR p. 3
I. Have Been Hungry. Carolyn M. Rodgers. HoIGO p.49
I have been leaping from floe

to floe. Naomi Long Madgett. PiLAF p.53
I have built my tower on the wings of a spider. Nikki Giovanni. MyH p.45
I Have Carried Sorrow. Joanne Jimason. NaABE p.30
I Have Changes so Much in This World. Carolyn M. Rodgers. HoIGO p.4
I have come down from the hills today. Pinkie Gordon Lane. MyFe p.24
I have come to catch birds. Anonymous. TYBP p.28
I have considered my reluctance to be a fear of death. Nikki Giovanni. CoCRD p.36
I Have Days (Rainy Days & Mondays) Naami Verano. ThHSD p.5
I have deferred the things I wanted most. Pinkie Gordon Lane. WiTh p.32
I have dug you a grave. Naomi Long Madgett. PhN p.81
I have forgotten you as one forgets at dawning. Helen Morgan Brooks. NNPUSA p.104; PoNe p.278; RoATW p.149
I have found my voice in the attic. Pinkie Gordon Lane. MyFe p.36
I have given you this Ashanti stool. Margaret Danner. DoOAT p.111; IrLa p.1
I have given you what I could not give my dearest love. Naomi Long Madgett. PhN p.92
I have gone into my eyes. Sonia Sanchez. LoP p.76
I have got old in a desert country. Lucille Clifton. DOBB p.54; MoCAP p.141
I Have Grown Weary. Julia Fields. GaBW p.304
I have just re turned from walk ing. Sonia Sanchez. LoP p. 15
I have just seen a beautiful thing. Angelina Weld Grimke. AmNP p.17; NeNRe p.366; PoBA p.15; PoN p.49
I have known many women. Patricia Parker. MoIB p.128
I have laughed these centuries when weaker creatures might have died beneath the blow. Naomi Long Madgett. PhN p.85
I have learned not to worry about love. Alice Walker. RePOP p.66
I have learned some few things. Lucille Clifton. GoNAE p.35
I have learned that love is not the whispered nothings of a love. Myra Estelle Morris. NegVo p.107
I have learned to be silent. Naomi Long Madgett. PhN p. 67; SoTPN p.19
I have learned your ways. E. Marie Newsome. RoATW p.150
I have lived in circles of solitude. Jayne Cortez. COAG p.11; Scar p.44
I have lived in the shadow of the first chance. Thulani Davis. AlTRGR p.4
I Have Looked Into my Father's Eyes. Sonia Sanchez. IvBAW p.67
I have lost my face. May Miller. ClAB p.31
I have lost track of time. Naomi Long Madgett. PiLAF p.41
I Have Made a Garden With Infinite care. Virginia Houston. NegVo p.78
I have mounted the corpse of my sorrow. Georgia Douglas Johnson. ALC p.68
I have my freedom. Toi Derricotte. EmDH p.26
I have never been contained. Mari Evans. IABW p.18; WhIAM p.5
I have nine guppies there were ten but the mother died shortly. Nikki Giovanni. MyH p.9
I have nine pretty smiling dolls. Floretta Howard. AmLNA p.53
I have not ever seen my father's grave. Audre Lorde. BTB p. 140; ChPON p.9; COAL p.4; FiCi p.13; MoCAP p.121; PoBA p.248; SiAS p.47; UNBP p.285
I have not like Einstein been an intellectual giant of the world. Naomi F. Faust.

PoBBl p.31
I have people. Kali Grosvenor. PBK p.20
I Have Robed Myself in the mentality of Motherhood. Joanne Jimason. NaABE p.11
I have sat in many thinking corners. S. Diane Bogus. WITM p.30
I Have Seen. Joanne Jimason. NaABE p.9
I have seen a new world from a new hill. Naomi Long Madgett. PhN p.55
I have seen many deaths. Eleanor Thomas-Grumbach. MoSu p.23
I have seen my people in a cave, digging. Joanne Jimason. NaABE p.9
I have seen them at many hours. Julia Fields. PoBA p.320; PoNe p.417
I have stepped into the mirror of my hatred. Wanda Coleman. MaDBL p.31
I have studied the tight curls on the back of your neck. Audre Lorde. ChPON p.63; FrLWP p.35
I have swung to the uttermost reaches of pain. Georgia Douglas Johnson. HWOP p.56
I have tasted alien mouths and felt the sinews of an arm. Mari Evans. IABW p.30
I have the greatest fun at night. Effie Lee Newsome. CaD p.58
I Have the Rolling Pin Mother Received When First She Wed. ** Gloria Oden. RESUR p.111
I have toiled in your corn fields. Georgia Douglas Johnson. BrBV p.33
I Have Walked a Long Time. Sonia Sanchez. LoP p.63
I have with me a mental bliss. Nola Richardson. WhOL p.57
I haven't done anything. Nikki Giovanni. CoCRD p.89
I haven't heard a robin sing. Naomi Long Madgett. PhN p.44; SoTPN p.25
I haven't written a poem in so long. Nikki Giovanni. CoCRD p.57
I haveta turn my television down sometimes cuz I can't stand to have white people/shout at me. Ntozake Shange. DaGe p.59
I Hear a Rumbling. ** Margaret Danner. CoAAAW p.369
I hear a wagon rumbling far away. Elma Stuckey. BiGa p.5
I hear myself drought caught. Audre Lorde. FiCi p.16
I hear the little black cricket. Effie Lee Newsome. GoS p.75
I hear you singing happily. Georgia Douglas Johnson. BrBV p.46
I heard a child cry in the night. May Miller. DeDF p. 96
I Heard a Young Man Saying. ** Julia Fields. BTB p.107; MoCAP p.149; NNPUSA p.110
I heard an organ pealing a soft refrain. Mae V. Cowdery. WLOV p.24
I Heard Myself Knocking. ** Marva Tatum Smith. MELVA p.1
I heard my young friend, you were seeking a wife. Frances E. W. Harper. RoATW p.90
I Heard the Angels Singin'. Anonymous. UNBP p.78
I heard the bugles blowing. Naomi Long Madgett. PhN p.63
I heard you singing to someone. Naomi Long Madgett. PhN p.52
I heard you today when you breezed by me. Carolyn M. Rodgers. HoIGO p.44
I heard your heart's soft tears. Helen C. Harris. EbR p.78
I here within myself centuries of self hate that know no way to destruct that know no way to break loose. Mae Jackson. BlSp p.91
I hold my honey and I store my bread. Gwendolyn Brooks. SPGB p.23; StIB p.48; WoOGB p.50
I Holler Hallelujah. Elma Stuckey. BiGa p.61
I hope that when I am dead that I shall lie. Jessie Redmond Fauset. ANP p.89; BANP p.

208; PoN p.67; PoNe p.69
I humbly bow beneath my cross. Lucy Mae Turner. BCF p.46
I is allus very happy. Lucy Mae Turner. BCF p.7
I is the total Black being spoken from the earth's inside. Audre Lorde. BTB p.141; ChPON p.10; COAL p.6; FiCi p.4; MoCAP p.121; NeBV p.291; PoBA p.244; SoS p.95
I just put all my trust in a fella I ain't seen. Elma Stuckey. BiGa p.72
I just turned a pan of scalding hot water on my arm. Isabella Maria Brown. PoNe p. 342
I keep on dying again. Maya Angelou. AnSIR p.18
I keep on movin': ain't gettin' nowhere. Elma Stuckey. BiGa p.65
I keep reaching back for the magic of those first few days. Saundra Sharp. RoATW p.137
I Keep the Tremor. Jayne Cortez. MoOP p.25
"I Ken Mek It." Bessie Woodson Yancey. EcFTH p.58
I kept a rendezvous with God one day, just he and I. Ruby Berkley Goodwin. NegVo p.63
I kept feeling all over my world for you. Carolyn M. Rodgers. HoIGO p.44
I kissed my lover in the storm. Thelma T. Clement. BTh p.22
I Kneel Down. Sonia Sanchez. IvBAW p.67
I Knew a Girl. Marva Tatum Smith. BeYM p.3
I knew that one day, a Thursday. Saundra Sharp. RoATW p.69
I Knew Then. May Miller. ClAB p.37
I knew you yesterday. Mary Bohanon. GaBW p.259
I know a tendril softly twined. Pauli Murray. DaTAOP p.85
I Know De Moonlight. Spiritual. BlP p.23
I know I haven't grown but I don't fit beneath the rose bush. Nikki Giovanni. CoCRD p.76
I know my love is seeking me. Georgia Douglas Johnson. ALC p.40
I know my upper arms will grow flabby. Nikki Giovanni. WoATM p.12
I know of an entertainer that went into a Black community. Mae Jackson. CaPWY p.8
I Know She Will Pray For Me. Sharon Bourke. UNBP p.375
I know that his eyes look into mine. Josephine D. (Henderson) Heard. MoGl p.31
I know the boundaries of my nation lie within myself. Audre Lorde. BlUn p.90
I know they want to make it. Jayne Cortez. Scar p.47
I Know Very Little About Love.** Melva Eloise Tatum. MELVA p.22
I know what it means to give birth to a child already dying. Naomi Long Madgett. PiLAF p.35
I know with pain the me that is I. Mari Evans. IABW p.19; WhIAM p.10
I know you love me better cold. Georgia Douglas Johnson. ALC p.13
I know you think of me when you are lonely. Naomi Long Madgett. PhN p.70
I Kumquat You. Patricia Parker. MoIB p.122
I laughed and no one heard. June Vanleer Williams. WiRYPS p.13
I Laughed, I Cried, I Ached Inside. Nola Richardson. WhOL p.29
I laughed then sat on a stump. June Vanleer Williams. WiRYPS p.3
I Laughed When I Wrote It. (Don't You Think It's Funny?) Nikki Giovanni. MyH p.59
I lay calm and let men jut their cities' cold feet. Helen F. Chappell. NegVo p.28
I lay down in my grave. Maya Angelou. OhPWFW p.62

I lay my head on a choppin' block. Elma Stuckey. BiGa p.46
I Lay Naked Against the Belly of the Earth. Joanne Jimason. NaABE p.5
I lay paralyzed with moorish fingers pressed firmly against my head. Jayne Cortez. NeBV p.236
I Lean Back and Feel the Warmth. Sonia Sanchez. IvBAW p.87
I leave all in thy hands, my God. Josephine D. (Henderson) Heard. MoGl p.98
I Leave These Things. Joanne Jimason. NaABE p.16
I left my baby standin in the back door cryin'. Anonymous. BlWOA p.887
I left my pain taped on two breasts. LoP p.87
I Like. Melva Eloise Tatum. MELVA p.24
I like brown babies bathed in the icy sun. Melva Eloise Tatum. MELVA p.24
I like it here just fine and I don't want no bail. Margaret Walker. BlP p.156; PFND p. 8; PoBA p.148;
I like love anonymous more than incorporated. June Jordan. ThTDID p.144
I like movies because people get to mug their faces in movies. Patricia Jones. BlSi p.251
I like the smell of new clothes. Naomi Long Madgett. PhN p.58
I like the way you look at things. Catherine L. Findley. EbR p. 64
I like things that are intense. Countess W. Twitty. EbR p. 146
I like this quiet place of lawns and trees well kept. Mae V. Cowdery. WLOV p.44
I like to see you lean back in your chair. Gwendolyn Brooks. BlP p.169; FaP p.15
I like to watch the fairies. Gertrude Parthenia McBrown. ReFNA p.53
I Listen For Yo. Sonia Sanchez. IvBAW p.85
I listened as Dionne Warwick sang I'll Never Fall in Love Again. Lyn. SiSH p.15
I live in a house of flowers. Judy Dothard Simmons. JuB p.5
I live in a house where birds fly in and out. Jodi Braxton. SoITM p.21
I Live in Music. Ntozake Shange. NaEd p.126
I Live in Subtraction. ** June Jackson. SCh p.26; ThTDID p.44
I lived in hell the other day. Georgia Douglas Johnson. ALC p.48
I long to fly feathers past your mouths or mine. June Jordan. SCh p.81; ThTDID p.162
I look around and see many things. Frances Garcia. ThHSD p.63
I Look at the Waves and Cry. Margaret Danner. DoOAT p.26
I look at you. Sandra Royster. WoTa p.18
I look into the eyes of one returning from distant lands. Mary Wilkerson Cleaves. EbR p.45
I looked death calmly in the face. Georgia Douglas Johnson. ALC p.22
I looked over Jordan, and what did I see. Anonymous. GoS p.61
I lost a poem once. Naomi Long Madgett. DeDF p.35; ExAE p.54
I lost my first dearest person. Thulani Davis. AlTRGR p.34
I Love... LaVerne Davis. GLOWC p.2
I Love Black Faces. Anita Scott Coleman. EbR p.51
I Love Somebody. Anonymous. AmLNA p.8
I love the birds that sing to me in the birth of Morning. LaVerne Davis. GLOWC p.2
I Love Thee. Josephine D. (Henderson) Heard. MoGl p.53
I Love Thee Yet. Josephine D. (Henderson) Heard. MoGl p. 95
I love those little booths at

Benvenuti's. Gwendolyn Brooks. AnA p.46; SPGB p. 59; UNBP p.174; WoOGB p. 118
I love to play upon the hill. Ruby Stevens. NegVo p.146
I love you because the earth turns round the sun. Nikki Giovanni. ThWRNW p.48
I Love You Don't.** Kali Grosvenor. PBK p.24
I love you for the puzzled way you smile. Naomi Long Madgett. PhN p.102
I love you for your browness. ANP p.128; BANP p.243; BlSi p.76; CaD p.157; DeDF p.61; PoBA p.81; VoFHR p.191
I Love You Sooner. S. Diane Bogus. WITM p.35
I love your hands. Angelina Weld Grimke. CaD p.44; NeNRe p.84; PoBA p.16; ReFNA p.25; RoATW p.3
I loves somebody, yes, I do. Anonymous. AmLNA p.8
I luv u! I love u! Ayo Sharpe. HoDo p.90
I made a change and all was new. C. Tillery Banks. HeTMWL p. 14
I made love to you at your every request. Nola Richardson. WhOL p.23
I made my children promises in wintry afternoons. Audre Lorde. ChPON p.53; FrLWP p.20
I may come to love him again. Naomi Long Madgett. PiLAF p. 18
I mean if I didn't know. Sharon Scott. JuBa p.172
I mean it's only natural that if water seeks its own level. Nikki Giovanni. BFBTBJ p.71
I mean we bees real bad. Sonia Sanchez. BrT p.141; TGWL p.87; WABP p.52
I meant to scrub my floors. Fareedah Allah. RoATW p.84
I meant to tell you this, Papa. Pinkie Gordon Lane. PoBBl p.15; WiTh p.11
I met a nice man. Thulani Davis. AlTRGR p.31
I met a squirrel one autumn day. Alvies M. Carter. AOS p.7
I Might be Lonely.** C. Tillery Banks. HeTMWL p.76
I miss thee, my mother, thy image is still the deepest impressed on my heart. Josephine D. (Henderson) Heard. MoGl p.114
I miss you this time every year. Naomi Long Madgett. PhN p.42
I mix my men and booze. Naomi Long Madgett. NeBV p.296; PiLAF p.56
I Move Into Loving. Judy Dothard Simmons. JuB p.16
I move on feeling and have learned to distrust those who don't. Nikki Giovanni. PoBA p.458
I Must Become a Menace to my Enemies. June Jordan. ThTDID p.144
I must give back to each the borrowed dreams. Naomi Long Madgett. OnATM p.18
I must go to La Costa. Ntozake Shange. DaGe p.49
I Must Have. Nola Richardson. WhOL p.27
I must have you for all of my misfortunes. Naomi Long Madgett. PhN p.20
I must love the questions themselves. Alice Walker. RePOP p.33
I Need a Place;** C. Tillery Banks. HeTMWL p.76
I need kai kai ah a glass of akpetesie. Jayne Cortez. COAG p.23; MoOP p.6
I needed to think me a thought one day. Ann Wallace. GLOWC p.32
I never did feel so blue. Lillian Tucker Lewis. HeD p.27
I never knew your loneliness. Mari Evans. IBAW p.43; WhIAM p.6
I never loved the rain till now. Naomi Long Madgett. PhN p.46
I Never Scream. Pinkie Gordon Lane. MyFe p.13
I no longer sleep in a bed. Jodi

Braxton. SoITM p.22
I offer my little sister up. Lucille Clifton. OrW p.49
I once drove to Atlantic City. Thulani Davis. AlTRGR p.36
I Once Knew a Man. Lucille Clifton. TwW p.30
I once knowed an ole sexion boss but he done been ladid low. Anonymous. BlP p.17
I once saw a gray beard. Barbara Jean Knight. PoBBl p.28
I once went down to de races. Lucy Mae Turner. BCF p.26
I only want to be there to kiss you. Nikki Giovanni. MyH p.67
I Only Watch the Bubbles. Nikki Giovanni. VaT p.41
I Paraplegic. Sonia Sanchez. IvBAW p.67
I passed by the house of the young man who loves me. Anonymous. MBP p.25
I peeped once through a holly wreath. Charlemae Rollins. ChG p.68
I perfumed and in gold knit, and Jeanne, serene like a face on an ivory cameo. Carole Gregory Clemmons. NiBPo p. 84
I Picked Up a Rock...** Melva Eloise Tatum. MELVA p.5
I piece together my childhood for my son. Sherley Williams. PePo p.71
I pirouette in my golden shoes. Mari Evans. NIGHT p.41
I pray for the sight of a hill. Katharine Beverly. NegVo p.14
I pretend I understand our silences. Pamela Cobb. InDM p.25
I rather like old gloomy days. Maurine L. Jeffrey. HeD p.23
I Reach For You. Margaret Danner. DoOAT p.101
I Refused to Be. Gertrude Blackwell Bailey. IfWCF p. 48
I rejoice that I know of no religion. Margaret Danner. DoOAT p.23
I Release Thee--With Love. Eleanor Thomas-Grumbach. MoSu p.21
I re'lect the driver man was sleeping very sound. Elma Stuckey. BiGa p.29
I Remember. Carolyn M. Rodgers. SoBB p.24
I Remember. Jayne Cortez. Scar p.49
I Remember. Mae Jackson. BOL p. 35; CaPWY p.14; PoBA p.498
I Remember. Nikki Giovanni. MyH p.19
I remember...January 1968. Mae Jackson. CaPWY p.14
I remember learning you jump in your sleep. Nikki Giovanni. MyH p.19
I remember sunshine. Safiya Henderson. CoAAAW p.135
I Remember That Day. Sharon Bourke. UNBP p.374
I remember the first time I dug it. Nia nSabe. ThHSD p.73
I remember the night he beat her. Carolyn M. Rodgers. HoIGO p.13; JuBa p.119
I remember the onion-like conversation we had. Linda Brown Bragg. LoSBM p.11
I remember through remains of my lip hanging cigarette. Jayne Cortez. Scar p.49
I remember the time he dared me to understand. Della Burt. BlSi p.162
I Remember When. Gwendolyn Williams. GLOWC p.54
I remember when I could not/did not/was not allowed to see your knees. S. Diane Bogus. WITM p.9
I Remember You. Melva Eloise Tatum. MELVA p.28
I remember you, Granddaddy, in shades of black and white. Harryette Mullen. TTW p.14
I remember you the way one remembers a bad meal this evening. Wanda Coleman. MaDBL p.29
I require bran bread with you. Linda Brown Bragg. LoSBM p. 5
I rest my deep within the wood.

Georgia Douglas Johnson. HWOP p.9
I retrace your bare feet. S. Carolyn Reese. BrT p.170 RoATW p.152
I rise up above my self like a fist flying. Lucille Clifton. GoNAE p.43
I rode into the golden yell. Gwendolyn Brooks. BeEa p.44; WoOGB p.342
I run away from beatin'. Elma Stuckey. BiGa p.23
I said I didn't like the look of tulips. Linda Brown Bragg. LoSBM p.8
"I," said the carver of bones. Margaret Danner. DoOAT p.92
I Said to Poetry.** Alice Walker. CoAAAW p.353
I said you cursed the God that made you. Pinkie Gordon Lane. WiTh p.10
I sailed in my dreams to the land of night. Gwendolyn B. Bennett. BlSi p.72; CaD p.158
I Salute. Margaret Danner. DoOAT p.67
I sat alone at my window. Josephine D. (Henderson) Heard. MoGl p.13
I sat there in the midst of ten thousand folk or more. Eloise Culver. GANIV p.68
I sat up in my attic high. Lucy Mae Turner. BCF p.33
I saw a man once. Johari Amini. ImIB p.2; UNBP p.352
I saw a rose and it soothes my soul. Jo Nell Rice. OnOW p. 9
I saw a screamer this morning. Y. W. Easton. CoAAAW p.103
I saw a tree with its bare branches lifted up in bunches. Carolyn M. Rodgers. HeAEG p.70
I Saw Beauty.** Clara H. Haywood. NegVo p.70
I saw green apples in a gilt gold cage. Linda Brown Bragg. LoSBM p.28
I saw her again. S. Diane Bogus. WITM p.27
I saw him beared, framed in a modern setting. Margaret Danner. PoCo p.19
I saw him yesterday. Josephine D. (Henderson) Heard. MoGl p.34
I saw Jesus on a Christmas tree. S. Diane Bogus. WITM p.46
I Saw No Gain at All in Any Gain. Margaret Danner. DoOAT p.100
I saw the morning coming in. Dorothy Randall. GLOWC p. 83; ThHSD p.41
I Saw Them Lynch. Carol Freeman. BlFi p.330; PoBA p.397
I saw you on my walk last night. Pearl Cleage Lomax. PoBA p.503
I saw you sitting there. Eleanor Thomas-Grumbach. MoSu p.10
I saw you there in that dark hole. Mae Jackson. CaPWY p.13
I saw you today. Sonia Sanchez. IvBAW p.47; LoP p.52
I saw your eyes like bumps of flint. Jayne Cortez. MoOP p.22
I saw your hands on my lips. Audre Lorde. ChPON p.7; COAL p.28; FiCi p.14; NNPUSA p.106
I say things to myself. Jayne Cortez. BlSi p.152; Scar p.23
I/Scattered Poems. Angela Jackson. VoDLM p.22
I search for seeds of remembered songs. Angela Jackson. VoDLM p.22
I See Chano Pozo. Jayne Cortez. COAG p.65
I see 'em whipped and branded too. Elma Stuckey. BiGa p. 33
I see her sit. Mariah Britton Howard. CoAAAW p.145
I see it. Anonymous. TYBP p.13
I See My Life. Sherley Williams. PePo p.85
I see skies more bright and blue than any skies beheld by you. Cora Ball Moten. GoS p.186; NegVo p.111
I see something in the tree. Mary Nell Nash. PoBBl p.30
I see the garden of Gethsemane.

Inez M. Thurman. NegVo p.149
I See the Long Pull of You. Johari Amini. LetGSM p.31
I see wonder in little things. Nikki Giovanni. MyH p.14
I see you. Pinkie Gordon Lane. MyFe p.41
I see you brown-skinned. Maya Angelou. AnSIR p.53
I see you in the silver. Effie Lee Newsome. PoN p.56; PoNe p.71
I see you now standing tall. Christine C. Johnson. FoM p.3
I see you return. Damali (Denise Burnett) IATWMB p.14
I see you standing there, son. Leatrice Emeruwa. BlGBG p.5
I see'd her in de springtime. Anonymous. AmLNA p.9; BlP p.16
I Seek. Katherine Cuestas. BTB p.76
I seek no token of you dear. Georgia Douglas Johnson. ALC p.65
I Seem to Be/But Now I Am. Rhonda Metz. GLOWC p.46
I seem to be evil, mean, ugly. Rhonda Metz. GLOWC p.46
I send a message my worthy chief. Josephine D. (Henderson) Heard. MoGl p.78
I shall be thunder. Lucia Mae Pitts. NeVo p.128
I shall hate you like a dart of singing steel. Gwendolyn B. Bennett. AmNP p.73; BANP p.246; BlSi p.73; CaD p. 160; PoBA p.82; RoATW p.113; VoFHR p.356
I shall leave you as I came. Laura E. Smith. NegVo p,143;
I shall make a song like your hair. Gwendolyn B. Bennett. BlSi p.74
I shall not sing a May song. Gwendolyn Brooks. BeEa p. 46; HoFTD p.136; MBP p.28; SPGB p.99; WoOGB p.344
I shall remember how we met and parted. Naomi Long Madgett. SoTPN p.14
I shall save my poems for the winter of my dreams. Nikki Giovanni. CoCRD p.82
I shall tell you how Nathaniel how the sage, devout young prophet gave his life to save his people. Ophelia Robinson. AmLNA p. 51
I shall write of the old men I knew. Alice Walker. PoBA p.471; RePOP p.2
I share this clot of blood with you. Pinkie Gordon Lane. WiTh p.34
I should like to creep through the long brown grasses. Angelina Weld Grimke. BlSi p.60; BlWOA p.627; CaD p. 42
I should write a poem. Nikki Giovanni. CoCRD p.68
I Sing. Ruby Berkley Goodwin. NegVo p.62
I sing a song from Brooklyn. Kattie M. Cumbo. GaBW p. 285; NiBPo p.60
I sing--for in my small dream-basket. Ruby Berkley Goodwin. NegVo p.62
I sing my song in a cycle. Sherley Williams. PePo p.42
I sing of a new American. Pauli Murray. DaTAOP p.71
I sing of slum scabs on city faces. Margaret Walker. FBPA p.112
I sing of youth, imperious, inglorious. Pauli Murray. DaTAOP p.51
I Sing This Song for Our Mothers. Sherley Williams. PePo p.79
I sip pink ladies in the afternoon. Naomi Long Madgett. PiLAF p.23
I sit a throne upon the times. Maya Angelou. JGM p.16
I Sit and Sew.** Alice Dunbar-Nelson. BlSi p.65; CaD p. 73; DuSAE p.145
I sit and sew - a useless task it seems. Alice Dunbar-Nelson. CaD p.73
I Sit and Wait For Beauty. Mae V. Cowdery. BlSi p.93; WLOV p.41
I sit at the desk. Wanda Coleman. MaDBL p.21

I sit in the fading twilight there. Josephine D. (Henderson) Heard. MoGl p.119
I slept the sleep of angels. Nola Richardson. WhOL p.55
I smile because I can. Naomi Long Madgett. PhN p.53; SoTPN p.20
I so admired you then. Alice Walker. RePOP p.43
I speak skimpily to you about apartments. Sonia Sanchez. HoC p.32; IvBAW p.13
I speak to you as a friend speaks. Audre Lorde. CaTR p.22; ChPON p.12; COAL p.33
I stand on my father's ground not breaking. Lucille Clifton. OrW p.79
I stand to-day on this historic ground. Josephine D. (Henderson) Heard. MoGl p.82
I stood in a meadow and all I should see was the green valley surrounding me. Dorothy Vena Johnson. PoN p.120; PoNe p.227
I stood still and was a mushroom on the forest green. Nikki Giovanni. BFBTBJ p.7; BrT p.48
I suppose living in a materialistic society luxury to some would be having more than what you need. Nikki Giovanni. WoATM p.31
I swear I ain't done what Richard told me bout jumpin round and stuff. Sherley Williams. BlSi p.254; PePo p.14
I take my freedom lest I die. Mari Evans. IABW p.75
I take my war machine and fire it. Daphne Diane Page. UNBP p.316
I takes up for my colored man. Fareedah Allah. BlSi p.174
I Talk to Myself. Ntozake Shange. NaEd p.17
I talked to a farmer one day in Iowa. Margaret Walker. FMP p.55; KAL p.144
I tarry in days shaped like the high staired street. Audre Lorde. ChPON p.80; NeHS p.10
I tell yo' 'bout 'Unk' Enoch Mann. Lucile D. Goodlett. WGC p.57
I tell you how dat hypocrite do. Anonymous. BlP p.9
I Thank God I'm Free at Las'. Spiritual. BlP p.31
I that had found the way so smooth. Jessie Redmond Fauset. CaD p.70
I think hands must be very important. Nikki Giovanni. ThWRNW p.16
"I Think I see Her." Jessie Redmond Fauset. AVAN p.194; BANP p.208; BlSi p.64; GoS p.165; NeNRe p.325; PoBA p.18
I think I see her sitting bowed and Black. Jessie Redmond Fauset. AVAN p.194; BANP p.208; BlSi p.64; GoS p.165; NeNRe p.325; PoBA p.18
I think I would like to remember you always. Lyn. SiSH p.18
I think it must be lonely to be God. Gwendolyn Brooks. BlEx p.545; BlVo p.462; MoCAP p.80; SPGB p.8; StIB p.13; WoOGB p.15
I think of a coffin's quiet when I sit in the world of my car. Audre Lorde. CaTR p.20; ChPON p.33; COAL p.24
I think we probably love each other. Carolyn M. Rodgers. BlSp p.182; RoATW p.103
I think you're rather like the wind. Naomi Long Madgett. PhN p.26
I thought I had run out of words. Pinkie Gordon Lane. WiTh p.58
I thought I might be in slug's pharoah waz singin. Ntozake Shange. DaGe p.67
I thought I saw white clouds. Linda B. Graham. GaBW p.313
I thought that love was a beautiful thing. June Vanleer Williams. WiRYPS p.18
I thought that missing you would fall at close of every day. Lois Royal Hughes. EbR p.90
I told my child God could make

worlds. Marion Cuthbert. SOC p.9
I told you the day I met you. NolaRichardson. WhOL p.69
I, Too, Am Not Perfect. Marva Eloise Tatum. BeYM p.30
I took a peek for the first time at the tiny brown mite on the bed. Constance Nichols. EbR 110
I touch your nose. Toi Derricotte. EmDH p.23
I touched sky today. Pinkie Gordon Lane. MyFe p.44
I tried so desperately to peer into your heart. Mattie T. Lakin. GaBW p.366
I tried to make you right-handed son. Pinkie Gordon Lane. WiTh p.32
I tried to pattern all my life like the petals of a rose. Lois Royal Hughes. EbR p.89
I tried to tell her. Naomi Long Madgett. FBPA p.97; PiLAF p.25
I tried to tell this way the twig is bent. Naomi Long Madgett. DeDF p.53
I tried to tell the doctor. Ntozake Shange. DaGe p.31
I turn to meet this vast land of bitter-sweet. Margaret Danner. ImOAAF p.1
I turned my thoughts inward today. Mae V. Cowdery. WLOV p.33
I use to die (D-I-E) Gwendolyn Williams. GLOWC p.54
I used to be a poet once. Naomi Long Madgett. OnATM p.26
I used to be dreamin' and schemin' bout you all the time. Pearl Cleage Lomax. RoATW p.108; WeDNNM p.9
I used to dream militant. Nikki Giovanni. EgT p.28; Rec p. 20; WoATM p.13
I Used to Wrap My White Doll Up. Mae Jackson. BOL p.72; CaPWY p.19; PoBA p.498
I usta wonder who I'd be. Nikki Giovanni. AfAWA p.772; BFBTBJ p.68; MoCAP p.169; NaPr p.23
I vision God standing on the heights of heaven. Anonymous. MBP p.1; TYBP p.196
I wait in this room. Marion Nicholes. LiS p.19
I wake sweet warm to ice blue veil draped darkness. Carolyn M. Rodgers. SoBB p. 16
I walk across noon with you today. Audre Lorde. FrLWP p.34
I walk in the morning light. Pinkie Gordon Lane. MyFe p. 23
I walk on bones. Lucille Clifton. GoNAE p.33
I walk through the churchyard. Naomi Long Madgett. ExAE p. 45
I walked thro' the street called Petticoat Lane on a Sunday morning. Alice McGee Smart. AmLNA p.63
I Wanna Make Freedom. Amina Baraka. CoAAAW p.72
I wanna take him in my arms. Jayne Cortez. FeAF p.16
I Want. Ann Wallace. GLOWC p.34
I want calm without the whiskey. Ann Wallace. GLOWC p.34
I want it to be clear for us that I am not letting go. Sharon Scott. JuBa p.173
I want me a home. Nayo. NeBV p.383
I want my body bathed again by southern suns. Margaret Walker. AfAWA p.520; FMP p.18
I want the chains. Amini Baraka. CoAAAW p.72
I Want to Die While You Love Me. ** Georgia Douglas Johnson. ALC p.42; AmNP p.22; BANP p.183; BlSi p.58; CaD p. 78; ITBLA p.155; KAL p.39; NeCa p.346; NeNRe p.75 RoATW p.157
I want to go to bed. Harryette Mullen. TTW p.38
I want to resign. Patricia Parker. MoIB p.61
I want to say these things to you. Ntozake Shange. NaEd p.139
I want to see the slim palm-trees. Gwendolyn B. Bennett. AmNP

p.73; BANP p.245; BlSi p.77
I Want to Sing. Nikki Giovanni. Rec p.48; WoATM p.30
I Want to Write.** Margaret Walker. OcJo p.30
I want to write an image like a log-cabin quilt pattern. Nikki Giovanni. WoATM p.47
I want wings. Laura E. Smith. NegVo p.143
I want you to stop, think and say a prayer. Carolyn Ogletree. TNV p.78
I wanta say just gotta say something bout those beautiful beautiful outasight black men. BFBTBJ p.77; BlP p.320; BrT p.57; EgT p.25
I wanted love that does not mean I believe in Hollywood. Pamela Cobb. InDM p.19
I wanted to be a nature poet. Thadious M. Davis. BlSi p. 279
I wanted to be free. Melva Eloise Tatum. MELVA p.16
I Wanted to Live in the Past Today. Melva Eloise Tatum. p.20
I wanted to love you. Carolyn M. Rodgers. SoBB p.21
I wanted to take your hand and run with you. Nikki Giovanni. MyH p.25
I wanted to write a poem that rhymes. Nikki Giovanni. BFBTBJ p.88; BlP p.321; BlWOA p.823; BrT p.57; NaPr p.28; TNV p.34; TYBP p.256
I was a man full growed. Sherley Williams. PePo p.79
I was a woman at war. Hazel L. Washington. EbR p.152
I was asleep when the urgent message came. Naomi Long Madgett. ExAE p.57
I was born in a Hotel. Lucille Clifton. OrW p.71
I was born in the Congo. Nikki Giovanni. EgT p.3; Rec p.37; WoATM p.22
I Was Born With Twelve Fingers.** Lucille Clifton. TwW p.4
I was christened Ebenezer. Lucy Mae Turner. BCF p.38
I was cooking her. Wanda Coleman. MaDBL p.119
I was in love with you. Naomi Long Madgett. PhN p.50
I was kissed once by a beautiful man. Alice Walker. ONC p. 51
I was not here when you called last night. Mari Evans. IABW p.31
I Was Not Really Left Behind. Mari Evans. NIGHT p.8
I was planning to call her. Jennifer Blackman Lawson. BlIMT p.20
I was sad, so very sad last night. Myntora J. Roker. NegVo p.137
I was sick and my motha called me. Carolyn M. Rodgers. BlSi p.180; HoIGO p.8; NaPr p.118; PoBA p.432; SoBB p.9; YoBBI p.48
I was sitting on a park bench one day. Olean Bess. MiFe p.17
I was sitting on the bridge writing a letter. Naomi Long Madgett. PhN p.64
I was walking a lonely road in tropical Africa. Stella Ngatho. PoBBl p.30
I was your fantasy come to flesh. Harryette Mullen. TTW p.45
I wasn't raised by no river. Sherley Williams. PePo p.35
I Watched Little Black Boys. Nayo. NeBV p.384
I wear no scars across my brow. Lois Royal Hughes. NegVo p. 81
I wear you in my heart. Julia Fields. NiBPo p.79
I Weep.** Angelina Weld Grimke. CaD p.45; DeDF p.29; MyNIB p.69; RoATW p.115
I weep--not as the young do noisily. Angelina Weld Grimke. CaD p.45; DeDF p. 29; MyNIB p.69; RoATW p.115
I weep these tears upon my bier. Georgia Douglas Johnson. EbAT p.35
I Welcome Lace. Margaret Danner. DoOAT p.42

I went all the way this time. Thulani Davis. AlTRGR p.48
I went back to my cabin home. Lucy Mae Turner. BCF p.32
I went down into the valley. Anonymous. AmLNA p.7
I went down to St. James Infirmary. Anonymous. BlWOA p.647
I went into my mother as some souls go into a church. Lucille Clifton. TwW p.17
I went looking for the southern cross. Naomi Long Madgett. PiLAF p.50
I went out in the world. Frenchy J. Hodges. BlW p.10
I went to a party out in Hollywood. Maya Angelou. OhPWFW p.5
I Went to the Valley but I Didn't go to Stay. Lucille Clifton. OrW p.79
I went up to New York las' week. Alice McGee Smart. AmLNA p. 64
I, who am used to rolling swell. Lucy Mae Turner. BCF p.34
I who encompass millions. Mari Evans. IABW p.17
I will always remember how much life is you. Melba Joyce Boyd. CaEADW p.9
I will be patient while my Lord punishes me for I have sinned against him. Fareedah Allah. BlSi p.167
I will be ready to stand for what is right. Gertrude Blackwell Bailey. IfWCF p.27
I will cock my ear. Joanne Jimason. NaABE p.16
I will have to forget your face. Lucille Clifton. OrW p.25
I will live. Naomi Long Madgett. DeDF p.85
I Will Look Up.** Josephine D. (Henderson) Heard. MoGl p.44
I will look with detachment on the signing of contracts. Pinkie Gordon Lane. BlSi p.228; MyFe p.29
I will no longer lightly walk behind. June Jordan. ThTDID p.144
I Will Not Let You Drive me to Write.** Gloria Oden. RESUR p.95
I will remember a time when "Amazing Grace" was all the rage in the South. Alice Walker. ONC p.41
I will sing you songs until your heart can hear their silences. Naomi Long Madgett. StBS p.30
I will take you down the years. Naomi Long Madgett. BlP p. 194
I will touch stone. Lucille Clifton. OrW p.31
I will track you down the years down the night. Naomi Long Madgett. AmLNA p.84; OnATM p.12; SiAS p.13
I will walk all day with you. Beatrice M. Murphy. RoCO p.9
I Wish. Risa Gerson. GLOWC p.33
I wish everyone could have their own field. Risa Gerson. GLOWC p.33
I wish for her fantastic hands. Lucille Clifton. CoAAAW p. 87
I wish I could have been oppressed by straightened hair. Nikki Giovannni. Rec p.39
I wish I could still stay. Sherley Williams. PePo p.43
I wish I had known this land before house infected the hills. Sherley Williams. PePo p.74
I wish I were a shadow. Nikki Giovanni. EgT p.13; Rec p.43
I Wish it Were Mid/Night Again. Sonia Sanchez. IvBAW p.77
I Wish That I Could Hate You.** Patricia Parker. MoIB p. 124
I wish that I could write. Jennifer Blackman Lawson. BlIMT p.52
I wish to own only the warmth of your skin. Alice Walker. RePOP p.59
I wished him dead. Nola Richardson. WhOL p.25

I witnessed the lynchings of Jonathan of George. Jayne Cortez. Scar p.30
I woke up this mornin' with the blues all around my bed. Anonymous. TYBP p.203
I woke up this morning and found my life had escaped me during the night. Dorothy Randall. ThHSD p.38
I woke up this morning my head was sore as a board. Gertrude "Ma" Rainey. UNBP p. 111
I, Woman. Irma McClaurin. BlSi p.197
I, Woman. Julia Fields. BlLi p.532; RoATW p.57
I Wonder. Georgia Douglas Johnson. ALC p.30
I wonder about the brother. Sharon Scott. JuBa P.175
I wonder--as I see them pass unheeded down the way. Georgia Douglas Johnson. ALC p.30
I Wonder How Many Matches it Would Take.** Patricia Parker. MoIB p.60
I wonder if the elephant is lonely in his stall. Gwendolyn Brooks. BeEa p.47; WoOGB p.345
I Wonder Why.** Bessie Woodson Yancey. EcFTH p.39
I wondered about it but now I know. Gertrude Blackwell Bailey. IfWCF p.28
I won't let marsa pat me jes' because I'm big and plump. Elma Stuckey. BiGa p.35
I wore a baseball cap. Naomi Long Madgett. BrT p.169; PiLAF p.24
I worked this strip to make the railroad track. Elma Stuckey. BiGa p.70
I would give you the blue-violet dreams of clouds. Mae V. Cowdery. WLOV p.51
I Would Like to be Serene.** Jayne Cortez. FeAF p.26; RoATW p.63
I would like to believe we loved each other once. Naomi Long Madgett. ExAE p.67
I would like to make a brief statement. Sharon Scott. JuBa p.176
I would like to scream but there is no one to hear. Carolyn Rodgers. JuBa p.122
I would not tell them why I had smashed the window with my hand. Carolyn M. Rodgers. JuBa p.110
I Would Prefer to Dispatch Myself.** Gloria Oden. RESUR p.143
I would rather be beautifully happy. Pinkie Gordon Lane. WiTh p.57
I Would Sunday cry on white sheets of a wedding. Jayne Cortez. FeAF p.8
I wouldn't coax the plant if I were you. Naomi Long Madgett. BlPo p.29; FBPA p.96; StBS p.21
I wove the fabric of my thoughts. Bessie Woodson Yancey. EcFTH p.1
I Write Because I Am Afraid of Dying. Thulani Davis. AlTRGR p.61
I Wrote a Good Omelet.** Nikki Giovanni. ThWRNW p.51
I wrote a poem for you. Nikki Giovanni. CoORD p.47
I wrote in San Francisco on a 4 by 12 board. Ntozake Shange. NaEd p.82
I wrote this poem because I feel there are very few flowers in this field we so dishonestly call life. Nikki Giovanni. BlSp p.74
Icarus. Pauli Murray. DaTAOP p. 80
Ice between me and the earth. June Jordan. PaNP p.96
Ice water click of windchimes tickled by a breeze. Harryette Mullen. TTW p.51
Icicles on Trees. Catherine L. Finley. EbR p.63
I'd Change the Colors I See. Harryette Mullen. TTW p.65
I'd like to see you lean back in your chair. Gwendolyn Brooks. BlP p.173
I'd really hate to go to bed. Effie Lee Newsome. GoS p.193

Identity. Johari Amini. ImIB p. 2; UNBP p.352
Idyl. Henrietta Cordelia Ray. EBAP p.143
Idyl: Sunrise. Henrietta Cordelia Ray. BlSi p.37
Idyl: Sunset. Henrietta Cordelia Ray. BlSi p.38
Idyll. Gladys M. Jameson. EbAT p.135
If a city takes its rhythms. Audre Lorde. ChPON p.79
If anybody has a little playmate will you spare him for me? Naomi Long Madgett. PhN p.13
If anything seemed unreal, it was you lying still. Vanessa Howard. ScWh p.44
If Crispus Attuck's statue took life to walk, he would wink his owl-eyes part lips and talk. Dorothy Vena Johnson. EbR p.91
If dead men died abruptly by a blow. Margaret Walker. FMP p.56
If ever a garden was Gethsemane. Anne Spencer. AmNP p.7; PoN p.54; PoNe p.65
If Ever You Should Walk Away. ** Lucia M. Pitts. EbR p.121
If ever you're feeling blue let's go to our native Congo. Stella Ngatho. PoBBl p.57
If Hair Makes Me Black, I Must Be Purple. Linda G. Hardnett. GaBW p.319
If He Let Us Go Now. Sherley Williams. PePo p.15
If here and now he but a timely span. Katharine Cater. AmNP p.140; PoN p.192; PoNe p.340
If I Asked: Is This James Brown or Clifford Jordan? Ntozake Shange. NaEd p.2
If I be you let me not forget. Lucille Clifton. OrW p.19
If I can't do what I want to do then my job is to not do what I don't want to do. Nikki Giovanni. CoCRD p.66
If I cda known youd be real. June Jordan. ThTDID p.78
If I could bend each yesterday and make it do my will. Frenchy J. Hodges. BlW p.11
If I could climb the mountains and rest on clouds that float. Nikki Giovanni. VaT p.45
If I Could Fly.** Kali Grosvenor. PBK p.57
If I could have spoken. Naomi Long Madgett. PhN p.71
If I Could Know. Josephine D. (Henderson) Heard. MoGl p. 92
If I could pass right back through time. Blossom Powe. MyNIB p.72
If I could read between the lines your hands make in the air. Linda Brown Bragg. LoSBM p.10
If I could ever write a poem as beautiful as u little 2/yr/old/brother, I wid laugh, jump, leap up and touch the stars. Sonia Sanchez. ItND p.18
If I could remember back to when I was an embryo. Pinkie Gordon Lane. WiTh p.7
If I do take somebody's word on it means I don't know. June Jordan. SCh p.36
If I ever do love again it will be for silver and gold. Naomi Long Madgett. OnATM p.30
...if I had a gun that would shoot.** Mari Evans. IABW p.36
If I had caught the tears I cried since you first broke my heart. Deborah Fuller Wess
If I had given myself to you. Lucy Mae Turner. BCF p.37
If I had it--you could get it. Negro Work Song, USA. MyNIB p.44
If I had known. Sonia Sanchez. IvBAW p.49; LoP p.50
If I live Sangaree. Anonymous. UNBP p.85
If I Must Know. Mae V. Cowdery. WLOV p.21
If I must know sorrow to live then burden my soul. Mae V. Cowdery. WLOV p.21

If I never know your touch again. Jennifer Blackman Lawson. BlIMT p.47
If I should hear tonight that you were dead. Lucia Mae Pitts. NegVo p.133
If I Stand in My Window. Lucille Clifton. BlP p.251; DOBB p.54
If I Take You. Angela Jackson. VoDIM p.11
If I understood you. Bessie Woodson Yancey. EcFTH p.13
If I were a painter it would be easier. Carolyn M. Rodgers. HoIGO p.39; TGWL p.84
If I were able to reverse the years. June Vanleer Williams. WiRYPS p.66
If I were blind and could not watch the late sun. Naomi Long Madgett. ExAE p.60
If I were sitting on the banks of the river I would write poems. Pinkie Gordon Lane. MyFe p.20
If I Were There. Jayne Cortez. FeAF p.8
If it comes on like a cave man I'll write it. Naomi Long Madgett. ExAE p.51
If It Were Possible to Place You in My Brain.** Patricia Parker. MoIB p.127
If Love Dies. Julia Fields. GaBW p.309; NiBPo p.70
If Love Were All. Naomi Long Madgett. OnATM p.37
If Mama Could See. Lucille Clifton. OrW p.69
If Mary came would Mary forgive, as mothers may. Gwendolyn Brooks. BeEa p.52; SPGB p. 102; WoOGB p.350
If music is the most universal language just think of me as one whole note. Nikki Giovanni. EgT p.35; WoATM p.29
If my garden oak spares one bare ledge. Anne Spencer. CaD p. 51
If Not in Summer.** Naomi Long Madgett. PiLAF p.36
If on this sphere a grim and final fate. Paul Murray. DaTAOP p.81
If only the day need not come when I must tell you. Naomi Long Madgett. BTB p. 148; CNAW p.772; StBS p. 57
If orange chiffon sadness flowed from my chin. Jayne Cortez. BlSi p.153
If possible, sleep through the morning three-thirties of the world. Gwendolyn Brooks. FaP p.22
If St. Louis took its rhythms from the river. Audre Lorde. NeHS p.47
If she could only break the glass. Toi Derricotte. EmDH p.17
If she don't hurry up and let me out of here. Gwendolyn Brooks. StIB p.34; WoOGB p.36
If she wore her dresses the same length as mine people would gossip. Nikki Giovanni. WoATM p.9
If some autumn you should see, out of season. Naomi Long Madgett. OnATM p.35
If the desert wind is not the image. S. Diane Bogus. WITM p.39
If The Drum is a Woman. Jayne Cortez. COAG p.57
If the Kamikazee circles up. Carole Gregory Clemmons. NiBPo p.89
If the shoe fits, it might be yours. Carolyn M. Rodgers. SoBB p.15
If the Shoe Fits, Wear It. Gertrude Blackwell Bailey. IfWCF p.18
If the world looked in a looking glass. Vanessa Howard. SoS p.2
If the world seems all against you. Bessie Woodson Yancey. EcFTH p.19
If There Be Sorrow.** Mari Evans. BlLi p.434; IABW p.16; KAL p.174; NNPUSA p.22; OnOW p.15; PoNe p.308; WhIAM p.3
If There Were Songs.** Naomi Long Madgett. PiLAF p.37

If they put you in a jack-in-the-box poet would you pop up poeming. Nikki Giovanni. BrT p.69; Rec p.40
If This Be a Dream.** Naomi Long Madgett. SoTPN p.28
If This Be Good-bye.** Ruby Berkley. EbR p.67
If this country is a bastard will the lowdown mother user. Maya Angelou. OhPWFW p.27
If this is peace this dead and leaden thing. Jessie Redmond Fauset. ANP p.89; BANP p. 207; PoN p.66; PoNe p. 68; VoFHR p.313
If this must be the destiny to which I have come, pour the wine faster and into a deeper cup. Naomi Long Madgett. PhN p.60
If This World Were Up Side Down.** Kali Grosvenor. PBK p.61
If to be a valentine is to be true as the beat of a heart. Margaret Danner. DoOAT p.46
If to do is to be take this lovely cat, here. Margaret Danner. DoOAT p.132; PoCo p.9
If today I follow death. Maya Angelou. JGM p.20
If trees could talk wonder what they'd say. Nikki Giovanni. Rec p.33; WoATM p.54
If we do is to be, take this lovely cat, here. Margaret Danner. IrLa p.5
If we hate the rush hour subways who ride them every day. Audre Lorde. ChPON p.83; NeHS p.13
If We Part Now.** Mae V. Cowdery. WLOV p.42
"If Winter Comes." Edna Gullins. NegVo p.66
If you are lucky to find a friend stick with through thick and thin. Olean Bess. MiFe p.3
If You Come Softly.** Audre Lorde. FiCi p.19
If you come as softly as wind within the trees. Audre Lorde. ChPON p.3; COAL p. 65
If you crawled and cringed I would not want you back. June Vanleer Williams. WiRYPS p.46
If you dislike me. Pauli Murray. DaTAOP p.30
If you don't get old. Gertrude Blackwell Bailey. IfWCF p. 31
If You Forget.** Eleanor McDuffie. NegVo p.103
If You Have Had Your Midnights. ** Mari Evans. NIGHT p.2
If You Live in West Virginia.** Bessie Woodson Yancey. EcFTH p.4
If you own your soul the mornings come heavy. Melba Joyce Boyd. CaEADW p.12
If you plant grain you get fields of flour. Nikki Giovanni. BrT p.68; Rec p.32
If you sang songs I could make a request. Nikki Giovanni. BFBTBJ p.91
If You Saw a Negro Lady.** June Jordan. SCh p.17; SoS p.54; ThTDID p.158
If you see a cycle of heavy blowing backward. Jayne Cortez. COAG p.53
If you take these capes of wet sheets and broken glass. Jayne Cortez. Scar p.42
If you want to be a writer. Marva Tatum Smith. BeYM p. 24
If Your Conscience is Free. Gertrude Blackwell Bailey. IfWCF p.29
If you've got the key then I've got the door. Nikki Giovanni. CoCRD p.92
Ife. Jayne Cortez. Scar p.31
Ile De La Tortue. Jodi Braxton. SoITM p.22
I'll always write a poem on the flowers of spring. Naomi Long Madgett. PhN p.27
I'll count life worth the living. Bessie Woodson Yancey. EcFTH p.21
"I'll get out of your life." Thulani Davis. AlTRGR p.15
I'll Give You What You Need. Marva Tatum Smith. BeYM p.

2
I'll paint Malcolms music on all yo walls. Angela Jackson. VoDLM p.21
I'll remember this night. May Miller. ClAB p.36
I'll sink my roots far down. Pauli Murray. DaTAOP p.91
I'll tell about the times. Pinkie Gordon Lane. WiTh p.26
I'll Walk the Tightrope.** Margaret Danner. BTB p.87; ITBLA p.219; KAL p.125; MoCAP p. 87
I'll wear me a cotton dress. Anonymous. BlP p.11
Illusion. Georgia Douglas Johnson. ALC p.18
Illusions. Georgia Douglas Johnson. HWOP p.50
Illusions of Visions. Jayne Cortez. FeAF p.31
I'm a big fat mama. Anonymous. BlWOA p.888
I'm a Dreamer. Kattie M. Cumbo. BlSi p.137
I'm-a goin' to tell you 'bout de comin' of de savior. Anonymous. AmLNA p.4
I'm a happy moile. Nikki Giovanni. BFBTBJ p.35
I'm a Rapper. Lois Elaine Griffith. CoAAAW p.110
I'm a real young boy jus sixteen years ol. Anonymous. BlWOA p.887
I'm a Round Town Gent. Anonymous. GoS p.17
I'm a Salesman. Marva Tatum Smith. BeYM p.9
I'm a Very Mixed Up Person.** Susan Robbins. GLOWC p.23
I'm a Worker. Jayne Cortez. FeAF p.14; NeBV p.234
I'm Alone. Nola Richardson. WhOL p.33
I'm alone in this crowded world of people. Nola Richardson. WhOL p.33
I'm bound. Bound with a thousand cords - never to be free. Ruth Brownlee. EbR p.96
I'm climbing, pulling my brother behind me. Gertrude Blackwell Bailey. IfWCF p.30
I'm folding up my little dreams. Georgia Douglas Johnson. BANP p.184; BlSi p.59; CaD p.79; GoS p.196; HWOP p.62; PoN p.60; PoNe p.81
I'm giving up on language. Nikki Giovanni. MyH p.31
I'm glad marse give me driver job. Elma Stuckey. BiGa p. 8
I'm glad that Henry Wandsworth took pen in hand. Eloise Culver. GANIV p.34
I'm goin down this road feelin bad. Anonymous. BlWOA p.461
I'm gon put a hex on you. Angela Jackson. VoDLM p.7
I'm gonna be about righteousness. Dolores Abramson. RoATW p. 79; ThHSD p.37
I'm Gonna Be Long Gone, Baby Blues.** Leatrice Emeruwa. BlGBG p.18
I'm gonna get me some mammy tape for your love. Sonia Sanchez. IvBAW p.93
I'm gonna shout, oh yes I am. Elma Stuckey. BiGa p.26
I'm gonna write me a poem like e.e. cummings today. Sonia Sanchez. HoC p.20; UNBP p. 73
I'm In The Middle. Sonia Sanchez. IvBAW p.73
I'm in the middle of you. Marva Tatum Smith. BeYM p.20
I'm Jo, the conju woman. Colleen McElroy. MuDLSG p. 23
I'm Just a Stranger Here, Heaven is My Home. Carole Gregory Clemmons. PoBA p.489
I'm leaving at five. Nikki Giovanni. MyH p.63
I'm mad about you. Leatrice Emeruwa. BlGBG p.26
I'm Me. Linda Brown Bragg. LoSBM p.29
I'm Not Jealous.** Nola Richardson. WhOL p.96
I'm Not Lonely. Nikki Giovanni. BFBTBJ p.32; BrT p.52
I'm Not Saying. Jayne Cortez. MoOP p.28
I'm Not Very Communicative.

Ntozake Shange. NaEd p.57
I'm on my way to Nana's house. Linda Brown Bragg. LoSBM p. 32
I'm playing word games with myself. Brenda Connor-Bey. CoAAAW p.76
I'm proud of myself. Juanita Brown. PoBBl p.44
I'm Really Very Fond.** Alice Walker. CoAAAW p.359
I'm So Tired of Hearing About Capitalist.** Patricia Parker. MoIB p.70
I'm sure that Spring is on the way. Beatrice M. Murphy. GoS p.25
I'm the best that ever done it. Maya Angelou. JGM p.30
I'm tired, days and nights to me. Georgia Douglas Johnson. HWOP p.31
I'm upset I'm angry I can't sit straight. Marva Tatum Smith. BeYM p.4
I'm what has gone out blithely and with noise. Gwendolyn Brooks. BeEa p.41. SPGB p.96; WoOGB p.339
I'm your momma, and I could always tell when you're doing somethin you ain't got no business. Harryette Mullen. HoDo p.72; TTW o,4
Image. Mari Evans. NIGHT p.41
Image in the Mirror. Peggy Susberry Kenner. JuBa p.92
Image Maker. Naomi Long Madgett. PiLAF p.21
Imagine now & know the old renegades in this room. Thulani Davis. AlTRGR p.51
Imagine what Mrs. Haessler would say. Margaret Danner. AfAWA p.634; ImOAAF p.3; IrLa p.26; MoCAP p.88; NNPUSA p.30; PoBA p.134; PoNe p.163
Immortality. Marion Cuthbert. SOC p.43
Impelled. Georgia Douglas Johnson. HWOP p.21
Imperfectus. Naomi Long Madgett. OnATM p.32
Imposition. Linda Brown Bragg. LoSBM p.11
Impossibilities. Josephine D. (Henderson) Heard. MoGl p. 102
Impossibility. Jamye H. Coleman. EbR p.52
Impressions. Naomi Long Madgett. ExAE p.62
Improvisation. Ntozake Shange. DaGe p.14
In a Bone White Frame. Margaret Danner. DoOAT p.70
In a Chicago Museum, these small bells of Benin are bringing their charm to a foreign scene. Margaret Danner. IrLa p.28
In a far-away wood their lived two monkeys. Lillian Brown. BTh p.63; EbAT p.151
In a lovely garden, filled with fair and bloomin flowers, stood a beautiful rose tree. Frances E. W. Harper. BlSi p.34
In a lower, slower mood you mock me. June Vanleer Williams. WiRYPS p.30
In a package of minutes there is this we. Gwendolyn Brooks. BlP p.179
In a press conference this afternoon the Secretary of Space Development confirmed earlier reports. June Jordan. CoAAAW p.183
In a quiet place of my mind, I remember you. Melva Eloise Tatum. MELVA p.28
In a Stream of Ink. Jayne Cortez. COAG p.90
In a Time.** Maya Angelou. JGM p.11
In Abscence. Naomi Long Madgett. PhN p.42
In Africa night walks into day. Nikki Giovanni. WoATM p.51
In Alaska we realize that stars are not the far away remote twinklers. Margaret Danner. DoOAT p.35
In amoratas, with an approbation bestowed his title. Gwendolyn Brooks. CNAW p.516
In an age of napalmed children with words like the enemy is whatever moves. Nikki

Giovanni. MyH p.54
In an ancient sky the sun blazed upon a woman. Damali (Denise Burnett) IATWMB p.9
In Babylon when Semiramis reigned. Naomi Long Madgett. PhN p.106
In balm iconic prague I offered my bosom to a wandering Arab student. Alice Walker. ONC p.66
In Between Time (Transcience) Marsha Ann Jackson. TNV p. 52
In canebrake dark my spirit came near breaking. Naomi Long Madgett. PiLAF p.12
In Case You Forget. Jodi Braxton. SoITM p.36
In Celebration of Blk/Men. Johari Amini. LetGSW p.25
In childhood's sunny day my heart was taught to love. Josephine D. (Henderson) Heard. EBAP p.262; MoGl p.14
In comparison to what my lot has been. Margaret Danner. DoOAT p.96
In curve scooped out and necklaced with light. Audre Lorde. ChPON p.17; COAL p. 32; FiCi p.7
In Dat Great Gettin' Up Mornin'. Anonymous. AmLNA p.4
In Emanuel's Nightmare: Another Coming of Christ. Gwendolyn Brooks. BeEa p.69; SPGB p. 107; WoOGB p.367
In English Lit., They Told Me Kafra was good. Patricia Parker. ChOM p.9; MoIB p. 48
In every town and village. Maya Angelou. AnSIR p.6
In front of Fifth Avenue Library on the Steps.** Frenchy J. Hodges. BlW p.29
In front of the bank building after six o'clock the gathering of the bay people begins. Nikki Giovanni. CoCRD p.29
In front of the City Hotel in Kumasi two horned snarls come at twilight. Audre Lorde. BlUn p.9
In gray, scarred Leningrad a tiny fist unsnapped to show crumpled head. Alice Walker. ONC p.46
In groves of green trees. Julia Fields. NBP p.49
In Higher Places. Eleanor Weaver. NegVo p.161
In Honor of David Anderson Brooks, My Father. Gwendolyn Brooks. SPGB p.69; WoOGB p.309
In honor of yr poise in the face of hungry lions. Ntozake Shange. NaEd p.68
In kinder garden I was handed wooden blocks. Nia nSabe. ThHSD p.69
In life one is always balancing. Nikki Giovanni. BFBTBJ p.90; MoCAP p.171
In lipstick and nail enamel ears pierced. Wanda Coleman. MaDBL p.99
In Little Rock the people bear babes. Gwendolyn Brooks. AfAWA p.581; AmNP p,142; BeEa p.32; BlEx p.546; BlVo p.466; BlWOA p.718; BTB p.52; CNAW p.521; ITSA p.242; MoCAP p.82; PoBA p.155; SPGB p.87; WoOGB p.330
In Love. Georgia Douglas Johnson. ALC p.48
In Love. June Jordan. SCh p. 43; ThTDID p.45
In love never tired of the forward to retreat. June Jordan. SCh p.43; ThTDID p. 45
In Margaret's Garden. Audre Lorde. BlUn p.47
In meiotic division, crossing over chromosones unlike. Carole Gregory Clemmons. NiBPo p.87
In me there is rage to defy. Alice Walker. RePOP p.61
In Memoriam: Martin Luther King, Jr. June Jordan. PoBA p. 305; SCh p.15; SoS p.115; ThTDID p.108
In Memorian of Mother. Josephine D. (Henderson) Heard. MoGl

p.114
In Memoriam: Omualowiba. Naomi Long Madgett. PiLAF p.49
In Memory of James M. Rathel. Josephine D. (Henderson) Heard. MoGl p.81
In Memory of the Hokey Pokey. Jennifer Blackman Lawson. BlITM p.30
In Memory of the Hon. Frederick Douglass, The Sage of Anacostia. Josephine D. (Henderson) Heard. MoGl p.125
In Miami the blood suckers came sucking in full speed. Jayne Cortez. COAG p.59
In my dry cell of love's heat here, in May. Gloria Oden. PoBA p.185
In My Life, Latin and Adolescence Came Along Together.** Gloria Oden. RESUR p.123
In My Own Quietly Explosive Here. June Jordan. SCh p.79; ThTDID p.3
In my season of ghosts I wear a crown of holes. Pinkie Gordon Lane. MyFe p.42
In my 22nd year I wrote my first poem. Melba Joyce Boyd. CaEADW p.2
In my younger years before I learned Black people aren't suppose to dream. Nikki Giovanni. BFBTBJ p.74; EgT p. 29; PoBA p.454
In my youth I was taught the law is good. Patricia Parker. MoIB p.139
In nineteen hundred and twenty-nine was born a prince of steel. Olean Bess. MiFe p.1
In other destinies of choice you could have some redheaded. Audre Lorde. BlUn p.69
In our church we don't --always-- be singing. Carolyn M. Rodgers. HeAEG p.81
In our infancy of action we were women of peace. Audre Lorde. BlUn p.83
In Our Last Virgin Hours. Pamela Cobb. InDM p.25
In perverted speaking, I lisping my longing for you. S. Diane Bogus. WITM p.26
In Populated Air Our Ancestors Continue.** Lucille Clifton. TwW p.60
In Pursuit. Naomi Long Madgett. PhN p.39
In Quest. Georgia Douglas Johnson. HWOP p.44
In reference to: International Women's Year. Leatrice Emeruwa. BlGBG p.22
In Response. Carolyn M. Rodgers. HeAEG p.76
In Retrospect. Maya Angelou. AnSIR p.49
In Robert's early manhood his people were not news. Eloise Culver. GANIV p.50
In Salem. Lucille Clifton. OrW p.3
In school today we studied joy. Nikki Giovanni. VaT p.55
In Search of Aunt Jemima. Naomi Long Madgett. ExAE p. 35
In Search of You. Naomi Long Madgett. PhN p.49
In secret seasons I have carefully hung spring. Jill Witherspoon Boyer. DrF p.9
In Shades of Van Gogh. Margaret Danner. DoOAT p.45
In Some Time Hence. Isabelle McClellan Taylor. EbR p.136
In sometime hence, in some well-doing year when we have done with war. Isabelle McClellan Taylor. EbR p.136
In some distant year should you come to me sons lovers. Tomi Carolyn Tinsley. EbR p,141
In Springtime. Naomi Long Madgett. SoTPN p.15
In sucn an armor he may rise and raid. Gwendolyn Brooks. BeEa p.48; IADB p.16; ITBLA p.217; PoBA p.157; SPGB p.100; WoOGB p.346
In the Art Institute of St. Valentine's Day. Margaret Danner. DoOAT p.38
In the back of the drawer. Angela Jackson. VoDLMP p.10
In the Baha'i Mirror. Margaret Danner. DoOAT p.40
In the bar they play songs about

outer space. Wanda Coleman. MaDBL p.59
In the bed of my mother's mother. Jodi Braxton. SoITM p.41
In the beginning there was no end. Sonia Sanchez. BluB p.59
In the Beginning Was the Sight. Johari Amini. LetGSW p.11; TGWL p.12
In the beginning was the word. Lucille Clifton. TwW p.51
In the Blue Room. Leatrice Emeruwa. BlGBG p.11
In the Blueness/Say Greens. Ntozake Shange. DaGe p.62
In the center of a harsh and spectrumed city all things natural are strange. Audre Lorde. BlUn p.61
In the clearing stands a three story white brick structure. Linda Piper. BlSi p.184
In the Courtroom. Sonia Sanchez. WABP p.34
In the December of my springs I long for the days. Nikki Giovanni. WoATM p.11
In the dream I saw him mount her. Sonia Sanchez. LoP p.6
In the earnest path of duty. Charlotte Forten Grimke. BlSi p.23
In the End Let All White Racists Thank the Holy Jackass. ** Julia Fields. NiBPo p.76
In the Evenings. Lucille Clifton. OrW p.83
In the Everyday Routine. Jayne Cortez. Scar p.9
In the faint sweet hush of the evening still. Ruby Stevens. NegVo p.145
In the far corner close by the swings. Linda B. Graham. GaBW p.313
In the hollow of a tree between the brances. Colleen Mc-Elroy. MuDLSG p.31
In the hours that passed you arrived/I lived hyponotized days at uncertainty is mercy. S. Diane Bogus. WITM p.21
In the house of my son I am hiding myself. June Jordan. ThTDID p.13
In the Inner City.** Lucille Clifton. DOBB p.52; MoCAP p.139
In the keyfood market on Broad-way a woman waits. Audre Lorde. ChPON p.86; NeHS p.17
In the last question I ask, the answer will not be different. Esther Louise. CoAAAW p.149
In the lightness of the breeze I heard your heart's soft tears. Helen C. Harris. EbR p.78
In the Line of Duty. Jayne Cortez. MoOp p.21
In the Mecca. Gwendolyn Brooks. BlLi p.414; ITM p.5; WoOGB p.377
In the Middle. Abbey Lincoln. CoAAAW p.188
In the middle of the nite is a blue thing. Ntozake Shange. DaGe p.62
In the Misty Hollow of the Morning. Vanessa Howard. ScWh p.43
In the Morning. Jayne Cortez. BlSi p.157; COAG p.28; MoOP p.46
In the Morning. Nola Richardson. WhOL p.43
In the night in my half hour Negro dreams I hear voices knocking at the door. Sonia Sanchez. BlFi p.254; IvBAW p.36; LoP p.30
In the revolution I, one of the 22 million overseas African. Mae Jackson. CaPWY p.14
In the rush for humanity they stole my name. Jennifer Blackman Lawson. BlIMT p.23
In the rusty pages of Gray's Anatomy in witchcraft and chewing gum. Audre Lorde. BlUn p.56
In the seat that we shared in the second grade. Audre Lorde. BlUn p.54
In the Shadows. Constance E. Berkley. PoBBl p.43
In the shadows of the waiting room. June Jordan. ThTDID p.190
In the shimmer darkness of early morning move with the melody

of dissonance. Linda Brown Bragg. LoSBM p.18
In the shower naked he bends. Wanda Coleman. MaDBL p.131
In the silence and the dark I fought with dragons. Georgia Douglas Johnson. ALC p.32
In the stark daylight of sanity. June Vanleer Williams. WiRYRS p.48
In the strange rooms. Julia Fields. GaBW p.306
In the street outside a school what the chidren learn possesses them. Audre Lorde. NeHS p.45
In the swamp dismal as fears. May Miller. ClAB p.32
In the Sweetness of Silent Death. Vanessa Howard. ScWh p.42
In the third grade I looked like a little dark Olive Oyl. Harryette Mullen. TTW p.3
In the time when white sands threatened. Mari Evans. NIGHT p.59
In the Times of My Heart.** June Jordan. SCh p.4; ThTDID p. 116
In the town where I was born there is a mound. Alice Walker. RePOP p.20
In the velvet beauty of your eyes I'm lost. Dorothy Lee Louise Shaed. NegVo p.140
In the wake of my departed. Mari Evans. IABW p.30
In the wintertime my father wears a hat. June Jordan. SCh p. 70; ThTDID p.19
In the wondrous light of a pair of brown eyes. Josephine D. (Henderson) Heard. MoGl p.36
In their tomb paintings the Greeks reveal what was important to them. June Jordan. ThTDID p. 187
In These Dissenting Times. Alice Walker. PoBA p.475; RePOP p. 2
In This August Heat.** Gloria Oden. RESUR p.69
In This Cold Day Who Throws the Stones. Mari Evans. NIGHT p.51
In this fly-by-day church through this hot July sermon. Harryette Mullen. TTW p.16
In This Garden.** TwW p.23
"In This House, There Shall Be No Idols." Carolyn M. Rodgers. JuBa p.110
In this life time we've shared a love profound. Eleanor Thomas-Grumbach. MoSu p.21
In this misty place where hunger finds us. Audre Lorde. BlUn p.70
In this new picture your smile has been to war. Audre Lorde. BlUn p.28
In this place of helmets and tar the anxious burblings of recreats buzz over us. Alice Walker. ONC p.45
In this room, holding hands, joining in the small talk. Sarah Webster Fabio. BlSi p.141; DOBB p.29
In this the way, my father. Josephine D. (Henderson) Heard. MoGl p.52
In Time. Marva Tatum Smith. BeYM p.19
In Vieques the ocean is closed on Mondays. June Jordan. PaNP p.63
In western skies rare radiance lies. Henrietta Cordelia Ray. BlSi p.38; EBAP p.144
In what coinage America. Virginia Houston. NegVo p. 78
In what had been a pathway in between our bed and a shared bathroom. Audre Lorde. COAL p.43
In wintertime I have such fun. Effie Lee Newsome. CaD p.59; GoS p.22
In workshops without light we have mad binds. Audre Lorde. BlUn p.87
In your wet season I painted violets. Sonia Sanchez. LoP p.91
In your youth you vow to love me. Mae V. Cowdery. WLOV p.32
Inamorata, with an approbation, bestowed his title. Gwendolyn Brooks. SoOM p.560; SPGB p.12; StIB p.24;

UNBP p.169; WoOGB p.26
Inaugural Rose. June Jordan. PaNP p.68
Incandescence Formless Form and the Soft Shuffle of Sound. Lucille Clifton. TwW p.52
Incarceration. S. Diane Bogus. WITM p.30
Inception of the Negro, The. Jo Nell Rice. GLOWC p.51; ThHSD p.65
Incessant. Naomi Long Madgett. PhN p.74
Incident. Mae Jackson. CaPWY p. 19
Incident in a Black Ghetto. Pinkie Gordon Lane. PoBBl p. 11; WiTh p.30
Incidentally. Leighla Lewis. NegVo p.95
Indelible. Jayne Cortez. Scar p.41
Independent Man, The. Gwendolyn Brooks. SPGB p.9; StIB p. 15; WoOGB p.17
Indian Summer. Wanda Coleman. MaDBL p.129
Indianapolis/Summer/1969/Poem. Sonia Sanchez. IvBAW p.21; NaPr p.131; WABP p.22; YoBBI p.365
Indictment. Dorothy C, Parrish. TNV p.89
Indifference. Josephine D. (Henderson) Heard. MoGl p.95
Indifference. Kattie M. Cumbo. GaBW p.290
Individual ideas - like breaths are waiting to be drawn. Margaret Danner. DoOAT p.11
Indulgent muse! my grov'ling mind inspire. Phillis Wheatley. PAL p.71; PPW p.36
Inevitably. Georgia Douglas Johnson. HWOP p.34
Inevitably. S. Diane Bogus. WITM p.22
Inevitably people go. S. Diane Bogus. WITM p.22
Infant eyes look out amazed upon the frowning earth, The. Georgia Douglas Johnson. BrBV p.44
Infinity doesn't interest me. June Jordan. ThTDID p.73
Inflation. Margaret Porter. CoAAAW p.264
Influenced-By-Benin Onyema of Touch, The. Margaret Danner. DoOAT p.93
Inheritance for Muffin. Margaret Danner. DoOAT p.76
Initiate, The. Georgia Douglas Johnson. BrBV p.76
Initiation. Jayne Cortez. FeAF p.3; PoBA p.345
Innocence. Anne Spencer. CaD p.51
Innocent Question. Frenchy J. Hodges. BlW p.18
Inquietude. Pauli Murray. BlSi p.92
Inquiry. Ntozake Shange. NaEd p.56
Inquisition, The. Bobbretta M. Elliston. PoBBl p.21
Insanity he would not have had to suffer, The. Pamela Cobb. InDM p.42
Insatiate. Mae V. Cowdery. WLOV p.56
Inside. C. Tillery Banks. HeTMWL p.26
Inside, Inside need to get it outside. Nola Richardson. WhOL p.63
Inside My Soul You Came.** C. Tillery Banks. HeTMWL p.66
Inside ourselves is where we want to be fed. Pamela Cobb. InDM p.22
Inside/Outside. Nola Richardson. WhOL p.63
Insistent rhythms feeding Black fingers. Mari Evans. IABW p.88
Insists blast me back from wherever I was on the plane of nod. Leatrice Emeruwa. BlGBG p.25
Instant Before Sleep. May Miller. ClAB p.13
Instantaneous.** Vivian Ayers. NNPUSA p.85
Insurgent, The. Mari Evans. FoM p.4; IABW p.75
Intellectualism. Nikki Giovanni. 63; EgT p.13
Interim. Clarissa Scott Delany. ANP p.129; CaD p.142; PoN p.96; PoNe p.181

Interim. Georgia Douglas Johnson. ALC p.11
Interim. Virginia Houston. NegVo p.77
Interlude. June Vanleer Williams. WiRYPS p.48
Interlude. Mae V. Cowdery. WLOV p.44
Interlude Revised. June Vanleer Williams. WiRYPS p.48
Intermission. Gwendolyn Brooks. AnA p.55; CNAW p.525; SoOM p.565; WoOGB p.119
Interracial. Georgia Douglas Johnson. EbR p.93; PoNe p. 77; RoATW p.98; TYBP p.210
Interview in Color. Delores Kendrick. TGWL p.61
Into Blackness Softly. Mari Evans. IABW p.26; PoBA p. 191
Into her mother's bedroom to wash the ballooning body. Gwendolyn Brooks. BeEa p.30; SPGB p.85; WoOGB p.328; YoBBI p.164
Into the garden of sorrow. Georgia Douglas Johnson. HWOP p.20
Into the topaz the crystalling signals of Manhattan. June Jordan. PaNP p.48
Into wars we were born. Naomi Long Madgett. PiLAF p.16
Intoxication. Edna White Hill. NegVo p.72
Intro. Pinkie Gordon Lane. WiTh p.41
Introduction (Queens of the Universe) Sonia Sanchez. BluB p.11
Introspection. Nikki Giovanni. CoCRD p.24
Invitation, The. Frenchy J. Hodges. BlW p.7
Invitation. Naomi Long Madgett. PhN p.54
Invitation. Ronda Davis. JuBa p.58
Invitation to my Friends, An. Ntozake Shange. NaEd p.146
Invitations. May Miller. ClAB p.17
Invocation. Helene Johnson. AmNP p.102; BANP p.282; PoN p.153; PoNe p.265; RoATW p.161
Invocation of the Creator. Anonymous. AfAV p.12
Involv'd in clouds of woe. Phillis Wheatley. EbAT p.77; PPW p.79
Iowa. Naomi Long Madgett. PiLAF p.38
Iowa Farmer. Margaret Walker. FMP p.55; KAL p.144
Iowa River runs swift tonight, The. Naomi Long Madgett. PiLAF p.38
Ira Aldridge, Shakespearean Actor, 1805-1867: New York. Eloise Culver. GANIV p.21
"Iron Man" sat with gone eyes, The. Thulani Davis. AlTRGR p.52
Irony. Mae Jackson. CaPWY p.10
Is a dimension of heavy minds. Barbara Jean Knight. PoBBl p.19
Is a man. who. sleeping on a hill. Alexis De Veaux. CoAAAW p.101
Is ah wukkin? Bessie Woodson Yancey. EcFTH p.48
Is Anybody Here? June Vanleer Williams. WiRYPS p.13
Is having a baby whose father disowns it a sin? Geraldine Peterson. PoBBl p.35
Is it possible to come with you and be away from you. Ntozake Shange. NaEd p.45
Is it possible to love so much? Sonia Sanchez. LoP p.101
Is it true the ribs can tell the kick of a beast from a lover's fist? Maya Angelou. AnSIR p.3
Is life itself but many ways of thought. Anne Spencer. BlSi p.71; CaD p.48
Is merry glory. Gwendolyn Brooks. SPGB p.123
Is not spendthrift of faith. Gwendolyn Brooks. BeEa p.51; WoOGB p.349
Is she the sage who will not slip. Georgia Douglas Johnson. HWOP p.16
Is that the Black/man can/not be/destroyed. Jackie Earley. BlSp p.62; RoATW p.31

Is the moment conscious that (with public prescription). Delores Kendrick. TGWL p.60
Is the total Black being spoken from the earth's inside. Audre Lorde. BlSi p.198; FiCi p.4; UNBP p.284; YoBBI p.313
Is There No Tangerine Witched Fire? Margaret Danner. DoOAT p.101
Is this my house, I ask? Naomi Long Madgett. AmLNA p.87; OnATM p.17
Is this the sea? Helene Johnson. ReFNA p.50
Is this the way, my father. Josephine D. (Henderson) Heard. MoGl p.52
Is thy sun obscured to-day. Josephine D. (Henderson) Heard. MoGl p.56
Is Wild Nigger Bill From Redpepper Hill. Anonymous. BlP p.7; UNBP p.89
Is yo eye so empty. Johari Amini. BlSp p.2; PoBA p. 292; RoATW p.28
Isaiah. Margaret Walker. PFND p.24
Isaiah LXII, 1-8. Phillis Wheatley. BlLi p.10; PAL p.82; PPW p.27
Isaiah was a man of the court. Margaret Walker. PFND p.24
I's eighty year old and my name is Boy. Elma Stuckey. BiGa p.2
Island Mary. Lucille Clifton. TwW p.40
Isn't Life.** Anonymous. GLOWC p.8
Isn't mendacity's way the paw sheating claw way. Margaret Danner. DoOAT p.49
Isolation. Georgia Douglas Johnson. AVAN p.208; HWOP p.29
It ain't mine, you say? Linda G. Hardnett. GaBW p.320
It ain't no mo cane on dis Brazis. Anonymous. BlWOA p.457
It be cold cold cold on you lip. Sherley Williams. PePo p.19
It be hot & then again not. Ntozake Shange. DaGe p.74
It came to me while musing on, first one thing then another. Bessie Woodson Yancey. EcFTH p.22
It came upon the noontide air. Josephine D. (Henderson) Heard. MoGl p.77
It comes in black and blue. Maya Angelou. OhPWFW p.8
It crawled away from 'neath my feet. Blanche Taylor Dickinson. CaD p.109
It does not impress me that I have a mind. Alice Walker. RePOP p.60
It Does Not Matter.** C. Tillery Banks. HeTMWL p.30
It doesn't hurt as much now. Patricia Parker. MoIB p.141
It fell and fell, that night. S. Diane Bogus. WITH p.68
It finally became apparent to her. Margaret Danner. DoOAT p.50
It Goes Deep. Jayne Cortez. Scar p.22
It Has Been a Long Time. Joanne Jimason. NaABE p.33
It has been four centuries. Kattie M. Cumbo. GaBW p.286; NiBPo p.45
It Has Been Remarked Upon.** Gloria Oden. RESUR p.53
It has rained for five days. Audre Lorde. BlUn p.33
It hasn't always been this way. Ntozake Shange. DaGe p.13
It is a blessed heritage to wear pain. Mae V. Cowdery. WLOV p.64
It is a waste of time hating a mirror or its reflection. Audre Lorde. ChPON p.43; FrLWP p.15
It is all blood and breaking. Lucille Clifton. Anne Spencer. BlSi p.70; EbAT p.94
It is dangerous for a woman to defy the Gods. Anne Snencer. BlSi p.70; BlWOa p.628; EbAT p.94; PoBA p.16
It is Deep. Carolyn M. Rodgers. AfAWA p.780; HoIGO p.11; NaPr p.121; SoBB p.12; YoBBI p.483

It is difficult to believe we ever talked. Sonia Sanchez. IvBAW p.29; LoP p.7
It is essential I remember ours was a fair exchange. Gloria Oden. PoBA p.186
It is Friday, we have come to the paying of the bills. Lucile Clifton. TwW p.16
It is midnight. Sonia Sanchez. BlFi p.250; BlP p.231; BrT p.136; HoC p.10; IvBAW p.4; PoBA p.286; UNBP p.271
It is my Sister's Ring I Wear.** Gloria Oden. RESUR p.23
It is New Year's Day. Margaret Danner. DoOAT p.73; IrLa p.22; PoBA p.137; PoNe p. 162
It is nice to think of love as poetry. Pinkie Gordon Lane. WiTh p.25
It is Not Important That You Do Not Say I Thank You.** C. Tillery Banks. HeTMWL p.46
It is not "peace at any price" to which the world now must aspire. Isabelle McClellan Taylor. EbR p.136
It is Not Unfair of Me to Say, I Think.** Gloria Oden. RESUR p.91
It is nothing to me, the beauty said. Frances E. W. Harper. EBAP p.32; PBFH p.42
It is politically incorrect to demand monogamous relationship. Patricia Parker. MoIB p.123
It is quite evident by now that Kennedys are kill able easily assassinated. Sonia Sanchez. WABP p.25
It is quite possible. Pauli Murray. DaTAOP p.61
It is rare that I find the time to write any more. Pearl Cleage Lomax. WeDNNM p.11
It is so important to record. Nikki Giovanni. BFBTBJ p.66
It is the Black God, Kali. Lucille Clifton. OrW p.47
It is the hybrid beginning. Mary Bohanon. GaBW p.262
It is the morning of our love. Gwendolyn Brooks. AfAWA p. 585; RIOT p.21
It is the sink of the afternoon. Audre Lorde. CaTR p.23
It is time for a poem. Pinkie Gordon Lane. WiTh p.44
It is too easy not to like Jesus. Alice Walkeer. RePOP p.24
It is When we Love.** Gloria Oden. RESUR p.25
It isn't the place nor the defacing of or refacing of Places. Margaret Danner. DoOAT p.108
It Just Ain't Right.** Theresa Thorpe. BTh p.62
It lay in the minds of a near two-third well meaning world. Margaret Danner. DoOAT p.57
It rains for the passenger who drinks too much. Linda Brown Bragg. LoSBM p.7
It saddens me so not to speak when you pass my way. Jacqueline Cox. AOS p.24
It seems so odd that we should have met. Georgiana Oliver. NegVo p.118
It Seems To Me. Edna L. Anderson. EbR p.1
It shall flash through coming ages. Frances E. W. Harper. EaNAW p.296
It sits on ass-phyxiated space. Melba Joyce Boyd. CaEADW p.25
It starts with a hand reaching out in the night. Nikki Giovanni. BFBTBJ p.15
It takes all kinds of people. D. T. Ogilvie. YoBBI p.515
It Takes Prayer and Patience.** Melva Eloise Tatum. MELVA p.13
It takes so little time to smile. June Vanleer Williams. WiRYPS p.11
It took 27 years to write this poem. Colleen J. McElroy BlSi p.286
It Was a Day. S. Diane Bogus. WITM p.62
It was a day when people lined up on Lake Shore Drive. S. Diane Bogus. WITM p.62

It was a season when even music was expensive. Sherley Williams. CoAAAW p.388
It was as if Gauguin had upset a huge paint pot. Margaret Danner. BrT p.39; DoOAT p. 53; ImOAAF p.10; MoCAP p.90; PoBA p.136
It was early, early one mornin'. Anonymous. TYBP p.201; UNBP p.103
It was fun traveling through the heart of this country. Jayne Cortez. COAG p.75
It was good for the Virgin Mary. Nikki Giovanni. Rec p.34
It was in Abomey that I felt the full blood of my father's wars. Audre Lorde. BlUn p.10
It was in the year of eighteen hundred and sixty-one. Anonymous. BLIA p.45; ITBLA p.123
It was just there in the middle of the thoroughfare. Kattie M. Cumbo. GaBW p.290
It was Mabbie without the grammar school gates. Gwendolyn Brooks. SPGB p.7; StIB p.12; WoOGB p.14
It was never relly about us. Thulani Davis. AlTRGR p.35
It was 1912 when the awful news got around. Anonymous. BlWOA p.651
It Was Not the Fashion in Our House to Kiss or Touch.** Gloria Oden. RESUR p.71
It was on the top of a hill beneath the glittering stars that I saw you. Georgia Holloway Jones. EbR p.98
It was running down to the great Atlantic. Lula Lowe Weeden. CaD p.228; MyNIB p.78
It was the beginning of me. Carolyn M. Rodgers. JuBa p. 122
It was the mace after they celled him. Mari Evans. NIGHT p.47
It was very pleasant not having you around this afternoon. Nikki Giovanni. MyH p.21
It Wasn't Just the Rain. Pam Brown. GLOWC p.44
It wasn't ready for the frost. Naomi Long Madgett. PiLAF p.28
It wasn't there. Naomi Long Madgett. PiLAF p.43
It wouldn't have been so bad if there had been a white rock group singing "Steal Away." Nikki Giovanni. MyH p.61
It wuz the first day of the first hour. Angela Jackson. VoDLM p.18
Itaparica is where Dona Flor took her two husbands. Ntozake Shange. DaGe p.24
It's a day for running out of town. Gwendolyn Brooks. BeEa p.61; WoOGB p.359
It's a drag sitting around for death. Nikki Giovanni. Rec p.15
It's a hell creeping back into the garden. Sarah Webster Fabio. BlSi p.139; DOBB p.31
It's a journey. Nikki Giovanni. ThWRNW p.47
It's a new day. Sonia Sanchez. ItND p.17
It's a New Kind of Day. Kali Grosvenor. PBK p.53
It's About You on the Beach. June Jordan. ThTDID p.66
It's All in the Name. Ester Louise. CoAAW p.199
It's All the Same. Thadious M. Davis. BlSi p.276
It's Christmas Day, I did not get the presents that I hoped for. Gwendolyn Brooks. ChG p.102
It's difficult to explain a good feeling. Patricia Parker. MoIB p.135
It's early in the morning and I am still awake. Olean Bess. MiFe p.5
It's funny that smells and sounds return. Nikki Giovanni. MyH p.33
It's Good Being Me.** Marva Tatum Smith. BeYM p.4
It's good to know when it's time to leave. Linda Brown Bragg. LoSBM p.10
It's got to end some time.

Nola Richardson. WhOL p.95
It's Happenin/But You Don't Know Abt It. Ntozake Shange. NaEd p.26
It's Hunt's catsup splattered over the country. Patricia Parker. DOBB p.110
It's insane & childish. Patricia Parker. MoIB p.130
It's intriguing to me that "Book Maker" is a gambling. Nikki Giovanni. ThWRNW p.13
It's me bathed and ashy smelling. Carolyn M. Rodgers. PoBA p. 432; SoBB p.34; UNBP p.345
It's morning again. Pearl Cleage Lomax. WeDNNM p.16
It's morning. We get up old. June Jordan. ThTDID p.137
It's not called soul food. Patricia Parker. MoIB p.67
It's not like the old days. Ntozake Shange. NaEd p.132
It's not that the world can ever be contained. Sherley Williams. PePo p.62
It's not the crutches we decry. Nikki Giovanni. CoCRD p.32
It's Nothing. Jayne Cortez. COAG p.19; Scar p.61
It's nothing this tragedy in our arms. Jayne Cortez. COAG p.19; Scar p.61
It's our anniversary. Lucia M. Pitts. EbR p.120
It's permissible to turn and fling, your legs. Barbara Mahone. Suga p.24
It's so hard to love people who will die soon. Nikki Giovanni. BFBTBJ p.33
It's the day of never. Abbey Lincoln. CoAAW p.189
It's the small deaths in the supermarket. Audre Lorde. BlUn p.64
It's Time (Repatriation... Africa)? Kattie M. Cumbo. NiBPo p.53
It's Tuesday night in ole possum face New York City. Jayne Cortez. Scar p.15
It's two o'clock in the morning. Leatrice Emeruwa. BlGBG p. 19
It's usually from the insides of the door that takes my peek at the sun. Gwendolyn Brooks. StIB p.33; WoOGB p.35
It's Wednesday night baby. Nikki Giovanni. Rec p.28
I've a little bunch of flowers. Josephine D. (Henderson) Heard. MoGl p.122
I've been a woman. Sonia Sanchez. IvBAW p.50; LoP p.55
I've been married to Bob Marley for at least 17 years. Ntozake Shange. DaGe p.71
I've been reduced to rubber tipped fingers. Wanda Coleman. MaDBL p.93
I've been to Canossa. Naomi Long Madgett. PhN p.41; SoTPN p.30
I've been waking up angry. Patricia Jones. HoDo p.77
I've cleaned house and the kitchen smells like pine. Harryette Mullen. TTW p.10
I've come back many times today. May Miller. BlSi p.112; ClAB p.29
I've come this far to freedom and I won't turn back. Naomi Long Madgett. BlP p. 197; BlSi p.128; MoCAP p. 93; NNPUSA p.39; OnOW p.41; PoNe p.38; SoS p.126; StBS p.63
I've ever lost were I thought at first for a long time. Sharon Scott. JuBa p.180
I've got a belly full of whiskey and a headful of gin. Anonymous. BlWOA p.465
I've got a wife an - a five lil chillun. Anonymous. BlWOA p.312
I've got the children to tend. Maya Angelou. AnSIR p.31
I've got to go now. Frenchy J. Hodges. BlW p.13
I've got two hundred dollars. Alice Walker. ONC p.72
I've had a man for fifteen years, give him room and board. Anonymous. BlWOA p.649
I've had tangled feelings lately about ev'rything. Carolyn M. Rodgers. BlP p.263

I've heard them all singing. Paulette Childress White. DeDF p.99; DeRi p.1
I've Learned to Sing. Georgia Douglas Johnson. EbR p.93; GoS p.29
I've lived through lessons sugaring them. Gwendolyn Brooks. Bec p.12
I've lost my mind, -- again. Marva Tatum Smith. BeYM p.26
I've noticed I'm happier when I make love. Nikki Giovanni. WoATM p.28
I've seen heaven, children. Elma Stuckey. BiGa p.67
I've stayed in the front yard all my life. Gwendolyn Brooks. HoFTD p.101; IADB p.11; PoBA p.153; SoOM p. 558; SPGB p.6; StIB p.10; WoOGB p.12
I've told myself a hundred times that it don't make sense. Carolyn Rodgers. HoIGO p.45
I've tried reading James Baldwin and Frantz Fanon. June Vanleer Williams. WiRYPS p.40
Ivory Tower. Naomi Long Madgett. OnATM p.27
Ivy. Georgia Douglas Johnson. ALC p.21
IWA: Portal of Redemption. Jodi Braxton. SoITM p.45

- J -

J, My Good Friend Another Foolish Innocent. Alice Walker. RePOP p.24
Jack. Gwendolyn Brooks. BeEa p.51
Jack and Dinah Want Freedom. Anonymous. BlP p.6
Jack Frost. Gertrude Parthenia McBrown. ReFNA p.54
Jack Frost is a painter. Gertrude Parthenia McBrown. ReFNA p.54
Jackass rared jackass pitched. Anonymous. MyNIB p.38
Jackie Robinson. Lucille Clifton. OrW p.77
Jackleg. Elma Stuckey. BiGa p. 74
Jackson, Mississippi. Margaret Walker. BrT p.151; FBPA p.110; PFND p.12
J'ai Peur (The Coward Speaks). Ariel Williams Holloway. BTh p.17
Jake. Mari Evans. BlSi p.143
Jake the best damn cap'n in the world. Mari Evans. BlSi p.143
Jamaica is an island full of bays. Margaret Walker. OcJo p.19
Jamaica, W. J. Haiku. Leatrice Emeruwa. BlGBG p.20
Jamaican woman, a gold gourd of God, The. Carolyn M. Rodgers. HeAEG p.3
James E. Durr sheet metal worker come down from Gary, Indiana. Mari Evans. NIGHT p.43
James Meredith, Courageous Student 1933- Mississippi. Eloise Culver. GANIV p.79
Jamie's Puzzle. Frances E. W. Harper. PBFH p.34
Jan E. Matzeliger, Inventor of the Shoe Lasting Machine, 1852-1889, Dutch Guiana. Eloise Culver. GANIV p.39
Jane. Elma Stuckey. BiGa p.49
Janis. Mari Evans. BlSi p.144
January 3, 1970. Mae Jackson. PoBA p.499
Jaybird. Anonymous. AmLNA p.7
Jaybird jump from lim' to lim, De. Anonymous. AmLNA p.7
Jazz. Carolyn M. Rodgers. JuBa p.113
Jazz Song. Charron Libscomb. NeJCL p.26
Jealousy. Gertrude Blackwell Bailey. IfWCF p.31
Jealousy will cloud your power of reasoning. Gertrude Blackwell Bailey. IfWCF p.31
Jeff Donaldson's Wall, Five Years Later. Margaret Danner. DoOAT p.126
Jeff, Gene, Geronimo, and bop, they cancel, cure and curry, Gwendolyn Brooks. ITM p.45; PoBa p.160; WoOGB p.417
Jennifer. Edith Loyd. BlIMT p. xii

Jennifer is a choreopoet. Edith Loyd. BlIMT p.xii
Jenny. Elma Stuckey. BiGa p.30
Jeremiad. Naomi Long Madgett. PhN p.101
Jeremiah. Margaret Walker. PFND p.23
Jeremiah, prophet of Jerusalem, is now a man whose name is Benjamin. Margaret Walker. PFND p.23
Jericho is on the inside. Blanche Taylor Dickinson. CaD p.106
Jerked to God. Dorothy Vena Johnson. NegVo p.85
"Jerry Johnson! haven't seen you since '65." Melba Joyce Boyd. CaEADW p.10
Jesse Owens, Olympic Star of 1936, 1913- . Alabama. Eloise Culver. GANIV p.74
Jessica, A Bird Who Sings. Nikki Giovanni. VaT p.37
Jessie Mitchell's Mother. Gwendolyn Brooks. BeEa p.30; SPGB p.85; WoOGB p.328; YoBBI p.164
Jessie Rufus. Lucile D. Goodlett. WGC p.26
Jest finished readen a book. Sonia Sanchez. BrT p.146; WABP p.66
Jesus Bell. May Miller. ClAB p. 12
Jesus Christ Can You Justify. Vanessa Howard. ScWh p.22
Jesus Must of Been Some Kind of Dude. Carolyn M. Rodgers. HoIGO p.63
Jesus, Saviour, Pilot Save. Josephine D. (Henderson) Heard. MoGl p.134
Jesus Was Crucified or It Must Be Deep. Carolyn M. Rodgers. BlSi p.180; HoIGO p.8; NaPr p.118; PoBA p.432; SoBB p.9; YoBBI p.481
Jewels. Lucy Mae Turner. BCF p. 54
Jibaro you are my spanish man. Frances Garcia. ThHSD p.63
Jim. Elma Stuckey. BiGa p.1
Joan did you never hear in the soft rushes of France. Lucille Clifton. TwW p.57
Job. Lucille Clifton. GoNAE p. 34
Job easy is the pride of God. Lucille Clifton. GoNAE p.34
Joe Louis, Boxing Champion, Alabama, 1914- . Eloise Culver. GANIV p.73
Joe Turner. Anonymous. BlWOA p.646
Joel. Margaret Walker. PFND p.26
Joel A Rogers, Historian, 1883-1966. Jamaica, B.W.I. Eloise Culver. GANIV p.60
Joel, that young prophet son of Pethuel. Margaret Walker. PFND p.26
Johann. Alice Walker. ONC p.63
John. Lucille Clifton. GoNAE p.3
John Cabot, out of Wilma once a Wycliffe, all white blue rose below his golden hair. Gwendolyn Brooks. BlP p. 175; BlPo p.26; NeBV p. 201; PoBA p.164; RIOT p. 9
John Hardy. Anonymous. BlWOA p.460
John Hardy stood at the gaming table. Anonymous. BlWOA p.460
John Henry. Anonymous. AfAV p. 121; AfAWA p.294; BlEx p. 2; BlP p.12; BlWOA p.463; HoFTD p.104; ITBLA p.122
John Henry told his captain, "well, a man ain't nothin' but a man. Anonymous. HoFTD p.104
John Henry was a li'l baby. Anonymous. BlEx p.2
John J. Maya Angelou. OhPWFW p.52
John. Look at our Mercy. Gwendolyn Brooks. Bec p.7
Johnny-Come-Lately. Leatrice Emeruwa. BlGBG p.14
Joining, Merging & Breaking Up. Carolyn M. Rodgers. HeAEG p.36
Jonah. Lucille Clifton. GoNAE p.36
Jonathan Sitting in Mud. Nikki Giovanni. VaT p.19
Joseph. Lucille Clifton. GoNAE p.39

Joseph, I am afraid of stars. Lucille Clifton. TwW p.38
Joshua Fit de Battle of Jericho. ** Anonymous. AfAWA p.104; BlP p.24
Journey, A. Nikki Giovanni. ThWRNW p.47
Journey to Babylon. Tyki Brown. ThHSD p.75
Journeystones. Audre Lorde. BlUn p.102
Joy. Clarissa Scott Delany. CaD p.140; PoN p.96; PoNe p.180
Joy. Georgia Douglas Johnson. ALC p.26; HWOP p.25
Joy, The. Harryette Mullen. TTW p.39
Joy. Nikki Giovanni. VaT p.55
Joy or Sorrow. Leanna F. Johnson. EbR p.95
Joy shakes me like the wind thst lifts a sail. Clarissa Scott Delany. CaD p.140; PoN p.96; PoNe p.180
Ju ba dis and Ju ba dat. Anonymous. BlWOA p.234
Juba. Anonymous. BlWOA p.234
Juba Dance. Anonymous. MBP p.14
Juba jump and Juba sing. Anonymous. MBP p.14
Juber. Anonymous. BlWOa p.236
Juber up and Juber down. Anonmous. BlWOA p.236
Judge Every One With Perfect Calm. Alice Walker. RePOP p.48
Judge Me Not. Eleanor Thomas-Grumbach. MoSu p.9
Judge Not. Josephine D. (Henderson) Heard. MoGl p.61
Judith dances on my wall. Harryette Mullen. TTW p.59
Judith's Blues. Judy Dothard Simmons. JuB p.20
Juice of a Lemon on the Trail of Little Yellow. June Jordan. SCh p.25; ThTDID p.18
July. Sonia Sanchez. IvBAW p. 28; LoP p.4
July and August in a city more people I do not know come in on the buses. Pamela Cobb. DeRi p.8; InDM p.14
July 4, 1974. June Jordan. ThTDID p.12
Jump Bad. Carolyn M. Rodgers. JuBa p.109
Jump City. Harryette Mullen. TTW p.26
Jump down. turn around to pick a bale of cotton. Anonymous. ITBLA p.121
Jump rope under my feet. Linda Brown Bragg. LoSBM p.30
Jumping. Linda Brown Bragg. LoSBM p.30
June. Bessie Woodson Yancey. EcFTH p.11
June-Bug's got de golden wing, De. Anonymous. AmLNA p.9; GoS p.15; MBP p.41
June Song, A. Charlotte Forten Grimke. DuSAE p.26
Jungle. Mary Carter Smith. PoNe p.389
Jungle colors fluted and starred. Marcella Caine. FoM p.8
Jungle Flowers. Marcella Caine. FoM p.8
Junkie in the Saddle. Jennifer Blackman Lawson. BlIMT p. 44
Junkie Lost/Junkie Found, Lyn. SiSH p.18
Junkie Monkey Real. Maya Angelou. AnSIR p.17
Jus' Livin'. Julia Gaillard. BTh p.42
Just a bit of ashes grey, grey ashes--spent. Georgia Douglas Johnson. ALC p.61
Just a New York Poem. Nikki Giovanni. MyH p.25
Just about everybody up north got a big mama down south. Jennifer Blackman Lawson. BlIMT p.3
Just As Our African Ancestors Did. Margaret Danner. DoOAT p.31
Just as the Del Vikings Stole My Heart. Ntozake Shange. NaEd p.55
Just as you think you're better now. Gwendolyn Brooks. BlP p.174; FaP p.17
Just Asked. Ruth Duckett Gibbs. GLOWC p.59
Just back from Minnesota/North Dakota. June Jordan. PaNP 60
Just Blues. Anonymous. BlWOA p.647

Just for a Time. Maya Angelou. AnSIR p.14
Just Like Job. Maya Angelou. AnSIR p.50
Just look at me. Mae Jackson. CoAAAW p.169
Just Taking Note--. Sharon Scott. JuBa p.172
Just the Two of Us. Sonia Sanchez. IvBAW p.75
Just think, imagine there will be no crevice. Margaret Danner. DoOAT p.113
Just Wanna Be. Sonia Sanchez. ItND p.16
Just when I thought I had gotten away my mother called me on the phone. Carolyn M. Rodgers. HoIGO p.77
Just yesterday a robin sang his happy little tune. Naomi Long Madgett. PhN p.21
Just You, Just Me. Sonia Sanchez. IvBAW p.81
Justice Allgood. Mari Evans. NIGHT p.42
Juvenile Suicide. Naomi Long Madgett. OnATM p.39

- K -

Kaleidoscope. Sonia Sanchez. LoP p.33
Kaleidoscope: Leaving Baton Rouge. Pinkie Gordon Lane. MyFe p. 17
Kali. Lucille Clifton. OrW p.37
Karamojans. Alice Walker. ONC p.20
Kat can play ball, man, The. Fareedah Allah. BlSi p.170
Katherine Ferguson Founder of a Sunday School, 1779-1854, New York. Eloise Culver. GANIV p.36
Katherine is warm. Melba Joyce Boyd. BlSi p.283; CaEADW p.29
Kathy (1) Wanda Coleman. MaDBL p.35
Kathy (2) Wanda Coleman. MaDBL p.37
Keep Faith. Gertrude Blackwell Bailey. IfWCF p.44
Keep On Singing. ** Naomi Long Madgett. PhN p.51
Keep Pushing. Nancy L. Arnez. RoCO p.18
Keep your eye on the sun. Anonymous. MyNIB p.45
Keller is the Swingest. Margaret Danner. DoOAT p.136
Keorapetse Kgositsile (Willie) Gwendolyn Brooks. BlP p.172
Kewpie. Margaret Danner. DoOAT p.134
Keyfood. Audre Lorde. ChPON p. 86; NeHS p.17
Kid Bruin. Gwendolyn Brooks. BeEa p.44; WoOGB p.342
Kid in the yellow organdy dress that's me. Wanda Coleman. MaDBL p.113
Kidnap Poem. Nikki Giovanni. BlP p.326; BrT p.66; EgT p.1; Rec p.23; WoATM p.29
Kids in the street. Yvonne Johnson. TNV p.58
Killing summer heat wraps up the city, A. Audre Lorde. ChPON p.105
Kin. Maya Angelou. AnSiR p.36
Kin. Naomi Long Madgett. ExAE p.19
Kind of Love, Some Say, A. Maya Angelou. AnSIR p.3
Kind of Man He is For Fred, The. Lucille Clifton. GoNAE p.29
Kind of place for sale big cities where no gateways wide, The. June Jordan. SCh p.73; ThTDID p.164
Kindly Leave Me Out. Nola Richardson. WhOL p.69
King Lives. Jill Witherspoon Boyer. DrF p.19
King still lives in come crowded bar. Jill Witherspoon Boyer. DrF p.19
King uv ancient Inca-Land Aztez lakes & Mali bush wuz hi-ho silver. Ntozake Shange. NaEd p.103
Kinship Ties. Jennifer Blackman Lawson. BlIMT p.23
Kiss, The. Alice Walker. ONC p. 51
Kiss me! and let the hours bloom triumphantly. Georgia

Douglas Johnson. ALC p.46
Kisses. Nikki Giovanni. VaT p. 33
Kissie Lee. Margaret Walker. BlSi p.95; FMP p.38
Kitchen is in readiness, The. Maya Angelou. OhPWFW p.66
Kitchenette Building. Gwendolyn Brooks. AfAAu p.80; BlALP p.101; BlP p.166; ITSA p. 200; PoN p.188; PoNE p.334; StIB p.2; SPGB p.3; WoOGB p.4
Knee-Deep. Bessie Woodson Yancey. NegVo p.170
"Kee-Dee!" and "Try It!" Bessie Woodson Yancey. EcFTH p.57
Knee-Grow, A. Mae Jackson. CaPWY p.10
Knit together firm a short triangular full body. June Jordan. ThTDID p.63
Know that amid your darkness I am bright. Naomi Long Madgett. OnATM p.45
Know that I am not by nature cruel. Sonia Sanchez. LoP p.34
Know the touch of a woman. Patricia Parker. MoIB p.97
Know This is True. Mary Bohanon. GaBW p.261
Know Yourself. Jayne Cortez. FeAF p.35
Knowing the Difference. Carolyn M. Rodgers. SoBB p.14
Knowledge and wisdom go hand-in-hand. Gertrude Blackwell Bailey. IfWCF p.25
Knowledge of life, its myriad complexities untapped. E. Sharon Gomillion. FoAAM p.9
Knoxville, Tennessee. Nikki Giovanni. BFBTBJ p.65; BlP p.322; BlSi p.237; BOL p.58; BrT p.55; EgT p.15; NaPr p.21; OnOW p. 45; PoBA p.450
Kob Antelope. Anonymous. AfAV p.12
Kwa Mama Zetu Waliotuzaa. Sonia Sanchez. CoAAW p.327; IvBAW p.99

- L -

LBJ: Rejoinder. June Jordan. SCh p.53; ThTDID p.108
La Bohem Brown. Gwendolyn Brooks. AfAWA p.585
La King What They Went to See Makes My Eyes Hungry, Audre Lorde. BlUn p.94
La, Lala, La, La. Margaret Danner. DoOAT p.129
La Terrorista. Harryette Mullen. TTW p.27
La Vie C'est La Vie. Jessie Redmond Fauset. NeNRe p.78
Laced in fitted tightly sewed up enmeshed into the image they've tried to mould me to. Lyn. SiSH p.16
Ladder of Life, The. Josephine D. (Henderson) Heard. MoGl p.97
Lady Bird.** Kali Grosvenor. PBK p.35
Lady Executive Looks at a Mangbetu Palm Wine Jug, The. Margaret Danner. DoOAT p.32; IrLa p.23
Lady in the Chair, The. Nikki Giovanni. VaT p.39
Lady justice is often blind. Dorothy Vena Johnson. NegVo p.83
Lady, Lady. Anne Spencer. BlSi p.72; PoBA p.72
Lady, lady, I saw your face. Anne Spencer. BlSi p.72; PoBA p.17
Lady Luncheon Club. Maya Angelou. AnSIR p.24
Lady of the Convent...The Avenue That Is. Dorothy Randall. ThHSD p.4
Lady Santa Ana why does the child cry? Anonymous. ChG p.81
Laid Off Blues. Nancy L. Arnez. RoCO p.17
Lake Michigan's Waves. Margaret Danner. DoOAT p.24
Lake Michigan's waves will claim their own. Margaret

Danner. DoOAT p.26
Lake Murry. Pinkie Gordon Lane. MyFe p.23
Lament. Akua Lezli Hope. CoAAAW p.141
Lament. Malkia M'Buzi. CoAAAW p.218
Lament. Naomi Long Madgett. PhN p.38
Lament. Portia Bird Daniel. NegVo p.44
Lament of Tantalus. Naomi Long Madgett. PhN p.61
Lament of the Slave. Anonymous. MBP p.54
Lamp Lights Into Its Prey, The. Harryette Mullen. TTW p.24
Lamp post light outside the front bedroom penetrated the curtained barrier, The. Jennifer Blackman Lawson. BlIMT p.46
Land is cold, The. Colleen J. McElroy. BlSi p.291
Land of flowers is dusty, The. Audre Lorde. COAL p.47
Land of Nod is a desert, The. Lucille Clifton. GoNAE p.31
Land will not always be foreign, The. Audre Lorde. ChPON p. 48
Landing Place. Wanda Coleman. MaDBL p.61
Landlady tendered me notice today, The. Margaret Danner. ImOAAF p.8
Langston. Mari Evans. BOL p.27
Langston Hughes. Gwendolyn Brooks. SPGB p.123
Langston Hughes. Julia Fields. NiBPo p.79
Langston Hughes a Man of the New Day. Margaret Danner. DoOAT p.82
Langston Hughes Made It. Margaret Danner. DoOAT p.84; IrLa p.6
Langston Hughes, Writer, Missouri, 1902-1967. Eloise Culver. GANIV p.65
Langston, I would like to tell you about your poems. Kali Grosvenor. PBK p.49
Laocoon. Georgia Douglas Johnson. BrBV p.30
Larger sin could not obtain, A. Nancy L. Arnez. RoCO p.20
Las' Sunday while I'se settin' on de bench beside de do'. Anonymous. DuSAE p.55
Las Turestas Negras Grande. Wanda Coleman. MaDBL p.128
Last Arms. Thulani Davis. AlTRGR p.21
Last Conversation, The. Colleen MeElroy. MuDLSG p.19
Last Dialog on the Left, A. June Jordan. CoAAAW p.182
Last Letter to the Western Civilization. D. T. Ogilvie. NPB p.95
Last Look. Naomi Long Madgett. PiLAF p.20
Last M. F. Carolyn M. Rodgers. SoBB p.37; UNBP p.346
Last man I loved couldn't believe in me. Maami Verano. RoATW p.153; ThHSD p.64
Last night after you sat across from me. S. Diane Bogus. WITM p.37
Last night I saw another year. Wanda Coleman. MaDBL p.94
Last night I watched yr face and touched you sleeping behind yr beard. Pearl Cleage Lomax. WeDNNM p.10
Last night I went out into the moonlight. Ylessa Dubonee. EbR p.60
Last night somewhere in the 90's I played bridge. Marion Nicholes. LiS p.21
Last Note to my Girls. Lucille Clifton. OrW p.29
Last of the Trees. May Miller. ClAB p.19
Last Poem for a Little While. June Jordan. SCh p.82; ThTDID p.132
Last Poem I'm Gonna Write About Us. Sonia Sanchez. IvBAW p.24; MoCAP p.136; RoATW p.135; WABP p.40
Last Quatrain of the Ballad of Emmett Till, The. Gwendolyn Brooks. BeEa p.26; PoBA p.155; SP B p.81; WoOGB p. 324
Last time I got married was yesterday. June Jordan. ThTDID p.71
Last time I was home to see my

mother we kissed, The. Nikki Giovanni. MyH p.6
Last Warehouse, The. May Miller. BTB p.152; ClAB p.41
Last Will of One Who Lived Alone. Toi Derricotte. EmDH p.26
Last year changed its seasons subtly. Maya Angelou. AnSIR p.49
Late. Naomi Long Madgett. PiLAF p.23
Late Annie in her bower lay. Gwendolyn Brooks. AnA p.10; SPGB p.34; WoOGB p.74
Late las' night I was a-makin' my rounds. Anonymous. AfAWA p.298
Late Lesson. Clara H. Haywood. NegVo p.70
Late October. Maya Angelou. JGM p.7
Late on Tomorrow. Jayne Cortez. FeAF p.29
Late that mad Monday evening I made mermaids come from the sea. Julia Fields. BTB p. 108; ITBLA p.275; KAL p.22; MoCAP p.150; NNPUSA p.78
Lately Everybody I Meet is a Poet. Lucille Clifton. GoNAE p.7
Later I'll Say I Spent My Life Loving a Great Man. Lucille Clifton. GoNAE p.5
Latin Night is Monday. Ntozake Shange. NaEd p.81
Laughing eyes followed the gold everywhere in our circle. Thadious M. Davis. BlSi p. 280
Laughter. Portia Lucas. BTh p. 37
Law, The. Patricia Parker. MoIB p.139
Law and Order. Jayne Cortez. Scar p.24
Lawd, De! Lucy Mae Turner. BCP p.62
Lawd, ah wuz down on my knees. Anonymous. UNBP p.78
Lawd, Dese Colored Chillum. Fareedah Allah. BlSi p.175
Lawd, hab mussy, muy kang done spole out and died. Frenchy J. Hodges. BlW p.19
Lawd, I'm goin' away for the summer. Anonymous. ITBLA p.121
Lawd is a spirit, great, glorious, and strong. Lucy Mae Turner. BCP p.62
Lawd is dead, The. Barbara Marshall. TNV p.70
Lawd, son, whut un go do with you? Betty Gates. UNBP p. 309
Laws of Motion, The. Nikki Giovanni. WoATM p.36
Laws of science teach us a pound of gold weighs as much as a pound of flour. Nikki Giovanni. WoATM p.36
Lay back women are cooking gold in their iron pots, The. Audre Lorde. BlUn p.107
Lay him down gently, lay him down slow. Margaret Burroughs. FoM p.22
Lay me Down. Elma Stuckey. BiGa p.64
Layen in the joint wondrin when ah mona raise. Mari Evans. NIGHT p.45
Le Soir. Georgia Douglas Johnson. ALC p.33
Lead. Jayne Cortez. PoBA p.343
Leader of the pack. Marion Nicholes. LiS p.19
Leaders, The. Gwendolyn Brooks. ITM p.45; PoBA p.160; WoOGB p.417
Leaf from freedom's golden chaplet fair, A. Henrietta Cordelia Ray. BlSi p.38; EBAP p.139
Lean Brown Back. Jill Witherspoon Boyer. DrF p.6
Leanna's Poem. Lucille Clifton. OrW p.7
Learning to lift myself higher. C. Tillery Banks. HeTMWL p.86
Learning to Read. Frances E. W. Harper. BlSi p.29; CNAW p.106; EBAP p.37
Learning to Spend Time With Myself.** C. Tillery Banks. HeTMWL p.2
Leave Me Alone! C. Tillery Banks. HeTMWL p.36
Leave my eyes alone. June Jordan. SCh p.20; ThTDID p.98

Leave the freeway at this point. Naomi Long Madgett. ExAE p. 24
Leave the sister and brotha with the yellow/gold red/orange streak in their hair. Carolyn M. Rodgers. SoBB p.14
Leave your footsteps in the sands of time. Gertrude Blackwell Bailey. IfWCF p.9
Leaves. Pinkie Gordon Lane. MyFe p.26
Leaves believe such letting go is love, The. Lucille Clifton. OrW p.43
Leaves are green, the world is new, The. Naomi Long Madgett. SoTPN p.15
Leaves are turning brown again, The. Naomi Long Madgett. PhN p.33
Leaves Blow Backward. June Jordan. SCh p.40; ThTDID p.162
Leaves blow backward with the wind behind them June Jordan. SCh p.40; ThTDID p.162
Leaves From a Loose-Leaf War Diary. Gwendolyn Brooks. SPGB p.50; WoOGB p.94
Leaves turn brown and fall, turn brown and fall. Naomi Long Madgett. OnATM p.49
"Lee." Eleanor Thomas-Grumbach. MoSu p.8
Left like water in glasses overnight in a cold house. Carole Gregory Clemmons. NiBPo p.85; PoBA p.489
Left right. left right. left right. Black innocence marches. Alicia Loy Johnson. NiBPo p.150
Leftist Orator in Washington Park Pleasantly Punishes the Grophers. Gwendolyn Brooks. BeEa p.66
Leg Cannulas for the Dialysis Machine. Pinkie Gordon Lane. WiTh p.42
Legacies. Nikki Giovanni. MyH p.5
Legacy. Jennifer Blackman Lawson. BlIMT p.4
Legend of the Holy Night When the Police Finally Held Fire. June Jordan. PaNP p.61
Lend a Hand. Josephine D. (Henderson) Heard. MoGl p.135
Leo-- she came roaring like a woooooooooman! S. Diane Bogus. WITM p.52
Leora. Elma Stuckey. BiGa p.48
Leslee, Les- the distance crackles between us. Sherley Williams. PePo p.21
Lesson, The. Katherine Dunham. GaBW p.299
Lesson, The. Maya Angelou. AnSIR p.18
Lesson of the Falling Leaves, The. Lucille Clifton. OrW p.43
Let Amicitia in her ample reign. Phillis Wheatley. EBAP p.111
Let go of the old hurts. C. Tillery Banks. HeTMWL p.68
Let it be alleys. Gwendolyn Brooks. BeEa p.49; BlP p. 167; SPGB p.101; WoOGB p. 347
Let it be Known. Margaret T. G. Burroughs. WhSIT p.14
Let me be buried in the rain. Helene Johnson. AmNP p.102; BANP p.282; PoN p.153; PoNe p.265; RoATW p.161
Let me Be Your Flute. Sonia Sanchez. IvBAW p.70
Let me believe my work is not a drudgery. June Vanleer Williams. WiRYRS p.60
Let me come into your days. Naomi Long Madgett. PiLAF p. 30
Let Me Come to You Naked.** Patricia Parker. ChOM p.34; MoIB p.120
Let me crook my arm around them. Mari Evans. IABW p.47
Let me, for you sisters, run down somethings about your lives. Dolores Abramson. ThHSD p.1
Let me hip you to the streets. Maya Angelou. JGM p.27
Let me learn now where beauty is. Anne Spencer. CaD p.48
Let me Live With Marriage. June Jordan. SCh p.35; ThTDID p.48
Let Me Not Hate.** Georgia Douglas Johnson. BrBV p.22

Let Me Not Lose My Dream.** Georgia Douglas Johnson. BrBV p.21
Let me steal gently from the marts of men when the sun is sending forth her rays. Constantia E. Riley. EbR p. 126
Let me strap the baby in the seat. Sherley Williams. PePo p.15
Let me touch the touch of gray. Nola Richardson. WhOL p.51
Let me wear the day. Sonia Sanchez. LoP p.71
Let my being whistle down the corridor of your mercy. Naomi Long Madgett. PiLAF p.32
Let my love be the soothing for that pain. June Vanleer Williams. WiRYPS p.23
Let my restless words flutter like autumn leaves over my grave. Naomi Long Madgett. ExAE p.56
Let not my faith in a higher power be judged by my fellow man. Eleanor Thomas-Grumbach. MoSu p.9
Let not sorrow burden your thoughts. Mae V. Cowdery. WLOV p.31
Let the Day Come. Jodi Braxton. SoITM p.19
Let the leaders of nations. Beatrice M. Murphy. TNV p. 139
Let the Light Enter. Frances E. W. Harper. NeCa p.296; PBFH p.71; PoN p.11; PoNe p.15
Let the r(evolution) come, uh. Carolyn M. Rodgers. TNV p. 112
Let the winds rise. Pinkie Gordon Lane. MyFe p.30
Let Them Come. Elma Stuckey. BiGa p.79
Let them come to us. Lucia M. Pitts. EbR p.117
Let Them Wear Pale Orchid Shoes. Margaret Danner. DoOAT p.81
Let There Be New Flowering. Lucille Clifton. OrW p.91
Let There Be Three Of Us. Lois Royal Hughes. NegVo p.80
Let uh revolution come. Carolyn M. Rodgers. BlSi p.183; HoIGO p.26; NaPr p.117; PoBA p.430; SoBB p.23
Let us be still. Gwendolyn B. Bennett. BlSi p.76
Let Us Be That Something. Mari Evans. NIGHT p.74
Let Us Begin the Real Word (for Elijah Muhammad who has begun) ** Sonia Sanchez. BrT p.145; WABP p.65
Let us not lose that voice that holds us together. Pinkie Gordon Lane. WiTh p.51
Let us poets put away our pens. Julia Fields. MoCAP p.151
Let us remove the shields from our eyes. Damali (Denise Burnett) IATWMB p.20
Let us run and clap our hands. Naomi Long Madgett. PhN p.57
Let us treasure our friends. Josephine D. (Henderson) Heard. MoGl p.105
Let your life be as a shinning light. Gertrude Blackwell Bailey. IfWCF p.23
Let your mind be like this porcupine fish. Margaret Danner. DoOAT p.75
Lethe. Georgia Douglas Johnson. CaD p.77
Let's be friends. Jeannette Adams. ThHSD p.30
Let's build bridges here and there. Georgia Douglas Johnson. EbR p.93; PoN p.59; PoNe p.78; TYBP p.210
Let's get together like sisters and brothers. Olean Bess. MiFe p.2
Let's give a hand to Joe now. Eloise Culver. GANIV p.73
Let's Keep in Touch. Naomi Long Madgett. PiLAF p.44
Let's Majeste. Maya Angelou. JGM p.16
Let's say "good-bye." Georgia Douglas Johnson. ALC p.12; AmLNA p.74; RoATW p.96
Letter, The. Beatrice M. Murphy. PoN p.162; PoNe p. 287
Letter. Judy Dothard Simmons. JuB p.15

Letter, A. Marva Tatum Smith. BeYM p.22
Letter. Pinkie Gordon Lane. PoBBl p.16; WiTh p.38
Letter for El-hajj Malik El-Shabazz. Carmin Auld Goul - bourne. FoM p.29
Letter for Jan. Audre Lorde. BlUn p.88
Letter From a Wife. S. Carolyn Reese. BrT p.170; PoNe p. 413; RoATW p.152
Letter in my mailbox says you've made it, A. Audre Lorde. ChPON p.75; NeHS p.75
Letter to a Blkwoman's Daughter. Johari Amini. LetGSW p.14
Letter To a Bourgeois Friend Whom Once I Loved (and Maybe Still Do If Love Is Valid) Nikki Giovanni. BFBTBJ p.29
Letter to an Aspiring Junkie. Maya Angelou. JGM p.27
Letter to Langston Huhes. PBK p.49
Letter to my Father...a Solidarity Long Overdue. Safiya Henderson. CoAAAW p.135
Letter to my Friend the Poet Ntozake Shange. June Jordan. PaNP p.60
Letter to my Sister. Angelina Weld Grimke. PoBA p.16
Letter to my Sister. Anne Spencer. BlSi p.70; CNAW p.240; AmNP p.19; ITBLA p.155; PoN p.51; PoNe p. 51; PoNe p.61
Letter to the Local Police. June Jordan. PaNP p.28
Letters cluttered on the table. Nola Richardson. WhOL p.79
Lettie. Elma Stuckey. BiGa p.3
Lewis Adams, Father of Tuskegee Institute (1881) - 1905. Alabama. Eloise Culver. GANIV p.42
Lexington/96 Street Stop. Jayne Cortez. Scar p.46
Libation hey sisters, we the color of our men. Johari Amini. BlSi p.192
Libations. Jayne Cortez. Scar p.30
Liberated Woman? Jennifer Blackwell Lawson. BlIMT p.10
Liberation/Poem. Sonia Sanchez. MoCAP p.135; NeBV p.337; WABP p.54
Liberty and Peace, A Poem. Phillis Wheatley. AVAN p. 31; BlSi p.13, EaNAW p.53; NeCa p.286; PAL p.55; PPW p.93
Library, The. Wanda Coleman. MaDBL p.52
Lie is sometimes masqueraded as the truth, The. Naomi Long Madgett. OnATM p.33
Life. Gertrude Blackwell Bailey. IfWCF p.32
Life. Naomi Long Madgett. OnATM p.21
Life aint all beer and skitties. Harryette Mullen. TTW p.23
Life & Positive. Carolyn M. Rodgers. HoIGO p.7
Life can be beautiful. Gertrude Blackwell Bailey. IfWCF p.32
Life Cycles. Nikki Giovanni. CoCRD p.52
Life doesn't frighten me. Maya Angelou. AnSIR p.45
Life For My Child is Simple.** Gwendolyn Brooks. AfAWA p. 583; WoOGB p.104
Life has become U coming from the night of all stars. Johari Amini. LetGSW p.30
Life I Led, The. Nikki Giovanni. WoATM p.12
Life is a Two-Way Experience. Vanessa Howard. ScWh p.40
Life is at 2 playing in a lofty room. Johari Amini. JuBa p.165; LetGSW p.13
Life is but a toy that swings on a bright gold chain. Naomi Long Madgett. OnATM p.21
Life is the Art of Drawing.** Carolyn Ogletree. TNV p.79
Life--it just happened to them. Carolyn M. Rodgers. HeAEG p.74
Life-Long, Poor Browning.** Anne Spencer. CaD p.49; NeCa p.352; PoN p.50; PoNe p.60
Life of God, The. Marion Cuthbert. SOC p.17

Life of Lincoln West, The. Gwendolyn Brooks. BrT p.33; FaP p.9; FBPA p.23
Life/Poem. Sonia Sanchez. BrT p. 142; WABP p.55
Life Styles. Marion Nicholes. LiS p.11
Life, to me, is a pattern of lace. Margaret Danner. DoOAT p.36
Life to the bigot is a whip. Dorothy Vena Johnson. EbR p.91; PoN p.120; PoNe p.226
Life was simple in the yesteryear. Naomi Long Madgett. Naomi Long Madgett. PhN p.17
Life was such a big piece of candy for a little boy. Naomi Long Madgett. OnATM p.39
Life was trembling faintly trembling faintly trembling. Frances E. W. Harper. CNAW p.102; ITBLA p.93; PBFH p. 17
Life we find is nevermore. Josephine D. (Henderson) Heard. MoGl p.69
Life's Like the Wind. Jane W. Burton. NegVo p.23
Life's not about the valiant stride. Jill Witherspoon Boyer. DeDF p.101; DrF p.7
Lifetime. Georgia Oliver. NegVo p.118
Light and Diplomatic Bird, A. Gwendolyn Brooks. WoOGB p.107
Light inside has flickered and died, The. Frenchy J. Hodges. BlW p.22
Light keeps on breaking. Lucille Clifton. OrW p.85
Light! more light! the shadows deepen. Frances E. W. Harper. NeCa p.296; PBFH p.71; PoN p.11; PoNe p.15
Light on My Mother's Tongue. Lucille Clifton. OrW p.73
Light That Came to Lucille Clifton Came a Shift of Knowing.** Lucille Clifton. TwW p.47
Lighten our darkness, we beseech thee, O Lord. Pauli Murray. DaTAOP p.38
Lighten up why is your hand so heavy. Lucile Clifton. GoNAE p.14
Lightly. Audre Lorde. BlUn p.95
Lights. W. Blanche Nivens. BTh p.44
Lights at Carney Point, The. Alice Dunbar-Nelson. DuSAE p.132
Like a fawn from the arrow, startled and wild. Frances E. W. Harper. AfAV p.82; NeCa p.294
Like a pot turned on the straw. Lucille Clifton. TwW p.37
Like a wild flame it leaps and speaks to the innermost portion of the soul. Dolores A. Brown. EbR p.15
Like a will-o'-the wisp in the night of a honeysuckele breeze. Nikki Giovanni. WoATM p.32
Like Bigger Thomas. Sonia Sanchez. IvBAW p.78
Like Breaths. Margaret Danner. DoOAT p.11
Like dives in the deeps of hell I cannot break this fearful spell. Frances E. W. Harper. PBFH p.40
Like he always said the things of Daddy will find him. Lucille Clifton. GoNAE p.28
Like how do you build on a tower of truths. Val Gray Ward. TGWL p.99
Like hungry birds searching a winter land. Carole Gregory Clemmons. TGWL p. 20
Like I mean doesn't it all come down to e/co/no/mics. Sonia Sanchez. IvBAW p.21; NaPr p.131; YoBBI p.365
Like I mean, don't it all come down to e/co/no/mics. Sonia Sanchez. WABP p.22
Like lonely fools our limbs do not combine. June Jordan. ThTDID p.44
Like most young girls, I used to fantasize. Eleanor Thomas-Grumbach. MoSu p.14
Like my mother and her grandmother before I paddle around the house. Nikki Giovanni. WoATM p.8
Like Rain Drops on a Windowpane. Margaret Danner. DoOAT p.45

Like the verseless, rhymeless, pointless, vision-writing of a poet gone creatively blind. S. Diane Bogus. WITM p.65
Like this jewel--studded carved-from-ivory, leopard. Margaret Danner. DoOAT p.139
Like Unto a Rose. Lois Royal Hughes. EbR p.89
Like Thunder Among tall Buildings. Margaret Danner. DoOAT p.40
Like you letting down your purple shadowed hair. Mae V. Cowdery. EbAT p.26; WLOV p.23
Lilacs. Gertrude Parthenia McBrown. EbR p.104
Lillies. Linda B. Graham. GaBW p.313
Limbo. Pamela Cobb. InDM p.17
Lineage. Margaret Walker. BlSi p.94; BOL p.58; DeRi p.14; KAL p.141; PoBA p.148
Lines. Ada. BlSi p.20
Lines Between Seekonk and Fairhaven. Sherley Williams. PePo p.34
Lines For My Mother. Margaret T. G. Burroughs. WhSIT p.11
Lines Suggested on Reading 'An Appeal to Christian Women of the South' by A. E. Grimke. Ada. BlSi p.17
Lines to a Nasturtium. Anne Spencer. AmLNA p.47; AmNP p.18; BlWOA p.627; CaD p.52; CNAW p.272; ITBLA p.155; NeCa p.354; PoN p.53; PoNe p.64
Lines to a Sophisticate. Mae V. Cowdery. WLOV p.50
Lines to Blood Brothers and Sisters. Margaret T. G. Burroughs. WhSIT p.15
Lines Written at the Grave of Alexandre Dumas. Gwendolyn B. Bennett. CaD p.159; PoN p.110
Linkage. Nikki Giovanni. ThWRNW p.25
Linseed Oil and Dreams. Judy Dothard Simmons. CoAAAW p. 332
Lion in Daniel's Den, The. Nikki Giovanni. Rec p.29; WoATM p.41
Lions and tigers dominate. Mary Carter Smith. PoNe p.389
Lip Love. June Vanleer Williams. WiRYPS p.22
Lip Service. Helen G. Quigless. TNV p.97
Liquor don't drown. Quandra Pretyman. BOL p.60
Listen. Gertrude Blackwell Bailey. IfWCF p.36
Listen after I have set the table. June Jordan. PaNP p.19
Listen brother love you love you love you love you dig me. Audre Lorde. ChPON p.76; NeHS p.24
Listen Children. Lucille Clifton. PoBA p.308
Listen children keep this in the place. Lucille Clifton. GoNAE p.9; PoBA p.3'08
Listen I have a complaint to make. Jayne Cortez. Scar p.41
Listen, I said, rocking to the tingle in my spine. Colleen McElroy. MuDLSG p.19
Listen is just a six-letter word. Gertrude Blackwell Bailey. IfWCF p.36
Listen, I'se talkin' to you Lawd. Frenchy J. Hodges. BlW p.19
Listen listen listen to me. Sonia Sanchez. HoC p.23
Listen to arks of filed down teeth. Jayne Cortez. Scar p.27
Listen to big Black at S.F. State. Sonia Sanchez. WABP p.48
Listen to the drum. Sherley Williams. PePo p.66
Listen to the lambs. Margaret Danner. DoOAT p.135
Listen why is your grandaddy's chopped up penis. Jayne Cortez. FeAF p.28
Listen, you a wonder. Lucille Clifton. TwW p.7
Listenen to big Black at S.F. State. Sonia Sanchez. BlP p.235
Listening for the sound of my own voice. Pinkie Gordon Lane. BlSi p.233

Listening to Jimmy Garrison (Pittsburgh, Pa.) Sonia Sanchez. LoP p.81
Listening. Pinkie Gordon Lane. MyFe p.18
Litany for Afro-Americans, A. Naomi Long Madgett. ExAE p. 40
Litany for Peppe. Nikki Giovanni. BFBTBJ p.57
Litany For Survival, A. Audre Lorde. BlUn p.31
Litany From the Dark People, A. Margaret Walker. OcJo p.35
Lithe and gay and debonair. Bessie Woodson Yancey. EcFTH p.35
Lithe mottled legs sprawled in final cradle. Mari Evans. NIGHT p.40
Little Anthony and the Imperials singer. Sonia Sanchez. WABP p.30
Little birches. Effie Lee Newsome. PoN p.8; PoNe p.72
Little birches haunt the hills, The. Effie Lee Newsome. PoN p.8; PoNe p.72
Little bird with tuneful throat. Josephine D. (Henderson) Heard. MoGl p.54
Little Black Boy.** Barbara Marshall. TNV p.69
Little (Black) Man. Anonymous. ThHSD p.26
Little Black Ones. Nilaja. ThHSD p.61
Little boy bowed his head, A. Bernadine Blessitt. NegVo p.15
Little boy Brown ridin to town. Jeanette Adams. ThHSD p.66
Little boy wears my mistakes, A. Audre Lorde. ChPON p.44; DeRi p.17; FrLWP p.17
Little Boys. Elma Stuckey. BiGa p.81
Little boys are like snowflakes. Nikki Giovanni. VaT p.17
Little Boy's Prayer. Bernadine Blessitt. NegVo p.15
Little Brown Boy. Helene Johnson. AmNP p.100; BANP p.279; CaD p.218; GoS p.112
Little brown boy, slim, dark, big-eyed. Helene Johnson. MyNIB p.140; NeNRe p.151; PoBA p.103; VoFHR p.183
Little Bru and little Chris every morning give a kiss. Nikki Giovanni. VaT p.39
Little child sat on the floor, A. Josephine D. (Henderson) Heard. MoGl p.57
Little Child Shall Lead Them. Frances E. W. Harper. PBFH p.19
Little Child Shall Lead Us...If We Dare to Follow, A. Nia nSabe. ThHSD p.69
Little Dandelion, The. Lula Lowe Weeden. CaD p.229
Little David play on yo'harp. Anonymous. GoS p.63; MBP p.80
Little David was a shepherd boy. Anonymous. GoS p.63; MBP p.80
Little firefly passed me by, A. Eleanor A. Thompson. BTh p. 47
Little Girl Speaking. Maya Angelou. OhPWFW o,64
Little girl was sitting near her mother's house one day, A. Eloise Culver. GANIV p.15
Little Girl's Dream World, A. Della Burt. BlSi p.162
Little, gray, desolate, they stand. Linda Brown Bragg. LoSBM p.6
Little Grey Leaves.** Esther Popel. ReFNA p.48
Little Helper. Edna Shaw. NegVo p.140
Little Hour of Sunshine. Georgia Douglas Johnson. HWOP p.49
Little kangaroos: think prefer to live in pouches. Nikki Giovanni. VaT p.35
Little King. Georgia Douglas Johnson. ALC p.55
Little More About the Brothers and Sisters, A. Sharon Scott. JuBa p.171
Little Poem, A. Linda Brown BTB p.54
Little Robin Red Breast. Lula Lowe Weeden. CaD p.228
Little Rooster, The. Anonymous. AmLNA p.8
Little sister, not all Black

people are ready. Audre Lorde. ChPON p.90; NeHS p. 33
Little Son. Georgia Douglas Johnson. AVAN p.209; BrBV p.49; CaD p.76; DeDF p.46
Little Sycamore, The. Anonymous. TYBP p.29
Little white boy, when you grow up, what do you want to be? Elma Stuckey. BiGa p.81
Little yellow looked at the banana tree. June Jordan. SCh p.25
Live and love; live and love. Valerie Tarver. TNV p.127
Live Celebration. Sarah Webster Fabio. TGWL p.34
Living in the Shadows. Carolyn M. Rodgers. HeAEG p.73
Living is too much effort. Mari Evans. IABW p.33; WhIAM p.
Living Water. Carolyn M. Rodgers. HoIGO p.79
Living waters. May Miller. ClAB p.7
Lo! for this dark terrestrial ball. Philis Wheatley. PAL p.62; PPW p.45
Lo! freedom comes. Phillis Wheatley. AVAN p.31; EaNAW p.53; PAL p.55; PPW p.93; NeCa p.286
Lo! the glorious dawn is breaking. Josephine D. (Henderson) Heard. MoGl p.65
Loafin'. Bessie Woodson Yancey. EcFTH p.48
Loam Norton. Gwendolyn Brooks. BlPo p.22; BlWOA p.721
Loam Norton considers Belsen and Dachan. Gwendolyn Brooks. BlPo p.22; BlWOA p.721
Lolotte, who attires my hair, lost her lover. Jessie Redmond Fauset. ReFNA p.38 NeNRe p.76
Lone man stood on the glory road, A. Pauli Murray. DaTAOP p.36
Loneliness For Nona. Colleen McElroy. MuDLSG p.13
Loneliness lies just there beyond heartbreak. Dorothy C. Parrish. TNV p.90
Lonely figure strode on, A. Eloise Culver. GANIV p.79
Lonely night, a deserted street, A. June Vanleer Williams. WiRYPS p.33
Lonely Particular. Alice Walker. RePOP p.40
Lonely poem is nothing special, A. Carolyn M. Rodgers. HeAEG p.25
Lonely sails unlivened by the wind. Eleanor C. Hunter. NegVo p.83
Lonely Sleepless Night, A. Olean Bess. MiFe p.5
Lonely Tulip Grower. Julia Alvarez. SoS p.11
Lonely wanderer, impatient seeker what if your driven heart screams pain. Pauli Murray. DaTAOP p.94
Lonely Woman. Jayne Cortez. NeBV p.233
Long Cotton Row. Elma Stuckey. BiGa p.4
Long Distance. Carole Gregory Clemmons. NiBPo p.85
Long green symbolized by gold is the shape esperanto. Margaret Danner. AfAWA p. 637; IrLa p.12
Long, grim years with iron tread move down the shuttered isle. Georgia Douglas Johnson. BrBV p.82
Long have I beat with timid hands upon life's leaden door. Georgia Douglas Johnson. BlALP p.44; BrBV p.55; CaD p.76; NeCa p.340; PoBA p.23; PoN p.587; PoNe p.76; VoFHR p.350
Long have I yearned and sought for beauty. Mae V. Cowdery. BlSi p.93; WLOV p.41
Long John Nelson and Sweetie Pie.** Margaret Walker. FMP p.47
Long-Live Skinner's Blues. Anonymous. BlWOA p.465
Long March, The. Alicia Loy Johnson. GaBW p.342; NiBPo p.150
Long Road Rhythm. Nzadi Zimele-Keita. CoAAAW p.398
Long way is often the short way,

The. Carolyn M. Rodgers. HeAEG p.37
Longing. Lillian Tucker Lewis. HeD p.27
Longing in California Poem. S. Diane Bogus. WITM p.28
Longings. Mae V. Cowdery. WLOV p.10
Look ahead but not without the glancing back, A. Pinkie Gordon Lane. WiTh p.34
Look at him layen there. Johari Amini. LetGSW p.12
Look at me and you will see I am Black and ugly as can be. Gertrude Blackwell Bailey. IfWCF p.56
Look at me 8th grade. Sonia Sanchez. HoC p.22; IvBAW p.12; PoBA p.288
Look at my Face. Carolyn M. Rodgers. JuBa p.122
Look at you so you finally made it. E. Sharon Gomillion. FoAAM p.14
Look at yourself and you will find the greatest enemy is oneself. Gertrude Blackwell Bailey. IfWCF p.33
Look i-n-t-o me----not merely at me. Dolores Abramson. RoATW p.83; ThHSD p.36
Look of him the beauty of the man, The. Lucille Clifton. GoNAE p.29
Look out, look out on yonder world. Naomi Long Madgett. PhN p.56
Look! she cried, I am not perfect. Alice Walker. RePOP p.42
Look Up. Gertrude Blackwell Bailey. IfWCF p.41
Look up the path from whence you came. Gertrude Blackwell Bailey. IfWCF p.41
Look up, dear one, nor be cast down. Josephine D. (Henderson) Heard. MoGl p.22
Looking. Gwendolyn Brooks. MyNIB p.64; SPGB p.24; StIB p.49; WoOGB p.51
Looking across the horizons wondering what tomorrow will bring. Eleanor Thomas-Grumbach. MoSu p.20
Looking at the pain/faces of people forever in the rain. Sandra Royster. WoTa p.5
Looking For a Country Under its Original Name. Colleen J. McElroy. BlSi p.290
Looks like to me folks ought to mind they own business. Carolyn M. Rodgers. CoAAAW p.314
Loomit. Adrienne Ingrum. CoAAAW p.152
Looped in each other's arc without thoughts of ending. Pinkie Gordon Lane. WiTh p. 55
Lord, don't set that sun on the long cotton row. Elma Stuckey. BiGa p.4
Lord God, I hear thy voice, I bow my head. Naomi Long Madgett. PhN p.119
Lord I Would Love Thee. Josephine D. (Henderson) Heard. MoGl p.98
Lord, In My Heart. Maya Angelou. OhPWFW p.32
Lord, on thy promise I rely. Josephine D. (Henderson) Heard. MoGl p.90
Lord, on thy promise I rely. Josephine D. (Henderson) Heard. MoGl p.135
Lord, teach me patience in a world of time. Naomi Long Madgett. PhN p.120
Lorraine Hansberry. Nikki Giovanni. ThWRNW p.13
Lost. Dorothy Lee Louise Shaed. NegVo p.140
Lost, The. Naomi Long Madgett. OnATM p.30
Lost Baby Poem, The. Lucille Clifton. BlSi p.247; GoNAE p.4; MoCAP p.141
Lost Cause. June Vanleer Williams. WiRYPS p.73
Lost Illusions. Georgia Douglas Johnson. ANP p.86; BANP p.182
Lost Love. Eleanor Thomas-Grumbach. MoSu p.18
Lost Muse, The. Naomi Long Madgett. OnATM p.26
Lost My Mind Again. Marva Tatum Smith. BeYM p.27
Lost Song. Naomi Long Madgett.

DeDF p.35; ExAE p.54
Lost Soul. Eleanor Thomas-Grumbach. MoSu p.12
Lost soul, roaming trying to find a home. Eleanor Thomas-Grumbach. MoSu p.12
Lot of slaves was always full of grief and strife, The. Eloise Culver. GANIV p.16
Lotsa Body & Cultural Heritage. Ntozake Shange. NaEd p.38
Lou had to leave her sickly child. Elma Stuckey. BiGa p.58
Lou's Room. Sandra Royster. WoTa p.12
Lou's room in the afternoon was crystal bottle. Sandra Royster. WoTa p.12
Love. Anonymous. MBP p.19; TYBP p.198
Love. Alice Walker. ONC p.17
Love. Carolyn M. Rodgers. HeAEG p.16
Love. Elaine Mitchell. AOS p.26
Love. Josephine D. (Henderson) Heard. MoGl p.102
Love. Kali Grosvenor. PBK p.26
Love. Lucy Mae Turner. BCF p.36
Love. Olean Bess. MiFe p.4
Love. Valerie Parks. NegVo p.123
Love Ain't Hip. Sandra Royster. BrA p.18; RoATW p.97; WoTa p.6
Love & Friendship are Words of People.** Patricia Parker. ChOM p.29; MoIB p.119
Love be a (single) message. Barbara Mahone. Suga p.31
Love calls me tonight. Georgia Douglas Johnson. ALC p.41
Love came again today like gusts of spring. Naomi Long Madgett. PhN p.122
Love comes from deep within. Olean Bess. MiFe p.4
Love, Considered. Pinkie Gordon Lane. WiTh p.25
Love Ends. Carolyn M. Rodgers. HeAEG p.26
Love Ends II, or Numbers Racket. Carolyn M. Rodgers. HeAEG p.15
Love From my Father. Carole Gregory Clemmons. NiBPo p.85; PoBA p.489
Love has two. Carole Gregory Clemmons. NiBPo p.88
Love, I adore your timid tenderness. Lucia Mae Pitts. NegVo p.128
Love in Wartime. Pauli Murray. DaTAOP p.99
Love is a funny thing. Anonymous. MBP p.19; TYBP p.198
Love: is a Human Condition. Nikki Giovanni. ThWRNW p.45
Love is a kind of terror. Harryette Mullen. TTW p.27
Love is a warm and strong and hopeful thing. Naomi Long Madgett. PiLAF p.21
Love is having a relationship that is meaningfull. Elaine Mitchell. AOS p.26
Love is life. Johari Amini. LetGSW p.28
Love is my Color. Kali Grosvenor. PBK p.18
Love is not the only face. Nikki Grimes. CoAAAW p.121
Love kisses spurned so long ago. Georgia Douglas Johnson. HWOP p.58
Love Letter. Carolyn Gregory Clemmons. BlSi p.185
Love Letters. Josephine D. (Henderson) Heard. MoGl p.52
Love, love, let's say "I love." Ann Wallace. GLOWC p.94
Love, Maybe. Audre Lorde. ChPON p.47; FrLWP p.47
Love Note. Gwendolyn Brooks. AmLNA p.89
Love Note I: Surely. Gwendolyn Brooks. SPGB p.57; StIB p.55; WoOGB p.57
Love person from love people, A. Lucille Clifton. OrW p.65
Love Poem. Audre Lorde. ChPON p.77; NeHS p.26
Love Poem. Carole Gregory Clemmons. NiBPo p.83
Love Poem. Pinkie Gordon Lane. MyFe p.41
Love Poem. Thulani Davis. AlTRGR p.35
Love Poem (for real) Nikki Giovanni. BFBTBJ p.33
Love Poem to an African Freedom Fighter, A. Rosemari

Mealy. CoAAAW p.221
Love Poem Written For Sterling Brown, A. Sonia Sanchez. IvBAW p.92
Love Poems. Marva Tatum Smith. BeYM p.20
Love Rejected. Lucille Clifton. BlP p.250
Love rejected hurts so much more. Lucille Clifton. BlP p.250
Love Song. Anonymous. TYBP p.28
Love Song. Anonymous. TYBP p.30
Love Song. Anonymous. TYBP p.30
Love Song. Anonymous. TYBP p.31
Love Song. Anonymous. TYBP p.31
Love Song for Summer. Mae V. Cowdery. WLOV p.52
Love Songs of an Outcast. Pinkie Gordon Lane. WiTh p.44
Love--The Beginning and the End. Carolyn Rodgers. HoIGO p.70
L-o-v-e, the beginning of evolution. Anonymous. GLOWC p. 98
Love, the top of the hill is the lower waiting place. Pinkie Gordon Lane. PoBBl p.13; WiTh p.46
Love thee? yes, I'm sure I love thee. Josephine D. (Henderson) Heard. MoGl p.66
Love Thoughts. Nikki Giovanni. ThWRNW p.59
Love Word, A. Lyn. SiSH p.14
Love. You Are. Sonia Sanchez. IvBAW p.82
Love you right back. Gwendolyn Brooks. FaP p.21
Lovelight. Georgia Douglas Johnson. AmNP p.23
Lovely Love, A. Gwendolyn Brooks. BeEa p.49; BlP p.167; SPGB p.10; WoOGB p.347
Lover/Brother. Nola Richardson. WhOL p.35
Lover of the mountains maker of the flame. Barbara Mahone. Suga p.32
Lovers and others cliche about the moon. Margaret Danner. DoOAT p.77
Lovers of the Poor, The. Gwendolyn Brooks. BeEa p.35; ITSA p.245; MoCAP p.83; SPGB p.90; WoOGB p.333
Lovers, sitting on a park bench, Claudia E. Jemmott. GaBW p.352
Lover's Song, A. Audre Lorde. FiCi p.22
Love's Miracle. Georgia Douglas Johnson. ALC p.9
Love's More Enduring Uses. Pauli Murray. DaTAOP p.79
Love's Roses I gathered, all dewy in May. Georgia Douglas Johnson. HWOP p.36
Love's Tendril. Georgia Douglas Johnson. HWOP p.61
Loving Beauty Is Loving God. Isabelle McClellan Taylor. EbR p.134
Lovesong to the Workshop. Dorothy Randall. ThHSD p.39
Loving. Pinkie Gordon Lane. WiTh p.55
Loving U Rite. Angela Jackson. VoDLM p.21
Loving you is Ecstasy to Me. Ntozake Shange. NaEd p.31
Loving You is Like Taking a ride on a magic carpet. C. Tillery Banks. HeTMWL p.49
Loving you is one continual dawn. Jennifer Blackman Lawson. BlIMT p.54
Loving you redeems this brokenhearted universe. Pamela Cobb. InDM p.37
Low cost children left in deserted street cars. Pamela Cobb. InDM p.11
Low Down Blues. Lucile D. Goodlett. WGC p.43
Loyal subject, thou, to that bright queen, A. Charlotte Forten Grimke. BlSi p.24
Lucy and her Girls. Lucille Clifton. TwW p.3
Lucy by Sam out of Thelma limps down a ramp. Lucille Clifton. TwW p.25
Lucy is the ocean. Lucille Clifton. TwW p.3
Lucy One-Eye. Lucille Clifton. OrW p.67
Lullaby. Cora Ball Moten. NegVo p.111
Lullaby. June Jordan. ThTDID p.78
Lullaby. Marion Nicholes.

LiS p.18
Lullaby. Naomi Long Madgett. OnATM p.23
Lullaby. Quandra Prettyman. BOL p.75; OnOW p.19
Luxury. Nikki Giovanni. WoATM p. 31
Luz. Wanda Coleman. MaDBL p.29
Lying here alone before dawn. Pinkie Gordon Lane. WiTh p.30
Lying, thinking last night. Maya Angelou. OhPWFW p.18
Lynch Fragment. Jayne Cortez. FeAF p.20
Lynch Fragment 2. Jayne Cortez. COAG p.16; Scar p.12
Lynching, The. Isabelle McClellan Taylor. EbR p.135
Lyric, A. Katie Kelly. BTh p.55
Lyric. Naomi Long Madgett. ExAE p.55
Lyric. Pamela Cobb. InDM p.21
Lyric, A. Wanda Coleman. MaDBL p.51
Lyric for Bessie Smith. Patricia Jones. HoDo p.13
Ma Lord ain't no stuck-up man. Anonymous. GoS p.64
Macee. Frances E. W. Harper. PBFH p.79
Macee dead! a thrilled sorrow through our hearts in sadness ran. Frances E. W. Harper. PBFH p.79
Madness One Monday Evening. Julia Fields. BTB p.108; MoCAP p.150
Madness One Morning. Julia Fields. ITBLA p.275; KAL p.221; NNPUSA p.78
Madness Without Head. Jayne Cortez. MoOP p.49
Madonna. Harryette Mullen. TTW p.60
Madwomen. Joanne Jimason. NaABE p.24
Maecenas, you, beneath the myrtle shade. Phillis Wheatley. PAL p.89; PPW p.3
Magalu. Helene Johnson. BlSi p.103; CaD p.223; PoBA p. 103; PoN p.152; PoNe p. 263
Maggie. Theresa Ford. NeJCL p. 23
Magi Call Him King, The. (A Christmas Song). Effie Lee Newsome. ChG p.69
Magic. Sonia Sanchez. IvBAW p. 32; LoP p.13
Magic my man is you. Sonia Sanchez. BlP p.233; BrT p. 137; IvBAW p.7; RoATW p.30
Magic of Black Poetry, The. Anonymous. MBP p.1
"Mah Lawd, mah Lawd, whut a dawn" dat wuz. Mary Bohanon. GaBW p.264
Mahalia Jackson Gospel Singer, Alabama, 19111-1972. Eloise Culver. GANIV p.71
Maiden, The. Audre Lorde. ChPON p.8; COAL p.34
Make it with the man if you can. Marion Nicholes. LiS p.17
Make me a grave where'er you will. Frances E. W. Harper. AfAWA p.98; ANP p.17; AVAN p.42; BlP p. 40; BlWOA p.225; CNAW p. 103; EaNAW p.292; EBAP p.36; NeCa p.296
Make the First Step. Gertrude Blackwell Bailey. IfWCF p. 22
Make Up. Nikki Giovanni. CoCRD 79
Make Up Your Mind. Beth Jackson. PoBBl p.59
Make Up Your Mind. Gertrude Blackwell Bailey. IfWCF p. 11
Make/n My Music. Angela Jackson. VoDLM p.8
Maker-of-sevens in the scheme of things. Anne Spencer. ANP p.123; BANP p.216; NeNRe p.79
Making It. Audre Lorde. CaTR p.24;
Making It. Jayne Cortez. Scar p.47
Making Love. Melva Eloise Tatum. MELVA p.9
Making of Poems, The. Lucille Clifton. TwW p.24
Making out. Leatrice Emeruwa. BiGBG p.8
Malcolm. Kattie M. Cumbo. BOL p.34; NiBPo p.65
Malcolm. Lucille Clifton.

GoNAE p.22
Malcolm. Sonia Sanchez. BlPo p.37; BrT p.25; FoM p.38; HoC p.14; IvBAW p.10; MoCAP p.134
Malcolm X. Gwendolyn Brooks. BlALP p.106; BlPo p.24; PoBA p.158; WoOGB p.411; YoBBI p.165
Malcolm X, a Lover of the Grass Roots. Margaret Danner. DoOAT p.71; FoM p.6; IrLa p.7
Malcolm X. (For Dudley Randall). Gwendolyn Brooks. CNAW p. 523; FoM p.3; ITM p.39; MBP p.88; TYBP p.236
Mama. Nora Blakely. TGWL p.14
Mama. Sandra Royster. WoTa p.20
"Mama, I Don't Know." Pam Brown. GLOWC p.26
Mama Knows. Sharon Scott. JuBa p.175
Mama! mama! tell me what's happening? Beatrice M. Murphy. RoCO p.12
Mama, mama when? Bobbretta M. Elliston. PoBBl p.21
Mama says ol Johnny-Mae she just triflin. Sandra Royster. WoTa p.20
Mama, she wasn't my mother. Sandra Royster. WoTa p.22
Mama, teacher say I gotta bring me fifty cent for the symphony next week. Naomi Long Madgett. PiLAF p.59
Mama Settles the Dropoout Problem. Betty Gates. UNBP p. 309
Mama slapped me. Nola Richardson. WhOL p.7
Mama spent pennies in uh gallon milk jar. Carolyn M. Rodgers. HoIGO p.33; NaPr p. 111
Mama's God. Carolyn M. Rodgers. HoIGO p.62
Mama's God never was no white man. Carolyn M. Rodgers. HoIGO p.62
Mame was singing at the Midnight Club. Gwendolyn Brooks. StIB p.38; WoOGB p.40
Man and Maid. Myra Estelle Morris. NegVo p.106
Man Behind the Woman, The. Wanda Coleman. MaDBL p.43
Man black in strength virility hardness, A. Johari Amini. ImIB p.10
Man Feeds Me, The. Marva Tatum Smith. BeYM p.26
Man, I am Trying to Love You. Sonia Sanchez. IvBAW p.69
Man is an alien in this world. Sonia Sanchez. IvBAW p.94
Man of courage, and despair shot because he was himself. Patricia. FoM p.31
Man of the Middle Class, A. Gwendolyn Brooks. BeEa p.41; SPGB p.86; WoOGB p.339
Man said don't give up, The. Thulani Davis. AlTRGR p.14
Man, standing in the shadows of a white marble building chipping at the stones earnestly, A. Carolyn M. Rodgers. BlP p.262; HoIGO p. 38; SoBB p.30
Man, them revolutionary niggers is all over the place. Sharon Scott. JuBa p.172
Man went forth with gifts, A. Gwendolyn Brooks. BOL p.28; BrT p.167; PoBA p.159
Man White, Brown Girl and All That Jazz. Gloria Oden. PoBA p.186
Man who loosed the bullet lives, The. Mari Evans. NIGHT p.39
Man whose height his fear improved, The. Gwendolyn Brooks. AfAAV p.81' BlEx p.548; ITM p.38; PoBA p. 158; WoOGB p.410
Man whose life was like a candle's flame, A. Margaret Walker. OcJo p.33
Mana Lucy she a witch. Lucile D. Goodlett. WGC p.51
Mandy. Elma Stuckey. BiGa p.56
Manicure. Gwendolyn Brooks. AnA p.53
Mannessahs. Carolyn M. Rodgers. CoAAAW p.312
Many a Thousand Die. Anonymous. BlWOA p.313
Many cages round me. Georgia Douglas Johnson. BrBV p.77
Many Die Here.** Gayl Jones.

BlSi p.210; SoS p.14
Many nostalgic guitars and violins are playing. Margaret Danner. DoOAT p.81
Many years ago there was a person that I wanted to be. Marva Tatum Smith. BeYM p.1
Map, The. Gloria Oden. AmNP p. 161; MoCAP p.97; NNPUSA p. 47; PoNe p.385
Map shows me where it is you are, I am here, The. Gloria Oden. AmNP p.158; ITBLA p.275; KAL p.185; NNPUSA p.91; PoNe p.383
Mari Pina & the B & G. Grill. Mari Evans. NIGHT p.16
Maria Pina Brown coffee voice pinched thin Jamaican edges. Mari Evans. NIGHT p.16
Marion (the addition of our years barely the sum of fourteen). Pinkie Gordon Lane. WiTh p. 12
Marian Anderson, Pennsylvania, 1908- . Eloise Culver. GANIV p.69
Marine Intrusion. Ntozake Shange. NaEd p.144
Market Street. Naomi Long Madgett. PhN p.88
Marrie dear the box is full. Mari Evans. AmNP p.164; BlWOA p.818; DaS p.510; ITBLA p.274
Married Woman Blues. Anonymous. BlWOA p.888
Marrow of my Bone. Mari Evans. BlP p.187; IABW p.32; WhIAM p.11
Marse shot the ground around his feet. Elma Stuckey. BiGa p.44
Martha. Audre Lorde. CaTR p.10; ChPON p.24; COAL p.53
Martha. Brenda Connor-Bey. CoAAAW p.78
Martha. Naomi Long Madgett. PhN p.73
Martha this is a catalog of days. Audre Lorde. CaTR p.10; ChPON p.24; COAL p.53
Martin Luther King, Jr. Gwendolyn Brooks. BOL p.28; BrT p.167; PoBA p.159
Martin Luther King, peaceful warrior for Civil Rights Nobel Peace Prize winner, 1929-1968, Georgia. Eloise Culver. GANIV p.77
Martyr of Alabama, The. Frances E. W. Harper. PBFH p.49
Mary. Lucille Clifton. GoNAE p.38
Mary, Don You Weep. Anonymous. BlWOA p.237
Mary Mary Astonished By God. Lucille Clifton. TwW p.41
Mary's Dream. Lucille Clifton. TwW p.36
Mask, The. Clarissa Scott Delany. CaD p.143; PoN p. 94; PoNe p.177; ReFNA p.43
Mask, The. Irma McClaurin. BlSi p.195
Mask, The. Nancy L. Arnez. RoCO p.23
Masks. Julia Fields. GaBW p. 304
Masks. Nikki Giovanni. VaT p. 53
Masquerade. Carolyn M. Rodgers. BlSi p.176; HoIGO p.54
Masquerade. Naomi Long Madgett. OnATM p.33
Massa say it was a good thing what I did, The. Jo Nell Rice. GLOWC p.51; ThHSD p.65
Massa sleeps in the feather bed. Millie Williams. MyNIB p.37
Master Charge Blues. Nikki Giovanni. Rec p.28
Master, Still the Tempest. Josephine D. (Henderson) Heard. MoGl p.97
Mate. Georgia Douglas Johnson. HWOP p.12
Material Beale Street has been stripped, The. Margaret Danner. DoOAT p.93
Maternity. Georgia Douglas Johnson. BrBV p.42
Mathematics. Katherine Dunham. GaBW p.300
Matilda At the Tuba. Lucy Mae Turner. BCF p.20
Matin Hymn. Josephine D. (Henderson) Heard. MoGl p.52
Matter of Money, A. Damali (Denise Burnett) IATWMB p.12
Matthew Cole. Gwendolyn Brooks.

STIB p.22; WoOGB p.24
Mattie dear the box is full. Mari Evans. BTB p.105; IADB p.56
Maud went to college. Gwendolyn Brooks. SPGB p.8; StIB p.14; WoOGB p.16
Maxie Allen. Gwendolyn Brooks. AnA p.4; WoOGB p.68
Maxie Allen Always Taught Her Stipendiary Little Daughter. Gwendolyn Brooks. AnA p.4; WoOGB p.68
Maxine I used to admire your talent. Audre Lorde. BlUn p.102
May. Bessie Woodson Yancey. EcFTH p.10
May 1, 1970. June Jordan.. ThTDID p.93
May I Return? Lucy Mae Turner. BCF p.40
May Lament. Naomi Long Madgett. PhN p.105
May 27, 1971: No Poem. June Jordan. ThTDID p.117
Maybe; if I could have sat at five or eight, upon his knee. S. Diane Bogus. WITM p.35
Maybe it was an omen. Jennifer Blackman Lawson. BlIMT p.48
Maybe the Birds. June Jordan. SCh p.14; ThTDID p.162
Maybe the birds are worried by the wind. June Jordan. SCh p.14; ThTDID p.162
Maybe you thought I would forget about the sunrise. June Jordan. ThTDID p.69
Me. Joanne Jimason. NaABE p.7
Me. Pinkie Gordon Lane. WiTh p.7
Me Alone. Lula Lowe Weeden. CaD p.227
Me & Steenie. Harryette Mullen. TTW p.7
Me and you be sisters. Lucille Clifton. OrW p.5
Me I drop my shovel fall at the foot of a tree. Joanne Jimason. NeABE p.7
Me? I never could keep my edges and kitchen straight. Carolyn M. Rodgers. SoBB p.14
Me, In Kulu Se & Karma. Carolyn M. Rodgers. PoBA p.432; SoBB p.34; UNBP p.345
Me nappy hair dream child sending Father's Day cards. Peggy Susberry Kenner. JuBa p.92
Me, the Tree. Eleanor Thomas-Grumbach. MoSu p.6
Mea Culpa. Katherine L. Cuestas. BTB p.76
Measure, The. Georgia Douglas Johnson. HWOP p.33
Mechanic, The. Colleen McElroy. MuDLSG p.11
Medgar Evers. Gwendolyn Brooks. AfAAu p.81; BlEx p.548; ITM p.38; PoBA p.158; WoOGB p.410
Medicine. Alice Walker. ONC p. 70
Meditation. Nora Davis. GLOWC p.10
Meditations of an Unwed Blk-Mother-To-Be. Linda Cousins. ThHSD p.48
Meet. Audre Lorde. BlUn p.33
Meeting, The. Elaine Brown. GLOWC p.95
Meeting After the Savior Came 4/4/68. Lucille Clifton. DOBB p.50
Meeting You Two Years Later.** Melva Eloise Tatum. MELVA p.3
Meeting meetings meetings rooms crowded spaces. Carolyn M. Rodgers. BlP p.266
Melodrama. Thulani Davis. AlTRGR p.33
Memba the time...we met at home. Angela Jackson. VoDLM p.12
Memo. June Jordan. PaNP p.82
Memo in Bronze. Pauli Murray. DaTAOP p.90
Memo to Daniel Pretty Moynihan. June Jordan. ThTDID p.117
Memoranda Toward the Spring of Seventy-Nine. June Jordan. PaNP p.74
Memorial. Naomi Long Madgett. PhN p.36
Memorial. Sonia Sanchez. BlSi p.242; HoC p.29
Memorial I. Audre Lorde. ChPON p.3; COAL p.65
Memorial II. Audre Lorde. ChPON p.5; COAL p.66; FiCi p.1
Memorial III From a Phone Booth on Broadway. Audre Lorde. ChPON p.88; NeHS p.31

Memorial For My Father. Margaret T. G. Burroughs. WhSIT p.12
Memorial IV. Audre Lorde. NeHS p.25
Memorial to Ed Bland. Gwendolyn Brooks. AnA p.vi; WoOGB p. 63
Memories are like dry bones. Carolyn M. Rodgers. HeAEG p.20
Memories: 1956. Jennifer Blackman Lawson. BlIMT p.35
Memories/The Red Bootee. Angela Jackson. VoDLM p.10
Memory. Georgia Douglas Johnson. HWOP p.46
Memory. Margaret Walker. AfAWA p.521; FMP p.56
Memory, The. Maya Angelou. AnSIR p.38
Memory. Sandra Royster. WoTa p.18
Memory, let me go. Ruth Brownlee Johnson. EbR p.97
Men. Maya Angelou. AnSIR p.11
Men and women long ago, The. Gwendolyn Brooks. AnA p.44; WoOGB p.108
Men are all Away, The. Nayo. YoBBI p.438
Men: beware the woman who thinks money will solve all her problems. Toi Derricotte. EmDH p.24
Men of careful turns, haters of forks in the road. Gwendolyn Brooks. BlALP p.102; WoOGB p.123
Men we let come into our lives, The. Pamela Cobb. InDM p.41
Menda City. Margaret Danner. DoOAT p.49
Men's Settlement House. Jayne Cortez. Scar p.58
Mention his name and they bristle or shake heads like steel, exhibiting a frowned face. Helen C. Quigless. FoM p.65
Mentor. Audre Lorde. ChPON p.67; NeHS p.27
Mentors. Gwendolyn Brooks. AfAWA p.578; BlWOA p.717; KAL p.156; PoN p.191; SPGB p.25; StIB p.51; WoOGB p.53
Mercenaries & Minstrels. Jayne Cortez. MoOP p.13
Mercenary like Rolf Steiner will split open your head with a bottle of I. W. Harper, A. Jayne Cortez. MoOP p.13
Merciful Hour, A. S. Diane Bogus. WITM p.21
Message. Pinkie Gordon Lane. MyFe p.36
Message to a Loved One Dead, A. Josephine D. (Henderson) Heard. MoGl p.78
Met a big Blk bad--mouthing Charley Cat. Leatrice Emeruwa. BlGBG p.8
Metamorphis. Helene Johnson. ReFNA p.50
Metamorphosis. Patricia Parker. MoIB p.132
Metarhetoric. June Jordan. ThTDID p.84
Mexico Entered the Door on the Wind. Wanda Coleman. MaDBL p.69
Micah. Margaret Walker. PFND p.27; UNBP p.166
Micah was a young man of the people. Margaret Walker. PFND p.27; UNBP p.166
Michael Be. Margaret Danner. DoOAT p.130
Michael is meaner that Hal who is keener. Nikki Giovanni. VaT p.19
Michigan Willows Do Not Weep. Margaret Danner. DoOAT p.19
Mid-Summer Thoughts. Pinkie Gordon Lane. MyFe p.43
Middle Age Syndrome, The. June Vanleer Williams. WiRYPS p.51
Middle of the Beginning, The. S. Diane Bogus. WITM p.37
Midnight. Henrietta Cordelia Ray. EBAP p.144
Midnight Carries Me South Along Illusion Ave. Wanda Coleman. MaDBL p.45
Midnight is no time for poetry. Julia Fields. AmNP p.183; ITBLA p.275; MoCAP p.149
Midnight Magnolias. Naomi Long Madgett. PhN p.98
Midnight Song. Pinkie Gordon Lane. MyFe p.20

Midnight streetlights beckon me. Naomi Long Madgett. PiLAF p. 39
Midnight Thoughts of the Two Whores. Pinkie Gordon Lane. WiTh p.29
Midtown manhattan honk beep. June Jordan. PaNP p.39
Midway. Naomi Long Madgett. BlP p.197; BlSi p.128; MoCAP p.93; NNPUSA p.39; OnOW p. 41; PoNe p.381; SoS p.126; StBS p.63
Migration. Carole Gregory Clemmons. NiBPo p.82; PoBA p. 489
Migration. Pinkie Gordon Lane. BlSi p.231; MyFe p.19
Militant is quietly armed and waiting, The. Marion Nicholas. LiS p.14
Military spending huge profits & death. Jayne Cortez. COAG p.104
Million-aire makes a thousand-aire. Mae Jackson. CaPWY p.12
Milton. Henrietta Cordelia Ray. BlSi p.39
Minds of Black men once hoveled hutlike under persecution's storms. Margaret Danner. DoOAT p.40
Mine ear was dull, my harp unstrung. Josephine D. (Henderson) Heard. MoGl p. 120
Mine is a single room in a large house & warm climate. Thulani Davis. AlTRGR p.23
Mine is no southern tradition. Beatrice M. Murphy. RoCO p. 11
Minature Potters & Significant Clays. Carolyn M. Rodgers. HeAEG p.74
Minority. Judy Dothard Simmons. CoAAAW p.330
Minute hand of a defective clock circles in perennial embrace, The. Naomi Long Madgett. ExAE p.23
Minutes From the Meeting. June Jordan. ThTDID p.81
Minutes swiftly throb and pass. Georgia Douglas Johnson. HWOP p.10
Miracle. Louise Blackman. EbR p.5
Mirror Poems, The. Toi Derricotte. EmDH p.17
Mirror thinks it has no self. Toi Derricotte. EmDH p.17
Mirrored. Georgia Douglas Johnson. HWOP p.14
Mirrors. Nikki Giovanni. ThWRNW p.22
Miscarriage. Pinkie Gordon Lane. WiTh p.34
Misconception. Naomi Long Madgett. SoTPN p.14
Miscreant. Bessie Woodson Yancey. EcFTH p.9
Misdemeanor. S. Diane Bogus. WITM p.51
Misery of Being, The. E. Sharon Gomillion. FoAAM p.6
Misfit. Claire Turner. NegVo p.156
Misfortune perched on his shoulder. Naomi Long Madgett. PiLAF p.19
Miss Brown. S. Diane Bogus. WITM p.40
Miss Brown came to church today. S. Diane Bogus. WITM p.40
Miss Lucy she is handsome. Anonymous. GoS p.18
Miss Marilyn a cooly pale moon maid. Sandra Royster. WoTa p.14
Miss Maime. Jodi Braxton. SoITM p.4
"Miss Moses" people called her. Eloise Culver. GANIV p.23
Miss Nancy's Geo'ge. Lucile D. Goodlett. WGC p.25
Miss Nancy's Geo'ge got a stugie down by de corners sto. Lucile D. Goodlett. WGC p.25
Miss Persephone. Harryette Mullen. HoDo p.101; TTW p.31
Miss Rosie. Lucille Clifton. BlSi p.248; DOBB p.51; MoCAP p.139; PoBA p.397
Miss Scarlet, Mr. Rhett and Other Day Saints. Maya Angelou. JGM p.28
Misse Got a Gold Chairn. Anonmous. BlWOA p.235

Missing Beat. Carolyn M. Rodgers. JuBa p.116
Missing in Action. S. Diane Bogus. WITM p.63
Missing Manuscript. Thulani Davis. AlTRGR p.30
Missing Missionaries, The. Margaret Danner. IrLa p.27
Missing the Warmth (Of Hands Gliding Over My Body). C. Tillery Banks. HeTMWL p.20
Missing You Is Like Spring. Sonia Sanchez. IvBAW p.86
Mission of the Flowers, The. Frances E. W. Harper. BlSi p.34
Missionaries in the Jungle. Linda Piper. BlSi p.184
Missionary Brings a Young Native to America, A. Helene Johnson. VoFHR p.350
Mississippi Born. Pearl Cleage Lomax. DeDF p.25
Mrs. Coley's three-flat brick isn't here any more. Gwendolyn Brooks. SPGB p.11; StIB p.23; WoOGB p.25
Mrs. Johnson Objects. Clara Ann Thompson. AVAN p.133; BlSi p.42
Mrs. Small. Gwendolyn Brooks. BeEa p.82; WoOGB p.324
Mrs. Small went to the kitchen for her pocket book. Gwendolyn Brooks. BeEa p.27; SPGB p.82; WoOGB p.324
Mistah me! Lucy Mae Turner. BCF p.58
Mistah Robert. Anonymous. BlWOA p.235
Mistah Rabbit, mistah rabbit, yo tales mighty white. Anonymous. BlWOA p.235
Mistah Skeeter. Lucy Mae Turner. BCF p.34
Mistah skeeter--jes' skeet, on away fum hyah! Lucy Mae Turner. BCF p.34
Mistakes. E. Sharon Gomillion. FoAAM p.23
Mistakes. Gertrude Blackwell Bailey. IfWCF p.37
Mistakes. Naomi Evans Vaughn. EbR p.149
Mistakes are made by everyone. IfWCF p.37
Mistakes are made by those to err. E. Sharon Gomillion. FoAAM p.23
Mister Banjo. Anonymous. MBP p.52
Mr. Nixon, you ran and won. Olean Bess. MiFe p.12
Mr. Roosevelt Regrets. Pauli Murray. DaTAOP p.34; PoBA p.109
Mr. Suggs is all that is left of the dreams. Mari Evans. NIGHT p.19
Mixed Media. Nikki Giovanni. MyH p.24
Mneme begin inspire, ye sacred nine. Phillis Wheatley. EBAP p.105; PAL p.80; PPW p.28
Mneme, begin: inspire ye sacred nine. Phillis Wheatley. PPW p.74
Moanin', Moanin'. Lucile D. Goodlett. WGC p.32
Mode of Communication, A. June Vanleer Williams. WiRYPS p.28
Models. Leatrice Emeruwa. BlGBG p.1
Modern mather sings for...Judith Lynn who is three. Mae V. Cowdery. WLOV p.48
Modern poet, were he attempting to record your virtues, The. Margaret Danner. DoOAT p.133
Modern Song. Anonymous. MBP p. 31
Modulations. Georgia Douglas Johnson. HWOP p.35
Moe Belle Jackson's husband whipped her good last night. Gwendolyn Brooks. StIB p.37; WoOGB p.39
Molly Means. Margaret Walker. AmNP p.130; BlSi p.96; DaS p.496; FMP p.33; KAL p.142; MoCAP p.74; PoN p.178; PoNe p.309
Moment in Paradise. Lucia Mae Pitts. NegVo p.129
Moment Left Behind, A. Patricia Parker. ChOMP p.27; MoIB p.38
Momma. Maami Verano. ThHSD p. 67
Momma had words for us. Harry-

ette Mullen. TTW p.5
Momma Momma Momma Momma Momma Mammy Nanny Granny Woman Mistress Sista. June Jordan. ThTDID p.27
Momma Sayings. Harryette Mullen. TTW p.5
Momma was cold cold cold. Maami Verano. ThHSD p.67
"Momma" we call you. Melba Joyce Boyd. CaEADW p.7
Momma Welfare Roll. Maya Angelou. AnSIR p.26
Mommy did you bring my flippers. Nikki Giovanni. VaT p.51
Mommy Mommy come and see what the strawmen left for me. Audre Lorde. ChPON p.73; NeHS p. 41
Mommy watches the Soap when I wash dishes. Nikki Giovanni. VaT p.41
Mona Lisa, A. Angelina Weld Grimke. BlSi p.60; BlWOA p.627; CaD p.42
Monday Morning Blues. Naomi Long Madgett. ExAE p.36
Monday night is latin night. Ntozake Shange. NaEd p.81
Money, But Also... Marva Tatum Smith. BeYM p.6
Money cannot buy you what you want. Audre Lorde. BlUn p. 99
Monkey and the lion got to talking one day, The. Anonymous. BlWOA p.650
Monkey Man. Naomi Long Madgett. OnATM p.59
Monkeyman. Audre Lorde. ChPON p.91; NeHS p.34
Monologue. Linda Brown Bragg. LoSBM p.8
Monte Carlo Blues. Anonymous. BlWOA p.888
Monticello. Lucille Clifton. OrW p.33
Monument in Black. Vanessa Howard. ScWh p.13; SoS p.3
Mood. Pinkie Gordon Lane. WiTh p.43
Mood, The. Quandra Prettyman. PoBA p.260.
Mood Indigo. Ntozake Shange. DaGe p.13
Moods. Georgia Douglas Johnson. BrBV p.32
Moon, The. Anonymous. MBP p.3
Moon Below Me, The. Naomi Long Madgett. PhN p.25; SoTPN p.18
Moon has be one a future haven for kings, The. S. Diane Bogus. WITM p.11
Moon is not two hours old, The. Helen F. Chappell. NegVo p.29
Moon lights the earth, The. Anonymous. MBP p.3
Moon lights the wooded death spot to the shame of the wode-spreading tree, The. Isabelle McDlellan Taylor. EbR p.135
Moon marked and touched by sun. Audre Lorde. BlUn p.4
Moon minded the sun goes farther from us. Audre Lorde. ChPON p.7; COAL p.31; FiCi p.10; SiAS p.46
Moon People Speak. Olean Bess. MiFe p.6
Moon Poem. Sandra Sharp. MBP p.5
Moon saw blowing wind breathe cold upon their dripping boughs. Catherine L. Findley. EbR p.63
Moon Shines Down, The.** Nikki Giovanni. CoCRD p.90
Moon, they say, called mantis, The. TYBP p.5
Moon was an old, old woman, tonight. Esther Popel. ReFNA p.47
Moonstalk. Harryette Mullen. TTW p.44
Moratorium means well what you think it means. June Jordan. SCh p.71; ThTDID p. 131
More Melodrama. Thulani Davis. AlTRGR p.34
Morn. Josephine D. (Henderson) Heard. MoGl p.54
Morning. Bernette Golden. TNV p.39
Morning After...Love, The. Kattie M. Cumbo. BlSi p.136
Morning colors burn bright. May Miller. ClAB p.24
Morning Coming In, The. Dorothy

Randall. GLOWC p.82; ThHSD p.41
Morning in the rain, the leaves like confetti are driven & pasted. Pamela Cobb. InDM p.39
Morning is a state of mind. Bernette Golden. TNV p.39
Morning Light (The Dew-Drier). Effie Lee Newsome. AmNP p.19; CaD p.55; NeNRe p.217; PoBA p.21; PoN p.55; PoNe p.70
Morning Meditation. Pearl Cleage Lomax. WeDNNM p.16
Morning on the mountains where the mist diffuses, The. June Jordan. PaNP p.10
Morning Snow Falling.** Sonia Sanchez. IvBAW p.75
Morning Song. Pearl Cleage Lomax. WeDNNM p.5
Mornings I got up early. Lucille Clifton. GoNAE p.3
Mornings. Alice Walker. ONC p.53
Mortality. Naomi Long Madgett. MoCAP p.92; NNPUSA p.23; PoBA p.182; PoNe p.382; StBS p.16
Mose. Elma Stuckey. BiGa p.32
Moses. Lucille Clifton. GoNAE p. 32
Most often I hardly know myself. S. Diane Bogus. WITM p.50
Most things are colorful things--the sky, earth, and sea. Anne Spencer. NeNRe p.46
Mother, The. Georgia Douglas Johnson. BrBV p.41
Mother, The. Gwendolyn Brooks. AfAWA p.579; BlP p.165; BlSi p.100; BlVo p.461; BlWOA p.715; MoCAP p.79; SoOM p.557; SPGB p.4; StIB p.3; WoOGB p.5
Mother. Josephine D. (Henderson) Heard. MoGl p.25
Mother. Leatrice Emeruwa. BlGBG p.2
Mother, The. Naomi Long Madgett. PiLAF p.26
Mother America. Hazel L. Washington. EbR p.151
Mother and Child. Elma Stuckey. BiGa p.27
Mother and Dad. Gertrude Blackwell Bailey. IfWCF p.20
Mother Bore my Three Sisters and Two Brothers.** Gloria Oden. RESUR p.47
Mother, dear mother, I'm dying. Patricia Parker. ChOM p.14; MoIB p.51
Mother, I Am Mad.** Lucille Clifton. TwW p.53
Mother of Nightmares, The. Harryette Mullen. TTW p.29
Mother Palm had plaited her daughter's hair for us. Nikki Giovanni. Rec p.7
Mother sat on the curve of her bed, The. Lateifa-Ramona Lahleet Hyman. CoAAAW p.150
Mother soothes her mantled child, The. Georgia Douglas Johnson. BrBV p.41
Mother was an Afr'an princess. Leatrice Emeruwa. BlGBG p. 2
Mothering Blackness, The. Maya Angelou. JGM p.18
Motherless Child. Anonymous. BLIA p.40; BlWOA p.239
Mothers. Nikki Giovanni. MyH p.6
Mothers cranking the machine, adding milk to make ice cream. Carole Gregory Clemmons. BlSi p.190
Mothers, go to school very unexpectedly. Gertrude Blackwell Bailey. IfWCF p. 18
Mother's Habits. Nikki Giovanni. BlSi p.236; WoATM p.25
Mother's Love, A. Josephine D. (Henderson) Heard
Mother's Treasures. Frances E. W. Harper. PBFH p.56
Moths. <u>See</u> Poems: Birmingham 1962-1964. Julia Fields
Mount Zion. Anonymous. AmLNA p.6
Mountain is earth's mouth, A. Mae V. Cowdery. WLOV p.13
Mountain Stream. Bessie Woodson Yancey. EcFTH p.6
Mountains at Night. Lucy Mae Turner. BCF p.53
Mountains lift their hoary heads on high, The. Lucy Mae Turner. BCF p.53

Mourners Bench. Elma Stuckey. BiGa p.71
Mournful winter's sky in its sorrow sobbed, A. Dorothy Lee Louise Shaed. NegVo p.140
Mournful Grace. Maya Angelou. JGM p.20
Mourning suns filter thru her. Regina Williams. CoAAAW p. 378
Mouth laced with gold stars with diamond centers, The. Thulani Davis. AlTRGR p.7
Move away from him she said. Carolyn M. Rodgers. HeAEG p.17
Move from the middle of the mirror, Grandmother. Margaret Danner. DoOAT p.40
Move in Closeness. Patricia Parker. MoIB p.97
Move in Darkness Know the Truth of a Woman. Patricia Parker. ChOM p.28
Move over, white boy, because I'm moving up. Gertrude Blackwell Bailey. IfWCF p.57
Movement in Black. Patricia Parker. MoIB p.86
Movement Song. Audre Lorde. ChPON p.63; FrLWP p.34
Movin' Nowhere. Elma Stuckey. BiGa p.65
Moving. Josephine D. (Henderson) Heard. MoGl p.106
Moving back into the sun. Pamela Cobb. InDM p.29
Moving constantly, some destiny calling out to me. Sonia Sanchez. BluB p.38
Moving In. Audre Lorde. ChPON p.63; FrLWP p.25
Moving out or the end of cooperative living. Audre Lorde. ChPON p.61; FrLWP p.22
Moving slowly...against time. Nikki Giovanni. ThWRNW p.38
Mozetta Lee. Sandra Royster. WoTa p.11
Ms. Claus. Toi Derricotte. EmDH p.49
Mud turtle settin' on de end of a log. Anonymous. BlP p.18
Muffin at the Baha'i Temple. Margaret Danner. DOOAT p.29
Muffin, His Baba and the Boneman. Margaret Danner. DoOAT p.95
Muffin on the Population explosion. Margaret Danner. DoOAT p.16
Muffle Jaw, I Remember You. Naomi Long Madgett. ExAE p. 17
Mulatto. Eleanor Weaver. NegVo p.162
Mulatto's Dilemma. Pauli Murray. DaTAOP p.33
Murder, The. Gwendolyn Brooks. StIB p.20; WoOGB p.22
Murder is as common as worms these days. S. Diane Bogus. WITM p.61
Murder self slowly. Linyatta. JuBa p.77
Murderer Awaiting Sentence. Ruby Stevens. NegVo p.145
Muderous intent with a deadly weapon. Rashidah Ismaili. CoAAAW p.162
Music. Alice Dunbar-Nelson. BlSi p.67
Music. Josephine D. (Henderson) Heard. MoGl p.55
Music comes to me from all corners of the room, The. Pinkie Gordon Lane. MyFe p. 17
Music From Home. Colleen McElroy. MuDLSG p.33
Music! lilting, soft and languorous. Alice Dunbar-Nelson. BlSi p.67
Mute-lipped-unquestioning grim-visaged fate. Georgia Douglas Johnson. ALC p.33
M'wezi wa baridi a coldness a white/ness. Mari Evans. NIGHT p.64
My Arkansas. Maya Angelou. AnSIR p.21; BlSi p.266
My babies: Black and shining jewel. Sandra Royster. WoTa p.9
My baby she found a brand new place to go. Anonymous. BlWOA p.888
My bed one-sided from me sleepin alone so mucha the time. Sherley Williams. PePo p. 11
My Birthright, Too. Margaret

Danner. UNBP p.231
My Black prince has come to me and I have to him. Alexis Yancey. AOS p.2
My Black sisters and brothers are dieing. Kali Grosvenor. PBK p.25
My Blk/ness like poetry is not to be deceived. Alicia Loy Johnson. CNAW p.769; GaBW p.340; NiBPo p.148
My blood sang to the music of pulsing heat when you came near me. Dorothy F. Blackwell. EbR p.6
My boat sails downstream. Anonymous. TYBP p.31
My body arching across your white place. Audre Lorde. CaTR p. 24
My body is weak and sickly. Elma Stuckey. BiGa p.21
My Body Waiting. Sonia Sanchez. IvBAW p.71
My bones a-creakin' on a creaky bed. Elma Stuckey. BiGa p. 64
My Boy. Georgia Douglas Johnson. BrBV p.46
My Boys. Lucille Clifton. OrW p.27
My boys beauty is numberless. Lucille Clifton. OrW p.27
My branch of thoughts is frail tonight. Blanche Taylor Dickinson. EbAT p.51
My breath leaves me. Patricia Parker. ChOM p.10; MoIB p.49
My Brother. Eloise Culver. GANIV p.80
My Brother Malcolm. Christine O. Johnson. FoM p.3
My brothers are rough tumble shake somersault crack bang! Linda Brown Bragg. LoSBM p.29
My Canary. Josephine D. (Henderson) Heard. MoGl p.54
My carnation is in the black wings of your being. S. Diane Bogus. WITM p.15
My Children Are Me. Vanessa Howard. ScWh p.21
My children are unique. Vanessa Howard. ScWh p.20
My children, my children, remember the day. Margaret T. G. Burroughs. WhSIT p.30
My children play with skulls. Audre Lorde. BlUn p.55
My children's voices sing in the midst of it all. Kattie M. Cumbo. NiBPo p.49
My Choice. Naomi Long Madgett. PhN p.14
My City Garden Plot. Lucy Mae Turner. BCF p.34
My colored child/hood wuz mostly music. Angela Jackson. VoDLM p.8
My conscience commissions me to take pen and paper. Damali (Denise Burnett) IATWMB p. 15
My contraceptive history pregnant with pain. Akua Lezli Hope. CoAAAW p.141
My daddy don't know the same lady I do. Carolyn M. Rodgers. HoIGO p.42
My daddy has paid the rent. Lucille Clifton. BlP p.250; DOBB p.52; MoCAP p.140; OnOW p.53; PoBA p.306
My daughter marks the day that Spring begins. Audre Lorde. ChPON p.39; FrLWP p.11
My days are filled with diets and charts. Mae V. Cowdery. WLOV p.48
My Dream About Being White. Lucille Clifton. CoAAAW p. 87
My dreams, my works, must wait till after hell. Gwendolyn Brooks. SPGB p.23; StIB p.48; WoOGB p.50
My eager waiting heart can bear no more. Josephine D. (Henderson) Heard. MoGl p.30
My ears have heard the battle drum. Anonymous. MyNIB p.16
My eye walked lightly over their faces until it stopped. Mari Evans. WhIAM p.8
My fairy godmother retired with the Brown vs Ferguson decision. Ntozake Shange. NaEd p.55
My Father. May Miller. ClAB p. 33

My father (back blistered) beat me because I could not stop crying. Alice Walker. ONC p.43
My father came in the darkness. Anonymous. TYBP p.9
My Father is a Retired Magician. Ntozake Shange. NaEd p.136
My father, it is surely a blue place and straight. Gwendolyn Brooks. ITBLA p.217; KAL p. 151; SPGB p.5; StIB p.9; WoOGB p.11
My fathers sits on benches. Maya Angelou. OhPWFW p.55
My favorite things is u/blowen yo/ favorite/things. Sonia Sanchez. UNBP p.274; WABP p.69
My Fear is What I Remember Most. ** Gloria Oden. RESUR p.79
My feet kiss the pavement on Castillo. Wanda Coleman. MaDBL p.128
My fellow eggs and apples rising acid. June Jordan. ThTDID p.92
My Fifth Trip to Washington Ended in Northeast Delaware. Audre Lorde. ChPON p.84; NeHS p.19
My Friend. Beth Hollender. GLOWC p.25
My friend--he is the most fabulous person. Beth Hollender. GLOWC p.25
My friend they don't care if you're an individualist. Jayne Cortez. CoAAAW p.90; COAG p.68
My friend was decently wild as a child. Gwendolyn Brooks. StIB p.16; WoOGB p.18
My friend, your face is showing. Pinkie Gordon Lane. BlSi p. 232; MyFe p.38
My Friends. Lucille Clifton. TwW p.28
My Frow Towards the City. Anonymous. ThHSD p.24
My Garden. Gertrude Blackwell Bailey. IfWCF p.35
My garden will be...a garden of love. Gertrude Blackwell Bailey. IfWCF p.35
My girls my girls my almost me mellowed in a brown bag. Lucille Clifton. OrW p.29
My God is a Rock in a Weary Land. Anonymous. UNBP p.79
My God is Everywhere. June Vanleer Williams. WiRYPS p.3
My God sometimes I cannot pray. Josephine D. (Henderson) Heard. MoGl p.61
My Grace is Sufficient. Josephine D. (Henderson) Heard. MoGl p.56
My Grandmama don't believe they walked in space. Thadious M. Davis. BlSi p.276
My Grandmother. Harryette Mullen. TTW p.12
My Grandmother Don't Believe They Walked in Space. Thadious M. Davis. BlSi p. 276
My Grandmother haunted the halls above Webster's Funeral Home. Toi Derricotte. EmDH p.42
My Grandmothers were strong. Margaret Walker. BlSi p.94; BOL p.59; DeRi p.14; FMP p. 25; KAL p.141; MoCAP p.77; PoBA p.148
My grandpa was a doughboy from Carolina. Ntozake Shange. NaEd p.54
My Guilt. Maya Angelou. JGM p.42
My guilt is "slavery's chains," too long. Maya Angelou. JGM p.42
My hair is springy like the forest grasses. Naomi Long Madgett. BlSi p.130; FBPA p.95; PiLAF p.54; PoBA p. 183
My Hands are Big and Tough.** Patricia Parker. MoIB p.43
My Hate. Leighla Lewis. NegVo p.96
My hatred for you is a beautiful thing. Beatrice M. Murphy. NegVo p.114
My heart is ever green. Carolyn M. Rodgers. HeAEG p.53
Hy heart is fresh cement. Patricia Parker. MoIB p.49
My heart is full of ghosts tonight. Mae V. Cowdery. WLOV p.54
My heart is incased in rubies

of red that are full of seeds of malice in man. Martha E. Lyons. EbR p.103
My heart is pregnant with a great dispair. Georgia Douglas Johnson. BrBV p.32
My heart that was so passionless. Jessie Redmond Fauset. CaD p. 70
My House. Nikki Giovanni. MyH p.67
My house is filled with simple fools. Beatrice M. Murphy. NegVo p.114
My husband sits buddha like. Sonia Sanchez. LoP p.3
My Jibaro Man. Frances Garcia. ThHSD p.63
My joy leaps with your ecstasy. Georgia Douglas Johnson. HWOP p.4
My Lady Ain't No Lady.** Patricia Parker. MoIB p.113
My Lai as Related to no Vietnam Alabama. Carolyn M. Rodgers. AfAWA p.776
My last defense is the present tense. Gwendolyn Brooks. BeEa p.18; SPGB p.74; WoOGB p.316
My Last Feeling This Way Poem. Mae Jackson. CoAAAW p.170
My last night of bondage. Naomi Long Madgett. PhN p.68
My Last Year in High School.** Gloria Oden. RESUR p.97
My legs swollen from pressing pedals. Jayne Cortez. FeAF p.14; NeBV p.234
My lfe hs bn abrev's since yr bust. Lyn SiSH p.25
My Life. Henrietta C. Parks. TNV p.84
My life is a bald headed match. Peggy Susberry Kenner. JuBa p.106
My lips were never meant to mold. Ruby Stevens. NegVo p.147
My Little 'Bout-Town Girl. ** Gwendolyn Brooks. BeEa p.14; SPGB p.70; WoOGB p.312
My Little Dreams. Georgia Douglas Johnson. BANP p.184; BlSi p.59; CaD p.79; GoS p.196; HWOP p.62; PoN p. 60; PoNe p.81
My little one when I am away from you. Margaret T. G. Burroughs. WhSIT p.10
My Lord, he calls me. Anonymous. AmLNA p.5
MY Lord, my Lord, long have I cried out to Thee. Maya Angelou. AnSIR p.50
My Lord, What a Mornin! Anonymous. BlLi p.112
My Love. Joanne Jimason. NaEBE p.37
My love I am sure that I have kissed the face of the moon. Joanne Jimason. NaEBE p.37
My love is a lotus blossom. Anonymous. TYBP p.28
My Lover is a Woman.** Patricia Parker. MoIB p.98
My Lover is a Fisherman. Gertrude Davenport. BTh p.51
My lover, my brother which one to me. Nola Richardson. WhOL p.35
My lover one is unique without a peer. Anonymous. TYPB p.31
My Mama Moved Among the Days.** Lucille Clifton. BlSi p. 248; DeDF p.16; MoCAP p. 139; PoBA p.308
My man don't try none of your jealous shit with me. Sonia Sanchez. HoC p.13
My man is Black, golden amber. Maya Angelou. JGM p.6
My Man Let Me Pull Your Coat. Mari Evans. BlVo p.480; IABW p.82
My man loved me so much he wanted to kill me. Jayne Cortez. Scar p.45
My man should've been a scientist. June Vanleer Williams. WiRYPS p.27
My Man Was Here Today, Fareedah Allah. RoATW p.84
My Mind. Eleanor Thomas-Grumbach. MoSu p.16
My mind is never silent. Eleanor Thomas-Grumbach. MoSu p.16
My Mistatke. Pamela Cobb. InDM p.40
My Mocking Bird. Josephine D. (Henderson) Heard. MoGl p.54
My Momma Moved Among the Days.

Lucile Clifton. DoBB p.50
My Mother. Kali Grosvenor. PBK p.43
My Mother. Eleanor A. Thompson. BTh p.43
My mother, bastared by southern greed. Toi Derricotte. EmDH p.40
My mother cried. Lyn. SiSH p.6
My mother had two faces and a frying pot. Audre Lorde. BlUn p.6
My mother her sad eyes worn as bark faces me in the mirror. Lucille Clifton. CoAAAW p.88
My mother is a never-failing light. Eleanor A. Thompson. BTh p.43
My mother is an indictment. Akua Lezli Hope. CoAAAW p.143
My mother is lovely. Kali Grosvenor. PBK p.43
My mother is so proud of me. Gertrude Blackwell Bailey. IfWCF p.49
My mother murdering me. June Jordan. ThTDID p.25
My mother told me that after he left us. Harryette Mullen. TTW p.18
My mother taught each one of us to pray. Audre Lorde. NeHS p.40
My mother warned me I'd perish in dirt. Harryette Mullen. TTW p.22
My mother was called Gertrude. Gertrude Blackwell Bailey. IfWCF p.20
My Mother's Blessing. Olean Bess. MiFe p.7
My mother's face is liquid. Angela Jackson. VoDLM p.15
My Mother's Kiss. Frances E. W. Harper. PBFH p.1
My mother's kiss, my mother's kiss, I feel its impress now. Frances E. W. Harper. PBFH p.1
My name is Black. Kathy Weathers. MyNIB p.159
My needing, really, my own sweet good. Gwendolyn Brooks. Ana p.15
My ol missus promise me. Anonymous. BlWOA p.235
My old man tells me I'm so full of sweet. Sonia Sanchez. HoC p.17; IvBAW p.5
My ole mistiss promise me. Anonymous. BlP p.5
My orgasm is like a delicate disc. S. Diane Bogus. WITM p.20
My Own, Naomi Long Madgett. OnATM p.18
My Own Sweet Good. Gwendolyn Brooks. AnA p.15; WoOGB p.79
My outward self is prim and staid. Marie E. Alexandre. NegVo p.12
My Path is Lighted by a Star.** Lucy Mae Turner. BCF p.55
My pathway lies through worse than death. Georgia Douglas Johnson. AmNP p.24; HoFTD p.102
My pen is my guardian. Jean. AOS p.4
My People. Kali Grosvenor. PBK p.20
My People are Black.** Kali Grosvenor. PBK p.23
My Poem. Lucille Clifton. OrW p.65
My Poem. Nikki Giovanni. BFBTBJ p.95; BlLi p.534; BlP p.319; BOL p.23; BrT p.58; NaPr p.29; NeBV p.250; PoBa p.453; TNV p.35; YoBBI p.476
My poor wealth had been spent thst afternoon off. Lucia M. Pitts. EbR p.121
My potential is greater now that his face has vanished. S. Diane Bogus. WITM p.1
My precious seed sown, from a little lad. Eleanor Thomas-Grumbach. MoSu p.8
My proper prudence toward his proper probe astonished their ancestral seemliness. Gwendolyn Brooks. BlWOA p.719; SPGB p.115
My Puertorican husband who feeds me. Sonia Sanchez. LoP p. 4
My questions concern the subject poetry. Ntozake Shange. NaEd p.56

My rag is red, my couch, where on I deal. Gloria Oden. AmNP p.161; NNPYSA p.47; PoNE p.385
My Rainy Day. Maurine L. Jeffery. HeD p.23
My roots are deep in southern life. Margaret Walker. FMP p.19
My Rug is Red. Gloria Oden. MoCAP p.97
My Sadness Sits Around Me.** June Jordan. BlP p.248; SCh o,30; ThTDID p.52
My Saucer Done Cracked. Elma Stuckey. BiGa p.66
My Sea of Tears. Deborah Fuller Wess. EbR p.159
My separate self must range from star to star. Pauli Murray. DaTAOP p.83
My Sister and I. Helen Morgan Brooks. NNPUSA p.109; PoNe p.274
My sister and I have been raised to hate genteelly. Audre Lorde. BlUn p.111
My sister has my hair my mouth my eyes and I presume her trustless. Audre Lorde. ChPON p.18; COAL p.14; FiCi p.3
My Sister is a Sister.** Kali Grosvenor. PBK p.47
My sisters do not write. Wanda Coleman. MaDBL p.40
My son awoke, yet unborn, to talk of the visions that he sees. S. Diane Bogus. WITM p.48
My own prince of peace in war like raiment. Marion Nicholes. LiS p.18
"My son," said father, "you are young." Eloise Culver. GANIV p.21
My Song. Naomi Long Madgett. OnATM p.23
My Soul. Marie E. Alexander. NegVo p.12
My soul cried out to you. Marsha Ann Jackson. TNV p. 53
My soul is a petal. Carole Gregory Clemmons. GaBW p.269
My soul is a stream that washes out to the sea at night. Joanne Jimason. HoDo p.27
My spirit leans in joyousness tow'rd thine. Ada. BlSi o,17
My sunlight came pre-packaged. Naomi Long Madgett. BlSi p.129; ExAE p.32
My sweet, red blood to snuff the yellow haze. Lois Augusta Cuglar. EbAT p.114
My teacher asked a pupil: "what is it you desire most?" Mary Bohanon. GaBW p.258
My Tears Don't Come Cheap Anymore. G. Tillery Banks. HeTMWL p.49
My Thoughts are Free.** Eleanor Thomas-Grumbach. MoSu p.11
My Thoughts Are I Love You. Vanessa Howard.
My throats a hungry saxaphone longing the cold train. Angela Jackson. VoDLM p.20
My Thumb in My Eye. Joanne Jimason. NeABE p.26
My time is nearly up. Vera Guerard. TNV p.46
My tired eyes unceasingly have searched the wide world through and through. Naomi Long Madgett. PhN p.49
My tongue whips blood through the ribs of a cobra. Jayne Cortez. FeAF o,20
My tower. Nikki Giovanni. MyH p.45
My trouble is I always try to save everything. Naomi Long Madgett. ExAE o,69
My Truth and my Flame. Margaret Walker. CoAAAW p.361
My uncle is a sergeant in the army now. Deborah Fuller Wess. EbR p.159
My Way's Cloudy. Anonymous. BiLi p.112
My window is his wall. Lucille Clifton. GoNAE p.18
My window opens out into the trees. Clarissa Scott Delany. PoBA o,71; ReFNA o,44
My windows and doors are barren. Naomi Long Madgett. ExAE p.29

My words shall drip like molten lava. Mae V. Cowdery. WLOV p.18
Myself. Juanita Brown. PoBBl p.44
Mysteries. Alice Walker. RePOP p.52
Mystery. Elma Stuckey. BiGa p. 24
Mystery That Surely is Present, The. Lucille Clifton. TwW p.33
Mystic Female, The. Pinkie Gordon Lane. MyFe p.11
Mystic land of wild, black nights, A. Ethel Coleman. NegVo p.39
Myth going around. Loretta Rodgers. RoATW p.81; ThHSD p.83

- N -

Naked. Mary Bohanon. GaBW p.262
Naked Against the Belly of the Earth. Joanne Jimason. NaABE p.1
Nam, The. Jill Witherspoon Boyer. DrF p.16
Name Change, A. Abbey Lincoln. CoAAAW p.189
Name Lightfoot implies a swift and heady, airy kind of flight, The. Margaret Danner. DoOAT p.135
Name Michael Brings the Whirr of Wings, The. Margaret Danner. DoOAT p.127
Name of the beast is man, The. Sonia Sanchez. BlWOA p.822; NBP p.114
Name of this poem is George Washington, The. June Jordan. BlP p.243; SCh p.76; ThTDID p.115
Names of the things, The. Lucille Clifton. GoNAE p.30
Naming, The. Toi Derricotte. EmDH p.45
Naomi. Gwendolyn Brooks. BeEa p.60; WoOGB p.358
Nappy Edges (A Cross Country Sojourn) Ntozake Shange BlSi p.268; NaEd p.86
Nat Turner, Ophelia Robinson. AmLNA p.51
Nat Turner, an Epitaph. Lucy Mae Turner. BCF p.64
Nat Turner was a slave who stood for a supreme great brotherhood. Lucy Mae Turner. BCF p.64
National Cemetery, Beaufort, South Carolina, The. Josephine D. (Henderson) Heard. MoGl p.82
National Security. Jayne Cortez. Scar p.42
Native. Naomi Long Madgett. BlVo p.476; MoCAP p.92; StBS p.19
Natives of America, The. Ann Plato. BlSi p.43; EBAP p. 118
Natural Aruba. Vanessa Howard. ScWh p.19
Natural Habitat of Things That Bite, The. Wanda Coleman. MaDBL p.58
Naturalism is easier than playing games. Vanessa Howard. ScWh p.19
Naturally. Audre Lorde. BlSi p.203; DeDF p.63; MoCAP p.122; NaPr p.65; NeHS p. 35; SoS p.87; UNBP p.283
Nature of Struggle, The. Pamela Cobb. InDM p.26
Nature of the beast is the man, The. Sonia Sanchez. HoC p. 17; IvBAW p.6
Nature of This Flower is to Bloom, The. Alice Walker. RePOP p.70
Nature tests those she would call hers. Patricia Parker. ChOM p.33; MoIB p.39
Naw, love ain't hip. Sandra Royster. BrA p.18; RoATW p.97; WoTa p.6
Naw, naw, little brother u don't shoot no-brother! Ronda M. Davis. BrT p.181
Nay, Captain, get you back into your bonds. Naomi Long Madgett. PhN p.109
Nay, do not blush! Frances E. W. Harper. AfAV p.83; RoATW p. 92

Nazarene. Pauli Murray. DaTAOP p.68
Nebulous. Nancy L. Arnez. RoCO p.23
Need: a Chorale of Black Women's Voices. Audre Lorde. ChPON p.111; CoAAAW p.191
Needed/poem/for my salvation, A. Sonia Sanchez. BrT p.140; WABP p.49
Negro Choir. Beatrice M. Murphy. RoCO p.13
Negro Church, The. Andrea Razafkerlefo. NeNRe p.378
Negro here. Gwendolyn Brooks. KAL p.152
Negro Hero. Gwendolyn Broooks. SPGB p.19; StIB p.30; WoOGB p.32
Negro in New York, A. Naomi Long Madgett. OnATM p.53
Negro Lullaby. Bessie Woodson Yancey. EcFTH p.50
Negro Soldier's Civil War Chant. Anonymous. BlP p.7
Negro Speaks of Night, A. Iola M. Brister. EbR p.14
Negro Spirituals. Eloise Culver. GANIV p.19
Negro Woman, The. Andrea Razafkeriefo. NeNRe p.363
Negro Woman, The. Bessie Woodson Yancey. EcFTH p.31
Negroes listen to me. Kattie M. Cumbo. NiBPo p.46
Neighbor! Pearl Cleage Lomax. WeDNNM p.15
Neighbors. Audre Lorde. CaD p.47; ChPON p.46; FrLWP p.26
Never!! Lyn. SiSH p.15
Never Again. Colleen McElroy. MuDLSG p.25
Never May My Thirst for Freedom. Sonia Sanchez. IvBAW p.72
Never mind if dawns refuse to waken you. Naomi Long Madgett. OnATM p.22; StBS p.27
Never, never, never. Lucia M. Pitts. EbR p.120
Never Take Fire From Women. Audre Lorde. BlUn p.111
Never tickle a prickled pickle. Nikki Giovanni. VaT p.29
Never Without Remembrance.** Naomi Long Madgett. PiLAF p.40.
Never would I seek to capture you with tempestous ardor. Mae V. Cowdery. WLOV p.50
New Address. Elma Stuckey. BiGa p.86
New Blues From a Brown Baby. Sandra Sharp. RoATW p.67
New Bones. Lucille Clifton. OrW p.17
New Calvary. Naomi Long Madgett. OnATM p.57
New Chapters For Our History. Rosemari Mealy. CoAAAW p.223
New Cologne, A. Jayne Cortez. **Scar p.19**
New Day. Naomi Long Madgett. BlSi p.130; ExAE p.37
New Direction. C. Tillery Banks. HeTMWL p.14
New Face. Alice Walker. RePOP p.66
New House. Naomi Long Madgett. PhN p.103
New Lady Godiva. Toi Derricotte. EmDH p.32
New Leaf. Naomi Long Madgett. OnATM p.36
New Leaf. Wanda Coleman. MaDBL p.122
New Like Magasaki Nice Like Nicene. June Jordan. SCh p.61; ThTDID p.130
New Love. Nancy L. Arnez. RoCO p.24
New Math, The. Vanessa Howard. ScWh p.15
New Name. Marva Tatum Smith. BeYM p.4
New Organ, The. Josephine D. (Henderson) Heard. MoGl p.68
New Pieta: for the Mother and Children of Detroit. June Jordan. SCh p.5
New pimp don't drive no cadillac, The. Marion Nicholes. LiS p.12
New Testament Remembered. Marva Tatum Smith. BeYM p.15
New World Coro. Ntozake Shange. DaGe p.52
New Year. Lucille Clifton. TwW p.25

New Year's Day. Audre Lorde. ChPON p.45; FrLWP p.19
New Year's Prayer. Ruby Berkley Godwin. EbR p.67
New York at 3 a.m. the yellow lamps spot light. Carolyn M. Rodgers. HeAEG p.40
New York City. Audre Lorde. ChPON p.73
New York City 1970. Audre Lorde. NeBV p.289; NeHS p.1
New York he was caught in a penitentiary of tears. Jayne Cortez. Scar p.46
New York I'm embellished by your face of plaster. Jayne Cortez. Scar p.38
New York won't you confess. Jayne Cortez. COAG p.14; Scar p.55
New Yorkers, The. Nikki Giovanni. CoCRD p.29
Newark, for now. Carolyn M. Rodgers. PoBA p.430
Newblack. Naomi Long Madgett. PiLAF p.60
Newer Cry, The. Pauli Murray. DaTAOP p.54
Newest Star, The. (A Memorial to W. E. B. DuBois, 1868-1963, Massachusetts) Eloise Culver. GANIV p.48
News. Elma Stuckey. BiGa p.87
News, The. Lucille Clifton. GoNAE p.11
Newspaper told the story, The. Carolyn M. Rodgers. HoIGO p.27
Next Spring. Naomi Long Madgett. OnATM p.38
Next to me a boy is wearing a red brocaded velvet jacket. June Jordan. ThTDID p.185
Next to not Having Beautiful Daughters.** Gloria Oden. RESUR p.119
Next to you I do nothing to perfect my safety. June Jordan. PaNP p.53
Niagra Falls. June Jordan. PaNP p.73
Nicodemus. Carolyn M. Rodgers. HeAEG p.61
Nicodemus Quartette: I. Mari Evans. NIGHT p.17
Nicodemus Quartette: II. Mari Evans. NIGHT p.19
Nicodemus Quartette: III. Mari Evans. NIGHT p.21
Nicodemus Quartette:IV. Mari Evans. NIGHT p.22
Nigger. Sonia Sanchez. BlP p. 232; HoC p.12
Nigger can you kill. Nikki Giovanni. BFBTBJ p.19; BlP p.318; BrT p.48; PoBA p. 451
Nigger, that word ain't shit to me. Sonia Sanchez. BlP p. 232; HoC p.12
Nigger, them grits was too soggy. Linda Cousins. ThHSD p.46
Nigger Who is Now Hunting You, The. Mari Evans. NIGHT p.67
Niggers with naturals still smoking pot. Sonia Sanchez. NaPr p.127
Nigguhs with naturals still smoken pot. Sonia Sanchez. BrT p.144; WABP p.63
Night. Bessie Woodson Yancey. EcFTH p.7
Night. Birdelle Wycoff Ransom. HeD p.34
Night. Josephine D. (Henderson) Heard. MoGl p.19
Night, The. Kattie M. Cumbo. NiBPo p.55
Night. Nikki Giovanni. WoATM p.51
Night Club Entrance. Iola M. Brister. NegVo p.16
Night is beautiful, The. Vanessa Howard. ScWh p.33
Night Letter #3. Ntozake Shange. NaEd p.47
Night of Death, The. Frances E. W. Harper. PBFH p.53
Night People. Colleen McElroy. MuDLSG p.9
Night Pumping Like an Otis Redding. Sonia Sanchez. IvBAW p.76
Night Rider. Naomi Long Madgett. StBS p.26
Night Rising. Pinkie Gordon Lane. PoBBl p.9; WiTh p.22
Night Seems to Cry, The. Vanessa Howard. ScWh p.53
Night Song. Katharine Beverly.

EbR p.3
Night Song. Pearl Cleage Lomax. WeDNNM p.10
Night turned over in her sleep. Mae V. Cowdery. WLOV p.12
Night was made for rest and sleep. Clarissa Scott Delany. ANP p. 129; CaD p.142; PoN p.96; PoNe p.181
Night Watch. Naomi Long Madgett. OnATM p.13
Night We Slept on the Beach, The. Harryette Mullen. TTW p.33
Night, you are upon us. Birdelle Wycoff Ransom. HeD p.34
Nightletters. June Jordan. PaNP p.53
Nightmare. Ann Wallace. GLOWC p.32
Nightstone. Audre Lorde. FiCi p.12
Nighttrains. Jayne Cortez. COAG p.38; MoOP p.43
Nikki-Rosa. Nikki Giovanni. BFBTBJ p.58; BlP p.48 BlSi p.233; EgT p.16; ITSA p.208; MoCAP p.169; NaPr p.22; NBP p.53: OnOW p.49 PoBA p.451; SoS p.22; YoBBI p.475
Nina. Mae Jackson. CaPWY p.8
Nina Simone. Carole Gregory Clemmons. GaBW p.270
9 Lines. Johari Amini. LetGSW p.12
Nine to Five. Jill Witherspoon Boyer. DrF p.17
1964 Valentine to my Grandson. Margaret Danner. DoOAT p.36
1965. Melba Joyce Boyd. CaEADW p.10
1977: Poem for Mrs. Fannie Lou Hamer. June Jordan. PaNP p.40
1978. June Jordan. PaNP p.24
Ninth Michael, The. Margaret Danner. DoOAT p.131
Niobe in Distress for her Children Slain by Apollo. Phillis Wheatley. EaNAW p.44; PAL p.94; PPW p.47
Nite paused, The. Sonia Sanchez. LoP p.75
Nitecaps I. Margaret Danner. DoOAT p.135
No Bargains Today. Peggy Susberry Kenner. JuBa p.94
No cold no snow--warmth. Kattie M. Cumbo. NiBPo p.58
No Dawns. Julianne Perry. PoBA p.516
No doubt she was a singerof naughty verse. Alice Walker. RePOP p.45
No Exit. Pamela Cobb. InDM p. 41
No Fixed Place. Alice Walker. RePOP p.65
No flaiming point of beauty is edge. Leighla Lewis. NegVo p.96
No Flowers. Elma Stuckey. BiGa p.71
No gorgeous coat has he. Josephine D. (Henderson) Heard. MoGl p.54
No Gusts of Wind Tickle Me. Ntozake Shange. NaEd p.106
No, I cannot turn from love. Sarah Webster Fabio. BlSi p.140; DOBB p.30
No I don't think you were chicken not to speak. Audre Lorde. BlUn p.88
No light entered the darkened room. Louise Blackman. EbR p.5
No lodge with banners flappin! Gwendolyn Brooks. StIB p. 36; WoOGB p.38
No Loser, No Weepers. Maya Angelou. JGM p.8
No Love. Marion Nicholes. LiS p.15
No love baby don't speak to me of love. Marion Nicholes. LiS p.15
No Love/Just Response. Nola Richardson. WhOL p.23
No matter what fools say, my marse was kind to me. Elma Stuckey. BiGa p.22
No mere gymnast you are he who gives. Julia Fields. GaBW p.302
No Mo Cane on Dis Brazis. Anonymous. BlWOA p.45
No mo meetings where u talk bout whitey. Sonia Sanchez. BlP p.235; WABP p.48
No More Auction Block.** Anonmous. BlEx p.8; BiLi p.114;

ITBLA p.98
No More Auction Block. Spiritual. BlP p.21
No more driver call for me. Anonymous. BlWOA p.313
No More Love Poems #1. Ntozake Shange. BlSi p.272
No more the chicken and the egg come. June Jordan. ThTDID p.93
No more the feel uf your hand. Mae V. Cowdery. WLOV p.29
No more the flow'ry scences of pleasure rise. Phillis Wheatley. PAL p.64; PPW p. 43
No More Ugly Days for Me.** C. Tillery Banks. HeTMWL p.4
No Need of Sound. Naomi Long Madgett. OnATM p.25
No Nina Simone tonight. Lyn. SiSH p.27
No, no, Bessie didn't smoke pot, not Bessie, nothing like that --just regular refers. Sherley Willimans. ChOSa p.117
No no no I am not doing my 'thing. Sharon Scott. JuBa p.174
No no no no. Maya Angelou. JGM p.38
No, nothing remains the same. Pinkie Gordon Lane. MyFe p. 45; WiTh p.54
No one can communicate to you. Lucy Smith. NNPUSA p.45
No one is left here to eat by my fire. Audre Lorde. FrLWP p. 31
No one is robbed of stone. Audre Lorde. FiCi p.12
No One Knows the Year. Mari Evans. NIGHT p.77
No one should feel peculiar living as they do. June Jordan. SCh p.9; ThTDID p. 165
No Poem Because Time is not a Name. June Jordan. ThTDID p.72
No Reservations. Nikki Giovanni. BrT p.64; Rec p.9; WoATM p.52
No Revival. June Vanleer Williams. WiRYPS p.71
No Sign Shall be Given. Marva Tatum Smith. BeYM p.2
No Simple Explanation. Jayne Cortez. COAG p.71
No sleep tonight not even after all the red and green pills. Sonia Sanchez. BlFi p.252; BlP p.233; BrT p.138; HoC p.14; IvBAW p.8
No sound falls from the morning sky. Maya Angelou. JGM p. 17
No Stars Tonight.** Naomi Long Madgett. PhN p.29; SoTPN p.27
No straight lines but drooping shoulders. Jodi Braxton. SoITM p.4
No such thing as a witch, just a woman, needing some love. Carolyn M. Rodgers. HoIGO p.41
No the two legg'd beasts that walk like me. Maya Angelou. JGM p.38
No they will not understand. Lucille Clifton. TwW p.28
No Time. Mae Jackson. CaPWY p.7
No Time. Marion Nicholes. LiS p.17
No Time for Poetry. Julia Fields. AmNP p.183; ITBLA p.275; MoCAP p.149
No Train of Thought. June Jordan. ThTDID p.112
No train of thought, April 4, 1969. June Jordan. SCh p. 64
No Violin At All. Margaret Danner. DoOAT p.50
No Way Out. June Vanleer Williams. WiRYPS p.4
No Way Out. Linda Curry. SoS p.8
No we didn't live in a one room shack. Jennifer Blackman Lawson. BlIMT p.33
No Wings. Elma Stuckey. BiGa p.5
No Woman's Land. Wanda Coleman. MaDBL p.26
Noblesse Oblige. Jessie Redmond Fauset. CaD p.67; NeNRe p.76; ReFNA p.38
Nobody can have as much fun as

while being so oblivious. Naomi Long Madgett. PiLAF p.58
Nobody cares when I am glad. Georgia Douglas Johnson. HWOP p.15
Nobody else can have as much fun. Naomi Long Madgett. NeBV p. 297
Nobody Knows da Trubble Ah See. Anonymous. BlEx p.4; BlLi p.111; BlWOA p.239
Nobody Knows the Trouble I See, Lord! Anonymous. AfAV p. 117
Nobody Knows Tomorrow, Margaret Danner. DoOAT p.124
Nobody knows what a dialysis machine is, really. Pinkie Gordon Lane. WiTh p.41
Nobody Likes to Read His Own Epitaph. Pinkie Gordon Lane. PoBBl p.14; WiTh p.14
Nobody Lives! Audre Lorde. BlUn p.65
Nobody mentioned war. Lucille Clifton. GoNAE p.22
Nobody needs you. Jodi Braxton. SoITM p.27
Nobody Riding the Roads Today.** June Jordan. BlP p.249; SCh p.41; ThTDID p.160
Nobody wants to die on the way. Audre Lorde. BlUn p.52
Nobody's Ever Heard.** Thulani Davis. AlTRGR p.22
Nocturnal Sounds. Kattie M. Cumbo. BlSi p.134; NiBPo p.57
Nocturne. Gwendolyn Bennett. ANP p.128; BANP p.244
Nocturne. Dorothy F. Blackwell. EbR p.6
Nocturne. Naomi Long Madgett. AfAWA p.690; BlALP p.111; DeDF p.67; StBS p.56
Nocturne. Pinkie Gordon Lane. BlSi p.233; MyFe p.18
Nocturne. Ylessa Dubonee. EbR p.61
Nocturne II: Still. Naomi Long Madgett. PiLAF p.39
Nomen. Naomi Long Madgett. BlSi p.129; ExAE p.32
Non-Monogamy is a Pain the Butt. Patricia Parker. MoIB p.114
Non-Poem. Carolyn M. Rodgers. SoBB p.15
None have gained a loftier recognition through the medium of the arts. Margaret Danner. DoOAT p. 31; IrLa p.4
Nonviolence. Lyn. SiSH p.8
Nonviolence (the words get harder and harder to say) Lyn. SiSH p.8
Noon Tide. Henrietta Cordelia Ray. EABP p.143
Nor shall I in sorrow repine. Georgia Douglas Johnson. BrBV p.38
Nor white nor Black shall habitate the earth. Georgia Douglas Johnson. AmLNA p.73
Nor, will anyone dare say. Sharon Scott. JuBa p.177
North Boun'. Ariel Williams Holloway. BANP p.288; BlSi p.57; BTh p.11; CaD p.201; GoS p.152; PoN p.144
North County: The Dream Realized. Sherley Williams. PePo p.74
Nostalgia. Mae V. Cowdery. WLOV p.22
Not a Suicide Poem. June Jordan. SCh p.9; ThTDID p.165
Not About Poems. Carolyn M. Rodgers. HeAEG p.25
Not all of me is there. Marva Tatum Smith. BeYM p.30
Not Blue. Kattie M. Cumbo. NiBPo p.56
Not by hammering the furious word. Pauli Murray. DaTAOP p.35; PoBA p.109
Not by way out hairdoos. Margaret T. G. Burroughs. BlSi p.120
Not Enough. Naomi Long Madgett. OnATM p.50
Not Enough Time to Say What I Could. C. Tillery Banks. HeTMWL p.28
Not even these would be enough to keep my constancy. Mae V. Cowdery. WLOV p.58
Not Everything One Says is Lyri-

cal. Marva Tatum Smith. BeYM p.28
Not for your tender eyes that shine. Georgia Douglas Johnson. HWOP p.18
Not I Alone. Naomi Long Madgett. AmLNA p.86; OnATM p.52
Not in a Name. Margaret Danner. DoOAT p.123
Not Juliet's words in truth can I repeat. Virginia Houston. NegVo p.76
Not less than this, beloved. Georgia Douglas Johnson. ALC p.43
Not Like Falling Leaves. Pinkie Gordon Lane. WiTh p.59
Not Looking. June Jordan. SCh p. 31; ThTDID p.50
Not looking now and then I find you here. June Jordan. SCh p.31; ThTDID p.50
Not more than we can bear. Nikki Giovanni. ThWRNW p.19
Not needing, really, my own sweet good. Gwendolyn Brooks. WoOGB p.79
Not only from the wise who have lived before us. Marion Cuthbert. SOC p.11
Not particularly the woman but especially the men. Carolyn M. Rodgers. HeAEG p.36
Not That Far. May Miller. BiSi p.113; ClAB p.43
Not That Now I Remember.** Gloria Oden. RESUR p.11
Not Wanted. Rosa Paul Brooks. AmLNA p.91
Not when leaves are brown and sere. Josephine D. (Henderson) Heard. MoGl p.59
Not wholly this or that. Georgia Douglas Johnson. BrBV p.59
Note From a Field Nigger. Mae Jackson. CaPWY p.17
Notes From the Childhood and the Girlhood. Gwendolyn Brooks. SPGB p.33
Notes on the Peanut. June Jordan. PaNP p.44
Notes Upon Vanessa's Promotion Ceremony. Leatrice Emeruwa. BlGBG p.20
Nothing and Something. Frances E. W. Harper. EBAP p.321 FBFH p.42
Nothing fills me up at night. June Jordan. PaNP p.55
Nothing from nothing is nothing. Katherine Dunham. GaBW p. 300
Nothing is colder than a dead love. Georgiana Oliver. NegVo p.117
Nothing is Right. Alice Walker. RePOP p.36
Nothing is sorry sameness a trap called no dream remembered. Audre Lorde. NeHS p.30
Nothing Makes Sense. Nikki Giovnni. MyH p.56
Nothing says that you must see me in the street. Audre Lorde. CaTR p.18; ChPON p. 23; COAL p.45
Nothing will keep us young. Sonia Sanchez. IvBAW p.20; WABP p.21
Nothing's too high to reach for. Alice D. Anderson. EbR p.1
Novembah Dusk. Lucile D. Goodlett. WGC p.27
November. Naomi Long Madgett. OnATM p.11
November/December (Echoing Voices of Remembrances) Kattie M. Cumbo. NiBPo p.58
Novitiates sing ave before the whipping post. Maya Angelou. JGM p.28
Now. Audre Lorde. ChPON p.88; NeHS p.20
Now. Margaret Walker. PFND p.9
Now Ain't That Love? Carolyn M. Rodgers. BlP p.260; BrT p.180; RoATW p.6
Now and at the Hour. Naomi Long Madgett. StBS p.50
Now and then she would shout in church. Elma Stuckey. BiGa p.70
Now, de Lawd said unto Jonah in the time of great distress. Ionie Daniels. NegVo p.44
Now I ain't got nothing against the church. E. Sharon Gomillion. FoAAM p.25
Now I am only aggravated. Judy Dothard Simmons. JuB p.8
Now I Understand.** Kattie M. Cumbo. NiBPo p.59

Now let me put my words to bed. Naomi Long Madgett. OnATM p.35
Now Let's Be Real. Carolyn M. Rodgers. SoBB p.18
Now like the pines intoning. Georgia Douglas Johnson. ALC p.59
Now Long Ago. Maya Angelou. OhPWFW p.12
Now look hyah nickle. Lucy Mae Turner. BCF p.57
Now Poem For Us. Sonia Sanchez. PoBA p.290; WABP p.67
Now rock the boat to a fare-thee-well. Audre Lorde. CaTR p. 3; ChPON p.19; COAL p.3; NaPr p.69; PoBA p.249
Now That I am Forever With Child. Audre Lorde. ChPON p.13; COAL p.21; FiCi p.6; PoBA p.246
Now that I am old I will never forget the young are no different than I was. Gertrude Blackwell Bailey. IfWCF p.42
Now that I have climbed the steep battlements of the universe. Pauli Murray. DaTAOP p.80
Now the fragrant petals shower downward. Elma Stuckey. BiGa p.88
Now the way of the mecca was on this wise. Gwendolyn Brooks. BlLi p.414
Now they go forth to war. Lucia M. Pitts. EbR p.117
Now thread my voice with lies. Maya Angelou. JGM p.21
Now we've made a child. Audre Lorde. CaTR p.17; ChPON p.15; COAL p.46; NaPr p. 681; PoBA p.247
Now who could take you off to tiny life in one room or in two rooms or in three. Gwendolyn Brooks. SPGB p.9; StIB p.14; WoOGB p.17
Now you are strong. Pauli Murray. DaTAOP p.31
Nowadays the Heroes. June Jordan. SCh p.8; ThTDID p.88
Nowadays the heroes go out looking for the cradle in the cold. June Jordan. SCh p. 8; ThTDID p.88
Nun. Toi Derricotte. EmDH p.27
Nursing Home, USA. June Vanleer Williams. WiRYPS p.52
Nyanu was appointed as my Lord. Alice Walker. BlSi p.223
NYC Love Poem. Carole Gregory Clemmons. NiBPo p.83
Nymph. Audre Lorde. SiAS p.43

- O -

O Black warrior, hurl a dark spear of song. Pauli Murray. DaTAOP p.16
O bretheren, my way, my way's cloudy. Anonymous. BlLi p. 112
O bring back the good old days. Sonia Sanchez. AfAA p.4
O come while youth's bright rosy veil. Georgia Douglas Johnson. HWOP p.59
O cruel mob--destroying crew. Lauretta Holman Gooden. HeD p.16
O dainty bud, I hold thee in my hand. Eva Jessye. ANP p.80
O, de ole nigger driver. Anonymous. BlWOA p.234
O, de spring is jes a promise. Bessie Woodson Yancey. EcFTH p.54
O' de wurl' ain't flat. Ariel Williams Holloway. BANP p. 288; BlSi p.57; BTh p.11; CaD p.200; GoS p.152; NeCa p.377; PoN p.144; PoNe p.257
O death! Whose sceptere trembling realms obey. Phillis Wheatley. PPW p.95
O do, Lawd, remember me. Anonymous. BlWOA p.240
O God--are you busy today? Valeria Parks. NegVo p.124
O, han' me down my 'cordion, chile. Bessie Woodson Yancey. EcFTH p.61
O, hungry heart, contend not with thy fate. Josephine D. (Henderson) Heard. MoGl p.43

O, hypocrisy, thou evil-minded, forked tongued and hydra-headed monster. Josephine D. (Henderson) Heard. MoGl p. 113
O I am so sad. Sonia Sanchez. IvBAW p.34; LoP p.28
O, I don't mean the house that you live in. Bessie Woodson Yancey. EcFTH p.15
O life, do not pass me by. Naomi Long Madgett. OnATM p.29
O love, you have shorn me, and rifled my heart. Georgia Douglas Johnson. HWCP p.53
O lovely form that has lain so long beneath my heart. Mae V. Cowdery. WLOV p.46
O man, behold your destiny. Margaret Walker. CoAAAW p.361
O, Mary, bearing blessed virgin's name. Josephine D. (Henderson) Heard. MoGl p.103
O Modern Song of the F.B.I. Sonia Sanchez. AfAA p.4
O, muse away--intrude not on this calm. Josephine D. (Henderson) Heard. MoGl p.123
O my brother I heard u come through my life. Johari Amini. JuBa p.167; LetGSW p.27
O night! when the light palls. Bessie Woodson Yancey. EcFTH p.7
O, po' sinner, o, now is yo' time. Spiritual. BlP p.29
O, poet gifted with the sight divine! Henrietta Cordelia Ray. BlSi p.39; EBAP p.139
O sacrificial throng whose lives build up. Georgia Douglas Johnson. BrBV p.88
O say can u see. Sonia Sanchez. NeBV p.338; WABP p.36
O shepherds, while you watch your flocks the wise men watch his star. Effie Lee Newsome. ChG p.69
O sing no more of pretty, useless things. Naomi Long Madgett. AmLNA p.85
O soldier of every nation. Mae V. Cowdery. WLOV p.66
O sorrowed and despairing one, I have listened. Pauli Murray. DaTAOP p.95
O, soul, why shouldst thou downcast be. Josephine D. (Henderson) Heard. MoGl p.46
O, that the holy angels would indite. Josephine D. (Henderson) Heard. MoGl p.41
O, the good things said of us when we are dead. Josephine D. (Henderson) Heard. MoGl p.121
O, the world was made for a boy. Bessie Woodson Yancey. EcFTH p.25
O this day like an orange. Sonia Sanchez. LoP p.99
O thou bright jewel in my aim I strive. Phillis Wheatley. BlWOA p.41; PAL p.91; PPW p.4
O thou whose exit wraps in boundless woe. Phillis Wheatley. PAL p.79; PPW p. 90
O, what white little lights at Carney's Point. Alice Dunbar Nelson. DuSAE p.132
O, wondrous depth to which my soul is stirr'd. Josephine D. (Henderson) Heard. MoGl p.55
O, ye poet who sings. Bessie Woodson Yancey. EcFTH p.29
Oak Tree. Gertrude Blackwell Bailey. IfWCF p.27
Oakland in February. Ntozake Shange. NaEd p.120
Oaxaca. Audre Lorde. ChPON p. 6; COAL p.10; FiCi p.17; SiAS p.41
Obeah. Pamela Cobb. InDM p.29
Obituary. Beatrice M. Murphy. RoCO p.10
Obituary. June Vanleer Williams. WiRYS p.81
Obituary for a Living Lady. Gwendolyn Brooks. StIB p.16; WoOGB p.18
Oblivion. Jessie Redmond Fauset. ANP p.89; BANP p.208; PoN p.67; PoNe p.69
Observation. Sonia Sanchez. LoP p.38
Observation on a Subway Train. Vanessa Howard. ScWh p.50
Observations of a Saturday Night

Crowd. Damali (Denise Burnett) IATWMB p.11
Observe Me. Black/male. Mari Evans. NIGHT p.53
Obviously, I must take two paintings. Margaret Danner. DoOAT p.70
October. Audre Lorde. ChPON p. 108
October Journey. Margaret Walker. AmNP p.132; BTB p.180; IADB p.28; OcJo p.11; PoBA p.146; PoN p.176; PoNe p.317
October 29, 1972 1:45 and On. Jodi Braxton. SoITM p.39
Octoroon, The. Georgia Douglas Johnson. AVAN p.209; BrBV p.36
Ode of Verses, An. Phillis Wheatley. PPW p.69
Ode on the birthday of Pompey Stockbridge. Philis Wheatley. EBAP p.111
Ode on the Occasion of the Inauguration of the Sixth President of Jackson State College. Margaret Walker. OcJo p.26
Ode to a Scotlandville Bus. Lois Miller. PoBBl p.27
Ode to Barbara. Olean Bess. MiFe p.9
Ode to Justice. Dorothy Vena Johnson. NegVo p.83
Ode to Neptune (1772) on Mrs. W----'s Voyage to England. Phillis Wheatley. PAL p.46; PPW p.35
Ode to Nixon. Olean Bess. MiFe p.12
Odessa. Ntozake Shange. NaEd p. 79
Odyssey. Mari Evans. NIGHT p.53
Odyssey. Naomi Long Madgett. PiLAF p.45
O'erwhelming sorrow now demands my song. Phillis Wheatley. PAL p.69; PPW p.38
Of all the places I have been. Marva Tatum Smith. BeYM p.15
Of all the ways in which this country prints its death upon me. Audre Lorde. ChPON p.68
Of De Witt Williams on his way to Lincoln Cemetery. Gwendolyn Brooks. BlWOA p.716; CNAW p.516; PoN p.189; SPGB p. 10; StIB p.21; WoOGB p.23
Of Death and Doom. Pauli Murray. DaTAOP p.81
Of Earth. Mae V. Cowdery. WLOV p.13
Of Faith: Confessional. June Jordan. SCh p.80; SoS p.70; ThTDID p.163
Of falling leaves and melting snows. Maya Angelou. OhPWFW p.35
Of Liberation. Nikki Giovanni. BFBTBJ p.45
Of New England Rock, 1976. Jodi Braxton. SoITM p.47
Of Night Song and Flight. June Jordan. ThTDID p.68
Of Our Love. Kattie M. Cumbo. GaBW p.290
Of Robert Frost. Gwendolyn Brooks. SPGB p.122
Of Sleep. Naomi Long Madgett. StBS p.20
Of Someone I Loved. Mae Jackson. CaPWY p.16
Of the furious who take today and jerk it out of joint. Gwendolyn Brooks. BrT p.37; FaP p.18
Of the world so beautiful the men and women. June Jordan. ThTDID p.91
Of two great truths we need to be so deeply clear. Marion Cuthbert. SoC p.37
Of us who darkly stand. Pauli Murray. DaTAOP p.27
Of what avail the tardy showers. Georgia Douglas Johnson. HWOP p.26
Off the track I blew and traveled. Carolyn M. Rodgers. HoIGO p.6; JuBa p.112
Offering. Georgia Douglas Johnson. ALC p.65
Offering of Paws, An. Wanda Coleman. MaDBL p.119
Offspring. Naomi Long Madgett. DeDF p.53; FBPA p.97; PiLAF p.25
Oft have I thought, since I have grown and grayed. Naomi Long Madgett. OnATM p.24
Oft times I invision myself as a

tree. Eleanor Thomas-Grumbach. MoSu p.6
Ofttimes I go into the cupboard of my mind and find upon its shelf a bowl of mistakes. Naomi Evans Vaughn. EbR p. 149
Ofttimes I wish that I could be like yonder rustling poplar tree. Mae V. Cowdery. WLOV p.14
Ogun's Friend. Jayne Cortez. NoOP p.22
Oh beautiful, Black martyr, cut down by guns held in Black hands. Joyce Whitsitt Lawrence. BrT p.23; FoM p. 20
Oh, Black man, why do you northward roam. Georgia Douglas Johnson. BrBV p.33
Oh, blow me worldward wind of my desire! Naomi Long Madgett. OnATM p.16
Oh Cordelia Brown. Anonymous. MBP p.57
Oh day! with sun glowing. Mae V. Cowdery. WLOV p.26
Oh, de ole sheep, dey know de road. Spiritual. BlP p.32
Oh, dey whupped him up de hill. Anonymous. BlLi p.32
Oh doctor, I have a pain in my heart. Anonymous. MBP p.31
Oh! for the veils of my far-away youth. Georgia Douglas Johnson. ALC p.18; ANP p.86; BANP p.182
Oh, Freedom.** Anonymous. MBP p. 53
Oh God, make me white and shining as a star. Mae V. Cowdery. WLOV p.47
Oh have you heard the lates'. Anonymous. ITBLA p.121
Oh! how I want you so. Nola Richardson. WhOL p.27
Oh how you used to walk. Maya Angelou. AnSIR p.14
Oh, I see myself as I was. Sherley Williams. CoAAAW p. 390
Oh, I shall sing my song from the deep heart of me. Naomi Long Madgett. OnATM p.23
Oh, I'm 10 Months Pregnant. Ntozake Shange. DaGe p.31
Oh! it is plain to see people are not the same as they used to be. Gertrude Blackwell Bailey. IfWCF p.14
Oh Lawd have mussy now upon us. Anonymous. BlP p.17
Oh like Atlanta parking lots insatiable and still collected kindly by the night love lies. June Jordan. SCh p. 35
Oh, little Christ, why do you sigh. Jessie Redmond Fauset. BANP p.206
Oh! Lord. Antionette T. Payne. TNV p.92
Oh love, when in trouble call unto me. Alvies M. Carter. AOS p.24
Oh Mary, Don't You Weep.** Anonymous. BLIA p.41; ITBLA p.97
Oh, Mary, what you gonna name that pretty little baby? Anonymous. ChG p.96; ITBLA p.97
Oh mother, mother, where is happiness? Gwendolyn Brooks. AnA p.32; SPGB p. 51; WoOGB p.96
Oh, my boys I'm bound to tell you. Anonymous. BlWOA p. 236
Oh, my fancy teens with a world of dreams. Georgia Douglas Johnson. HWOP p. 37
Oh, my lover is a fisherman. Gertrude Davenport. BTh p. 51
Oh Night of Love.** Georgia Douglas Johnson. ALC p.5
Oh nightingale that lures my soul to slumber. Naomi Long Madgett. SoTPN p.9
Oh nimber, nimber will-o! Anonymous. BlP p.19
Oh, nobody knows da trubble ah see. Anonymous. BlWOA p. 239
Oh, say, can't you see. Bobbretta M. Elliston. PoBBl p.21
Oh, sing no more of pretty, useless things. Naomi Long

Madgett. OnATM p.27
Oh stand erect defiant tree! Pauli Murray. DaTAOP p.66
Oh, take my hand for one more time. Naomi Long Madgett. PhN p.34
Oh, the blue blue bloom. Effie Lee Newsome. CaD p.56
Oh the sad little dreams of the dim yesteryear. Georgia Douglas Johnson. ALC p.29
Oh they go, this youth the world over. Pauli Murray. DaTAOP p.53
Oh, we must set our little boats adrift. Naomi Long Madgett. PhN p.59
Oh, when--a mah blood runs chilly an col ize got to go. Anonymous. BlWOA p.238
Oh, when I come to die. Spiritual. BlP p.28
Oh, when this earthly tenement shall join its kindred clay. Ada. BlSi p.19
Oh will you wear red? Anonymous. BlP p.11
Oh--Yeah! Sharon Scott. JuBa p. 176
Oh yeah, I know they call you king. Elma Stuckey. BiGa p. 38
Oh, you crazy girls from Laredo. Harryette Mullen. TTW p.53
Oh You Tender, Lovely Scrubwoman. Pinkie Gordon Lane. WiTh p. 35
Oh you who bore us in pain and joy. Mae V. Cowdery. WLOV p. 9
Oh Zaki tan ke parlay lot you who hear tell the others. Audre Lorde. ChPON p.101
Ohnedaruth. Angela Jackson. VoDLM p.20
OK, so she got back the baby. June Jordan. ThTDID p.65
Okay. Sharon Scott. JuBa p.173
Okay "Negroes." June Jordan. BlP p.243; SCh p.48; ThTDID p.102
Okay "Negroes" American Negroes looking for milk. June Jordan. BlP p.243; SCh p.48; ThTDID p.102
Okra to Greens Again (Special Delivery). Ntozake Shange. DaGe p.64
Okra to Greens: A Historical Perspective of Sound/Downtown. Ntozake Shange. DaGe p.67
Okra to Greens/An Aside On Amsterdam Avenue. Ntozake Shange. DaGe p.68
Ol' Ant Kate, She Died So Late. Anonymous. BlWOA p.646
Ol Fashion Lady, An. Ntozake Shange. NaEd p.66
Old. Gertrude Blackwell Bailey. IfWCF p.31
Old age is more than just a notion. June Vanleer Williams. WiRYPS p.54
Old black bull come down de hollow. Anonymous. BlWOA p.235
Old Black ladies carryin shopping bags full of more shopping bags. Elouise Loftin. PoBA p.515
Old Black mamma lived in a shoe. Lotus Schaefer. PoBBl p.59
Old Black Men. Georgia Douglas Johnson. CaD p.77; DeDF p.45; PoBA p.21; PoN p.58; PoNe p.77; VoFHR p.358
Old Days, The. Audre Lorde. BlUn p.93
Old folks I'm convinced have their own communication system. Jennifer Blackman Lawson. BlIMT p.16
Old Hen Cackled, The. Anonymous. AmLNA p.8
Old home, I'm leaving thee today, our sweet relations end. Josephine D. (Henderson) Heard. MoGl p.106
Old Jim Crow. Anonymous. AfAV p.196; NeNRe p.54
Old Jonah. Ionie Daniels. NegVo p.44
Old King Cotton. Elma Stuckey. BiGa p.38
Old Laughter. Gwendolyn Brooks. AnA p.44; WoOGB p.108
Old Man, The. Barbara Jean Knight. PoBBl p.28
Old Man. Elma Stuckey. BiGa p. 73

Old man at the corner table wears the face you will grow into. Naomi Long Madgett. ExAE p. 61
Old Man Know-All. Anonymous. BlP p.9
Old man you ain't always been good. Elma Stuckey. BiGa p.73
Old-Marrieds, The. Gwendolyn Brooks. AmNP p.141; PoBA p.154; PoN p.190; StIB p. 1; WoOGB p.3
Old marsa's wife done run away. Elma Stuckey. BiGa p.50
Old Marse John.** Anonymous. TYBP p.198
Old Mary. Gwendolyn Brooks. BeEa p.18; SPGB p.74; WoOGB p.316
Old Massa I am dying now. Josephine D. (Henderson) Heard. MoGl p.124
Old Men, The. Ntozake Shange. NaEd p.65
Old men and women quilt their legs in the shade, The. Sonia Sanchez. IvBAW p.28; LoP p.4
Old men meet round 2:00 maybe ten to, The. Ntozake Shange. NaEd p.65
Old men still drowse on gray park benches. Naomi Long Madgett. PiLAF p.15
Old Men Used to Sing, The. Alice Walker. PoBA p.476; RePOP p.3
Old Molly Means was a hag and a witch. Margaret Walker. AmNP p.130; BlSi p.96; DaS p.496; FMP p.33; KAL p.141; MoCAP p.74; PoN p.178; PoNe p.309
Old Movies. Thulani Davis. AlTRGR p.46
Old people should die first. Carole Gregory Clemmons. NiBPo p.89
Old people will tell you that after each battle, don't care who won, The. Sherley Williams. PePo p.66
Old People Working (Garden Car) Gwendolyn Brooks. SPGB p.125
Old Relative. Gwendolyn Brooks. AnA p.8; SPGB p. 34; WoOGB p.72
Old Scars. Nola Richardson. WhOL p.53
Old Section Boss, The. Anonymous. BlP p.17
Old slippery Slim, you cold snake. Harryette Mullen. TTW p.24
Old Spice. Margaret Danner. DoOAT p.80
Old stillness of your body excites a madness, The. Alice Walker. RePOP p.58
Old Stormer. May Miller. ClAB p.18
Old Tennis Player. Gwendolyn Brooks. SPGB p.125
Old Warrior Terror, The. Alice Walker. RePOP p.47
Old Wine. Naomi Long Madgett. StBS p.51
Old Woman and Young Child at a Wedding Reception. Jennifer Blackman Lawson. BlIMT p.17
Old woman I can see you huddled in your window. Pearl Cleage Lomax. DeDF p.58
Old woman in me walks patiently to the hospital, An. Carole Gregory Clemmons. BlSi p. 185
Old Women, The. Naomi Long Madgett. ExAE p.33
Old women worn out mamas ride subways in the night. Leatrice Emeruwa. BlGBG p.22
Old Words. Sonia Sancchez. CoAAAW p.322; IvBAW p.43; LoP p.46
Old Yalluh Hammuh were a guy I knowed long time ago. Margaret Walker. FMP p.40
Ole Abe (God's bless' is ole soul) Anonymous. BlP p.7
Ole Aunt Dinah, she's jes lak me. Anonymous. BlP p.6
Ole Hen She Cackled, De. Anonymous. AmLNA p.8
Ole Ma'am Pattie settin' in de sun. Lucile D. Goodlett. WGC p.49
Ole Ma'am Pattie stew huh broth.

Lucile D. Goodlett. WGC p.58
Ole Man Jollie.** Lucile D. Goodlett. WGC p.69
Ole man know-all, he come 'round. Anonymous. BlP p.9
Ole marse has got a pointed nose. Elma Stuckey. BiGa p.7
Ole marse, he thrown me on the bed. Elma Stuckey. BiGa p. 51
Ole marse is pot belly man. Elma Stuckey. BiGa p.56
Ole marse look at de pallet. Elma Stuckey. BiGa p.36
Ole missus is a vile one. Elma Stuckey. BiGa p.47
Ole missus were a sorry sight. Elma Stuckey. BiGa p.30
Ole Nigger Driver, De. Anonymous. BlWOA p.234
Ole Sheep Day Know de Road, De. Spiritual. BlP p.32
Ole woman sittin' in de do'. Julia Gaillard. BTh p.42
Omega. Georgia Douglas Johnson. HWOP p.27
Omega ran to witness him. Gwendolyn Brooks. SPGB p.126
On a Birthday. Gendolyn Bennett. HeD p.2
On a Bright Day Next Week.** Maya Angelou. JGM p.26
On a Colored Doll. Floretta Howard. AmLNA p.53
On a day when we were dark. Carolyn M. Rodgers. HeAEG p.23
On a Diverse Deviations. Maya Angelou. JGM p.19
On a Letter I Received. Dorothy Lee Louise Shaed. NegVo p. 139
On a Monday Afternoon. June Jordan. ThTDID p.192
On a Narrow Street. Naomi Long Madgett. PhN p.90
On a New Year's Eve. June Jordan. ThTDID p.73
On a Night of the Full Moon. Audre Lorde. CaTR p.25; ChPON p.20; COAL p.19
On a snug evening I shall watch her fingers. Gwendolyn Brooks. AfAWA p.577; BlWOA p.716; SPGB p.24; StIB p. 50; WoOGB p.52
On a Sunday morning it begins to rain. Anonymous. BlWOA p. 463
On a Thursday Evening. June Jordan. ThTDID p.193
On Aging. Maya Angelou. AnSIR p.48
On Becoming Successful. Ntozake Shange. NaEd p.102
On being asked to leave a place of honor for one of comfort, preferably in the northern suburbs. Alice Walker. ONC p.45
On Being Brought From Africa to Phillis Wheatley. AfAV p. 28; AfAWA p.18; AmLNA p. 22; BlALP p.10; BlLi p.10; BlWOA p.41; CNAW p.11; EBAP p.100; ITSA p.13; KAL p.7; PAL p.92; PPW p.7; TYBP p.205
On Being Head of the English Department. Pinkie Gordon Lane. BlSi p.228; MyFe p.29
On Being High. Abbey Lincoln. CoAAAW p.187
On Black or brown white folks frown. Gertrude Blackwell Bailey. IfWCF p.11
On bone-bruised afternoons when my eyes tighten like the neck ties gripping my people. Melba Joyce Boyd. CaEADW p.47
On Busing. Carolyn M. Rodgers. HeAEG p.77
On Contemporary Issues. Ridhiana. GLOWC p.55
On death's domain intent I fix my eyes. Phillis Wheatley. AVAN p.30; BlSi p.14; PAL p.68; PPW p.39
On Declining Values. June Jordan. ThTDID p.190
On Democracy. Naomi Long Madgett. PhN p.63
On Diverse Deviation. Maya Angelou. BlSi p.267
On Divine Adaptation to an Age of Disbelief. June Jordan. ThTDID p.189
On Dreams. Frenchy J. Hodges. BlW p.29
On Finding Arts Extended Gallery

and You. Margaret Danner. ImOAAF p.12
On 5 Compositions of Roscoe Mitchell. Thulani Davis. AlTRGR p.55
On Freedom. Phillis Wheatley. ITSA p.13
On Friendship. Phillis Wheatley. EBAP p.111
On Genessaret. Josephine D. (Henderson) Heard. MoGl p.28
On Hearing "The Girl with the Flaxen Hair." Nikki Giovanni. BFBTBJ p.4
On Heaven Street at One A.M. Wanda Coleman. MaDBL p.98
On Holidays in the Best Tradition. June Jordan. ThTDID p.16
On Imagination. Phillis Wheatley. AfAWA p.15; AVAN p.28; BlSi p.16; CNAW p.13; EaNAW p.42; EBAP p.170; PAL p.76; PoN p.7; PoNe p. 9; PPW p.29
On Jealousy. Patricia Parker. MoIB p.130
On Learning. Mae Jackson. CoAAAW p.169
On Lonely Nights. Nola Richardson. WhOL p.85
On Major General Lee (1776) Phillis Wheatley. PAL p.53
On Midsummer's Eve. Audre Lorde. COAL p.38
On Moral Leadership as a Political Dilemma (Watergate, 1973) June Jordan. ThTDID p.141
On my bedroom wall hang a poster. Nikki Giovanni. MyH p.24
On my Blk/ness. Alicia Loy Johnson. CNAW p.769; GaBW p.340; NiBPo p.148
On My First Trip to Mississippi. Linda Brown Bragg. LoSBM p.22
On My Happy/Matrimonal Condition. June Jordan. ThTDID p.71
On My Stand. Sharon Scott. JuBa p.173
On my Way to Nana's House. Linda Brown Bragg. LoSBM p. 32
On, nightingale that lures my soul to slumber. Naomi Long Madgett. PhN p.30
On Not Calling on Cranes in the Night. Thulani Davis. AlTRGR p.5
On Not Sending Love Letters to Cranes. Thulani Davis. AlTRGR p.6
On one never-to-be-forgotten day, we launched a sky. Ruby Berkley Goodwin. EbR p.70
On Parting. Naomi Long Madgett. PhN p.37
On Philosophy. Barbara Marshall. TNV p.70
On preparing for grazing in another galazy, siziling orange from his lust. Carole Gregory Clemmons. NiBPo p.87
On Reaching Forty. Maya Angelou. OhPWFW p.7
On Recollection. Phillis Wheatley. EBAP p.105; PAL p.80; PPW p.28
On Seeing an Old Friend. Sandra Royster. BrA p.14; RoATW p.75; WoTa p.19
On seeing Black Journal and watching Negro leaders "Give Aid and Comfort to the Enemy" to Quote Richard Nixon. Nikki Giovanni. MyH p.61
On Seeing my Limitations Outside of the U.S. S. Diane Bogus. WITM p.68
On Seeing Pharoah Sanders Blowing. Sonia Sanchez. HoC p.23
On Snobbery. Carole Gregory Clemmons. NiBPo p.88
On such a cold night my bones feel loose inside my skin. Harryette Mullen. TTW p.28
On summer afternoons I sit quiescent by you in the park. Jessie Redmond Fauset. BANP p.205; CaD p.69; NeNRe p.78; PoN p.65; PoNe p.67
On That One Day. Naomi F. Faust. PoBBl p.32
On the Aluminum. June Jordan. ThTDID p.80
On the Asphalt. Wanda Coleman. MaDBL p.49
On the Birth of Bomani. Lucille

Clifton. OrW p.9
On the bite of a kola nut I was so high the clouds blanketing Africa. Nikki Giovanni. MyH p.47
On the Black Poet Reading his Poems in the Dark. June Jordan. THTDID p.63
On the Capture of General Lee. Phillis Wheatley. PPW p.87
On the Church. E. Sharon Gomillion. FoAAM p.25
On the corner of Newberry and 14th Place. Marion Nicholes. LiS p.11
On the corner they go to the stud. Wanda Coleman. MaDBL p.100
On the Day When Nobody Smiled. Margaret Danner. DoOAT p.71
On the Death of a Young Gentleman. Phillis Wheatley. PAL p.87; PPW p.11
On the Death of a Young Lady of Five Years of Age. Phillis Wheatley. ITBLA p.28; PAL p.88; PPW p.10
On the Death of Allen's Son. Lucille Clifton. TwW p.11
On the Death of Boochie by Starvation. Mari Evans. NIGHT p.31
On the Death of Dr. Samuel Marshall (1771). Phillis Wheatley. PAL p.39; PPW p. 40
On the Death of J. C. an Infant. Phillis Wheatley. PAL p.64; PPW p.43
On the Death of Lisa Lyman. Della Rurt. BlSi p.163
On the Death of Rev. Dr. Sewell (1769). Phillis Wheatley. PAL p.34; PPW p.7
On the Death of the Rev. Mr. George Whitefield (1770). Phillis Wheatley. BlWOA p. 40; C AW p.11; EaNAW p.37; EBAP p.101; PAL p.36; PPW p. 69
On the Death of the Rev'd Dr. Sewall 1769. Phillis Wheatley. PPW p.64
On the Dismission of a School Term. Ann Plato. ANP p.12
On the edge of his tongue; it was the one word he dared not speak. Abbey Lincoln. CoAAAW p.187
On the far south side niggers slept in used white folks houses. Marion Nicholes. LiS p.12
On the harbor freeway heavy traffic 6 p.m. home to the pad. Wanda Coleman. MaDBL p.27
On the Ile De Goree, M. Diop elegant in steel-gray cardigan bowed his greeting. Thadious M. Davis. BlSi p. 277
On the Loss of Energy. June Jordan. ThTDID p.93
On the morning you woke beside me. Alice Walker. ONC p. 55
On the Murder of Two Human Being Men, Denver A. Smith and His Unidentified Brother, at Southern University, Baton Rogue, Louisiana, 1972. June Jordan. ThTDID p.119
On the Occasion of the Open-Air Formation of the Olde Tymers' Walking and Nature Club. Gwendolyn Brooks. BeEa p.58; WoOGB p.356
On the Paradox in Rhyme. June Jordan. ThTDID p.66
On the Real World: Meditation # 1. June Jordan. CoAAAW p.180
On the road to Damascus to slay the Christians Saul saw the light. Nikki Giovanni. Rec p.29; WoATM p.41
On the Sinking of a Great Liner. May Miller. ClAB p.9
On the Spirit of Mildred Jordan. June Jordan. ThTDID p.26
On the Train. Wanda Coleman. MaDBL p.63
On the Twenty-Fifth Anniversary of the United Nations: 1970. June Jordan. ThTDID p.91
On this bus to oblivion I bleed in the seat numb silent rider. Wanda Coleman. MaDBL p.25
On This Louisiana Day.** Pinkie

Gordon Lane. MyFe p.16
On Thursday Nights Entertainment was the Use to Which the Hall Was Put.** Gloria Oden. TiTBi p.13
On Virtue. Phillis Wheatley. BlWOA p.41; PAL p.91; PPW p.4
On Watching a World Series Game. Sonia Sanchez. NeBV p.338; WABP p.36
On Working White Liberals. Maya Angelou. JGM p.44
On Your Love. June Jordan. ThTDID p.52
Once. Alice Walker. BlSi p.213; ONC p.23; PoBA p.474
Once. Carolyn Rodgers. SoBB p. 17
Once a Lady Told Me. Nikki Giovanni. WoATM p.8
Once a snow flake fell on my brow. Nikki Giovanni. MyH p.10
Once after a meeting you left your glasses behind the couch. Lyn. SiSH p.21
Once Again. Mae Jackson. CaPWY p.14
Once again I float down the enchanted streets of my town. Naomi Long Madgett. OnATM p. 19
Once Again the Poets. Mari Evans. NIGHT p.59
Once, ages ago it seems I had a son. Portia Bird Daniel. NegVo p.43
Once and Future Dead Who Learn, The. Lucille Clifton. TwW p.20
Once I asked for one lone petal of a rose. Ruth E. J. Sarver. EbR p.128
Once I Was Chaste. Sonia Sanchez. IvBAW p.83
Once I was immortal beside an ocean. Audre Lorde. ChPON p.8; COAL p.34; SiAS p.43
Once I wrote a poem about the bus. Damali (Denise Burnett) IATWMB p.17
Once made a fairy rooster from mashed potatoes. Alice Walker. RePOP p.16
Once, the canyons say there was but one cloud. Nzadi Zimele-Keita. CoAAAW p.396
Once there was a man sitting in a corner. Mae Jackson. CaPWY p.14
Once upon a dreary evening in the midst of the world's despair. Gladys Marie Parker. EbR p.112
Once Upon a Road. Jayne Cortez. COAG p.75
Once upon a time, I a poet, transformed myself into a poem. Wanda Coleman. MaDBL p.97
Once upon a time there were three black lines. Kali Grosvenor. BlSp p.105
Once, When Georgia Was Readying her Return to College.** Gloria Oden. RESUR p.61
Once when I walked into a room my eyes would seek out the one or two Black faces. Audre Lorde. BlUn p.112
Once when I was so high I saw myself. Barbara Mahone. Suga p.20
Once you are Black you can never be blacker. D. T. Ogilvie. YoBBI p.515
1. Akua Lezli Hope. CoAAAW p. 143
One. Carolyn M. Rodgers. BlP p.261
One and the Many. Naomi Long Madgett. OnATM p.11
One April. Lucia M. Pitts. EbR p.120
One by one, distant lamps glimmered. Naomi Long Madgett. PiLAF p.48
One cloven foot raised. May Miller. ClAB p.18
One Day. Georgia Douglas Johnson. ALC p.27
Ond day a long time ago. Katherine Cuestas. BTB p.75;
One day and a sleep ago few things were on my mind. Frenchy J. Hodges. BlW p.14
One day I slipped in the snowy gutter of Brighton Beach. Audre Lorde. ChPON p.70
One day Marilyn marched beside me. Alice Walker. ONC p.37

One day on a hill. May Miller. ClAB p.37
One day she saw them coming into the garden. June Jordan. PaNP p.79
One day while strolling down the street I met a six-year old. Bessie Woodson Yancey. EcFTH p.33
One day you gonna walk in this house and I'm gonna have on a long African gown. Nikki Giovanni. BFBTBJ p.38; BrT p.54; NaPr p.25; RoATW p. 125
One drop of midnight in the dawn of life's pulsating stream. Georgia Douglas Johnson. AVAN p.209; BrBV p.36
One Eyed King. S. Diane Bogus. WITM p.11
One foot down, then hop! Maya Angelou. JGM p.48
105th and Euclid Street Peddler's Song, A. Leatrice Emeruwa. BlGBG p.27
125th Street and Aboney. Audre Lorde. BlUn p.12
One innocent spring your voice meant to me. Maya Angelou. OhPWFW p.12
One is never enough for me. Lucille Clifton. OrW p.7
One lovely summer afternoon when balmy breezes blew. Josephine D. (Henderson) Heard. MoGl p.47
One Man's Confession on Brotherhood. Naomi F. Faust. PoBBl p.31
One Mind. Pamela Cobb. InDM p. 33
One Minus One Minus One. June Jordan. ThTDID p.25
One More Black Belt Gone. Mari Evans. NIGHT p.23
One More Poem for Dolphy. Ntozake Shange. NaEd p.132
One More Round. Maya Angelou. AnSIR p.33
One Mornin' Soon. Anonymous. UNBP p.78
One need not be a student of E.S.P. to receive these vibes. Margaret Danner. DoOAT p.94
One night lost in a lifetime. Linda Brown Bragg. LoSBM p.9
One o' these days I lay cotton sack down. Elma Stuckey. BiGa p.6
"One of the Least of These, My Little One." Georgia Douglas Johnson. BrBV p.44
One of these days I'm gonna write a real performance poem. Harryette Mullen. TTW p.54
One ounce of truth benefits like ripples on a pond. Nikki Giovanni. MyH p.38
1 Poem 2 Voices a Song. Sherley Williams. PePo p.77
One poises, poses, at track, or range, or river. Gwendolyn Brooks. BeEa p.57
One Saturday's afternoon I ran up some stairs. Maami Verano. ThHSD p.66
One Sided Dialog. June Jordan. ThTDID p.65
One thing sure do shock me I seen marse on his knees. Elma Stuckey. BiGa p.24
One Thousand Nine Hundred & Sixty Eight Winters. Jackie Earley. BlSp p.65; MBP p. 93; SoS p.127
One Wants a Teller in a Time Like This. Gwendolyn Brooks. WoOGB p.116
One Who So Hated the War.** Thulani Davis. AlTRGR p.19
One winter, the cold twisted the bodies of our old folks. Zelma Smith. HoDo p.97
One woman say a good man make her want to shout. Carolyn M. Rodgers. CoAAAW p.315
One Year to Life on the Grand Central Shuttle. Audre Lorde. ChPON p.83; NeHS p.13
One's not a man one's not a woman grown. Gwendolyn Brooks. WoOGB p.116
One's who live in the desert, The. Lucille Clifton. TwW p.26
Ones who turn face to wall and die. Wanda Coleman. MaDBL

p.110
Only a little scrap of blue preserved with loving care. Frances E. W. Harper. PBFH p.19
Only hungers left are the hungers allowed us, The. Audre Lorde. ChPON p.93; NeHS p.50
Only in This Way. Margaret Burroughs. BlSi p.120
Only my own room is gray. June Jordan. ThTDID p.166
Only nothing limits the world. June Jordan. ThTDID p.45
Only our hearts will argue hard. June Jordan. ThTDID p.59
Only Somg I'm Singing, The. Nikki Giovanni. MyH p.16
Only Successful Heart Transplant, The. June Jordan. SCh p.57
Only the casket left. Charlotte Forten Grimke. DuSAE p.258
Only the minutes, not the years, are ours. Naomi Long Madgett. OnATM p.31
Only thing that you can ever be is what you are, The. Jennifer Blackman Lawson. BlIMT p.50
Only to keep his little bear he kills his cities. Lucille Clifton. GoNAE p.1
Only to Sleep. S. Diane Bogus. WITM p.16
On'ry Weathah. Bessie Woodson Yancey. EcFTH p.62
Onward to her distinction o'er the stream the Hannah sped. Frances E. W. Harper. PBFH p.15
Ooh, My Abyssinian Kitten, be Fun Again. Margaret Danner. DoOAT p.138
Opaque eyes of hollow rooms peep between venetian blinds. Melba Joyce Boyd. CaEADW p. 33
Ope! ye everlasting doors. Georgia Douglas Johnson. BrBV p. 24
Oppossum. Pinkie Gordon Lane. MyFe p.25
Oppression. Nikki Giovanni. Rec p.39
Optimist, The. Anonymous. GLOWC p.8
Optimist fell ten stories, The. Anonymous. GLOWC p.8
Or. June Jordan. SCh p.34; ThTDID p.161
Or like Atlanta parking lots insatiable and still. June Jordan. ThTDID p.161
Orange. Linda B. Graham. GaBW p.314
Orange as an orange tree. Linda B. Graham. GaBW p.314
Orange Chiffon. Jayne Cortez. BlSi p.153; Scar p.51
Orchard Street. Jayne Cortez. Scar p.14
Oriflamme. Jessie Redmond Fauset. ANP p.89; AVAN p.194; BANP p.207; BlSi p.64; NeNRe p.325; PoBA p.18
Original. Ragged-round. Gwendolyn Brooks. BlALP p.106; BlPo p.24; CNAW p.523; FoM p.3; ITM p.39; PoBA p.158; TYBP p.243; WoOGB p.411; YoBBI p.165
Oriki Erinle. Anonymous. TYBP p.11
Oriki: for James Mark Essex and the Others. Mari Evans. NIGHT p.64
Orisha. Jayne Cortez. BlSi p. 151; Scar p.29
Oronde. Paulette Childress White. DeDF p.15
Orphan, yes, but not an orphan. Linyatta. JuBa p.77
Other acquainted years sidle with modest decorum. Maya Angelou. OhPWFW p.7
Other loves I have known. Bessie Calhoun Bird. BlSi p.82
Other Year. May Miller. ClAB p.39
Otis I really love you. Kali Grosvenor. PBK p.48
Otto. Gwendolyn Brooks. ChG p. 102
Our ancestors called thee by other names. Naomi Long Madgett. ExAE p.40
Our best singers can't really sing. Val Ferdinand. NeBV p.375
Our birth and death are easy hours, like sleep and food and drink. Margaret Walker.

FMP p.58
Our Black People. Kali Grosvenor. PBK p.21
Our Black people are your and my people. K. Grosvenor. PBK 21
Our Blackness did not Come to us Whole. Linda Brown Bragg. LoSBM p.14
Our Bodies Made Rain. Sonia Sanchez. IvBAW p.76
Our boys had crossed the ocean. Eloise Culver. GANIV p.74
Our Children are Our Children. Geraldine L. Wilson. CoAAAW p.394
Our Cups are Full. Naomi Long Madgett. PhN p.62
Our Days are Numbered. Alicia Loy Johnson. BrT p.176
Our Detroit Conference (for Don L. Lee). Nikki Giovanni. BFBTBJ p.8
Our eyes caught the gun going across the counter. Wanda Coleman. MaDBL p.85
Our faces are the light & dark window panes. Carolyn M. Rodgers. HeAEG p.78
Our fadder, which are in heaben! Anonymous. BlP p.5
Our heart for rent. Tomi Carolyn Tinsley. EbR p.142
Our hearts are filled with pride to-day. Josephine D. (Henderson) Heard. MoGl p.15
Our Here. Frances E. W. Harper. PBFH p.15
Our language is tactile. Ntozake Shange. DaGe p.52
Our Lives. Sharon Scott. JuBa p.174
Our mothers, when asked may speak of us. Carolyn M. Rodgers. HeAEG p.47
Our moulting days are in their twilight stage. Margaret Danner. AmNP p.153; BlP p. 149; BlPo p.20; BlWOA p. 816; DoOAT p.47; IrLa p. 14; MoCAP p.88; NNPUSA p. 29; PoBA p.134; UNBP p.229
Our Need. Margaret Walker. FMP p.57
Our own shadows disappear. June Jordan. PaNP p.42
Our Richard Allen in his early youth. Josephine D. (Henderson) Heard. MoGl p.74
Our separate winding ways we trod. Georgia Douglas Johnson. HWOP p.12
Our Story. Jill Witherspoon Boyer. DrF p.18
Our sweat drops bit the land with urgency. Jayne Cortez. FeAF p.18
Our Task. Henrietta Cordelia Ray. AVAN p.152
Our Teenagers. Olean Bess. MiFe p.8
Our theme this morning is the wounds of Jesus. Anonymous. BLIA p.32
Our victories at this time seem so minute. Rosemari Mealy. CoAAAW p.221
Our World is Our.** Kali Grosvenor. PBK p.39
Our Your Friend Charlie was a glorious blaze. Maya Angelou. JGM p.34
Out in de 'tater field down side de lane. Lucile D. Goodlett. WeB p.22
Out in the Desert.** Josephine D. (Henderson) Heard. MoGl p.70
Out My Street. Bessie Woodson Yancey. EcFTH p.34
Out of Heaven.** Naomi Long Madgett. StBS p.23
Out of her womb of pain my mother spat me. Audre Lorde. ChPON p.35; COAL p.27
Out of my flesh that hungers and my mouth that knows. Audre Lorde. CaTR p.26; ChPON p.20; COAL p.19
Out of my navel a beanstalk grows up to the moon. Harryette Mullen. TTW p.44
Out of My Way. Gertrude Blackwell Bailey. IfWCF p.57
Out of the dark raw earth of blood and water. Julia Fields. PoBA p.329; PoNe p.420
Out of the marketplace where would I go? June Jordan. SCh p.61; ThTDID p.130
Out of Time. Naomi Long Mad-

gett. PiLAF p.28
Out upon the deep old ocean. Josephine D. (Henderson) Heard. MoGl p.28
Outcast, The. Josephine D. (Henderson) Heard. MoGl p.25
Outcast from her home in Syria. Frances E. W. Harper. OBFH p.9
Outside. Audre Lorde. BlUn p.61
"Ouu gee whiz hey charlie look." Saundra Sharp. MBP p.5
Over. Naomi Long Madgett. OnATM p.43
Over and over I read the dear letters. Josephine D. (Henderson) Heard. MoGl p.112
Over the ambassador bridge--an arc of perpetual pregnancy. Toi Derricotte. DeDF p.42; EmDH p.44
Over the warts on the bumpy, half plastered wall. Margaret Danner. BTB p.87; DoOAT p.65; IrLa p.17; KAL p.128; PoBA p.138
Overdose of Lovers, An. Wanda Coleman. MaDBL p.53
Overture. Carolyn M. Rodgers. HeAEG p.67
Ox in De Ditch. Lucile D. Goodlett. WGC p.30
Oxford is a Legend.** Margaret Walker. PFND p.13
Oya. Audre Lorde. ChPON p.91; NeHS p.39
Oyster man! Oyster man! Anonymous. ITBLA p.125
Oyster Man's Cry. Anonymous. ITBLA p.125

- P -

Pa. Alice McGee Smart. AmLNA p.64
Pack Rat. Naomi Long Madgett. ExAE p.69
Page one and I enter a land where the tangerine sun smoulders down on the lowlands. Margaret Danner. ImOAAF p.13; PoCo p.12
Pages From Life. Georgia Douglas Johnson. HWOP p.18
Pain, like fertilizer can be used for growth. Patricia Parker. MoBI p.133
Pain-sharp gnawing comes like a storm-fed mountain flood. Lenora Gillison. EbR p.66
Painted cocks ride halo round and round in the dinner plate. May Miller. ClAB p. 42
Painted Lady, The. Margaret Danner. BlP p.152; DoOAT p.78; IrLa p.21
Painted Lady is a small African butterfly, The. Margaret Danner. BlP p.152; DoOAT p.78; IrLa p.21
Painter, The. Gertrude Parthenia McBrown. ReFNA p.54
Painting Myself a New Mirror. Harryette Mullen. TTW p.65
Palace. Dorothy Vena Johnson. GoS p.79
Palace at Four A.M., The. Jodi Braxton. SoITM p.21
Pale and cold moons in retreat. May Miller. ClAB p.10
Pale dressed evening star. Dorothy Vena Johnson. GoS p.185
Palm Sunday. Lucille Clifton. GoNAE p.42
Palm Sunday (we) duck underneath umbrellas. June Jordan. ThTDID p.61
Paltry surrealism can't account for it. Harryette Mullen. TTW p.55
Pansy. Effie Lee Newsome. CaD p.56
Papa. Joanne Jimason. NaABE p.8
Papa he was a conjure man. JoAnne Jimason. NaABE p.8
Papa's not too hard to understand. Colleen McElroy. MuDLSG p.4
Paper is neither kind nor cruel. Audre Lorde. CaTR p.9; ChPON p.32; COAL p.49
Paperweight. Audre Lorde. ChPON p.32; COAL p.49
Pappy's Last Song. Maurine L. Jeffrey. HeD p.24
Para Maria Sandra. Patricia Parker. MoIB p.133

Parable. Thulani Davis. AlTRGR p.8
Parades what do we care for parades. Jayne Cortez. FeAF p.17
Paradox. Angelina Weld Grimke. CaD p.43
Paradox. Carolyn M. Rodgers. HeAEG p.27
Paradox, A. Georgia Douglas Johnson. ALC p.19
Paradox. June Vanleer Williams. WiRYPS p.21
Paradox. Pauli Murray. DaTAOP p.85
Paradox. S. Diane Bogus. WITM p.4
Paraphernalia For a Suicide: a Revelation of Life. Lateifa-Ramona Lahleet Hyman. CoAAAW p.150
Parasitosis. Ronda Davis. JuBa p.61
Parasitosis is a white disease. Ronda Davis. JuBa p.61
Parental Lament. June Vanleer Williams. WiRYPS p.5
Parents: People Like Our Marriage Maxie and Andrew, The. Gwendolyn Brooks. AnA p.6; SPGB p.33; WoOGB p.70
Parody. Georgia Douglas Johnson. ALC p.19
Parting. Audre Lorde. BlUn p. 68
Parting, The. Josephine D. (Henderson) Heard. MoGl p.19
Parting Hymn, A. Charlotte Forten Grimke. BlSi p.22
Parting Kiss, The. Josephine D. (Henderson) Heard. MoGl p. 16
Parts of me fall and shatter. Julia Fields. NiBPo p.72
Pass down the aisle of buried years to-night. Georgia Douglas Johnson. BrBV p.101
Passing. Ruby Stevens. NegVo p.145
Passing ever, early, late, no fond foot steps seek my gate. Georgia Douglas Johnson. ALC p.4
Passing for Black. Colleen McElroy. MuDLSG p.23
Passing men in the street who are dead. Audre Lorde. ChPON p.47; FrLWP p.32
Passing of F.D.R., The. Pauli Murray. DaTAOP p.36
Passing of the Ex-slave, The. Georgia Douglas Johnson. BrBV p.35
Passing the Sirens. Naomi Long Madgett. PhN p.109
Passing Time. Maya Angelou. OhPWFW p.11
Passive Resistance. Margaret Danner. DeDF p.95; DoOAT p.98; IrLa p.18; PoCo p. 5; UNBP p.231
Past. Sonia Sanchez. BluB p. 21; IvBAW p.53
Past is a tune in your ear, The. Barbara Mahone. Suga p.12
Pastels. Julia Fields. GaBW p.306
Pastorale. Mae V. Cowdery. WLOV p.63
Patent Leather. Gwendolyn Brooks. StIB p.11; WoOGB p.13
Paths that lead to freedom was lighted long ago, The. Eloise Culver. GANIV p.78
Pathways: From Mother to Mother. Audre Lorde. BlUn p.71
Patience. Nikki Giovanni. CoCRD p.78
Patriach, The. Margaret Danner. PoCo p.19
Patricia's Poem. June Jordan. PaNP p.19
Paul Robeson. Gwendolyn Brooks. BrT p.38; FaP p.119; PoBA p.165
Paul Robeson, Baritone, 1895- New Jersey. Eloise Culver. GANIV p.68
Paul Was Saul. June Jordan. ThTDID p.196
Paula the Cat.** Nikki Giovanni. VaT p.25
Paused from the resting long summer and with the quiet gulls. Julia Fields. NiBPo p.69
Pavlov. Naomi Long Madgett. BlP p.196; StBS p.58
Pavonine Watch, A. Sherley Williams. PePo p.46
Pay Day. Lucy Mae Turner.

BCF p.60
Pay day! yo' fame hab ne'er been sung. Lucy Mae Turner. BCF p.60
Peace. Georgia Douglas Johnson. BrBV p.71; HWOP p.9
Peace and Principle. Isabelle McClellan Taylor. EbR p.136
Peace on a thousand hills and dales. Georgia Douglas Johnson. BrBV p.71
Peaches. Musu Ber. YoBBI p.519
Peaches in open markets in Brownsville. Musu Ber. YoBBI p.519
Peacock Poems. Sherley Williams. PePo p.57
Peacock Poems: I, The. Sherley Williams. PePo p.43
Peacock Poems: 2, The. Sherley Williams. PePo p.41
Peacock Poems 3, The. Sherley Williams. PePo p.48
Peacock Song, The. Sherley Williams. PePo p.67
Pearl Sheba. Jayne Cortez. FeAF p.6
Peeing in the men's john and cursing loud. Jennifer Blackman Lawson. BlIMT p.10
Peep squir'l, ying-ding-did-lum. Anonymous. UNBP p.88
Peep Squirrel. Anonymous. UNBP p.88
Peerless Boom of Innocence, The. Georgia Douglas Johnson. HWOP p.3
Peeved petulant, silence tugged when I paused there. Dorothy F. Blackwell. EbR p.5
Pegasus. Jodi Braxton. SoITM p. 37
Pendulum. Georgia Douglas Johnson. HWOP p.56
Pent. Georgia Douglas Johnson. HWOP p.17
Penitent Considers Another Coming of Mary, A. Gwendolyn Brooks. BeEa p.52; SPGB p.102; WoOGB p.350
Pennsylvania Dutch Country. Sonia Sanchez. LoP p.20
Penny-Ante. Colleen McElroy. MuDLSG p.6
Pensando En La Muerte. Harryette Mullen. TTW p.55
People. Carole Gregory Clemmons. NiBPo p.87
People always sd they were dirty 4 letter words. Anonymous. ThHSD p.2
People awe me who can leave their doors open. Carolyn M. Rodgers. HeAEG p.43
People die from loneliness. Carolyn M. Rodgers. BlP p.261
People Gather, The. Mari Evans. BlSi p.143
People I used to hate I hate no more. Bessie A. Cobb. NegVo p.35
People just ain't for real. Vanessa Howard. ScWh p.50
People keep telling me to put my feet on the ground. Ntozake Shange. NaEd p.129
People know, The. Sharon Scott. JuBa p.171
People of Atlantis, The. Harryette Mullen. TTW p.32
People of Gleaming Cities and of the Lion's and the Leopard's Brood. Sharon Bourke. UNBP p.374
People of today have a lot of book learning. Gertrude Blackwell Bailey. IfWCF p. 25
People of Unrest. Margaret Walker. FMP p.27
People Protest in Sprawling Lightless Ways. Gwendolyn Brooks. WoOGB p.122
People say they have a hard time. Lucille Clifton. DOBB p.53; PoBA p.306
People who have no children can be hard. Gwendolyn Brooks. AnA p.35; BlWOA p.717; DaS p.500; SPGB p.52; WoOGB p.99
People Will Be People. Gertrude Blackwell Bailey. IfWCF p. 14
Pepper and salt, vinegar in the face. Anonymous. MBP p.27
Peppermint Candy March, The.** Effie Lee Newsome. ChG p. 74
Perception. Catherine L. Findley. EbR p.64

Perchance the friend who cheered the early years. Josephine D. (Henderson) Heard. MoGl p.61
Perfection. Alice Walker. RePOP p.41
Perhaps. Lucille Clifton. TTW p.54
Perhaps, I snapped shut my mouth too late. Esther Louise. CoAAAW p.200
Perhaps it is because I saw the first one while I was still in swaddling clothes. Margaret Danner. DoOAT p.127
Perhaps it was the bleak street. Audre Lorde. NaPr p.68
Perhaps, when Shakespeare lived a rose by any other term might smell as sweet. Ruth Duckett Gibbs. GLOWC p.40
Persephone, you were one of those girls who give rape a bad name. Harryette Mullen. HoDo p.101; TTW p.31
Personae Poem (For Sylvia Henderson). Nikki Giovanni. BFBTBJ p.1
Personal Letter No. 2. Sonia Sanchez. HoC p.32; IvBAW p.13
Personal Letter No. 3. Sonia Sanchez. IvBAW p.20: WABP p.21
Personality Sketch: Bill, A. Ronda Davis. JuBa p.63
Personals. Leatrice Emeruwa. BlGBG p.4
Perspective. Georgia Douglas Johnson. BrBV p.61
Pervade the womb of time. Johari Amini. ImIB p.12
Petals of the Faded Rose, The. Georgia Douglas Johnson. HWOP p.35
Pete. Elma Stuckey. BiGa p.50
Pete at the Zoo. Gwendolyn Brooks. BeEa p.47; WoOGB p.345
Peter, the fiery one. Marva Tatum Smith. BeYM p.19
Petulance is purple happiness pink. Mari Evans. WhIAM p. 9
Pheasant arrives Flemish coloring that burns, The. June Jordan. ThTDID p.194
Phenomenal Woman. Maya Angelou. AnSIR p.8
Phillis. Naomi Long Madgett. ExAE p.40
Phillis Wheatley (Poetess, 1753-1784, Senegal, West Africa). Eloise Culver. GANIV p.15
Phillis's reply to the Answer in our Last by the Gentleman in the Navy. Phillis Wheatley. PPW p.86
Phoenix. Carolyn M. Rodgers. JuBa p.112
Photograph. Quandra Prettyman. PoBA p.258
Photography. Nikki Giovanni. CoCRD p.67
Phraseology. Jayne Cortez. BlSi p.152
Pianissimo. Naomi Long Madgett. PhN p.82
Piano After War. Gwendolyn Brooks. AfAWA p.577; BlWOA p.716; SPGB p.24; StIB p.50; WoOGB p.52
Piano keys sit stiff and stark, The. Naomi Long Madgett. ExAE p.53
Pick a Bale of Cotton. Anonymous. ITBLA p.121
Pickin Em Up and Layin Em Down. Maya Angelou. OhPWFW p.3
Picture, The. Jeanette Adams. RoATW p.72; ThHSD p.34
Pictures from a school window. Naomi Long Madgett. PhN p. 22
Pied Piper. Patricia Parker. MoIB p.58
Pig feet, chicken ham and rice they're okay. E. Sharon Gomillion. FoAAM p.11
Pig will be a pig, A. Katherine Jackson. BTh p.63; EbAT p.135
Pilgrimage, The. Josephine D. (Henderson) Heard. MoGl p. 93
Pineapple. Harryette Mullen. TTW p.35
Pineapple is armored flower. Harryette Mullen. TTW p.35
Pioneer, she blazed a trail of light, A. Georgia Douglas Johnson. BrBV p.98

Pirouette. Audre Lorde. ChPON p. 7; COAL p.28; FiCi p.14; NNPUSA p.106
Pisces Bath. Barbara Mahone. Suga p.30
Pit is a covered hole, A. Patricia Parker. MoIB p.104
Pit Stop. Patricia Parker. MoIB p.104
Pitch in and Help Out. Gertrude Blackwell Bailey. IfWCF p.16
Pitch sun-child drowns in the Mississippi. Patricia Parker. ChOM p.15; DOBB p.111; MoIB p.55
Pity a Poor Boy. Anonymous. BlWOA p.461
Pity for him who suffers from his waste. Audre Lorde. FiCi p.20; PoBA p.248
Pity Me. Clara Haywood. NegVo p.71
Pity the poor who hate. Pauli Murray. DaTAOP p.22
Pity us, the poets. Lucia Pitts. EbR p.122
Pizen. Jodi Braxton. SoITM p.14
Plagiarism For a Trite Love Poem. Carolyn M. Rodgers. NaPr p. 117; RoATW p.26; SoBB p.20
Plain Truth. Jayne Cortez. COAG p.87
Plaint of the Madonna, The. Lucy Mae Turner. BCF p.46
Planes fly patterns. Nikki Giovanni. ThWRNW p.59
Plane's motor roars like a forest fire, The. Pinkie Gordon Lane. WiTh p.17
Plans. Helen Morgan Brooks. NNPUSA p.107; PoNe p.274
Play House. Mae Jackson. CaPWY p.15
Play me a game like blind man's dance. Maya Angelou. AnSIR p.47
Playing the Invisible Saxaphone En El Combe De Las Estrellas. Harryette Mullen. TTW p.54
Playpoets gather round the table. Wanda Coleman. MaDBL p.81
Plea. Edna White Hill. NegVo p.72
Plea, A. Mary Bohanon. GaBW p. 263
Plea. Nancy L. Arnez. RoCO p.24
Plea for my Heart's Sake. Naomi Long Madgett. PhN p.70
Please. Mae Jackson. BlSp p.90
Please Don't Wites. Kali Grosvenor. PBK p.16
Please excuse this letter. Beatrice M. Murphy. PoN p. 162; PoNe p.287
"Please, Muffin, please say "I am not." Margaret Danner. DoOAT p.82
Please send me a miracle by noon tomorrow. Beatrice M. Murphy. RoCO p.14
Pledge. Georgia Douglas Johnson. ALC p.44
Pledge of Allegiance. Beatrice M. Murphy. ReCO p.9
Pledge of Allegiance. Mae Jackson. CaPWY p.14
Plentiful sacrifice and believers in redemption are all that is needed. Audre Lorde. ChPON p,22; COAL p.37
Plow a restin' in de sun. Bessie Woodson Yancey. EcFTH p.60
Plum Ripens, The. Pinkie Gordon Lane. WiTh p.28
Plum ripens, my darling, The. Pinkie Gordon Lane. WiTh p.28
Po Laz'us. Anonymous. BlWOA p. 458
Poem. Blanche Taylor Dickinson. ANP p.130; CaD p.107
Poem. Charlotte Forten Grimke. BlSi p.23
Poem, A. Elaine Bethel. BTh p. 34
Poem. Georgiana Oliver. NegVo p.117
Poem. Helene Johnson. MyNIB p.140; NeNRe p.151
Poem. Helene Johnson. AmNP p. 100; BANP p.279; CaD p.218 PoBA p.103; VoFHR p.183
Poem. Julia Fields. MoCAP p. 151
Poem. Katherine Cuestas. BTB p.75; SoS p.85
Poem. Nikki Giovanni. CoCRD p.36; WoATM p.32
Poem. Pearl Cleage Lomax. WeDNNM p.11
Poem. Pearl Cleage Lomax.

WeDNNM p.13
Poem. Pearl Cleage Lomax. RoATW p.29
Poem. Sonia Sanchez. HoC p.22; IvBAW p.12; PoBA p.288
Poem About a Night Out: Michael: Goodbye for a While. June Jordan. PaNP p.31
Poem about beauty, blackness, poetry (and how to be all three) A. Linda Brown Bragg. LoSBM p.16
Poem about intelligence for my brothers and sister, A. June Jordan. PaNP p.37
Poem About My Rights. June Jordan. PaNP p.86
Poem About Police Violence. June Jordan. PaNP p.34
Poem About the Head of a Negro. June Jordan. PaNP p.9
Poem About Vieques, Puerto Rico, A. June Jordan. PaNP p.63
Poem Against the State. June Jordan. ThTDID p.123
Poem Addressed to Women. Frances E. W. Harper. ANP p.15
Poem at Thirty. Sonia Sanchez. BlFi p.250; BlP p.231; BlSi p.245; BrT p.136; HoC p.10; IvBAW p.4; PoBA p.286; UNBP p.271
Poem at 3:00 A.M. Pinkie Gordon Lane. WiTh p.30
Poem/Because it Came as a Surprise to Me. Nikki Giovanni. Rec p.38
Poem/Ditty-Bop. Carolyn M. Rodgers. JuBa p.126
Poem Extract. Pinkie Gordon Lane. MyFe p.42
Poem for a Bassist. Judy Dothard Simmons. JuB p.13
Poem for a Friend. Jennifer Blackman Lawson. BlIMT p.38
Poem for a Lady Whose Voice I Like. Nikki Giovanni. Rec p.45; WoATM p.21
Poem...For a Lover. Mae V. Cowdery. WLOV p.51
Poem for a Poet. Audre Lorde. CaTR p.20; ChPON p.33; COAL p.24; NaPr p.72
Poem for all the Children, A. SCh p.73; ThTDID p.164
Poem for all the Men in the World, A. Mae Jackson. CoAAAW p. 169
Poem (For Anna Hedgeman and Alfreda Duster). Nikki Giovanni. MyH p.53
Poem For Aretha. Nikki Giovanni. BlP p.327; BrT p.61; PoBA p.454; WoATM p.15
Poem (For BMC No.1). Nikki Giovanni. BFBTBJ p.7; BrT p. 48
Poem (For BMC No.2). Nikki Giovanni. BFBTBJ p.10
Poem (For BMC No.3). Nikki Giovanni. BFBTBJ p.13
Poem for Black Boys. Nikki Giovanni. BlP p.325; EgT p.11
Poem for Blackboys in Floppy Tie-Die Hats Who Try to Relate to Sisters on Off-Nights. Jodi Braxton. SoITM p.28
Poem for Brother/for the Nation. Carolyn M. Rodgers. HoIGO p.30
Poem for Carol, A. Nikki Giovanni. EgT p.19; MyH p.8
Poem (For Dudley Randall). Nikki Giovanni. BFBTBJ p.9
Poem for Ed and Archie, A. Nikki Giovanni. CoCRD p.70
Poem (For Ema). Nikki Giovanni. CoCRD p.74
Poem for Etheridge. Sonia Sanchez. BlP p.239; WABP p. 41
Poem For Flora. Nikki Giovanni. EgT p.9; PoBA p.456; Rec p.42; WoATM p.10
Poem for Granville Ivanhoe Jordan, November 4, 1890-December 21, 1974. June Jordan. ThTDID p.20
Poem for Heroes, A. Julia Fields. NiBPo p.68
Poem for Larry Ridley. Judy Dothard Simmons. UNBP p.364
Poem for Lloyd. Nikki Giovanni. Rec p.15
Poem for Lois: An Elegy. Pinkie Gordon Lane. MyFe p.30
Poem for Michael. Pearl Cleage Lomax. WeDNNM p.7
Poem for Michael, A. Vanessa Howard. ScWh p.36
Poem for my Family: Hazel Griffin and Victor Hernandez

Cruz. June Jordan. BlP p. 245; SCh p.54; ThTDID p. 104
Poem for my Father, A. Sonia Sanchez. BlP p.236; BrT p.139; IvBAW p.17; WABP p. 14
Poem for my Love. June Jordan. ThTDID p.70
Poem for my Nephew. Nikki Giovanni. EgT p.13; Rec p.43
Poem for my Pretty Man. June Jordan. ThTDID p.65
Poem for my Sisters. Lucille Clifton. GoNAE p.28
Poem for Nana. June Jordan. BlSi p.148; PaNP p.1
Poem for Neighbors. Pearl Cleage Lomax. WeDNNM p.14
Poem (for Nina). Nikki Giovanni. MyH p.46
Poem For Nina Simone to Put Some Music to and Blow Our Niggu/ Minds. Sonia Sanchez. WABP p.60
Poem (For PCH). Nikki Giovanni. BFBTBJ p.12
Poem for Positive Thinkers, A. Barbara Mahone. PoBA p.473; Suga p.23
Poem for Some Black Women. Carolyn M. Rodgers. BlSi p. 176; HoIGO p.47
Poem for South African Women. June Jordan. PaNP p.42
Poem for Stacia. Nikki Giovanni. MyH p.14
Poem for Sterling Brown, A. Sonia Sanchez. CoAAAW p.317; IvBAW p.91
Poem (For TW). Nikki Giovanni. BFBTBJ p.6
Poem for the New Year, A. Leatrice Emeruwa. BlGBG p. 16
Poem for the Poet Alexis DeVeaux. June Jordan. PaNP p.6
Poem for Unwed Mothers. Nikki Giovanni. Rec p.34
Poem for Weedie, A. S. Diane Bogus. WITM p.36
Poem for Women in Rage, A. Audre Lorde. ChPON p.105
Poem for Young People, A. Jennifer Blackman Lawson. BlIMT p.16
Poem From the Empire State. June Jordan. BlP p.248; SCh p.65
Poem in Celebration of the Recovery of Mrs. R. Buckminster Fuller, June 1967. June Jordan. ThTDID p.45
Poem (No Name No.1). Nikki Giovanni. BFBTBJ p.13
Poem (No Name No.2). Nikki Giovanni. BFBTBJ p.19; BOL p. 9
Poem (No Name No.3). Nikki Giovanni. BFBTBJ p.24; BlLi p. 533; BrT p.50
Poem No. 1. Carolyn M. Rodgers. HeAEG p.78
Poem No. 1. Sonia Sanchez. LoP p.3
Poem No. 1. Toi Derricotte. EmDH p.37
Poem No. 2. Sonia Sanchez. LoP p.5
Poem No. 2 for Inaugural Rose. June Jordan. PaNP p.85
Poem No. 3. Sonia Sanchez. IvBAW p.30; LoP p.10
Poem No. 4. Sonia Sanchez. IvBAW p.31; LoP p.11
Poem No.5. Sonia Sanchez. LoP p.24
Poem No. 6. Sonia Sanchez. LoP p.36
Poem No. 7. Sonia Sanchez. IvBAW p.39; LoP p.42
Poem No. 8. Sonia Sanchez. IvBAW p.50; LoP p.55
Poem No. 9. Sonia Sanchez. LoP p.56
Poem No. 10. Sonia Sanchez. LoP p.57
Poem No. 11. Sonia Sanchez. LoP p.65
Poem No. 12. Sonia Sanchez. LoP p.70
Poem No. 13. Sonia Sanchez. LoP p.72
Poem No. 14. Sonia Sanchez. LoP p.75
Poem No. 15. Sonia Sanchez. LoP p.101
Poem of Angela Yvonne Davis. Nikki Giovanni. BlSp p.74; PoBA p.458
Poem of Friendship, A. Nikki Giovanni. CoCRD p.88

Poem of Personal Greeting for Fidel. June Jordan. PaNP p.14
Poem of Praise, A. Sonia Sanchez. IvBAW p.94
Poem Off Center, A. Nikki Giovanni. CoCRD p.39
Poem on my Fortieth Birthday to my Mother Who Died Young. Lucille Clifton. TwW p.14
Poem on the Assassination of Robert F. Kennedy, A. Nikki Giovanni. ThWRNW p.31
Poem on Turning Sound. Jodi Braxton. SoITM p.32
Poem Re You and Another Brother in the Fall. Sonia Sanchez. LoP p.17
Poem to Ethel and Chenese, A. Olean Bess. MiFe p.10
Poem to James Brown, A. Olean Bess. MiFe p.11
Poem to Myself, A. Elaine Taylor. HoDo p.102
Poem to the Mass Communications Media. June Jordan. SCh p. 81; ThTDID p.162
Poem Toward the Bottom Line. June Jordan. PaNP p.75
Poem Towards a Final Solution. June Jordan. CoAAAW p.183
Poems About Playmates. Ronda Davis. JuBa p.59
Poems be clickin' forth out my fingers now. Thulani Davis. AlTRGR p.62
Poems: Birmingham 1962-1964. Julia Fields. PoBA p.320; PoNe p.417
Poems Come In, The. Linda Brown Bragg. LoSBM p.5
Poems for Black Boys (With Special Love to James). Nikki Giovanni. BFBTBJ p.50
Poems for Malcolm. Carolyn M. Rodgers. UNBP p.347
Poems For the Lonely. Mae Jackson. BlSp p.91
Poems Gotta Come Outta My Crotch, De? Ntozake Shange. NaEd p.103
Poems to my Father. Pinkie Gordon Lane. MyFe p.49; WiTh p.8
Poet, The. Alice D. Anderson. EbR p.1
Poet, The. Lucille Clifton. OrW p.61
Poet, The. Mae Jackson. CaPWY p.5
Poet After Surgery. Wanda Coleman. MaDBL p.88
Poet asks, and Phillis can't refuse, The. Phillis Wheatley. PAL p.93; PPW p.60
Poet Deserts His Ivory Tower, The. Naomi Long Madgett. AmLNA p.85
Poet-In. Sandra Royster. WoTa p.7
Poet Questions His Immortality, A. Claire Turner. NegVo p.156
Poet Speaks, The. Georgia Douglas Johnson. AmNP p.22
Poetry. Georgia Douglas Johnson. HWOP p.46
Poetry. Nikki Giovanni. WoATM p.56
Poetry is a Tressel. Nikki Giovanni. WoATM p.35
Poetry is motion graceful as a fawn. Nikki Giovanni. WoATM p.56
Poetry Makes Unlikely Bedmates.** Gloria Oden. RESUR p.15
Poets. Lucia M. Pitts. EbR p. 122
Poets Beyond the Blues. Naomi Long Madgett. ExAE p.45
Poets love to rave of summer. Bessie Woodson Yancey. EcFTH p.8
Poet's Plea, A. June Vanleer Williams. WiRYPS p.60
Poet's Query. Mae V. Cowdery. WLOV p.59
Poet's Vision, The. Carolyn M. Rodgers. HoIGO p.68
Point of No Return. Mari Evans. NNPUSA p.19
Point of View. Naomi Long Madgett. ExAE p.39
Pointing to the middle of your forehead where a white stripe (you say) marks the face. June Jordan. PaNP p.71
Points of View. Margaret Danner. DoOAT p.96
Poised, cool, serene, apart,

magic is thy subtle art. Bessie Woodson Yancey. EcFTH p.12
Policeman is a pig, A. Sonia Sanchez. HoC p.19; PoBA p.288
Ponce De Leon. Naomi Long Madgett. PiLAF p.43
Pond Lament. May Miller. ClAB p.21
Pool Players, The. Gwendolyn Brooks. BTB p.51; IADB p.5; ITBLA p.217; MBP p. 96; TYBP p.245
Poor Girl. Maya Angelou. OhPWFW p.14
Poor Loser. Nola Richardson. WhOL p.61
Poor pale-eyed, thrice--gulping amazed. Gwendolyn Brooks. BeEa p.66; WoOGB p.364
Poor Renaldo. Naomi Long Madgett. BTB p.148; StBS p. 25
Pop dat pill. Ann Wallace. GLOWC p.56
Poplar Tree. Mae V. Cowdery. WLOV p.14
Poppa Chicken. Margaret Walker. CNAW p.529; FMP p.36
Poppa was a sugah daddy. Margaret Walker. CNAW p.529; FMP p.36
Portrait. Audre Lorde. BlUn p.51
Portrait. Carolyn M. Rodgers. HoIGO p.33; NaPr p.111
Portrait. Pinkie Gordon Lane. WiTh p.31
Portrait of a White Nigger. Carolyn M. Rodgers. AfAWA p.777
Portrait of a Woman Artist. Safiya Henderson. CoAAAW p. 131
Positives. Johari Amini. LetGSW p.29; PoBA p.291
Positives, positives, aiń u sumthin. Johari Amini. LetGSW p.29; PoBA p.291
Possession. Sandra Royster. WoTa p.18
'Possum-Huntin'. Bessie Woodson Yancey. EcFTH p.55
Post-Script. Naomi Long Madgett. StBS p,53
Post War Ballad. Dorothy Vena Johnson. EbR p.91
Posted. Elma Stuckey. BiGa p. 53
Posthumous. Georgia Douglas Johnson. HWOP p.26
Postmortem. Naomi Long Madgett. ExAE p.46
Postscript. Pinkie Gordon Lane. WiTh p.57
Potter, The. Anonymous. TYBP p.47
Poverty Blues. Nancy L. Arnez. RoCO p.17
Power. Audre Lorde. BlUn p. 108
Power and the Glory, The. S. Diane Bogus. WITM p.32
Praise due to Gwen Brooks. Cynthia M. Conley. TGWL p.22
Praise the Rat-infested Rooftop. Vanessa Howard. ScWh p.2
Pray for the Lovers.** Jayne Cortez. FeAF p.7; RoATW p.120
Prayer. Gertrude Blackwell Bailey. IfWCF p.45
Prayer. Isabella Maria Brown. NNPUSA p.61; PoNe p.341
Prayer. Lucille Clifton. GoNAE p.14
Prayer, A. Yolande Zealy. OnOW p.3
Prayer for a Hill. Katharine Beverly. NegVo p.14
Prayers to the God That. Anonymous. TYBP p.28
Praying primarily and fervently in a wind storm. Carolyn M. Rodgers. HeAEG p.11
Preacher Kyo Siam, De. Lucile D. Goodlett. WGC p.61
Preacher Man. Elma Stuckey. BiGa p.57
Preacher Ruminates Behind the Sermon, The. Gwendolyn Brooks. BlEx p.545; BlVo p.46; MoCAP p.80; SPGB p.8; StIB p.13; UNBP p. 169; WoOGB p.15
Preaching from the bigness of his skull bowing to flowers between butts. Jayne Cor-

tez. FeAF p.31
Precarious. Lyn. SiSH p.27
Precious night-blooming cereus you flowered once in Mississippi. Thadious M. Davis. BlSi p.277
Precious Offering, A. June Vanleer Williams. WiRYPS p.23
Precious Things. Anonymous. TYBP p.198
Precocious Curiosity. Linda Brown. BTB p.54
Predictable, the easy lie that swings back like a boomerang. Naomi Long Madgett. PiLAF p.13
Preferences. Margaret Danner. DoOAT p.57
Prejudice. Georgia Douglas Johnson. BrBV p.29; NeNRe p. 24; PoBA p.23
Prejudice. Margaret Danner. DoOAT p.106
Prelude to Nothing. Sonia Sanchez. IvBAW p.35; LoP p.29
Prelude to Spring. Pauli Murray. DaTAOP p.78
Presence. Pauli Murray. DaTAOP p.89
Present. Sonia Sanchez. BluB p. 41; CoAAAW p.325; IvBAW p. 60
Present Age, The. Frances E. W. Harper.
President, The. Gertrude Blackwell Bailey. IfWCF p.50
President is a man just like you and me. Gertrude Blackwell Bailey. IfWCF p.50
President Lincoln's Proclamation of Freedom. Frances E. W. Harper. EaNAW p.296
President talks about peril, The. June Jordan. SCh p.53; ThTDID p.108
Pressed against the windowpane. June Vanleer Williams. WiRYPS p.10
Pretending. Brenda Connor-Bey. CoAAAW p.76
Pretending to be in control of a fated journey's ride. Jennifer Blackman Lawson. BlIMT p.44
Pretty women wonder where my secret lies. Maya Angelou. AnSIR p.8
Price, The. Bessie Woodson Yancey. EcFTH p.23
Price to pay for a lovely garden is work. Julia Fields. GaBW p.303
Prickled Pickles Don't Smile. Nikki Giovanni. VaT p.29
Primer for Blacks. Gwendolyn Brooks. CoAAAW p.82
Prince Harlem. Lois Elaine Griffith. CoAAAW p.110
Princeling. Mari Evans. BlSp p.71; IABW p.81
Priscilla Assails the Sepulchre of Love. Gwendolyn Brooks. BeEa p.65; WoOGB p.363
Prison-house in which I live is falling to decay, The. Frances E. W. Harper. PBFH p.33
Prisoner. Maya Angelou. OhPWFW p.49
Prisoners, The. Naomi Long Madgett. PiLAF p.29
Private Letter to Brazil. Gloria Oden. AmNP p.158; ITBLA p.275; KAL p.185; NNPUSA p.91; PoNe p.383
Privilege, The. May Miller. ClAB p.26
Procession. May Miller. ClAB p.4; CNAW p.360
Proclamation/From Sleep, Arise. Carolyn M. Rodgers. JuBa p.117
Prodigal. Pamela Cobb. InDM p. 13
Proem on Africa. Margaret T. G. Burroughs. WhSIT p.20
Professors. Jill Witherspoon Boyer. DrF p.22
Progress, The. Gwendolyn Brooks. AmLNA p.90; SPGB p.28; StIB p.57; WoOGB p.59
Progress Report. Audre Lorde. ChPON p.51; FrLWP p.13
Prologue. Audre Lorde. ChPON p.58; FrLWP p.43
Promise, The. E. Sharon Gomillion. FoAAM p.12
Promise. Georgia Douglas Johnson. BrBV p.54
Promise, The. Jayne Cortez. FeAF p.18
Promise, The. Johari Amini.

BlFi p.195; CoAAAW p.51
Promise. Lucia Mae Pitts. NegVo p.131
Promises of Freedom. Anonymous. BlP p.5
Proof. Bessie Calhoun Bird. BlSi p.83
Prophecy. Pauli Murray. DaTAOP p.71
Prophets, The. Marva Tatum Smith. BeYM p.18
Prophets Came, The. Marva Tatum Smith. BeYM p.18
Prophets for a New Day. Nargaret Walker. BlP p.160; BrT p. 150; PFND p.22
Prophet speaks his images disseminate, The. Johari Amini. BlP p.230
Proposal for Brothers and Sisters, A. Jeanette Adams. ThHSD p.30
Proposition. Leatrice Emeruwa. BlGBG p.13
Proud? perhaps-and yet I cannot say with surety. Georgia Douglas Johnson. BrBV p.42
Proud to Be. Gertrude Blackwell Bailey. IfWCF p.49
Proverb. Naomi Long Madgett. OnATM p.15
Proving. Georgia Douglas Johnson. ALC p.10; CaD p.77; RoATW p.10
Psalm of Deliverance. Pauli Murray. DaTAOP p.41
Pulitzer prises, lavish appointments, laurels everywhere. Maxine Hall Elliston. TGWL p.33
Pulkha. Juanita M. Dickerson. NegVo p.52
Pullin me in off the corner to wash my face. Mari Evans. AfAWA p.683; BlP p.183; BlVo p.481; BlWOA p.818; DaS p.512; PoBA p.188; IABW p.77; UNBP p.250; WhIAM p.19
Pulling out of the old scarred skin. Harryette Mullen. TTW p.37
Puppet Player, The. Angelina Weld Grimke. CaD p.46
Purchase. Naomi Long Madgett. PhN p.58
Pure in heart shall see God, The. Frances E. W. Harper. PBFH p.28
Pure Intention, A. Margaret Danner. DoOAT p.57
Purple. Linda B. Graham. GaBW p.313
Purple as violets. Linda B. Graham. GaBW p.313
Purple red and gold sands endless stretching. Wanda Coleman. MaDBL p.61
Purring of the refrigerator turned cantankerous with might, The. S. Diane Bogus. WITM p.23
Push Back the Catastrophes. Jayne Cortez. COAG p.102
Pusher, The. Maya Angelou. OhPWFW p.40
Put it Right Here or Keep It Out There. Anonymous. BlWOA p.649
Put my Black Father on the Penny. Vanessa Howard. ScWh p.13; SoS p.3
Put your hands to the plow. Gertrude Blackwell Bailey. IfWCF p.55
Put your shoulders to the task. Gertrude Blackwell Bailey, IfWCF p.38
Pygmies are Pygmies Still, Though Perch on Alps. Gwendolyn Brooks. AnA p.14; PoNe p.336; SPGB p.3; WoOGB p.78
Pyramus and Thisbe. Naomi Long Madgett. PhN p.106

- Q -

QPP, The. Alice Walker. RePOP p.49
Quality of Change, The. Carolyn M. Rodgers. HeAEG p.63
Quarrel, The. Josephine D. (Henderson) Heard. MoGl p. 34
Quarrel. Pauli Murray. DaTAOP p.57
Quarter century ago, on a March morning, bleak and wild, A. Josephine D. (Henderson)

Heard. MoGl p.63
Quarter past midnight and the sea the dark blue music does not belong to me. June Jordan. ThTDID p.57
Quartet. Sherley Williams. PePo p.71
Quarto Centennial of the Birth of Bishop Richard Allen. Josephine D. (Henderson) Heard. MoGl p.41
Quatrains. Gwendolyn B. Bennett. CaD p.155
Queen Anne's Lace. June Jordan. ThTDID p.81
Queen of fatality, she determines the destiny. Lucille Clifton. OrW p.37
Queen of the Blues. Gwendolyn Brooks. StIB p.38; WoOGB p.40
Queen of the image and maker of beautiful words. Pinkie Gordon Lane. WiTh p.39
Queens of the Universe. Sonia Sanchez. BlSp p.186
Query. Georgia Douglas Johnson. HWOP p.16
Query. Virginia Houston. NegVo p.78
Quest. Georgia Douglas Johnson. HWOP p.11
Quest. Naomi Long Madgett. AmLNA p.84; BlP p.194; OnATM p.12; StBS p.13
Quest for Self. June Vanleer Williams. WiRYPS p.83
Questing. Anne Spencer. CaD p. 48
Question. Georgia Douglas Johnson. BrBV p.75
Question, The. Josephine D. (Henderson) Heard. MoGl p.17
Question authority question: why should trees or rivers or even stars. Alexis De Veaux. CoAAAW p.98
Question of where the flood would take us sits at our table, The. Jill Witherspoon Boyer. DrF p.12
Question To a Mob. Lauretta Holman Gooden. HeD p.16
Questioning. May Miller. ClAB p.24
Questions. Patricia Parker. MoIB p.79
<u>Questions For Anne</u>, Did your poems write you like nightmares. Toi Derricotte. EmDH p.47
Questions, Questions. June Vanleer Williams. WiRYPS p.59
Quick and the Dead, The. Linda Brown Bragg. LoSBM p.20
Quick wet wind blew in last night, A. Sandra Royster. WoTa p.18
Quicksand. Kathy Elaine Anderson. NeJCL p.27
Quiet afternoon the speaker dull the New Testament washed out. Alice Walker. ONC p.47
Quiet Arrogance. Marva Tatum Smith. BeYM p.26
Quiet Poem, A. Pinkie Gordon Lane. MyFe p.12
Quietly pacifist peaceful always die, The. Alice Walker. RePOP p.49
Quietly the world lay sleeping. Josephine D. (Henderson) Heard. MoGl p.58
Quilt. Effie Lee Newsome. CaD p.58
Quit hanging on the corner, man. Blossom Powe. GLOWC p.80; MyNIB p.70
Quite firmly did you stand. Georgia Douglas Johnson. BrBV p.97
Quite like the small fowl that sacrificed his claim of grace to you. Margaret Danner. DoOAT p.126
Quiet rays of the sun filter through piled clouds. Damali (Denise Burnett) IATWMB p.21
Quo Vadis. Countess W. Twitty. EbR p.149
Quoits. Effie Lee Newsome. CaD p.59; GoS p.22

- R -

Race. Naomi Long Madgett. PhN p.76; SoTPN p.10
Race-Prejudice in America.

Ruby Berkley Goodwin. NegVo p.63
Race Question, The. Naomi Long Madgett. AfAWA p.691; BlP p.196; BlVo p.477; MoOAD p. 93; StBS p.54
Race results, U.S.A., 1966. Sarah Webster Fabio. BrT p. 171
Rage. Alice Walker. RePOP p.61
Ragman, The. Naomi Long Madgett. PiLAF p.19
Railman's Story, The. Bessie Woodson Yancey. EfFTH p.42
Railroad Bill. Anonymous. BlWOA p.459
Railroad Bill, he a mighty bad coon. Anonymous. BlWOA p. 459
Railroad Section Leader's Song. Anonymous. BlWOA p.465
Rain. Elma Stuckey. BiGa p.59
Rain. Nikki Giovanni. Rec p.14; WoATM p.34
Rain Ditch. Pinkie Gordon Lane. WiTh p.36
Rain drops falling down on my head. Mae Jackson. CaPWY p.10
Rain, how I love thy dull, accented beat! Naomi Long Madgett. PhN p.78
Rain is falling steadily, The. Georgia Douglas Johnson. HWOP p.17
Rain is God's sperm falling. Nikki Giovanni. Rec p.14; WoATM p.34
Rain is in Our Heads, The. Carolyn Rodgers. AfAWA p. 778; NaPr p.113
Rain on 71st Street. Dorothy Randall. ThHSD p.40
Rain, rain upon my window. Naomi Long Madgett. PhN p.75
Rain-slick summer streets was never really deserted. Sherley Williams. PePo p.26
Rain Tastes Lovely Like You, The. ** Sonia Sanchez. IvBAW p. 83
Rain/Wish. Louise Blackman. EbR 4
Rainbow Roun Mah Shoulder. Anonymous. BlWOA p.64
Rainbows. Nikki Giovanni. VaT p. 45
Rain's falling somewhere in London, The. Naomi Long Madgett. PhN p.69
Rains softly come like the cries of a newborn baby, The. Sonia Sanchez. LoP p.56
Raise a "Rucus" To-night. Anonymous. BlP p.10; BlWOA p. 235
Raising of Lazarus, The. Lucille Clifton. GoNAE p.41
Ralph Bunche, Nobel Peace Prize Winner (1955) Michigan, 1904-1971. Eloise Culver. GANIV p.57
Ramadan--Hot Night. Marion Nicholes. LiS p.12
Ran against walls without breaking. Lucille Clifton. OrW p.77
Rap continues with the bad dude in the lead, The. Mae Jackson. BlSp. p.90
Rape. Jayne Cortez. CoAAAW p. 89; COAG p.63
Rape is Not a Poem. June Jordan. PaNP p.79
Rapping With Opportunity. Wanda Coleman. MaDBL p.20
Rat-fink baby buddy palomine. Naomi Long Madgett. NeBV p. 297
Rat-fink buddy before you. Naomi Long Madgett. PiLAF p.57
Rationale or she drove me crazy, The. June Jordan. PaNP p. 11
Rattle those chains restless spirit of neon. Wanda Coleman. MaDBL p.37
Raymond Melvin Brooks. Gwendolyn Brooks. Bec p.3
Re Entry. Mari Evans. NIGHT p. 4
Re: Joan Baez. Leatrice Emeruwa. BlGBG p.10
Reach Out. Gertrude Blackwell Bailey. IfWCF p.46
Reach out to help the falling one. Gertrude Blackwell Bailey. IfWCF p.46
Reaching Back. Saundra Sharp. RoATW p.137
Readin' 'riting & 'rithmetic are taught in every school.

Beth Jackson. PoBBl p.54
Reading Won't Make It. June Vanleer Williams. WiRYPS p.40
Real cool, the real thing, we are and you. Sarah Webster Fabio. TGWL p.37
Real estate real estate land for sale! Marva Tatum Smith. BeYM p.9
Real Sport. Bessie Woodson Yancey. EcFTG p.25
Reality. Yvette Johnson. TNV p. 56
Reality snaps against the frosted panes. May Miller. ClAB p. 20
Realization. Mattie T. Lakin. GaBW p.366
Realizing That Revolution will not Take Place By Telephone. June Jordan. ThTDID p.137
Reason I Like Chocolate, The. Nikki Giovanni. VaT p.49
Reason why I do it though I fail and fail. Lucille Clifton. TwW p.24
Reason Why I'm Lonely, The. Naomi Long Madgett. PhN p. 13
Reassurance. Alice Walker. RePOP p.33
Rebel. Elma Stuckey. BiGa p. 31
Rebel, The. Mari Evans. AmNP p.163; DeDF p.87; IABW p. 76; IADB p.4; MyNIB p.102 PoBA p.187
Rebellious Living Against the Elemental Church. Alice Walker. RePOP p.70
Rebirth. Paula Giddings. RoATW p.66
Rebirth. Sonia Sanchez. BluB p.45; IvBAW p.62
Rebolushinary X-mas/Eastuh Julie 4/Etc, Etc. Etc. Etc. Carolyn M. Rodgers. JuBa p.113
Rebuked. Elma Stuckey. BiGa p. 37
Rebus, By J. B.,A. Phillis Wheatley. PAL p.92
Recall. Georgia Douglas Johnson. HWOP p.19
Recapitulation. Virginia Houston. NegVo p.78
Reception, The. June Jordan. ThTDID p.47
Recessional. Georgia Douglas Johnson. ALC p.67; CaD p.79; PoN p.60; PoNe p.89
Recipes. Harryette Mullen. TTW p.51
Reckoning, The. Naomi Long Madgett. KAL p.177; StBS p.22
Reckoning A. M. Thursday After an Encounter Between a Saw Dust Sack and a Silly. Linyatta. JuBa p.77
Recollection To Miss A-----M____, Humbly Inscribed by the Authoress. Phillis Wheatley. PPW p.74
Recollections Toward a Stream. Carolyn M. Rodgers. HeAEG p.35
Recompense. Bessie Woodson Yancey. EcFTH p.20
Recompsense. Georgia Douglas Johnson. HWOP p.45
Record For My Friends, A. Sherley Williams. CoAAAW p.388
Records. Nikki Giovanni. BFBTBJ p.66
Recreation. Audre Lorde. BlUn p.81
Recurrent Dream. Sonia Sanchez. LoP p.32
Red bulbs click on. Colleen McElroy. MuDLSG p.28
Red-gold sun sinking to rest at day's end, The. Esther Popel. ReFNA p.49
Red Pepper Poet, The. Jayne Cortez. COAG p.53
Red Queen, The. Wanda Coleman. MaDBL p.31
Red queen flops face down, The. Colleen McElroy. MuDLSG p. 6
Red rose dark red with velvet. Patricia Jones. HoDo p.13
Redemption. Pauli Murray. DaTAOP p.100
Refiner's Gold, The. Frances E. W. Harper. PBFH p.58
Reflection. C. Tillery Banks. HeTMWL p.58
Reflection. Naomi Long Madgett. ExAE p.61
Reflections. Vanessa Howard.

SoS p.2
Reflections/On a Golden Anniversary. Nikki Giovanni. ThWRNW p.42
Reflections on April 4, 1968. Nikki Giovanni. BFBTBJ p.54; UNBP p.279
Reflections on the Reeferlution. Barbara Mahone. Suga p.16
Reflections, Written on Visiting the Grave of a Venerated Friend. Ann Plato. BlSi p. 46; EBAP p.115
Refugee. Naomi Long Madgett. OhATM p.56; PhN p.89; PoN p.207; PoNe p.379; StBS p. 28
Refugee Mother. Geraldine L. Wilson. CoAAAW p.394
Refusal. Maya Angelou. AnSIR p. 13
Refuse me the right to kill. S. Diane Bogus. WITM p.2
Refuse to refuse the racket. Gwendolyn Brooks. SPGB p.125
Regret. Lucy Mae Turner. BCF p. 37
Rehearsed quite early as early as gold pouring into sun. Carole Gregory Clemmons. NiBPo p.86
Reincarnation. Mae Jackson. PoBA p.498
Rejection. Naomi Long Madgett. PhN p.52
Release. Beatrice M. Murphy. NegVo p.114
Release Time. Audre Lorde. ChPON p.72; NeHS p.37
Relevant is Different Points on the Circle. Audre Lorde. ChPON p.55; FrLWP p.30
Religion. Elma Stuckey. BiGa p. 43
Reluctant Spring. Naomi Long Madgett. ExAE p.50
Remember. Elma Stuckey. BiGa p. 34
Remember. Georgia Douglas Johnson. PoN p.57; PoNe p.75
Remember. Jennifer Blackman Lawson. BlIMT p.24
Remember Not. Helene Johnson. BANP p.28; PoN p.153; PoNe p.264; RoATW p.95
Remember not the promises we made. Helene Johnson. BANP p.281; PoN p.153; PoNe p.264; RoATW p.95
Remember Times. Carolyn M. Rodgers. JuBa p.117
Remember...when Black was a word. Jennifer Blackman Lawson. BlITM p.24
Remembered Rhythms (The Individuals). Mari Evans. IABW p. 88
Remembering. Maya Angelou. JGM p.10
Remembering Fannie Lou Hamer. Thadious M. Davis. BlSi p. 277
Remembering my father's drum. Nikki Giovanni. EgT p.7
Remembering Willie. Mari Evans. NIGHT p.47
Remembrance. Jayne Cortez. Scar p.32
Remembrance. Maya Angelou. AnSIR p.5
Recontre. Jessie Redmond Fauset. CaD p.70
Rendezvous . Lois Royal Hughes. EbR p.89
Rendezvous With God. Ruby Berkley Goodwin. NegVo p.63
Renewal of Strength. Frances E. W. Harper. PBFH p.33
Repeat that magic mutha-word. Naomi Long Madgett. PiLAF p. 60
Replacing Faith. Lyn. SiSH p.9
Reply. Naomi Long Madgett. OnATM p.33
Reply, The. Pamela Cobb. InDM p23
Report. Frances E. W. Harper. RoATW p.90
Reports. Mariah Britton Howard. CoAAAW p.145
Representing the Universe. Alice Walker. CoAAAW p.360
Reprobate. Dorothy Lee Louise Shaed. NegVo p.139
Repulse. Georgia Douglas Johnson. HWOP p.15
Request. Barbara Marshall. TNV p.71
Request. Maya Angelou. OhPWFW p.27
Requiem. Georgia Douglas Johnson. EbAT p.35

Requiem. Lucia Mae Pitts. NegVo p.133
Requiem. Naomi Long Madgett. ExAE p.56
Requiem. Nell Chapman. EbR p.30
Requiem for a Newsman. June Vanleer Willims. WiRYPS p.79
Rescue Mission. Marion Nicholes. LiS p.19
Reservation. Johari Amini. ImOK p.7
Resignation. Josephine D. (Henderson) Heard. MoGl p.98
Resignation. Katharine Beverly. NegVo p.14
Resignation. Nikki Giovanni. ThWRNW p.48
Resistance. Pamela Cobb. InDM p.20
Response, A. Nikki Giovanni. CoCRD p.87
Resolution. Georgia Douglas Johnson. BrBV p.78
Resolution. Jennifer Blackman Lawson. BlITM p.29
Resolve. Pinkie Gordon Lane. WiTh p.34
Response to the Visiting Poets' Names, A. Carole Gregory Clemmons. NiBPo p.86
Resting. Josephine D. (Henderson) Heard. MoGl p.80
Recurrection. Mae V. Cowdery. WLOV p.60
Resurrection of the daughter. Ntozake Shange. NaEd p.90
Retaliation. Tomi Carolyn Tinsley. EbR p.142
Retort. Ruth Duckett Gibbs. GLOWC p.20
Retrospect. Georgia Douglas Johnson. HWOP p.58
Retrospect. Josephine D. (Henderson) Heard. MoGl p.13
Retrospect. Pearl Cleage Lomax. DeDF p.58
Retrospection. Georgia Douglas Johnson. ALC p.35; ReFNA p.27
Retrospection of a Black Woman. Naomi Evans Vaughn. NegVo p.160
Retrospective on Selection. June Vanleer Williams. WiRYPS p.66
Return. Audre Lorde. FiCi p.23
Return, The. Georgia Douglas Johnson. ALC p.59; HWOP p.60
Return, The. Jessie Redmond Fauset. CaD p.70
Return. Johari Amini. BlSi p. 194
Return. Naomi Long Madgett. OnATM p.39
Return is not a way of going forward after all. June Jordan. ThTDID p.56
Returned Letters, The. Josephine D. (Henderson) Heard. MoGl p.112
Returning Spring. Pauli Murray. DaTAOP p.91
Revelation. Blanche Taylor Dickinson. CaD p.107
Revelation. Carole Gregory Clemmons. BlSi p.185
Revelation. June Vanleer Williams. WiRYPS p.18
Revelations (The Night Greens Went Off With That Hussy, Rutabaga). Ntozake Shange. DaGe p.69
Rev. Andrew Brown, Over the Hill To Rest. Josephine D. (Henderson) Heard. MoGl p.56
Reverend is Gwine to de Big 'Soc'ation.** Lucy Mae Turner. BCF p.56
Reverie & In My Father's House Towards Hallelujahs & Freedom. Carolyn M. Rodgers. HeAEG p.71
Reverses. Maya Angelou. OhPWFW p.64
Review. Georgia Douglas Johnson. ALC p.17
Review From Staten Island. Gloria Oden. ITBLA p.275; KAL p.182; MoCAP p.95; NNPUSA p.90
Revolution. Angela Jackson. VoDLM p.13
Revolution. Damali (Denise Burnett) IATWMB p.16
Revolution is dead said little Willie to Joe, The. Carolyn M. Rodgers. HoIGO p.2
Revolution is one Form of Social Change. Audre Lorde. ChPON p.68; NeHS p.38
Revolution is Resting, The. Carolyn M. Rodgers. HoIGO

Revolution Man Black.** Linda Goss. RoATW p.23
Revolutionary Dreams. Nikki Giovanni. EgT p.28; Rec p.20; WoATM p.13
Revolutionary Music. Nikki Giovanni. BFBTBJ p.75; BrT p. 75; EgT p.33; UNBP p.280
Revolutionary Petunias. Alice Walker. BlSi p.212; RePOP p.29
Revolutionary Requiem in Five Parts, A. Johari Amini. LetGSW p.20
Reynaldo's dead and gone whereever people go who never loved a song. Naomi Long Madgett. BTB p.148
Rhetoric of Langston Hughes, The. Margaret Danner. BlSi p. 133; DoOAT p.85; FBPA p. 49
Rhythm. Georgia Douglas Johnson. HWOP p.37
Rhythm & Blues. Jayne Cortez. FeAF p.12
Rhythm and Blues. Mae Jackson. BOL p.63
Rhythm and blues ain't what it use to be. Mae Jackson. CaPWY p.9; PoBA p.496
Rhythm and blues sired you. Sarah Fabio. UNBP p.243
Rhythmatic Sounds. Loretta Rodgers. ThHSD p.82
Rhythms of a House. C, Tillery Banks. HeTMWL p.16
Richard Allen, Founder of the A.M.E. Church 1760-1831, Pennsylvania. Eloise Culver. GANIV p.16
Richard Penniman When His Mama and Daddy Died. Lucille Clifton. GoNAE p.26
Richard the White-hearted has got to be the only flunky. Linda Brown Bragg. LoSBM p.21
Riddle, The. Georgia Douglas Johnson. PoBA p.23
Ride the swing season. Audre Lorde. COAL p.38
Riders to the Blood Red Wrath. Gwendolyn Brooks. BlWOA p. 719; SPGB p.115
Riding behind a fast truck trucking for the other side of town. Edith Brandon Humphrey. HoDo p.35
Riding the Bus Home. Jill Witherspoon Boyer. DrF p.13
Rig up de cane pole an' dig up de red worm. Lucile D. Goodlett. WGC p.29
Right good jolly boy am mistah me, A. Lucy Mae Turner. BCF p.58
Right On. Beth Jackson. PoBBl p.54
Right on what? Beth Jackson. PoBBl p.54
Right On: White America. Sonia Sanchez. NaPr p.124; PoBA p.287; YoBBI p.368
Right on: white America 1. Sonia Sanchez. WABP p.25
Right on: white America 2. Sonia Sanchez. WABP p.26
Right on white: America 3. Sonia Sanchez. BOL p.42; SoS p.104; WABP p.27
Right on: white America 4. Sonia Sanchez. WABP p.28
Rt. Rev. Richard Allen. Josephine D. (Henderson) Heard. MoGl p.74
Right-to-Lifer in Grand Forks, North Dakato, A. June Jordan. PaNP p.95
Right to make my dreams come true, The. Georgia Douglas Johnson. BrBV p. 23
Rigmarole: Puzzles For Children. Elma Stuckey. BiGa p.82
Ring-Around-The Rosy. Kattie M. Cumbo. NiBPo p.54
Ring, Hammer, Ring! May Miller. ClAB p.4; CNAW p.360
Riot. Gwendolyn Brooks. BlP p. 175; BlPo p.26; NeBV p.20; PoBA p.164; RIOT p.9
Riot: 60's. Maya Angelou. JGM p.34
Rip Off. Ronda M. Davis. BrT p.181
Rise Up Fallen Fighters (Okra Takes Up With a Rastafari Man/She Can't Hold Back/ She Say Smilin'). Ntozake Shange. DaGe p.71
Rise Up, Shepherd and Follow.

Anonymous. ChG p.
Risin (for n-Nn and all our bruthas goin through changes/ real. Nia nSabe. ThHSD p. 74
Rising, The. Jayne Cortez. FeAF p.37; NeBV p.236
Rising. Jodi Braxton. SoITM p. 46
Rites for Cousin Vit, The. AnA p.45; BlP p.167; CNAW p. 520; SPGB p.58; WoOGB p.109
Rites of Passage. Audre Lorde. CaTR p.3; ChPON p.19; COAL p.3; NaPr p.69; PoBA p. 249
Ritual of Earpiercing, The. Harryette Mullen. TTW p.8
Ritual of the lovin blk. Barbara Mahone. Suga p.16
Rituals. Nikki Giovanni. MyH p.13
Rivah's a Black Mare. Lucile D. Goodlett. WGC p.19
Riven Quarry, The. Gloria Oden. PoBA p.185
Roaches are winning Mr. Exterminator, The. May Miller. BTB p.152; ClAB p.41
Road, The. Helene Johnson. AmNP p.100; BANP p.280; BlSi p.80; CaD p.221; GoS p.176; PoN p.154; PoNe p. 266; ReFNA p.50
Road to Anywhere. Dorothy Vena Johnson. EbR p.92
Roadmap. Harryette Mullen. TTW p.42
Roaring Third. Helen Johnson. NegVo p.87
Roasting Grasshoppers. Pinkie Gordon Lane. WiTh p.25
Roasting grasshopper meant making an oven out of fist-sized rocks. Pinkie Gordon Lane. WiTh p.25
Robert G. Shaw. Henrietta Cordelia Ray. BlSi p.37; EBAP p.140
Robert S. Abbott Founder of Chicago Devender Newspaper (1905) 1870-1940, Georgia. Eloise Culver. GANIV p.50
Robin Red Breast. Lula Lowe Weeden. CaD p.228
Robin's Poem, A. Nikki Giovanni. BrT p.68; Rec. p.32
Rock About My Saro Jane. Anonymous. BlWOA p.312
Rock, for ages, stern and high stood flowin 'gainst the earth and sky, A. Frances E. W. Harper. ANP p.16; PBFH p.36
Rock Thrown Into the Water Does Not Fear the Cold, A. Audre Lorde. BlUn p.9
Rocking Her White Feet. Sonia Sanchez. IvBAW p.78
Rogue & Jar: 4/27/77. Thulani Davis. AlTRGR p.52
Roland Hayes Singer, 1887- Georgia. Eloise Culver. GANIV p.59
Roll, Jordan Roll.** Anonymous. AfAWA p.106
Rolling, rushing, raftling, hushing waves race for shore. Carolyn Coleman. PoBBl p.27
Rolls are on the radiator rising, The. Naomi Long Madgett. ExAE p.14
Roman Poem Number Eight. June Jordan. ThTDID p.55
Roman Poem Number Eleven. June Jordan. ThTDID p.58
Roman Poem Number Fifteen. June Jordan. ThTDID p.61
Roman Poem Number Five. June Jordan. ThTDID p.16
Roman Poem Number Four. June Jordan. ThTDID p.182
Roman Poem Number Fourteen. June Jordan. ThTDID p.59
Roman Poem Number Nine. June Jordan. ThTDID p.56
Roman Poem Number One. June Jordan. ThTDID p.166
Roman Poem Number Seven. June Jordan. ThTDID p.184
Roman Poem Number Seventeen. June Jordan. ThTDID p.187
Roman Poem Number Six. June Jordan. ThTDID p.183
Roman Poem Number Sixteen: sightseer. June Jordan. ThTDID p.185
Roman Poem Number Ten. June Jordan. ThTDID p.57
Roman Poem Number Thirteen. June Jordan. ThTDID p.59

Roman Poem Number Three. June Jordan. ThTDID p.181
Roman Poem Number Twelve. June Jordan. ThTDID p.180
Roman Poem Number Two. June Jordan. ThTDID p.53
Romance. Georgia Douglas Johnson. ALC p.55
Romance of Antar, The. Anonymous. MBP p.66
Rome Fell. Gertrude Blackwell Bailey. IfWCF p.24
Rondeau. Jessie Redmond Fauset. NeNRe p.79; ReFNA p.38
Room was a red glow, The. Carolyn M. Rodgers. NaPr p.112; PoBA p.431; TNV p.113
Room With the Tapestry Rug, The. Nikki Giovanni. ThWRNW p.57
Rooming Houses are Old Women.** Audre Lorde. CaTR p.7; ChPON p.19; COAL p.7
Rooms are More Than Room. Carolyn M. Rodgers. HeAEG p.42
Roots. Lucille Clifton. OrW p. 21
Rose and ivory roses open among us. June Jordan. PaNP p.26
Rose Bush, The. Nikki Giovanni. CoCRD p.76
Rose Solitude. Jayne Cortez. COAG p.36; MoOP p.40
Rosebuds though you were flowers. Jennifer Blackman Lawson. BlIMT p.22
Roses After Rain. Georgia Douglas Johnson. HWOP p.45
Rotting murders are fresh blood clots in our brains. Carolyn M. Rodgers. AfAWA p.778; NaPr p.113
Round, A. Carolyn M. Rodgers. HeAEG p.37
Round and round I've paced these walls of sorrow. Pauli Murray. DaTAOP p.79
Round of Grief, The. June Jordan. ThTDID p.40
Round Table, The. Peggy Susberry Kenner. JuBa p.99
Round table will not tell, The. Peggy Susberry Kenner. JuBa p.99
'Round the Neighborhood. Floretta Howard. AmLNA p.53
Rout. Mari Evans. IABW p.50
Rubber stamp day, A. Pinkie Gordon Lane. WiTh p.42
Rudolph Reed Was Oaken. Gwendolyn Brooks. BeEa p.62; SoS p.46; SPGB p.110; WoOGB p.360
Run from me. Nola Richardson. WhOL p.75
"Run 'long, Sheppy, shame on you!" Bessie Woodson Yancey. EcFTH p.56
Run, Nigger, Run! Anonymous. BlP p.5
Run, nigger, run, the paddyroll get you. Anonymous. MyNIB p.36
Run to the kitchen and shout in the window. Fannie Berry. MyNIB p.48
Runaway. Elma Stuckey. BiGa p. 23
Running gag about carnations. Wanda Coleman. MaDBL p.123
Running to Gone. Esther Louise. CoAAAW p.200
Rut, The. Naomi Long Madgett. OnATM p.34
Ruth. Colleen J. McElroy. BlSi p.286
Ruth. Pauli Murray. DaTAOP p.40
Ruth Rev. S. Diane Bogus. WITM p.42

- S -

SOS. Anonymous. AfAA p.1
Sabbath Bells. Josephine D.(Henderson) Heard. MoGl p.32
Sacrifice. Alexis. AOS p.8
Sacrifice. Audre Lorde. ChPON p.93; NeHS p.50
Sacrifice. Pamela Cobb. InDM p. 27
Sad Me. Jacqueline Cox. AOS p. 24
Sadie and Maud. Gwendolyn Brooks. SPGB p.8; StIB p.14; WoOGB p.16
Sadie the cleaning lady: I ain't stud'n her. Leatrice Emeruwa. BlGBG p.4
Sadie's Playhouse. Margaret Danner. BTB p.87; DoOAT p.65; IrLa p.17; KAL p.128; PoBA

p.138
Safari. Sonia Sanchez. ItND p. 21
Safeguard. Beatrice M. Murphy. NegVo p.115
Sahara. Audre Lorde. BlUn p.16
Sailor/le marin/tells me "there is no violence in Haiti, The." Ntozake Shange. DaGe p.33
St. James Infirmary Blues. Anonymous. BlWOA p.647
St. Louis/such a colored town. Ntozake Shange. BlSi p.268; NaEd p.86
Saint Malcolm. Johari Amini. BlP p.230
St. Vanentine's Day Poem. Pinkie Gordon Lane. MyFe p.42
Saintly congregation of Calvary Baptist Church in Birmingham (white) hold their Sunday-morning services in a fine edifice. Naomi Long Madgett. OnATM p.57
Sale began--young girls were there, The. Frances E. W. Harper. AfAV p.81; AfAWA p.96; BlP p.39; CNAW p.101; EBAP p.32; KAL p.13; NeCa p.295; PoN p.10; PoNe p.14; TYBP p.205
Salia. Lucile D. Goodlett. WGC p.50
Salia totes a white chile. Lucile D. Goodlett. WGC p.50
Sally. Elma Stuckey. BiGa p.45
Sally: Twelfth Street. Naomi Long Madgett. NeBV p.286; PiLAF p.56
Salt. Lucille Clifton. OrW p.11
Salt and Sand. Naomi Long Madgett. PiLAF p.63
Salt bread and broom be still. Audre Lorde. ChPON p.63; FrLWP p.25
Sambas and Things. Jill Witherspoon Boyer. DrF p.15
Same Death Over and Over to Lullabies are for Children, The. Audre Lorde. BlUn p.64
Sammy Chester Leaves "Godspell" and Visits Upward Bound on a Lake Forest Lawn, Bringing West Africa. Gwendolyn Brooks. Bec p.13
Sammy Lou of Rue sent to his reward. Alice Walker. BlSi p.212; RePOP p.29
Samuel Allen's Soul Dances. Margaret Danner. DoOAT p. 64
San Juan. June Jordan. SCh p. 38; ThTDID p.49
Sanctus. Naomi Long Madgett. PiLAF p.18
Sand evy'where over Janis sweepin. Mari Evans. BlSi p.144; NIGHT p.29
Sand, sifting thru a broken hour glass. Patricia Ford. PoBBl p.36
Sand Sifting Thru My Toes. Eleanor Thomas-Grumbach. MoSu p.24
Sand swirls a halo. Geraldine L. Wilson. CoAAAW p.394
Sandy. Olean Bess. MiFe p.13
Sandy's Poem. Melba Joyce Boyd. CaEADW p.42
Sangaree. Anonymous. UNBP p.85
Sapling. Yvette Johnson. TNV p.57
Sarah Street. Naomi Long Madgett. OnATM p.19
Sassafras Tea. Effie Lee Newsome. CaD p.56' GoS p.8
Sassafras tea is read and clear. Effie Lee Newsome. CaD p. 56; GoS p.8
Sassy. Lucy Mae Turner. BCF p. 11
Sat in the sun hands hung between her legs. Elouise Loftin. PoBA p.514
Satori. Gayl Jones. BlSi p.210; SoS p.15
Saturday Afternoon, When Chores are Done. Harryette Mullen. TTW p.10
Saturday Afternoons, While School Was in Session.** Gloria Oden. TiTBi p.20
Saturday Night at the Parsonage. Naomi Long Madgett. ExAE p. 14
Saturdays. Jayne Cortez. Scar p.9
Save the Boys. Frances E. W. Harper. PBFH p.40
Say, bud, ya got a cigarette? Naomi Long Madgett. PhN p. 89; PoN p.207; PoNe p.379

Say, heav'nly muse, what king, or mighty God. Phillis Wheatley. BlLi p.10; PAL p.82
Say Hello to John. Sherley Williams. BlSi p.254; PePo p.14
Say, muse divine, can hostile scenes delight. Phillis Wheatley. PAL p.74; PPW p. 32
Say not the age is hard and cold. Frances E. W. Harper. PBFH p.6
Say skinny manysided tall on the ball. Lucille Clifton. TwW p.9
Say that he was legend. Pauli Murray. DaTAOP p.68
Say That I Am. Paulette Childress White. DeDF p.68
Say that I am beautiful. Paulette Childress White. DeDF p.68
Say to them, say to the down-keepers. Gwendolyn Brooks. FaP p.23
Say you brother! Barbara Marshall. TNV p.68
Says I be's so crazy insane. Joanne Jimason. NaABE p.20
Scaling your words like crags I found silence. Audre Lorde. ChPON p.67; NeHS p.27
Scar. Audre Lorde. BlUn p.48
Scarity in oil and gas can bring about a cold spell. Nikki Giovanni. CoCRD p.84
Scared? are responsible Negroes running scared? Nikki Giovanni. BFBTBJ p.323; BlP p.323
Scars and Stripes. Elma Stuckey. BiGa p.33
Scavenger winds bowel blown of industry hug the space between the here and theres. S. Diane Bogus. WITM p.59
Schemin'. Pearl Cleage Lomax. RoATW p.108; WeDNNM p.9
Schizophrenia. Judy Dothard Simmons. JuB p.21
School of Beauty's a tavern now, The. Gwendolyn Brooks. SPGB p.5; StIB p.5; WoOGB p.7
Schoolhouse, The. Mari Evans. NIGHT p.38
Scorn not my lowly station on this earth. Naomi Long Madgett. OnATM p.60
Scorn Not My Station. Naomi Long Madgett. OnATM p.60
Scorpio People. Nola Richardson. WhOL p.45
Scrapbooks. Nikki Giovanni. MyH p.33
Scream, The. May Miller. DeDF p.33
Screams. Jayne Cortez. FeAF p.16
'Scuse me, white folks I'se old and dull. Elma Stuckey. BiGa p.49
Sea Horse.** Anonymous. MBP p. 60
Sea is calling you, The. Melba Joyce Boyd. CaEADW p.17
Sea Purge. May Miller. ClAB p. 25
Sea shell is a palace, A. Dorothy Vena Johnson. GoS p.179
Sea Sounds. Carolyn Coleman. PoBBl p.27
Searching, The. Alice S. Cobb. BlSi p.146
Searching. Melva Eloise Tatum. MELVA p.7
Searching...searching for anything I can find. Melva Eloise Tatum. MELVA p.7
Seascape: Union Pier. Naomi Long Madgett. PiLAF p.32
Seasonal Note. Naomi Long Madgett. ExAE p.64
Seasoning. Audre Lorde. BlUn p.35
Seasons/changes moods the things of this earth are the things that gives us pleasure. Carolyn M. Rodgers. HoIGO p.76
Seasons Have to Pass. Naomi Long Madgett. OnATM p.37
2nd Ave. & 12th St. Sonia Sanchez. AfAA p.2
Second hand sights, like crumpled mud-smudged postcards. Carolyn M. Rodgers. PoBA p. 430
Second man I love, The. Carole Gregory Clemmons. PoBA p. 488

Second Meeting. Angela Jackson. VoDLM p.12
2nd Rap. Nikki Giovanni. BrT p. 68; EgT p.37; Rec p.31
Second Sermon on the Warpland, The. Gwendolyn Brooks. BLIA p.335; BlP p.171; ITM p.51; PoBA p.163; WoOGB p.423
Second Spring. Audre Lorde. ChPON p.3; COAL p.69; FiCi p.8
Secret, The. Bessie Woodson Yancey. EcFTH p.36
Secret. Gwendolyn B. Bennett. BlSi p.74; CaD p.155
Secret Hours Ere Dawn, The. Lucy May Turner. BCF p.23
Secret Seasons. Jill Witherspoon Boyer. DrF p.9
Sectional Touchstone. Lillie Kate Walker Benitez. UNBP p.313
Secured by sooted windows and amazement. Maya Angelou. AnSIR p.22
Security on #406. Jodi Braxton. SoITM p.27
Seduction. Jo Ann Hall-Evans. BlSi p.192
Seduction. Nikki Giovanni. BFBTBJ p.38; BrT p.54; NaPr p.25; RoATW p.125
"See America First." the tour guide cried. Frenchy J. Hodges. BlW p.25
See Dee Gread Big Sweet Pertaters. Anonymous. ITBLA p.125
See how dark the night settles on my face. Naomi Long Madgett. AfAWA p.690; BlALP p.111; DeDF p.67; StBS p. 56
See Michie banjo there. Michie Banjo. Anonymous. MBP p.52
Seed Abe Lincoln wid my eyes. Elma Stuckey. BiGa p.62
Seeds. Carolyn M. Rodgers. HeAEG p.45
Seeing blue things: you, Marion. Pinkie Gordon Lane. MyFe p. 32
Seeing Eye-Dog, A. Sandra Sharp. RoATW p.64
Seeing/Remembering. Pinkie Gordon Lane. MyFe p.32
Seemingly, I shall never forget this night. Alicia Loy Johnson. TGWL p.52
Seems my one child had a habit. June Vanleer Williams. WiRYPS p.4
Seems We Got Detoured. June Vanleer Williams. WiRYPS p.46
Sees the man in the wood. Lucille Clifton. OrW p.89
Seldom Seen. Margaret Danner. DoOAT p.73
Sellin' Time. Anonymous. BlWOA p.234
Selling Melvina. Elma Stuckey. BiGa p.41
Selling my soul is not the question. Wanda Coleman. MaDBL p.22
Senate Man. Colleen McElroy. MuDLSG p.14
Senegalese girls (dazzling carriers of carriage) gracing their yards of sheer mboubous. Margaret Danner. IrLa p.27
Senses of Heritage. Ntozake Shange. NaEd p.54
Senses of Insecurity. Maya Angelou. OhPWFW p.17
Sensitivity is so deeply patterned in the spirit. Margaret Danner. DoOAT p. 131
Sensuous. Melva Eloise Tatum. MELVA p.24
'Sensuous' Lion, The. Margaret Danner. DoOAT p.60
Sensuous sloe eyed soft lipped. Jo Ann Hall-Evans. BlSi p.192
Sent to prison last week about a brother I almost killed. S. Diane Bogus. WITM p.51
Sentiment. Thelma T. Clement. BTh p.22
Sentimental Woman. Barbara Mahone. Suga p.24
Separation. Audre Lorde. ChPON p.85; NeHS p.29
Separation. Georgia Douglas Johnson. ALC p.8
Sepia Fashion Show. Maya Angelou. BlSi p.267; JGM p.45

September Lament. Naomi Long Madgett. OnATM p.49
Sepulchure. Georgia Douglas Johnson. ALC p.68
Sequel. Mae V. Cowdery. WLOV p.43
Sequel No. 1. Pinkie Gordon Lane. WiTh p.10
Sequel No. 2. Pinkie Gordon Lane. WiTh p.11
Sequel No. 3. Pinkie Gordon Lane. PoBBl p.15; WiTh p.11
Sequelae. Audre Lorde. BluB p. 25
Sequences. Sonia Sanchez. IvBAW p.40; LoP p.43
Sergeant Jerk. Deborah Fuller Wess. EbR p.159
Serious Lessons Learned. Ntozake Shange. NaEd p.110
Sermon on the Warpland, The. Gwendolyn Brooks. BlP p.170; ITM p.49; PoBA p.163; WoOGB p.421
Service. Bessie Woodson Yancey. EcFTH p.19
Service. Georgia Douglas Johnson. BrBV p.87; CaD p.75
Service, Please. Myrtle Campbell Gorham. EbR p.71
Sessions. Wanda Coleman. MaDBL p.70
Setting/Slow Drag. Carolyn M. Rodgers. JuBa p.122
Seven Months and six letters ago we packed it away in the cellar. Carolyn Gregory Clemmons. NiBPo p.83
7/2. Audre Lorde. NaPr p.68
7:25 Trolley, The. Mari Evans. IABW p.55
Seventh Sense, The. Audre Lorde. ChPON p.40; FrLWP p.18
'70s, The. Lucille Clifton. GoNAE p.8
Seventy-One Years Have Gathered.** Sonia Sanchez. IvBAW p.84
Several Propostions in the Middle of the Mile. Ntozake Shange. NaEd p.37
Sewer Plant Grows in Harlem or I'm a Stranger Here Myself When Does the Next Swan Leave, A. Audre Lorde. NeHS p.9
Sewerplant Grows in Harlem or I'm a Stranger Here Myself Here Myself When Does the Next Swan Leave, A. Audre Lorde. ChPON p.69
Sex is good but not enough. Wanda Coleman. MaDBL p.73
Sexual Privacy of Women on Welfare. Pinkie Gordon Lane. BlSi p.230; MyFe p.38
Shades of eve are falling fast, The. Evelyn Watson. AmLNA p.78
Shades of eve are quickly closing in, The. Josephine D. (Henderson) Heard. MoGl p.19
Shades of the gloaming around me are stealing, The. Georgia Douglas Johnson. HWOP p.55
Shadow & Veil. Thulani Davis. AlTRGR p.4
Shadows. Helen F. Clarke. EbR p.40
Shadows. Pinkie Gordon Lane. WiTh p.53
Shadows in the Light. Elma Stuckey. BiGa p.91
Shadows of our Colored bodies play on the wall. Charron Lipscomb. NeJCL p.26
Shadows of the body blue and not blue, The. June Jordan. PaNP p.6
Shadows on the wall. Maya Angelou. AnSIR p.45
Shadows, shadows, hug me round. Georgia Douglas Johnson. PoBA p.22
Shaft of light--a soul forlorn, A. Juanita M. Dickinson. NegVo p.52
Shah of Iran was overthrown, The. June Jordan. PaNP p.76
Shake hands with loneliness. Jennifer Blackman Lawson. BlIMT p.43
Shakespeare. Henrietta Cordelia Ray. EBAP p.140
Shall I die shall I die a sweet/ death. Sonia Sanchez. BrT p.142; WABP p.55
Shall I Light a Candle?** Judy Dothard Simmons. JuB p.18
Shall I say, "My son, you are branded in this country pageantry." Georgia Douglas Johnson. BrBV p.45; DuSAE p.143; NeNRe p.380

Shall we forget with each returning year. Josephine D. (Henderson) Heard. MoGl p.110
Shame on you. Dorothy C. Parrish. TNV p.89
Shango is an animal like the gorilla. Anonymous. TYBP p. 12
Shango is the death who kills money with a big stick. Anonymous. TYBP p.12
Shango I. Anonymous. TYBP p.12
Shango II. Anonymous. TYBP p.12
Sharon Will be No/Where on Nobody's Best-Selling List. Sharon Scott. JuBa p.177
Shattered Dreams. Frenchy J. Hodges. BlW p.75
Shattered Mirror. Mae V. Cowdery. WLOV p.55
Shattereing silence a gun full of bullets. Wanda Coleman. MaDBL p.50
Shd I have said like the lady & Ben W. Ntozake Shange. NaEd p.35
She called to say she thought she died. Regina Williams. CoAAAW p.379
She came down to get him. Mari Evans. NIGHT p.23
She came from the East a fair young bride. Frances E. W. Harper. PBFH p.63
She came home running. Maya Angelou. JGM p.18
She can't wait for you to knock. Sandra Rogers. CoAAAW p.316
She captured aura bold of yellow sun. Leatrice Emeruwa. BlGBG p.4
She caught a chicken and wrung its neck. Elma Stuckey. BiGa p.76
She chases dreams that flitter this way and that. Jennifer Blackman Lawson. BlIMT p.15
She clear her throat and spit in soup. Elma Stuckey. BiGa p.45
She coaxes her fat in front of her. Naomi Long Madgett. BlSi p.130; ExAE p.37
She crawls in it for the only refuge allowed her. Wanda Coleman. MaDBL p.21
She didn't like to think in abstracts. Nikki Giovanni. CoCRD p.24
She Didn't Want Her Friends to Know. Naomi Evans Vaughn. NegVo p.160
She didn't want his love. Beatrice M. Murphy. NegVo p.117
She doesn't flow into a room. Patricia Parker. MiIB p.113
She dragged me from the backyard. Angela Jackson. VoDLM p.9
She emptied her purse on the table. Elma Stuckey. BiGa p.75
She-Feelings Poems # 1. S. Diane Bogus. WITM p.20
She gives herself to a burning man. Nzadi Zimele-Keita. CoAAAW p.398
She goes to different bars. Patricia Parker. MoIB p.154
She got her mama's ways. Lucille Clifton. OrW p.67
She got so drunk she didn't know herself. Thulani Davis. AlTRGR p.46
She had always been called "Healthy". Theresa Ford. NeJCL p.23
She had not found herself a hard pillow. Angelina Weld Grimke. AmNP p.15
She had on sandals. Vanessa Howard. ScWh p.45
She has not found herself a hard pillow. Angelina Weld Grimke. EbAT p.67
She hears Donne, Blake, n' Browning. Leatrice Emeruwa. BlGBG p.1
She hugged me and kissed me. Anonymous. AmLNA p.9; BlP p.16
She hung inside the window. Melba Joyce Boyd. CaEADW p.27
She, in dowdy dress and dumpy. Quandra Prettyman. PoBA p. 259
She Insists On Me. Lucille Clifton. OrW p.49
She is beautiful! Corinne Lytle. NegVo p.103
She is Dreaming. Lucille Clifton. OrW p.53

She just took off. Jennifer Blackman Lawson. BlIMT p.5
She kept it in a black green felt-lined box. Wanda Coleman. MaDBL p.96
She lay there missing. Leatrice Emeruwa. BlGBG p.13
She leaned her head upon her hand. Frances E. W. Harper. BlSi p.27; EaNAW p.294; EBAP p.34; PBFH p.44
She lies down a mess on white paper under glass. June Jordan. ThTDID p.188
She lived in a shingled shell. Melba Joyce Boyd. CaEADW p. 30
She loves me I know. Wanda Coleman. MaDBL p.33
She loves you, you love me. June Vanleer Williams. WiRYPS p. 19
She moves through darkness. Pamela Cobb. InDM p.16
She often wondered why people spoke of gaining years as turning. Nikki Giovanni. CoCRD p.85
She picked up her ticket yesterday. Jill Witherspoon Boyer. DrF p.15
She realized she wasn't one of life's winners. Nikki Giovanni. CoCRD p.52
She said the Jehovan Witness man gave her the cane to walk with. Gayl Jones. BlSi p.205
She sees the little things that you'd pass by. Alice D. Anderson. EbR p.1
She sighed beneath the stars her weary lays. Naomi Long Madgett. OnATM p.25
She sings looks young carries visions of pop tunes. Colleen McElroy. MuDLSG p.21
She sits ebony skinned drawing sun rays. Patricia Parker. MoIB p.58
She smelled him right away. Alexis De Veaux. CoAAAW p. 99
She stood before the multitude. Eloise Culver. GANIV p.71
She stood hanging wash before sun. Carole Gregory Clemmons. NBP p.56; NiBPo p.82; PoBA p.489
She stood in mental greyness. Margaret Danner. DoOAT p.45
She stood there like a Inca statue. Amina Baraka. CoAAAW p.73
She stood there, resting all of her weight against the doorway. Dorothy Randall. ThHSD p.4
She stops at the gas station. Toi Derricotte. EmDH p.32
She swayed from the barre. Ntozake Shange. NaEd p.108
She tries to knit the hole in his hand. Melba Joyce Boyd. CaEADW p.20
She tripped and fell against a star. Anne Spencer. CaD p. 57
She turned to me and said the weather's bad. Carolyn M. Rodgers. HeAEG p.54
She Understands Me. Lucille Clifton. OrW p.51
She wait they come when can word mask. Jodi Braxton. SoITM p.45
She waited on the 7th floor. Ntozake Shange. BlSi p.273; NaEd p.61
She walked along the crowded street. Blanche Taylor Dickingson. CaD p.107
She walks the dead leaf path. Jennifer Blackman Lawson. BlIMT p.4
She walks up astrological stairs. Wanda Coleman. MaDBL p.111
She wanted pretty fine china. Wanda Coleman. MaDBL p.116
She wanted to be a blade of grass. Nikki Giovanni. CoCRD p.71
She wants a man she can just unfold when she needs him. Harryette Mullen. TTW p.42
She was a symphony in lace and gold. Iola M. Brister. NegVo p.16
She was afraid of men. Maya Angelou. OhPWFW p.43
She was Black and solid moonshine. Elma Stuckey. BiGa p.77

She was just like me. Thulani Davis. AlTRGR p.49
She was not easy to have. Thulani Davis. AlTRGR p.8
She was the perfect woman. Wanda Coleman. MaDBL p.75
She was touched by the seeming insanity. Margaret Danner. DoOAT p.78
She wished of him a lover's kiss. Maya Angelou. OhPWFW p.20
Shedding My Years. Sonia Sanchez. IvBAW p.77
Shedding Skin. Harryette Mullen. TTW p.37
Shepherd. Elma Stuckey. BiGa p.25
She's Free! Frances E. W. Harper. BlSi p.32
She's got whiskers bout quarter inch long. Ntozake Shange. NaEd p.66
Shine and the Titantic. Anonymous. BlWOA p.651
Shining Ground, The. Pamela Cobb. InDM p.24
Ship a chain, a distant, A. Sherley Williams. PePo p.57
Ships? sure I'll sail them. Maya Angelou. AnSIR p.52
Shooting Star. Jayne Cortez. FeAF p.34
Shore against me I shake with wetness. Wanda Coleman. MaDBL p.133
Shores that tide in and harbor keller. Margaret Danner. DoOAT p.136
Short essay of affirmation explaining why (with apologies to the Federal Bureau of Investigation). Nikki Giovanni. BFBTBJ p.21
Short magic is a kiss in the street. Sonia Sanchez. IvBAW p.32; LoP p.13
Short Note to my Very Critical and Well-Beloved Friends and Comrades, A. June Jordan. PaNP p.78
Short Poem. Sonia Sanchez. HoC p.17; IvBAW p.5
Short Poem # 1. S. Diane Bogus. WITM p.6
Short Poem # 3. S. Diane Bogus. WITM p.27
Short Poem for Us Slick Ones. Sonia Sanchez. IvBAW p.72
Short Song From My Heart. June Jordan. ThTDID p.63
Shorty George. Anonymous. BlWOA p.460
Should this final poem be sad? Pinkie Gordon Lane. WiTh p.56
Should you, my love, while you pursue my sons. Phillis Wheatley. BlP p.38; ITSA p.13
Shoulders broad and squared and strong. Naomi Long Madgett. PiLAF p.62
Shoulders sag. The pull of weighted needling. Maya Angelou. AnSIR p.17
Shout. Carolyn M. Rodgers. HeAEG p.33
Shout Along, Children. Anonymous. BlWOA p.241
Show me no mirages in this death. Margaret Danner. DoOAT p.46
Shrine to What Should Be. Mari Evans. NNPUSA p.77
Shuddering. Harryette Mullen. TTW p.28
Siam at de meetin' house dress up fine. Lucile D. Goodlett. WGC p.32
Siam at De Radio. Lucile D. Goodlett. WGC p.33
Siam wuz sick fo' two long mont's. Lucile D. Goodlett. WGC p.61
Sick man looks at flowers. Gwendolyn Brooks. SPGB p.124
Sidewalk. Wanda Coleman. MaDBL p.124
Sight. Cora Ball Moten. GoS p.186; NegVo p.111
Sight of paroding man or little chubby boys of four. Mae V. Cowdery. WLOV p.66
Sighted a black tornado of flying feces. Peggy Susberry Kenner. JuBa p.98
Signals. Johari Amini. PoBA p.292; RoATW p.28; BlSp p.2
Signifying Monkey, The. Anonymous. BlWOA p.650
Signs. Audre Lorde. FrLWP p.31
Signs. Beatrice M. Murphy. GoS p.25

Signs of Spring. Bessie Woodson Yancey. EcFTH p.45
Signs of the End. Sonia Sanchez. BluB p.51
Silence. Naomi Long Madgett. PhN p.67; SoTPN p.19
Silence hangs about us so thickly, The. S. Diane Bogus. WITM p.17
Silence of the brooding night, The. Georgia Douglas Johnson. HWOP p.22
Silence polishing the streets to rain. June Jordan. SCh p. 80; SoS p.70; ThTDID p.163
Silence slipping around like death. Angelina Weld Grimke. CaD p.36; NeCa p.343; PoN p. 47; PoNe p.54
Silent City Cries Today, The. Vanessa Howard. ScWh p.6
Silk-like thoughts gently thread the horizons of their minds. Jennifer Blackman Lawson. BlIMT p.14
Silver Cell, The. Mari Evans. IABW p.18; WhIAM p.5
Silver Cord, The. Naomi Long Madgett. ExAE p.23
Silver Creek, Mississippi. Thulani Davis. AlTRGR p.44
Silver Lace. Melba Joyce Boyd. CaEADW p.17
Silver one year was a broomstick from the kitchen. Naomi Long Madgett. ExAE p.20
Simple. Naomi Long Madgett. FBPA p.93; PiLAF p.55; PoBA p.182
Simplicity you said no excess. Sonia Sanchez. LoP p.83
Sin, A? Geraldine Peterson. PoBBl p.35
Since dawn broke on the planet earth. Eloise Culver. GANIV p.57
Since I don't want to trip over your silence. Audre Lorde. BlUn p.85
Since it has become fashionable to wear a caduce. S. Diane Bogus. WITM p.42
Since I've found out, that you really don't care. Carolyn M. Rodgers. HeAEG p.62
Since Malcolm died that old Aardvark has got a sort of fame. Julia Fields. NiBPo p.75
Since naturally Black is naturally beautiful I must be proud. Audre Lorde. BlSi p.203; DeDF p.63; MoCAP p.122; NaPr p.65; NeHS p. 35; SoS p.87; UNBP p.283
Since 1619. Margaret Walker. FMP p.26
Since the song the winter's way. Helen C. Harris. EbR p.79
Since you wrote a poem explaining the color of Black. Carolyn M. Rodgers. BlP p. 265; SoBB p.22
Sing a song of colored folk. Claire Turner. NegVo p.156
Sing me a song for a Negro. Naomi Long Madgett. PhN p. 100
Sing Soft and Low.** Naomi Long Madgett. SoTPN p.24
Sing your song to Jesus. Beatrice M. Murphy. RoCO p.13
Singer, The. Colleen McElroy. MuDLSG p.21
Singer Will Not Sing, The. Maya Angelou. AnSIR p.27
Sinners, gamblers, whores and such. Elma Stuckey. BiGa p.74
Sinners were coaxed to sit up front, The. Elma Stuckey. BiGa p.74
Sips of Wine. Nola Richardson. WhOL p.37
Sis wears a mask. Nikki Giovanni. VaT p.53
Sissy. Elma Stuckey. BiGa p.35
Sister. Marion Nicholes. LiS p.14
Sister Charity. Colleen McElroy. MuDLSG p.17
Sister, Morning is a Time for Miracles. Audre Lorde. ChPON p.109
Sister Outsider. Audre Lorde. BlUn p.106
Sisters! I love you. Gwendolyn Brooks. CoAAAW p.84
Sisters, I saw it today. Sonia Sanchez. BlSp p.186
Sisters its time to be veiled again. Marion Nicholes. LiS p.17

Sisters, we fear each other. Barbara Mahone. Suga p.26
Sit-Ins. Margaret Walker. PFND p.10
Sit where the light corrupts your face. Gwendolyn Brooks. ITM p.5; WoOGB p.377
Sitten near my window at my typewritter. Carolyn M. Rodgers. SoBB p.21
Sitting here listening to the beat. Loretta Rodgers. ThHSD p.82
Sitting Here, Listening to You.** Patricia Parker. MoIB p.126
Sitting in a candle lit room warm from tip top top. Carolyn M. Rodgers. BlSp p.176
Sitting on the stone gray church steps cupped in expensive shrubbery. Carolyn M. Rodgers. SoBB p.36; UNBP p.344
Sitting there on the assembly line piecing together frocks all alike. Carolyn M. Rodgers. CoAAAW p.313
Six Stories High, She Stands Flooded.** Gloria Oden. RESUR p.141
6:30. Carolyn M. Rodgers. SoBB p.16
16. Tell me why he is no longer in school. Carolyn M. Rodgers. HoIGO p.30
Sketch. Delores Kendrick. TGWL p.60
Sketching in the Transcendental. June Jordan. PaNP p.47
Skies o'ercast and fierce wind blow, The. Josephine D. (Henderson) Heard. MoGl p.61
Sky, The. Anonymous. MBP p.6; TYBP p.8
Sky at night is like a big city, The. Anonymous. MBP p.6; TYBP p.8
Sky Diving. Nikki Giovanni. ThWRNW p.46
Sky is heavy, it is raining stars, The. Anonymous. TYBP p.24
Sky Pictures. Effie Lee Newsome. GoS p.177
Sky was blue, so blue that day, The. Angelina Weld Grimke. BlSi p.63; CaD p.45; PoN p. 97; PoNe p.55
Skyline of New York does not excite me, The. Gloria Oden. ITBLA p.275; KAL p.182; MoCAP p.95; NNPUSA p.90; PoBA p.184
"Slackahs". Bessie Woodson Yancey. EcFTH p.56
Slave and the Iron Lace, The. Margaret Danner. AmNP p.157; BlP p.154; DoOAT p.103; UNBP p.229; YoBBI p.103
Slave Auction, The. Frances E. W. Harper. AfAV p.81; AfAWA p.96; BlP p.39; CNAW p.101; EBAP p.32; KAL p.13; PoN p.10; PoNe p.14; TYBP p.205;
Slave Marriage Ceremony Supplement. Anonymous. BlP p.16
Slave Mother, The. Frances E. W. Harper. AfAWA p.97; BlWOA p.225; EBAP p.31
Slave Mother's Crime, The. Josephine D. (Henderson) Heard. MoGl p.129
Slave Ritual. Carolyn M. Rodgers. HoIGO p.15
Slave Song. Anonymous. MyNIB p.45
Slave Song. Susie Melton. MyNIB p.46
Slavery. S. Diane Bogus. WITM p.30
Slavery Chain. Anonymous. BlLi p.115
Slavery chain done broke at last, broke at last, broke at last. Anonymous. BlLi p.115
Slaves couldn't go to school. Eloise Culver. GANIV p.30
Sleep. Lucy Mae Turner. BCF p.57
Sleep, Child. Judy Dothard Simmons. JuB p.19
Sleep, child your bright brown eyes are closed. Judy Dothard Simmons. JuB p.19
Sleep early rise early breakfast, prep, departure late. S. Diane Bogus. WITM p.29
Sleep, love, sleep, just such peace. Quandra Prettyman. BOL p.75; OnOW p.19
Sleep, mah lil' lamb sleep! EcFTH p.50
Sleep, restful sleep. Lucy Mae

Turner. BDF p.57
Sleeping With Mr. Death. Toi Derricotte. EmDH p.13
Slender, shy, and sensitive young girl is woman now, The. Margaret Walker. OcJo p.34; TGWL p.95
Slight breeze soft cool shadowed woods, A. Johari Amini. ImIB p.4
Slim sentinels stretching last arms about a slumbrous moon. Helene Johnson. BlSi p.81
Slow mist rises up, A. Pamela Cobb. InDM p.24
Slow wand'ring came the sightless sire and she, great soul Antigone. Henrietta Cordelia Ray. BlSi p.40; EBAP p.141
Slumbering Bats. Pinkie Gordon Lane. PoBBl p.7; WiTh p.13
Slumbering Passion. Josephine D. (Henderson) Heard. MoGl p.23
Small and glowing in this cold place of brick cement. June Jordan. ThTDID p.16
Small as a mustard seed from the Nile and nubile kingdom. June Jordan. PaNP p.61
Small Bells of Benin, The. Margaret Danner. BrT p.39; ImOAAF p.2; IrLa p.28
Small brown girl began to sing, A. Eloise Culver. GANIV p. 69
Small Comment. Sonia Sanchez. BlWOA p.822; HoC p.17; IvBAW p.6; NBP p.114
Small Contradiction, A. Patricia Parker. MoIB p.123
Small green spring puffs of breath balloon into absurs enormities. Naomi Long Madgett. ExAE p.17
Small Slaughter, A. Audre Lorde. BlUn p.100
Small sounds come from outside the window. Julia Alvarez. SoS p.11
Small Time Profundity. S. Diane Bogus. WITM p.58
Small Time Profundity # 2. S. Diane Bogus. WITM p.8
Small Wind. Naomi Long Madgett. PiLAF p.32
Smell of Lebanon, The. Alice Walker. ONC p.66
Smile please today I saw the angels. Thulani Davis. AlTRGR p.47
Smiles do not always echo cheer. Georgia Douglas Johnson. HWOP p.51
Smiling Sunshine Sammy, magic is your mirth! Bessie Woodson Yancey. EcFTH p.36
Smoke kaleidoscope my people create, A. Damali (Denise Burnett) IATWMB p.11
Smooth surfaces are easy. Barbara Mahone. Suga p.27
Smothered Fires. Georgia Douglas Johnson. BlSi p.59; HWOP p.32
Snake hear an' er lizard tail/ hoo-doo, A. Jodi Braxton. SoITM p.15
Snatches of a Day. Patricia Parker. MoIB p.72
Snow. Dorothy Lee Louise Shaed. NegVo p.140
Snow has left Mount Mitchell, The. Audrey Johnson. BTh p.39
Snow in October. Alice Dunbar-Nelson. ANP p.85; BlSi p.66; CaD p.71
Snow piles on the city covering all it touches. Lyn. SiSH p.31
Snowflakes. Nikki Giovanni. VaT p.17
Snuffed out, choked in its infancy. June Vanleer Williams. WiRYPS p.14
So bitterly we parted. Mae Jackson. CaPWY p.16
So Black great great grandmomma they tell me you pushed a baby carriage. Jodi Braxton. SoITM p.3
So Brooklyn has become a holy place. June Jordan. ThTDID p.121
So Close They Come so Close. Lucille Clifton. GoNAE p. 20
So detached and cool she is. Clarissa Scott Delany. CaD p.143; PoN p.94; PoNe p.177; ReFNA p.43
So he said: you ain't got no

talent. Nikki Giovanni. Rec p.45; WoATM p.21
So here come I home again. Lucille Clifton. GoNAE p.42
So how come we can't touch when we hurt most? Patricia Parker. MoIB p.103
So I met this man who was a publisher when he was young. Nikki Giovanni. BFBTBJ p.9
So I Say! June Vanleer Williams. WiRYPS p.46
So innocent and strange to wounds. May Miller. ClAB p. 19
So I've found me at last. Daphne Diane Page. UNBP p.316
So just because my skin is Black you think you are better than me. Beth Jackson. PoBBl p.58
So like a boundless, soundless sea the miracle of love to me. Georgia Douglas Johnson. ALC p.9
So Long. Jayne Cortez. Scar p.45
So many elbows on the bandstand. Jayne Cortez. COAG p.90
So Many Feathers. Jayne Cortez. BlSi p.155; COAG p.33; MoOP p.18
So many weary years I've crept. Lucy Mae Turner. BCF p.40
So much I hates 'bout slavery time. Elma Stuckey. BiGa p.55
So Much of Me.** Ann Wallace. GLOWC p.108
So Much of What I Did Today.** Melva Eloise Tatum. MELVA p.11
So much of what we say. Marva Tatum Smith. BeYM p.22
So much rain. Sonia Sanchez. LoP p.15
So near is my desire. Naomi Long Madgett. PhN p.83
So now it is your time to leave me. Naomi Long Madgett. PhN p.48; SoTPN p.23
So piercing like burning pain. Marva Tatum Smith. BeYM p. 16
So Quickly it Ends. June Vanleer Williams. WiRYPS p.14
So, so afraid--an inner terror gnaws at my innards. June Vanleer Williams. WiRYPS p. 51
So they kicked him off the beach. Wanda Coleman. MaDBL p.46
So This is Our Revolution. Sonia Sanchez. BrT p.146; NaPr p.127; WABP p.63
So Tired. Virginia Williams. GaBW p.427
So We've Come at Last to Freud. Alice Walker. ONC p.61; RoATW p.87
So you are herded like sheep. June Vanleer Williams. WiRYPS p.69
So, You've Grown Up.** Marva Tatum Smith. BeYM p.7
So you've reached your thirty-eighth birthday. Josephine D. (Henderson) Heard. MoGl p.37
Soap toilet paper a grocery list begins a poem. Margaret Porter. CoAAAW p.263
Soft lamp shinin and me alone in the night. Sherley Williams. PePo p.25
Soft Man, The. Gwendolyn Brooks. StIB p.7; WoOGB p.9
Soft pink clouds float lazily on a calm cerulean sea. Portia Bird Daniel. NegVo p.44
Soft poems are so hard to write. Lyn. SiSH p.14
Soft Soap. Lucile D. Goodlett. WGC p.24
Soft the stars are meeting. Sharon Bourke. UNBP p.376
Soft velvet royal red fragrant honest thorny prickly ouch. Jennifer Blackman Lawson. BlITM p.28
Soft words he's blowing in my ear. Wanda Coleman. MaDBL p.87
Soft you day, be velvet, soft, my true love. Maya Angelou. JGM p.4
Softly, now, or mammy'll ketch us round. Lucy Mae Turner. BCF p.35

Sojourner Truth, Freedom Fighter, 1797-1883, New York. Eloise Culver. GANIV p.25
"Sojourner Truth," she named herself. Eloise Culver. GANIV p.25
Solace. Clarissa Scott Delany. AmNP p.59; CaD p.14; PoBA p.71; PoN p.94; PoNe p. 178; ReFNA p.44
Solace. Josephine D. (Henderson) Heard. MoGl p.83
Soldier. Georgia Douglas Johnson. BrBV p.68
Solemly they gathered in oak paneled offices overlooking the Hudson, the Trinity, the Moskva, the Yungting. Mari Evans. IABW p.44
Solidarity Day, 1968. June Jordan. SCh p.50; ThTDID p.110
Soliloquy. Dorothy C. Parrish. TNV p.90
Soliloquy. Lucile D. Goodlett. WGC p.35
Solitaire. Naomi Long Madgett. OnATM p.32
Solo. Jayne Cortez. FeAF p.41
Solo full of quivering flesh, A. Jayne Cortez. FeAF p.41
Solomon. Lucille Clifton. GoNAE p.33
Solomòn Mahlangu freedom fighter from Mamelodi. Jayne Cortez. COAG p.101
Solstice. Audre Lorde. BlUn p. 117
Solution. Lyn. SiSH p.18
Solution # 9 "To Touch You." Mariah Britton Howard. CoAAAW p.147
Some Body Call. Carolyn M. Rodgers. HoIGO p.13
Some Compromise. Nola Richardson. WhOL p.65
Someday I shall be dead. Georgia Douglas Johnson. ALC p.66
Some day I shall be glad that it was mine to be. Georgia Douglas Johnson. BrBV p.61
Some day I shall write a poem for you. Lucia Mae Pitts. NegVo p.131
Some day the poet and warrior who grapple in my brain. Pauli Murray. DaTAOP p.70
Some day this form must crumble. Claire Turner. NegVo p.156
Some Dreams Hang in the Air. Lucille Clifton. OrW p.87
Some faces pass by as dissipating clouds. Damali (Denise Burnett) IATWMB p.14
Some fo'ks lib in houses grand. Lucy Mae Turner. BCF p.40
Some folks are always complaining nothing is ever right. Gertrude Blackwell Bailey. IfWCF p.16
Some folks are getting mighty smart. Elma Stuckey. BiGa p.84
Some folks can live while others die. Elma Stuckey. BiGa p. 82
Some Hands are Lovelier. Mae V. Cowdery. WLOV p.40
Some have their many jewels. Lucy Mae Turner. BCF p.54
Some Jesus has come to me. Lucille Clifton. GoNAE p.40
Some Light to Hold in my Hands. Harryette Mullen. TTW p.21
Some Men. Ntozake Shange. DaGe p.37
Some/men don't know anything abt that. Ntozake Shange. DaGe p.37
Some Men of Beauty. Carolyn M. Rodgers. HoIGO p.53
Some men on the street look at me. Pamela Cobb. InDM p.17
Some of you in our country say that you are more American. Margaret Burroughs. WhSIT p.16
Some mortal has said that beyond the sky reigns rest and eternal peace. Naomi Long Madgett. PhN p.24
Some of my loneliiest hours have been with you. Saundra Sharp. RoATW o,67
Some other witches, those more deeply dipped. Margaret Danner. DoOAT p.52
Some People. June Jordan. ThTDID p.195
Some people despise me. June Jordan. ThTDID p.195
Some rise by easy stages. Josephine D. (Henderson) Heard.

MoGl p.97
Some say he's from Georgia. Anonymous. BLIA p.43; BlWOA 463; GoS p.34; ITBLA p.122
Some small island birthed her. Nikki Giovanni. Rec p.30; WoATM p.19
Some Smooth Lyrics For a Natural People. Alicia Loy Johnson. TGWL p.55
Some spoke of a third world. Mae Jackson. CaPWY p.k2
Some things are very dear to me. Gwendolyn B. Bennett. AmNP p.75; BANP p.243; CaD p. 161; ITBLA p.218; PoBA p.82
Some things you white folks say ain't funny. June Vanleer Williams. WiRYPS p.65
Some time turns inside out. Audre Lorde. ChPON p.88; NeHS p.31
Some times I dream bout u & me. Sonia Sanchez. IvBAW p.24; MoCAP p.136; RoATW p.135; WABP p.40
Some times the road gets so thick. Melba Joyce Boyd. CaEADW p.19
Some Uses for Them Not Stated. Nikki Giovanni. Rec p.41
Some would rather know volcanoes. June Jordan. ThTDID p.81
Some years the Mississippi rose up so high. Thulani Davis. AlTRGR p.44
Somebody Call. Carolyn M. Rodgers. JuBa p.119
Somebody come and carry me into a seven-day kiss. June Jordan.
Somebody coming in blackness like a star. Lucille Clifton. GoNAE p.37
Somebody's Calling Your Name. Jennifer Blackman Lawsonn. BlIMT p.48
Somehow a child got lost in the piano. Judy Dothard Simmons. JuB p.13
Somehow to find a still spot in the noise was the frayed inner want. Gwendolyn Brooks. BeEa p.13; WoOGB p.311
Someone Sweet Angel Child. Sherley Williams. ChOSa p.117
Something About a Little Kid. S. Diane Bogus. WITM p.49
Something about this boy has spelled my tongue. Lucille Clifton. GoNAE p.39
Something Else. June Vanleer Williams. WiRYPS p.34
Something fresh and newly seen in placing this leg over. Jodi Braxton. SoITM p.35
Something has passed between us more than blood. Naomi Long Madgett. ExAE p.19
Something in You Speaks to Me.** Gloria Oden. RESUR p.41
Something Lost. Nola Richardson. WhOL p.11
Something should be said now for my mother. Margaret T. G. Burroughs. WhSIT p.11
Something to be Said for Silence. Nikki Giovanni. WoATM p.40
Something turned you it was a movement (like the dull round earth). Pamela Cobb. InDM p.28
Something's Changed. Nola Richardson. WhOL p.89
Something's changed inside. Nola Richardson. WhOL p.89
Sometimes. Jennifer Blackman Lawson. BlIMT p.46
Sometimes. Joanne Jimason. NaABE p.23
Sometimes. Nikki Giovanni. Rec p.43; WoATM p.53
Sometimes a right white mountain. Effie Lee Newsome. CaD p.57; GoS p.177
Sometimes a vision flashes out to me of more abundant life that is to be.
Sometimes I cool out on this world. Ronda Davis. JuBa p. 60
Sometimes I Feel Like a Motherless Child. Anonymous. AfAWA p.102. BLIA p.40; BlLi p.113; BlWOA p.239:
Sometimes I feel like I just get in everybody's way. Nikki Giovanni. BFBTBJ p.63; EgT p.13
Sometimes I feel so bad. Alice Walker. CoAAAW p.354

Sometimes I get the feeling that I have been here before. Mae Jackson. PoBA p.498
Sometimes I see you leaning there in the doorway. Jill Witherspoon Boyer. DrF p.8
Sometimes I sit and I wonder. Bernadette Simmons. ThHSD p.36
Sometimes I spit on the rain. Joanne Jimason. NaABE p.23
Sometimes I Think of Maryland. Jodi Braxton. SoITM p.6
Sometimes it's like this. Harryette Mullen. TTW p.61
Sometimes it is painful you know. Carolyn M. Rodgers. HoIGO p. 68
Sometimes it seems as though some puppet player. Angelina Weld Grimke. CaD p.46
Sometimes it's hard to write a poem about the revolution. Mae Jackson. CaPWY p.5
Sometimes My Husband Acts Just Like a Man.** Patricia Parker. ChOM p.3; DOBB p.111; MoIB p.32
Sometimes My Past Closes In.** C. Tillery Banks. HeTMWL p. 78
Sometimes the poems becomin so bad. Sharon Scott. JuBa p. 178
Sometimes the whole world of women seems a landscape of red blood. Lucille Clifton. OrW p.53
Sometimes we could feel the impending close. Johari Amini. CoAAAW p.51
Sometimes we find we have nothing to give. Nikki Giovanni. TNV p.33
Sometimes We Pray With Our Tears. ** C. Tillery Banks. HeTMWL p.60
Sometimes, when I become others of my people. Sharon Bourke. UNBP p.375
Sometimes when I wake up. Nikki Giovanni. Rec p.43; WoATM p.53
Sometimes when the lost links of our togetherness turn up. S. Diane Bogus. WITM p.24
Sometimes you hear a question like "what is your responsibility as an unwed mother." Nikki Giovanni. MyH p.29
Somewhere. Wanda Coleman. MaDBL p.28
Somewhere in London. Naomi Long Madgett. PhN p.69
Somewhere in the City. Naomi Long Madgett. OnATM p.44
Somewhere it being yesterday. Lucille Clifton. TwW p.39
Somewhere there was a piano playing. Nikki Giovanni. CoCRD p.41
Somewhere you live and I am many years away. Patricia Parker. ChOM p.13; MoIB p.31
Son of A. Wanda Coleman. MaDBL p.15
Son of a race, whose dusky visage shows. Georgia Douglas Johnson. BrBV p.94
Son to His Father, A. Naomi Long Madgett. OnATM p.24
Song. Audre Lorde. CaTR p.5; ChPON p.11; COAL p.15
Song. Gwendolyn B. Bennett. BlSi p.73
Song. Lucille Clifton. GoNAE p.13
Song. Millie Williams. MyNIB p.37
Song. Pauli Murray. BlSi p.92
Song About the Paddyrollers. Anonymous. MyNIB p.36
Song boat swaying in the cane brake. Anonymous. ThHSD p.24
Song For a Negro. Naomi Long Madgett. PhN p.100
Song For a Season. Naomi Long Madgett. StBS p.29
Song For a Thin Sister. Audre Lorde. ChPON p.78; NeNS p.36
Song for Kwame. Jayne Cortez. Scar p.34
Song for Many Movements, A. Audre Lorde. BlUn p.52
Song For NewArk, A. Nikki Giovanni. ThWRNW p.61
Song For Nkazi or the Final Ironies. Thulani Davis. AlTRGR p.15

Song for the Dead, III. Anonymous. TYBP p.13
Song for the Old Ones. Maya Angelou. OhPWFW p.55
Song for the Sun That Disappeared Behind the Rain Clouds. Anonymous. TYBP p.5
Song From Brooklyn, A. Kattie M. Cumbo. GaBW p.285; NiBPo p. 60
Song in the Front Yard, A. Gwendolyn Brooks. HoFTD p. 101; IADB p.11; PoBA p. 153; SoOM p.558; SPGB p.6; StIB p.10; WoOGB p.12
Song of a Dancer. Harryette Mullen. TTW p.58
Song of Dambisa-Luwewe. Anonymous. MyNIB p.15
Song of Mary, A. Lucille Clifton. TwW p.39
Song of Names and Faces, A. Audre Lorde. FrLWP p.34
Song of Sojourner Truth, A. June Jordan. PaNP p.49
Song of the Highway, The. Pauli Murray. DaTAOP p.62
Song of the Poor Man. Anonymous. TYBP p.49
Song of the Sinner. Georgia Douglas Johnson. ALC p.60
Song to the Runaway Slave. Anonymous. BlP p.8
Song of the Warriors. Anonymous. MyNIB p.16
Song to a Phantom Nightingale. Naomi Long Madgett. PhN p.30
Song to Some Other Men. Thulani Davis. AlTRGR p.31
Song: The Rev. Mu Bugwu Dickinson ruminates behind the sermon. Gwendolyn Brooks. FaP p.22
Song to Jackie Robinson, Baseball Hall of Fame, Cairo, Georgia, 1919-1972. Eloise Culver. GANIV p.73
Songless Lark, The. Audre Lorde. COAL p.67
Songs don't sing any more, The. Naomi Long Madgett. ExAE p. 55
Songs for the People. Frances E. W. Harper. EBAP p.30; PBFH p.69
Songs to the Dialysis Machine. Pinkie Gordon Lane. WiTh p. 41
Sonia, you beautiful Black sister. Pinkie Gordon Lane. PoBBl p.16; WiTh p.38
Sonnet. Alice Dunbar-Nelson. ANP p.86; BANP p.164; BlSi p.65; CaD p.72; PoBA p.12; PoN p.41; PoNe p.46; ReFNA p.32
Sonnet. Naomi Long Madgett. PhN p.78
Sonnet-Ballad, The. Gwendolyn Brooks. AnA p.32; SPGB p. 51; WoOGB p.96
Sonnet I. Gwendolyn B. Bennett. PoBA p.82
Sonnet II. Gwendolyn B. Bennett. PoBA p.82
Sonnet for June. Edythe Mae Gordon. NegVo p.65
Sonnet to Byron. Naomi Long Madgett. OnATM p.29; PhN p.110
Sonnet to the Mantled. Georgia Douglas Johnson. BrBV p.15
Sonnet to Those Who See But Darkly. Georgia Douglas Johnson. BrBV p.16
Sonora Desert Poem. Lucille Clifton. TwW p.26
Sonnet to a Negro in Harlem. Helene Johnson. AmNP p.102; BANP p.281; CaD p.217; EbAT p.148; NeNRe p.152; VoFHR p.182
Sonnets I. Gwendolyn B. Bennett. AmNP p.74; CaD p.160; ITBLA p.218; PoN p.109; PoNe p. 206
Sonnets II. Gwendolyn B. Bennett. AmNP p.75; BANP p.244; CaD p.161; ITBLA p.218
Sons of slaves and daughters of masters all come up from the ocean together. Lucille Clifton. GoNAE p.13
Soon as the sun forsook the eastern main. Phillis Wheatley. AmLNA p.26; CNAW p.13; EaNAW p.41; PAL p.83; PPW p.26; ReFNA p.5
Soon One Mawnin. Anonymous. BlWOA p.238
Sooner or later air hisses from the punctured balloon. Naomi Long Madgett. PiLAF p.

52
Sophisticated Postscript for a Five-Page Letter. Helen F. Chappell. NegVo p.29
Sopranosound, Memory of John. Sharon Bourke. UNBP p.376
Sorceress gave it to me, A. Anita Scott Coleman. NegVo p.36
Sorrow came to me. Beatrice M. Murphy. NegVo p.115
Sorrow Home. Margaret Walker. FMP p.19
Sorrow is a Woman. Joanne Jimason. NaEBE p.19
Sorrow Singers. Georgia Douglas Johnson. BrBV p.27
Sorry 'Bout That. Linda Cousins. ThHSD p.46
Sortin-Out. Amini Baraka. CoAAAW p.73
Soul. Barbara Simmons. BlFi p. 304
Soul. Leatrice Emeruwa. BlGBG p.14
Soul Food Goes Elite. E. Sharon Gomillion. FoAAM p.8
Soul-Home Feeling. Damali (Denise Burnett). IATWMB p.12
Soul is the ability to "git down." Leatrice Emeruwa. BlGBG p.14
Soul Suffering. Edna Gullins. NegVo p.67
Soulfolk, think a minute. Margaret Burroughs. BlSi p.118
Souls of Black Men. Naomi Evans Vaughn. NegVo p.161
Sound of Music, The. Carolyn M. Rodgers. SoBB p.21
Sounds Like Pearls. Maya Angelou. JGM p.22
Sounds of the city can keep a crane up all night, The. Thulani Davis. AlTRGR p.5
South Africa ain't the only place they lock Blacks into camps at night. Alice Lovelace. HoDo p.31
South Carolina Chain Gang Song. Anonymous. ITBLA p.121
South of success and east of gloss and glass are sandals. Gwendolyn Brooks. BlPo p.24; BlWOA p.721
South Paw Baby. Pinkie Gordon Lane. WiTh p.32
South: The Name of Home. Alice Walker. ONC p.39
Southeast Arkansas. Maya Angelou. OhPWFW p.54
Southeast Corner. Gwendolyn Brooks. SPGB p.5; StIB p. 5; WoOGB p.7
Southern Belle. Elma Stuckey. BiGa p.47
Southern Blues. Anonymous. BLIA p.48; BlWOA p.648; ITBLA p.124
Southern Negro Heart Cry. Valerie Parks. NegVo p.124
Southern Road, A. Helene Johnson. VoFHR p.360
Southern Song. Margaret Walker. AfAWA p.520; FMP p.18
Southern University. Pinkie Gordon Lane. MyFe p.23
Souvenir. Naomi Long Madgett. HWOP p.49; NeBV p.297; PiLAF p.42
Soweto Song. Amini Baraka. CoAAAW p.70
Soweto when I hear your name I think about you. Jayne Cortez. CoAAAW p.95; COAG p.44; MoOP p.61
Sowing. Audre Lorde. CaTR p. 23
Space. Nikki Giovanni. CoCRD p. 72
Spacin. Ronda Davis. JuBa p.61
Span of Life, The. Josephine D. (Henderson) Heard. MoGl p.109
Spark no more, A. Katie Kelly. BTh p.55
Sparrow is a Bird, A. Margaret Danner. DoOAT p.97; IrLa p.15; PoCo p.7
Sparrow's Fall, The. Frances E. W. Harper. DuSAE p.18; PBFH p.21
Spaulding and Francois. Gwendolyn Brooks. SPGB p.126
Spawning to Bring Forth. Carolyn M. Rodgers. HeAEG p.9
Speak earth and bless me with what is richest. Audre Lorde. NeHS p.26
Speak the Truth to the People. Mari Evans. CoAAAW p.107; IABW p.91; UNBP p.253
Speak Without Words. Barbara Mahone. Suga p.28

Speaking of Death and decay it hardly matters. Alice Walker. ONC p.79
Speaking of Loss. Lucille Clifton. TwW p.12
Speaking of Naomi's in the bible. Margaret Danner. DoOAT p.123
Speckled frogs leap from my mouth. Audre Lorde. CaTR p.26; ChPON p.24; COAL p.48; NaPr p.66
Spectacle of evening color binds me to you, A. Jodi Braxton. SoITM p.36
Spectre rises unseen by masses sensed, The. Johari Amini. ImIB p.1
Spectrum. Mari Evans. BlP p. 186; WhIAM p.9
Speech to the young. Speech to the progress toward. Gwendolyn Brooks. FaP p.23
Spell of Dawning, The. Lucy Mae Turner. BCF p.45
Spelled Backwards. Anonymous. GLOWC p.98
Speretual 'Oman, De. Lucile D. Goodlett. WGC p.55
Speretual 'oman come from toun, A. Lucile D. Goodlett. WGC p.55
Spin me a Dream. Helen C. Harris. EbR p.78
Spin me a dream, weaver of my soul. Helen C. Harris. EbR p.78
Spirit and the mind, yes--a prelude. Pinkie Gordon Lane. WiTh p.47
Spirit Flowers. Della Burt. BlSi p.161
Spirit flowers are our lives. Della Burt. BlSi p.161
Spirits of the abnormally born live on in water. Audre Lorde. ChPON p.108
Spirits we are live like leaves bowing trees, The. Carolyn M. Rodgers. HeAEG p.82
Spitpolished bronze immovable gleamed by Kansas heat. Mari Evans. NIGHT p.22
Splash for my love, A. Barbara Mahone. Suga p.30
Split, The. Melba Joyce Boyd. CaEADW p.30
Splitz. Wanda Coleman. MaDBL p.85
Spook Village. Lucy Mae Turner. BCF p.15
Spose I say I know yr leaky. Ntozake Shange. DaGe p.68
Spring. Carole Gregory Clemmons. PoBA p.488
Spring. Pinkie Gordon Lane. MyFe p.44
Spring comes slowly. Rosemari Mealy. CoAAAW p.222
Spring Dawn. Ethel Caution. ReFNA p.52
Spring has not arrived. June Jordan. ThTDID p.58
Spring in Carolina. Audrey Johnson. BTh p.39
Spring in St. Louis. Naomi Long Madgett. PhN p.44; SoTPN p.25
Spring is Here! Oliva M. Hunter. BTh p.33
Spring is the harshest blurring the lines of choice. Audre Lorde. FiCi p.9
Spring Lament. Mae V. Cowdery. WLOV p.45
Spring laughs at winter. Mae V. Cowdery. WLOV p.49
Spring of Joy. Vera Guerard. TNV p.47
Spring People. Audre Lorde. CaTR p.6; ChPON p.16; COAL p.21
Spring Poem in Winter. Mae V. Cowdery. WLOV p.49
Spring Song. Lucille Clifton. GoNAE p.45
Spring III. Audre Lorde. FiCi p.9
Spring's earliet suggestion was a curling, stretching rope of slime. Naomi Long Madgett. StBS p.15
Springtide. Georgia Douglas Johnson. HWOP p.54
Springtime. Georgia Douglas Johnson. ALC p.39
Spurned Friendship. Anita Anderson. PoBBl p.50
Squirrel in Man, The. Alvies M. Carter. AOS p.7
Stackalee. Anonymous. BLIA p. 45; ITBLA p.123
Stackerlee and de Debbil. Anon-

ymous. BlWOA p.460
Stackerlee he tol de debbil, say "Come on, less have some fun." Anonymous. BlWOA p.460
Stagolee. Anonymous. TYBP p.201; UNBP p.103
Stairway Left Standing. May Miller. ClAB p.23
Stand! E. Sharon Gomillion. FoAAAM p.19
Stand Tall. Gertrude Blackwell Bailey. IfWCF p.54
Stand tall, Blackman. Gertrude Blackwell Bailey. IcWCF p.54
Stand up nigger, get on your feet. E. Sharon Gomillion. FoAAM p.19
Stand up, thou mighty monarch, stand. Josephine D. (Henderson) Heard. MoGl p.116
Standing By. Naomi Long Madgett. OnATM p.45
Standing on 127th the smell of collards. Mari Evans. BOL p.27
Standing with the brothers talking shit and swapping spit. Colleen McElroy. MuDLSG p. 17
Stanton Street. Jayne Cortez. Scar p.40
Star Gazing. Jill Witherspoon Boyer. DrF p.10
Star Journey. Naomi Long Madgett. BlP p.195; OnATM p.40; StBS p.52
Starbound. Wanda Coleman. MaDBL p.111
Stare from your pillow into the sun. Margaret Walker. FMP p.27
Stark winter tree stalks of shredded branches stab the sky, The. June Vanleer Williams. WiRYPS p.62
Starlight night and you and me, A. Leighla Lewis. NegVo p.95
Stars, The. Nikki Giovanni. VaT p.47
Stars by night are the candles which light up my soul, The. Henrietta C. Parks. TNV p. 84
Stars Dwindle, The. Audre Lorde. ChPON p.85
Stars have their price. Naomi Long Madgett. OnATM p.37
Stars on high, flickering now, The. Naomi Long Madgett. PhN p.18
Stars shine again, The. C. Tillery Banks. HeTMWL p.58
Startled Waves Began to Recede, The. Margaret Danner. DoOAT p.26
State has no case against freedom, The. Thulani Davis. AlTRGR p.58
Statement on Conservation, A. Nikki Giovanni. CoCRD p.84
Status Symbol. Mari Evans. AfAWA p.682; BLIA p.348; BlVo p.479; IABW p.68; IADB p.92; ITSA p.248; MyNIB p.100
Stay beautiful with your strength. Pinkie Gordon Lane. MyFe p.32
Staying and not staying. Wanda Coleman. MaDBL p.73
Steal Away. Anonymous. AmLNA p.5; BLIA p.42; BlLi p. 112; ITBLA p.97
Steal away, steal away, steal away to Jesus! Anonymous. AfAWA p.105; BLIA p.42; BlP p.27; ITBLA p.97
Steal Away to Jesus. Anonymous. AfAWA p.105; BlP p.27
Stealin' Grub. Lucy Mae Turner. BCF p.35
Steam rises over my nose. Wanda Coleman. MaDBL p.109
Steam Song. Gwendolyn Brooks. Bec p.8
Steeled behind big sounds twanged from livid guitars. Sarah Webster Fabio. DOBB p.32
Stench of stale urine over powers you, The. June Vanleer Williams. WiRYPS p.52
Stephen. Wanda Coleman. MaDBL p.133
Stephen's Hair. Wanda Coleman. MaDBL p.126
Stero Abstract. Frenchy J. Hodges. BlW p.10
Sterile radiators steamless clankings sent roaches surrying away. Lyn. SiSH

p.29
Stick the fingers inside the chink. Alice Walker. RePOP p.38
Still are there wonders of the dark and day. Angelina Weld Grimke. BlSi p.61
Still do I Keep My Look, My Identity. Gwendolyn Brooks. SPGB p.23; StIB p.47; WoOGB p.49
Still I Rise. Maya Angelou. AnSIR p.41; BlSi p.265
Still, it is dear defiance now to carry. Gwendolyn Brooks. AmNP p.140; PoN p.190; SPGB p.28; StIB p.56; WoOGB p.58
Still let me find your guarded eyes. Naomi Long Madgett. StBS p.53
Still Life: Lady With Birds. Quandra Prettyman. PoBA p. 259
Stirrings. Harryette Mullen. TTW p.38
Stockpiling. Jayne Cortez. COAG p.79
Stockpiling of frozen trees in the deep freeze of the earth, The. Jayne Cortez. COAG p. 79
Stokley and Mirea I wish you happiness. Kali Grosvenor. PBK p.45
Stoker's Chant, The. Anonymous. BlWOA p.236
Stone/cold/daylight. Sonia Sanchez. BlP p.239; WABP p.41
Stood Up. Nancy L. Arnez. RoCO p.21
Stop again! This engine must have a bit of oil. Eloise Culver. GANIV p.40
Stop sending duns to my house. Elma Stuckey. BiGa p.86
Stop smoking...air pollution. Carolyn M. Rodgers. HeAEG p.79
Storm. Alice Walker. RePOP p.62
Storm, The. Naomi Long Madgett. PhN p.119; SoTPN p.12
Storm Poem, A. Lucille Clifton. OrW p.13
Storm rushed in his eye, A. Nancy L. Arnez. RoCO p.21
Story Books on a Kitchen Table. Audre Lorde. ChPON p.35; COAL p.27
Story For the Remainder. Johari Amini. CoAAAW p.51
Story is about yesterday, The. Carolyn M. Rodgers. JuBa p.125
Story of a Very Broken Lady, The. Toi Derricotte. EmDH p.14
Story of the Rebellion, A. Frances E. W. Harper. PBFH p.60
Story/Riff, The. Carolyn M. Rodgers. JuBa p.125
Storyville, New York 7/27/77. Thulani Davis. AlTRGR p.51
Straight black hair piled high on her head. Mae Jackson. CaPWY p.10
Straight lines erased all curving on that day of stun. Margaret Danner. DoOAT p.71
Straight Talk. Nikki Giovanni. MyH p.31
Strain of Music. Mae V. Cowdery. WLOV p.24
Strange. Julia Fields. GaBW p.307
Strange atoms we unto ourselves. Georgia Douglas Johnson. AmNP p.23
Strange summer sun shines round our globe of circumstances. Margaret Walker. PFND p.31
Strange to a sensing motherhood. Georgia Douglas Johnson. BrBV p.95
Strange town filled with weird things, A. Kathy Sterling. MyNIB p.157
Stranger, The. Eleanor Thomas-Grumbach. MoSu p.10
Strategy. Bessie Woodson Yancey EcFTH p.52
Straw Bosses. E. Sharon Gomillion. FoAAM p.21
Strawberry Patches. Nikki Giovanni. VaT p.23
Stream, The. Lula Lowe Weeden. CaD p.228; MyNIB p.78
Streams of viewer, swarms of gazers pass the bier and hesitate. June Vanleer Williams. WiRYPS p.79
Street Called Petticoat Lane,

The. Alice McGee Smart. AmLNA p.63
Street Demonstration. Margaret Walker. BlP p.156; PFND p. 7
Street in Bronzeville, A. Gwendolyn Brooks. SPGB p.3; WoOGB p.3
Street Lady. Mari Evans. NIGHT p.30
Street Scene. Leatrice Emeruwa. BlGBG p.23
Streets are sweating again, The. Dorothy Randall. ThHSD p.40
Strength with which you face today. Jennifer Blackman Lawson. BlIMT p.41
Stricken Deer, The. Josephine D. (Henderson) Heard. MoGl p. 94
Stri-i-ke One! the call comes through the air. Lucy Mae Turner. BCF p.10
Strike out in the dark and blind me. Naomi Long Madgett. PhN p.111
Striptease. Harryette Mullen. TTW p.45
Stroke across a nervous thigh with a hesitating hand, A. Carole Gregory Clemmons. NiBPo p.88
Strong Men, Riding Horses.** Gwendolyn Brooks. BeEa p.15; KAL p.158; PoBA p.157; SPGB p.71; WoOGB p.313
Strong women know the taste of their own hatred. Audre Lorde. BlUn p.51
Struggle of Class. Rashidah Ismaili. CoAAAW p.166
Struggle of class etched across the richness of my flesh. Rashidah Ismaili. CoAAAW p. 166
Struggle Stsggers Us, The. Margaret Walker. FMP p.58
Studies of a Honeypeach Philosopher of Art. Margaret Danner. DoOAT p.77
Stunned by her Desires.** Gloria Oden. RESUR p.127
Styx Before Crossing. Naomi Long Madgett. PhN p.72; SoTPN p. 21
Subconsciously I think of you. Vanessa Howard. ScWh p.35
Substitution. Anne Spencer. BlSi p.71; CaD p.46
Subterfuge. Countess W. Twitty. EbR p.147
Success. Dorothy Vena Johnson. EbR p.92
Success does not seem to have spoiled Gwen Brooks. Cynthia M. Conley. TGWL p.22
Success is like a blazing flame of meteoric light. Dorothy Vena Johnson. EbR p.92
Such a Peculiar World. June Vanleer Williams. WiRYPS p.27
Such simple things can make me know a deep exultant joy. Mae V. Cowdery. WLOV p.63
Such trivial things. Beatrice M. Murphy. TNV p.141
Suck in that sweet herb. Sandra Royster. WoTa p.17
Sudden Sight, The. Mari Evans. WhIAM p.8
Suddenly life is so easy because of you-me-us. C. Tillery Banks. HeTMWL p.80
Suddenly rain begins to dot the windshield. Naomi Long Madgett. ExAE p.65
(Suddenly) there you were. Pinkie Gordon Lane. WiTh p.49
Suffer the Children. Audre Lorde. FiCi p.20; PoBA p. 248
Suffused in April twilight I lie beside you. Pauli Murray. DaTAOP p.100
Sugarfields. Barbara Mahone. PoBA p.473; Suga p.13
Sugarman. Margaret Porter. CoAAAW p.262
Suicide. Alice Walker. ONC p. 74
Suicide Poem # 3. Jodi Braxton. SoITM p.20
Suite of Assassinations, The. Carolyn M. Rodgers. SoBB p. 25
Sullen and dark as an angry mood that envelop a treacherous soul. Rosa Paul Brooks. AmLNA p.90
Summary. Sonia Sanchez. BlFi

p.252; BlP p.233; BrT p.138; HoC p.14; IvBAW p.8
Summer. Mae Jackson. CaPWY p.16
Summer comes, The. Helene Johnson. BlSi p.79; CaD p.223; PoN p.152; PoNe p.263
Summer Day. Naomi Long Madgett. OnATM p.13
Summer: Falling in Love. May Miller. ClAB p.36
Summer Has Sped. Sonia Sanchez. IvBAW p.84
Summer heat lies like a stone. May Miller. ClAB p.38
Summer in between and I have not learned to talk about it. Mae Jackson. CaPWY p.16
Summer is waving her hand sadly. Naomi Long Madgett. SoTPN p. 29
Summer Matures. Helene Johnson. BlSi p.81; CaD p.217; PoN p.150; PoNe p.261
Summer matures brillant scorpion appears. Helene Johnson. BlSi p.81; CaD p.217; PoNe p.261
Summer-Moon. Bessie Woodson Yancey. EcFTH p.12
Summer Oracle. Audre Lorde. BlSi p.201; CaTR p.4; PoBA p.245; SoS p.88
Summer rains like my blood cries lover my lover. Audre Lorde. BlUn p.101
Summer Story, A. Angela Jackosn. VoDLM p.9
Summer/time T.V./ (is witer than ever). Sonia Sanchez. WABP p.30
Summer Words For a Sister Addict. Sonia Sanchez. BlSi p.246
Summer Words Of a Sistuh Addict. Sonia Sanchez. BlP p.237; IvBAW p.23; NaPr p.126; WABP p.35
Summers summers summers afternoons ripe peaches. Wanda Coleman. MaDBL p.107
Sun, The. Nikki Giovanni. VaT p.43
Sun burned darkest red into your skin. Pamela Cobb. PoBA p. 118
Sun goes slowly down the golden ladder. Ethel Caution. ReFNA p.52
Sun Heals, A.** Johari Amini. JuBa p.168. LetGSW p.26
Sun make me whole again. Audre Lorde. BlUn p.44
Sun people gods and goddesses kings and queens ba-a-a-d. Anonymous. ThHSD p.23
Sun shines so brightly on the hill. Audre Lorde. COAL p.67
Sun was shinning down on a cabin dull and gray, The. Eloise Culver. GANIV p.52
Sun, you be here and I'll be gone. Susie Melton. MyNIB p.46
Sunday. Patricia Parker. MoIB p.56
Sunday Afternoon. Naomi Long Madgett. PhN p.47
Sunday Chicken. AnA p.7; SPGB p.33; WoOGB p.71
Sunday clothes and parlor pipes, lily-scented hair. Naomi Long Madgett. PhN p.47
Sunday/Evening at Gwen's. Sonia Sanchez. TGWL p.86; WABP p.58
Sunday School. Alice Walker. PoBA p.489; RePOP p.11
Sunday strollers along a sewage-chocked Schuylkill. Sarah E. Wright. PoBA p.212
Sundays are Special (Letter Poem) Sandra Sharp. RoATW p.69
Sundays of Satin-Legs Smith, The. Gwendolyn Brooks. SoOM p. 560; SPGB p.12; StIB p.24; UNBP p.169; WoOGB p.26; CNAW p.516
Sundown. Elma Stuckey. BiGa p.28
Sundown Sigh. Melba Joyce Boyd. CaEADW p.12
Sunflower Sonnet Number One. June Jordan. ThTDID p.77
Sunflower Sonnet Number Two. June Jordan. ThTDID p.77
Sunflowers and Saturdays. Melba Joyce Boyd. BlSi p.281; CaEADW p.3
Sunny. Naomi Long Madgett. BrT p.169; PiLAF p.24
Sunny South. Lucy Mae Turner.

BCF p.7
Sunny South With Fragrant Breeze. Lucy Mae Turner. BCF p.7
Sunrise. Henrietta Cordelia Ray. EABP p.143
Sunrise. Pinkie Gordon Lane. WiTh p.58
Sunrise Poems. Colleen McElroy. MuDLSG p.31
Sun's goin' down, heavenly Lord, The. Elma Stuckey. BiGa p.28
Sunset. Ethel Caution. ReFNA p. 52
Sunset. Georgia Douglas Johnson. ALC p.21
Sunset. Henrietta Cordelia Ray. EBAP p.144
Sunset by the lake. Pinkie Gordon Lane. MyFe p.23
Sunset of the City, A. Gwendolyn Brooks. BeEa p.39; SPGB p.94; WoOGB p.337
Sunsets are so pretty. Nikki Giovanni. VaT p.43
Sunshine After Cloud. Josephine D. (Henderson) Heard. MoGl p.23
Sunshine After Rain. Vera E. Guerard. TNV p.47
Sunshine after rain leaves my soul filled with mist of happiness and remembrance, The. Vera E. Guerard. TNV p.47
Sunshine days ole marsa nice. Elma Stuckey. BiGa p.59
Sunstill. Joanne Jimason. NaABE p.35
Sunstroke. Sandra Royster. EoTa p.5
Super Thought. Frenchy J. Hodges. BlW p.11
Supercool--know everything made love to me. Anonymous. AOS p.8
Supper Time. Elma Stuckey. BiGa p.40
Suppliant, The. Georgia Douglas Johnson. BlALP p.44; BrBV p.55; CaD p.76; NeCa p.340; PoBA p.23; PoN p.58; PoNe p.76; VoFHR p.350
Supply. Bessie Woodson Yancey. EcFTH p.17
Suppose they had cheated me out of my Black-ness. Carolyn M. Rodgers. JuBa p.117
Supposing we could just go on and on as two. June Jordan. ThTDID p.77
Supposition. Naomi Long Madgett. PhN p.71
Supremacy. Leanna Johnson. EbR p.95
Supremacy. Lenora Gillison. EbR p.66
Supreme. Georgia Douglas Johnson. HWOP p.43
Supremes done gone and sold their soul. Sonia Sanchez. BlSi p.242; HoC p.29
Suppression. Jayne Cortez. NeBV p.236
Sure slavery time was rough. Elma Stuckey. BiGa p.3
Surely. Gwendolyn Brooks. AmLNA p.89
Surely you stay my certain own. Gwendolyn Brooks. AmLNA p. 89; SPGB p.27; StIB p.55; WoOGB p.57
Surrealist and Omega. Gwendolyn Brooks. SPGB p.126
Surrender. Angelina Weld Grimke. CaD p.38; NeCa p.342; ReFNA p.25
Survival Poem. Pinkie Gordon Lane. MyFe p.46
Survivors, The. Naomi Long Madgett. ExAE p.31
Susie Lou. Lucile D. Goodlett. WGC p.58
Suspect is Black & in his early 20's, The. Ntozake Shange. NaEd p.118
Suspended. Mary Bohanon. GaBW p.263
Suspension. Audre Lorde. ChPON p.8; COAL p.41; FiCi p.24; SiAS p.45
Swaziland. Nikki Giovanni. WoATM p.46
Sweeping like the whirlwind over the desert. Jane W. Burton. NegVo p.23
Sweet and calm the breezes stealing o'er the quiet sabbath day. Josephine D. (Henderson) Heard. MoGl p.32
Sweet and low sounds the organ.

Jeannette V. Miller. NegVo p.104
Sweet butterfly once and now. S. Diane Bogus. WITM p.6
Sweet Ethel. Linda Piper. BlSi p.183
Sweet Ethel was a roaming gal. Linda Piper. BlSi p.183
Sweet Land of Everything to Thee I Sing. Bobbretta M. Elliston. PoBBl p.21
Sweet Mama Wanda Tells Fortunes For a Price. Wanda Coleman. MaDBL p.79
Sweet Otis Suite. Anasa Jordan. CoAAAW p.176
Sweet Potato Man. Anonymous. ITBLA p.125
Sweet Rough Man. Gertrude "Ma" Rainey. UNBP p.111
Sweet Sally took a cardboard box. Gwendolyn Brooks. AnA p.41; SPGB p.56; WoOGB p.105
Sweet-tongued birds have left, The. May Miller. ClAB p.40
Sweeter far than lyric rune. Georgia Douglas Johnson. HWOP p.61
Sweetest Thing, The. Anonymous. MBP p.102; TYBP p.7
Swift little-thoughts come a-nesting in my brain. Frenchy J. Hodges. BlW p.7
Swift melting into yesterday, The tortured hordes of ebon-clay, The. Georgia Douglas Johnson. BrBV p.35
Swift the years have sped away. Josephine D. (Henderson) Heard. MoGl p.87
Swing Low, Sweet Chariot.** Anonymous. AfAV p.118; BlEx p.4; BlWOA p.239; GoS p.61
Swing out, time, use the arrow for the arc. Marion Cuthbert. SOC p.43
Swing sweet rhythm charcoal toes. Mari Evans. BlSp p.71; IABW p.81
Sybil Warns Her Sister. Anne Spencer. EbAT p.94
Sylvester Expelled. Naomi Long Madgett. PiLAF p.13
Sympathy. Georgia Douglas Johnson. HWOP p.4
Sympathy Note to a Friend. Jennifer Blackman Lawson. BlIMT p.41
Symphonies. Esther Popel. ReFNA p.49
Syncopating Rhythm. Frenchy J. Hodges. BlW p.20
Syncopating rhythm please echo home to me. Frenchy J. Hodges. BlW p.20
Synecdoche/Asbury Park in October. Ntozake Shange. DaGe p.61
Synopsis. June Vanleer Williams. WiRYPS p.9

- T -

TCB. Sonia Sanchez. WABP p.59; YoBBI p.367
T.V. Kali Grosvenor. PBK p.34
T.V. is a fake. Kali Grosvenor. PBK p.34
TV is Easy Next to Life. June Jordan. PaNP p.22
Tadpoles are legless and never learn to curtsy. Audre Lorde. BlUn p.71
Take a note and spin it. Nikki Giovanni. EgT p.31; Rec p.24; WoATM p.14; YoBBI p.478
Take dis hammer--hahn! take it to da cap'n han'h. Anonymous. BlWOA p.464
Take my hand and be my guide. Gertrude Blackwell Bailey. IfWCF p.45
Take my hand and lead me to the promised land. Lyn. SiSH p.20
Take my share of soul food. Julia Fields. MoCAP p.154
Take off your hat. Anonymous. TYBP p.17
Take the A Train. Ntozake Shange. DaGe p.18
Take this rose and share with me. Rosemari Mealy. CoAAAW p.223
Take Time Out. Maya Angelou. OhPWFW p.59
Take Yo Time, Miss Lucy. Anon-

ymous. GoS p.18
Takers, The. Nikki Grimes. CoAAAW p.121
Takes Time. Gwendolyn Brooks. AfAWA p.584
"Takes time," grated the gradualist. Gwendolyn Brooks. AfAWA p.584
Taking a Solo/a Poetic Possibility/a Poetic Imprative. Ntozake Shange. NaEd p.2
Taking Care. June Jordan. PaNP p.92
Taking Sides. Elma Stuckey. BiGa p.36
Tale of the Newborn with Tapering Nails, The. Margaret Danner. DoOAT p.105
Talisman, A. Frenchy J. Hodges. BlW p.7
Talk erbot yo' fine french pastry. Bessie Woodson Yancey. EcFTH p.40
Talkin bout wite folks and they so-called sole singers. Carolyn M. Rodgers. SoBB p.19
Tall man and myself tonight we will not sleep together. June Jordan. PaNP p.90
Tall man without clothes beautiful like a statue. Alice Walker. ONC p.20
Tall palm tree sixty feet high, The. Anonymous. TYBP p.28
Tall poetic loud Black angry proud. Kattie M. Cumbo. BOL p.12; NiBPo p.44
Tall, straight birches starkly etched against the sky. Gladys M. Jameson. EbAT p.135
Talluh Hammuh. Margaret Walker. FMP p.40
Tally. May Miller. CNAW p.361
Tangles on my baby's head are curious and beautiful, The. Paulette Childress White. DeDG p.15
Tanka. Fatimah Afif. CoAAAW p.47
Tapping. Jayne Cortez. COAG p.17; Scar p.62
Taps. Georgia Douglas Johnson. AVAN p.209; BrBV p.70
Tar Paper Bungalow. Lucy Mae Turner. BCF p.40
Taste of Time, The. S. Diane Bogus. WITM p.66
Tater Field. Lucile D. Goodlett. WGC p.22
Teach Me to Sing. June Jordan. ThTDID p.64
Teacher. Audre Lorde. ChPON p. 53; FrLWP p.20
Teacher. Margaret Walker. FMP p.44
Teacher. Naomi Long Madgett. PiLAF p.22
Teacher was a bad man, The. Margaret Walker. FMP p.44
Tear it out of the history books! Pauli Murray. DaTAOP p.26
Tears. Josephine D. (Henderson) Heard. MoGl p.99
Tears. Maya Angelou. JGM p.12
Tears. Naomi Long Madgett. PhN p.86
Tears. Pauli Murray. DaTAOP p.75
Tears and a Dream. Marsha Ann Jackson. TNV p.53
Tears and Kisses. Georgia Douglas Johnson. HWOP p.28
Tears don't flow, The. June Vanleer Williams. WiRYPS p.77
Tears flowing backwards past my ears. Jennifer Blackman Lawson. BlIMT p.39
Tears I shed that flow quite free, The. Nola Richardson. WhOL p.19
Tears of Disguise. Nola Richardson. WhOL p.19
Tears, salt tears, fit emblem of my grief. Josephine D. (Henderson) Heard. MoGl p. 99
Tears the crystal rags viscious tatters of a worn-through soul. Maya Angelou. JGM p. 12
Telephone, The. Maya Angelou. OhPWFW p.8
Telephone Call. Pinkie Gordon Lane. MyFe p.44
Telephone company is harassing me in my sleep, The. Ntozake Shange. NaEd p.47
Telephone unanswered parties unserved. Pinkie Gordon Lane. PoBBl p.8; WiTh p.27
Telephones & other false gods. Ntozake Shange. NaEd p.73

Television on TV tray by the bed stead, The. Wanda Coleman. MaDBL p.47
Television/Poem. Sonia Sanchez. WABP p.24
Tell Me. Jayne Cortez. COAG p. 106
"Tell me a story, father, please." Ann Plato. BlSi p.43; EBAP p.118
Tell me about soul. Barbara Simmons. BlFi p.304
Tell me, christians, worn and Weary. Josephine D. (Henderson) Heard. MoGl p.136
Tell me is there anything lovelier. Angelina Weld Grimke. ANP p.86; CaD p.36; CNAW p.30
Tell me, smart children of the southland. Jessie Redmond Fauset. EbAT p.27
Tell me something what you think would happen. June Jordan. PaNP p.34
Tell me that the plutonium sludge in your corroded torso is all a dream. Jayne Cortez. COAG p.106
Tell the fair dreamer, now that dreams are over. Naomi Long Madgett. OnATM p.14
Tell us about that shaking ensemble of itching flesh. Jayne Cortez. Scar p.52
Telling It All. Elma Stuckey. BiGa p.55
Temperance Poem. Josephine D. (Henderson) Heard. MoGl p. 92
Temptation. Katharine Beverly. NegVo p.14
Ten cents you're bowing for old Black man. Sonia Sanchez. AfAA p.2
10:15 A.M. - April 29, 1969 Poem. Sonia Sanchez. WABP p.39
Ten Years to the Day My Brother Milton Died.** Gloria Oden. RESUR p.37
Tenacity was my youth. Carolyn M. Rodgers. HeAEG p.10
Tender is the night. Mary Bohanon. GaBW p.256
Tending in the Great House. Elma Stuckey. BiGa p.58
Tenebris. Angelina Weld Grimke. CaD p.40; PoBA p.15; PoN p.49; PoNe p.58
Tennyson's Poems. Josephine D. (Henderson) Heard. MoGl p. 51
Tent Revival. Harryette Mullen. TTW p.16
Tequila Sunrise. Wanda Coleman. MaDBL p.113
Testament. Carolyn M. Rodgers. HeAEG p.39
Testament. Lucille Clifton. TwW p.51
Testimonials. Julia Fields. BlLi p.530
Testimony. Carolyn M. Rodgers. BlP p.261
Testimony of an Eye-Witness. Pamela Cobb. InDM p.11
Thank God for Little Children.** Frances E. W. Harper. PBFH p.47
Thank God for tears when cold hearts turn to stone. Naomi Long Madgett. PhN p. 86
Thank You. Marva Tatum Smith. BeYM p.25
Thank you for letting me walk with you. Marva Tatum Smith. BeYM p.25
Thank You Lord. Maya Angelou. AnSIR p.53
Thanksgiving Day. Jennifer Blackman Lawson. BlIMT p. 42
Thanksgiving is a good time to stuff a T.W.A. Ambassador turkey flight to Las Vegas. June Jordan. ThTDID p.16
Thanksgiving 1969. Dear God I thank you for the problems that are mine. June Jordan. SCh p.82; ThTDID p.32
That cool chick down on Calumet. Gwendolyn Brooks. StIB p. 11; WoOGB p.13
That Day. Beth Jackson. PoBBl p.51
That dusky child upon your knee is breath of God's eternity. Georgia Douglas Johnson. BrBV p.47
That fool myself at yesterday

collapsed apart. June Jordan. ThTDID p.156
That Hill. Blanche Taylor Dickinson. CaD p.109
That Hypocrite. Anonymous. BlP p.9
That I may Gird to Meet Dry Death. Margaret Danner. DoOAT p.46
That is the way God made you. Gwendolyn Brooks. HoFTD p. 76; ITM p.35; WoOGB p.407
That man over there say a woman needs to be helped into carriages. Sojurner Truth. BlSi p.24
That phone call, the one that you wait for. Carole Gregory Clemmons. NiBPo p. 85
That Rider. May Miller. ClAB p. 11
That song it sing the sweetness like a good song car. Gwendolyn Brooks. Bec p.8
That Stagelee was an all-right lad. Margaret Walker. FMP p.35
That the Negro church possesses extraordinary power. Andrea Razafkeriefo. NeNRe p.378
That time we all heard it. Gwendolyn Brooks. BrT p.38; FaP p.19; PoBA p.165
That We May Be. Damali (Denise Burnett) IATWMB p.20
That which is inside of me screaming beating about for exit or entry. Audre Lorde. CaTR p.8; NaPr p.70
That's a Summer Storm. Kattie M. Cumbo. NiBPo p.61
That's all I could think of in that moment. Melva Eloise Tatum. MELVA p.24
That's me, I am there. June Jordan. ThTDID p.192
Thee sacrosance, thee sweet, thee crystalline. Gwendolyn Broks. SPGB p.26; StIB p. 53; WoOGB p.55
Theft. Esther Popel. ReFNA p. 47
Their eyes accuse me. Carolyn M. Rodgers. HeAEG p.76
Their Fathers. Nikki Giovanni. CoCRD p.48
Their gaze uplifting from shoals of despair. Georgia Douglas Johnson. BrBV p.16
Their hair, pomaded faces jaded. Maya Angelou. BlSi p.267; JGM p.45
Their hearts pump kool-aid. Jill Witherspoon Boyer. DrF p.18
Theme With Variations. Anita Scott Coleman. NegVo p.36
Then. Kathleen Reed. PoBBl p. 29
Then and Now. Franes E. W. Harper. PBFH p.75
Then I remember watching year after year. Pinkie Gordon Lane. MyFe p.26
Then in comes. Marva Tatum Smith. BeYM p.12
Then in comes chatty Charlene. Marva Tatum Smith. BeYM p.12
Then in walks a lady sedately dressed. Marva Tatum Smith. BeYM p.12
Then It Was. June Jordan. RoATW p.7; SCh p.37; ThTDID p.49
Then it was our eyes locked slowly on the pebble wash. June Jordan. SCh p.37
Then off they took you, off to the jail. Gwendolyn Brooks. StIB p.42; WoOGB p.44
Then there was the day I knew for the first time. Beth Jackson. PoBBl p.51
Then there's the rare being who goes to church. Marva Tatum Smith. BeYM p.13
Then this is the truth. June Jordan. PaNP p.75
Then when the three chillun looked round an' round. Leona Lyons. NegVo p.99
Theodore R, the III finally got past Aunt Clelia Uncle Dan and the heavy glassed front door. Mari Evan. IABW p.42
Therapy. Audre Lorde. BlUn p.63
There ain't no pay beneath the sun. Maya Angelou. AnSIR p. 33
There Are Blk/Puritans.** Sonia Sanchez. WABP p.17
There are cloudlets and things

of cool silver in our dream. Gwendolyn Brooks. SPGB p.126
"There are dreams that need rest." Sharon Scott. JuBa p.173
There are five people in this room. Margaret Walker. CoAAAW p.360
There are highways in the soul. Georgia Douglas Johnson. HWOP p.8
There are holes in her walls. Joanne Jimason. NaABE p.27
There are moments I want to share with you. Eleanor Thomas-Grumbach. MoSu p.22
There are no reservations for the revolution. Nikki Giovanni. BrT p.64; Rec p.9; WoATM p. 52
There are no simple explanations. Jayne Cortez. COAG p.71
There Are No Words. Jennifer Blackman Lawson. BlIMT p.52
There are Old Ladies. Joanne Jimason. NaABE p.10
There are running feet on my roof's top. Pinkie Gordon Lane. MyFe p.18
There Are Seeds to Sow. Bernette Golden. TNV p.40
There are so many girls now in the street who look like Noelle. Audre Lorde. NeHS p.42
There are so many roots to the tree of anger. Audre Lorde. ChPON p.49; FrLWP p.49
There are some poems that you just don't want to write. Mae Jackson. CoAAAW p.170
There are sounds which shatter the stateness of lives. Nikki Giovanni. CoCRD p.78
There are tears sweet, refreshing like dewdrops that rise. Georgia Douglas Johnson. HWOP p.28
There are things lovely and dangerous still. June Jordan. ThTDID p.68
There are things sadder than you and I. Sonia Sanchez. LoP p. 54
There Are Times. Claudia E. Jemmott. GaBW p.354
There are Times That the Smell of You. Sonia Sanchez. IvBAW p.87
There are times when I feel like being alone. Eleanor Thomas-Grumbach. MoSu p.3
There are two kinds of us in the world. Linda Brown Bragg. LoSBM p.20
There had been death. June Jordan. PaNP p.31
There had been quiet all that afternoon. Gwendolyn Brooks. BeEa p.69; SPGB p.107; WoOGB p.367
There have been brothers whose rhythms I nver knew. Mari Evans. NIGHT p.44
There he is. E. Sharon Gomillion. FoAAM p.22
There is a deep brooding in Arkansas. Maya Angelou. AnSIR p.21; BlSi p.266
There is a Girl Inside. Lucille Clifton. TwW p.8
There is a hunger after associated with pain. Nikki Giovanni. MyH p.2
There is a Lady. Marva Tatum Smith. BeYM p.1
There is a leaf hung high in the orchard. May Miller. ClAB p.3
There is a light that comes on. Carolyn M. Rodgers. HeAEG p.16
There is a little lightning in his eyes. Gwendolyn Brooks. SPGB p.122
There is a strange man attached to my backbone. Audre Lorde. ChPON p.91; NeHS p.34
There is a thin wall. Mari Evans. BlVo p.478
There is a tree, by day. Angelina Weld Grimke. CaD p.40; PoBA p.15; PoN p.491; PoNe p.58
There is a Woman in This Town. Patricia Parker. BlSi p. 240; MoIB p.154
There is a woman with a mountain of stones. Mariah Britton Howard. CoAAAW p.145
There is always something of the child in us. Nikki Giovanni. CoCRD p.54
There is an old story. Nikki

Giovanni. ThWRNW p.39
There is escape from loneliness and fearing. Naomi Long Madgett. PhN p.19
There is in this world something. Anonymous. MBP p.102
There is law, too, for our ways one with another. Marion Cuthbert. SOC p.25
There is much sorrow in your eyes. Margaret Danner. ImOAAF p.12
There is no beauty to the world I see. Mari Evans. BlLi p. 434; IABW p.79; KAL p.173; WhIAM p.20
There is no need to flirt with him today. Saundra Sharp. RoATW p.64
There is no peace with you. Jesse Redmond Fauset. PoN p.65; PoNe p.66; RoATW p.118
There is no solitude like the death of a sinner. Adrienne Ingrum. CoAAAW p.152
There is No Title: Only Echoes. Johari Amini. CoAAAW p.50
There is no wounded knee in America. Jayne Cortez. Scar p.21
There is noise outside my window. Pinkie Gordon Lane. MyFe p. 44
There is Nothing. Melva Eloise Tatum. MELVA p.26
There is nothing familiar about this house. Naomi Long Madgett. PhN p.103
There is nothing in my mind. Melva Eloise Tatum. MELVA p.26
There is nothing...that can be said. Nikki Giovanni. ThWRNW p.34
There is reason for disrespect. Rashidah Ismaili. CoAAAW p. 164
There is something caught in my throat. Ntozake Shange. DaGe p.14
There is something magic something tragic about the house across the street. Naomi Long Madgett. PhN p.22
There is something to be said for silence. Nikki Giovanni. WoATM p.40
There is the yet undone. Mari Evans. NIGHT p.4
There It Is. Jayne Cortez. CoAAAW p.90; COAG p.68
There they are. Gwendolyn Brooks. BlALP p.104; PoBA p.159; WoOGB p.416; ITM p. 44
There they stand together like Moses standing with Aaron. Margaret Walker. PFND p.16
There was a large one lying on its side. Pinkie Gordon Lane. PoBBl p.17; WiTh p. 18
There was a time. Mae Jackson. CaPWY p.8
There was grief within our household because of a vacant chair. Frances E. W. Harper. PBFH p.34
There was once a time when all that was on my mind was the thought of being free. Eleanor Thomas-Grumbach. MoSu p.19
There was one among us who rose. Pauli Murray. DaTAOP p.69; PoBA p.110
There Was One Night.** Naomi Long Madgett. PhN p.80; SoTPN p.13
There Was This Michael From My Motherland.** Margaret Danner. DoOAT p.129
There wasn't any hot water for the teapot. June Jordan. ThTDID p.83
There were bizarre beginnings in old lands for the making of me. Margaret Walker. FMP p.15
There were fields where once we walked among the clover. Nikki Giovanni. BFBTBJ p.10
There were hours and many of valor and many were those of suspense. Emily Jane Greene. EbR p.73
There were probably more Indians. June Jordan. SCh p.66; ThTDID p.88
There were three who sat and drank of wine. Pauli Murray. DaTAOP p.77

There you were, sitting across the room frowning at me. Carolyn M. Rodgers. HoIGO p.41
There's a blackbird in my tree. Jennifer Blackman Lawson. BlIMT p.31
There's a long-legged girl in San Francisco. Maya Angelou. OhPWFW p.3
There's a mighty battle raging. Josephine D. (Henderson) Heard. MoGl p.135
There's a quiet little spot that is all the world to me. Josephine D. (Henderson) Heard. MoGl p.120
There's a Raindrop.** Lisa McCann. GLOWC p.9
There's a Sampson, lying, sleeping in the land. Josephine D. (Henderson) Heard. MoGl p.71
There's a soft rosy glow o'er the whole world to-day. Georgia Douglas Johnson. HWOP p.25
There's a star in the East on Christmas morn. Anonymous. ChG p.97
There's a tender bud I'm saving. W. Blanche Nivens. BTh p. 60
There's an alley with my name on it. Wanda Coleman. MaDBL p.28
There's an herb I rub on my eyelids. Harryette Mullen. TTW p.58
There's laughter that comes tumbling out. Portia Lucas. BTh p.37
There's music in the measured tread of those returned from the dead. Georgia Douglas Johnson. BrBV p.69
There's no return to virtue's state. Josephine D. (Henderson) Heard. MoGl p.102
There's nothing certain. Georgia Douglas Johnson. ALC p.26
There's nothing in the world that clings. Georgia Douglas Johnson. HWOP p.34
There's nothing like seeing the familiar and living in it. Patricia Jones. HoDo p.74
There's nothing quite so beautiful. Beatrice M. Murphy. RoCO p.9
There's Peggy and Polly and Nancy Kenneth and Jimmy and Ray. Bessie Woodson Yancey. EcFTH p.34
There's Tony, he's the fruit man's boy. Floretta Howard. AmLNA p.53
These are tales told in darkness. Sherley Williams. CoAAAW p. 383
These are the Alternatives. Pamela Cobb. InDM p.35
These are the Times. Jayne Crotez. Scar p.21
These Autumn Trees. Sonia Sanchez. IvBAW p.73
These Beast and the Benin Bronze. Margaret Danner. ImOAAF p. 11; KAL p.126
These bunioned feet and corn-topped toes gonna take a rest. Jennifer Blackman Lawson. BlIMT p.26
These daughters are bone. Lucille Clifton. OrW p.15
These Days. Joanne Jimason. NaABE p.3
These Days. S. Diane Bogus. WITM p.61
These days fat pigeons coo. Wanda Coleman. MaDBL p.80
These days I have taken to sitting in solitude. Joanne Jimason. NaABE p.3
These days when you do say hello. Audre Lorde. ChPON p.51; FrLWP p.13
These fell miasmic rings of mist, with ghoulish menace bound. Georgia Douglas Johnson. AmNP p.24; BrBV p.29; NeNRe p.24; PoBA p. 23
These hips are big hips. Lucille Clifton. TwW p.6
These kisses are clandestine. Ntozake Shange. NaEd p.26
These paths are dark now. Naomi Long Madgett. PhN p.98
These things I hold for all the world to see. Katharine

Beverly. EbR p.3
These witches don't use brooms to engineer. Margaret Danner. DoOAT p.52
These Words Stained With Red. Sonia Sanchez. IvBAW p.74
They adorn themselves lovingly and go forth. Mari Evans. IABW p.86
They ain't gonna never get rap. Nikki Giovanni. BrT p.68; EgT p.37; Rec p.31
They always play it different in New York. Thulani Davis. AlTRGR p.55
They appeared and their reaching put the guns to our bony shoulders. Mari Evans. NIGHT p.51
They are Calling Me. Gertrude Parthenia McBrown. ReFNA p. 54
They are Coming. Josephine D. (Henderson) Heard. MoGl p. 72
They are embosomed in the sod. Georgia Douglas Johnson. BrBV p.70
They are not for us any more. Margaret Walker. CoAAAW p. 372
They are ours fighting mothers. Geraldine L. Wilson. CoAAAW p.394
They are young. Naomi Long Madgett. ExAE p.33
They asked the how of ghettoed intelligence. Johari Amini. ImIB p.6
They built a schoolhouse. Mari Evans. NIGHT p.38
They call me mentally retarded. Jennifer Blackman Lawson. BlIMT p.45
They called grateful meetings did grateful dances to the pulse of grateful drums. Mari Evans. IABW p.66
They Came Again in 1970 in 1980. Jayne Cortez. COAG p.82
They came in ships. Patricia Parker. MoIB p.86
They Came Knocking on my Door at 7 A.M. Wanda Coleman. MaDBL p.48
They come to catch the stars. Helen G. Quigless. TNV p.94
They charge me with humility. Anita Scott Coleman. EbR p. 51
They Clapped. Nikki Giovanni. MyH p.51
They clapped when we landed. Nikki Giovanni. MyH p.51
They come to knead my flesh. Nikki Grimes. CoAAAW p.121
They Crucified My Lord.** Anonymous. AfAWA p.107
They crucified my Lord. Spiritual. BlP p.29
They don't like to see you with yo tail draggin low. Sherley Williams. PePo p.67
They Don't Understand. Nola Richardson. WhOL p.7
They dunked me in the creek. Alice Walker. RePOP p.23
They eat beans mostly this old pair. Gwendolyn Brooks. BeEa p.16; BlEx p.546; BlSi p.101; KAL p.159; ITBLA p. 217; MoCAP p.81; PoBA p. 154; SoS p.23; SPGB p.72; TYBP p.245; WoOGB p.314
They found Billy squashed in a corner. Lyn. SiSH p.19
They gave me the wrong name. Naomi Long Madgett. BlVo p. 476; OnATM p.55; PoBA p.183; StBS p.62
They get to Benvenuti's. Gwendolyn Brooks. AnA p.46; SPGB p.59; UNBP p.174; WoOGB p.110
They had a rebellion in Washington this year. Nikki Giovanni. BFBTBJ p.57
They had a warrant for my arrest. Wanda Coleman. MaDBL p.48
They had broken teeth and billy club ears. Alice Walker. PoBA p.478; RePOP p.9
They had it together and they laid it out easy. Mari Evans. BlSi p.143; NIGHT p.28
They had never had one in the house before. Gwendolyn Brooks. BeEa p.53; SPGB p. 103; WoOGB p.351
They had supposed their formula was fixed. Bwendolyn Brooks. SPGB p.25; StIB p.52; WoOGB

p.54

They have breasts shaped like papayas. Jayne Cortez. COAG p.94

They have dreamed as young men dream. Georgia Douglas Johnson. CaD p.77; DeDF p.45; PoBA p.21; PoN p.58; PoNe p.77; VoFHR p.356

They have fenced in the dirt road that once let to Wards Chapel. Alice Walker. RePOP p.12

They have fled like the green of the heath and the hill. Naomi Long Madgett. PhN p.36

They have sed u will die in this nite room of tubes. Sonia Sanchez. BlP p.236; PoBA p. 289; WABP p.29

They heard the south wind sighing. Frances E. W. Harper. BlSi p.33; FBFH p.4

They need something to believe in. Mari Evans. NIGHT p.74

They padlocked school doors. Pauli Murray. DaTAOP p.42

They rubbed the roots. Mari Evans. NIGHT p.31

They said, "wait." Naomi Long Madgett. BlALP p.111; StBS p.60

They saw you, child. Leatrice Emeruwa. BlGBG p.10

They Say. Beatrice M. Murphy. RoCo p.13

They say: "Black women are primitive; living on their emotions." Beatrice M. Murphy. RoCO p.13

They say it snoops down at midnight. Jayne Cortez. MoOP p.49

They say jab the pencils. Jayne Cortez. COAG p.87

They say that a poem is a beautiful thought expressed. Elaine Bethel. BTh p.34

They say, that I should not use the word muthafucka anymo. Carolyn M. Rodgers. SoBB p. 37; UNBP p.346

They say, "There's a race problem!" June Vanleer Williams. WiRYPS p.38

They say they can't control me. Elma Stuckey. BiGa p.48

They say, "wait," well, I waited. Naomi Long Madgett. BlP p.197

They say you are not for me. Alice Walker. RePOP p.64

They seem to smile as others smile. Georgia Douglas Johnson. BrBV p.37

They shall see Him the crimson flush. Frances E. W. Harper. PBFH p.28

They sleep who know a regulated place. June Jordan. PoBA p.305

They sprout from the earth like grass. Patricia Ford. PoBBl p.59

They stood, those two, against a mammoth well. Ariel Williams Holloway. BTh p. 16

They Take a Little Nip. Alice Walker. PoBA p.479; RePOP p.10

They take stations in the broken doorways. Mari Evans. IABW p.49

They tell me Joe Turner's come and gone. Anonymous. BlWOA p.646

They tell me that I am beautiful. Nikki Giovanni. MyH p.16

They tell me time will soon erase the bitterness within my heart. Beatrice M. Murphy. NegVo p.115

They tell me you are a far-away God who acts as a recorder and a judge. Etholia Arthur Robinson. EbR p.127

They thought me fool. Sonia Sanchez. AfAA p.3; LoP p. 14

They told the story better. Elma Stuckey. BiGa p.68

They told me when I came that sex was like drinking water. Alexis. AOS p.8

They took away the windmill. Vanessa Howard. ScWh p.54

They trample on my sensitivity. Wanda Coleman. MaDBL p.26

They tried to force Solomon Mahlangu to swallow. Jayne Cortez. COAG p.101

They wait like darkness not becoming stars. June Jordan. PoBA p.303; SCh p.5; ThTDID p.103
They Went Home.** Maya Angelou. JGM p.3
They Went to Church. Marva Tatum Smith. BeYM p.11
They were going to have so much fun in the summer. Gwendolyn Brooks. BeEa p.50; WoOGB p. 348
They were like fish meal poppin in a greasy cracklin hot at sunrise. Jayne Cortez. PoBA p.343
They were women then. Alice Walker. PoBA p.476; RePOP p.5
They Who Feel Death.** Alice Walker. ONC p.44
They will blow from your mouth one morning. Lucille Clifton. TwW p.45
They winged his spirit. Jayne Cortez. FeAF p.9
They Wuz Off to See the Wizard.** Ava Saunders. ThHSD p.45
They'll say we was only sleeping round wid each other. Carolyn Rodgers. SoBB p.17
They're brooding in Rosedale. Jayne Cortez. COAG p.26; MoOP p.8
They've done something to daffodils. June Dothard Simmons. JuB p.19
Thief. Alice Walker. RePOP p.59
Thieves give more to blue than hardness does. Jill Witherspoon Boyer. DrF p.21
Thin-Sliced. Mari Evans. IABW p. 24
Thine Own. Josephine D. (Henderson) Heard. MoGl p.51
Thing Burn of Darkness, A. Martha E. Lyons. EbR p.103
Things begin again on home land. Johari Amini. BlSi p.194
Things is Changing. Mari Evans. IABW p.74
Things Said When he Was Gone. Blanche Taylor Dickinson. EbAT p.51
Think About It. Gertrude Blackwell Bailey. IfWCF p.13
Think of me only as a bird. Coston Vale. NegVo p.159
Think of sweet and chocolate. Gwendolyn Brooks. AnA p.19; BlSi p.102; SPGB p.38; WoOGB p.83
Think of yourself as a novel. Colleen McElroy. MuDLSG p.34
Thinning hair estee laundered deliberate sentences. Nikki Giovanni. MyH p.53
Third Face, The. Melba Joyce Boyd. CaEADW p.36
Third Sermon on the Warpland, The. Gwendolyn Brooks. BlP p.176; RIOT p.11
Thirst. Gertrude Blackwell Bailey. IfWCF p.40
Thirteens, The (Black). Maya Angelou. JGM p.46
Thirteens, The (White). JGM p. 47
Thirty Eight Year of My Life, The. Lucille Clifton. OrW p. 93
Thirty turbine boilers thought the Lord couldn't sink it. May Miler. ClAB p.9
This a Rap on yo Do'. Sherley Williams. PePo p.47
This ain't the beginning. Sherley Williams. PePo p.41
This basket is heavy. Linda Brown Bragg. LoSBM p.6
This breast is so prim a pink background for your minute ivory curves. Margaret Danner. DoOAT p.88
This Child is the Mother. Gloria Oden. BlSi p.123
This City-Light. Sherley Williams. CoAAAW p.390
This coil spiraling itself to an infernal blue heaven. Pinkie Gordon Lane. WiTh p.21
This cool night is strange. Gwendolyn Bennett. BANP p.244; ANP p.128
This country might have been a pioneer land. Sonia Sanchez. BOL p.42; MoCAP p.135; NaPr p.124; PoBA p.287; SoS p. 104; WABP p.27
This first bright day has broken the back of winter. Audre Lorde. BlUn p.38

This garden too pleasant the moon too near pools of water a void. Helen Quigless. NBP p. 102
This generation of bruthas be already just like all the others--unready! Leatrice Emeruwa. BlGBG p.7
This heart conditioned on severity. Sonia Sanchez. LoP p.89
This here's a tale of a sho-nuff man. Margaret Walker. FMP p. 49
This house was gay once. Naomi Long Madgett. OnATM p.41
This house will not stand forever. Audre Lorde. BlUn p. 115
This humming does have the hum of birds. Pinkie Gordon Lane. WiTh p.42
This I have made my sacred vow. Lucia Mae Pitts. NegVo p.133
This is a cultured kewpie. Margaret Danner. DoOAT p.134
"This is a funny world," said Muffin. Margaret Danner. DoOAT p.60
This is a memorial to my father. Margaret T. G. Burroughs. WhSIT p.12
This is a quiet poem. Pinkie Gordon Lane. MyFe p.12
This is a Sad-Ass Poem for a Black Woman to be Writing. Sherley Williams. PePo p.18
This is a shining city gay and bright. Naomi Long Madgett. PhN p.91; SoTPN p.91
This is a simple poem. Audre Lorde. BlUn p.48
This is a trip that strangers make. June Jordan. ThTDID p.167
This is an African Worm. Margaret Danner. BlP p.151; DoOAT p.86; PoCo p.11; UNBP p.230
This is best letters are dangerously handled. Thulani Davis. AlTRGR p.6
This is CTR Reed. Mari Evans. NIGHT p.24
This is how I came to be loved. Audre Lorde. ChPON p.70; NeHS p.15
This is how it is or can be. Carolyn M. Rodgers. CoAAAW p.313
This is It. Elma Stuckey. BiGa p.61
This is My Century...Black Synthesis of Time. Margaret Walker. CoAAAW p.361
This is my country. Mary Wilkerson Cleaves. EbR p.46
This is my mother, America. Hazel L. Washington. EbR p. 151
This is My Vow. Lucia Mae Pitts. NegVo p.133
This is No Promised Land. Carolyn M. Rodgers. HoIGO p.28
This is not about romance & dream. Thulani Davis. AlTRGR p.53
This is Not for John Lennon. Nikki Giovanni. ThWRNW p.19
This is not what I meant to keep. Naomi Long Madgett. NeHV p.297; PiLAF p.42
This is one way to die. Naomi Long Madgett. StBS p.20
This is powerful country. Sonia Sanchez. LoP p.20
This is really the story of a sista who was very too-ga-tha. Sherley Williams. BlSi p.255; PePo p.50
This is September, 'see the red leaves flying, flying. Naomi Long Margaret. PhN p. 38
This is Silence. Pamela Cobb. InDM p.12
This is the City. Yvette Johnson. TNV p.58
This is the Religion my Father Taught Me. Pamela Cobb. InDM p.34
This is the surest death of all the deaths I know. Naomi Long Madgett. MoCAP p.92; NNPUSA p.23; PoNe p.382; StBS p.16
This is the sweet death. Naomi Long Madgett. PoBA p.182
This is the time of the crit, the creeple, and the make-iteer. Gwendolyn Brooks. Bec p.6

This is the urgency; Live! Gwendolyn Brooks. BLIA p.335; BlP p.171; ITM p.51; PoBA p.163; WoOGB p.423
This is the way to the highlands. Pinkie Gordon Lane. MyFe p. 11
This is too beautiful a day to walk alone. Mary Wilkerson Cleaves. EbR p.46
This is what you told me once. Alice Walker. ONC p.59
This is where poor Percy died. Gwendolyn Brooks. StIB p.20; WoOGB p.22
This Island Now (Jamaica). Kattie M. Cumbo. NiBPo p.62
This Kind of Artist.** Margaret Danner. DoOAT p.59
This kiss as soft as cotton. Lucille Clifton. GoNAE p.38
This land will not always be foreign. Audre Lorde. FrLWP p.37
This Little Light of Mine.** Kali Grosvenor. PBK p.28
This Little Senufo Bird. Margaret Danner. DoOAT p.34; IrLa p.3
This little Senufo tribal bird reminds me of Picasso's lofty Chicago lady. Margaret Danner. DoOAT p.34; IrLa p.3
This of that and the that of this, The. Naomi Long Madgett. StBS p.22; KAL p.177
This love is a rich cry over the deviltries and the death. Gwendolyn Brooks. Bec p.10
This Man. Joanne Jimason. NaABE p.13; SCh p.10
This Man. June Jordan. ThTDID p.157
This man he carries the ocean in his pocket. Joanne Jimason. NaABE p.13
This mirror that reflects me, cool, serene, knows nothing of the turmoil in my mind. Ylessa Dubonnee. EbR p.60
This moment is precious. Sarah E. Wright. BTB p.185; PoNe p.270
This Morning. Lucille Clifton. OrW p.39
This morning I recognized the portrait. Pamela Cobb. InDM p.13
This morning this morning I met myself. Lucille Clifton. OrW p.39
This morning this old way worn woman came tipping along. Carolyn M. Rodgers. HeAEG p.48
This of that and the that of this, The. Naomi Long Madgett. KAL p.177; StBS p.22
This old whistle could not blow. June Jordan. SCh p.10; ThTDID p.157
This one lie down on grass. Lucille Clifton. TwW p.34
This palm wine jug of curves yet long and slender head. Margaret Danner. DoOAT p. 32; IrLa p.23
This quiet province of schizophrenia. Jodi Braxton. SoITM p.25
This savory mouthful mine. Mari Evans. IABW p.48
This spirit-choking atmosphere with deadly serpent-coil. Georgia Douglas Johnson. BrBV p.30
This Sun is Hot. Anonymous. BlP p.9
This sun touched Benin. Malkia M'Buzi. CoAAAW p.218
This Treasured Book. Pinkie Gordon Lane. WiTh p.23
This two-toned sandalwood stick was of pencil height. Margaret Danner. DoOAT p.118; IrLa p.2
This Winter Day. Maya Angelou. OhPWFW p.66
This woman is Black. Audre Lorde. ChPON p.111; CoAAAW p.191
This woman thinks we're De Beauvoir & Jean-Paul/never forget/I'ma spic & yr a colored girl. Ntozake Shange. NaEd p.35
This woman vomiting her hunger over the world. Sonia Sanchez. CoAAAW p.325; IvBAW p.60

Thistles are accorded reverence in Africa. Margaret Danner. DoOAT p.12
Those barbed-wire summers over which our memories dare not climb. Naomi Long Madgett. ExAE o,66
Those black out lines in living flesh every day pressed to the window panes. Sarah Wright. BTB p.184
Those Boys That Ran Together. Lucille Clifton. DOBB p.53; PoBA p.307
Those of us who are left are ganging for one last fight. Thulani Davis. AlTRGR p.21
Those Summers I Was Fourteen and Fifteen. Gloria Oden. RESUR p.87
Those things which you so laughing call hands. Nikki Giovanni. MyH p.18
Those were the days of winking at a Funeral. Alice Walker. PoBA p.476; RePOP p.4
Those Who Can, Do. Marva Tatum Smith. BeYM p.24
Thou art not near me, but I see thine eyes. Josephine D. (Henderson) Heard. MoGl p. 53
Thou Lovest Me. Josephine D. (Henderson) Heard. MoGl p. 35
Thou monstrous gift and rainbow-linted thine. Josephine D (Henderson) Heard. MoGl p.68
Though battles are nearing an end, fires still exist. E. Sharon Gomillion. FoAAM p.27
Though change has passed upon thy heart for me. Josephine D. (Henderson) Heard. MoGl p.95
Though I do wonder why you intrigue me. Nikki Giovanni. CoCRD p.74
Though I should weep with the judgment, how would it serve. Georgia Douglas Johnson. BrBV p.68
Though no words, given in token exchange. Jennifer Blackman Lawson. BlIMT p.40
Though the long night the long trucks running the road. June Jordan, PaNP p.36
Though thou did'st hear the tempest from a far. Phillis Wheatley. PAL p.70; PPW p. 37
Though you are a continent and two seasons away. Jo Ann Hall-Evans. BlSi p.191
Though you are ever more and ever more returning. Naomi Long Madgett. OnATM p.39
Thou your love claims me. Mae V. Cowdery. WLOV p.53
Thought. Leatrice Emeruwa. BlGBG p.7
Thought, A. Marva Tatum Smith. BeYM p.16
Thoughts. Kathy Sterling. MyNIB p.157
Thoughts of the girl he left behind. Iola M. Brister. NegVo p.16
Thoughts On the Works of Providence. Phillis Wheatley. EBAP p.101; PAL p.42; PPW p.19
Thoughts run tonight. Pinkie Gordon Lane. MyFe p.41
Thoughts While Driving. Nola Richardson. WhOL p.57
Thousand Ways, A. Nòla Richardson. WhOL p.40
Thrall. Georgia Douglas Johnson. HWOP p.23
Thralldom. Georgia Douglas Johnson. ALC p.7
Three Bills. Pinkie Gordon Lane. MyFe o,29
Three Bills I knew. Pinkie Gordon Lane. MyFe p.29
3 Day New York Blues. Jayne Cortez. Scar p.15
Three Dollars Cash. Alice Walker. PoBA p.477; RePOP p.6
Three faces...mirrored in the muddy streams of living. Margaret Walker. BlP p.158; BrT p.152
Three o'clock in the morning when most people were asleep. Olean Bess. MiFe p.13

Three of us in the bar was red shimmering. Carolyn M. Rodgers. JuBa p.113
Three of us went to the top of the city, The. June Jordan. BlP p.248; SCh p.65
Three Poems For Gwendolyn Brooks. Delores Kendrick. TGWL p.60
Three poems for my daughter. Mae V. Cowdery. WLOV p.47
Three Poems for Nat Nakasa. Kattie M. Cumbo. NiBPo p.64
Three/Quarter Time, Nikki Giovanni. ThWRNW p.52
Three Scenes For all Men. May Miller. DeDF p.97
Three Stars: "Fleming Feather." June Jordan. PeNP p.30
3-31-70. Gayl Jones. BlSi p.205
Three times have I known tears. Pauli Murray. DaTAOP p.75
Three Trees. Wanda Coleman. MaDBL p.105
Three yr old sistuh going on forty. Sonia Sanchez. LoP p.66
Threnody. Naomi Long Madgett. PhN p.75
Through airy roads he wings his instant flight. Phillis Wheatley. PAL p.75; PPW p.31
Through my veins pulses the sweet perfume of magnolias. Naomi Long Madgett. PhN p. 97
Through random doors we wandered into passages disguised as paradise. Naomi Long Madgett. BlSi p.128; ExAE p. 47
Through the dirt of my windows it is sometimes difficult to relate. Vanessa Howard. ScWh p.17
Through the green clover and white-tipped violets. Nikki Giovanni. VaT p.23
Through the Holly Wreath. Effie Lee Newsome. ChG p. 68
Through the Inner City to the Suburbs. Maya Angelou. AnSIR p.22
Through the long night and weary day. Josephine D. (Henderson) Heard. MoGl p. 86
Through the long winter. Audre Lorde. NNPUSA p.20
Through the moil and the gloom they have issued to the steps of the upwinding hill. Georgia Douglas Johnson. BrBV p.54
Through the Varied Patterned Lace. Margaret Danner. DoOAT p.114; IrLa p.11
Through thickest glooms look back, immortal shade. Phillis Wheatley. PAL p.39; PPW p.40
Through winter's chill, stay. Naomi Long Madgett. StBS p. 29
Through you I entered Heaven and hell. Georgia Douglas Johnson. ALC p.70
Throughout the storm and party. Alice Walker. RePOP p.62
Throwing out the flowers. Gwendolyn Brooks. AnA p.11
Thrust of the thirty-eight side became evident last night, The. Margaret Walker. DoOAT p.89
Thus she had lain sugar can sweet. Maya Angelou. OhPWFW p.28
Thy various works, imperial queen, we see. Phillis Wheatley. AfAWA p.15; AVAN p.28; BlSi p.16; CNAW p.13; EaNAW p.42; EBAP p.107; PAL p.76; PoN p.7; PoNe p.9; PPW p.29
Thy weary feet have pressed once more thy native soil. Josephine D. (Henderson) Heard. MoGl p.31
Thy Will, O Lord, Not Mine. Josephine D. (Henderson) Heard. MoGl p.108
Tied-dyed woman wrapped in Ife blues. Fatimah Afif. CoAAAW p.47
Tight grip but loose reins hold in harness. Sarah Webster Fabio. TGWL p.34
Tim and Johnny run by hoping to play. June Jordan. ThTDID p.180
Time. Sherley Williams. PePo

p.21
Time Aint Long, De. Bessie Woodson Yancey. EcFTH p.61
Time Ain't Long As It Has Been. Carolyn M. Rodgers. HeAEG p.81
Time and Tide. Hazel Washington Lamarre. PoNe p.360
Time Comes When You Know. Wanda Coleman. MaDBL p.72
Time Heals All Wounds. Nola Richardson. WhOL p.21
Time I dropped your almost body down, The. Lucille Clifton. BlSi p.247; GoNAE p.4; MoCAP p.141
Time is an old washerwoman. Naomi Long Madgett. ExAE p.27
Time is No Thief. Naomi Long Madgett. OnATM p.31
Time is Now, The. Mari Evans. NIGHT p.62
Time is Now, The. Naomi Long Madgett. OnATM p.46
Time moves on leaden wings. Josephine D. (Henderson) Heard. MoGl p.105
Time Somebody Told Me.** C. Tillery Banks. HeTMWL p.12
Time to wipe away ths slime from inner rooms of thinking. Margaret Walker. PFND p.9
Time was, I was confined to one small spot. Ruby Berkley Goodwin. NegVo p.63
Time would not wait on me. Hazel Washington Lamarre. PoNe p.360
Timepiece. Audre Lorde. BlUn p.69
Times and Things Have Changed. Josephine D. (Henderson) Heard. MoGl p.137
Times are very different now. Josephine D. (Henderson) Heard. MoGl p.137
Times Change and We Change With Them or We Seem to Have Lost Touch With Each Other. Audre Lorde. NeHS p.42
Time's Flight. Josephine D. (Henderson) Heard. MoGl p. 105
Times-Square-Shoeshine-Composition. Maya Angelou. JGM p. 30
Timing. Audre Lorde. BlUn p. 83
Timing. Elma Stuckey. BiGa p. 70
Tin cans alleys stretch themselves out to gather. Carolyn M. Rodgers. HeAEG p.73
Tiny electrical coffee pot take a long time to make, The. June Jordan. ThTDID p.182
Tired. Georgia Douglas Johnson. HWOP p.31
Tired poem/slightly negative/ more positive. Carolyn M. Rodgers. BlSp p.178
Tires are blackbirds on the rack. Colleen McElroy. MuDLSG p.11
Tiretracks covered their skulls. Joanne Jimason. NaABE p.24
'Tis Difficult. Ethel Brown. BTh p.50
'Tis difficult to read man's face aright. Ethel Brown. BTh p.50
'Tis queer, it is, the ways of man. Angelina Weld Grimke. CaD p.39
'Tis sabbath, and a lovely calm. Josephine D. (Henderson) Heard. MoGl p.104
'Tis the octoroon ball! Rosalie Jonas. BlSi p.55
Tivoli. Naomi Long Madgett. PiLAF p.48
To--. Isabelle H. Monroe. NegVo p.106
To a Brown Boy. Naomi Long Madgett. PhN p.102
To a Child That Was. Mari Evans. IABW p.43; WhIAM p.6
To a Clergyman on the Death of His Lady. Phillis Wheatley. PAL p.84; PPW p.24
To a Critic. Bessie Woodson Yancey. EcFTH p.1
To a Dark Girl. Gwendolyn B. Bennett. ANP p.128; BANP p.243; BlSi p.76; CaD p. 157; DeDF o,61; PoBA p. 81; VoFHR p.191
To a Dark Moses. Lucille Clifton. OrW p.35
To a Dream City, in Departing. Naomi Long Madgett. PhN p.

92
To a Few of the Most Lovely. Margaret Danner. DoOAT p.124
To a Fountain. Lucy Mae Turner. BCF p.259
To a Freedom Fighter. Maya Angelou. JGM p.33
To a Friend. Jayne Cortez. Scar p.16
To a Gentleman and Lady on the Death of the Lady's Brother and Sister, and a Child of the Name of Avis, Aged One Year. Phillis Wheatley. AVAN p.30; BlSi p.14; PAL p.68; PPW p.69
To a Gentleman of the Navy (For the Royal American Magazine). Phillis Wheatley. PPW p.81
To a Gentleman on his Voyage to Great Britain for the Recovery of his health. Phillis Wheatley. EbAT p.79; PAL p.66; PPW p.41
To a Girl Who Knew What Side her Bread was Buttered On. Audre Lorde. ChPON p.5; COAL p. 70; FiCi p.11; SiAS p.42
To a Gone Era. Irma McClaurin. BlSi p.196
To a hungry man she's his watermelon. Angela Jackson. VoDLM p.16
To a Husband. Maya Angelou. JGM 14
To a Lady and Her Children on the Death of her son and Their Brother. Phillis Wheatley. PAL p.69; PPW p.38
To a Lady on her Coming to North America with Her Son, for the Recovery of Her Health. Phillis Wheatley. PAL p.71; PPW p.36
To a Lady on Her Remarkable Preservation in a Hurricane in North Carolina. Phillis Wheatley. PAL p.70; PPW p. 37
To a Lady on the Death of her Husband. Phillis Wheatley. PAL p.38; PPW p.12
To a Lady on the Death of Three Relations. Phillis Wheatley. PAL p.86; PPW p.23
To a Jealous Cat. Sonia Sanchez. HoC p.13
To a Man. Maya Angelou. JGM p.6
To a Man With Wings. Naomi Long Madgett. PhN p.118
To a Mounted Ivory Masque Pin. Margaret Danner. DoOAT p.88
To a Nickel. Lucy Mae Turner. BCF p.57
To a Nigerian Student of Metallurgy. Margaret Danner. ImOAAF p.13; PoCo p.12
To a Poet I Knew: Johari Amini. Sonia Sanchez. LetGSW p.24; PoBA p.291
To a Reactionary. Mae Jackson. CaPWY p.6
To a Rosebud. Eva Jesse. ANP p.80
To a Spaniard, Dying. Norma Lopez Garcia. NeJCL p.28
To a Winter Squirrel. Gwendolyn Brooks. HoFTD p.76; ITM p. 35; WoOGB p.407
To a Woman. Harryette Mullen. TTW p.1
To a Woman Poet That I Know. Pinkie Gordon Lane. MyFe p. 33
To a Wounded Bird. Hilda Preer. BTh p.36
To a Young Blood. Blossom Powe. GLOWC p.80; MyNIB p.70
To Abraham Lincoln. Georgia Douglas Johnson. BrBV p.90
To All Brothers. Sonia Sanchez. BrT p.136; LoP p.95; RoATW p.65
To All Brothers: From All Sisters. Sonia Sanchez. LoP p.95
To All Sisters. Sonia Sanchez. BlFi p.255; HoC p.27; PoBA p.290
To All Sisters. Sonia Sanchez. HoC p.22
To An Icicle. Blanche Taylor Dickinson. CaD p.110
To Anita. Sonia Sanchez. BlSp p. 190; ItND p.8
To an Avenue Sport. Helen Johnson Collins. PoN p.193; PoNe p.346
To Any Negro Youth. Beatrice M. Murphy. RoCO p.7
To Atlanta University--Its Founders and Teachers. Georgia Douglas Johnson. BrBV p.101

To Autumn. Naomi Long Madgett. SoTPN p.17
To awaken in the morning with arms around my waist. Nola Richardson. WhOL p.43
To Be....Dolores Abramson. ThHSD p.37; RoATW p.79
To Be a Woman.** Jackie Earley. RoATW p.53
To Be Black in America.** Nancy L. Arnez. RoCO p.16
To be dust to be dust I want to be dust. Wanda Coleman. MaDBL p.106
To Be in Love.** Gwendolyn Brooks. RoATW p.11; SPGB p. 120
To be or not to be. Kathleen Reed. PoBBl p.29
To Be: Go Touch...To Feel: A Hair, The Warmth. S. Diane Bogus. WITM p.16
To Beat the Child Was Bad Enough, Maya Angelou. AnSIR p.30
To Bell-like flowers in Belle Isle. Margaret Danner. PeCo p.22
To Bill. Naomi Long Madgett. PhN p.79
To Bishop Allen's Memory. Josephine D. (Henderson) Heard. MoGl p.110
To Bishop H. Turner, D.D, LL.D. Josephine D. (Henderson) Heard. MoGl p.100
To Bishop Turner. Josephine D. (Henderson) Heard. MoGl p. 116
To Blk/Record/Buyers. Sonia Sanchez. HoC p.26; UNBP p. 272
To Bobby Seale. Lucille Clifton. GoNAE p.24; PoBA p.308
To Boston City, one morning. Eloise Culver. GANIV p.11
To Captain H--D, Of the 65th Regiment. Phillis Wheatley. PAL p.74; PPW p.32
To Carry Out an Act of Love. Joanne Jimason. NaABE p.6
To Chuck. Sonia Sanchez. HoC p.20; UNBP p.273
To Clarissa Scott Delany. Angelina Weld Grimke. AmNP p. 15; EbAT p.67
To Clements' Ferry. Josephine D. (Henderson) Heard. MoGl p.47
To climb a hill that hungers for the sky. Helene Johnson. CaD p.219; PoN p.151; PoNe p.262; RoATW p.162
To cultivate in ev'ry noble mind. Phillis Wheatley. PAL p.65; PPW p.42
To dance in the light of moon. Mae V. Cowdery. WLOV p.10
To Darnell and Johnny. Melba Joyce Boyd. CaEADW p.9
To Death. Lois Royal Hughes. NegVo p.82
To Desi as Joe as Smoky the Lover of 115th Street. Audre Lorde. NeHS p.5
To Die Once One Wakes Must be Glad. Alice Walker. ONC p. 76
To Don at Salaam. Gwendolyn Brooks. BlP p.12; FaP p.16
To Egypt. Gloria Davis. DeDF p.71; NBP p.46
To Emilie Bigelow Hapgood--Philanthropist. Georgia Douglas Johnson. BrBV p.96
To Etta Moten. Margaret Danner. DoOAT p.133
To F.S.I. Claire Turner. NegVo p.155
To Fanon, Culture Meant Only One Thing - An Environment Shaped to Help Us & Our Children Grow Shaped by Ourselves in Action Against the System That Enslaves Us. Sonia Sanchez. WABP p.50
To George. Pinkie Gordon Lane. WiTh p.27
To get my freedom I would chance my life. Elma Stuckey. BiGa p.52
To grow up in a father's image idolizing. Naomi Long Madgett. PiLAF p.20
To Gwen. Carolyn M. Rodgers. HoIGO p.39
To Gwen,/No Luv. Carolyn M. Rodgers. TGWL p.84
To Gwendolyn Brooks the Creator in the Beginning - Words. Barbara A. Reynolds. TGWL p. 83
To Harriet Tubman: A Plea. Lyn.

SiSH p.20
To have set my eyes upon you. Kattie M. Cumbo. NiBPo p.48
To hell with Ezra Pound. Toi Derricotte. EmDH p.37
To Henry Lincoln Johnson--Lawyer. Georgia Douglas Johnson. BrBV p.97
To His Excellency General Washington. Phillis Wheatley. BiLi p.11; BlWOA p.43
To His Honor the Lieutenent Governor, On The Death of His Lady, March 24, 1773. Phillis Wheatley. PAL p.47; PPW p. 55
To James Weldon Johnson. Georgia Holloway Jones. EbR p.98
To Jill. Naomi Long Madgett. OnATM p.21
To Joan. Lucille Clifton. TwW p.57
To John Brown. Georgia Douglas Johnson. BrBV p.89
To John Oliver Killens in 1975. Gwendolyn Brooks. Bec p.7
To Judith Lynn on Her First Birthday. Mae V. Cowdery. WLOV p.47
To Judith Lynn..Who is Just Two. Mae V. Cowdery. WLOV p.47
To Keep the Memory of Charlotte Forten Grimke. Angelina Weld Grimke. BlSi p.61
To Kenny. Sonia Sanchez. ItND p.9
To Keorapetse Kgositsile (Willie). Gwendolyn Brooks. FaP p.14
To Koala, Who Will Soon be Extinct. Carole Gregory Clemmons. NiBPo p.86
To L. Julianne Perry. PoBA p. 516
To live and not to be thine own. Josephine D. (Henderson) Heard. MoGl p.51
To live believe in no one. Sonia Sanchez. LoP p.53
To Live With Father.** Gloria Oden. RESUR p.65
To love a man wholly love him feet first. Alice Walker. ONC p.68
To love, to lose, and then to find. Naomi Long Madgett. OnATM p.43
To Maqui. Margaret Danner. DoOAT p.126
To March. Naomi Long Madgett. PhN p.43
To Marie, In Flight. Audre Lorde. ChPON p.78; NeHS p.44
To Market, To Market To Buy a Fat Pig.** Marva Tatum Smith. BeYM p.26
To Martha:: a New Year. Audre Lorde. BlUn p.46
To Mary Church Terrell--Lecturer. Georgia Douglas Johnson. BrBV p.98
To May Howard Jackson--Sculptor. Georgia Douglas Johnson. BrBV p.99
To Melancholy. Naomi Long Madgett. OnATM p.35
To Merle. Lucille Clifton. TwW p.9
To mend the human heart before eighteen ninety three yet have the sick one live was still a mystery. Eloise Culver. GANIV p.41
To Mr. and Mrs.-----On the Death of Their Infant Son. Phillis Wheatley. PPW p.95
Ro Morani/Mungu. Sonia Sanchez. BlSp p.188; ItND p.7
To Mother and Steve. Mari Evans. BlP p.184; IABW p.20; PoBA p.191; RoATW p.140; UNBP p.251; WhIAM p.22
To Mrs. Bishop Lee. Josephine D. (Henderson) Heard. MoGl p.105
To Mrs. Leonard, on the Death of Her Husband. Phillis Wheatley. PPW p.71
To Ms. Ann. Lucille Clifton. OrW p.25
To My Children. Sandra Royster. WoTa p.9
To My Country. Naomi Long Madgett. OnATM p.61
To My Daughter the Junkie On a Train. Audre Lorde. ChPON p.79; NeHS p.5
To My Father. Henrietta Cordelia Ray. BlSi p.38; EBAP p.139
To My Father. Josephine D. (Henderson) Heard. MoGl p.114

To My Friend. Josephine D. (Henderson) Heard. MoGl p.107
To My Friends. Sandra Royster. WoTa p.17
To My Grandmother. Mae Smith Johnson. ANP p.112; NeNRe p.364
To My Lost Love. Naomi Long Madgett. PhN p.21
To My Mother. Naomi Long Madgett. PhN p.84
To My Sister, Ethel Ennis, Who Sang "The Star Spangled Banner" at the Second Inauguration of Richard Milhous Nixon, January 20, 1973. June Jordan. ThTDID p.139
To My Sisters Out There. Dolores Abramson. ThHSD p.1
To My Son. Georgia Douglas Johnson. NeNRe p.380
To My Vegetarian Friend. Patricia Parker. MoIB p.67
To Non-African American Brothers and Sisters. Margaret T. G. Burroughts. WhSIT p.16
To Otis Redding. Kali Grosvenor. PBK p.48
To P.J. (2 Yrs Old Who Sed Write a Poem For Me in Portland, Oregon). Sonia Sanchez. ItND p.18
To Poets Who Have Rebelled. Pauli Murray. DaTAOP p.58
To poor and humble farmers, was born near Christmas Night. Eloise Culver. GANIV p.55
To Reggie. Frenchy J. Hodges. BlW p.14
To Richard R. Wright--Instructor. Georgia Douglas Johnson. BrBV p.94
To Ridley Torrance--Playwright. Georgia Douglas Johnson. BrBV p.93
To Robert Peters. Pinkie Gordon Lane. PoBBl p.11; WiTh p.16
To Roger Wilson's Harlequin. Margaret Danner. ImOAAF p. 12
To S.M. a Young African Painter on Seeing His Work. Phillis Wheatley. BlSi p.15; EaNAW p.51
To Samuel Coleridge Taylor, Upon Hearing His Sometimes I Feel Like a Motherless Child. Georgia Douglas Johnson. BrBV p.95
To Scipio Moorhead, a Young African Painter, On Seeing His Works. Phillis Wheatley. EBAP p.110; ITBLA p.29; PAL p.58; PPW p.54
To See a Man Cry Is Like Watching Animals.** Patricia Parker. ChOM p.6; MoIB p.35
To see you standing in the sagging bookstore door. Margaret Danner. AfAWA p.635; IrLa p.19; MoCAP p.89; NNPUSA p.31; PoBA p.135
To show the lab'ring bosum's deep intent. Phillis Wheatley. BlSi p.15; EaNAW p. 51; EBAP p.110; ITBLA p. 29; PAL p.58; PPW p.54
To Some Who Are Prone to Criticize. Claire Turner. NegVo p.156
To Singers of Song. Pinkie Gordon Lane. MyFe p.32
To smell the sting of rotting brownstones. Pamela Woodruff Hill. UNBP p.318
To Some Millions Who Survive Joseph E. Mander Senior. Sarah E. Wright. PoBA p.212
To Someone I Met on 125th Street 1966. Mae Jackson. CaPWY p.13
To Soulfolk. Margaret Burroughts. BlSi p.118
To speak/a test of silence. Ntozake Shange. NaEd p.123
To spin a tale of Africa takes devoted heart and hands. Eloise Culver. GANIV p.62
To Sunshine Sammy. Bessie Woodson Yancey. EcFTH p.36
To Swinehearts, From Dachau With Love. Judy Dothard Simmons. JuB p.8
To The Artist Who Just Happens to be Black. Jayne Cortez. FeAF p.28
To the Bronze Head. Margaret Danner. IrLa p.13
To the Bronze Masque. Margaret Danner. DoOAT p.121
To the church house the fashion-plate goes. Marva Tatum

Smith. BeYM p.11
To The Dunbar High School: A Sonnet. Angelina Weld Grimke. ANP p.87; ReFNA p.24
To the Evangelist. Linda Brown Bragg. LoSBM p.21
To the First of August. Ann Plato. BlSi p.45; EBAP p. 117
To the Freedom Riders. Eloise Culver. GANIV p.78
To the Girl Who Lives in a Tree. Audre Lorde. ChPON p.75; NeHS p.21
To the Hon'ble Thomas Hubbard Esq: on the Death of Mrs. Thankfull Leonard (1773). Phillis Wheatley. PAL p.59; PPW p.77
To the Honorable T. H. Esq. on the Death of His Daughter. Phillis Wheatley. PAL p.61; PPW p.46
To the King's Most Excellent Majesty (1768). Phillis Wheatley. PAL p.34; PPW p.6
To the Man in the Yellow Terry. Alice Walker. ONC p.49
To the Martyred. Georgia Douglas Johnson. BrBV p.88
To the Memory of Inez Milholland. Georgia Douglas Johnson. BrBV p.100
To the Memory of J. Horace Kimball. Ada. BlSi p.21
To the Nature Lovers. Vanessa Howard. ScWh p.17
To the Negro Intellectuals. Mae Jackson. CaPWY p.9
To the northern pearl sheba woman. Jayne Cortez. FeAF p.6
To the Negro Farmers of the United States. Alice Dunbar-Nelson. DuSAE p.240
To the Oppressors. Pauli Murray. DaTAOP p.31
To the Original Poet. Wanda Coleman. MaDBL p.84
To the Plow. Gertrude Blackwell Bailey. IfWCF p.55
To the Rev. Dr. Thomas Amory, on Reading His Sermons on Daily Devotion in Which that Duty is Recommended and Assistance. Phillis Wheatley. PAL p.65; PPW p.42
To the Rev. Mr. Pitkin, on the Death of His Lady (1772). Phillis Wheatley. PAL p.40; PPW p.76
To the Right Honorable William, Earl of Dartmouth. Phillis Wheatley. BlP p.38; NeCa p.284
To the Right Honorable William, Earl of Dartmouth, His Majesty's Secretary of State for North America. Phillis Wheatley. EaNAW p.39; KAL p.4; PAL p.73; PPW p. 33; ReFNA p.6; TYBP p.204
To the Singer. Helen C. Harris. EbR p.79
To the Sisters. Loretta Rodgers. RoATW p.81; ThHSD p.83
To the Unborn and Waiting Children. Lucille Clifton. TwW p.17
To the University of Cambridge, in New England. Phillis Wheatley. AfAWA p.17; BlALP p.10; BlWOA p.41; CNAW p.10; EaNAW p.36; EBAP p.99; PAL p.33; PPW p. 5;
To the University of Cambridge, wrote in 1767. Phillis Wheatley. PPW p.63
To the Veterans of Future Wars. Mae V. Cowdery. WLOV p.66
To the White Man. Valerie Tarver. TNV p.130
To "The You."** Margaret Danner. DoOAT p.61
To Thelma Who Worried Because I Couldn't Cook. Lucille Clifton. TwW p.13
To Those of My Sisters Who Kept There Naturals. Gwendolyn Brooks. CoAAAW p.84
To those who after listening to the ugly truths. Margaret Danner. DoOAT p.124
To Time. Georgia Douglas Johnson. ALC p.15
To Turn From Love. Sarah Webster Fabio. BlSi p.140; DOBB p.30
To Usward. Gwendolyn B. Bennett. BlSi p.76
To W.E.B. DuBois--Scholar. Georgia Douglas Johnson. BrBV p.92

To W.L.G. on Reading His Chosem Queen. Charlotte Forten Grimke. BlSi p.24
To walk in the muck of uncertainty. Henrietta C. Parks. TNV p.85
To whatever you incline, your final choice here must be handling. Gwendolyn Brooks. StIB p.8; WoOGB p.10
To Whittier. Josephine D. (Henderson) Heard. EBAP p.262; MoGl p.14
To Whom it Does Concern Blue is My Favorite Color. LaVerne Davis. GLOWC p.39
To whom should I speak today? Anonymous. TYBP p.26
To William Stanley Braithwaite. Georgia Douglas Johnson. BlALP p.44; BrBV p.91
To Wives (Of Artists). Judy Dothard Simmons. JuB p.11
To You. Linda G. Hardnett. GaBW p.320
To You. Marva Tatum Smith. BeYM p.23
To You. Ruby Stevens. NegVo p. 147
To You/Who Almost Turned/Me On. Sonia Sanchez. IvBAW p.48; LoP p.51
To Youth. Josephine D. (Henderson) Heard. MoGl p.28
Toast to Colored Girls, A. Bessie Woodson Yancey. EcFTH p.29
Today. Margaret Walker. FBPA p.112; FMP p.28
Today. Wanda Coleman. MaDBL p. 127
Today and Tomorrow. Naomi Long Madgett. OnATM p.28
Today, at dawn, or nearly. Margaret Danner. DoOAT p.124
Today blackness lay backing & rooting. Carolyn M. Rodgers. HoIGO p.1
Today I Am a Homicide in the North of the City. Wanda Coleman. MaDBL p.25
Today I am tired of sabbaths. Sonia Sanchez. IvBAW p.40; LoP p.43
Today I am 24. Mae Jackson. PoBA p.499
Today I Became the Age Your Father Was.** Gloria Oden. RESUR p.129
Today I had a talk with my dog. Patricia Parker. MoIB p.71
Today I heard my heart screeching like a subway train. Audre Lorde. ChPON p.21; COAL p.29
Today I saw a thing of arresting poignant beauty. Alice Dunbar-Nelson. ANP p.85; BlSi p.66; CaD p.71
Today I smile a prayer of Thanksgiving. Jennifer Blackman Lawson. BlITM p.29
Today I walked a thousand miles and missed not one. Naomi Long Madgett. PhN p.39
Today is forest green. Thulani Davis. AlTRGR p.29
Today is me and friend girl macking. Wanda Coleman. MaDBL p.127
Today is Ours.** Anonymous. GLOWC p.91
Today oh! Oh today oh! Oh today oh! Anonymous. MBP p.55
Today on This Day. Jayne Cortez. FeAF p.5
Today on this day of old boots filled with sores. Jayne Cortez. Scar p.58
Today Requires a Lace of Truths. Margaret Danner. DoOAT p.41
Today requires a stronger lace. Margaret Danner. DoOAT p.41
Today your life will be wasted riding on a bus. Pamela Cobb. InDM p.13
Today's Pimp. Marion Nicholes. LiS p.12
Together. Carolyn M. Rodgers. BlSp p.176
Tokens For "T". Esther Louise. CoAAAW p.201
Told my sweet mama to leave me alone. Carolyn M. Rodgers. HoIGO p.1
Toleration. Coston Vale. NegVo p.159
Tom. Elma Stuckey. BiGa p.46
Tomorrow. Gertrude Blackwell Bailey. IfWCF p.32
Tomorrow. Olean Bess. MiFe p.14
Tomorrow is like a shining star.

Olean Bess. MiFe p.14
Tomorrow Will Surely Come. Gertrude Blackwell Bailey. IfWCF p.32
Tomorrow's Men. Georgia Douglas Johnson. GoS p.51
Tommy's Mommy. Nikki Giovanni. VaT p.51
Tongues. Pauli Murray. DaTAOP p.61
Tonight fate and I run swiftly. Naomi Long Madgett. PhN p.76; SoTPN p.10
Tonight I left a white cross on a grave. Naomi Long Madgett. PhN p.65
Tonight it is the wine. Alice Walker. ONC p.75
Tonight the machinery of shadow moves into the light. June Jordan. SCh p.39; ThTDID p.11
Tonight the whooping moan of invading blues. Jayne Cortez. MoOP p.16
Tonight when you spread your pallet of magic I escaped. Maya Angelou. JGM p.15
Too dumb to know. Marva Tatum Smith. BeYM p.23
Too foraging to blue-print or deploy. Gwendolyn Brooks. BeEa p.60; WoOGB p.358
Too frail to soar, a feeble thing. Frances E. W. Harper. DuSAE p.18; PBFH p.21
Too Late. Naomi Long Madgett. PhN p.66
Too many tears with the blood have been wasted. Damali (Denise Burnett) IATWMB p. 16
Too many times I caressed the night. Pinkie Gordon Lane. WiTh p.29
Too much to wait a life out. Pinkie Gordon Lane. PoBBl p.14; WiTh p.14
Tortured History of Non-Love, A. Pamela Cobb. InDM p.47
Toss your gay heads. Angelina Weld Grimke. BlSi p.61
Totality. Mae V. Cowdery. WLOV p.33
Touch me, touch me, little cool grass fingers. Angelina Weld Grimke. BlWOA p.627; CaD p.38; NeNRe p.85; ReFNA p.24
Touch of Gray. Nola Richardson. WhOL p.51
Touch Poem 5. Carolyn M. Rodgers. CoAAAW p.313
Touch. Translation Poem 4. Carolyn M. Rodgers. CoAAAW p.312
Touche. Jessie Redmond Fauset. BlSi p.63; CaD p.66
Toughest gal I ever did see was a gal by the name of Kissie Lee. Margaret Walker. BlSi p.95; FMP p.38
Tour America! Patricia Parker. MoIB p.69
Touring. Audre Lorde. BlUn p. 36
Toward a City That Sings. June Jordan. PaNP p.48
Toward a Personal Semantics. June Jordan. SCh p.36
Toward Spring. Carolyn M. Rodgers. HeAEG p.20
Toward the deep clear waters that you are my dry roots yearn. Naomi Long Madgett. PiLAF p.31
Toward the end of twenty minutes we come to a still standing archway. June Jordan. ThTDID p.53
Town-folks tink dey's awful smaht, huh? Bessie Woodson Yancey. EcFTH p.46
Toy Poem. Nikki Giovanni. BrT p.69; Rec p.40
Tracings. May Miller. ClAB p. 20
Trade a king's freedom for a barrel of molasses. Pauli Murray. DaTAOP p.21
Traditional statement about a traditional situation with a new response, A. Sherley Williams. PePo p.37
Trail. May Miller. ClAB p.22
Trail Ridge Road. Pinkie Gordon Lane. WiTh p.21
Trailing night's sand-sitted stars. Georgia Douglas Johnson. HWOP p.7
Train, The. Anonymous. TYBP p. 9

Train is gone, The. Jodi Braxton. SoITM p.39
Train-Man's Call, The. Bessie Woodson Yancey. EcFTH p.38
Train Ride, A. Carolyn M. Rodgers. HoIGO p.32
Translation. Anne Spencer. BANP p.218
Translation. Carolyn M. Rodgers. HeAEG p.82
Translation. S. Diane Bogus. WITM p.10
Transpositions. Georgia Douglas Johnson. HWOP p.51
Traveler, The. Maya Angelou. AnSIR p.35
Traveling Light. Elma Stuckey. BiGa p.60
Traveling Together Side by Side. C. Tillery Banks. HeTMWL p. 82
Traveller take heed for journeys undertaken in the dark of the year. Margaret Walker. AmNP p.132; BTB p.180; IADB p. 28; OcJo p.11; PoBA p.146; PoN p.176; PoNe p.317
Treacherous sands had caught our boat, The. Frances E. W. Harper. PBFH p.60
Treading air eyes wide against the horror. Mari Evans. IABW p.50
Treasure. Georgia Douglas Johnson. ALC p.34
Tree. Harryette Mullen. TTW p. 62
Tree of Heaven. Naomi Long Madgett. DeDF p.85; StBS p.55
Tree Poem, The. Paulette Jones. TGWL p.58
Tree talk and windsong are the language of my mother. Barbara Mahone. PoBA p.473; Suga p.14
Tree Tall Woman.** Harryette Mullen. TTW p.63
Tree--that lives & feeds & feels. Patricia Parker. ChOM p.30; MoIB p.151
Tree...to...B. H. Mae V. Cowdery. WLOV p.25
Tree Women Quest for Sun.** Malkia M'Buzi. CoAAAW p.219
Trees. Toi Derricotte. EmDH p. 39
Trees Are Laughing, The. Sonia Sanchez. IvBAW p.72
Trees are never felled...in summer. Nikki Giovanni. ThWRNW p.31
Trees At Night. Helene Johnson. BlSi p.81
Trembling November winds, steam whistling in tenement pipes. Kattie M. Cumbo. BlSi p.134; NiBPo p.57
Triangle. Roslyn Greer. TNV p. 44
Tribute to Duke. Sarah Webster Fabio. UNBP p.243
Trick, Maybe, The. June Vanleer Williams. WiRYPS p.29
Tricked Again. Ridhiana. NBP p.111
Trifle. Georgia Douglas Johnson. AmNP p.21; HoFTD p.20
Trilogy - Untitled. Carolyn M. Rodgers. HoIGO p.44
Triology: To My Unborn Children. Pinkie Gordon Lane. WiTh p. 32
Trinity: a Dream Sequence. Naomi Long Madgett. StBS p. 30
Trip on the Staten Island Ferry, A. Audre Lorde. ChPON p.87; NeHS p.18
Tripart. Gayl Jones. BlSi p. 209; SoS p.13
Triple Benison, The. Henrietta Cordelia Ray. AVAN p.153
Trivia. Beatrice M. Murphy. TNV p.141
Trolley cars was rolling and the passengers all white, The. June Jordan. PaNP p.49
Trollop Maiden, The. Audre Lorde. BlUn p.116
Troost Express. Damali (Denise Burnett) IATWMB p.17
Tropical Dance. Ntozake Shange. NaEd p.127
Trousers of Wind.** Anonymous. TYBP p.48
Trudge over the hill, autumn. Naomi Long Madgett. PhN p. 37
True Import of Present Dialogues: Black vs Negro, The. Nikki Giovanni. BFBTBJ p.19; BlP p.318; BrT p.48; PoBA p.

451
True Worshipper, The. Marva Tatum Smith. BeYM p.13
Truism. Josephine D. (Henderson) Heard. MoGl p.102
Trumpet. Elma Stuckey. BiGa p. 93
Trust me no more. Patricia Parker. ChOM p.8; MoIB p. 37
Trusting Thee. Josephine D. (Henderson) Heard. MoGl p. 90
Truth. Frances E. W. Harper. ANP p.16; PBFH p.36
Truth. Gwendolyn Brooks. AnA p. 50; SPGB p.62; WoOGB p.114
Truth. Josephine D. (Henderson) Heard. MoGl p.22
Try...Later. Eleanor Thomas-Grumbach. MoSu p.22
Try to Understand Papa. Colleen McElroy. MuDLSG p.4
Trying to see you my eyes grow confused. Audre Lorde. BlUn p.63
Tuck dreams from sight in star-dust. Katharine Beverly. EbR p.4
Tulips. W. Blanche Nivens. BTh p.60
Tulips were smiling in the spring. W. Blanche Nivens. BTh p.60
Tumbling blue and brown tulips that leap into frogs. Sonia Sanchez. LoP p.33
Tumultuous mountains arch in defiance against the sky. Mae V. Cowdery. WLOV p.64
Tune For Two Fingers. Mari Evans. NIGHT p.58
Tune in Your Car, The. Barbara Mahone. Suga p.12
Turbulence of pain is o'er, The. Ruby Stevens. NegVo p.145
Turn away in the wind. May Miller. ClAB p.11
Turn not away thy face. Josephine D. (Henderson) Heard. MoGl p.85
Turned around found you gone. Sonia Sanchez. LoP p.17
Turned sideways in the sky the pelvis bone is an outlandish shape. Harryette Mullen. TTW p.56
Turning. Lucille Clifton. OrW p.63
Turning (I Need a Better Title). Nikki Giovanni. CoCRD p.85
Turning into my own. Lucille Clifton. OrW p.63
Turquoise sea licks softly french kisses, The. Leatrice Emeruwa. BlGBG p. 20
Turtle's Song, The. Anonymous. BlP p.18
Twas a fearful night--the tempest raved. Frances E. W. Harper. EBAP p.29; PBFH p. 35
Twas a night of dreadful horror. Frances E. W. Harper. PBFH p.52
Twas Brief. Nola Richardson. WhOL p.91
Twas brief the time we met last year, The. Nola Richardson. WhOL p.91
Twas mercy brought me from my pagan land. Phillis Wheatley. AfAV p.28; AfAWA p. 18; AmLNA p.22; BlALP p. 10; BlWOA p.41; CNAW p.11; EBAP p.100; ITSA p.13; KAL p.7; PAL p.92; PPW p. 7; TYBP p.205
Tween Itaparica & Itapua. Ntozake Shange. DaGe p.24
12 Gates to the City. Nikki Giovanni. PoBA p.457; Rec p.35
24 Hours Up. Wanda Coleman. MaDBL p.132
25 years/the art ensemble. Ntozake Shange. NaEd p.31
Twenty Grand, The. Naomi Long Madgett. PiLAF p.58
Twenty Grand (Saturday Night on the Block) The. Naomi Long Madgett. NeBV p.297
21 Lines. Johari Amini. LetGSW p.30
Twenty-one years of my life you have been the lost color in my eye. Lucille Clifton. TwW p.15
Twice a Child. Naomi Long Madgett. DeDF p.54
Twice burned bitches never learn. Wanda Coleman. MaDBL p.53

Twin stars through my purpling pane. Angelina Weld Grimke. CaD p.46
Twinight earth my flesh quakes. Wanda Coleman. MaDBL p.83
Twinkling Gown. Dorothy Vena Johnson. GoS p.189
Twist spinning into love. Vanessa Howard. ScWh p.40
Two. Naomi Long Madgett. PiLAF p.34
2½ Poems Making Whole. Sherley Williams. PePo p.19
2 B Blk. Val Ferdinand. NeBV p.377
Two ants at bay. Pauli Murray. DaTAOP p.57
Two Black Men on the Front Page. Damali (Denise Burnett) IATWMB p.14
Two Countries. Jill Witherspoon Boyer. DrF p.5
Two countries sweetly confide. Jill Witherspoon Boyer. DrF p.5
Two Dedications. Gwendolyn Brooks. PoBA p.161; WoOGB p.412
Two deer and a fawn hidden in the greener parts. Pamela Cobb. InDM p.34
Two For Malcolm. Patricia. FoM p.31
2:48 P.M. Ava Sanders. ThHSD p.5
Two-Gun Buster and Trigger Slim. Margaret Walker. FMP p.42
Two-Gun Buster was a railroad hand. Margaret Walker. FMP p.42
Two liddle niggers all dressed in white (Radise a rucus tonight) Anonymous. BlP p.10
Two little children sit by my side. Frances E. W. Harper. PBFH p.56
Two Love Poems. Pinkie Gordon Lane. WiTh p.28
Two mules for sale and one Black boy. Elma Stuckey. BiGa p. 53
Two mornings ago you left my little house. Alice Walker. ONC p.57
Two Nuns By the Sea. S. Diane Bogus. WITM p.9
Two Poems. Pinkie Gordon Lane. MyFe p.k4
Two Poems From Barbados. Nikki Giovanni. Rec p.7
Two Poems From Trinity: a Dream Sequence. Naomi Long Madgett. KAL p.178
Two shining women, I will not betray you. Lucille Clifton. TwW p.31
Two things have sorrowed me this day. Pauli Murray. DaTAOP p.88
Two Thousand People Came to His Funeral When Father Died.** Gloria Oden. RESUR p.51
Two times they call us from the field. Elma Stuckey. BiGa p.9
Two trees breathe the same sweet air. Mae V. Cowdery. WLOV p.40
221-1424 (San/Francisco/Suicide/ Number. Sonia Sanchez. WABP p.12
Two Views of the 3R's. Beth Jackson. PoBBl p.54
Tyrone married her this afternoon. June Jordan. SCh p. 6; ThTDID p.46

- U -

U bet u wer left ther to die. Johari Amini. LetGSW p.24; PoBA p.291
U Can Run, But U Can't Hide. Carolyn M. Rodgers. SoBB p. 39
U Name This One. Carolyn M. Rodgers. BlSi p.183; HoIGO p.26; NaPr p.117; PoBA p. 430; SoBB p.23; TNV p.112
Ugliest little boy that everyone ever saw. Gwendolyn Brooks. BrT p.33; FaP p.9; FBPA p. 23
Ugly. Gertrude Blackwell Bailey. IfWCF p.56
Ugly Art. Melba Joyce Boyd. CaEADW p.38
Ugly honkies, or the election game and how to win it. Nikki Giovanni. BFBTBJ p.81

Uhuru. Mari Evans. IABW p.87
Uhuru in the O. R. June Jordan. SCh p.57; ThTDID p.144
Uhuru Uberalles! (and the sound of weeping). Mari Evans. IABW p.44
Unburying the Bird. Toi Derricotte. EmDH p.51
Uncertainty. Elma Stuckey. BiGa p.90
Uncertainty. Henrietta C. Parks. TNV p.85
Uncle Bull-Boy. June Jordan. PoBA p.304; SCh p.13; SoS p. 28; ThTDID p.14
Uncle Enoch know a heap about how come de moon. Lucile D. Goodlett. WGC p.23
Uncle Gabriel. Anonymous. BlWOA p.236
Uncle Tom. Eleanor A. Thompson. BTh p.12
Uncle Tom was just a slave man. Eleanor A. Thompson. BTh p.12
Uncles. Alice Walker. PoBA p. 478; RePOP p.9
Uncle Ike's Rooster. Anonymous. DuSAE p.55
Unconquerable Dust. Pauli Murray. DaTAOP p.92
Under the bronze-lipped Jesus bell midnight answers. May Miller. ClAB p.12
Under the Edge of February. Jayne Cortez. BlSi p.153; Scar p.10
Under the urination of astronauts and the ejaculation of polluted sparrows. Jayne Cortez. COAG p.103
Underground Railroad, The. Eloise Culver. GANIV p.27
Underneath the veneer of smooth cool. Carolyn M. Rodgers. HeAEG p.41
Undersized: Throw It Back! June Vanleer Williams. WiRYPS p. 47
Unemployment Monologue. June Jordan. PaNP p.46
Unencouraged Lingering. Frenchy J. Hodges. BlW p.13
Unfinished Song. Naomi Long Madgett. PhN p.122
Unfunny Situation. Carolyn M. Rodgers. SoBB p.26
Unity. Ann Wallace. GLOWC p.104
Universality. Nikki Giovanni. BFBTBJ p.64
Unk' Enoch Mann. Lucile D. Goodlett. WGC p.57
Unknown Soldier. Mae V. Cowdery. WLOV p.66
Unknowns. Kattie M. Cumbo. NiBPo p.63
Unless you remind me. Naomi Long Madgett. BlP p.196; StBS p.58
Unlike Me. Nola Richardson. WhOL p.83
Unlike you I wait. Nola Richardson. WhOL p.83
Unrepentant. Countess W. Twitty. EbR p.147
Unseemly as a marvelous an astral renegade. June Jordan. ThTDID p.81
Until I Was Eight or Nine.** Gloria Oden. RESUR p.103
Until. Myntora J. Roker. NegVo p.137
Until They Have Stopped. Sarah E. Wright. PoBA p.215
Untitled. Ada. BlSi p.19
Untitled. Amma Khalil. HoDo p. 80
Untitled. Amanda Ambrose. MyNIB p.151
Untitled. Anonymous. ThHSD p.2
Untitled. Carolyn M. Rodgers. HoIGO p.6
Untitled. Daphne Diane Page. UNBP p.316
Untitled. Jennifer Blackman Lawson. BlIMT p.39
Untitled. Johari Amini. BlSp p. 4; JuBa p.169; LetGSW p.19
Untitled. Nikki Giovanni. MyH p.27
Untitled. Pamela Cobb. InDM p. 38
Untitled. Pearl Cleage. WeDNNM p.8
Untitled. Rosemari Mealy. CoAAAW p.222
Untitled. Sharon Scott. JuBA p. 179
Untitled. Stella Ngatho. PoBBl p.30
Untitled. Wanda Coleman. MaDBL p.11
Untitled. Wanda Coleman. MaDBL

p.75
Untitled--A Political Contribution. Carolyn M. Rodgers. HeAEG p.56
Untitled (For Margaret Danner). Nikki Giovanni. MyH p.38
Untitled (Hi Ronda). Sharon Scott. JuBa p.178
Untitled No. Hurt. Carolyn M. Rodgers. SoBB p.21
Untitled No. 1. Carolyn M. Rodgers. HeAEG p.28
Untitled (No.1). Mae Jackson. CaPWY p.11
Untitled I. Mari Evans. NIGHT p.5
Untitled II. Mari Evans. NIGHT p.6
Untitled No. 4. Carolyn M. Rodgers. HeAEG p.18
Untitled Poem. Linda Cousins. RoATW p.27
Untitled Poem. Patricia Ford. PoBBl p,36
Untitled. To Smell the Stink of Rotting Brownstones. Pamela Woodruff Hill. UNBP p.318
Unuttered Prayer. Josephine D. (Henderson) Heard. MoGl p. 61
Unwelcomed confinement cold sterile room. Jennifer Blackman Lawson. BlIMT p.42
Up on a hill on a windless day I watch the year slip lowly into a gray perspective. Pinkie Gordon Lane. MyFe p. 13
Up rising: a day in the history of revolutionary warfare. Pamela Cobb. InDM p.43
Up the dark stairs to the top floor of the tenement house. Pinkie Gordon Lane. WiTh p. 31
Up the shaken stairway back four hundred years. June Jordan. PaNP p.9
Up tight you're right. Nola Richardson. WhOL p.61
Uplifted and aloof, her lips, face, gestures, quote her pride. S. Diane Bogus. WITM p.3
Upon Being Black One Friday Night in July. Johari Amini. ImIB p.8; UNBP p.354
Upon Finding a False Friend. Lycurgus J. Alee. NegVo p. 9
Upon his dull ear fell the stern command. Carrie Williams Clifford. BlSi p.82
Upon Looking At Love. Dolores A. Brown. EbR p.15
Upon the Grass. Henrietta Cordelia Ray. EBAP p.143
Upstairs on the third floor of the 135th Street Library. Helene Johnson. BlSi p.78; CaD p.221; GoS p.126; NeNRe p.213; PoBA p.104
Upstart. Elma Stuckey. BiGa p.42
Uptight, tense, expecting a ring of a telephone. June Vanleer Williams. WiRYPS p.73
Urgency. Sarah E. Wright. BTB p.185; PoNe p.270
Urgency/to know taste touch smell others gossip? Wanda Coleman. MaDBL p.86
Us. S. Diane Bogus. WITM p.29
Us sint de preacher down t' town. Lucile D. Goodlett. WGC p. 30
Use of the word I is totally unjustifiable so. Ntozake Shange. NaEd p.138
Use to Be When My Fuel Tank Hit "E" I Could Fill Up at Most Any Station. C. Tillery Banks. HeTMWL p.52
Used to know a man who sold it hot. Wanda Coleman. MaDBL p.45
Using, A. Mariah Britton Howard. CoAAAW p.145
Utility. Marion Nicholes. LiS p.20
Utopia. Georgia Douglas Johnson. BrBV p.48
Utopia. Johari Amini. BlP p.230

- V -

Vacant Lot, The. Gwendolyn Brooks. SPGB p.11; StIB p. 23; WoOGB p.25
Vacant lots abundant with debris,

The. Vanessa Howard. ScWh p. 4
Vacation End. May Miller. ClAB p.34
Vacation Time. Nikki Giovanni. VaT p.15
Vacationing clerk is on her way to Santa Barbara, The. Wanda Coleman. MaDBL p.95
Vacuumous, the sun sets in yr mouth. Toi Derricotte. EmDH p.27
Val. Gwendolyn Brooks. MyNIB p.99
Valediction to Shuffling. Jennifer Blackman Lawson. BlITM p.26
Valentine. Margaret Danner. DoOAT p.46
Valentine (Nineteen Sixty Six). Margaret Danner. DoOAT p.36
Values. Georgia Douglas Johnson. ALC p.31; ANP p.87; ReFNA p.26
Vanished Road, The. Georgia Douglas Johnson. BrBV p.83
Vashti. Frances E. W. Harper. BlSi p.27; EaNAW p.294; EBAP p.34; PBFH p.44
Veil, The. Lois Royal Hughes. NegVo p.81
Veiled Again. Marion Nicholes. LiS p.17
Venerable Black women you of yesterday. Margaret T. G. Burroughs. WhSIT p.24
Venon. Naomi Long Madgett. PhN p.111
Ventus Memoriae. Naomi Long Madgett. PhN p.26
Verdure sleeps in winter, The. Georgia Douglas Johnson. BrBV p.80
Verse From a Fragmentary Marriage. June Jordan. PaNP p. 39
Very acme of my woe, The. Georgia Douglas Johnson Douglas. AVAN p.209; BrBV p.49; CaD p.76; DeDF p.46
Very fine conga of sweat, A. Jayne Cortez. COAG p.65
Very friendly prison this is, A. Gayl Jones. BlSi p.209; SoS p.13
Very proud he barely asked directions to a nearby hotel. Alice Walker. ONC p.69
Very Simple Wish, A. Nikki Giovanni. WoATM p.47
Very soon the yankee teachers came down and set up schools. Frances E. W. Harper. BlSi p.29; CNAW p.106; EBAP p. 37
Via Dolorosa. Naomi Long Madgett. PhN p.37; SoTPN p.11
Vibes. Margaret Danner. DoOAT p.94
Victim of Slavery. Vanessa Howard. ScWh p.14
Vie c'est la Vie, La. Jessie Redmond Fauset. BANP p.205; CaD p.69; PoN p.65; PoNe p.67
Viejas Locas. Harryette Mullen. TTW p.53
Vietnam addenda. Audre Lorde. ChPON p.85; NeHS p.46
View from Rosehill Cemetery: Vicksburg. Alice Walker. RePOP p.25
Virgil. Pearl Cleage Lomax. WeDNNM p.12
Vignettes. Pinkie Gordon Lane. WiTh p.49
Violet. Naomi Long Madgett. StBS p.59
Violet was beautiful at four. Naomi Long Madgett. StBS p. 59
Virgin Mary had a Baby Boy.** Anonymous. BLIA p.41; ChG p.95
Virginia. Elouise Loftin. PoBA p.514
Virginia. Naomi Long Madgett. PhN p.97
Virgo Stella slips out. Wanda Coleman. MaDBL p.16
Virtue. Josephine D. (Henderson) Heard. MoGl p.102
Vision, The. Elma Stuckey. BiGa p.67
Vision, A. Sarah Collins Fernandis. AVAN p.212
Visions. Eleanor Thomas-Grumbach. MoSu p.6
Visions like butter flies floating in my head. Eleanor Thomas-Grumbach. MoSu p.7

Vision's no longer appear, The. Marva Tatum Smith. BeYM p.21
Visit of the Professor of Aesthetics. Margaret Danner. AfAWA p.635; IrLa p.19; MoCAP p. 89; NNPUSA p.31; PoBA p.135
Visit to a City Out of Time. Audre Lorde. ChPON p.79; NeHS p.47
Visit to Gettysburg, A. Lucille Clifton. OrW p.31
Visitor to my patio who think he is, A. Pinkie Gordon Lane. MyFe p.25
Visitors, The. May Miller. ClAB p.42
Vive Noir. Mari Evans. AfAWA p. 684; BlLi p.435; BOL p.50; CNAW p.765; IABW p.70; NeBV p.245; PoBA p.188; UNBP p.247
Voice has gone out of the wilderness, The. Julia Fields. FoM p.33; YoBBBI p.398
Voodoo. Ethel Coleman. NegVo p. 39
Voodoo/Love/Magic. Angela Jackson. VoDLM p.7
Voodoo on the Un-assing of Janis Joplin: Warning to Ole Tom. Carolyn M. Rodgers. JuBa p. 115
Vowels...are a part of the English language. Nikki Giovanni. ThWRNW p.55

- W -

WAC. Beatrice M. Murphy. RoCO p.9
Wail. Mari Evans. WhIAM p.13
Waiting. Naomi Long Madgett. PhN p.23
Waiting. Pinkie Gordon Lane. MyFe p.15
Waiting for her Man Too Long. Sandra Rogers. CoAAAW p.316
Waiting for Paul. Wanda Coleman. MaDBL p.59
Waiting for the Next Star to Fall. Harryette Mullen. TTW p.19
Waiting for the subway a buster Puerto Rican lulling in liquor. Melba Joyce Boyd. CaEADW p.38
Waiting--for what? June Vanlee Williams. WiRYPS p.48
Waiting out the Days. Pinkie Gordon Lane. WiTh p.51
Wake Up! Brothers and Sisters. E. Sharon Gomillion. FoAAAM p.5
Walk, God's Chillun. Lucile D. Goodlett. WGC p.37
Walk into the soft soft, A. Sherley Williams. PePo p.16
Walk Like Freedom. Carolyn M. Rodgers. HeAEG p.54
Walk, Talk, Chicken With Your Head Pecked. Anonymous. UNBP p.89
Walk Together, Children. Anonymous. AmLNA p.4; BlP p.1
Walk within thy own heart's temple, child, and rest. Georgia Douglas Johnson. HWOP p.38
Walking Down Park. Nikki Giovanni. Rec p.21; WoATM p. 49
Walking his hall--a wonder explore shelves behind eyes. Wanda Coleman. MaDBL p.52
Walking Our Boundaries. Audre Lorde. BlUn p.38
Walking the Dog. Pinkie Gordon Lane. WiTh p.8
Walking with you shuts off shivering. Gwendolyn Brooks. Bec p.14
Wall, The. Gwendolyn Brooks. BlPo p.24; BlWOA p.721; CNAW p.524; ITM p.42; PoBA p.161; PoNe p.338; WoOGB p.414
Wall of normalcy wraps your body. Patricia Parker. MoIB p.87
Walls are awash with framed color, The. Pinkie Gordon Lane. MyFe p.45
Walls of Jericho, The. Blanche Taylor Dickinson. CaD p.106
Walter Bradford. Gwendolyn Brooks. BlP p.174; FaP p. 17
Wanda in Worryland. Wanda Coleman. MaDBL p.23
Wanderer, The Pauli Murray. DaTAOP p.93

Wanderer Reclaimed, The. Josephine D. (Henderson) Heard. MoGl p.111
Want to really touch you. Mariah Britton Howard. CoAAAW p.147
Wanted him to stay a little boy. S. Diane Bogus. WITM p.36
Wanting to stomp down Eighth Avenue snow. June Jordan. PaNP p.68
Wantongold Dream. Thulani Davis. AlTRGR p.7
War Widow. Pauli Murray. DaTAOP p.66
Warm me with your fingertips. Mari Evans. IABW p.24
Warning. Alice Walker. ONC p.68
Warning For All Loveless, Though on the Case Sistuhs Who Would be Mothers. Nia nSabe. ThHSD p.80
Warriors Prancing, Women Dancing. ** Nioma Rashidd. NBP p.107
Wars the generations the wars in spring, The. Julia Fields. NiBPo p.74
Was ever there so exquisite a hate as mine? Leighla Lewis. NegVo p.96
Was it really you all the time? Naomi Long Madgett. BlP p. 195
was it yesterday. Sonia Sanchez. IvBAW p.33; LoP p.25
Washerwoman. Naomi Long Madgett. ExAE p.27
Washington D.C. was seized by a nation of war heroes. Pamela Cobb. InDM p.15
Washiri (Poet). Kattie M. Cumbo. BOL p.12; NiBPo p.44
Wasn't That A Mighty Day.** Anonymous. ChG p.94
Wass sat...Nonnie. Linda Brown. BTB p.54
Waste. Beatrice M. Murphy. NegVo p.117
Wasted. June Jordan. ThTDID p. 82
Wasted flow of water hiding, A. Jayne Cortez. NeBV p.233
Wasting time checking heels. Nola Richardson. WhOL p.59
Watch Out. Jayne Cortez. FeAF p.27
Watch out for the woman whose body is bloated with tears. Jayne Cortez. FeAF p.27
Watch Out God is on the TV. June Jordan. ThTDID p.189
Watch Your English. Anonymous. GLOWC p.19
Watcher, The. Georgia Douglas Johnson. BrBV p.82
Watching. Wanda Coleman. MaDBL p.47
Watching a Parade in Harlem 1970. Jayne Cortez. FeAF p.17
Watching you frown at your feet in the mirror. Alice Walker. ONC p.56
Watermelon Vendor's Cry. Anonmous. ITBLA p.125
Watermelon! Watermelon! red to the rind. Anonymous. ITBLA p.125
Way, A. Carolyn M. Rodgers. HoIGO p.43
Way down South, there's an old, old Blackman. Ariel Williams Holloway. BTh p.31
Way I Feel, The. Nikki Giovanni. WoATM p.28
Way I hear tell Aunt Jennie tapdanced on the hood of her husband's car. Colleen McElroy. BlSi p.288
Way is long and rough, my God, The. Josephine D. (Henderson) Heard. MoGl p.93
Way It Was, The. Lucille Clifton. GoNAE p.3
Way of Things, The. Mari Evans. WhIAM p.14
Way-Out Morgan. Gwendolyn Brooks. BlPo p.23; BlWOA p.720
Way They Feel, The. Wanda Coleman. MaDBL p.87
Way we talk is we never finish a sentence, The. Harryette Mullen. TTW p.7
Ways O' Men, The. Angelina Weld Grimke. CaD p.39
Waz, adverse to thinking got transplant. Peggy Susberry Kenner. JuBa p.94
Wd you like to make love tonite. Ntozake Shange. DaGe p.70
We. Nikki Giovanni. MyH p.65
We a Bad People. Sonia Sanchez. TGWL p.87
We a BaddDDD People. Sonia San-

chez. BrT p.141; WABP p.52
We all start as a speck. Nikki Giovanni. Rec p.11
We all used to play hide n' go seek. Jennifer Blackman Lawson. BlITM p.30
We am gethered men an' bred'ren. Bessie Woodson Yancey. EcFTH p.44
We are a new people. Sonia Sanchez. ItND p.28
We are all a part of the self same tree--the bark and the limbs are all skin. Eve Lynn. ChG p.98
We are all heroes living in the frozen space of time. Pamela Cobb. InDM p.20
We are all imprisoned in the castle of our skins. Nikki Giovanni. MyH p.46
We are alone in the beginning and the end. Jill Witherspoon Boyer. DrF p.13
We are caught beneath a tight skin of water. Harryette Mullen. TTW p.32
We are Farmers. Nancy L. Arnez. RoCO p.18
We are Gatherers of Bamboo Songs. Sonia Sanchez. IvBAW p.82
We are landless dream farmers. Jill Witherspoon Boyer. DrF p.14
We are like a field. Nikki Giovanni. ThWRNW p.58
We are Muslim Women.** Sonia Sanchez. BluB p.57
We are No Longer Afraid. Joanne Jimason. NaABE p.34
We are Not Alone. Beatrice M. Murphy. RoCO p.12
We are not lovers. Nikki Giovanni. CoCRD p.88
We are psyche to psyche. Julia Fields. GaBW p.304
We are some of us born for the water. Lucille Clifton. TwW p.29
We are spendthrifts with words. Pauli Murray. DaTAOP p.82
We Are the Dead. Sonia Sanchez. CoAAAW p.322; IvBAW p.43; LoP p.46
We are the screeeeeamers. Sonia Sanchez. WABP p.61
We are things of dry hours and the involuntary plan. Gwendolyn Brooks. AfAAu p.80; BlALP p.101; BlP p.166; ITSA p.200; PoN p.188; StIB p.2; WoOGB p.4
We are two scars in a dead woman's belly. Lucille Clifton. TwW p.10
We ask for peace. Angelina Weld Grimke. CaD p.38; NeCa p.342; ReFNA p.25
We Be. Gonna Be. Sonia Sanchez. IvBAW p.78
We Black dead end kids striving struggling to win identity. Vanessa Howard. ScWh p.18
We Black People Should. Kali Grosvenor. PBK p.37
We Black/woooman have been called many things. Sonia Sanchez. BluB p.11
We can be anything we want. Sonia Sancez. ItND p.23
We can know Surely. Marion Cuthbert. SOC p.11
We come to the border again. Ntozake Shange. NaEd p.112
We competed for hurts. Carolyn M. Rodgers. HeAEG p.26
We corner ourselves into loud bars. Pamela Cobb. InDM p.44
We could never climb you. Wanda Coleman. MaDBL p.105
We could walk happily through rustling leaves. Kattie M. Cumbo. NiBPo p.47
We cried out. Angela Jackson. VoDLM p.13
We Dance Like Ella Riffs. Carolyn M. Rodgers. NaPr p.112; PoBA p.431; TNV p.113
We didn't think nothin of stalking silver death. Ronda Davis. JuBa p.59
We die, welcolming bluebeards to our darkening closets. Maya Angelou. JGM p.13
We Disappear To Dance. Vanessa Howard. ScWh p.23
We do not know what day will be our last. Josephine D. (Henderson) Heard. MoGl p.105
We don't want the days to become

stale. Pinkie Gordon Lane. WiTh p.51
We drink the bitter cup. Naomi Long Madgett. PhN p.101
We entered silence before the clock struck. Audre Lorde. ChPON p.8; COAL p.41; FiCi p.24; SiAS p.45
We entered the dark house that day, Papa. Pinkie Gordon Lane. WiTh p.8
We Face the Future. Georgia Douglas Johnson. BrBV p.67
We forgot to water the plantain shoots. Audre Lorde. BlUn p. 117
We gave you food we did not want. Nancy L. Arnez. RoCO p.15
We go back to who we were. Carolyn M. Rodgers. JuBa p.117
We gon be outa sight Black/men. Sonia Sanchez. ItND p.17
We got to the point of balloons all of us. June Jordan. PaNP p.17
We grow up my love. Sonia Sanchez. LoP p.19
We had a nice time together. Jayne Cortez. COAG p.97
We had gathered for the love-feast on the time appointed night. Josephine D. (Henderson) Heard. MoGl p.38
We had planned it. Jill Witherspoon Boyer. DrF p.10
We Had Slept in the Old Beds too Long.** Margaret Danner. DoOAT p.113
We Have Been Believers.** Margaret Walker. AfAWA p.523; BTB p.179; CNAW p.530; FMP p.16; MoCAP p.76; PoBA p. 145; PoN p.180; PoNe p.312; SoS p.130
We have been believers believing in the Black gods of an old land. Margaret Danner. AfAWA p.523; BTB p.179; CNAW p.530; FMP p.16; MoCAP p.76; PoBA p.145; PoN p.180; PoNe p.312; SoS p.130
We have brought back our summer souvenirs. Naomi Long Madgett. PiLAF p.44
We Have Had/Stand Ins. Vanessa Howard. ScWh p.24
We have never stopped being Africans. Sharon Bourke. UNBP p.374
We have no passions left to love the spring. Audre Lorde. ChPON p.3; COAL p.69; FiCi p.8
We have not forgotten the market square. Pauli Murray. DaTAOP p.20
We have not, up to now, known each other. Sherley Williams. PePo p.18
We have screamed and we have filled our lungs. Mari Evans. NIGHT p.62
We have spent the year talking in profuse & varied silences to people. Carolyn M. Rodgers. HeAEG p.63
We have sung the sorrow songs. Mari Evans. NIGHT p.61
We have taken the best leaves and the best roots. Lucille Clifton. OrW p.9
We, his purple an' linen, too. Anonymous. TYPB p.197
We knew how to order. Gwendolyn Brooks. SPGB p.22; StIB p.46; WoOGB p.48
We knew it could not last. Katharine Beverly. NegVo p. 14
We knew well the morning sun had not warmed the earth. Naomi Faust. DeDF p.103
"We know a secret." said the flowers. Bessie Woodson Yancey. EcFTH p.37
We know growing up is sometimes hard. Olean Bess. MiFe p. 8
We know the official puke of official appointees. Jayne Cortez. Scar p.24
We know you by your dance Carolina Kingston. Jayne Cortez. MoOP p.52
We Launched a Ship. Ruby Berkley Goodwin. EbR p.69
We Lay There Ageless. Jodi Braxton. SoITM p.41
We lay there drained of time. May Miller. CNAW p.361
We leaped in a wind. May Miller. ClAB p.21

We leave thy courts to-day. Josephine D. (Henderson) Heard. MoGl p.18
We lift a song to you across the day. Georgia Douglas Johnson. BrBV p.89
We Lift Our Voices. Mae V. Cowdery. WLOV p.67
We, like shades that were first conjured up. Margaret Danner. AfAWA p.638; BlP p.152; DoOAT p.117; PoCo p.15
We love for love. Colleen McElroy. MuDLSG p.30
We made strong poems for each other. Audre Lorde. ChPON p.46; FrLWP p.26
We make up our faces for lots of reasons. Nikki Giovanni. CoCRD p.79
We may sigh o'er the heavy burdens. Frances E. W. Harper. PBFH p.90
We meet in golden circles. Sandra Royster. WoTa p.7
We met in the digest. Nikki Giovanni. BFBTBJ p.8
We Might as Well Stop Now. Nola Richardson. WhOL p.95
We mourn to-day o'er our sister dead. Josephine D. (Henderson) Heard. MoGl p.80
We move like puppets in so many old shoes. Lotus Schaeffer. PoBBl p.59
We must say it all. Alice Walker. CoAAAW p.356
We Need a God Who Bleeds Now.** Ntozake Shange. DaGe p.51
We now know why the fish swims away. Carolyn M. Rodgers. HeAEG p.9
We only want to laugh at poetry. Carolyn M. Rodgers. SoBB p.26
We Pass. Beatrice M. Murphy. TNV p.139
We plan, we scheme, we mold our children's lives. June Vanleer Williams. WiRYPS p.5
We programmed fo death/die/on each day. Sonia Sanchez. WABP p.33
We Raise De Wheat. Anonymous. BlP p.3
We reach for destinies beyond what we come to know. Alice Walker. RePOP p.69
We Real Cool.** Gwendolyn Brooks. AfAWA p.580; BeEa p.17; BlVo p.465; BlWOA p.718; BTB p.51; CNAW p.521; HoFTD p.106; IADB p.5; ITBLA p.217; ITSA p.206; MBP p.96; MoCAP p.81; MyNIB p.76; PoBA p.157; SPGB p.73; TYBP p.245; UNBP p.176; WoOGB p.315
We remember our Brother Amicar Cabral. Jayne Coetez. Scar p.32
We rise up early and we work. Lucille Clifton. TwW p.35
We said, if it should rain, why should we care? Naomi Long Madgett. PhN p.62
We Saw Beyond Our Seeming.** Maya Angelou. JGM p.36
We saw them, Joanne. Pinkie Gordon Lane. PoBBl p.8; WiTh p.15
We say so much for mother dear. Bessie Woodson Yancey. EcFTH p.32
We sell it to the rich, we sell it to the poor. Anonymous. ITBLA p.125
We shall go playing in the woods again! Gwendolyn Brooks. BeEa p.58; WoOGB p.356
We shall never tell the world. Kattie M. Cumbo. GaBW p.290
We Shall Overcome.** Anonymous. BlEx p.6
We skim our surfaces. Naomi Long Madgett. PiLAF p.45
We stand accused. Mari Evans. NIGHT p.48
We stand befo u plain of Bl/ woooomen. Sonia Sanchez. WABP p.45
We stand mute! Georgia Douglas Johnson. HWOP p.5
We stayed through finger drifts and drifts to bury trees. June Jordan. PaNP p.95
We stood in a circle and we loved. Dorothy Randall. ThHSD p.39
We stood there waiting on the corners. Nikki Giovanni. MyH p.65
We Stumbled each Other's Line.**

Sonia Sanchez. IvBAW p.86
We suffer heat lying down. Wanda Coleman. MaDBL p.129
We swam in the rain-filled gulley. Pinkie Gordon Lane. WiTh p.37
We take place in what we believe. Pamela St. John. PoBA p.347
We talk of light things you and I in this small house. Sonia Sanchez. IvBAW p.98
We tend to fear old age. Nikki Giovanni. CoCRD p.44
We the Black Woman. Femi Funmi Ifetayo (Regina Micou) RoATW p.76
We took the trip together. Naomi Long Madgett. ExAE p.39
We touched land. May Miller. BlSi p.113; ClAB p.43
We trace the pow'r of death from tomb to tomb. Phillis Wheatley. PAL p.86; PPW p.23
We trekked into a far country. Anne Spencer. BANP p.218
We us the Black woman. Femi Funmi Ifetayo. (Regina Micou) RoATW p.76
We use Ardena here. Gwendolyn Brooks. AnA p.53; WoOGB p. 117
We used to gather at the high window. Quandra Prettyman. IADB p.56; PoBA p.260
We wake on the wrong side of morning. May Miller. BTB p. 152
We went there to confer on the possibility of Blackness of Blackness. Nikki Giovanni. BFBTBJ p.30
We were born in a poor time. Audre Lorde. BlUn p.106
We were entwined in red rings. Maya Angelou. AnSIR p.36
We were not raised to look in a grown person's mouth. Sherley Williams. CoAAAW p. 386
We were pals in old Virginny. Bessie Woodson Yancey. EcFTH p.42
We were so stricken by school. Sonia Sanchez. LoP p.18
We were the vanquished. Pauli Murray. DaTAOP p.44
We were waiting at the station. Josephine D. (Henderson) Heard. MoGl p.16
We Will Be. Anonymous. ThHSD p.23
We will be no generashuns to cum. Johari Amini. BlSp p.4; JuBa p.169; LetGSW p.19
We, women only after leaving our homes do we begin to understand. Pamela Cobb. InDM p.33
We wonder what the horoscope did show. Henrietta Cordelia Ray. EBAP p.140
We would sing a song to the fair young June. Charlotte Forten Grimke. DuSAE p.26
We would sit there on tall stools. Mari Evans. WhIAM p.14
We wuz comin' fum de meetin. Bessie Woodson Yancey. EcFTH p.57; NegVo p.170
Weaponed Woman. Gwendolyn Brooks. DeDF p.88; SPGB p.125
Wearing Glasses. Lyn. SiSh p.21
Wearing his equality like a too-small shoe. Vilma Howard. NNPUSA p.58
We'd like to tell you about the Negro and his songs. Eloise Culver. GANIV p.19
Wed poem before Thanksgiving. Sonia Sanchez. WABP p.18
Wedding, The. June Jordan. SCh p.6; ThTDID p.46
Wedding Anniversary, The. Josephine D. (Henderson) Heard. MoGl p.87
Wednesday. Jennifer Blackman Lawson. BlIMT p.47
Wednesdays, Father Gave the Parsonage His Attention.** Gloria Oden. TiTBi p.9
Weeks After Mother Died.** Gloria Oden. RESUR p.145
Weeks tumble over each other. Naomi Long Madgett. ExAE p. 64
Weeksville Women. Elouise Loftin. PoBA p.515
Weeps out of Kansas country something new. Gwendolyn

Brooks. PoN p.191. PoNe p. 335
Weeps out of Western country something new. Gwendolyn Brooks. AnA p.3; BlSi p. 102; WoOGB p. 67
Welcome, The. Y.W. Easton. CoAAAW p.103
Welcome Home. Josephine D. (Henderson) Heard. MoGl p.31
Welcome Home, My Prince. Sonia Sanchez. LoP p.58
Welcome to Hon. Frederick Douglass. Josephine D. (Henderson) Heard. MoGl p.15
Welfare Days. Naomi Long Madgett. PhN p.17
Well--A Shorty George, he ain' no fren of mine. Anonymous. BlWOA p.460
We'll begin with a box. Anonymous. GLOWC p.19
Well I have almost come to the place where you fell. Lucille Clifton. TwW p.14
Well I wanted to braid my hair. June Jordan. ThTDID p.39
Well, life has been a baffled vehicle. Gwendolyn Brooks. DeDF p.88; SPGB p.125
Well number-two baby is that change ain' nowhere. June Jordan. ThTDID p.23
Well, She Ask Me in de Parlor. Negro Work Song, USA. MyNIB p.40
Well, she ask me-whuk-in de parlor-whuk. Negro Work Song, USA. MyNIB p.40
We'll Soon Be Free. Anonymous. BlWOA p.312
Well then let it all go to hell. June Jordan. ThTDID p.97
Well, this'll make you laugh. Anonymous. BlWOA p.888
Well, white man, are you confused? Valerie Tarver. TNV p.130
Well, your honor, it was late. June Jordan. PaNP p.11
Welt. Georgia Douglas Johnson. ALC p.16; BANP p.183
W'en I jah my cellah do. Bessie Woodson Yancey. EcFTH p.58
We're back to square one. Wanda Coleman. MaDBL p.130
We're gathered here to tell our tales. Elma Stuckey. BiGa p.10
We're hoping to be arrested. Margaret Walker. BlP p.156; PFND p.7
Were I but able to turn back time. June Vanleer Williams. WiRYPS p.47
Were I but perfect. June Vanleer Williams. WiRYPS p.21
Were I not Black you would not turn and stare at me. Iola M. Brister. EbR p.13
Were I to remember a happy time. June Vanleer Williams. WiRYPS p.34
Were is My Head Going.** Kali Grosvenor. PBK p.62
Were it mine to select a woman. Andrea Razafkeriefo. NeNRe p.363
We're not learnen to be paper boys (for the young brothas who sell Muhammad Speaks). Sonia Sanchez. ItND p.27
We're summer flying over the bay. May Miller. CLAB p. 34
We're wending the trail of the vanishing road. Georgia Douglas Johnson. BrBV p. 83
Were you a leper bathed in wounds. Georgia Douglas Johnson. ALC p.10; CaD p.77; RoATW p.10
Were you Dere? Anonymous. BlWOA p.240
Were You There When They Crucified My Lord. Spiritual. BlP p.30
Wes cradling his ax. Mari Evans. NIGHT p.10
West, The. Bessie Woodson Yancey. EcFTH p.5
West Coast Episode. June Jordan. ThTDID p.62
"West Side," screamed Sammy Chester. Gwendolyn Brooks. Bec p.13
West Virginia. Bessie Woodson Yancey. EcFTH p.2
Weusi Resurrection, The. Maami Verano. ThHSD p.65
Wet Thursday. Wanda Coleman.

MaDBL p.68
We've Come Such a Long Way.** C. Tillery Banks. HeTMWL p. 64
What a Joke! Nola Richardson. WhOL p.13
"What a waste of a beautiful girl"?! D. T. Ogilvie. NBP p.95
What a white woman got? Sonia Sanchez. HoC p.27
What am I ready to lose in this advancing summer. Audre Lorde. BlUn p.35
What America needs is a democratic lesson. Carolyn M. Rodgers. AfAWA p.776
What anger in my hard-won bones. Audre Lorde. CaTR p.6; ChPON p.16
What angers in my hard-won bones of heritage of water. Audre Lorde. COAL p.21
What are differences dear. Pinkie Gordon Lane. WiTh p.53
What bid do I hear for this comely wench? Elma Stuckey. BiGa p.41
What business have these grizzled faces now with those flown breezes? Naomi Long Madgett. StBS p.17
What can I, a poor Black woman, do to destroy America? Nikki Giovanni. UNBP p.279
What can I say. Alicia L. Johnson. BrT p.176
What can I say? Dorothy Lee Louise Shaed. NegVo p.139
What can I say to you valentine. Margaret Danner. DoOAT p.36
What can you tell me now that I know you. Mae Jackson. CaPWY p.9
What candidate ever ran. Ruth Duckett Gibbs. GLOWC p.59
What cannot be committed to memory, this can save. Quandra Prettyman. PoBA p. 258
What Color is Black? Barbara Mahone. Suga p.18
What Color is Lonely. Carolyn M. Rodgers. BlP p.265; SoBB p. 22
What day yo say. Lije? Linda Cousins. ThHSD p.47
What de bus gon do. Carolyn M. Rodgers. HeAEG p.77
What Declaration. June Jordan. SCh p.29; ThTDID p.51
What declaration can I make to clear this room of strangers leaving quickly as an enemy might come? June Jordan. SCh p.29; ThTDID p.51
What Deeper Sin? Nancy L. Arnez. RoCO p.20
What differences does it make, now that the snows are falling? Naomi Long Madgett. OnATM p.46
What Do I Care For Morning.** Helene Johnson. CaD p.210
What do I know of you? Sonia Sanchez. IvBAW p.85
What do we teach our young ones? Katherine Dunham. GaBW p. 299
What do you mean no no no no. Audre Lorde. BlUn p.98
What do you think of us in fuzzy endeavor. Gwendolyn Brooks. SPGB p.124
What does it matter? Alice Walker. ONC p.52
What Does One Say To The Mad. Pinkie Gordon Lane. WiTh p.45
What germ cell harkened back to. Leatrice Emeruwa. BlGBG p. 24
What happened in Benin? Margaret Danner. DoOAT p.121; IrLa p.13
What Happens. June Jordan. BlP p.249; SCh p.69
What happens to reliability after today? Naomi Long Madgett. PiLAF p.14
What happens when the dog sits on a tiger. June Jordan. BlP p.249; SCh p.69
What Happing To The Heroes. Kali Grosvenor. PBK p.33
What I do with my life is strictly my own affair. June Vanleer Williams. WiRYPS p.15
What I might've said, might've been. Thulani Davis. AlTRGR p.38

What I remember about that day is boxes stacked across the walk. Lucille Clifton. DOBB p.51
What, I wonder, but not for long. Margaret Danner. UNBP p.231
What if sound ceased and waves of air no longer volatile. Pinkie Gordon Lane. MyFe p. 15
What if you saw me lying there like stone. Naomi Long Madgett. StBS p.50
What in the World. Carolyn M. Rodgers. HeAEG p.79
What is a blk poem & /or what is it that we writing. Val Ferdinand. NeBV p.378
What is a Negro? Nancy L. Arnez. RoCO p.19
What is God? Ethelia Arthur Robinson. EbR p.127
What is it About Me. Sonia Sanchez. IvBAW p.80
What is Love? Myra Estelle Morris. NegVo p.107
What is Real? June Vanleer Williams. WiRYPS p.59
What is This Reference To: or We Must Get Together Sometime Soon. June Jordan. PaNP p. 83
What is what sometimes is specifically what is need. Carolyn M. Rodgers. CoAAAW p.312
What it Means. Pinkie Gordon Lane. WiTh p.53
What it means to be an "N". Frenchy J. Hodges. BlW p.25
What language is it in when my bed is/too big cuz yr not in it. Ntozake Shange. DaGe p.64
What Liberation Front? Patricia Parker. MoIB p.71
What loves I hold who never recognize their own captivity! Naomi Long Madgett. PiLAF p.29
What matters though love's dream shall pass. Georgia Douglas Johnson. ALC p.34
What means this host advancing. Josephine D. (Henderson) Heard. MoGl p.24
What My Child Learns of the Sea.* * Audre Lorde. ChPON p.14; COAL p.21; FiCi p.5; MyNIB p.85; NBP p.85; PoBA p.247
What need Have I for Memory.** Georgia Douglas Johnson. CaD p.80; HWOP p.47
What Order? Carole Gregory Clemmons. NiBPo p.89
What Ovid Taught Me. Alice Walker. ONC p.52
What Peter Said. Naomi Long Madgett. PhN p.55
What! Roses growing in a meadow. Effie Lee Newsome. CaD p. 59
What sacrifice so great! Josephine D. (Henderson) Heard. MoGl p.56
What shall I give my children? Gwendolyn Brooks. BlALP p. 102; BlP p.166; ITSA p. 201; MoCAP p.80
What Shall I Tell My Children Who Are Black. Margaret T. G. Burroughs. WhSIT p.8
What should I write a poem about. Nikki Giovanni. VaT p.15
What song shall I sing you. Sonia Sanchez. CoAAAW p. 317; IvBAW p.91
What stopped the ticking of the clock? Nancy L. Arnez. RoCO p.24
What the Finger Writes. Alice Walker. RePOP p.63
What the Mirror Said. Lucille Clifton. TwW p.7
What thousand-eyed wind swept through your stone. Pinkie Gordon Lane. WiTh p.21
What Time is It?** Mari Evans. NIGHT p.36
What Uncaring Creator on This Earth. Vanessa Howard. ScWh p.46
What was Inez supposed to do for the man who declared war on her body. Jayne Cortez. CoAAAW p.89; COAG p.63
What was not pleasant was not the hush that coughed. Gwendolyn Brooks. AnA p.9; WoOGB p.73
What we decided is you save

your own self. Lucille Clifton. DOBB p.50
What We Know. Nzadi Zimele-Keita. (Michelle McMichael) CoAAAW p.399
What we think is love. Pamela Cobb. InDM p.40
What will we do when there is nobody left to kill? June Jordan. BlSi p.148; PaNP p.1
What word is there that can compare. Josephine D. (Henderson) Heard. MoGl p.127
What words suffice to tell you of the love I feel for you. Isabelle H. Monroe. NegVo p. 106
What would a little girl think. Nikki Giovanni. ThWRNW p.25
What Would I Do White. June Jordan. SCh p.47; ThTDID p.103
What Yo' Gwine to do When Yo' Lamp Burn Down? Spiritual. BlP p.29
What you Gonna Name That Pretty Little Baby. Anonymous. ChG p.96; ITBLA p.97
What you have to realize is about private property. June Jordan. ThTDID p.119
What You Say. Colleeen McElroy. MuDLSG p.16
What you say when somebody tell you he gon leave. Carolyn M. Rodgers. HeAEG p.19
Whatchu gonna do wid all them ho-mo-ny grits. Ntozake Shange. NaEd p.70
What'd you get Black Boy. Pauli Murray. DaTAOP p.34; PoBA p.109
Whatever became of that beautiful dream? Jun Vanleer Williams. WiRYPS p.44
Whatever Happened to Black America? Or: The Setzuan Invisibility Black and Blue. Jodi Braxton. SoITM p.25
Whatever Shall I do With my dead. Ntozake Shange. NaEd p.98
What's happening to the heroes. Kali Grosvenor. BlSp p.106
What's in a name? Josephine D. (Henderson) Heard. MoGl p. 22
What's in a Word? Ruth Duckett Gibbs. GLOWC p.40
What's the difference between a poet. Marva Tatum Smith. BeYM p.8
When... Frenchy J. Hodges. BlW p.11
When-a mah blood runs chilly an col. Anonymous. BlWOA p. 238
When a woman can walk down gold street. Ntozake Shange. NaEd p.145
When all my body has. Gwendolyn Brooks. FaP p.21
When all the cards are in. Nikki Giovanni. BrT p.65; Rec p. 27
When Ana was pregnant with Cielo the doctor listened to her stomach. Harryette Mullen. TTW p.8
When and where did you first confront loneliness? Pinkie Gordon Lane. MyFe p.38
When April's here and meadows wide. Jessie Redmond Fauset. NeNRe p.79; ReFNA p. 38
When Bennie was a teen-age boy, each household had a clock. Eloise Culver. GANIV p.13
When Brothers Forget.** Jill Witherspoon Boyer. DeRi p. 2; DrF p.20
When can I, a poor Black woman, do to destroy America. Nikki Giovanni. BFBTBJ p.54
When daddy died, as we rode home. Thulani Davis. AlTRGR p.59
When desire is gone and love is fled and you needs mostly pity me. Clara Haywood. NeVo p.71
When divers sorts of people want to know about me. Carolyn M. Rodgers. HeAEG p.38
When face to face we stand. Angelina Weld Grimke. CaD p.43
When fingers can move like hosiery. Carolyn M. Rodgers. HeAEG p.15
When first he tasted of the cup. Mary Bohanon. GaBW p.257

When first you sang a song to me. Gwendolyn B. Bennett. CaD p.197
When from earth my lonely bark shall be launched upon the wave. Josephine D. (Henderson) Heard. MoGl p.134
When God said "I'll make me a man." Anonymous. MBP p.7
When grown-up at parties are laughing. Gwendolyn Brooks. MyNIB p.99
When handed a lemon, make lemonade. Gwendolyn Brooks. Bec p.12
When he Came Home From Her He Poured. Sonia Sanchez. IvBAW p.38; LoP p.42
When he comes on top of me. June Jordan. ThTDID p.66
When hit come ter de question er de female vote, de ladies an' de cullud folks is in de same boat. Rosalie Jonas. BlSi p.56
When I am cold and buried deep away. Edythe Mae Gordon. NegVo p.66
When I Am Dead. Georgia Douglas Johnson. CaD p.80; HWOP p.42; KAL p.120
When I am dead, withould, I pray, your blooming legacy. Georgia Douglas Johnson. CaD p.80; HWOP p.42; KAL p.120
When I am gone. Josephine D. (Henderson) Heard. MoGl p.84
When I am woman then I shall be wife of your eyes. Sonia Sanchez. LoP p.70
When I asked him about it he said he had to do that. Carolyn M. Rodgers. HoIGO p.15
When I blow open green bottles straight across hump of a frozen tongue. Jayne Cortez. COAG p.38; MoOP p.42
When I came back after a few days away. June Jordan. ThTDID p.195
When I came to New York used to work at a factory on Twenty-Senond Street. Brenda Connor-Bey. CoAAAW p.78
When I consider how this frozen field will hold within its harrowed breast. Pauli Murray. DaTAOP p.78
When I delight to sip of wind. Nola Richardson. WhOL p.37
When I Die. Gwendolyn Brooks. StIB p.36; WoOGB p.38
When I die. Mari Evans. AmNP p.163; IABW p.76; IADB p.4
When I Die. Nikki Giovanni. MyH p.36
When I die, I hope no one who ever hurt me cries. Nikki Giovanni. MyH p.36
When I die I'm sure I will have a big funeral. Mari Evans. DeDF p.87; MyNIB p.102; PoBA p.187
When I do come, perhaps you will not recognize me. Naomi Long Madgett. OnATM p.28
When I Drink I Scream.** Patricia Parker. MoIB p.110
When I feel her jump up and dance I hear the music! Lucille Clifton. TwW p.5
When I felt your warm touch. Sonia Sanchez. LoP p.69
When I first saw you blooming the color was now. Audre Lorde. BlUn p.47
When I Grow. Kali Grosvenor. PBK p.59
When I Grow. Kali Grosvenor. PBK p.60
When I Grow Up.** Gertrude Blackwell Bailey. IfWCF p.51
When I grow up I want the world to be peaceful. Kali Grosvenor. PBK p.60
When I grow up I hope to be just half as great as Booker T. Eloise Culver. GANIV p.43
When I grow up I want to see bueuty. Kali Grosvenor. PBK p.59
When I grow up I'm going to Africa. Linda Brown Bragg. LoSBM p.31
When I hear Marian Anderson sing, I am a stuffless kind of thing. Gwendolyn Brooks. OnOW p.23

When I hear robins singing that all relinquished things shall come again. Naomi Long Madgett. OnATM p.38
When I hear some woman say she has finally decided you can spend time with other women. June Jordan. PaNP p.82
When I Learned That Mother Was Slain in the Bedroom.** Gloria Oden. RESUR p.43
When I look at my skin gleaming in the candlelight. Carolyn M. Rodgers. HeAEG p.18
When I look at Wilfredo Lam's Paintings. Jayne Cortez. COAG p.94
When I Look at You. Sonia Sanchez. IvBAW p.85
When I make love to you. Patricia Parker. MoIB p.102
When I met your ass in the air amplified. Jayne Cortez. FeAF p.35
When I Nap.** Nikki Giovanni. MyH p.23
When I or Else.** June Jordan. SCh p.32; ThTDID p.51
When I pat this floor with my tap. Jayne Cortez. COAG p.17; Scar p.62
When I pound on that great door. May Miller. ClAB p.7
When I read your poems I see the woman in you. Pinkie Gordon Lane. PoBBl p.9; WiTh p.6
When I remember is green in the trees. Lucille Clifton. GoNAE p.36
When I Return Home.** Sonia Sanchez. IvBAW p.81
When I rise above the earth. Georgia Douglas Johnson. BrBV p.62
When I Rise Up. Georgia Douglas Johnson. BrBV p.62
when I Rite. Margaret Porter. CoAAAW p.263
When I See Black. Kali Grosvenor. PBK p.17
When I stepped off the plane I knew I was home. Sonia Sanchez. BluB p.45; IvBAW p. 62
When I Think. Jayne Cortez. Scar p.125
When I Think About Myself.** Maya Angelou. JGM p.25
When I thought about you hiding away up in the hills. June Jordan. PaNP p.14
When I wake up another God-given morning. Frenchy J. Hodges. BlW p.11
When I Was a Child.** Jacqueline Copps. ThHSD p.31
When I was a child I knew red miners. Margaret Walker. AfAWA p.522; BOL p.72; FMP p.53; KAL p.145; MoCAP p.77; PoBA p.145
When I was a child, I was ashamed of Africa. Margaret T. G. Burroughs. WhSIT p. 20
When I Was A Child I Was Punished.** Patricia Parker. MoIB p.152
When I Was a Little Girl. Olean Bess. MiFe p.16
When I was a little girl Christmas was exquisite. Gwendolyn Brooks. Bec p.9
When I was a younger woman groovin' from my first crib. Carolyn M. Rodgers. SoBB p.24
When I was growing up my mother taught me the way. Olean Bess. MiFe p.7
When I was just a little girl. Pam Brown. GLOWC p.44
When I was little I thought them funny. Paulette Childress White. DeDF p.98
When I was six or so I washed an old blind lady's dirty apron. Julia Field. GaBW p.307
When I was very little though it's still true today. Nikki Giovanni. EgT p.19; MyH p.8
When I Was Very Small.** Gloria Oden. RESUR p.101
When I was very very young she told me. Sharon Scott. JuBa p.175
When I Was Young.** Naomi Long Madgett. OnATM p.43; PhN p.87; SoTPH p.16
When I was young and gay the

whirl spun me a cacoon. Nia nSabe. ThHSD p.71
When I was young I used to say: Romance will come riding by. Georgia Douglas Johnson. ALC p.55
When I was young I used to watch behind the curtains. Maya Angelou. AnSIR p.11
When I was young, my Mama used to ask me, "Boy, where are you goin' to live?" Pam Brown. GLOWC p.26
When I watch you wrapped up like garbage. Lucille Clifton. BlSi p.248; DOBB p.51; MoCAP p.139; PoBA p.307
When I Went Off to College.** Gloria Oden. RESUR p.81
When I Went to Paris.** Kali Grosvenor. PBK p.55
When I went to sleep last night Mr. Frost dressed the world in white. Gertrude Parthenia McBrown. ReFNA p.54
When I Would Die! Josephine D. (Henderson) Heard. MoGl p.59
When I write I like to write. Nikki Giovanni. ThWRNW p.61
When I write I think of my friends. Ntozake Shange. NaEd p.80
When in nineteen-thirty-seven, Etta Moten, sweetheart of our Art Study Group kept her promise. Margaret Danner. BlP p.149; BrT p.40
When in Rome. Mari Evans. AmNP p.164; BlWOA p.818; BTB p. 105; DaS p.510; IABW p.56; ITBLA p.274
When in the morning's misty hour. Ann Plato. EBAP p.116
When Israel was in Egypt's land. Anonymous. AfAV p.114; BlEx p.7; MBP p.79
When it rain five days an' de skies turned dark as night. Anonymous. AfAWA p.303
When Jesus called Peter, James and John, they were fishing. Marva Tatum Smith. BeYM p.19
When Jesus was leaving this sin-accursed land. Josephine D. (Henderson) Heard. MoGl p.62
When John Henry was a little fellow, you could hold him in the palm of your hand. Anonymous. AfAV p.121; AfAWA p.294; BlP p.12
When life is young, without a care. Georgia Douglas Johnson. HWOP p.52
When lilac and asparagus home come and gone. May Miller. ClAB p.16
When love and solitaire within your chamber. Georgia Douglas Johnson. HWOP p.14
When, Love, I Need Thee Most. Josephine D. (Henderson) Heard. MoGl p.109
When love is a shimmering curtain before a door of chance. Maya Angelou. BlSi p.267; JGM p.19
When love's brief dream is done. Georgia Douglas Johnson. PoN p.57; PoNe p.75
When love's triumphant day is done, go forward! Georgia Douglas Johnson. ALC p.47
When Mahalia Sings. Quandra Prettyman. IADB p.56; PoBA p.260
When Mary last night's nondoings turn daylight into noon. S. Diane Bogus. WITM p.7
When Mother Died.** Gloria Oden. RESUR p.77
When Mother Was Eleven Her Mother Died.** Gloria Oden. RESUR p.39
When Mother Was Over Forty-Five. ** Gloria Oden. RESUR p.57
When Mother Would Leave to Visit. ** Gloria Oden. RESUR p.55
When Mother's Mother Died.** Gloria Oden. RESUR p.63
When Mrs. Martin's Booker T. Gwendolyn Brooks. StIB p.6; WoOGB p.8
When My Oldest Brother, Buddy (And My Father's Namesade) Died.** Gloria Oden. RESUR p.33
When my poems and my dreams the spirit. Jodi Braxton. SoITM p.19
When My Uncle Willie Saw. Carol Freeman. BlFi p.331; BlLi p.525

When one has lived 'tis not so hard to fold the hands. Georgia Douglas Johnson. ALC p. 69
When Our Changing Bodies Meet and Merge.** Gloria Oden. RESUR p.85
When Roland sang at concerts he sang of things most dear. Eloise Culver. GANIV p.59
When she stabbed him it was not the folded leather. Mari Evans. NIGHT p.30
When she was little and colored. Nikki Giovanni. EgT p.9; PoBA p.456; WoATM p.10
When souls of Black men upward fly to mansions in the pearly sky. Naomi Evans Vaughn. NegVo p.161
When summer comes some other year and your fair head rests on my bosim in an infant angel's sleep. Naomi Long Madgett. OnATM p.22
When the African Arts, home again, became hosts of the hour. Margaret Danner. BlSi p.133; DoOAT p.112; FBPA p. 50
When the bell rings or you hear the knocking at the door. June Jordan. CoAAAW p.181
When the day has laid itself out. Patrice Wilson. NeJCL p.9
When the Green Lies Over the Earth.** Angelina Weld Grimke. CaD p.41; NeCa p.342; PoN p.48; PoNe p.56
When the ladder to success is broken they all tell you, "use the stairs." Helen F. Clarke. EbR p.41
When the man is busy making niggers it doesn't matter much what shade you are. Audre Lorde. ChPON p.68; NeHS p.38
When the nurse came in and said, "It's a girl." Olean Bess. MiFe p.9
When the people knew you that other time. Alice Walker. RePOP p.40
When the pin-headed Yale boy composes memos in the rear office. Melba Joyce Boyd. CaEADW p.36
When the Saints Come Marching In. Audre Lorde. ChPON p. 22; COAL p.37
When the spirit is strong there's no hope that's too high. From The Lillies of The Field. MyNIB p.50
When the sun comes back and the first quail call. Anonymous. AfAV p.120
When the sun dips hot blood-sauce on your flesh. Joanne Jimason. NaEd p.36
When the sun spins and rises in the west. Sonia Sanchez. BluB p.51
When there is no longer love. Mae V. Cowdery. WLOV p.59
When Those Who Are Precious Die. ** Gloria Oden. RESUR p.19
When through the winding cobbled streets of time. Georgia Love. IADB p.103; NNPUSA p.69
When time has rocked the present age to sleep. Georgia Douglas Johnson. BlALP p. 44; BrBV p.91
When tokens were thirty cents and telephone bills seventy-five units. Esther Louise. CoAAAW p.201
When Two-Year Olds Talk in Their Sleep. S. Diane Bogus. WITM p.48
When u left, because I did not call exactly at the hour u specified. Carolyn M. Rodgers. SoBB p.39
When war's red banner trailed along the sky. Henrietta Cordelia Ray. BlSi p.37; EABP p.140
When we are closest to death. Pamela Cobb. InDM p.18
When We Are Dead. Josephine D. (Henderson) Heard. MoGl p. 121
When we come rider our green horses against the tenement dust. Sonia Sanchez. ItND p.22
When we count out our gold at the end of the day. Geor-

gia Douglas Johnson. BrBV p.87; CaD p.75
When we look at ourselves we see ourselves through eyes which have been schooled to see as comely only the opaque. Margaret T. G. Burroughs. WhSIT p.18
When winter's royal robes of white from hill and vale are gone. Charlotte Forten Grimke. BlSi p.22
When you chart your course. Barbara Marshall. TNV p.71
When You Come To Me.** Maya Angelou. JGM p.9
When You Died. Christine Johnson. FoM p.71
When you disappeared the night sat in my mouth. Ntozake Shange. DaGe p.69
When you get up in the morning what the hell do you see? Frenchy J. Hodges. BlW p. 25
When You Have Forgotten Sunday: The Love Story. Gwendolyn Brooks. BlP p.168; SoOM p.559; StIB p.18; WoOGB p.20
When you have hung the keys on the wall. Toi Derricotte. EmDH p.13
When You Left. Sonia Sanchez. IvBAW p.76
When you lie again in the street of forgetfulness. Pinkie Gordon Lane. MyFe p.33
When you party to hearty then kill-off your brother or somebody. E. Sharon Gomillion. FoAAM p.17
When you perceive my fears aimed at an utter lack of self-esteem. June Vanleer Williams. WiRYPS p.82
When You Read This Poem. Pinkie Gordon Lane. BlSi p.229
When you see him you are sparkled by his particular grace of bearing. Margaret Danner. DoOAT p.82
When you see me sitting quietly like a sack left on the shelf. Maya Angelou. AnSIR p.48
When you see them on a freeway hitching rides wearing beads. Maya Angelou. OhPWFW p.59
When you show me that those colors carry special meaning in your head. Barbara Mahone. PoBA p.473; Suga p.15
When you sleep in the circle of my arms. Harryette Mullen. TTW p.64
When you told of Paul and his letter to Roman Christians. Frenchy J. Hodges. BlW p. 15
When You Walk Into the Sun and its Searing Rays Blind Your Eyes Warm Your Face. Naomi Long Madgett. OnATM p.61
When you were here in wonderful Detroit. Margaret Danner. BlP p.153; IrLa p.9; PoCo p.20
When your spring-vital rains refreshed my own parched season. Naomi Long Madgett. StBS p.51
Whenever I arrive you're there waiting. Wanda Coleman. MaDBL p.124
Whenever I go (those days) the tide seems low. June Jordan. ThTDID p.123
Whenever I Lift My Eyes To Bliss.** Georgia Douglas Johnson. HWOP p.40
Where? Georgia Douglas Johnson. HWOP p.30
Where are my people? Gloria Davis. DeDP p.71; NBP p.46
Where are the brave men, where are the strong men? Georgia Douglas Johnson. BrBV p.75; NeNRe p.379
Where are the Prayers. Josephine D. (Henderson) Heard. MoGl p.132
Where are you going barefoot boy. Marion Nicholes. LiS p.16
Where are your heroes, my little Black ones. Nikki Giovanni. BFBTBJ p.50; BlP p.325; EgT p.11
Where contemplation finds her sacred spring. Phillis

Wheatley. PAL p.40; PPW p. 76
Where contempation finds her sacred spring. Phillis Wheatley. PAL p.84; PPW p.24
Where did they go the writers. Mari Evans. NiGHT p.49
Where did you come from, mother and why. Yvonne Gregory. AmNP p.153
Where did you go to maaaannn. Sonia Sanchez. LoP p.36
Where Do School Days Go? Josephine D. (Henderson) Heard. MoGl p.57
Where Do We Go?** Naomi Long Madgett. OnATM p.42
Where Do You Go?** Marva Tatum Smith. BeYM p.2
Where Do You Go To Become a Non-Citizen. Patricia Parker. MoIB p.61
Where Do You Live? Bessie Woodson Yancey. EcFTH p.15
Where does fear go. Marva Tatum Smith. BeYM p.17
Where/from/here r what else then r we talking bout. Val Ferdinand. NeBV p.377
Where God stands is always morning. Marion Cuthbert. SOC p.17
Where grew the tangled brush. Josephine D. (Henderson) Heard. MoGl p.94
Where Hast Thou Gleaned? Josephine D. (Henderson) Heard. MoGl p.91
Where Have You Gone.** Mari Evans. BlP p.186; BlSp p. 68; CoAAAW p.106; IABW p. 35; ITBLA p.274; NNPUSA p. 105; PoN p.30; RoATW p. 105; TYBP p.254; WhIAM p. 15
Where have you gone, my mother? Naomi Long Madgett. PiLAF p. 49
Where I Live. Wanda Coleman. MaDBL p.13
Where I'd Like To Be. Marva Tatum Smith. BeYM p.15
Where is my pegasus. Jodi Braxton. SoITM p.37
Where is the love that might have been. Georgia Douglas Johnson. ALC p.61
Where life is a luxury and death a dark dream. Pinkie Gordon Lane. WiTh p.41
Where shall I hide ths sweet bastard? Pinkie Gordon Lane. MyFe p.31
Where the Mississippi meets the Amazon. Ntozake Shange. NaEd p.28
Where to go when I have already been there and aback again. Sonia Sanchez. WABP p.18
Where was I, mother, in the photograph? Naomi Long Madgett. ExAE p.11
Where We Belong, A Duet. Maya Angelou. AnSIR p.6
Whereas. June Jordan. SCh p.32
Whereas Judas hung himself I despise bravura. June Jordan. SCh p.33; ThTDID p.157
Whereas the outrageous violation of human rights under that racist regime persists. June Jordan. CoAAAW p.182
Wherever we live, it's right to forgive. Anonymous. AfAV p. 196; NeNRe p.54
Which calls forth the muse? Leanna F. Johnson. EbR p.95
While an intrinsic ardor prompts to write the muses promise to assist my pen. Phillis Wheatley. AfAWA p.17; BlALP p.10; BlWOA p.41; EaNAW p.36; PPW p.63
While deep you morn beneath the cypress-shade. Phillis Wheatley. PAL p.61; PPW p.46
While Everyone Wears Black That's Chic in Spring. Margaret Danner. DoOAT p.27
While Henry was painting or modeling with clay. Eloise Culver. GANIV p.49
While I was in the middle of the night. Lucille Clifton. GoNAE p.44
While it lasts I am peaceful. Naomi Long Mzdgett. OnATM p.51
while Love is Unfashionalble. Alice Walker. RePOP p.68
While others chant of gay

elysian scenes. Phillis Wheatley. EbAT p.79
While hireling scribblers prostitute their pen. Phillis Wheatley. EBAP p.111
While I was in the middle of the night. Lucille Clifton. GoNAE p.44
While it is true (though only in a factual sense). Nikki Giovanni. BFBTBJ p.16
While raging tempest shake the shore. Phillis Wheatley. PAL p.46; PPW p.35
While Sitting in the Airport Waiting Room. Pinkie Gordon Lane. MyFe p.45
While some "rap" over this turmoil. Margaret Danner. BlSi p.133; DoOAT p.85; FBPA p. 49
While thus you mourn beneath the cypress shade. Phillis Wheatley. PAL p.59; PPW p.77
While working towards the Ph.D degree. Pinkie Gordon Lane. PoBBl p.8; WiTh p.27
Whimper Baby. Lucile D. Goodlet. WGC p.56
Whine: Depalm Avenue, The. Wanda Coleman. MaDBL p.89
Whisper at twilight, a sigh through the night, A. Georgia Douglas Johnson. HWOP p. 57
Whisper Together Brethern.** Mari Evans. IABW p.89
"Whispers of The Child, The." Eleanor Thomas-Grumbach. MoSu p.5
Whistlin' Sam. Bessie Woodson Yancey. EcFTH p.35
White America is saying stand up & be counted. Sonia Sanchez. WABP p. 26
Whi/te Boys Gone. Val Ferdinand. NeBV p.374
White-Collar Job. Myra Estelle Morris. NegVo p.108
White Cross. Naomi Long Madgett. OnATM p.22; StBS p.27
White eyes wave across the aisle. MaDBL p.51
White Fear. Nannie M. Travis. EbR p.142
White folks always sitting around comparing their knots. Colleen McElroy. MuDLSG p.16
"White folks is white," says Uncle Jim. Naomi Long Madgett. DeDF p.89
White lies the town beneath. Bessie Woodson Yancey. EcFTH p.38
White man is nocturnal, The. Nikki Giovanni. PoBA p.457; Rec p.35
White man sent me the everything card, The. Nikki Giovanni. Rec p.41
White man tells me he told a white woman, A. June Jordan. PaNP p.70
White men looking at beautiful Black women. Loretta Rodgers. RoATW p.78; ThHSD p.82
White men opening doors for her. Harryette Mullen. TTW p.12
White men's children spread over the earth. Georgia Douglas Johnson. PoBA p.23
White plus white equals one. Vanessa Howard. ScWh p.15
White preacher like a mangy dog. Elma Stuckey. BiGa p.57
White stare splits the air, A. June Jordan. MyNIB p.93
White Things. Anne Spencer. NeNRe p.46
White Troops Had Their Orders But the Negroes Looked Like Men. Gwendolyn Brooks. SPGB p.25; StIB p.52; WoOGB p.54
Whither? Georgia Douglas Johnson. HWOP p.10
Who Am I. Frances Garcia. ThGSD p.62
Who Am I. Kali Grosvenor. PBK p.18
Who Am I Thinkin Of. Ntozake Shange. NaEd p.80
Who Are You. Sonia Sanchez. IvBAW p.84
Who are you, Black girl that you should walk through these Virginia pathways free. Naomi Long Madgett. PhN p.98
Who are you that your name come broken by the speeding cars. Audre Lorde. NeHS p.5

Who, But You, Can Tether the Tone of a Thief. Margaret Danner. DoOAT p.136

Who Can be Born Black.** Mari Evans. IABW p.93; NIGHT p. 76; OnOW p.5; WhIAM p.24

Who comes to have gone unbreathing. S. Diane Bogus. WITM p.4

Who dat nigger in a deer I spy? Anonymous. BlWOA p.236

Who Gives. May Miller. ClAB p. 15

Who hath not built his castles in the free and open air. Georgia Douglas Johnson. HWOP p. 50

Who is a purity. Carolyn M. Rodgers. HeAEG p.30

Who is My Brother? Pinkie Gordon Lane. BlSi p.232; MyFe p. 38

Who is my neighbor? Josephine D. (Henderson) Heard. MoGl p.38

Who is Setting These Priorities. Ntozake Shange. NaEd p.100

Who is that cigar mouthed man beside the chimney in khaki pants. Margaret Porter. CoAAAW p.262

Who likes to glitter. Jayne Cortez. COAG p.86

Who Look at Me. June Jordan. ThTDID p.2

Who made you? was always the question. Alice Walker. RePOP p.11

Who Said It Was Simple. Audre Lorde. ChPON p.49; FrLWP p. 39

Who sneaks and creeps and peeps down corners. Lois Miller. PoBBl p.27

Who taught thee conflict with the pow'rs of night. Phillis Wheatley. PAL p.87; PPW p. 11

Who this bone man is. Margaret Danner. DoOAT p.92

Who walked and blinked at sunlight on the snow. Linda Brown Bragg. LoSBM p.27

Who was it held me on her knee? Josephine D. (Henderson) Heard. MoGl p.25

Who were you, really? Naomi Long Madgett. ExAE p.46

Who wobbles through the breeze like a chiffon palm leaf. Carolyn M. Rodgers. HoIGO p.7

Who Would Encompass Millions.** Mari Evans. WhIAM p.12

Who would have the sky any color but blue. Mrs. J. W. Hammond. ANP p.82

Who would paint a people black or white. June Jordan. ThTDID p.2

Who would who could understand that. Carolyn M. Rodgers. BlP p.260; BrT p.180; RoATW p.6

Who you be remembering lil Jimmy Garrison. Sonia Sanchez. LoP p.81

Who-Zen John, Who-Za. Anonymous. BlWOA p.235

Whole depends on rain, The. Sonia Sanchez. LoP p.24

Whole point of writing you is pointless, The. Nikki Giovvanni. BFBTBJ p.29

Whom we love, whose actions are rooted in our common rage. Sherley Williams. PePo p.76

Whore. S. Diane Bogus. WITM p. 7

Whores. Margaret Walker. FMP p.54

Who's gonna make all that beautiful Blk/rhetoric. Sonia Sanchez. IvBAW p.18; MoCAP p.137; NaPr p.128

Whose broken window is a cry of art. Gwendolyn Brooks. ITM p.36; WoOGB p.408

Whose Fault. Nola Richardson. WhOL p.59

Whose knees were so wedded to your trade. Pinkie Gordon Lane. WiTh p.35

Whose Terms. Nola Richardson. WhOL p.76

Whoso Gives Freely Shall Freely Receive. Josephine D. (Henderson) Heard. MoGl p.62

Whut a Dawn. Mary Bohanon. GaBW p.264

Why. Georgia Douglas Johnson. BrBV p.80

Why? Melba Joyce Boyd. BlSi p. 283; CaEADW p.29
Why? Olean Bess. MiFe p.15
Why? Sonia Sanchez. IvBAW p.27; LoP p.1
Why am I alone? Katherine L. Cuestas. BTB p.76
Why are people always rushing. Olean Bess. MiFe p.15
Why are they mean? Kali Grosvenor. PBK p.27
Why are white folks so mean. Kali Grosvenor. PBK p.27
Why did the pilgrims discouver this country? Kali Grosvenor. PBK p.37
Why Do I Love This Country? Mary Wilkerson Cleaves. EbR p.46
Why do people always choose Saturdays to wit out. Jayne Cortez. Scar p.9
Why do people believe in some old sign. Anonymous. BlWOA p. 887
Why do people say "let's make love"? Melva Eloise Tatum. MELVA p.9
Why do the tears start? Naomi Long Madgett. PhN p.105
Why do they descend into the crotch of the city. Leatrice Emeruwa. BlGBG p.14
Why Do You Stare. Pinkie Gordon Lane. MyFe p.42
Why do you wish to give me over to someone else? Alice Walker. ONC p.58
Why does this flamingo continually frame so well. Margaret Danner. DoOAT p.67
Why don't you go & integrate. Ntozake Shange. NaEd p.102
Why Don't you love us? Nancy L. Arnez. RoCO p.15
Why I don't get high on shit. Sonia Sanchez. WABP p.57
Why I Like Movies. Patricia Jones. BlSi p.251
Why must I string my hate like Japanese lanterns. Sonia Sanchez. IvBAW p.27; LoP p.1
Why stand aghast, this weeping, wondering throng? Josephine D. (Henderson) Heard. MoGl p.75
Why question St. Paul's wisdom? Judy Dothard Simmons. JuB p.22
Why they closing down Alcatraz & considering closing Sing Sing. Sonia Sanchez. WABP p.19
Why would a robin think that a sparrow was made to fly. Margaret Danner. DoOAT p. 97; IrLa p.15; PoCo p.7
Why would anybody build a monument to the Civil War? June Jordan. PaNP p.90
Whys of the Black Child, The. E. Sharon Gomillion. FoAAM p.11
Widow With a Moral Question. Helene Johnson. VoFHR p. 416
Wierd sister the black witches know that. Lucille Clifton. OrW p.3
Wife. Lucille Clifton. TwW p. 29
Wife-Woman, The. Anne Spencer. ANP p.123; BANP p.216; NeNRe p.79
Wilberforce. Josephine D. (Henderson) Heard. MoGl p.63
Wild Flowers. Nikki Giovanni. ThWRNW p.58
Wild lions have no need to purr. Naomi Long Madgett. OnATM p.25
Wild Negro Bill. Anonymous. BlP p.7; UNBP p.89
Wild Roses. Effie Lee Newsome. CaD p.59
Wild trees have bought me, The. Audre Lorde. CaTR p.5; ChPON p.11; COAL p.15
Will, The. Alexis Yancey. AOS p.1
Will. Alice Walker. RePOP p.60
Will be the days I go unchildrened. Lucille Clifton. GoNAE p.8
Will e'er there come a time? Joseph8ne D. (Henderson) Heard. MoGl p.115
Will the Luna Moth Sigh. Margaret Danner. DoOAT p.62
Will the power go off this winter. S. Diane Bogus. WITM p.66
Will to make it sometimes over-

comes the saneness, The. Alexis Yancey. AOS p.1
Will You Come? Lyn. SiSH p.24
Will you have the chance to be strong as the wind? Anonymous. ThHSD p.26
William Leon Hansberry Historian of Ancient Africa, 1894-1965, Mississippi. Eloise Culver. GANIV p.62
Willie. Maya Angelou. AnSIR p. 28
Willie at the Golden Grill came straight from work to drink tequilla. June Jordan. PaNP p.20
Willie was a man without fame. Maya Angelou. AnSIR p.28
Willow, The. Georgia Douglas Johnson. HWOP p.52
Wilma Rudolph, Olympic Star, 1940- . Tennessee. Eloise Culver. GANIV p.75
Wilmington, Delaware. Nikki Giovanni. BFBTBJ p.26; BrT p. 51; NaPr p.26
Wilmington is a funni Negro. Nikki Giovanni. BFBTBJ p.26; BrT p.51; NaPr p.26
Wimmin. Carolyn M. Rodgers. CoAAAW p.315
Wind, The. L. Doretta Lowery. BTh p.51
Wind. Naomi Long Madgett. PhN p. 112
Wind, a jolly old lady in brown, The. L. Doretta Lowery. BTh p.51
Wind blew my father from the south to the north, The. Carolyn M. Rodgers. HoIGO p.58
Wind Blows, The.** Mae V. Cowdery. WLOV p.5
Wind-flutes sighing through the trees. Cora Ball Moten. NegVo p.111
Wind is a tall, bare-headed beggar, The. Naomi Long Madgett. PhN p.112
Wind is eating the world again, The. Lucille Clifton. OrW p. 13
Wind kissed the rose, The. Olivia M. Hunter. BTh p.33
Wind led me here and stillness holds me, The. Pinkie Gordon Lane. WiTh p.16
Wind the clock and feed the cat. Naomi Long Madgett. OnATM p. 34
Wind Thoughts. Pinkie Gordon Lane. WiTh p.16
Wind through the gathered people. Sherley Williams. PePo p.16
Wind whine, 'de fish blow, De. Lucile Goodlett. WGC p.56
Windless Hour. May Miller. ClAB p.14
Window Pictures. Sarah E. Wright. BTB p.184
Winds of Orisha, The. Audre Lorde. ChPON p.48; FrLWP p.37
Windy Rain. Kali Grosvenor. PBK p.54
Windy rain my old silly umbrella tries walking backwards. Kali Grosvenor. PBK p.54
Wine of life was sweet, The. Naomi Long Madgett. OnATM p.38
Winged women was saying "full of grace" and like. Lucille Clifton. TwW p.36
Wings. Laura E. Smith. NegVo p.143
Wings Against the Blue. Harryette Mullen. TTW p.56
Winking at a Funeral. Alice Walker. RePOP p.4
Wintah black and de wintah bittah, De. Lucile Goodlett. WGC p. 35
Winter. Bessie Woodson Yancey. EcFTH p.8
Winter. Nikki Giovanni. CoCRD p.81
Winter--aback sweeps the inward eye. Georgia Douglas Johnson. HWOP p.19
Winter--and like its snow your coldness chilled me. Dorothy Lee Louise Shaed. NegVo p. 139
Winter birds are flying from the North, The. Pinkie Gordon Lane. BlSi p.231; MyFe p.19
Winter Colder Than the Last, A. Linda Brown Bragg. LoSBM p. 11
Winter Night's Song. Leatrice

Emeruwa. BlGBG p.26
Winter Poem. Nikki Giocanni. MyH p.10
Winter Sonnet. Linda Brown Bragg. LoSBM p.27
Winter Storm, The. Nikki Giovanni. CoCRD p.41
Winter Twilight, A. Angelina Weld Grimke. CaD p.46; NeCa p.343; PoBA p.16; PoN p.47; PoNe p.54
Winter's Morn. Rosa Paul Brooks. AmLNA p.90
Wisdom. Gertrude Blackwell Bailey. IfWCF p.25
Wise: Having the Ability to Perceive and Adopt the Best Means for Accomplishing an End. Lucille Clifton. GoNAE p.21
Wise one said--set aside no day, The. Thelma Lamar. PoBBl p. 41
Wish, A. Eleanor A. Thompson. BTh p.47
Wish, The. Elma Stuckey. BiGa p.7
Wish on Line, The. Sherley Williams. CoAAAW p.392
Wit and laughter thy tears cannot shatter the remorse of years. Jamye H. Coleman. EbR p.52
Witches. Margaret Danner. DoOAT p.52
Witches II. Margaret Danner. DoOAT p.52
Wite/motha/fucka. Sonia Sanchez. WABP p.59; YoBBI p.367
With a hand more feeling than the one with which you sought my comfort. S. Diane Bogus. WITM p.28
With angry brow and stately tread. Josephine D. (Henderson) Heard. MoGl p.26
With but one life full certified. Georgia Douglas Johnson. BrBV p.78
With button eyes and cotton skin. Effie Lee Newsome. GoS p.99
With doubt, you ask what love is. Nola Richardson. WhOL p.39
With grace she rose when her name was called. Arlene Howard Benton. BTh p.61
With kisses I'll awake you love. Georgia Douglas Johnson. ALC p.44
With Malice Toward None. Carolyn M. Rodgers. HeAEG p.38
With No Immediate Cause. Ntozake Shange. NaEd p.114
With or Without You.** Naomi Long Madgett. OnATM p.24
With pinched checks hollow and wan. Josephine D. (Henderson) Heard. MoGl p.25
With praise of you I bring song and psalter. Edythe Mae Gordon. NegVo p.65
With springtime my father comes alive. May Miller. ClAB p. 33
With sympathy hands do motherone, take them in. S. Diane Bogus. WITM p.4
With the first blush of morning, my soul is a wing. Georgia Douglas Johnson. HWOP p.44
With the invention of the door man changed the western world. Thulani Davis. AlTRGR p.18
With the last whippoorwill call of evening settling over mountains. Margaret Walker. PFND p.74; PoBA p.149
With the Sun-Fear Leaves Me.** Patricia Parker. ChOM p.31; MoIB p.53
With you I pressed the rose you brought me. Sonia Sanchez. LoP p.23
With your breath upon my cheek there is no spring nor autumn. Mae V. Cowdery. WLOV p.52
With Your Permission. Barbara Mahone. Suga p.27
Withdrawal. Linda Brown Bragg. LoSBM p.10
Within my casement came one night the fairy moon. Henrietta Cordelia Ray. BlSi p.39; EBAP p.142
Within our house of flesh we wear a web of time. Margaret Walker. PFND p.31
Within our love the world looks like a reasonable easy plan. June Jordan. ThTDID p.63
Within the cage he ramped and

and raged. Constance Holley. PoN p.322
Within the day a seventh time I touch the pale wood antelope. May Miller. CNAW p.359
Within the temple of our heart your sacred memory dwells a part. Georgia Douglas Johnson. BrBV p.90
Within your pulsing day there must be little space. Georgia Douglas Johnson. ALC p. 8
Without. Naomi Long Madgett. ExAE p.60
Without expectation there is no end. Audre Lorde. BlSi p. 201; CaTR p.4; COAL p.11; MoCAP p.123; PoBA p.245; SoS p.88
Without meaning to, of course, but it is inevitable. Pinkie Gordon Lane. WiTh p.55
Without Name. Naomi Long Madgett. PhN p.83
Without Name. Pauli Murray. AmNP p.106; DaTAOP p.74; PoBA p.108; PoN p.159; PoNe p.270; RoATW p.14
Without Someone. Lyn. SiSH p.28
Without someone is waking up in the morning with an ache in your stomach. Lyn. SiSH p. 28
Without your lean brown back and baths together I take what's left. Jill Witherspoon Boyer. DrF p.6
Woes of flesh are naught. Georgia Douglas Johnson. BrBV p.76
Woke up early this morning. Leatrice Emeruwa. BlGBG p.17
Woke up this morning evil and black. Pearl Cleage Lomax. WeDNNM p.8
Woman. Audre Lorde. BlUn p.82
Woman. Elouise Loftin. PoBA p. 514
Woman. Naomi Long Madgett. PhN p.85
Woman. Nikki Giovanni. CoCRD p.71
Woman. Pinkie Gordon Lane. PoBBl p.9; WiTh p.6
Woman. Sonia Sanchez. IvBAW p. 55
Woman and Her Thang, The. Wanda Coleman. MaDBL p.96
Woman and Man. Pauli Murray. DaTAOP p.67
Woman and the Roses, The. Harryette Mullen. TTW p.57
Woman At War, A. Hazel L. Washington. EbR p.152
Woman/Child? Nola Richardson. WhOL p.14
Woman/Dirge For Wasted Children, A. Audre Lorde. BlUn p.66
Woman don't stand up straight, The. Ntozake Shange. DaGe p.57
Woman Eater. Wanda Coleman. MaDBL p.86
Woman finds it hard to give for/ give/a man. Carolyn M. Rodgers. HoIGO p.46
Woman in the Moon. S. Diane Bogus. WITM p.1
Woman in Travail bulging with the unborn. Pauli Murray. DaTAOP p.67
Woman Me. Maya Angelou. BlSi p.264; OhPWFW p.51
Woman Perception Poem # 1. S. Diane Bogus. WITM p.3
Woman Perception Poem # 2. S. Diane Bogus. WITM p.3
Woman Poem. Nikki Giovanni. BlSi p.234
Woman Power. Nikki Giovanni. BFBTBJ p.78
Woman power is Black power. Audre Lorde. ChPON p.88; NeHS p.20
Woman Rocking Her White Hair. Sonia Sanchez. IvBAW p.77
Woman Speaks, A. Audre Lorde. BlUn p.4
Woman Statement # 1. S. Diane Bogus. WITM p.2
Woman Thing, The. Audre Lorde. BlSi p.204; CaTr p.19; ChPON p.14; COAL p.9; NaPr p.67
Woman Walk/n Down a Mississippi Road. Angela Jackson. VoDLM p.18
Woman when we met on the solace. Audre Lorde. BlUn p.33

Woman who left the house this morning, The. June Jordan. PaNP p.24
Woman Who Lives in the Botantical Gardens, The. Alexis De Veaux. CoAAAW p.101
Woman who made me look down, A. Sonia Sanchez. IvBAW p.80
Woman whose color of life is like the sun. Sonia Sanchez. IvBAW p.68
Woman with a burning flame deep covered through the years, A. Georgia Douglas Johnson. BlSi p.59; HWOP p.32
Woman With Flower. Naomi Long Madgett. BlPo p.29; FBPA p.96; StBS p.21
Woman with hoe in hand, and baby on your back. Alice M. Jones. RoATW p.61; YoBBI p.435
Woman With Water/Melon Thighs. Angela Jackson. VoDLM p.16
Woman Work. Maya Angelou. AnSIR p.31
Womanhood, The. Gwendolyn Brooks. BlALP p.102; SPGB p.52
Womanhood. Sonia Sanchez. BluB p.38
Womanhood XV, The. Gwendolyn Brooks. BlALP p.102
Woman's Song, A. Colleen J. McElroy. BlSi p.291
Womanslaughter. Patricia Parker. MoIB p.141
Women. Alice Walker. PoBA p. 476; RePOP p.5
Women. Judy Dothard Simmons. JuB p.12
Women clutch their men, The. Carolyn M. Rodgers. HeAEG p. 28
Women Gather, The. Nikki Giovanni. WoATM p.4
Women had few words, The. Pauli Murray. DaTAOP p.64
Women in My Life, The. Wanda Coleman. MaDBL p.40
Women in Politics. Myra Estelle Morris. NegVo p.108
Women of Dan Dance With Swords in Their Hands to Mark the Time When They Were Warriors, The. Audre Lorde. BlUn p.14
Women of my Color. Wanda Coleman. MaDBL p.24
Women were raped. Mae Jackson. CaPWY p.11
Women who build nations learn to love. Audre Lorde. ChPON p.40; FrLWP p.18
Womens I. Sandra Royster. WoTa p.11
Womens II. Sandra Royster. WoTa p.12
Womens III. Sandra Royster. WoTa p.14
Wonder. Maya Angelou. OhPWFW p.22
Wonder Woman, The. Nikki Giovanni. MyH p.28
Wonders do not confuse. Gwendolyn Brooks. BeEa p.67; BlVo p.461; WoOGB p.365
Won't be no colorless undeveloped babies. Linda Cousins. ThHSD p.48
Won't you come again, my friend? Helene Johnson. VoFHR p.416
Won't you play house with me. Mae Jackson. CaPWY p.15
Woods and fields are calling me, The. Gertrude Parthenia McBrown. ReFNA p.54
Word For Me...Also, A. Nikki Giovanni. ThWRNW p.55
Word Game. Wanda Coleman. MaDBL p.97
Word Poem. Nikki Giovanni. BFBTBJ p.39; BOL p.9; EgT p.22; PoBA p.450
Wordless kiss, a stifled sigh, A. Georgia Douglas Johnson. HWOP p.13
Words. Bernette Golden. TNV p. 42
Words. Helen Morgan Brooks. NNPUSA p.104; PoNe p.278; RoATW p.149
Words. Pauli Murray. DaTAOP p.82
Words. Sonia Sanchez. LoP p. 18
Words are not what people read. Carolyn M. Rodgers. HeAG p. 45
Words dance polka through rays of electricity. Julia Fields. NiBPo p.73
Words "eye", The. Helen G. Quigless. TNV p.97
Words For a Motet. Linda Brown

Bragg. LoSBM p.18
Words for Geoffrey and Stephanie Hamilton. Sonia Sanchez. ItND p.10
Words for Kali and Poochie. Sonia Sanchez. ItND p.9
Words for our chidren (from their many parents). Sonia Sanchez. WABP p.61
Words marching together like the soldiers. June Vanleer Williams. WiRYPS p.81
Words massing images of sacred exclusion glacial crust words Unfeeling untouching unmeaning. Barbara A. Reynolds. TGWL p.83
Words that I speak, The. Bernette Golden. TNV p.42
Words! Words! Jessie Redmond Fauset. CaD p.65
Work. Thulani Davis. AlTRGR p. 60
Work it Out. Sarah Webster Fabio. DoBB p.32
Work Song. Anonymous. MBP p.56
Work Two Ways, Baby. Sherley Williams. PePo p.29
Workers Rose on May Day or Postscript to Karl Marx, The. Audre Lorde. ChPON p.85; NeHS p.14
World had steeled itself for death that day, The. Nell Chapman. EbR p.30
World I see, The. Mari Evans. KAL p.173
World is mine, The. Naomi E. Buford. EbR p.16
World is moving close to me. The. Linda Curry. SoS p.8
World is Not a Pleasant Place to Be, The.** Nikki Giovanni. MyH p.15
World is wakened by the sun-lit skies, The. W. Blanche Nivens. BTh p.44
Would I might mend the fabric of my youth. Georgia Douglas Johnson. BANP p.183
World they say keeps trying to drown you, The. Carolyn M. Rodgers. HeAEG p.59
Worldling, The. Naomi Long Madgett. OnATM p.16
Worm crawls with purpose, The. May Miller. ClAB p.26
Worse is not knowing if I do take somebody's words, The. June Jordan. ThTDID p.196
Would I might mend the fabric of my youth. Georgia Douglas Johnson. ALC p.16
Would it be safe to wash this quilt? Harryette Mullen. TTW p.13
Would it please you if I strung my tears in pearls for you to wear? Naomi Long Madgett. AfAWA p.691; BlP p.196; BlVo p.477; MoCAP p.93; StBS p.54
Would that I could believe. Lyn. SiSH p.9
Would you like to but can't take the time. Mae Jackson. CaPWY p.7
Would You Please Return my Pulse? Sonia Sanchez. IvBAW p.74
Would You Regret?** Josephine D. (Henderson) Heard. MoGl p.89
Wouldn't you agree the best curve she has now think. Audre Lorde. NaPr p.77
Wounded Heart, The. Josephine D. (Henderson) Heard. MoGl p.86
Wounds of Jesus, The. Anonymous. BLIA p.32
Wow...Yr Just Like a Man! Ntozake Shange. NaEd p.13
Wreaths of lillies and immortelles, scattered upon each silent mound. Alice Dunbar-Nelson. DuSAE p.251
Wrinkles of your brow and the silver of your hair are plain to see. Naomi Long Madgett. PhN p.84
Write Me a Poem. Pinkie Gordon Lane. PoBBl p.12; WiTh p, 48
Writer of rock songs writer of work songs at a wearer. Jodi Braxton. SoITM p.42
Writers, The. Mari Evans. NIGHT p.49
Writing a Poem.** Naomi Long Madgett. PiLAF p.11
Written on the Last of April.

Naomi Long Madgett. PhN p. 48; SoTPN p.23
Wrong side of morning, The. May Miller. BTB p.152

- Y -

Y'all know who I'm talkin' bout. E. Sharon Gomillion. FoAAM p.21
Yall out there looooken so coool. Sonia Sanchez. BlP p.240; WABP p.43
Y'all talken' crazy. Elma Stuckey. BiGa p.37
Yalla Gal. Lucile D. Goodlett. WGC p.42
Yalla gal, it's spring time. Lucile D. Goodlett. WGC p.42
Ye martial pow'rs, and all ye tuneful nine. Phillis Wheatley. BlALP p.11; PAL p.101; PPW p.13
Yeah: A Grind Poem. Lyn. SiSH p.24
Yeah billie, if someone had loved u like u shd have been loved. Sonia Sanchez. NaPr p.125
Yeah...But. Nikki Giovanni. Rec p.44
Yeah, my man got no place else to go. Sonia Sanchez. IvBAW p. 48; LoP p.51
"Yeah" she said, "my man's gone too." Nikki Giovanni. MyH p.11
Yeah, they hang you up. Sonia Sanchez. BlP p.231; BrT p. 136; RoATW p.65
Year runs long enough from force momentum trips the memory, A. June Jordan. SCh p.64; ThTDID p.112
Yeah Tomorrow/Tomorrow.** C. Tillery Banks. HeTMWL p.10
Yeah-you can really tell where a people is at. Carolyn M. Rodgers. JuBa p.114
Year 1978. left right, left right. left right. Black innocence marches, The. Alicia Loy Johnson. GaBW p. 342; NiBPo p.150
Year or So Before She Died, A.** Gloria Oden. RESUR p.137
Years of frustration, of futility. Thelma Parker Cox. TNV p.29
Years will fall through our fingers. Nzadi Zimele-Keita. CoAAAW p.399
Yeh billie if someone had loved u like u shud have been loved. Sonia Sanchez. WABP p.41
Yeh, yeh, yeh, yeh, yeh, yeh, yeh, yeh, yeh, yeh taught them to wear big naturals. Sonia Sanchez. WABP p.60
Yellow sickly yellow is the day's light. Countess W. Twitty. EbR p.148
Yes. Thulani Davis. AlTRGR p. 39
Yes, Ethiopia yet shall stretch her bleeding hands abroad. Frances E. W. Harper. EaNAW p.293
Yes, he turned and he walked. Elaine Brown. GLOWC p.95
Yes, I did suffer. Naomi Long Madgett. OnATM p.48
Yes, I goes down to Mis' Mary's. Lucy May Turner. BCF p.20
Yes. I'm grounded. Harryette Mullen. TTW p.62
"Yes, I'm guilty," the woman said. Josephine D. (Henderson) Heard. MoGl p.129
Yes, my hair is straight. Linda G. Hardnett. GaBW p.319
Yess uh, Mr. Jedge, suh dat de truf sh' nuf. Lucile D. Goodlett. WGC p.64
Yesterday. Vanessa Howard. ScWh p.52
Yesterday a world was born. Marsha Ann Jackson. TNV p. 52
Yesterday the sun shone bright. Vanessa Howard. ScWh p.52
Yesterday While Walking Down the Avenue. V. Howard. ScWh p.25
Yesterday's Sculpture. Pinkie Gordon Lane. MyFe p.13
Yo/smile green as an African morning. Sonia Sanchez. LoP p.65
Yolande the Panda.** Nikki Giovanni. VaT p.27

Yolk-colored tongue perched beneath a burning sky. Helene Johnson. VoFHR p.360
You. C. Tillery Banks. HeTMWL p.80
You. Carolyn M. Rodgers. HeAEG p.41
You. Tyki Brown. ThHSD p.71
You, a poet. Mae Jackson. CaPWY p.19
You always use yours and save that last little bit of privacy. Jodi Braxton. SoITM p.38
You and Me. Jo Nell Rice. OnOW p.9
You appeared in every feast every crime. Jayne Cortez. Scar p.34
You are a double-dipped copper-bottomed pot. Margaret Danner. DoOAT p.85
You are a gourmet of self expression. S. Diane Bogus. WITM p.53
You are a miracle of love. Mae V. Cowdery. WLOV p.47
You are a tall dark tree. Mae V. Cowdery. WLOV p.25
You are a tree. Claire Turner. NegVo p.155
You Are Amble.** Sonia Sanchez. IvBAW p.73
You are as sweet as magnilia milk. Ntozake Shange. NaEd p.37
You are Black. Helen F. Clarke. EbR p.41
You are disdainful and magnificent. Helene Johnson. AmNP p.102; BANP p.28; CaD p. 217; EbAT p.148; NeNRe p. 152; VoFHR p.182
You are holy young black God as you reconstruct pyramids for our minds. Sonia Sanchez. ItND p.9
You are like this French Provincially curved African V for Freedon King. Margaret Danner. ImOAAF p.12
You are sick and old. Gwendolyn Brooks. SPGB p.124
You are somewhere in the city. Naomi Long Madgett. OnATM p. 44
You Are Sucha Fool. Ntozake Shange. DaGe p.28
You are the earth. Pauli Murray. DaTAOP p.92
You are the one. Lucille Clifton. OrW p.35
You Are There. Nikki Giovanni. CoCRD p.82
You are two-faced but comrade you are fair. Elma Stuckey. BiGa p.90
You Ask What Love Is. Nola Richardson. WhOL p.39
You be sittin sowewhere thinkin. Lyn. SiSH p.10
You Bet On Me. Marva Tatum Smith. BeYM p.29
You came into my life filled with joy. Eleanor Thomas-Grumbach. MoSu p.18
You came so softly. Paul Murray. DaTAOP p.89
You came the tapestries of love. Georgia Douglas Johnson. ALC p.19
You came to me this morning. Louise Blackman. EbR p.4
You came, too. Nikki Giovanni. BFBTBJ p.5
You Came With Shells. June Jordan. ThTDID p.79
You can beat down the crabs on your hairs. Jayne Cortez. Scar p.17
You can call me Herbie Jr. or Ashamah Kazaam. June Jordan. PaNP p.46
You can look any man straight in the eye. Gertrude Blackwell Bailey. IfWCF p.29
You can sigh o'er the sad-eyed Armenian. Frances E. W. Harper. ANP p.15; BlSi p.31; PBFH p.72
You cannot hurt me any more. Georgia Douglas Johnson. ALC p.57; RoATW p.1236
You cannot live here and bend my heart. Sonia Sanchez. LoP p.8
You Can't Be Sure of Anything These Days.** Patricia Parker. ChOMP p.7; MoIB p.36
You Can't Shake Hands With a Fist.** Debbie Whitely. GLOWC p.60

You carry your greatness unconsciously. Margaret Danner. DoOAT p.73
You cd just take what he's got for you. Ntozake Shange. NaEd p.50
You chatter of your "white supremacy." Leanna. F. Johnson. EbR p.95
You claim you don't want to hurt me. Nola Richardson. WhOL p. 71
You cover the kisses of sailors and soldiers. Jayne Cortez. Scar p.19
You come to me and twist my soul with pain. Edna Gullins. NegVo p.67
You danced a magnetic dance. Jayne Cortez. BlSi p.155; COAG p.33; MoOP p.18
You did not clock the falling of the leaves. Audre Lorde. FiCi p.23
You didn't send for them. Jayne Cortez. COAG p.82
You Do Not Know the High Prayer. Sonia Sanchez. IvBAW p.83
You done what you done. June Jordan. ThTDID p.11
You drink a bitter draught. Maya Angelou. JGM p.33
You fill me up so much when you touch me. Ntozake Shange. NaEd p.28
You gave me your hand. Georgia Douglas Johnson. ALC p.20; RoATW p.116
You get on a train and say goodbye to places, people. Naomi Long Madgett. PhN p.94
You go to school everyday, but in your classroom you never stay. Gertrude Blackwell Bailey. IfWCF p.17
You got shoes, I got shoes. Anonymous. BlEx p.5
You had better cool it, Grandmother. Margaret Danner. DoOAT p.95
You Had to Go to Funerals. Alice Walker. PoBA p.478; RePOP p.7
You Have Always Been Walking Around.** C. Tillery Banks. HeTMWL p.62
You have an education. Kattie M. Cumbo. NiBPo p.53
You have made fine sound. Pinkie Gordon Lane. PoBBl p.11; WiTh p.16
You have no word for soldiers to enjoy. Gwendolyn Brooks. MyNIB p.64; SpGB p.24; StIB p.49; WoOGB p.51
You Have Pierced Me so Deeply. Sonia Sanchez. IvBAW p.86
You Have Stamped Your Hour on Me. Sonia Sanchez. IvBAW p.71
You have taught me how to dress without awakening the whole world. Mae Jackson. CoAAAW p.169
You have to come with me to this place. Ntozake Shange. NaEd p.146
You have two hands absolutely lean and clean. June Jordan. ThTDID p.66
You Hear About Them. Wanda Coleman. MaDBL p.110
You intend no doubt to give me nothing. Alice Walker. RePOP p.57
You Judge a Man by the Silence he Keeps. Wanda Coleman. MaDBL p.60
You keep saying you were always there. Sonia Sanchez. LoP p.57
You knew not the depth of her sorrow. Bessie Woodson Yancey. EcFTH p.31
You Know. Jayne Cortez. CoAAAW p.92; COAG p.41; MoOP p.58
You know I sure would like to write a blues. Jayne Cortez. CoAAAW p.92; COAG p.41; MoOP p.58
You know it's really cold when you wake up hurtin. Sherley Williams. PePo p.48
You know me--I'm that nigger. Mari Evans. NIGHT p.67
"You know what," said Muffin." Margaret Danner. DoOAT p.29
You look at me with children in your eyes. Alice Walker. ONC p.62
You lovely creature of the sky. Hilda Preer. BTh p.36

You Made it Rain. Fareedah Allah. BlSi p.173
You made me a slave and kept me a slave. Dorothy Parrish. TNV p.87
You Make the Feel-in' Good.** C. Tillery Banks. HeTMWL p. 24
You May Bury Me in De Eas'. Anonymous. BlLi p.111
You may choose to sleep with eagles. Nola Richardson. WhOL p.45
You may sing of the north with its chilly frost. Bessie Woodson Yancey. EcFTH p.5
You may write me down in history. Maya Angelou. AnSIR p.41; BlSi p.265
You Me Us...Moving Towards Something.** C. Tillery Banks. HeTMWL p.22
You meet a really far out man. Patricia Parker. MoIB p.36
You 'mind me of the winter's eve. Mae Smith Jackson. ANP p.112; NeNRe p.364
You Must Give Before You Get. Bessie Woodson Yancey. EcFTH p.18
You need the untranslatable ice to watch. Gwendolyn Brooks. BlSi p.111; SPGB p.50; WoOGB p.94
You needn' sen' my gal hoss apples. Anonymous. UNBP p.90
You never know...when you meet. Nikki Giovanni. ThWRNW p.42
You only wanted to chat awhile. Jennifer Blackman Lawson. BlIMT p.18
You opened my eyes. Kattie M. Cumbo. BOL p.34; NiBPo p. 65
"You ought to do a book, miss me. Judy Dothard Simmons. CoAAAW p.331
You oughta remember them kids. Johari Amini. ImIB p.13
You probably could put their names to them. Gloria Oden. AmNP p.160; KAL p.183; MoCAP p.96; RoATW p.143
You reached in to pull my mind out of the mire of four centuries to tell me I am beautiful. Paula Giddings. RoATW p.66
You rise--detached. June Vanleer Williams. WiRYPS p.55
You said don't write me a love poem. Pearl Cleage Lomax. RoATW p.29; WeDNNM p.13
You said: in Morocco they make deliberate mistakes. June Jordan. PaNP p.53
You said, "Now take your shoes off." Gwendolyn Brooks. BeEa p.59; WoOGB p.357
You saw the vision in the face of clay. Georgia Douglas Johnson. BrBV p.99
You said you love. Nola Richardson. WhOL p.31
You said you're crying. Tomi Carolyn Tinsley. EbR p.142
You say all the right things. June Vanleer Williams. WiRYPS p.22
You say I'm as cold as ice. Nikki Giovanni. CoCRD p.87
You say that you believe in democracy for everybody. Margaret Burroughs. BlSi p. 121; FBPA p.45
You say yes and I say yes... alas. Mari Evans. NNPUSA p.19
You see boy is universal. Nikki Giovanni. BFBTBJ p.64
You see my whole life is tied up to happiness. Nikki Giovanni. BFBTBJ p.78; BlSi p.234
You see so many graveyard around these little towns. Carolyn M. Rodgers. HeAEG p.68
You see traits in me. June Vanleer Williams. WiRYPS p. 84
You should slice the lying tongue of love. June Jordan. ThTDID p.82
You stand out in your passport. Jayne Cortez. MoOP p.44
You Still Don't Know Their Names. Rita Brady Keifer. NeJCL p.8
You sweet Black semitic angles seemless cape. Jodi Braxton. SoITM p.30
You take these fingers bid them

soft. Patricia Parker. MoIB p.132
You talked of the sun and moon. Carolyn M. Rodgers. NaPr p. 117; RoATW p.26; SoBB p.20
You Taught Me Love.** Frederica Katheryne Bunton. EbR p.17
You there, ain't your mama never taught you no manners. Jodi Braxton. SoITM p.28
You think you need me. Carolyn M. Rodgers. BlSi p.176; HoIGO p.54
You threw sand in my hair. Naomi F. Faust. PoBBl p.32
You tip inside my mind. C. Tillery Banks. HeTMWL p.26
You, too, are of the godless lot they say. Margaret Danner. DoOAT p.101
You Took This World Away From Us. Kali Grosvenor. PBK p.25
You trembled like an egg. Pinkie Gordon Lane. WiTh p.9
You understand how very often you are the one. Carolyn M. Rodgers. HoIGO p.57
You used to ricochet down the street at evening time. Pinkie Gordon Lane. MyFe p. 49; WiTh p.8
You used to say "June." June Jordan. PaNP p.40
You vowed eternal love to me today. Ruby Berkley Goodwin. NegVo p.61
You walk downstairs to see this man. June Jordan. ThTDID p. 183
You want me and I want you. Nola Richardson. WhOL p.67
You want me and your cake too. Nola Richardson. WhOL p.65
You wear wigs of fulfillment. Judy Dothard Simmons. JuB p. 12
You were a mistake my mother told me. Patricia Parker. ChOM p.17; MoIB p.19
You were a sophist. Gwendolyn B. Bennett. BlSi p.75; CaD p. 156
You Were Gone.** Nikki Giovanni. ThWRNW p.60
You were made of white clay. Naomi Evans Vaughn. NegVo p. 160
You Were Never Miss Brown to Me. Sherley Williams. CoAAAW p. 386
You were our first brave ones to defy their dissonance of hate with your silence. Margaret Walker. PFND p.11
You weren't even a revolutionary. Julianne Perry. PoBa p.516
You who descend river by river. Anonymous. MBP p.39
You who have held love. Valerie Parks. NegVo p.123
You will be alone at last. Lucille Clifton. TwW p.43
You will bloom in a family of flowers. Lucille Clifton. TwW p.32
You will enter morning without error. Lucille Clifton. TwW p.42
You Will Not Put Out My Light. C. Tillery Banks. HeTMWL p.72
You with your bullshit niggerish ways want to destroy me. Nikki Giovanni. BFBTBJ p. 98; BrT p.60
You would not recognize yourself if I should tell you. Naomi Long Madgett. KAL p.178
You wouldn't want a poem, would you? Naomi Long Madgett. PiLAF p.33
You wrap the thickest silence of ten years. Linda Brown Bragg. LoSBM p.9
You Wrote, "It is From Love I Ask the Devil In."** Gloria Oden. RESUR p.49
Young Africans. Gwendolyn Brooks. BrT p.37; FaP p.18
Young and the Old, The. Gertrude Blackwell Bailey. IfWCF p.42
Young Angry Men. Patricia Ford. PoBBl p.59
Young ash craven never near to gold. June Jordan. SCh p. 12; ThTDID p.156
Young/black girl. Sonia Sanchez. BluB p.26; IvBAW p.57
Young Blackland Beautiful In Pursuit of Ancient Freedom Dreams. Mari Evans. IABW p.85

Yourng body light as winter sunshine, A. Maya Angelou. AnSIR p.30
Young Boy Blues. Anonymous. BlWOA p.887
Young David: Birmingham, A. Helen. Morgan Brooks. PoNe p. 276
Young Girl Crying in the Street. Jennifer Blackman Lawson. BlIMT p.45
Young Heroes. Gwendolyn Brooks. BlP p.172
Young Katy's heart was breaking. Eloise Culver. GANIV p.36
Young marse, you come to beat me. Elma Stuckey. BiGa p.42
Young Men Dream.** Marva Tatum Smith. BeYM p.3
Young sweet thing moving across the floor. Colleen McElroy. MuDLSG p.9
Young Voices Cry, The. Mae V. Cowdery. WLOV p.9
Young Wisdom. Mae V. Cowdery. WLOV p.32
Young Womanhood. Sonia Sanchez. BluB p.30
Your beach air yields an arrowhead of quartz. Jodi Braxton. SoITM p.47
Your beauty is a thunder. Maya Angelou. JGM p.37
Your Children. Gertrude Blackwell Bailey. IfWCF p.43
Your children are what we make them. Gertrude Blackwell Bailey. IfWCF p.43
Your dolor de cabeza you blame on me. Harryette Mullen. TTW p.50
Your Eyes. Georgia Douglas Johnson. ALC p.45
Your eyes are widely open flowers. Alice Walker. RePOP p.52
Your eyes--dark pools, so calm and deep. Georgia Douglas Johnson. ALC p.45
Your Eyes Like Cups of Wine. Vanessa Howard. ScWh p.30
Your Eyes Sparkle With Approval.** C. Tillery Banks. HeTMWL p.56
Your face (with its inverted new moon cast of pain carved on the lips). Margaret Danner. DoOAT p.101
Your hand in my hand. Lucy Mae Turner. BCF p.36
Your Hands. Angelina Weld Grimke. CaD p.44; NeNRe p. 84; PoBA p.16; ReFNA p.25; RoATW p.3
Your hands easy weight, teasing the bees. Maya Angelou. AnSIR p.5
Your hands move across the table. Naomi Long Madgett. OnATM p.32
Your heart was an alter. Beatrice M. Murphy. NegVo p.113
Your innocence Tells on you in Early Morning. Jodi Braxton. SoITM p.35
Your lashes leave me naked in the square. Audre Lorde. NeHS p.23
Your Life. Gertrude Blackwell Bailey. IfWCF p.23
Your lightest breath may fan my cheek. Georgia Douglas Johnson. ALC p.58
Your love was a port. Sonia Sanchez. LoP p.61
Your loving late in coming. Sonia Sanchez. LoP p.85
Your momma kissed the chauffeur. Maya Angelou. JGM p.47
Your momma took to shouting. Maya Angelou. JGM p.46
Your mouth filled with words of pain. Mae Jackson. CaPWY p.8
Your name scrawled on a bit of paper moves me. Alice Walker. RePOP p.63
Your night is here so sleep little one. Marion Nicholes. LiS p.18
Your skin like dawn. Maya Angelou. OhPWFW p.11
Your smile, delicate rumor of peace. Maya Angelou. BlSi p. 264; OhPWFW p.51
Your Songs. Gwendolyn Bennett. CaD p.197
Your speaking silence floods the air. Pinkie Gordon Lane. MyFe p.42
Your subjects hope, dread sire. Phillis Wheatley. PAL p.34; PPW p.6

Your Task. Gertrude Blackwell Bailey. IfWCF p.38
Your voice at times a fist. Maya Angelou. JGM p.14
Your voice keeps ringing down the day in accents soft and mild. Georgia Douglas Johnson. ALC p.7
Your voice sister tells me another child has come. Pearl Cleage Lomax. DeDF p.25
Your World. Georgia Douglas Johnson. AmNP p.23; HoFTD p.170
Your world is as big as you make it. Georgia Douglas Johnson. AmNP p.23; HoFTD p.170
You're drunken of the cup of joy. Dorothy Lee Louise Shaed. NegVo p.139
"You're like one of the family." June Vanleer Williams. WiRYPS p.72
You're like the skinny fold. Harryette Mullen. TTW p.1
You're mad? I'm the one who's mad. Nola Richardson. WhOL p.81
You're Not Here. Nola Richardson. WhOL p.29
Yourself. Gertrude Blackwell Bailey. IfWCF p.33
Youth. Georgia Douglas Johnson. BANP p.182; GoS p.77; HWOP p.24; PoN p.57; PoNe p.74
Youth apathetic, youth energetic, breeding children before they are striplings. Pauli Murray. DaTAOP p.53
Youth, bloody with flags. Pauli Murray. DaTAOP p.51
Youth Cult, The. Judy Dothard Simmons. JuB p.22
Youth, 1933. Pauli Murray. DaTAOP p.51
Youth to Age. Pauli Murray. DaTAOP p.50
Youth who boasts of its strong personality. Pauli Murray. DaTAOP p.52
Youth's Progeny. Georgia Douglas Johnson. ALC p.29
You've got another love and I know it. Maya Angelou. OhPWFW p.14
You've heard about this railroad; its runs were late at night. Eloise Culver. GANIV p.27
You've just got to dig Sly and the Family Stone. Nikki Giovanni. BFBTBJ p.75; BrT p.55; EgT p.33. UNBP p.280
Yr hips n sequin slippers scamper in the night. Ntozake Shange. NaEd p.68
Yuh Lookin Good. Carolyn M. Rodgers. BlP p.266
Yusef touches silence. Mari Evans. NIGHT p.9

- Z -

Za Ki Tan Ke Palay Lot. Audre Lorde. ChPON p.101
Zetta used to call her man "Pig." Sandra Royster. WoTa p.11
Zimbabwe and we are one. Safiya Henderson. CoAAAW p.134
Zip e Duden Duden. Anonymous. BlWOA p.236
Zoom (The Commodores). Thulani Davis. AlTRGR p.36
Zorro Man, A. Maya Angelou. JGM p.5
Zulu King arrived at the new basin, The. Josephine Copeland. GoS p.125
Zulu King: New Oreans (at Mardi Gras(, The. Josephine Copeland. GoS p.125

AUTHOR INDEX

ABRAMSON, DOLORES
- Can She Go With You?
- I Am
- To Be...
- To My Sisters Out There

ADAMS, JEANETTE
- And We Shall Eat to Live
- Contemplatin
- Picture, The
- Proposal for Brothers and Sisters

ADA
- Lines
- Lines Suggested on Reading 'An Appeal to Christian Women of the South' by A. E. Grimke
- To the Memory of J. Horace Kimball
- Untitled

AFIF, FATIMAH
- Tanka

ALBA, NANINA
- Be Daedalus
- For Malcolm

ALEE, LYCURGUS J.
- Upon Finding a False Friend

ALEXANDER, MARGARET see WALKER, MARGARET

ALEXANDRE, MARIE E.
- My Soul

ALEXIS
- Sacrifice

ALLAH, FAREEDAH
- Ballad for the Brother
- Cinderella
- Funky Football
- Generation Gap, The
- Hush Honey
- Lawd, Dese Colored Chillun
- My Nan Was Here Today
- You Made It Rain

ALVAREZ, JULIA
- Lonely Tulip Grower

AMA, FAYOLA KAMARIA
- For 'Mamie'

AMINI, JOHARI
- About Communication
- About Man
- And Then...
- Before and After
- Black Expression
- Black Sun
- Black Writer, A
- Brother...
- Celebration, A
- Ceremony
- Childhood
- Coronach
- Faux-Semblant
- For Gwendolyn Brooks - A Whole & Beautiful Spirit
- Harpy
- Hear Our Silence
- I am Too Past Youth
- I See the Long Pull of You
- Identity
- In Celebration of Blk/Men
- Letter to a Blkwoman's Daughter
- 9 Lines
- Posititives
- Promise, The
- Reservation
- Return
- Revolutionary Requiem in Five Parts
- Saint Malcolm
- Signals
- Story for the Remainder
- Sun Heals, A
- There is no Title: Only Echoes

To a Poet I Know
21 Lines
Untitled
Upon Being Black One Friday Night in July
Utopia

ANDERSON, ALICE D.
Poet, The

ANDERSON, ANITA
Spurned Friendship

ANDERSON, EDNA
It Seems to Me

ANDERSON, KATHY ELAINE
Quicksand

ANGELOU, MAYA
Accident
Africa
After
Ain't That Bad?
Alone
America
Artful Pose
Black Ode
Bump d' Bump
California Prodigal
Call Letters, Mrs. V. B.
Calling of Names, The
Chicken - Licken
Child Dead in Old Seas
Come, And Be my Baby
Communication I
Communication II
Conceit, A
Country Lover
Couple, The
Detached, The
Elegy
Faces
For Us, Who Dare not Dare
Gamut, The
Greyday
Harlem Hopscotch
Here's to Adhering
How I Can Lie to You
I Almost Remember
In a Time
In Retrospect
John J
Junkie Monkey Real
Just for a Time
Just Like Job
Kin
Kind of Love, Some Say, A
Lady Luncheon Clud
Late October
Lesson, The
Let's Majeste
Letter to an Aspiring Junkie
Life Doesn't Frighten Me
Little Girl Speaking
Lord, in my Heart
Mama Welfare Roll
Memory, The
Men
Miss Scarlet, Mr. Rhett and Other Latter-Day Saints
Mourning Grace
My Arkansas
My Guilt
No Loser, No Weeper
No No No No
Now Long Ago
On a Bright Day, Next Week
On Aging
On Diverse Deviations
On Reaching Forty
On Working White Liberals
One More Round
Passing Time
Phenomenal Woman Pickin em up and Layin' em Down
Poor Girl
Prisoner
Pusher, The
Refusal
Remembering
Remembrance
Request
Reverses
Riot: 60's
Sense of Insecurity
Sepia Fashion Show
Singer Will not Sing, The
Song for the Old Ones
Sounds Like Pearls
Southeast Arkansas
Still I Rise
Take Time Out
Tears
Telephone, The
Thank You Lord
They Went Home
Thirteens (Black), The
Thirteens (White), The
This Winter Day
Through the Inner City to the Suburbs

Times-Square-Shoeshine-Composition
To a Freedom Fighter
To a Husband
To a Man
To Beat the Child Was Bad Enough
Traveler, The
We Saw Beyond the Seeming
When I Think About Myself
When You Come To Me
Where we Belong, A Duet
Willie
Woman Me
Woman Work
Wonder
Zorro Man, A

ANONYMOUS
All God's Chillen Got Shoes
Another Man Don Gon
Background Blues
Backwater Blues
Bad Man Ballad
Ballit of de Boll Weevil, De
Bed Bug
Bedbug
Big Fat Mama, A
Black Woman
Blessing Without Company
Blues Come from Texas, The
Brothers Sent to the Nam
Cala Vendor's Cry
Casey Jones
Charlie's Rhyme
Chuck Will's Widow Song
"Crab Man"
Creation of Man, The
Crucifixion
Deep River
Did You Feed My Cow?
Didn't my Lord Deliver Daniel?
Dink's Blues
Dis Hammer
Dis Werl Mos Done
Disgrace
Dives and Laz'us
Do, Lawd
Don Wid Driber's Dribin'
Down in the Lonesome Garden
Dry Bones
Easy Rider
Everybody Talkin' 'Bout Heaven
Fattening Frogs for Snakes
Flop, The
Fogyism
Follow the Drinkin'-Gourd
Frankie Baker
Free at Las'
Freed Slave Song
Freedom
Garvey
Gen'el Jackson
Gimme Dat ol' Time Religion
Go Down Moses
Go Down, Old Hannah
Go Tell it on the Mountain
Go'Way From my Window
God (A Folk Sermon)
God of War, The
God's Gonna Set Dis World on Fire
Going Down the Road
Gonna Shout
Good Mornin' Blues
Good Morning, Captain
Gospel Train, The
He Never Said a Mumbling Word
He Paid me Seven
How Long Blues
I am a Spiritual Alcoholic
I got a Home in Dat Rock
I got the Blues
I Heard the Angels Singin
I Love Somebody
I vision God
I'll Wear me a Cotton Dress
I'm a Round-Town Gent
In Dat Great Gittin' Up Mornin'
Invocation of the Creator
Isn't Life Peculiar?
Jack and Dinah Want Freedom
Jaybird
Joe Turner
John Henry
Joshua fit de Battle of Jericho
Juba
Juba Dance
Juber
Just Blues
Kob Antelope
Little (Black) Man
Little David, Play on Yo' Harp
Little Rooster, The
Long-Line Skinner's Blues
Love (Folk)
Many a Thousand Die
Married Woman Blues

Mary, Don You Weep
Misse Got a Gold Chain
Mistah Rabbit
Mistah Banjo
Monte Carlo Blues
Motherless Child
Mount Zion
My Frow Towards the City
My God is a Rock in a Weary Land
My Lord, What a Morning
My Way's Cloudy
Negro Soldier's Civil War Chant
No Mo Cane on Dis Brazis
No More Auction Block
Nobody Knows de Trouble I See
Oh Freedom
Oh, Mary, Don't You Weep
Ol' Ant Kate, She Died So Late
Old Hen Cackled, The
Old Jim Crow
Old Man Know-All
Old Marse John
Old Section Boss, The
Ole Nigger Driber, De
Optimist, The
Oyster Man's Cry
Peep Squirrel
Pick a Bale of Cotton
Pity a Poor Boy
Po Laz'us
Precious Things
Promises of Freedom
Put it Right Here or Keep it out There
Quoits
Railroad Bill
Railroad Section Leader's Song
Rainbow Roun Mah Shoulder
Raise a "Rucus" To-Night
Rise Up, Shepherd and Follow
Rock About my Saro Jane
Roll, Jordan, Roll
Run, Nigger, Run
St. James Infirmary Blues
Sangaree
Sellin' Time
She Hugged me and Kissed Me
Shine and the Titantic
Shorty George
Shout Along, Chillen
Signifying Monkey, The
Slave Marriage Ceremony Supplement
Slave Song
Slavery Chain
Sometimes I feel like a Motherless Child
Song About the Paddyrollers
Song of the Warriors
Song to the Runaway Slave
Soon one Mawnin
SOS
South Carolina Chain Gang Song
Southern Blues
Spelled Backwards
Stackalee
Stackerlee and de Debbil.
Stagolee
Steal Away
Steal Away to Jesus
Stoker's Chant, The
Sweet Potato Man
Swing Low, Sweet Chariot
Take Yo' Time, Miss Lucy
That Hypocrite
This Sun is Hot
Today is Ours
Turtle's Song, The
Uncle Gabriel
Uncle Ike's Roosters
Untitled
Virgin Mary Had a baby Boy
Walk, Talk, Chicken with your Head Pecked
Walk Together Children
Wasn't That a Mighty Day
Watch Your English
Watermelon Vendor's Cry
We Raise de Wheat
We Shall Overcome
We Will Be!
We'll Soon be Free
Were you Dere?
What You Gonna Name That Pretty Little Baby
When-a-Mah Blood Runs Chilly an Col
Who-zen John, Who-za
Wild Negro Bill
Wounds of Jesus, The
You May Bury me in de Eas'
Young Boy Blues
Zip e Duden Duden

ARNEZ, NANCY L.
Birmingham
Brown Child's Prayer, A
Discord
Keep Pushing

Laid Off Blues
Mask, The
Nebulous
New Love
Plea
Poverty Blues
Stood Up
To Be Black in America
What Deeper Sin?
What is a Negro?
Why Don't you Love Us?

BAILEY, GERTRUDE BLACKWELL
African American
Black is not the Man
Black you Are
Blackman Get Off that Corner
Blackman Has done his Part, The
Blind
Cities Crumble
Climbing
Common Sense
Death
Decisions
Drop-Out
Flowers
Footsteps
Future
Great Cities Crumble
Healing Stream
I Refuse to Be
If the Shoe Fits, Wear It
If Your Conscience is Free
Jealousy
Keep Faith
Life
Listen
Looking
Make the First Step
Make Up Your Mind
Mistakes
Mother and Dad
My Garden
Oak Tree
Old
Out of My Way
People Will be People
Pitch in and Help Out
Prayer
President, The
Proud to Be
Reach Out
Stand Tall
Think About It
Thirst
To the Plow
Tomorrow
Ugly
When I Grow Up
Wisdom
Young and the Old, The
Your Children
Your Life
Your Task
Yourself

BANKS, C. TILLERY
Brown Silky Eyes Flashing Stories at Me
Don't Touch me Now!
Door Opens, A
Free Yourself
Going Cold Turkey on Your Ass
Goodbye can be a Hello
I Don't Pretend to Understand
I Might be Lonely
I need a Place
Inside
Inside my Soul you Came
It does not Matter
It is not Important That You do not Say I Thank You
Learning to Lift Myself Higher
Learning to Spend Time With Myself
Leave me Alone!
Loving you is Taking a Ride on a Magic Carpet
Missing the Warmth (of hands Gliding over my Body)
My Tears Don't Come Cheap Anymore
New Direction
No More Ugly days for Me
Not Enough time to say What I Could...
Reflection
Rhythms of a House
Sometimes my Past Closes In...
Sometimes we Pray with our Tears
Time Somebody Told Me
Traveling Together Side by Side
Use to be When my Fuel Tank Hit "E"...

We've Come Such a Long Way
Yeah Tomorrow/Tomorrow
You
You Have Always Been Walking Around
You Make the Feel-in' Good
You Me Us...Moving Towards Something
You will not put out my Light
Your eyes Sparkle with Approval

BARAKA, AMINA
Haiti
I Wanna Make Freedom
Sortin-Out
Soweto Song

BARNETT, DENISE see DAMALI

BAXTER, BARBARA ANNE
"Grow in Hope and Grace"

BELL, VERA
Ancestor on the Auction Block

BENITEZ, LILLIE KATE WALKER
In my eye and Heart and all About the Same Blood

BENNETT, GWENDOLYN
Advice
Fantasy
Hatred
Heritage
Lines Written at the Grave of Alexandre Dumas
Nocturne
On a Birthday
Quatrains
Secret
Song
Sonnet I
Sonnet II
To a Dark Girl
To Usward
Your Songs

BENTON, ARLENA HOWARD
Disappointment

BER, MUSU
Peaches

BERKLEY, CONSTANCE E.
Glowchild
In the Shadows

BERRY, FANNIE
Freed Slave Song

BERRY, JOSIE CRAIG
And Death went Down

BESS, OLEAN
Black Power in the Making
Black Prince, A
Freedom at Last
Friend, A
Lonely Sleepless Night, A
Love
Moon People Speak
My Mother's Blessing
Ode to Barbara
Ode to Nixon
Our Teenagers
Poem to Ethel and Chenese, A
Poem to James Brown, A
Sandy
Tomorrow
When I was a Little Girl
Why

BETHEL, ELAINE
Poem

BEVERLY, KATHARINE
Dreams are so Pale
Night Song
Prayer for a Hill
Resignation
Temptation

BIRD, BESSIE CALHOUN
Proof

BLACKMAN, LOUISE
Miracle
Rain Wish

BLACKWELL, DOROTHY F.
Crescendo
Echo
Nocturne

BLAKELY, NORA
Mama

BLESSITT, BERNADINE
Little Boy's Prayer

BOGUS, S. DIANE
About our Silences
About the Birds and the Be's

All, The
And When the Fire Won't go Out
Beatitude, A
Blind, Cripple and Crazy
Calculated Passion
Chained Still
Chronicle
Concern for our Total Enviroment
Consciousness
Contagion
Copy Right
Crusade
Dream Like Daniel's, A
For E
For Marty
Franklin on U. S. History
Gabble
Ghosts of our Parting, The
God's Exteamination or Society's Souvernirs
I Find no Evil or Three Images & Trust
I Love you Sooner
Incarceration
Inevitably
It was a Day
Longing in California Poem
Merciful Hour, A
Middle of the Beginning, The
Misdemeanor
Miss Brown
Missing in Action
On Seeing my Limitations Outside of the U.S.
One Eyed King
Only to Sleep
Paradox
Poem for Weedie, A
Power and the Glory, The
Ruth Rev.
She Feelings Poem #1
Short Poem #1
Short Poem #3
Small Time Profundity
Small Time Profundity #2
Something About a Little Kid
Taste of Time, The
These Days
Translation
Two Nuns by the Sea
Us
When Two-Year Olds Talk In Their Sleep
Whore
Woman in the Moon
Woman Perception Poem #2
Woman Statement #1

BOHANON, MARY
Black can be Beautiful
Bought and Paid For
Complete Fulfillment
Earth Bosom
Fear Not
Gone
Good God, A
Know This is True
Naked
Plea, A
Suspended
Whut a Dawn

BOURKE, SHARON
I Know she will Pray for Me
I Remember that Day
People of Gleaming Cities, and the Lion's and the Leopard's Brood
Sopranosound, Memory of John

BOYD, MELBA JOYCE
Beer Drops
Cat Eyes
Check the Traps
Dead Wood
Detroit Renaissance
Even When the Moon Don't Shine
Faint Violets
Fingertips and Quiet Moments
For Momma
Gramma Wynn
Grandma's Hands
1965
Sandy's Poem
Silver Lace
Split, The
Sundown Sigh
Sunflowers and Saturdays
Third Face, The
To Darnell and Johnny
Ugly Art
Why?

BOYER, JILL WITHERSPOON
Anniversary
Backstage
But I Say
Detroit City
Detroit Summers

Dream Farmer
For Mama
For my Friends at the Boy's Training School
King Lives
Lean Brown Back
Nam, The
Nine to Five
Our Story
Professors...
Riding the Bus Home
Sambas and Things
Secret Seasons
Star Gazing
Two Countries
When Brothers Forget

BRACEY, JUDITH
Contentment
I Can Be Somebody

BRAGG, LINDA BROWN
Between Trains it Rains
Black Decision at Sundown
Bran Bread
Catch a Snowflake
Don't Honey Me (A Love Song to Black Men)
Going to Africa
Green Apples
Green Arbor, A
Hesitation
I'm Me
Imposition
Jumping
Monologue
On my First Trip to Mississippi
On my way to Nana's House
One Night Lost in a Lifetime
Our Blackness did not Come to us Whole
Poem about Beauty, Blackness, Poetry (and how to be all three) A
Poems Come In, The
Precocious Curiosity
Quick and the Dead, The
This Basket is Heavy
To the Evangelist
Winter Colder than the Last, A
Winter Sonnet
Withdrawal
Words for a Motet

BRAXTON, JODI
Black Sheba
Call Her Back
Contact Contract
Conversion
Devil Will Have You, The
Do you Know Jesus, His Only Son, Our Lord?
Full Moon Chanson
Home: Sea to Sea
Hoo-Dooism
Ile De La Tortue
In Case you Forget
Iwa: Portal of Perception
Let the Day Come
Miss Maime
October 29, 1972 - 1:45 And On
Of New England Rock, 1976
Palace at Four A.M., The
Pegasus
Pizen
Poems for Blackboys in Floppy Tie-Die Hats
Poem on Turning Around
Rising
Security on #406
Sometimes I Think of Maryland
Suicide Poem #3
We Lay There Ageless
Whatever Happened to Black America? Or: The Setzuan Invisibility Black and Blues
Your Innocence tells On You in Early Morning

BRISTER, IOLA M.
Epigram
Negro Speaks of Night, A
Night Club Entrance
Thoughts of the Girl He Left Behind

BROOKS, GWENDOLYN
Andre
Anniad, The
Annie Allen
Appendix to the Anniad (Leaves From a Loose-Leaf War Diary)
Artists' and Models' Ball, The
As Seen by Disciplines
Aspects of Love, Alive in the Ice and Fire, An

At the Hairdresser's
Ballad of Chocolate Mabbie, The
Ballad of Late Annie, The
Ballad of Pearl May Lee
Ballad of Rudolph Reed, The
Ballad of the Light-eyed Little Girl
Battle, The
Bean Eaters, The
Beauty Shoppe
Bessie of Bronzeville Visits Mary and Norman at a Beach-House in New Buffalo
Beverly Hills, Chicago
Big Bessie Throws her son Into the Street
Birth in a Narrow Room, The
Black Wedding Song, A
Blackstone Rangers, The
Boy Breaking Glass
Boy Died in my Alley, The
Bronzeville Man with a Belt in the Back
Bronzeville Mother Loiters in Mississippi, Meanwhile, a Mississippi Mother Burns Bacon, A
Bronzeville Woman in a Red Hat
Callie Ford
Chicago Defender Sends a Man to Little Rock, The
Chicago Picasso, The
Children of the Poor, The
Contemplation of Suicide: The Temptation of Timothy, The
Crazy Woman, The
Date, The
"Do not be Afraid of No"
Downtown Vaudeville
Egg Boiler, The
Elegy in a Rainbow
Empty Woman, The
End of the Day, The
Estimable Mable
Exhaust the Little Moment
Explorer, The
First Fight, Then Fiddle
Firstly Inclined to take What is Told
Five Men Against theme "My Name is Red Hot. Yo Name Ain Doodley Squat
Flags
For Clarice it is Terrible Because with This He takes away all the Popular Songs and the Moonlights and Still Night Hushes and the Movies with Star-eyed Girls
Friend
From The Children of the Poor
Funeral
Gang Girls
Garbage Man: The Man With the Orderly Mind
Gertrude
Ghost at the Quincy Club, The
"God Works in a Mysterious Way"
Hattie Scott
Horses Graze
Hunchback Girl: She Thinks of Heaven
I Love Those Little Booths at Benvenuti's
In Emanuel's Nightmare: Another Coming of Christ
In Honor of David Henderson Brooks, My Father
In the Mecca
Independent Man, The
Intermission
Jack
Jessie Mitchell's Mother
Keorapetse Kgositsile (Willie)
Kid Brain
Kid Bruin
Kitchenette Building
La Bohem Brown
Langston Hughes
Last Quatrain of the Ballad of Emmett Till, The
Leaders, The
Leaves from a Loose-leaf War Diary
Leftist Orator in Washington Park Pleasantly Punishes the Gropers
Life for my Child is Simple, and is Good
Life of Lincoln West, The
Light and Diplomatic Bird, A
Loam Norton
Looking
Love Note
Love Note I: Surely
Love Note II: Flags
Love You Right Back

Lovely Love, A
Lovers of the Poor, The
Malcolm X
Man of the Middle Class, A
Martin Luther King, Jr.
Matthew Cole
Maxie Allen
Medgar Evers
Memorial to Ed Bland
Men of Careful Turns, Haters of Forks in the Road
Mentors
Mother, The
Motto
Mrs. Small
Murder, The
My Dreams, My Works, Must Wait Till After Hell
My Little 'Bout-Town Gal
My Own Sweet Good
Naomi
Negro Hero
Notes From the Childhood and the Girlhood
Obituary for a Living Lady
Of De Witt Williams on his Way to Lincoln Cemetery
Old Laughter
Old Lem
Old-Marrieds, The
Old Mary
Old People Working (Garden, Car)
Old Relative
Old Tennis Player
On the Occasion of the Open-Air Formation of the Olde Tymers' Walking and Nature Club
One Wants a Teller in a Time Like This
Otto
Parents: People Like Our Marriage Maxie and Andrew
Patent Leather
Paul Robinson
Pentinent Considers Another Coming of Mary, A
People Protest in Sprawling Lightless Ways
Pete at the Zoo
Piano at War
Preacher Ruminates Behind The Sermon, The
Primer for Blacks
Priscilla Assails the Sepulchre of Love
Progress, The
"Pygmies are Pygmies Still, Though Perch on Alps
Queen of the Blues
Raymond Melvin Brooks
Riders to the Blood - Red Wrath
Riot
Rites for Cousin Vit, The
Sadie and Maud
Sammie Chester Leaves "Godspell" and Visits Upward Bound on a Lake Forest Lawn, Bringing West Africa
Second Sermon on the Warpland, The
Sermon on the Warpland, The
Sick Man Looks at Flowers
Slim in Hell
Soft Man, The
Song in the Front Yard, A
Song: the Rev. Mobugwu Dickinson Ruminates Behind the Sermon
Sonnet Ballad, The
Southeast Corner
Spaulding and Francois
Speech to the young, Speech to the Progress-Toward
Steam Song
Still do I keep my Look, My Identity
Street in Bronzeville, A
Strong Men, Riding Horses
Sun Came, The
Sunday Chicken
Sundays of Satin-Legs Smith, The
Sunset of the City, A
Surely
Surrealist and Omeaga, A
Takes Time
Third Sermon on the Warpland, The
Throwing out the Flowers
To a Winter Squirrel
To Be in Love
To Don at Salaam
To John Oliver Killens in 1975
To Keorapetse Kgositsile (Willie)
To Those of my Sisters Who Kept Their Naturals
Truth
Two Dedications

Vacant Lot, The
Val
Wall, The
Walter Bradford
Way-Out Morgan
We Real Cool
Weaponed Woman
What Shall I Give my Children
When Handed a Lemon: Make Lemonade
When I Die
When Mrs. Martin's Booker T
When you have Forgotten Sunday: The Love Story
White Troops had Their Orders but the Negroes Looked Like Men, The
Womanhood, The
Womanhood XV
Young Africans
Young Heroes

BROOKS, HELEN MORGAN
Words

BROOKS, ROSA PAUL
Not Wanted
Winter's Morn

BROWN, DELORES A.
Upon Looking at Love

BROWN, ELAINE
Meeting, The

BROWN, ETHEL
'Tis Difficult

BROWN, ISABELLA MARIA
Another Day
Prayer

BROWN, JUANITA
Myself

BROWN, LILLIAN
Disillusion

BROWN, LINDA
Blackness Is...
Little Poem, A
Precocious Curiosity

BROWN, PAM
It Wasn't Just the Rain
"Mama, I Don't Know"

BROWN, TYKI
Journey to Babylon
You

BUFORD, NAOMI E.
Heritage

BUNTON, FREDERICA KATHERYNE
You Taught me Love

BURROUGHS, MARGARET
Apology to my Little Daughter for Apparent Neglect
Beautiful Black and Beloved
Beauty of Black, The
Black Pride
Brother Freedom
Drum Major of the Freedom Parade, The
Everybody But Me
For Eric Toller
Homage to Black Madonnas
Let it be Known
Lines for my Mother
Lines to Blood Brothers and Sisters
Memorial for my Father
Only in this Way
Proem on Africa
To Non-African American Brothers and Sisters
To Soul Folk
What Shall I Tell My Children who are Black

BURT, DELLA
Little Girl's Dream World, A
On the Death of Lisa Lyman
Spirit Flowers

BURTON, JANE W.
Life's Like the Wind

CAINE, MARCELLA
Jungle Flower

CARTER, ALVIES
Call Unto Me
Squirrel in Man, The

CATER, CATHARINE
Here and Now

CAUTION, ETHEL
Sunset

CHAPMAN, NELL
Bread on the Water
Requiem

CHAPPELL, HELEN F.
Flood Song
For the Lips of one Grown Weary
Sophisticated Post Script for a Five-Page Letter

CLARKE, HELEN F.
Shadows
You are Black

CLEAVES, MARY WILKERSON
April Longing
Black Soldier
Why do I love This Country

CLEMENT, THELMA T.
Crimson Rose, A
Desire
Sentiment

CLEMMONS, CAROLE GREGORY
Aria
Black Children
Black Eurydice
Black Poet to Saint Exupèry, A
Bull, The
Conjugation
Cosmic Attack on Poets, The
David
For Dr. Coffin Who Loves
Freedom Song for the Black Woman, A
Ghetto Love Song
Greater Friendship Baptist Church, The
I'm Just a Stranger Here, Heaven is my Home
Long Distance
Love From my Father
Love Has Two
Love Letter
Love Poem
Migration
Nina Simone
NYC Love Poem
On Snobbery
People
Response to the Visiting Poets Names, A
Revelation
To Koala, Who Will Soon Be Extinct
What Order?

CLIFFORD, CARRIE WILLIAMS
Black Draftee From Dixie, The

CLIFTON. LUCILLE
Adam and Eve
Admonitions
Africa
After Kent State
Angels
Anna Speaks of the Childhood of Mary Her Daughter
Apology (to the Panthers)
Astrologer Predicts at Mary's Birth, The
At Last we Killed the Roaches
August the 12th
Aunt Agnes Hatcher Tells
Being Property One Myself
Bodies Broken on the Trail of Tears, The
Breaklight
Cain
Ca'line's Prayer
Calling of the Disciples, The
Calming Kali
Carver, The
Come Home from the Movies
Coming of Kali, The
Confession
Conversation with my Grand-son Waiting to be Con-ceived
Cutting Greens
Daddy 12/02 - 5/69
Daniel
Driving Through New England by Broken Barns and Pastures
Earth
Easter Sunday
Eldridge
Explanations
February 13, 1980
1st, The
For de Lawd
For Her
For Her Hiding Place in Whiteness
For the Bird who Flew A-

gainst our Window one Morn. ing and Broke his Natural Neck
For the Blind
For the Lame
For the Mad
For the Mute
Forgiving my Father
Friends Come
God Send Easter
God Waits for the Wandering World
God's Mood
Good Friday
Good Times
Harriet
Her Love Poem
Holy Night
Homage to my Hair
Homage to my Hips
How he is Coming Then
I am High on the Man Called Crazy
I am not Done Yet
I am Running into a New Year
I once Knew a Man
I was Born in a Hotel

I was Born with Twelve Fingers
I Went to the Valley but I Didn't go to Stay
If I Stand in my Window
If Mama Could See
In Populated Air Our Ancestors Continue
In Salem
In the Evenings
In the Inner City
In this Garden
Incadescence Formless Form
Island Mary
Jackie Robinson
Job
John
Jonah
Joseph
Kali
Last Note to my Girls
Lately Everybody I Meet is a Poet
Later I'll Say I Spent my Life Loving a Great Man
Leanna's Poem
Lesson of the Falling Leaves, The
Let There be New Flowering
Light on my Mother's Tongue
Light that Came to Lucille Clifton, The
Listen Children
Lost Baby Poem, The
Love Rejected
Lucy and her Girls
Lucy one-Eye
Making of Poems, The
Malcolm
Mary
Mary Mary Astonished by God
Mary's Dream
Meeting after the Saviour Came 4/4/68, The
Miss Rosie
Monticello
Morning Mirror
Moses
Mother, I am Mad
My Boys
My Dream About Being White
My Friends
My Mama Moved Among the Days
My Poem
Mystery That Surely Is Present, The
New Bones
New Year
News, The
On the Birth of Bomani
On the Death of Allen's Son
Once and Future Dead, The
Palm Sunday
Perhaps
Poem for my Sisters
Poem on my Fortieth Birthday to my Mother who Died Young
Poet
Prayer
Raising of Lazarus, The
Richard Penniman When his Mama and Daddy Died
Roots
Salt
70's, The
She Insists on Me
She is Dreaming
She Understands Me
Sisters
So Close They Come So Close
Solomon
Some Dreams Hand in the Air
Song

Song of Mary, A
Sonora Desert Poem
Speaking of Loss
Spring Song
Storm Poem, A
Testament
There is a Girl Inside
Thirty Eighth Year of my Life
This Morning
Those Boys that Ran Together
To a Dark Moses
To Bobby Seale
To Joan
To Merle
To Ms. Ann
To the Unborn and Waiting Children
To Thelma who Worried Because I Couldn't Cook
Turning
Visit to Gettysburg, A
Way it Was
What the Mirror Said
Wife
Wise: Having the Ability to Perceive and Adopt the Best Means for Accomplishing an End

CLINTON, DOLORES
Heritage

COBB, ALICE S.
Angela Davis
Searching, The

COBB, BESSIE
Change

COBB, PAMELA
Aliens, The
Autobiography
Axis
Centripetal Forces
Complot
Cultural Isolation
Earth Changes & We Move With It
Earth Mother
Evolution
Footnote to a Part of Life That is Now History
In Our Last Virgin Hours
Limbo
Lyric
My Mistake
Nature of Struggle, The
No Exit
Obeah
One Mind
Prodigal
Race
Reply, The
Resistance
Sacrifice
Shining Ground, The
Testimony of an Eye-Witness
These are the Alternatives
This is Silence
This is the Religion my Father Taught Me
Torturted History of Non-Love, A
(Untitled)
Up Rising: A Day in the History of Revolutionary Warfare

COLEMAN, ANITA SCOTT
America Negra
Black Faces
Colorist, The
Hands
Humility
Theme with Variations

COLEMAN, CAROLYN
Sea Sounds

COLEMAN, ETHEL
Voodoo

COLEMAN, JAMYE HARRIS
Impossibility
Swing of Life, The

COLEMAN, WANDA
About Flowers
Accounts Payable
After His Flight
Art in the Court of the Blue Fag (1)
Art in the Court of the Blue Fag (2)
Art in the Court of the Blue Fag (3)
Art in the Court of the Blue Fag (4)
Art in the Court of the Blue Fag (5)
Art in the Court of the Blue Fag (6)

At the Top
Aunt Jessie
Beaches: Why I Don't Care for Them
Beserk on Hollywood Boulevard
Beyond Sisters
Black Dust
Black Woman's Hole
Blind Betty
Breast Examination
Coffee
Collage
Cousin Mary
Dear Little Boy
Decor
Deuce of Cups, The
Doctor Spider
Dog Suicide
Doing Battle with the Wolf
Drone
Emotional Con Meets a Virginal Ideal, The
Gay Bar
Ghetto
His Eye into This Room
His Old Flame Lady Venice
Indian Summer
Kathy (1)
Kathy (2)
Landing Place
Las Turistas Negros Grande
Library, The
Luz
Lyric
Man Behind the Woman, The
Mexico Entered the Door on the Wind
Midnight Carries me South along Illusion Ave.
Natural Habitat of Things That Bite
New Leaf
No Woman's Land
Offering of Paws, An
On Heaven Street at one A.M.
On the Asphalt
On the Train
Overdose of Lovers, An
Poet After Surgery
Rapping with Opportunity
Red Queen, The
Sessions
Sidewalk
Somewhere
Son of A
Splitz
Starbound
Staying and Not Staying
Stephen
Stephen's Hair
Sweet Mama Wanda Tells Fortunes for a Price
Tequila Sunrise
They Came Knocking on my Door at 7 A.M.
Three Trees
To the Original Poet
Today
Today I am a Homicide in the North of the City
24 Hours Up
Untitled
Untitled
Waiting for Paul
Wanda in Worryland
Watching
Way They Feel, The
Wet Thursday
Where I Live
Woman and Her Thang, The
Woman Eater
Woman of Cups, The
Women in My Life, The
Women of My Color
Word Game
You Hear About Them
You Judge a Man by the Silence He Keeps

COLLINS, HELEN JOHNSON
To an Avenue Spirit

COLLINS, JEAN
Darwin Evolved

CONLEY, CYNTHIA
Praise Due to Gwen Brooks

CONNOR-BEY, BRENDA
Dancer, The
Martha
Pretending

COPELAND, JOSEPHINE
Zulu King: New Orleans (At Mardi Gras), The

COPPS, JACQUELINE
When I was a Child

CORTEZ, JAYNE
Acceptance Speech

African Night Suite
Alberta Alberta
America 1973
And Always
And Another Look at You
And From Your Mouth
Appearances
Assets
Back Home in Benin City
Big Fine Woman from Ruleville
Bleeker Street
Blood Suckers
Blues, A
Bowery Street
Bricks
Brooding
Call the Night
Carolina Kingston
Chocolate
Collage for Romare Bearden
Commitment
Complicity
Consultation
Do You Think
Drums Everywhere Drums
Drying Spit Blues
Everything is Wonderful
Expenditures Economic Love Song 1
Feathers
Festivals & Funerals
Firespitters
Flame
For Real
For the Brave Young Students in Soweto
For the Poets
Give me the Red on the Black of the Bullet
Grinding Vibrato
Herald Square
Here I Am
Homicide 1973
I am New York City
I and I
I Forgot to Remember
I Keep the Tremor
I Remember
I See Chango Pozo
I Would like to be Serene
If I Were There
If the Drum is a Woman
Ife Night
Illusions of Visions
I'm a Worker
I'm not Saying
In a Stream of Ink
In the Everyday Routine
In the Line of Duty
In the Morning
Indelible
Initiation
It Goes Deep
It's Nothing
Know Yourself
Lato on Tomorrow
Law and Order
Lead
Lexington 196 Street Stop
Libations
Lonely Woman
Lynch Fragment
Lynch Fragment 2
Madness Without Head
Making It
Men's Settlement House
Mercenaries & Minstrels
National Security
New Cologne, A
Nighttrains
No Simple Explanations
Ogun's Friend
Once Upon a Road
Orange Chiffon
Orchard Street
Orisha
Pearl Sheba
Phraseology
Plain Truth
Pray for the Lovers
Promise, The
Push Back the Catastrophes
Rape
Red Pepper Poet, The
Remembrance
Rhythm & Blues
Rising, The
Rose Solitude
Saturdays
Screams
Shooting Star
So Long
So Many Feathers
Solo
Solomon Mahlangu Freedom Fighter from Mamelodo
Song for Kwame
Stanton Street
Stockpiling
Suppression
Tapping
Tell Me

There it Is
These are the Times
They Came Again in 1970 in 1980
3 Day New York Blues
To a Friend
To the Artist who Just Happens to be Black
Today on this Day
Under the Edge of February
Watch Out
Watching a Parade in Harlem 1970
When I Look at Wilfredo Lam's Paintings
When I Think
You Know

COUSINS, LINDA
Dialogue with Lije
I can luv Blkman
Meditations of an Unwed Mother-to-be
Sorry 'Bout That
Untitled Poem

COWDERY, MAE V.
Advice to the Lovelorn
And so it is With Love
Contrast
Dawn Cities
Denial
Dusk
Each Night
Exultation
Farewell
Feast
For a New Mother
Four Poems After the Japanese
Goal
God is Kind
Haunted
Having Had You
Heritage
I Sit and Wait for Beauty
If I Must Know
If We Part Now
Insatiate
Interlude
Lamps
Lines to a Sophisticate
Longings
Love Song for Summer
Nostalgia
Of Earth
Pastorale
Poem...for a Lover
Poet's Query
Poplar Tree
Resurrection
Sequel
Shattered Mirror
Some Hands are Lovelier
Spring Lament
Spring Poem in Winter
Strain of Music
Three Poems for my Daughter
To the Veterans of Future Wars
Totality
Tree...to...B.H.
Unknown Soldier
We Lift our Voices
Wind Blows, The
Young Voices Cry, The
Young Wisdom

COX, THELMA PARKER
Evolution
Frustration, a Heritage

CUESTAS, KATHERINE L.
I Seek
Mea Culpa
Poem

CUGLAR, LOIS AUGUSTA
Consecration

CULVER, ELOISE
Abraham Lincoln
Benjamin Banneker
Booker T. Washington
Crispus Attucks
Dr. Carter G. Woodson
Dr. Charles R. Drew
Dr. Daniel Hale Williams
Elijah J. McCoy
Frederick Douglass
Dr. George Washington Carver
Harriet Tubman
Henry O. Tanner
Henry Wadsworth Longfellow
Ira Aldridge
James Meredith
Jan E. Matzeliger
Jesse Owens
Joe Louis
Joel A. Rogers
Katherine Ferguson

Langston Hughes
Lewis Adams
Mahalia Jackson
Marian Anderson
Martin Luther King
Dr. Mary M. Bethune
My Brother
Negro Spirituals
Newest Star, The
Paul Robeson
Phillis WHeatley
Ralph Bunche
Richard Allen
Robert S. Abbott
Roland Hayes
Sojourner Truth
Song to Jackie Robinson
To the Freedom
Underground Railroad
Dr. W. E. B. DuBois
William Leo Hansberry
Wilma Rudolph

CUMBO, KATTIE M.
African Beauty Rose
Age
All Hung Up
Anatomy of Frustration
Another Time, Another Place
Bahamas I
Bahamas II
Black Future
Black Goddess
Black Sister
Call for Black Unity, A
Ceremony
Consumed (For Brother LeRoi)
Domestics
I'm a Dreamer
Indifference
It's Time (Repatriation... Africa)?
Morning After...Love, The
Night, The
Nocturnal Sounds
Not Blue
November/December (Echoing Voices of Remembrances)
Now I Understand
Of our Love
Ring-Around-The-Rosy
Song From Brooklyn, A
That's a Summer Storm
This Island Now (Jamaica)
Three Poems for Nat Nakasa
Unknowns

CURRY, LINDA
Death Prosecuting
For Nina Simone Wherever You Are
No Way Out

CUTHBERT, MARION VERA
Great Laws, The
Great Truths
I and Me
Immortality
Life of God. The
We can Know Surely

DAMALI (DENISE BURNETT)
Angela
Black Disabled Veteran, The
Calm, The
Euclid Street
His Hands
I Am
Matter of Money, A
Observations of a Saturday Night Crowd
Revolution
Soul-Home Feeling
That we May Be
Troost Express
Two Black Men on the Front Page

DANIEL, PORTIA BIRD
God Gave me a Son
Lament

DANIELS, IONIE
Old Jonah

DANNER, MARGARET
Africa, Drifting Through Me Sings
Alaska
AMSAC
America Coach of Aesthetics, An
And he Carves These "Dudes"
And Through the Caribbean Sea
And to Their Friends
As a Businessman
As Critic
At Home in Africa
At Home in Dakar
Be Like This Porcupine Fish
Be Michael
Beale Street (Of the Mind)

Reaffirmed
Beautiful? You are the Most
Belle Isle
Best Loved of Africa
Beth
Black on the Back of Black
Black Power Language
Boneman
Boneman and my Senufo Masque, The
Bridge of Friendship and Understanding
By Their Fruits
Captive Artist, The
Chicago Art Scene 1967 Just as our African Ancestors Did
Christmas Soiree, The Missing Object of African Art
Citizens of the World
Convert, The
Cultural Cathedrals
Dance of the Abakweta, The
Detroit Michigan
Dipped Deeply into the Full Ocean
Down of the Thistle, The
Elevator Man Adheres to Form, The
Endangered Species, The
Endowed
Etta Moten's Attic
Far From Africa: Four Poems
Fifth Michael, The
Flamingo
For Beauty
For Mrs. Lightfoot
For Muffin
For There's no end to the Suffering a Female Will Bear for Beauty
From Esse to Handy to Hayes
Garnishing the Aviary
Gold is the Shade Esperanto
Goodbye David Tamunemi West
Grandson is a Hoticeberg, A
Her Blood, Drifting Through Me, Sing
Here and in That Same Light
Home
I Follow the Green Man
I Look at the Waves and Cry
I Reach for You
I Salute:
I Saw no Gain at all in Any Gain
I Welcome Lace
I'll Walk the Tightrope
In a Bone White Frame
In Shades of Van Gogh
In the Art Institute on St. Valentine's Day
In the Baha'I Mirror
Influenced-By-Benin Onyema of Touch
Inheritance for Muffin
Is There no Tangerine Witched Fire
Jeff Donaldson's Wall, Five Years Later
Just as Our African Ancestors Did
Keller is the Swingingest
Kewpie
La, Lala, La, La
Lady Executive Looks at a Mangbetu Palm Wine Jug, The
Lake Michigan's Waves
Langston Hughes A Man of the New Day
Langston Hughes Made It
Let Them Wear Pale Orchid Shoes
Like Breaths
Like Rain Drops on a Window pane
Like This Jewel-Studded, Carved-From-Ivory, Leopard
Like Thunder Among Tall Buildings
Malcolm X, a Lover of the Grass Roots
Mendacity
Michigan Willows Do not Weep
Missing Missionaries, The
Muffin at the Baha'i Temple
Muffin, His Baba and the Boneman
Muffin on the Population Explosion
My Birthright, Too
Name Michael Brings the Whirr of Wings, The
1964 Valentine to my Grandson
Ninth Michael, The
Nitecaps I
No Violin at All
Nobody Knows Tomorrow
Not in a Name

Old Spice
On Finding Arts Extended Gallery and You
On the Day When Nobody Smiled
Ooh, My Abyssinian Kitten, Be Fun Again
Painted Lady, The
Passive Resistance
Patriarch, The
Points of View
Preferences
Prejudice
Pure Intention, A
Rhetoric of Langston Hughes
Sadie's Playhouse
Samuel Allen's Soul Dances
Seldom Seen
'Sensuous Lion, The
Slave and the Iron Lace, The
Small Bells of Benin, The
Sparrow is a Bird, A
Startled Waves Began to Recede, The
Studies of a Honey Peach Philosopher of Art
Tale of the Newborn with Tappering Nails, The
That I May Gird to Meet My Death
There was this Michael From My Motherland
These Beasts and the Benin Bronze
This is an African Worm
This Kind of Artist
This Little Senufo Bird
This Two-Toned Stork of a Hairpin, This Comb
Through the Varied Patterened Lace
To a Few of the Most Lovely
To a Mounted Ivory Masque Pin
To a Nigerian Student of Metallurgy
To Etta Moten
To Maqui
To Rodger Wilson's Harlequin
To the Bronze Head
To the Bronze Mosque
To "The You"
Today Requires a Lace of Truths
Valentine
Valentine (Nineteen Sixty Six)
Vibes
Visit of the Professor of Aesthetics, The
We had Slept in the Old Beds Too Long
While Everyone Wears Black That's Chic in Apring
Who, But You Can Tether the Tone of a Thief
Will the Luna Moth Sigh
Witches
Witches II
You are a Double-Dipped Copper-Bottomed Pot

DAVENPORT, GERTRUDE
My Lover is a Fisherman

DAVIS, GLORIA
To Egypt

DAVIS, LA VERNE
I Love...
To Whom it Does Concern Blue is my Favorite Color

DAVIS, NORA
Meditation

DAVIS, RONDA
Debra: an Africanese Name Reading on the Sound of Debra
I am Here to Announce
Invitation
Parasitosis
Personality Sketch: Bill, A
Poems About Playmates
Rip-Off
Spacin

DAVIS, THADIOUS M.
Asante Sana, Te Te
Double Take at Relais De L'espadon
It's All the Same
"Honeysuckle was the Saddest Color of All, I Think"
Remembering Fannie Lou Hamer

DAVIS, THULANI
Acquittal
All the Renegade Ghosts Rise
At Times one can Know
C. T. at the Five Spot
Celine - Celine

Childhood
Cicatrix
Colors of the Spirit
Consulting Oracles
Could you Get the Door?
Delirium
Delirium No. 4
Desire 1
For Janet Gaillard
Forest Green
Goes Without Saying
He Didn't Give up He was Taken
I Write Because I am Afraid of Dying
Last Arms
Love Poem
Melodrama
Missing Manuscript
More Melodrama
Nobody's Ever Heard
Old Movies
On 5 Compositions of Roscoe Mitchell
On Not Calling on Cranes in the Night
On not Sending Love Letters to Cranes
One Who so Hated the War
Parable
Rogue & Jar: 4/27/77
Shadow & Veil
Silver Creek, Mississippi
Song for Nkazi or the Final Ironies
Song to Some Other Man
Storyville, New York 7/27/77
Wantongold Dream
Work
Yes
Zoom (The Commodores)

DELANY, CLARISSA SCOTT
Interim
Joy
Mask, The
Solace

DERRICOTTE, TOI
Divorce
Doll Poem
Empress of the Death House, The
Feeding, The
Face/ As it Must Be/ Of Love, The
From a Group of Poems Thinking About Anne Sexton on the Anniversary of Her Death
Funeral Parade, The
Last Will of one Who Lived Alone
Mirror Poems, The
Ms. Claus
Naming, The
New Lady Godiva
Nun
Poem No. 1
Sleeping With Mr. Death
Story of a Very Broken Lady
Trees
Unburying the Bird

DE VEAUX, ALEXIS
... And Then she Said
French Doors: a Vignette
Woman Who Lives in the Botanical Gardens, The

DICKERSON, JUANITA M.
Pulkha

DICKINSON, BLANCHE TAYLOR
Four Walls
Poem
Revelation
That Hill
Things said when He Was Gone
To an Icicle
Walls of Jericho, The

DUBONEE, YLESSA
Departure
Nocturne

DUNHAM, KATHERINE
Babies of Biafra, The
Lesson, The
Mathematics

EARLEY, JACKIE
Gospel Truth, The
One Thousand Nine Hundred & Sixty-Eight Winters
To Be a Woman

EASTON, Y. W. (YVONNE WATKINS)
Welcome, The

ELLISTON, BOBBRETTA M.
Brother, Brother I Dearly

Love Thee But...
Inquisition, The
Sweet Land of Everything to Thee I Sing

ELLISTON, MAXINE HALL
For Gwen

EMERUWA, LEATRICE
Bell Jangles...Jars Loud, The
Bitter Lemon
Black Girl, Black Girl
Blues
Blues Poem, A
Dear Dorothy: In Loving Memoriam
Elevens
Fad
First Date
For What-sa-Name
I'm Gonna Be Long Gone, Baby
In Reference to: International Women's Year
In the Blue Room
It's Two O'Clock in the Morning
Jamaica, W. I. Haika
Johnny-Come-Lately
Making Out
Models
Mother
Notes Upon Vanessa's Promotion Ceremony
105th and Euclid Street Peddler's Song, A
Personals
Poem for the New Year, A
Proposition
Re: Joan Baez
Soul
Street Scene
Thought
Thoughts
Winter Night Song

EVANS, MARI
Alarm Clock, The
And the Hotel Room Held Only Him
...And the Old Women Gathered
Apologia
beaTrice Does the Dinner
Black Jam for dr. Negro
Black Queen Blues
Blues in B^b
Boss Communication
Brother...the Twilight
Cage Alive with the Vibrations, The
Cell Block
Come Sunday
Conceptuality
Conflict
Curving Stonesteps in the Sun
Daufuskie
Daufuskie (Four Movements)
Daufuskie: Jake
Daufuskie: Janis
Daufuskie: The People Gather
Days of my Mindlessness, The
Do we Be There Waiting
Early in the Mornin'
El Hajj Malik Shabazz
Emancipation of George-Hector (A colored Turtle)
Escape
Eulogy for all our Murdered Children
Expendables, The
Eyes Gentled at the Corners So
Face on the Sunwarmed Granite
Flames
Forever Vagrant and Unowned
Friday Cadies of the Pay Envelope
Good Assassination Should Be Quiet, A
Great Civil Rights Law (A. D. 1964)
Grits and Rice Grains
Hegira
Here--Hold my Hand
Homecoming
How Far Away is Not Soon
How Will you Call Me, Brother
I am a Black Woman
I am not Lazy
I CAn no Longer Sing
I Was Not Really Left Behind
I Who Would Encompass Millions
...if i had a Gun that would Shoot
If There be Sorrow
If you Have Had Your Midnights
Image

In the Wake of My Departed
In This Cold Day Who Throws the Stones
Insurgent, The
Into Blackness Softly
Janis
Jake
Justice All Good
Langston
Let Us be That Something
Maria Pina & the B & G Grill
Marrow of my Bone
My Man let me Pull Your Coat
Nicodemus Quartette:I
Nicodemus Quartette;II
Nicodemus Quartette:III
Nicodemus Quartette:IV
Nigger Who is Now Hunting You, The
No One Knows the Year
Odyssey
On the Death of Boochie By Starvation
Once Again the Poets
One More Black Belt Gone
Oriki: for James Mark Essex and the Others
People Gather, The
Point of No Return
Princeling
Re Entry
Rebel, The
Remembering Willie
Root
Schoolhouse, The
7:25 Trolley, The
Shrine to What Should Be
Silver Cell, The
Speak the Truth to the People
Spectrum
Status Symbol
Street Lady
Sudden Sight, The
Thin-Sliced
Things is Changing
This is CTR Reed
Time is Now, The
To a Child That Was
To Mother and Steve
Tune for Two Fingers
Uhuru
Uhuru Ube Rallies (... and the Sound of Weeping)
Untitled I
Untitled II
Vive Noir
Wail
Way of Things, The
What Time is It?
When in Rome...
Where Have you Gone?
Whisper Together Brethren
Who Can be Born Black
Who Would Encompass Millions
World I See, The
Writers, The
Young Black and Beautiful in Pursuit of Ancient Freedom Dreams, The

FABIO, SARAH WEBSTER
All Day We've Longed for Night
Back into the Garden
Black Man's Feast
Bronzeville Breakthrough
Evil is no Black Thing
Live Celebration
Race Results, U.S.A., 1966
To Turn from Love
Tribute to Duke
Work it Out

FAUSET, JESSIE REDMOND
Christmas Eve in France
Dead Fires
Dining Afflatus
Enigma
Fragment
La Vie C'est La Vie
Noblesse Oblige
Oblivion
Oriflamme
Rencontre
Return, The
Rondeau
Touche
Words! Words!

FAUST, NAOMI
Danny Takes the Bus
On That One Day
One Man's Confession of Brotherhood

FERDINAND, VAL
Blues (in two parts) The
Food For Thought
2 B Blk
Whi/te Boys Gone

FERNANDIS, SARAH COLLINS

Vision, A

FIELDS, JULIA
Aarkvark
Accident Edgecombe General Hospital May 16, 1968
Alabama
Ambrosia
And Beauty's All Around
Black Students
Boats in Winter
Chopin Deciphered
Dancer, The
Death in Autumn
Eulogy for Philosophers
Flowers
For Malcolm X
Generations, The
High on the Hog
I Have Grown Weary
I Heard a Young Man Saying
I, Woman
If Love Dies
In the End Let All White Racists Thank the Holy Jackass
Langston Hughes
Madness one Monday Evening
Masks
No Time for Poetry
Pastels
Poem
Poem for Heroes, A
Poems: Birmingham 1962-1964
Strange
Testimonials
Untitled Poem

FINDLEY, CATHERINE L.
Icicles on Trees
Perception

FORD, PATRICIA
Young Angry Men

FORD, THERESA
Maggie

FREEMAN, CAROL S.
Christmas Morning I
Gift

GAILLARD, JULIA
Jus' Livin'

GARCIA, FRANCES
Blood is Thicker than Water, But.........
My Jibaro Man
Who Am I

GARCIA, NORMA LOPEZ
To a Spaniard, Dying

GATES, BETTY
Mamma Settles the Dropout Problem

GEE, LETHONIA
Black Music Man
By Glistening Dancing Seas

GERSON, RISA
I Wish

GIBBS, RUTH DUCKETT
Colors
Just Asked
Retort
What's in a Word?

GIDDINGS, PAULA
Rebirth

GILLISON, LENORA
Supremacy

GIOVANNI, NIKKI
Adulthood
Adulthood (For Claudia)
Adulthood II
Africa
Africa I
Africa II
Age
Alabama Poem
All I Gotta Do
Alone
Always There are Children
And Another Think
And Sometimes I Sit
Atrocities
Autumn Poems
Balances
Beautiful Black Men
Because
Beep Beep Poem, The
Being and Nothingness
Black Judgement
Black Power
Black Separatism
Boxes

Butterfly, The
Cancers
Categories
Certain Peace, A
Charles White
Choices
Communication
Concerning one Responsible Negro With too Much Power
Conversation
Cotton Candy on a Rainy Day
Covers
Crutches
Cultural Exchange
Cyclops in the Ocean, The
Dance Committee, The (Concerning Jean-Leon Destine)
December of my Springs, The
Detroit Conference of Unity and Art (For HRB)
Dragon Fly, The
Dreams
Drum, The
Each Sunday
Eagles
Ego Tripping
Ever Want to Crawl
Everytime It Rains
Fascinations
Fishy Poem, A
Flying Underground
For a Lady of Pleasure now Retired
For a Poet I Know
For an Intellectual Audience
For Gwendolyn Brooks
For Harold Logan
For Saundra
For the Masai Warriors
For Theresa
For Two Jameses
Forced Retirement
From a Logical Point of View
Funeral of Martin Luther King, Jr.
Game of Games, The
Geni in the Jar, The
Good Night
Great Pax White, The
Gus
Habits
Hampton, Virginia
Hands: For Mother's Day
Harvest
Her Cruising Car
Historical Footnote to Consider only when all Else Fails, The
House Cleaning
Houses
How do you Write a POem?
I am She
I Laughed when I Wrote It (Don't You Think It's Funny
I Only Watch the Bubbles
I Remember
I Want to Sing
I Wrote a Good Omelet
I'm Not Lonely
Intellectualism
Introspection
Jessica, A Bird Who Sings
Jonathan Sitting in Mud
Journey, A
Joy
Just a New York Poem
Kidnap Poem
Kisses
Knoxville, Tennessee
Lady in the Chair, The
Laws of Motion, The
Legacies
Letter to a Bourgeoise Friend Whom I Loved (And Maybe Still do if Love is Valid)
Life Cycles
Life I Led, The
Linkage
Lion in Daniel's Den, The
Litany for People, A
Lorraine Hansberry
Love is a Human Condition
Love Poem (For Real)
Love Thanks
Luxury
Make Up
Masks
Master Charge Blues
Mirrors
Mixed Media
Moon Shines Down, The
Mothers
Mother's Habit
My House
My Poem
My Tower
New Yorkers, The
Night
Nikki-Rosa
No Reservations

Nothing Makes Sense
Of Liberation
On Hearing "The Girl with the Flaxen Hair)
On Seeing Black Journal and Watching Nine Negro Leaders "Give Aid and Comfort to The Enemy" To Quote Richard Nixon
Once a Lady Told Me
Only Song I'm Singing, The
Oppression
Our Detroit Conference (For Don L. Lee)
Patience
Paula the Cat
Personae Poem (For Sylvia Henderson)
Poem
Poem (Because it Came as a Surprise To Me, A)
Poem for a Lady Whose Voice I Like
Poem (For Anna Hedgeman and Alfreda Duster)
Poem For Aretha
Poem For Black Boys
Poem (For BMC No. 1)
Poem (For BMC No. 2)
Poem (For BMC No. 3)
Poem For Carol, A
Poem (For Dudley Randall)
Poem for Ed and Archie
Poem (For Ema)
Poem For Flora
Poem for Lloyd
Poem for My Nephews
Poem (For Nina)
Poem (For PCH)
Poem For Stacia
Poem (For TW)
Poems for Unwed Mothers
Poem (No Name No.1)
Poem (No Name No.2)
Poem (No Name No.3)
Poem of Angela Yvonne Davis
Poem of Friendship, A
Poem Off Center
Poem on the Assassination of Robert F. Kennedy, A
Poetry
Poetry is a Tressel
Prickled Pickles Don't Smile
Rain
Rainbows
Reason I Like Chocolate, The
Records
Reflections/On A Golden Anniversary
Reflections on April 4, 1968
Resignation
Response
Revolutionary Dreams
Revolutionary Music
Rituals
Robin's Poem
Room With the Tapestry Rug, The
Rose Bush, The
Scrapbooks
2nd Rapp
Seduction
Short Essay of Affirmation Explaining Why (With Apologies to the Federal Bureau of the Investigation)
Sky Diving
Snowflakes
Some Uses for them not Stated
Something to be Said For Silence
Sometimes
Song for New-ark, The
Space
Stars
Statement on Conservation, A
Straight Talk
Strawberry Patches
Sun, The
Swaziland
That Day
Their Fathers
They Clapped
This is not for John Lennon
Three/Quarters Time
Tommy's Mommy
Toy Poem
True Import of Present Dialogue, Black vs. Negro, The
Turning (I Need a Better Title)
12 Gates to the City
Two Poems from Barbados
Ugly Honkies or the Election Game and How to Win It
Untitled
Untitled (For Margaret Danner)
Universality

Vacation Time
Very Simple Wish, A
Walking Down Park
Way I Feel, The
We
When I Die
When I Nap
Wild Flowers
Wilmington, Delaware
Winter
Winter Poem
Winter Storm, The
Woman
Woman Gather, The
Woman Poem
Wonder Woman, The
Word for Me...Also, A
Word Poem
World is not a Pleasant Place To Be
Yeah...But...
Yolandé The Panda
You Are There
You Came Too
You Were Gone

GOLDEN, BERNETTE
Morning
There are Seeds to Sow
Words

GOMILLION, E. SHARON
Am I Not a Human Being?
Be Cool Brother
Before Very Long
Black Woman
Dem Black Executives
Genocide Is
He Ain't My Idol
Misery of Being, The
Mistakes
On The Church
Promise, The
Soul Food Goes Elite
Straw Bosses
Wake Up Brothers and Sisters
Why of the Black Child, The

GOODEN, LAURETTA HOLMAN
Dream of Revenge, A
Question to a Mob

GOODLETT, LUCILLE D.
Angie Saves Her Man
'Bout De Moon
Conjuh Bag
Coon Song
Cotton Pickin'
Dead 'oman's Eyes
Fiddle in de Win'
Fishin'
Fox Fish
Hawg Killin'
Hush, Chillun
Jessie Rufus
Low Down Blues
Miss Nancy's Geo'ge
Moanin' Moanin'
Novembah Dusk
Ole Man Jollie
Ox in de Ditch
Preacher Kyo Siam, De
Rivah's a Black Mare
Salia
Siam at de Radio
Soft Soap
Soliloquy
Speretual 'Oman, De
Susie Lou
'Tater Field
Unk' Enoch Mann
Walk, God's Chillun
Whimper, Baby
Yalla Gal

GOODWIN, RUBY BERKLEY
Anxiety
Guilty
I Dream Alone Again
I Sing
If This be Good-bye
New Year's Prayer
Race-Prejudice in America
Rendezvous with God
We Launched A Ship

GORDON, EDYTHE MAE
Buried Deep
Sonnet for June

GORHAM, MYRTLE CAMPBELL
Service, Please

GOSS, LINDA
Revolution Man Black

GOULBOURNE, CARMIN AULD
Letter for El-Hajj Malik El-Shabazz

GRAHAM, LINDA B.
Blackbird, The

Lilies
Orange
Purple

GREENE, EMILY JANE
He's Coming Home at Last

GREER, ROSLYN
Triangle

GREGORY, CAROLE see CLEMMONS, CAROLE GREGORY

GREGORY, YVONNE
Christmas Lullaby for a New-born Child

GRIFFITH, LOIS ELAINE
Prince Harlem

GRIMES, NIKKI
Definition
Fragments: Mouse Trap
Takers, The

GRIMKE, ANGELINA WELD
At April
Black Fingers, The
Dawn
Dusk
Eyes of Regret, The
For the Candle Light
Grass Fingers
Greeness
Hushed by the Hands of Sleep
I Weep
Mona Lisa, A
Paradox
Puppet Playsr, The
Surrender
Tenebris
To Clarissa Scott Delany
To Keep the Memory of Charlotte Forten Grimke
To the Dunbar High School: a Sonnet
Ways o' Men, The
When the Green lies Over the Earth
Winter Twilight, A
Your Hands

GRIMKE, CHARLOTTE FORTEN
Charles Sumner
June Song, A
Parting Hymn, A
Poem
To W. L. G. on Reading his 'Chosen Queen

GROSVENOR, KALI
Black Is
Black is Black
Circles
Colmbes Didn't Discover this World
Do Subways Race
For Nina Simone
For Stokely Carmichael
I Love You Don't
If I Could Fly
If this World Were up side Down
It's a New Day
Lady Bird
Letter to Langston Hughes
Love
My Mother
My People
My People are Black
My Sister is a Sister
Our Black People
Our World is Our
Please Don't Wites
T.V.
This Little Light of Mine
To Otis Redding
We Black People Should
Were is my Head Going
What Happing to the Heroes
When I Grow
When I Grow
When I see Black
When I went to Paris
Who am I
Why are they Mean
Windy Rain
You took this World Away From Us

GUERARD, VERA
At Sea
Spring of Joy

GULLINS, EDNA
"If Winter Comes"
Soul Suffering

HALL-EVANS, JO ANN
Cape Coast Castle Revisited
Seduction

HAMMOND, MRS. J. W.
Optimist, The

HARDNETT, LINDA G.
If Hair Makes me Black, I Must Be Purple
To You

HARPER, FRANCES ELLEN WATKINS
Advice to the Girls
Appeal to my Country Women, An
Building, The
Burdens of All, The
Burial of Sarah, The
Bury me in a Free Land
Crocuses, The
Death of the Old Sea King
Dedication Poem
"Do not Cheer, Men are Dying," said Capt. Phillips, in the Spanish-American War
Double, Standard, A
Dying Bondman, The
Eliza Harris
Ethiopia
Fifteenth Amendment
"Fishers of Men"
Go Work in my Vineyard
God Bless our Native Land
Going East
Grain of Sand, A
He "Had not Where to Lay his Head"
Hermit's Sacrifice, The
Home, Sweet Home
Jamie's Puzzle
Learning to Read
Let the Light Enter
"Little Child Shall Lead Them, A"
Maceo
Martyr of Alabama, The
Mission of the Flowers
Mother's Treasures
Night of Death
Nothing and Something
Our Hero
"Poem Addressed to Women"
Present Age, The
President Lincoln's Proclamation of Freedom
Pure in Heart Shall see God
Refiner's Gold, The
Renewal of Strength
Report
Save the Boys
She's Free!
Slave Auction
Slave Mother, The
Songs for the People
Sparrow's Fall, The
Story of the Rebellion, A
Thank God for Little Children
Then and Now
Truth
Vashti

HARRIS, HELEN C.
I Heard your Heart's Soft Tears
Spin me a Dream
To the Singer

HARRISON, EDNA L.
First Lady

HAYWOOD, CLARA H.
Garden Ghosts
I am Too Much Loved
I Saw Beauty
Late Lesson
Pity Me

HEARD, JOSEPHINE D. (HENDERSON)
Admiration
Advance of Education, The
Ambition
"And it Shall Come to Pass"
Assurance
Bereft
Birth of Jesus, The
Birth of Time, The
Bishop James A. Shorter
Black Elm, The
Black Sampson, The
City by the Sea, The
Chorus
Could you Tell me a Falsehood
Day After Conference, The
December
Deception
Decoration, Day
Deserted Wife, The
Do You Think?
Doing
Dream, A
Dying Slave's Request, The
Earthquake of 1886, The
Easter Morn
Epitaph, An

Eternity
Faded Flowers
Fame
Farewell to Allen University
First Flakes that Fell on Mother's Grave, The
Forgetfulness
Forsaken
Friendship
General Robert Smalls
God is Near Thee
Gone
Good Bye
Graystone Crest, Logan Station, Philadelphia, Pa.
Happy Heart, A
He Comes not To-night
He Hath Need of Rest
He That Cometh to me I Will in no wise cast Out
Heart-Hungry
Hope
Hope Thou in God
Hypocrisy
I Love Thee
I Love Thee Yet
I Will Look Up
If I Could Know
Impossibilities
In Memoriam of Mother
In Memory of James M. Rathel
In Memory of the Hon. Frederick Douglass, The Saga of Anacostia
Indifference
Jesus, Savior, Pilot, Save
Judge Not
Ladder of Life, The
Lend a Hand
Lord I Would Love Thee
Love
Love Letters
Master, Still the Tempest
Matin Hymn
Message to a Lover One Dead, A
Morn
Mother
Mother's Love, A
Moving
Music
My Canary
My Grace is Sufficient
My Husband's Birthday
My Mocking Bird
National Cemetery, Beaufort, South Carolina
New Organ, The
Night
On Genessaret
Out in the Desert
Outcast, The
Parting, The
Parting Kiss, The
Pilgrimage, The
Quarrel, The
Quarto-Centennial of the Birth of Bishop Richard Allen
Question, The
Resignation
Resting
Retrospect
Returned Letters, The
Rev. Andrew Brown, Over the Hill to Rest
Rt. Rev. Richard Allen
Sabbath Bells
Slave Mother's Crime, The
Slumbering Passion
Solace
Span of Life, The
Stricken Deer, The
Sunshine After Cloud
Tears
Temperance Poem
Tennyson's Poems
"They Are Comin"
Thine Own
Thou Lovest Me
Thy Will, O Lord, Not Mine
Times and Things Have Changed
Time's Fluent
To Bishop Allen's Memory
To Bishop H. Turner, D. D., LL.D
To Bishop Turner
To Clements' Ferry
To Mrs. Bishop Lee
To My Father
To My Friend
To Whittier
To Youth
Truism
Trusting Thee
Truth
Unuttered Prayer
Virtue
Wanderer Reclaimed, The
We do not Know what Day Will Be our Last

Wedding and Anniversary, The
Welcome Home
Welcome to Hon. Frederick Douglass
When I Would Die!
When Love, I Need the Most
When we are Dead
Where are the Prayers
Where do School Days End?
Where Hast Thou Gleaned?
Who is My Neighbor?
Who so Gives Freely Shall Freely Receive
Wilberforce
Will E'er There Come a Time?
Would You Regret?
Wounded Heart, The

HENDERSON, SAFIYA
Harlem/Soweto
Letter to my Father...A Solidarity Long Overdue
Portrait of a Woman Artist

HILL, EDNA WHITE
Plea

HILL, PAMELA WOODRUFF
Untitled (To Smell the Stink of Rotting Brownstone)

HODGES, FRENCHY
Black Haika
Black Memorial Day, A
Black Wisdom
Elegy Written in America
Grasshopper Word, The
Hills, The
In Front of Fifth Avenue Library on the Steps
Innocent Question
Invitation
Listen, I'se Talkin' to You, Land
On Dreams
Shattered Dreams
Stereo Abstract
Super Thought
Syncopating Rhythm
Talisman
To Reggie
Unencouraged Lingering
What it Means to be an "N"
When

HOLLAR, CONSTANCE
Caged Mongoose, The

HOLLENDER, BETH
My Friend

HOLLOWAY, ARIEL WILLIAMS
Apples
Black Magician, The
Glory
Jai Peur (The Coward Speaks)
North Boun'

HOLMES, ETHLYNNE E.
Butterfly
Happiness

HOPE, AKUA LEZLI
August
Lament
1

HOUSTON, VIRGINIA
Couplet
For H. M. G.
Fugit Amor
Interim
Query
Recapitulation

HOWARD, FLORETTA
On a Colored Doll
'Round the Neighborhood

HOWARD, MARIAH BRITTON
Reports
Solution #9 To Touch You
Using

HOWARD, VANESSA
Abandoned
After the Rain
Agnew Rushes into the Waiting Room
America an Overdeveloped/Animosity Stamping out the Dreams
Blind are we Who Cannot tell the Bitter from the Sweet
Calmness hits the Careless Streets
Carelessly
Caressing Caresses
Cars Screech, Sirens Roar with Discontentment
Corner Coffee Klatch Begins, The
Dark so Dark
Dead End Kids

Don't Tell me You Don/t Understand
For My Children
For My Grandpa
Gifts of America
He Lay in the Alley
He Stood a Tall Silhouette of Love
I am Frightened that / the Flame of Hate/ Will Burn Me
I am Waiting
In the Misty Hollow of the Morning
In the Sweetness of Silent Death
Jesus Christ can you Justify
Life is a Two-Way Experience
Monument in Black
My Thoughts are I Love You
Natural Aruba
New Math, The
Night is Beautiful, The
Night Seems to Cry, The
Observations on a Subway Train
Poem for Michael, A
Praise the Rat-Infested Rooftop
Reflections
Silent City Cries Today, The
Subsconsciously / I Think of You
They Took Away the Wind Mill
To the Nature Lovers
Victims of Slavery
We Disappear to Dance
We Have had / Stand Ins
What Uncaring Creator on This Earth
Yesterday
Yesterday While Walking Down the Avenue
Your Eyes Like Cups of Wine

HOWARD VILMA
Citizen, The

HUGHES, LOIS ROYAL
I Could Not Know
Let There be Three of Us
Like Unto a Rose
Rendezvous
To Death
Veil, The

HUMPHREY, EDITH BRANDON
Good Friday's Garbage

HUNTER, ELEANOR C.
Frustration

HUNTER, KATHERINE JACKSON
Congenital

HUNTER, OLIVÁ M.
Spring is Here!

HYMAN, LATEIFA-RAMONA
Parahernalia for a Suicide: A Revelation of Life

IFETAYO, FEMI FUNMY
We the Black Woman

INGRUM, ADRIENNE
Friday the 13th Candlelight March
Loomit

ISMAILI, RASHIDAH
Dialogue
Murderous Intent with a Deadly Weapon
Struggle of Class

JACKSON, ANGELA
Because we Failed for a Child who Died from an Overdose of Heroin
Beginning for New Beginnings
Carve/n
Foreword
I/Scattered Poems
If I Tole You
Lovin u Rite
Make/n My Music
Memories/The Red Bootee
Ohnedaruth
Revolution
Second Meeting
Summer Story, A
Voo Doo/Love/Magic
Woman Walk/n Down a Mississippi Road
Woman with Water/Melon Thighs

JACKSON, BETH
Make Up Your Mind
Right On
That Day
Two Views of the 3 R's

JACKSON, KATHERINE
Congenital

JACKSON, MAE
All Praises due to Allah
Aretha
Black Genesis
Blues Today, The
Capitalism
Cool Breeze
Counteraction
For Some Poets
For the Count
He was Sad
I Remember
I Used to Wrap my White Doll Up
Incident
Ivory
January 3, 1970
Knee-Grow, A
My Last Feeling this Way Poem
Nina
No Time
Note From a Field Nigger
Of Someone I Loved
On Learning
Once Again
Play House
Please
Pledge of Alligence
Poem for all the Mens in the World, A
Poems for all the Lonely
Poet, The
Reincarnation
Summer
There was a Time
To a Reactionary
(To Someone I met on 125th Street, 1966)
To the Negro Intellectuals
Untitled (No.1)

JACKSON, MARSHA ANN
In Between Time (Transcience)
Tears and a Dream

JAMESON, GLADYS M.
Idyll

JEAN
Brother
For You

JEFFREY, MAURINE L.
My Rainy Day
Pappy's Last Song

JEMMOTT, CLAUDIA E.
City Park
Falling
There are Times

JESSYE, EVA
To a Rosebud

JIMASON, JOANNE
After the Rain
Be a Whale on a Searock
Bitches Brew
Darkness and a Blueslady
He Climbs Inside
I am a Mad Dog
I Hate
I Have Carried Sorrow
I Have Robed Myself in the Mentality of Motherhood
I Have Seen
I Lay Naked Against the Belly of the Earth
I Leave These Things
It Has Been a Long Time
Madwoman
Me
My Love
My Thumb in my Eye
Naked Against the Belly of the Earth
Papa
Sometimes
Sorrow is a Woman
Sunstill
There are Old Ladies
These Days
This Man
To Carry out an Act of Love
We are no Longer Afraid

JOHNSON, ALICIA LOY
Black Lotus/ A Prayer
Black Poetry Day, A
Blue/Black Poems (Or Call Them by Their Rightful Names)
Day of Peace a Day of Peace
Enemy of Man, The
Gathering of Artists, A
Long March, The
Our Days are Numbered
Some Smooth Lyrics for a

Natural People

JOHNSON, AUDREY
Spring in Carolina

JOHNSON, CHRISTINE CLAYBOURNE
My Brother Malcolm

JOHNSON, DOROTHY VENA
Crystal Shreds
Epitaph for a Bigot
Green Valley
Jerked to God
Ode to Justice
Palace
Post War Ballad
Road to Anywhere
Success
Twinkling Gown

JOHNSON, GEORGIA DOUGLAS
Afterglow
Aliens
Amour
Armageddon
Armor
Attar
Autumn
Benediction
Black Recruit
Black Woman
Bondage
Break, Break My Heart
Brotherhood
Calling Dreams
Celibacy
Common Dust
Concord
Conquest
Contemplation
Cosmopolite
Courier
Credo
Cross, The
Curtain
Dawn
Dead Days
Dead Leaves
Deluge
Delusion
Despair
Desire
Destiny
Devastation
Divide
Dreams of the Dreamer, The
Eclipse
Ecstasy
Elevation
Emblems
Envoys
Escape
Estrangement
Eventide
Faith
Fantasy, A
Fiction
Finality
Finis
Footsteps
Foredoom
Foregather
Fusion
Gethsemane
Gilead
Glamour
Gloamtide
Good-Bye
Gossamer
Guardianship
Heart of a Woman, The
Hegira, The
Homing Braves
Hope
How My Heart Sinks
Husks
I Closed my Shutters Late Last Night
I Want to Die While You Love Me
I Wonder
Illusions
Impelled
In Love
In Quest
Inevitably
Initiate
Interim
Interracial
Isolation
I've Learned to Sing
Ivy
Joy
Laocoon
Le Soir
Let Me Not Hate
Let me Not Lose my Dream
Lethe
Little King
Little Son
Lost Illusion
Love Light

Love's Miracle
Love's Tendril
Mate
Maternity
Measure, The
Memory
Mirrored
Modulation
Moods
Mother, The
My Boy
My Little Dreams
Octoroon, The
Offering
Oh Night of Love
Old Black Men
Omega
"One of the Least of These, My Little One"
Pages from Life
Paradox
Parody
Passing of the Ex-Slave, The
Peace
Pendulum
Pent
Perspective
Pledge
Poet Speaks, The
Poetry
Posthumous
Prejudice
Promise
Proving
Query
Quest
Question
Recall
Recessional
Recompense
Remember
Repulse
Requiem
Resolution
Retrospect
Retrospection
Return, The
Review
Rhythm
Riddle, The
Romance
Separation
Sepulchre
Service
Shall I Say "My Son, You're Branded?"
Smothered Fires
Soldier
Song of the Sinner
Sonnet to the Mantled
Sonnet to Those Who See But Darkly
Sorrow Singers
Souvenir
Spring Tide
Springtime
Sunset
Suppliant, The
Supreme
Sympathy
Taps
Tears and Kisses
Thrall
Thralldom
Tired
To Abraham Lincoln
To Atlanta University - It's Founders and Teachers
To Emille Bigelow Hapgood - Philanthropist
To Henry Lincoln Johnson - Lawyer - Georgia
To John Brown
To Mary Church Terrell - Lecturer
To May Howard Jackson - Sculptor
To My Son
To Richard R. Wright - Instructor
To Ridgely Torrence - Playwright
To Samuel Coleridge Taylor, Upon Hearing his Sometimes I Feel Like a Motherless Child
To the Martyred
To the Memory of Inez Milholland
To Time
To W. E. B. DuBois - Scholar
To William Stanley Braithwaite
Tomorrow's Men
Transpositions
Treasure
Trifle
Utopia
Values
Vanishing Road, The
Watcher, The
We Face the Future

Welt
What Need Have I for Memory?
When I Am Dead
When I Rise Up
Whene'er I Lift my Eyes to Bliss
Where
Whither!
Why?
Willow, The
Your Eyes
Your World
Youth
Youth's Progeny

JOHNSON, HELENE
Bottled: New York
Fulfillment
Invocation
"Little Brown Boy'
Magalu
Metamorphism
Missionary Brings a Young Native to America, A
Poem
Remember Not
Road, The
Roaring Third
Sonnet to a Negro in Harlem
Southern Road, A
Summer Matures
Trees at Night
What do I Care for Morning
Widow with a Moral Obligation

JOHNSON, LEANNA F.
Joy of Sorrow
Supremacy

JOHNSON, MAE SMITH
To my Grandmother

JOHNSON, RUTH BROWNLEE
Chained
Cords

JOHNSON, YVETTE
Ghetto
Reality
Sapling
This is the City

JONAS, ROSALIE
Ballade Des Belles Milatraisse
Brother Baptis' on Woman Suffrage

JONES, ALICE H.
For Sapphire, My Sister

JONES, BARBARA see ODARA

JONES, GAYL
Deep Song
Many Die Here
Satori
3-31-70
Tripart

JONES, GEORGIA HOLLOWAY
Enchantment
To James Weldon Johnson

JONES, JYMI
He Said she Said she Said He Said

JONES, PATRICIA
Getting Up
Going Home
I Done Got so Thirsty That My Mouth Waters at the Thought of Rain
Lyric for Bessie Smith
Why I Like Movies

JONES, PAULETTE
Tree Poem, The

JONES, SYLVIA see BARAKA, AMINI

JORDAN, ANASA
Sweet Otis Suite

JORDAN, JUNE
Abandoned Baby
About Enrique's Drawing
About Long Distance on Saturday
About the Reunion
After all is Said and Done
After Reading the Number One Intellectual American Best Seller, Future Shock, All About Change is Where We're At
Ah, Momma
All the World Moved
Alla Tha's All Right, But
And Who Are You?
Blue Ribbons for the Baby Girl
Bus Window

Calling it Quits
Calling on all Silent Minorities
Cameo No. I
Cameo No. II
Case in Point
Clock on Hancock Street
Current Events
Ecology
En Passant
Evidently Looking at the Moon Requires a Clean Place to Stand
Excerpts From a Verse Diary of Somebody Trying to Get Into Gear
Exercise in Quits
Explanation Always Follows, An
Fibrous Ruin
Firing Burst His Head
For Beautiful Mary Brown: Chicago Rent Strike Leader
For C.G; Because David Came in Hot and Crying From the News
For Christopher
For Dave: 1976
For Ethelbert
For Li'l Bit
For Michael Angelo Thompson (October 25, 1969 - March 23, 1973
For my Brother
For my Jamaican Sister or a Little Bet Lost on the Island of Manhattan
For My Mother
For Somebody to Start Singing
For the Poet: Adrienne Rich
47,000 Windows
Found Poem
Fragments From a Parable (Of the 1950's)
Free Flight
From America: A Poem in Process
From an Uprooted Condition
From Inside the Continum
From the Talking Back of Miss Valentine Jones
From the Talking Back of Miss Valentine Jones: Poem # One
From Who Look at Me
Getting Down to Get Over
Grand Army Plaza
"Hey, Baby: You Married?"
I am Untrue Yet I
I Celebrate the Sons of Malcolm
I Live in Subtraction
I Must Become a Menace to my Enemies
If you saw a Negro Lady
In Love
In Memoriam: Martin Luther King, Jr.
In My Own Quietly Explosive Here
In the Times of my Heart
Inaugural Rose
It's About You: On the Beach
Juice of a Lemon on the Trail of Little Yellow
July 4, 1974 (Washington, D. C.)
Last Dialog on the Left, A
Last Poem for a Little While
Leaves Blow Backward
Legend of the Holy Night When the Police Finally Held Fire
Let me Live with Marriage
Letter to My Friend the Poet Ntozake Shange
Letter to the Local Police
Lullaby
May 1, 1970
May 27, 1971: No Poem
Maybe the Birds
Memo
Memo to Daniel Pretty Moynihan
Memoranda Toward the Spring of Seventy-Nine
Metarhetoric
Minutes From the Meeting
Morning on the Mountains, The
My Sadness Sits Around Me
New Like Nagasski Nice Like Nicene
New Pieta: For the Mothers and Children of Detroit, The
Newport Jazz Festival: Saratoga Springs and Especially about George Benson and Everyone Who Was Listening
Niagara Falls
Night Letters
1978

1977: Poem for Mrs. Fannie Lou Hamer
No Poem Because Time is Not a Name
No Train of Thought
Nobody Riding the Roads Today
Not a Suicide Poem
Not Looking
Notes on the Peanut
Nowadays The Heroes
Of Faith: Confessional
Of Nightsong and Flight
Okay "Negroes"
On a Monday Afternoon
On a New Year's Eve
On a Thursday Evening
On Declining Values
On Divine Adaptation to the Age of Disbelief
On Holidays in the Best Tradition
On Moral Leadership as a Political Dilemma (Watergate, 1973)
On my Happy/Matrimonial Condition
On the Aluminum
On the Black Poet Reading His Poems in the Park
On the Loss of Energy (And Other Things)
On the Murder of Two Human Being Black Men, Denver A. Smith and His Unidentified Brother, at Southern University, Baton Rogue, Louisiana, 1972
On the Paradox in Rhyme
On the Real World: Meditation #1
On the Spirit of Mildred Jordan
On the Twenty-Fifth Anniversary of the United Nations: 1970
On Your Love
One Minus One Minus One
One Sided Dialog
Or
Patricia's Poem
Poem About a Night Out: Michael: Goodbye for A While
Poem About Intelligence for my Brothers and Sisters, A
Poem About My Rights
Poem About Police Violence
Poem About the Head of a Negro
Poem About Vieques, Puerto Rico, A
Poem Against the State
Poem for all the Children, A
Poem for Granville Ivanhoe Jordan, November 4, 1890-December 21, 1974
Poem for my Family: Hazel Griffith and Victor Hernandez Cruz
Poem for my Love
Poem for my Pretty Man
Poem for Nana
Poem for South African Women
Poem for the Poet Alexis De Veaux
Poem from the Empire State
Poem in Celebration of the Recovery of Mrs. R. Buckminster Fuller, June 1967
Poem #2 for Inaugural Rose
Poem of Personal Greeting for Fidel
Poem to the Mass Communications Media
Poem Toward the Bottom Line
Poem Towards a Final Solution
Queen Anne's Lace
Rape is not a Poem
Rationale, or She Drove Me Crazy, The
Realizing that Revolution Will not Take Place by Telephone
Reception
Right-to-Lifer in Grand Rapids, North Dakota, A
Roman Poem Number One
Roman Poem Number Two
Roman Poem Number Three
Roman Poem Number Four
Roman Poem Number Five
Roman Poem Number Six
Roman Poem Number Seven
Roman Poem Number Eight
Roman Poem Number Nine
Roman Poem Number Ten
Roman Poem Number Eleven
Roman Poem Number Twelve
Roman Poem Number Thirteen
Roman Poem Number Fourteen
Roman Poem Number Fifteen
Roman Poem Number Sixteen

Roman Poem Number Seventeen
Round of Grief, The
San Juan
Short Note to my Very Critical and Well-Beloved Friends and Comrades
Short Song from my Heart
Sketching in the Transcendental
Solidarity Day, 1968
Some People
Song of Sojourner Truth
Sunflower Sonnet Number One
Sunflower Sonnet Number Two
Taking Care
Then it Was
This Man
To my Sister, Ethel Ennis, Who Sang "The Star Spangled Banner" at the Second Inauguration of Richard Milhous Nixon, January 20, 1973
Toward a City that Sings
Toward a Personal Semantics
TV is Easy Next to Life
Uhuru in the O. R.
Uncle Bull Boy
Unemployment Monologue
Verse from a Fragmentary Marriage
Wasted
Wedding, The
West Coast Episode
What Declaration
What Happens
What is this in Reference To? Or We Must Get Together Sometime Soon
What Would I Do White?
When I or Else
Whereas
Who Look at Me
You Came With Shells

KALI, MARA MUJA TU
Grass Roots

KEIFER, RITA BRADY
You Still Don't Know Their Names

KELLY, KATIE
Lyric, A

KENDRICK, DELORES
Agony and the Bone
Interview in Color
Sketch
Three Poems for Gwendolyn Brooks

KENNER, PEGGY SUSBERRY
Black Taffy
Comments
Image in the Mirror
No Bargains Today
Round Table, The

KHALIL, AMMA
Untitled

KING, HELEN H.
For Gwendolyn Brooks

KNIGHT, BARBARA JEAN
Black
Old Man, The

KUNJUFU, JOHARI M see AMINI, JOHARI

LAKIN, MATTIE T.
Realization

LALANDE, ATHELSTON
Friendship

LAMAR, THELMA
Holy Day

LAMARRE, HAZEL WASHINGTON
Time and Tide

LANE, PINKIE GORDON
After the Quarrel
Afterthought, An
Apprehension
Awakening
Back Again
Backward Look, A
Baton Rouge
Baton Rouge #2
Beyond Words
Children
Coffee Hour
College Teacher
Communication
Dedication
Dialysis Machine Called the Artificial Kidney, The
Despair

Elegy: Marion
Epileptic
Eulogy on the Death of Trees
Finis
Finis
Flight
For a Future's Treasury
For Bill
For Gwendolyn Brooks
For You
Ghetto Song
Griefs of Joy
Gulls
Hallet's Peak
His Body is an Eloquence
Hum of the Dialysis Machine, The
I Never Scream
Incident in a Black Ghetto
Intro
Kaleidoscope: Leaving Baton Rogue
Lake Murry
Leaves
Leg Cannulas for the Dialysis Machine
Letter
Listenings
Love, Considered
Love Poem: Thoughts Run Tonight
Love Poem (To ---)
Love Songs of an Outcast
Loving
Me
Message
Mid-Summer Thoughts
Midnight Song
Midnight Thoughts of the Town Whore
Migration
Miscarriage
Mood
Mystic Female, The
Night Rising
Nobody Likes to Read His Own Epitaph
Nocturne
Not Like Falling Leaves
Oh You Tender, Lovely Scrubwoman
On Being Head of the English Department
On this Louisiana Day
Opossum
Plum Ripens, The
Poem at 3:00 A.M.
Poem Extract
Poem for Lois: An Elegy
Poems to my Father
Portrait
Postscript
Quiet Poem, A
Rain Ditch
Resolve
Roasting Grasshopper
St. Valentine's Day
Seeing: Remembering
Sequel No. 1
Sequel No. 2
Sequel No. 3
Sexual Privacy of Women on Welfare
Shadows
Slumbering Bats
Songs to the Dialysis Machine
South Paw Baby
Southern University
Spring
Sunrise
Survival Lane
Telephone Call
This Treasured Book
Three Bills
To a Woman Poet That I Know
To George
To Robert Peters
To Singers of Song
Trail Ridge Road
Trilogy: to my Unborn Children
Two Love Poems
Two Poems
Vignettes
Waiting
Waiting Out the Days
Walking the Dog
What Does one Say to the Mad
What it Means
When you Read this Poem
While Sitting in the Airport Waiting Room
While Working Towards the PH.D Degree
Who is My Brother?
Why Do You Stare
Wind Thoughts
Woman
Write me a Poem
Yesterday's Sculptors

LATIMER, BETTE DARCIE
For William Edward Burghardt DuBois on his Eightieth Birthday

LATTIMORE, JEWEL C see AMINI, JOHARI

LAWRENCE, JOYCE WHITSITT
From a Bus
For Malcolm

LAWSON, JENNIFER BLACKMAN
Acquaintance
Afterwards
Ain't No Blues Song
Apology to an Old Man Who Only Wanted to Chat
Bidding, The
Big Mama
Black Woman Portrait, A
Black Woman to Black Man: I
Black Woman to Black Man: II
Carla
Children
Classy Lady
Composition in Four Parts
De Facto Toilets
Dear Edith
Dedication for Joyce Carol Thomas, A
Ella Mae
Family: Growing Up
Gene
Going Home
Hello Woman!
In Memory of the Hokey Pokey
Kinship Ties
Legacy
Liberated Woman?
Memories: 1956
Old Woman and Young Child at a Wedding Reception
Poem for a Friend
Poem for Young People, A
Remember
Resolution
Somebody's Calling Your Name
Sometimes
Sympathy Note to a Friend
Thanksgiving Day
There are no Words
Valediction to Shuffling
Untitled
Wednesday
Young Girl Crying in the Street

LEWIS, LEIGHLA
Chrysis
Incidentally
My Hate

LEWIS, LILLIAN TUCKER
Longing

LINCOLN, ABBEY
I am the Weaver
In the Middle
Name Change, A
On Being High

LINYATTA
Fragment Reflection I
Reckoning A.M. Thursday After an Encounter Between a Sawdust Sack And a Silly

LIPSCOMB, CHARRON
Jazz Song

LOFTIN, ELOUISE
Virginia
Weeksville Women
Woman

LOMAX, PEARL CLEAGE
Conversion
Glimpse
Mississippi Born
Moving Meditation
Morning Song
Neighbor 1
Night Song
Poem
Poem
Poem for Michael
Poem for Neighbors
Retrospect
Schemin'
Untitled
Vigil

LONG, NAOMI CORNELIA see MADGETT, NAOMI LONG

LORDE, AUDRE
About Religion
After a First Book
Afterimages
Afterlove

All Hallows Eve
American Cancer Society or There is More Than one Way to Skin a Coon
And Don't Think I Won't be Waiting
And Fall Shall Sit in Judgment
And What About the Children
Anniversary
Artisan
As I Grow up Again
At First I Thought you were Talking About
Ballad for Ashes
Ballad from Childhood
Barren
Bazaar
Bees
Between Ourselves
Bicentennial Poem # 21,000, 000
Birthday Memorial to Seventh Street. A
Black Mother Woman
Black Unicorn, The
Blackstudies
Bloodbirth
Bridge Througn My Window
Brother Alvin
Brown Menace or Poem to the Survival of Roaches, The
But What can you Teach My Daughter
Cable to Rage or I've Been Talking on This Street Corner a Hell of a Long Time
Chain
Change of Season
Child Shall Lead, A
Chorus
Coal
Conclusion
Coniagui Women
Contact Lenses
Conversation in Crisis
Coping
Dahomey
Day They Eulogized Martha, The
Dear Toni Instead of a Letter of Congratulation Upon Your Book and Your Daughter Whom You say you are Raising to be a Colored Little Sister
Death Dance for a Poet
Digging
Dozens, The
Dream/ Songs From the Moon of Beulah Land
Dreams Bite
Echo
Equinox
Eulogy
Eulogy for Alvin Frost
Even
Evening News, The
Fallen, The
Family Resemblance, A
Fantasy and Conversation
Father Son and Holy Ghost
Father, The Year
Father, The Year is Fallen
Fog Report
For Assata
For Each of You
For My Singing Sister
For the King and Queen of Summer
From Inside an Empty Purse
From the Greenhouse
From the House of Yemanja
Future Promise
Gemini
Generation
Generation II
Ghost
Good Mirrors are Not Cheap
Hanging Fire
Hard Love Rock
Hard Love Rock # II
Harriet
How Can I Love...
"I Die for all Mysterious Things"
If You come Softly
In Margaret's Garden
Journeystones
Key Food
Letter for Jan
Lightly
Litany for Survival, A
Love Maybe
Love Poem
Lover's Song, A
Maiden, The
Kaking It
Martha
Meet
Memorial I
Memorial II

Memorial III From a Phone Booth on Broadway
Memorial IV
Mentor
Monkeyman
Moon-Minded the Sun
Movement Song
Moving In
Moving Out on the End of Cooperative Living
My Fifth Trip to Washington Ended in Northeast Delaware
Naturally
Need: A Choral of Black Women's Voices
Neighbors
Never Take Fire from a Woman
New Year's Day
New York City
Nightstone
Now
Now That I am Forever with Child
Nymph
Oaxaca
October
Old Days, The
On a Night of the Full Moon
On Midsummer's Eve
125th Street and Alomey
One Year to Life on the Grand Central Shuttle
Outside
Oya
Paperweight
Parting
Pathways: From Mother to Mother
Pirouette
Poem for a Poet, A
Poem for Women in Rage, A
Portrait
Power
Progress Report
Prologue
Recreation
Release Time
Relevant is Different Points on the Circle
Return
Revolution is one Form of Social Change
Rites of Passage
Rock Bottom into the Water Does Not Fear the Cold, A
Rooming Houses are Old Women
Sacrifice
Sahara
Same Death Over and Over or Lullabies are for Children
Scar
School Note
Seasoning
Second Spring
Separation
Sequelae
7/2
Seventh Sense, The
Sewerplant Grows in Harlem or I'm a Stranger Here Myself When Does the Next Swan Leave
Signs
Sister, Morning is a Time for Miracles
Sister Outsider
Small Slaughter, A
Solstice
Song
Song for a Thin Sister
Song for Many Movements, A
Song of Names and Faces, A
Songless Lark, The
Sowing
Spring People
Spring III
Story Books on a Kitchen Table
Suffer the Children
Summer Oracle
Suspension
Teacher
Therapy
Timepiece
Times Change and we Change with Them or We Seem to Have Lost Touch With Each Other
Timing
To a Girl who Knew What Side her Bread was Buttered On
To Desi as Joe as Smoky the Lover of 115th Street
To Marie, In Flight
To Martha: A New Year
To My Daughter the Junkie on a Train
To the Girl Who Lives in a Tree

Touring
Trip on the Staten Island Ferry
Trollop Maiden, The
Vietnam Addenda
Visit to a City Out of Time
Walking our Boundaries
What my Child Learns of the Sea
When the Saints Come Marchin In
Who Said it Was Simple
Winds of Orisha, The
Woman
Woman/Dirge for Wasted Children
Woman Speaks, A
Woman Thing, The
Women of Dan Dance with Swords in Their Hands to Mark the Time When Were Warriors
Workers Rose on May Day or Postscript to Karl Marx, The
Za Ki Tan Ke Parlay Lot

LOUISE, ESTHER
Enough
For Us
It's All in the Name
Running to Gone
Tokens For "T"

LOVELACE, ALICE
Ain't the Only Place

LOWERY, L. DORETTA
As a Goldfish see the World
Wind, The

LOYD, EDITH
Jennifer

LUCAS, PORTIA
Laughter

LUTHER, CAROL see BER, MUSU

LYN
Abbreviation
Blizzard
Communication
Dare to Struggle--Dare to Win
Define Revolution
Ecology Home-Style
Final Indignity, The
Home Coming Mass: General Hospital
Junkie Lost/Junkie Found
Love Word, A
Never!!
Nonviolence
Precarious
Replacing Faith
Solution
To Harriet Tubman, A Plea
Wearing Glasses
Without Someone
Yeah: A Grand Poem

LYNN, EVE (EVELYN C. REYNOLDS)
God's Christmas Tree

LYONS, LEONA
Faith

LYONS, MARTHA E.
Thing Born of Darkness, A

LYTLE, CORINNE
Behold the Bride

MCBROWN, GERTRUDE PARTHENIA
Happy Faces
Jack Frost
Lilacs
Painter, The
They are Calling Me

MCCANN, LISA
There's a Raindrop

MCCLAURIN, IRMA
I, Woman
Mask, The
To a Gone Era

MCDUFFIE, ELEANOR
If You Forget

MCELROY, COLLEEN
Amen Sister
Caledonia
Contemplate
Dance, The
Family Portrait
For Love
Gra'ma
Last Conversation, The
Loneliness For Nona

Looking for a Country Under its Original Name
Mechanic, The
Music From Home
Never Again
Night People
Passing for Black
Penny-Ante
Ruth
Senate Man
Singer, The
Sister Charity
Sunrise Poems
Try to Understand Papa
What You Say
Woman's Song, A

MCMICHAEL, MICHELLE see ZIMELE-KEITA, NZADI

MCNEIL, DEE DEE
Doorway That We Hide Behind, The

MADGETT, NAOMI LONG
Achievement
Advent
After
After Hours
After Parting
Afterglow, The
Afterthought
Again
Alabama Centennial
Album: Photo 2
Always
Anonymous Witness
April in Your Eyes
Arrival
Association
Atonement
Autumn Night
Autumnal
Awakening
Bad Penny
Because I Can
Beginning and End
Biography
Black: A Chant for Children
Black Woman
Bordentown School
Boy, The
Brothers at the Bar
Canossa
Catastrophe
Circus
City, The
City Nights
City Thought
Clock
Confession of a Sinner
Congenital
Conquest
Convent Hall
Cross
Culturally Deprived
Darn Near Dark
Deacon Morgan
Dedication
Deep
Departure of Summer
Destiny
Discards
Divorcee, The
Do not Pass Me By
Dream Boats
Dream Sequence, Part 9
Dreams
Driving Along Interstate 94
Dusk
Early News Report
Echoes
Elaine
Eliza
Encounter
End of Summer
Epitaph
Escape # 1
Escape # 2
Exits and Entrances
Family Portrait
Fantasia
Fantasy of a Fool
Fences
Fifth Street Exit, Richmond
For a Child
For One so Brief and Lovely Day
From a Train
From a Tenement Window
From Generation to Generation
From Seven Days Prayer
From the Shelter
Funeral
Glimpses of Africa
Good News
Grand Circus Park
Heart-Blossom
Heaven
Her Story
Heritage

High Noon
Homage
How Shall I Face the Dawn?
If Love Were All
If Not in Summer
If There Were Songs
If This Be a Dream
Image Maker
Imperfectus
Impressions
In Absence
In Memoriam: Omualowiba
In Pursuit
In Search of Aunt Jemima
In Search of You
In Springtime
Incessant
Invitation
Iowa
Ivory Tower
Jeremiad
Juvenile Suicide
Keep on Singing
Kin
Lament
Lament of Tantalus
Last Look
Late
Let's Keep in Touch
Life
Litany for Afro-Americans, A
Lost, The
Lost Muse, The
Lost Song
Lullaby
Lyric
Market Street
Martha
Masquerade
May Lament
Memorial
Midnight Magnolias
Midway
Misconception
Monday Morning Blues
Monkey Man
Moon Below Me, The
Mortality
Mother, The
Mufflejaw, I Remember You
My Choice
My Own
My Song
Native
Negro in New York, A
Never Without Remembrance
New Calvary
New Day
New House
New Leaf
Newblack
Next Spring
Night Rider
Night Watch
No Need of Sound
No Stars Tonight
Nocturne
Nocturne II: Still
Nomen
Not Enough
Not I Alone
November
Now and at the Hour
Now Below Me, The
Odyssey
Of Sleep
Offspring
Old Wine
Old Women, The
On a Narrow Street
On Democracy
On Parting
One and the Many
Our Cups are Full
Out of Heaven
Out of Time
Over
Packrat
Passing the Sirens
Pavlov
Phillis
Pianissimo
Pictures from a School Window
Plea for my Heart's Sake
Poet Deserts His Ivory Tower, The
Poets Beyond the Blues
Point of View
Ponce De León
Poor Renaldo
Post-Script
Postmortem
Prisoners, The
Proverb
Purchase
Pursuit
Pyramus and Thisbe
Quest
Race
Race Question, The
Ragman, The
Reason Why I'm Lonely, The

Reckoning, The
Reflection
Refugee
Rejection
Reluctant Spring
Reply
Requiem
Return
Rut, The
Sally: Twelfth Street
Salt and Sand
Sanctus
Sarah Street
Saturday Night at The Parsonage
Scorn not my Station
Seascape: Union Pier
Seasonal Note
Seasons Have to Pass
September Lament
Silence
Silver Cord, The
Simple
Sing Soft and Low
Small Wind
Solitaire
Somewhere in London
Somewhere in the City
Son to His Father, A
Song for a Negro
Song for a Season
Song to a Phantom Nightingale
Sonnet
Sonnet to Byron
Souvenir
Spring in Saint Louis
Standing By
Star Journey
Storm, The
Styx Before Crossing
Summer Day
Sunday Afternoon
Sunny
Supposition
Survivors, The
Sylvester Expelled
Teachers
Tears
There was one Night
Threnody
Time is no Thief
Time is Now, The
Tivoli
To a Brown Boy
To a Dream City in Departing
To a Man With Wings
To Autumn
To Bill
To Jill
To March
To Melancholy
To My Country
To My Lost Love
To My Mother
Today and Tomorrow
Too Late
Tree of Heaven
Trinity: A Dream Sequence
Twenty Grand, The
Twice a Child
Two
Two Poems from Trinity: A Dream Sequence
Unfinished Song
Venom
Ventus Memoriae
Via Dolorosa
Violet
Virginia
Waiting
Washerwoman
Welfare Days
What Peter Said
When I was Young
Where do we Go?
White Cross
Wind
With or Without You
Without
Without Name
Woman
Woman with Flower
Worldling, The
Writing a Poem
Written on the Last of April

MAHONE, BARBARA
Beachscape
Childhood/in the Grass
Colors for Mama
Drummer King
El Becomes a Subway in my Lifetime, The
First Meeting (Japanese Style)
For Every (One)
Grandmother
Hard Freeze, The
Love of our Brothers, The
Pisces, Bath
Poem for Positive Thinkers,

A
Reflection on the Reeferlution
Sentimental Women
Speak Without Words
Sugarfields
Tune in the Ear, A
What Color is Black?
With Your Permission

MALCOLM, BARBARA see NAYO

MANUAL, LOUISE see VALE, COSTON

MARSHALL, BARBARA
Colonized Mind
Little Black Boy
On Philosophy
Request

M'BUZI, MALKIA
Lament
Tree Women Quest for Sun...

MEALY, ROSEMARI
Love Poem to an African Freedom Fighter, A
New Chapters for our History
Untitled

MELTON, SUSIE
Slave Song

METZ, RHONDA
I Seem to be/But Now I Am

MEYER, JUNE
All the World Moved

MICOU, REGINA see IFETAYO, FEMI FUNMI

MILLER, JEANNETTE V.
Church Lets Out

MILLER, LOIS
Ode to a Scotlanville Bus

MILLER, MAY
Accordingly
Bole Tally
Calvary Way
Candle
Child in the Night
Count
Did You Hear
For a Young Friend Seeking Identity
Gift From Kenya
Green Leaf
History
I Knew Then
Instant Before Sleep
Invitations
Jesus Bell
Last of the Trees
Last Warehouse, The
Living Waters
My Father
Not That Far
Old Stormer
On the Sinking of a Great Liner
Other Year
Pond Lament
Privilege, The
Procession
Questioning
Scream
Sea Purge
Stairway Left Standing
Summer: Falling in Love
Tally
That Rider
Three Scenes for all Men
Tracings
Trail
Vacations End
Visitors, The
Who Gives
Windless Hour
Wrong Side of Morning

MITCHELL, GWENDOLYN
Black-Bearded Poet

MONEOW, ISABELLE H.
To—

MOORE, ALICE RUTH
Chalmette

MORGAN, MITCHELENE
Bridge of Love—A Child

MORRIS, MYRA ESTELLE
Man and Maid
What is Love?
White-Collar Job
Women in Politics

MOSEKA, AMINATA see LINCOLN, ABBEY

OTEN, CORA BALL
Dream Market
Lullaby
Sight

ULLEN, HARRYETTE
Affirmation
After the Rain
Alabama Memories
Anatomy
Astronaut of Innerspace, The
Aura
Bete Noire
Black Woman Never Faints, A
Circle of Arms
Country Boy
Dance She Does, The
Easter Colors
El Mal Ojo
Eyes in the Back of Her Head
Father (Part I)
Floorwax Mother
For my Grandfather, Lowell Paxter Mitchell
He Reads my Body like a Poem
Heritage
Invisible Saxophone, The
Joy, The
Jump City
La Terrorista
Lamp Lights Into its Prey, The
Madonna
Me & Steenie
Miss Persephone
Momma Sayings
Moon Stalk
Mother of Nightmares, The
My Grandmother
Night We Slept on the Beach, The
Painting Myself a New Mirror
Pensando En La Muerte
People of Atlantis, The
Pineapple
Playing the Invisible Saxaphone en el Combe De Las Estrellas
Recipes
Ritual of Ear Piercing
Road Map
Saturday Afternoon, When Chores are Done
Shedding Skin
Shuddering
Some Light to Hold in my Hands
Song of a Dancer
Stirrings
Strip Tease
Tent Revival
To a Woman
Tree
Tree Tall Woman
Viejas Locas
Waiting for the Next Star to Fall
Wings Against the Blue
Woman and the Roses, The

MURPHY, BEATRICE M.
Anniversary
Deadlines for Miracles
Demonstrators, The
Disclaimer
Even Among Thieves
Evicted
Guest, The
Hatred
Letter, The
Negro Choir
Obituary
Pledge of Allegiance
Release
Safeguard
Signs
They Say
To Any Negro Youth
WAC
Waste
We Are Not Along
We Pass

MURRAY, PAULI
Aloofness
Anguish
Collect for Poplarville
Color Trouble
Conflict
Conquest
Conscription--1940
Counsel
Dark Testament
Death of a Friend
Dinner for Three
Empty of Seed
For Mack C. Parker
For Pan
Harlem Riot, 1943
Hate
Icarus
Inquietude
Love in Wartime

Love's More Enduring Uses
Memo in Bronze
Mr. Roosevelt Regrets
Mulatto's Dilemma
Nazarene
Newer Cry, The
Of Death and Doom
Paradox
Passing of F.D.R., The
Prelude to Spring
Presence, A
Prophecy
Psalm of Deliverance
Quarrel
Redemption
Returning Spring
Ruth
Song
Song of the Highway, The
Tears
To Poets who Have Rebelled
To the Oppressors
Tongues
Unconquerable Dust
Wanderer, The
War Widow
Without Name
Woman and Man
Words
Youth, 1933
Youth to Age

NASH, MARY NELL
Compassion

NAYO
Bedtime Story
Black Woman Throws a Tantrum
Easy Way Out
First Time I was Sweet Sixteen
I Watched Little Black Boys
Men are All Away, The

NEGRO WORK SONG, USA
Baby Mine
Day I Lef' My Home, The
Well She Ask me in De Parlor

NELSON, ALICE DUNBAR
April is on the Way
I Sit and Sew
Lights at Carney's Point, The
Music
Snow in October
Sonnet
To the Negro Farmers of the United States

NEWSOME, E. MARIE
Freedom
!!!He!!!

NEWSOME, EFFIE LEE
Artic Tern in a Museum
Baker's Boy
Bats
Cotton Car, The
Cricket and the Star, The
Little Birches
Magi Call Him King, a Christmas Song
Morning Light, the Dewdrier
Pansy
Peppermint Candy March, The
Quilt
Quoits
Sassafras Tea
Sky Pictures
Wild Roses

NGATHO, STELLA
Children of Lumumba
Untitled

NSABE, NIA
Little Child Shall Lead Us... If we Dare to Follow, A
Risin (for n-N-n and all our Bruthas Goin Through Changes/Real)
T Be Growin Still
Warning for all Loveless, Though on the Case Sistuhs Who Would be Mothers

ODARA (Barbara Jones)
Alafia

ODEN, GLORIA CATHERINE
After Mother was Buried
Although he Returned to the Parsonage
As Other Women give Birth to Children
"...As When Emotion Too far Exceeds its Cause" Elizabeth Bishop
Before I Started School
Brown as the Field
Carousel, The

Church Services Began at Eleven on Sunday
Cornelia, Hands Around the Shoulders
Cover me with you Nakedness
Every Monday, Father took the Train to New York City
Few Years after Father Died, A
Friday, Father set Aside for Attention to the Church
He was Twenty When he Died
However Brief their Acquaintance with my Father
I do not Sleep Nights Though
I have the Rolling Pin Mother Received when first She Wed
I will not let you Drive me to Write
I Would Prefer to Dispatch Myself
In my Life, Latin and Adolescence came Along Together
In this August Heat
It has been Remarked Upon
It is my Sister's Ring
It is not Unfair of me to Say, I Think
It is When we Love
It was not the Fashion in our House to Kiss or Touch
Mother bore my Three Sisters and Two Brothers
My Fear is What I Remember Most
My Last Year in High School
Next to not Having Beautiful Daughter
Not That now I Remember
On Thursday Nights Entertainment was the use to Which the Hall was Put
Once, When Georgia was Readying her Return to College
Poetry makes Unlikely Bedmates
Saturday Afternoons While School was in Session
Six Stories High, She Stands Flowers
Something in you Speaks to Me
Stunned by her Desires
Ten Years to the Day my Brother Milton Died
This Child is the Mother
Those Summers I was Fourteen and Fifteen
To Live with Father
Today I Became the age your Father Was
Two Thousand People Came to his Funeral when Father Died
Until I was Eight or Nine
Wednesdays —Father gave the Parsonage his Attention
Weeks after Mother Died
When I Learned that Mother was Slain in the Bedroom
When I was Very Small
When I went off to College
When Mother Died
When Mother was Eleven her Mother Died
When Mother was over Forty-Five
When Mother Would Leave to Visit Georgia
When Mother's Mother Died
When my Oldest Brother, Buddy (And my Father's Namesake) Died
When our Changing Bodies Meet and Merge
When Those who are Precious Die
Year or so Before She Died, A
You Wrote, "It is From Love I Ask the Devil In."

OGILVIE, D. T.
Black Thoughts
Dudu Ni Dudu
Entkeni Le Sero
Formula
Gangan
Last Letter to the Western Civilization

OGLETREE, CAROLYN
Formula
Life is the Art of Drawing

OLIVER, GEORGIANA
Blind Street
Life Time
Poem

OVERBY, BEATRIS
Dust
Hands

PAGE, DAPHNE DIANNE

Untitled (I take/my War Machine)
Untitled (So/I've Found Me/At Last)

PARKER, GLADYS MARIE
Dream, The

PARKER, PATRICIA
As you Entered my Life
Autumn Morning
Best Friends
Bitch! I want to Scream
Blow Hot Soul Sister
Boots are Being Polished
Brother, I Don't Want to Hear About How my Real Enemy is the System
Cop-Out
Dialogue
Exodus (To my Husbands, Lovers)
Family Tree, A
For Donna
For Michael on his Third Birthday
For the Straight Folks Who Don't Mind Gays
For the White Person who Wants to Know how to be my Friend
For Willyce
From Cavities of Bones Spun
From Deep Within
From the Cavities of Bones
Fuller Brush Day
Gente
Goat Child
Group
Have you ever Tried to Hide?
I am a Child of America
I Followed a Path
I Have
I Have a Dream
I Have a Solitary Lover
I Kumquat You
I Wish that I Could Hate You
I Wonder how Many Matches it Would Take
If it were Possible to Place you in my Brain
I'm so Tired of Hearin About Capitalist
In English Lit., They Told me Kafka was Good
Law, The
Let me Come to You
Love & Friend Ship are Words of People
Metamorphosis
Moment Left Behind, A
Move in Darkness Know the Touch of a Woman
Movement in Black
My Hands are big and Tough
My Lady ain't no Lady
My Lover is a Woman
Non-Monogamy is a Pain in the Butt
On Jealousy
Para Maria Sandra
Pied Piper
Pit Stop
Questions
Sitting Here Listening to You
Small Contradiction, A
Snatches of a Day
Sometimes my Husbands Acts Just like a Man
Sunday
There is a Woman in this Town
To my Vegetarian Friend
To see a Man Cry
Tour America!
What Liberation Front?
When I Drink I Scream
When I was a Child I Was Punished
Where do you go to Become a Non-Citizen?
With the Sun-Fear Leaves Me
Womans Laughter
You Can't be Sure of Anything These Days

PARKS, HENRIETTA C.
My Life
Uncertainty

PARKS, VALERIE
Love
Southern Negro Heart Cry

PARRISH, DOROTHY C.
etc. etc. etc.
Hush Now
Indictment
Soliloquy

PATRICIA

Two for Malcolm

PAYNE, ANTOINETTE
Oh! Lord

PERRY, JULIANNE
No Dawns
To L

PETERSON, GERALDINE
Sin, A?

PIPER, LINDA
Missionaries in the Jungle
Sweet Piper

PITTS, LUCIA MAE
Afternoon Off
Challenge
Declaration
Let Them Come to Us
Moment in Paradise
Never, Never, Never
One April
Poets
Promise
Requiem
This is my Vow

PLATO, ANN
Advice to Young Ladies
Forget me Not
Natives of America, The
On the Dismission of a School Term
Reflections, Written on Visitating the Grave of a Venerated Friend
To the First of August

POPEL, ESTHER
Little Grey Leaves
Synphonies
Theft

PORTER, LINDA
As a Basic

PORTER, MARGARET
Inflation
Sugarman
When I Rite

PORTER, SHARON
Colors

POWE, BLOSSOM
Child of Another Crime
To a Young Blood

PREER, HILDA
To a Wounded Bird

PRETTYMAN, QUANDRA
Birth of the Poet, The
Blues
Crawl into Bed
Lullaby
Mood, The
Photograph
Still Life: Lady with Birds
When Mahalia Sings

QUIGLESS, HELEN
At the Ebony Circle
Circled by a Horsefly
Concert
Days After
Lip Service

RAINEY, GERTRUDE "MA"
Sweet Rough Man

RANDALL, DOROTHY
Black Mayflower
Lady of the Convent...The Avenue That Is
Lovesong to the Workshop
Morning Coming In, The
Rain on 71st Street

RANSOM, BIRDELLE WYCOFF
Night

RASHIDD, NIEMA
Warriors Prancing, Women Dancing

RAY, HENRIETTA CORNELIA
Antigone and Oedipus
Dawn of Love, The
Dawn's Carol
Idyl
Idyl: Sunrise
Idyl: Sunset
Milton
Our Task
Robert G. Shaw
Shakespeare
To My Father
Triple Benison, The

RAZAFKERIEFO, ANDREA
Negro Church, The
Negro Woman, The

REED, KATHLEEN
Then

REESE, SARAH CAROLYN
Letter from a Wife

REYNOLDS, BARBARA A.
To Gwendolyn Brooks the Creator of the Beginning—Words

RICE, JO NELL
God Called an Angel
Inception of the Negro, The
You and Me

RICHARDSON, NOLA
Africa
After
After you Change Me
As Simple as That
Best For Me, The
Cluttered Letters
Could I?
Deshackled
Doubled Dealing
Even Though
Funny, That I Live
Glimpses
He Comes
I Hate Goodbye
I Must Have
I'm Alone
I'm Not Jealous
In the Morning
Inside/Outside
Kindly Leave me Our
Lover/Brother
No Love/Just Response
Old Scars
On Lonely Nights
Poor Loser
Scorpio People
Sips of Wine
Some Compromise
Something Lost
Something's Changed
Tears of Disguise
They Don't Understand
Thoughts While Driving
Thousand Ways, A
Time Heals all Wounds
Touch of Gray
Twas Brief
Unlike Me
We Might as well Stop Now
What a Joke!
Whose Fault
Whose Terms
Woman/Child
You ask What Love Is
You're Not Here

RIDHIANA
On Contemporary Issues
Tricked Again

RILEY, CONSTANTIA E.
Adieu

ROBBINS, SUSAN
I'm a Very Mixed up Person

ROBINSON, OPHELIA
Black Boy
Nat Turner

RODGERS, CAROLYN M.
After Such Knowledge what Forgiveness
All the Clocks
(An Aside)
& Bearers
And When the Revolution Came
And While we are Waiting
Aunt Dolly
Black Heart as Ever Green, The
Black Licorice
Bloodlines
Blue
Breakthrough
Brief Synopsis, A
Broadway Uptown
C. C. Rider
Children of Their Sin (An Exorcise)
City Limits
Common Poem, A
Contemporay/Psalm
Convergence
Do Tell Faith/The Divine Natural
Earth Bound
Earth is not the World, Nor All the Beauty
Earth is not the World, Nor All its Beauty Poem II
East and West of New Haven/

The Heart, as Evergreen
East of New Haven
Esther, as Lead
Feminism
Folk
For Lillie
For O.--Two --Two Hung Up
For the Others
5 Winos
Food for Thought
For H. W. Fuller
For Muh' Dear
For Our Fathers
For Sapphires
For Sistuhs Wearin Straight Hair
For Some Black Men
For Women
47th & Vincennes/Chicago
From Space to Time
Gary Tyley Poems, The
Greek Crazeology
Group Therapy
Historical Poem, A
How I Got Ovah
How I Got Ovah II/It is Deep II
I Have Been Hungry
I Have Changed so Much in this World
I Remember
In Response
"In This House, There Shall be no Idols"
It is Deep
Jazz
Jesus Must of Been some Kind of Dude
Jesus was Crucified, or It Must Be Deep
Joining, Merging & Breaking Up, The
Jump Bad
Knowing the Difference
Last M. F., The
Life & Positive
Living in the Shadows
Living Water
Look at My Face
Love
Love Ends
Love Ends II or Numbers Racket
Love-The Beginning and the End
Mama's God
Mannessahs
Masquerade
Me, in Kulu Se & Karma
Minature Potters & Significant Clays
Missing Beat
My Lai as Related to No.
Neward, for Now (68)
Nicodemus
No Such Thing as a Witch/ Just a Woman, Needing Some Love
Non-Poem
Not About Poems
Now Ain't That Love?
Now Let's Be Real
On Busing
Once
One
Overture
Paradox
Phoenix
Plagiarism for a Trite Love Poem
Poem/Ditty-Bop
Poem for Brother/for the Nation
Poem for Some Black Women
Poem for Malcolm
Poem No. 1
Poet's Vision, The
Portrait
Portrait of a White Nigger
Proclamation/From Sleep, Arise
Quality of Change, The
Rain is in our Heads, The
Rebolushinary X-Mas/Eastuh Julie 4/Etc, Etc. Etc. Etc. Etc.
Recollections, Towards a Stream
Remember Times
Reverie & in my Father's House Towards Hallelujahs & Freedom, A
Revolution is Resting, The
Rooms are More Than
Round, A
Seeds
Setting/Slow Drag
Shout
6:30
Slave Ritual
Somebody Call
Some Me of Beauty

Sound of Music, The
Spawning-to Bring-Forth
Story/Riff, The
Suite of Assasinations, The
Testament
Testimony
This is no Promised Land
Time Ain't Long as it has Been
Tired Poem/Slightly Negative/
More Positive
To Gwen
To Gwen, Mo Luv
Together
Touch Poem 5
Touch Translation Poem 4
Towards Spring
Train Ride
Translation
Triology-Untitled
U Can Run, But U Can't Ride
U Name This One
Unfunny Situation
Untitled
Untitled-A Political Contribution
Untitled No. Hurt
Untitled No. 1
Untitled No. 4
Voodoo on the Un-Assing of Janis Joplin: Warning: To Ole Tom
Walk Like Freedom
Way, A
We Dance Like Ella Riffs
What Color is Lonely
What in the World
Wimmin
With Malice Toward None
You
Yuh Lookin Good

RODGERS, LORETTA
Beautiful Black Me
Rhythmatic Sounds
To the Sisters

ROGERS, SANDRA
Waiting for her man Too Long

ROKER, MYNTORA J.
Until

ROLLINS, CHARLEMAE
Through the Holly Wreath

ROYSTER, SANDRA
Bad Johnny
Desert Island
Lou/s Room
Love Ain't Hip
Mama
Memory
Miss Mary
Mozetta Lee
On Seeing an Old Friend
Poet-In
Possession
Sunstroke
To My Children
To My Friends
Womens I
Womens II
Womens III
Thoughts After Work

SALAAM, KALAMU see FERDINAND, VAL

SANCHEZ, SONIA
And it Will be Ours
After the Fifth Day
Agrionia
And the Joy
Another of the Clowns is Dead
Answer to Yr/Question of am I Not Yo/Woman Even if U Went on Shit Again
Apology
At the Center of Me
Autumn
Away from you These Sheets are Mummy Tapes
Baby, You are Sweet
Ballad
Ballad for Sterling Street, A
Because
Before I Travel to You
Black Magic
Blk/Rhetoric
Blk/Rhetoric (for Killebrew Keeby, Icewater Baker, Gary Adams and Omar Shabazz)
Blk/Woman/Speaks, A
Blk/Woooomen/Chant
Blues
Cause we are Carving
Change Us
Chant for Young/Brothas & Sistuhs, A
City Songs

Now Poem For Us
Observation
Old Words
On Seeing Pharoah Sanders Blowing
On Watching a World Series Game
Once I was Chaste
Our Bodies Made Rain
Past
Pennsylvania Dutch Country
Personal Letter no.2
Personal Letter no.3
Poem
Poem at Thirty
Poem for Etheridge
Poem for my Father, A
Poem for Nina Simone to put Some Music to and Blow our Nigguh/Minds, A
Poem for Sterling Brown
Poem no.1
Poem no.2
Poem no.3
Poem no.4
Poem no.5
Poem no.6
Poem no.7
Poem no.8
Poem no.9
Poem no.10
Poem no.11
Poem no.12
Poem no.13
Poem no.14
Poem no.15
Poem of Praise, A
Poem Re you and Another Brother in the Fall
Prelude to Nothing
Present
Queens of the Universe
Questions
Rebirth
Recurrent Dream
Right on White America
Right on White America #1
Right on White America #2
Right on White America #3
Right on White America #4
Rocking her White Feet
Safari
2nd Ave. & 12th St.
Sequences
Seventy-One Years Have Gatg- ered
Shedding my Years
Short Poem
Short Poem for us Black Ones
Signs of the End
Small Comment
So Much Rain
So This is Our Revolution
Summary
Summer Has Sped
Summer/time T.V. (is witer than ever)
Summer Words of a Sistuh Addict
Sunday/Evening at Gwen's
TCB
Television/Poem
10:15 A.M.--April 29, 1969
There are Blk/Puritans
There are Times That the Smell of You
These Autumn Trees
These Words Stained with Red
To a Jealous Cat
To All Brothers
To All Brothers: From all Sisters
To All Sisters
To Anita
To Blk/Record/Buyers
To Chuck
To Fanon, Culture Meant Only One Thing--an Environment Shaped to help us and Our Children Grow, Shaped by Ourselves in Action Against the System that Enslaved Us
To Kenny
To Morani/Mungu
To P.J.(2 Yrs Old Who Sed Write a Poem for me in Portland, Oregon)
To You/Who Almost Turned/Me On
Trees are Laughing, The
22-1424 (San/Francisco/ Suicide/Number
We a Bad People
We a badddDDD People
We are Gatherers of Bamboo Songs
We are Muslim Women
We Be. Gonna Be
We Can Be
We Not Learnen to be Paper Boys (For the Young

Brothas who Sell Muhammad Speaks)
We Stumbled into Each Other's Life
Welcome Home/My Prince
Wed Poem Before Thanksgiving
What Do I Know of You?
What is it About Me
When I Look at You
When I Return Home
When We Come
When You Left
Who Are You
Why
Why I Don't Get High on Shit
Woman
Woman. Rocking her White Hair
Womanhood
Words
Words for Geoffrey and Stephanie Hamilton
Words for Kali and Poochie
Words for Our Children (From Their Many Parents)
Would You Please Return my Pulse?
You are Amble
You Do Not Know the High Prayer
You Have Pierced me Deeply
You Have Stamped Your Hour On Me
Young/Black/Girl
Young Womanhood

SANDERS, AVA
Dear Daddy
They Wuz Off to See the Wizard
2:48 P.M.

SAUNDERS, RUBY C. see ALLAH FAREEDAH

SCHAEFFER, LOTUS
Old Black Mama Lived in a Shoe

SCOTT, SHARON
Between me and Anyone Who can Understand
Come on Home
Discovering
For Both of Us
For Gwen
Just Taking Note
Little More About the Brothers and Sisters, A
Mama Knows
Oh---Yeah!
Okay--
On My Stand
Our Lives
Sharon Will be No/Where On Nobody's Best-Selling List
Untitled
Untitled (Hironda)

SHAED, DOROTHY LEE LOUISE
Before Autumn Leaves Turn Gold
For a Discontented Soul
Lost
On a Letter Received
Reprobate
Snow

SHANGE, NTOZAKE
About Atlanta
Advice
& She Bleeds
& Then
Beach with Okra & Greens/On Their Honeymoon/Banda, Abao, Curacao
Black Night in Haiti, Palais National, Port-Au-Prince, A
Bocas: A Daughter's Geography
Chicago in San Francisco & A Poet
Crooked Woman/Okra Meets Greens in Strange Circumstances
Cross Oceans into my Heart
Dark Phases
Ego
Elegance in the Extreme
Expirese Girl Wanted
Fame on all Fours
Fiction/Non-Fiction Okras's Intellect Addresses Greens' Mind)
Five
Flying Song
For All My Dean & Loved Ones
For Marian
Frank Albert & Viola Benzena Owens
From Okra to Greens/A Differ-

ent Love Poem/We Need a Change
From Okra to Greens: A Personal Invitation (Reconciliation in Casablanca)
Get it & Feel Good
Hsnds & Holding
Jijo de las Americas
I Had Five Nose Rings
I Live in Music
I Talk to Myself
I'm Not Very Communicative
Improvisation
In Honor of Yr Poise in the Face of Hungry Lions
In the Blueness/Says Greens
Inquiry
Invitation to my Friends, An
It's Happening/But You Don't Know About It
Just as the Del Vikings Stole My Heart
Latin Night is Monday
Lotsa Body & Cultural Heritage
Loving You is Ecstasy to Me
Marine Intrusion
Mood Indigo
My Father is a Retired Magician
Nappy Edges
Nappy Edges (A Cross Country Sojourn)
New World Coro
Night Letter #3
No Gusts of Wind Tickle Me
No More Love Poems #1
Oakland in February
Odessa
Oh, I'm 10 Months Pregnant
Okra to Greens: A Historical Perspective of Sound/ Downtown
Okra to Greens Again (Special Delivery)
Okra to Greens/An Aside on Amsterdam Avenue
Ol Fashion Lady, An
Old Men, The
On Becoming Successful
One More Poem for Dolphy
Poems Gotta come Outta my Crotch, De?
Resurrection of the Daughter
Revelations (The Night Greens Went Off With That Hussy Rutagaba)
Rise Up Fallen Fighters Cora Takes Up With a Rastafari Man/She Cant Hold Back/ She say Smilin')
Senses of Heritage
Serious Lessons Learned
Several Propositions in the Middle of the Nite
Some Men
Suspect is Black & in his Early 20's, The
Synecdoche/Asbury Park in October
Take the A Train
Takin a Solo/A Poetic Possibility/A Poetic Imperative
Telephones & Other False Gods
This Woman Thinks we're de Beauvoir & Jean-Paul/ Never Forget/I'ma & Yr a Colored Girl
Tropical Dance
Tween Itaparica & Itapua'
We Need a God Who Bleeds Now
Where the Mississippi Meets the Amazon
Who am I Thinkin of
Who is Setting these Priorities
With no Immediate Cause
Wow...Yr Just Like a Man!
You are Such a Fool

SHARP, SAUNDRA
Moon Poem
New Blues from a Brown Baby
Reaching Back
Seeing Eye-Dog, A
Sundays are Special (Letter Poem)

SHARPE, AYO
Black Joy

SHAW, DORIS ANN
Emotions of the Blacks

SHAW, EDNA
Little Helper

SIMMONS, BERNADETTE

Get Involved

SIMMONS, BARBARA
Soul

SIMMONS, JUDY DOTHARD
Answer, The
Daffodils
Darling, Don't Be
Equal Opportunity
Generations
I Move into Loving
Judith's Blues
Letter
Linseed Oil and Dreams
Minority
Poem for a Bassist
Poem for Larry Ridley
Schizophrenia
Shall I Light Candles
Sleep, Child
To Swineherds, From Dachau With Love
To Wives (Of Artists)
Women
Youth Cult, The

SMART, ALICE MCGEE
Street Called Petticoat Lane, The
Pa

SMITH, LAURA E.
Exitus
Wings

SMITH, LUCY
Face of Poverty

SMITH, MARY CARTER
Club Woman
Jungle

SMITH, MARVA TATUM
Chatty Charlene, The
Critic, The
Difference, The
Doing
Fashion-Plate, The
Fear to Freedom
Fool, The
From the Infinite Bottom to the Infinite Top
God's Promise
How Can I Find the Words
I Don't Worry too Much
I Knew a Girl
I, Too, am not Perfect
I'm a Salesman
In Time
It's Good Being Me
Letter, A...
Lost My Mind Again
Love Poems....
Man Feeds Me, The
Money, But Also....
New Name
New Testament Remembered
No Sign Shall be Given
Not Everything one Say is Lyrical
Prophets, The
Quiet Arrogance
So, You've Grown Up
Thank You
There is a Lady
They Went to Church
Those Who Can, Do
Thought, A
To Market, to Market to Buy a Fat Pig
To You
True Worshipper, The
Where Do You Go?
Where I'd Like to Be
You Bet on Me
Young Men Dream

SMITH, ZELMA
Bully of the Brazos

SPENCER, ANNE
At the Carnival
Before the Feast of Shushan
Creed
Dunbar
For Jim, Easter Eve
I Have a Friend
Innocence
Lady, Lady
Life-Long, Poor Browning
Lines to a Nasturtium, A Lover Muses
Neighbors
Questing
Substitution
Sybil Warn her Sister
Translation
White Things
Wife-Woman, The

SPIRITUALS

Crucifixion
Deep River
Dere's No Hiding Place Down Here
Get on Board, Little Children
Give me Jesus
Go Down Moses
I Got a Home in Dat Rock
I Know de Moonlight
I Thank God I'm Free at Las'
No More Auction Block
Joshua Fid de Battle of Jericho
Ole Sheep Dey Know de Road, De
Steal Away to Jesus
Were You There When They Crucified my Lord
What Yo' Gwine to do When Yo' Lamp Burn Down?

STERLING, KATHY
Thoughts

STEVENS, RUBY
Hill, The
Murderer Awaiting Sentence, A
Passing
To You

STEVENS, SANDRA E.
Black Is

STUCKEY, ELMA
Beulah
Big Gate, The
Boy
Burying Ground
Cannonball
Collection
Cracked Saucer
Daylight Saving Time
Driver
Duke
Egg in Each Basket, An
Enancipation Proclamation
Enslaved
Family or Freedom
Feeding the Pastor
Flight
For W. E. B. DuBois
Good Masters
Gambler
Hallelujah
Hezekiah
His Hands
House Niggers
I Been There
Jackleg
Jane
Jenny
Jim
Lay me Down
Leora
Let Them Come
Lettie
Little Boys
Long Cotton Row
Mandy
Mose
Mother and Child
Mourners Bench
Movin' Nowhere
Mystery
New Address
News
No Flowers
No Wings
Old King Cotton
Old Man
Pete
Posted
Preacher Man
Rain
Rebel
Rebuked
Religion
Remember
Rigmarole: Puzzle for Children
Runaway
Sally
Scars and Stripes
Selling Melvina
Shadows in the Light
Shepherd
Sissy
Southern Belle
Sundown
Supper Time
Taking Sides
Telling it All
Tending in the Great House
This is It
Timing
Tom
Traveling Light
Trumpet
Upstart
Uncertain
Vision, The
Wish, The

TARVER, VALERIE
Differences
To the White Man

TATE, ELEANORA E.
African Madness

TATUM, MELVA ELOISE
For Moments
Hard to be Free
I Heard Myself Knocking
I Know Very Little About Love
I Like
I Picked Up a Rock...
I Remember You
I Wanted to Live in the Past
Today
It Takes Prayer and Patience
Making Love
Meeting You Two Years Later
Searching...
Sensuous
So Much of What I Did Today...
There is Nothing...

TAYLOR, ELAINE
Poem to Myself, A

TAYLOR, ISABELLE MCCLELLAN
In Some Time Hence
Loving Beauty is Loving God
Lynching, The
Peace and Principle

TERRY, LUCY
Bars Fight

THOMAS, BEVERLY
I

THOMAS, LINDA
Birth

THOMAS-GRUMBACH, ELEANOR
Accept Me
Black Woman
Bronzed Knight, The
Coping-I Just Can't Cope
Floating Thru the Galazy
Freedom/A State of Mind
Girl with the Ebony Eyes, The
Horizons
I
I Realease Thee-With Love
Judge Me Not
"Lee"
Lost Love
Lost Soul
Me, The Tree
Moonrise Sunset
My Mind
Sand Sifting Thru my Toes
Stranger, The
Try......Later
Visions
"Whispers of the Child, The"

THOMPSON, CLARA ANN
His Answer
Mrs. Johnson Objects

THOMPSON, ELEANOR A.
My mother
Uncle Tom
Wish, A

THORPE, THERESA
It Just Ain't Right

THURMAN, INEZ M.
Easter

TINSLEY, TOMI CAROLYN
Classified Ad
Cynic
I am Man
Retaliation

TOURE, AISHAH SAYYIDA MALI
For Love to Survive

TRAVIS, NANNIE M.
Dark Hands
White Fear

TRUTH, SOJOURNER
Ain't I A Woman

TURNER, CLAIRE
Creation
Misfit
Poet Questions his Immortality
To F.S.I.
To Some Who are Prone to
Criticize

TURNER, DORIS see LINYATTA

TURNER, LUCY MAY
Apple Trees by the River
Bird is Singing, A
Birth of Memory, The

'Bout Cullud Folkses
Curiosity
Deserted Cabin, The
Dog Catcher, The
Ebony
Evahbody's Got Trubbles
Eve
Flyin'
God's Gwine to Take all my Trubbles Away
How Come Dat?
Jewels
Lawd, De!
Love
Matilda at the Tuba
May I Return?
Mistah Me!
Mistah Skeeter
Mountains at Night
My City Garden Plot
My Path is Lighted by a Star
Nat Turner, an Epitaph
Pay Day
Pliant of the Madonna, The
Regret
Reverend is Gwine to be Big 'Soc'ation
Sassy
Secret Hours Ere Dawn, The
Sleep
Spell of Dawning, The
Spook Village
Stealin' Grub
Stri-i-ke One!
Sunny South
Tar Paper Bungalow, De
To a Fountain
To a Nickel

TWITTY, COUNTESS W.
Dali Fantasy
Defeat
Dusk Thoughts
High Tide
Quo Vadis
Subterfuge
Unrepentant

VALE, COSTON
Flight
Toleration

VAUGHN, NAOMI
Barren
Camouflauge
Mistakes
Retrospection of a Black Woman
Souls of Black Man

VERANO, MAAMI
Grass Man
I Have Days (Rainy Days & Mondays)
Momma
Weusi Resurrection, The

WALKER, ALICE
African Images
And Await the Answers
And His Fingers Peeled
And in the Hourly Making
And When She Thought of Him
Ballad of the Brown Girl
Baptism
Be Nobody's Darling
Beyond What
Black Mail
Black Prince, The
Burial
Burning Sharp
But She Was Known to Be
Clutter-Up People
Compulsory Chapel
Democratic Order, Such Things in Twenty Years I Understood, The
Each One, Pull One
Eagle Rock
Early Losses: A Requiem
Ending
Enemy
Excuse
Exercises on Themes From Life
Expect Nothing
Family Of
For my Sister Molly Who in the Fifties
Forbidden Things
Gift
Gift He Gave Unknowing, The
Girl Who Died # 1, The
Girl Who Died # 2/For d.p, The
He Said Come
Hymn
I Said to Poetry
I'm Really Very Fond
In These Dissenting Times
J. My Good Friend (Another Foolish Innocent)

Johann
Judge Every One With Perfect Calm
Karamojans
Kiss
Lonely Particular
Lost my Voice? Of Course/ for Beanie
Medicine
Mysteries
Nature of This Flower is to Bloom
New Face
No Fixed Place
Nothing is Right
Old Men Used to Sing, The
Old Warrior Terror, The
On Being Asked to Leave a Place of Honor for one of Comfort, Preferably in the Northern Suburbs
Once
Perfection
QPP, The
Rage
Reassurance
Representing the Universe
Revolutionary Petunias
Smell of Lebanon, The
So We've Come at Last to Freud
South: the Name of Home
Storm
Suicide
Sunday School, Circa 1950
They Take a Little Nip
Thief
Three Dollars Cash
To Die Before One Wakes Must Be Glad
To the Man in the Yellow Terry
Uncles
View from Rosehill Cemetery, Vicksburg
Warning
What Ovid Taught Me
What the Finger Writes
While Love is Unfashionable
Will
Winking at a Funeral
Women
You had to go to Funerals

WALKER, MARGARET

Amos—1963
Amos (Postcript—1968)
At the Lincoln Monument in Washington August 28, 1963
Bad-Man Stagolee
Ballad of the Free, The
Ballad of the Hoppy Toad, The
Big John Henry
Birmingham
Childhood
Dark Blood
Dear are the Names that Charmed me in my Youth
Delta
Elegy
Epitaph for my Father
Fanfare, Coda, and Finale
Five Black Men....
For Andy Goodman--Michael Schwerner--and James Cheney
For Gwen
For Malcolm X
For Mary McLeod Bethune
For My People
For Paul Laurence Dunbar
Girl Held Without Bail
Gus, the Lineman
Harriet Tubman
Hosea
How Many Silent Centuries Sleep in my Sultry Veins
I Hear a Rumbling...
I Want to Write
Iowa Farmer
Isaiah
Jackson, Mississippi
Jeremiah
Joel
Kissie Lee
Lineage
Litany From the Dark People, A
Long John Nelson and Sweetie Pie
Memory
Micah
Molly Means
My Truth and my Flame
Now
October Journey
Ode on the Occasion of the Inauguration of the Sixth President of Jackson

Our Need
Oxford is a Legend
People of Unrest
Poppa Chicken
Prophets for a New Day
Since 1619
Sit-Ins
Sorrow Home
Southern Song
Street Demonstration
Struggle Staffers Us, The
Teacher
They Who Feel Death
This is my Century...Black Synthesis of Time
Today
Two Gun Buster and Trigger Slim
We Have Been Believers
Whores
Yalluh Hammuh

WALLACE, ANN
C'mon Now
Free as a Bird
Go On
I Want
Nightmare
So Much of Me
Unity

WANGARA, MALAIKA AYO see AMINI, JOHARI

WARD, VAL GRAY
Gwen Brooks, A Pyramid

WASHINGTON, HAZEL L.
Mother America
Woman at War, A

WATSON, EVELYN
Dream World

WEAVER, ELEANOR
In Higher Places
Mulatto

WEEDEN, LULA LOWE
Dance
Have You Seen It
Little Dandelion
Me Alone
Robin Red Breast
Stream, The

WEISS, EDNA MAE
Commencement

WESS, DEBORAH FULLER
My Sea of Tears
Soldiers

WHEATLEY, PHILLIS
Answer, The
Answer to the Rebus, by the Author of These Poems
Elegial Poem on the Death of that Celebrated Divine, and Eminent Servant of Jesus Christ, the late Reverend, and Pious George Whitefield
Elegy Sacred to the Memory of Dr. Samuel Cooper (1784)
Elegy to Miss Mary Moorhead, on the Death of her Father, the Rev. Mr. John Moorhead
Farewell to America, A
Farewell to America (1773) to Mrs. S. W., A
Funeral Poem on the Death of C. E. an Infant of Twelve Months
Goliath of Gath (I Samuel, Chap. XVII)
His Excellency General Washington
Hymn to Humanity, An (To S. P. G. Esq.)
Hymn to the Evening, An
Hymn to the Morning, A
Isaiah LXIII 1-8
Liberty and Peace
Niobe in Distress for her Children Slain by Apollo, From Ovid's Metamorphoses, Book VI, and From a View of the Painting of Mr. Richard Wilson
Ode of Verses on the Much-Lamented Death of the Rev. Mr. George White-field
Ode on the Birthday of Pompey Stockbridge, An
Ode to Neptune
On Being Brought From Africa to America
On Freedom

On Friendship
On Imagination
On Major General Lee (1776)
On Recollection
On the Capture of General Lee
On the Death of a Young Gentleman
On the Death of a Young Lady of Five Years Old
On the Death of Dr. Samuel Marshall (1771)
On the Death of J. C. and Infant
On the Death of Rev. Dr. Sewell (1769)
On the Death of the Rev. Mr. George Whitefield, 1770)
On the Death of the Rev. Mr. George Whitefield (1776)
On the Death of the Rev'd Dr. Sewall 1769
On Virtue
Phillis' Reply to the Answer in our Last by the Gentleman in the Navy
Recollection to Miss A--M-- Humbly Inscribed by the Authoress
To a Clergyman on the Death of His Lady
To a Gentleman and Lady on the Death of Her Son and Their Brother
To a Gentleman and Lady on the Death of the Lady's Brother and Sister, and a Child of the Name Avis, Aged One Year
To a Gentleman of the Navy (For the Royal American Magazine)
To a Gentleman on His Voyage to Great Britain for the Recovery of His Health
To a Lady and Her Children, on the Death of Her Son and Their Brother
To a Lady on her Coming to North America with Her Son, for the Recovery of Her Health
To a Lady on her Remarkable Preservation in a Hurricane in North Carolina
To a Lady on the Death of her Husband
To a Lady on the Death of Three Relations
To Captain H---D, of the 65th Regiment
To His Excellency General Washington
To His Honor the Lieutenant Governor, on the Death of His Lady March 24, 1773
To Maecenas
To Mrs. Leonard on the Death of Her Husband
To Mr. and Mrs.--, On the Death of Their Infant Son
To S, M. a Young African Painter on Seeing His Works
To the Honorable T. H. Esq. on the Death of His Daughter
To the Hon'ble Thomas Hubbard, Esq. on the Death of Mrs. Thankfull Leonard
To the King's Most Excellent (1768)
To the Rev. Dr. Thomas Amory, on Reading His Sermons on Daily Devotion, in Which That Duty is Recommended and Assisted
To the Rev. Mr. Pitkin on the Death of His Lady (1772)
To the Right Honorable William, Earl of Dartmouth
To the Right Honorable William, Earl of Dartmouth His Majesty's Principal Secretary of State for North America, Etc.
To the University of Cambridge, of New England
To the University of Cambridge, Wrote in 1767

WHITE, PAULETTE CHILDRESS
Big Maybelle
Humbled Rock
Oronde
Say That I Am

WHITELY, DEBBIE
You Can't Shake Hands With a Fist

WIGGINS, BERNICE LOVE
Church Folks

WILEY, ELECTA
Power of Power, The

WILLIAMS, GWENDOLYN
I Remember When

WILLIAMS, JUNE VANLEER
All Right, Mama
Analysis
Behind the Curtain
Bend to Spring
Bus Trip-Rest Stop-1950
Contradictory Values
Cook's Job Available
Delusion
Demon: Possessed
Different Points of View
Don't Die in January
Episode
Fakery
Family Member (You Must Be Putting me On), A
Finale
Forfeiture
Ghetto Daybreak
GI Gratitude
Grief Unexplained
How Long to Live
How Old Did You Say?
Interlude
Interlude Revised
Is Anybody Here?
Lip Love
Lost Cause
Middle Age Syndrome, The
Mode of Communication, A
My God is Everything
No Revival
No Way Out
Nursing Home, USA
Obituary
Paradox
Parental Lament
Poet's Plea, A
Precious Offering, A
Quest for Self
Questions, Questions
Reading Won't Make It
Requiem for a Newsman
Retrospection on Selection
Revelation
Seems we Got Detoured
So I Say!
So Quickly It Ends
Something Else
Such a Peculiar World
Synopsis
They Say, "There's A Race Problem!"
Trick, Maybe, The?
Undersized: Throw it Back!

WILLIAMS, LUCY ARIEL see HOLLOWAY, ARIEL WILLIAMS

WILLIAMS, MILLIE
Song

WILLIAMS, REGINA
Asylum
For our Life is a Matter of Faith
I am Not my Sister's Keeper: I am My Sister

WILLIAMS, SHERLEY
Any Woman's Blues
Blues is Something to Think About
C/o Ambush c/o Mike
Collateral Adjective
Communion in a Small Room
Drivin' Wheel
Empress Brand Trim: Ruby Reminisces, The
Finding of a Nest the Coming to a Roost, The
Flo Show
Folding of the Feathers the Counting of the Birds, The
For Ronald King our Brother
From "The Iconography of Childhood"
House of Desire, The
I See My Life...
I Sing This Song for our Mothers
If He Let Us Go Now
Lines Between Seekonk and Fairhaven
Listen to the Drum
North County, The Dream Realized
1 Poem 2 Voices, a Song

Pavonine Truth, A
Peacock Poems: 1, The
Peacock Poems: 2, The
Peacock Poems: 3, The
Peacock Song
Quartet
Record for my Friends, A
Say Hellow to John
Someone Sweet Angel Child
This a Rap on Yo Do
This City-Light
This is a Sad-Ass Poem for a Black Woman to be Writing
Time
2½ Poem Making Whole
Walk into the Soft Soft
Wishon Line, The
You Were Never Miss Brown to Me

WILLIAMS, VIRGINIA
So Tired

WILSON, GERALDINE L.
Our Children are our Children
Refugee Mother

WILSON, PATRICE M.
February
Garden, The

WITHERSPOON, NAOMI LONG see MADGETT, NAOMI LONG

WRIGHT, SARAH E.
To Some Millions who Survive Joseph E. Mander, Senior
Until They Have Stopped

YANCEY, ALEXIS
4 Ever
Will, The

YANCEY, BESSIE WOODSON
After a Visit to the Home of Ex-Slaves
Ambassador
An't Milissy's Tater Pies
Assets
Backslidin'
Be a Good Sport
Below de Line
Calling Me
Comradery
Contentment
Dad
Disciplinarian, The
Disillusionment
Dreams
Fall-Time
Forward Ethiopia
Fros' is on de Punkin, De
Give Him a Chance
Harmony
"I Ken Mek It"
I Wonder Why
If You Live in West Virginia
June
Knee-Deep
"Knee-Deep!" And "Try It!"
Loafin'
May
Miscreant
Mountain Stream
Negro Lullaby
Negro Woman, The
Night
On'ry Weathah
Out My Street
'Possum-Huntin'
Price, The
Railman's Story, The
Real Sport
Recompense
Secret, The
Service
Signs ob Spring
"Slackahs"
Strategy
Summer-Moon
Supply
Time Aint Long, De
To a Critic
To Sunshine Sammy
Toast to Colored Girls, A
Train-Man's Call, The
West, The
West Virginia
Where Do You Live?
Whistlin' Sam
Winter
You Must Give Before you Get

ZEALY, YOLANDE
Prayer, A

ZIMELE-KEITA, NZADI
Birds of Paradise
Long Road Rhythm
What We Know

SUBJECT INDEX

ABBOTT, ROBERT S.
Robert S. Abbott. Eloise Culver

ABBREVIATIONS
Mother, The. Gwendolyn Brooks
U Name This One. Carolyn M. Rodgers

ABSCENCE
In Absence. Naomi Long Madgett

ACCIDENTS
Accident Edgecome General Hospital May 16, 1968 Julia Fields

ADAMS, LEWIS
Lewis Adams. Eloise Culver

ADOLESCENCE
Hanging Fire. Audre Lorde
In my life, Latin and Adolescence Came Along Together. Gloria Oden
Our Teenagers. Orlean Bess

ADULTHOOD
Adulthood (For Claudia) Nikki Giovanni
When I Grow Up. Gertrude Blackwell Bailey

ADVERTISING
Classified Ad. Tomi Carolyn Tinsley

ADVICE
Advice. Gwendolyn B. Bennett

AFRICA
Africa. Maya Angelou
Africa I. Nikki Giovanni
Africa II. Nikki Giovanni
Africa, Drifting Through me Sings. Margaret Danner
African Images. Alice Walker
African Night Suite. Jayne Cortez
Children of Lumumba. Stella Ngatho
Ego-Tripping. Nikki Giovanni
Far From Africa: Four Poems. Margaret Danner
For Us, Who Dare Not Dare. Maya Angelou
Glimpses of Africa. Naomi Long Madgett
Going to Africa. Linga Bragg Brown
Goodbye David Tamuncemi West. Margaret Danner
Her Blood, Drifting Through Me, Sings. Margaret Danner
It's Time (Repatriation... Africa)? Katie M. Cumbo
Old Laughter. Gwendolyn Brooks
People of Gleaming Cities and of the Lion's and the Leopard's Brood. Sharon Bourke
Proem on Africa. Margaret T. G. Burroughs
Return. Johari Amini
Song of the Warriors. Anonymous
Soweto Song. Amina Baraka
They Clapped. Nikki Giovanni
To S. M., A Young African

Painter, On Seeing His Works. Phillis Wheatley
Untitled. Stella Ngatho
William Leon Hansberry. Eloise Culver

AFRICAN--TRIBES
Dahomey. Audre Lorde

AFRO HAIR STYLES
Naturally. Audre Lorde
Oh---Yeah! Sharon Scott
3-31-70. Gayl Jones

AGED
Age. Kattie M. Cumbo
Age. Nikki Giovanni
Apology to an Old Man Who Only Wanted to Chat. Jennifer Blackman Lawson
Episode. June Vanleer Williams
How Old Did You Say? June Vanleer Williams
Now Poem For Us. Sonia Sanchez
Old. Gertrude Blackwell Bailey
Old Man, The. Barbara Jean Knight
Ole Men, The. Ntozake Shange
On Aging. Maya Angelou
Poem for Young People, A. Jennifer Blackman Lawson
They Take a Little Nip. Alice Walker
Young and the Old, The. Gertrude Blackwell Bailey
Youth to Age. Pauli Murray

AGRICULTURE
I'm Around-Town Gent. Anonymous
Iowa Farmer. Margaret Walker

AIRPLANES
Flight. Pinkie Gordon Lane
On Holidays in the Best Tradition. June Jordan

AIRPORTS
While Sitting in the Airport Waiting Rooom. Pinkie Gordon Lane

ALABAMA
Alabama. Julia Fields
Alabama Centennial. Naomi Long Madgett
Alabama Memories. Harryette Mullen
Alabama Poem. Nikki Giovanni
Birmingham. Margaret Walker

ALASKA
Alaska. Margaret Danner

ALCOHOLISM
5 Winos. Carolyn Rodgers
Make the First Step. Gertrude Blackwell Bailey

ALDRIDGE, IRA
Ira Aldridge. Eloise Culver

ALLEN, RICHARD
Quarto Centennial or the Birth of Bishop Richard Allen. Josephine D. (Henderson) Heard
Rt. Rev. Richard Allen. Josephine D. (Henderson) Heard
Richard Allen. Eloise Culver
To Bishop Allen's Memory. Josephine D. (Henderson) Heard

ALLEN, SAMUEL
Samuel Allen's Soul Dances. Margaret Danner

ALLEN UNIVERSITY
Farewell to Allen University. Josephine D. (Henderson) Heard

ALLEYS
Somewhere. Wanda Coleman

ALONE
Alone. Maya Angelou
Alone. Nikki Giovanni
Certain Peace, A. Nikki Giovanni
World is Not a Pleasant Place to Be, The. Nikki Giovanni

ALPHA KAPPA ALPHA SORORITY
Greek Crazeology. Carolyn Rodgers

AMBITION
Out of My Way. Gertrude Blackwell Bailey

AMERICA
America. Maya Angelou
America, An Overdeveloped/ Animosity Stamping Out of the Dreams. Vanessa Howard
America Negra. Anita Scott Coleman
Black Memorial Day. Frenchy J. Hodges
Farewell to America (1773) To Mrs. S. W. A. Philis Wheatley
Final Solution. Sonia Sanchez
Gifts of America. Vanessa Howard
Great Cities Crumble. Gertrude Blackwell Bailey
Natives of America, The. Ann Plato
Right On: White America, Sonia Sanchez
Sweet Land of Everything to Thee I Sing. Bobbretta M. Elliston
To My Country. Naomi Long Madgett

AMOEBA
Love: Is a Human Condition. Nikki Giovanni

ANCESTORS
Generations. Judy Dothard Simmons
On My First Trip to Mississippi. Linda Brown Bragg

ANDERSON, MARIAN
Gertrude. Gwendolyn Brooks
Marian Anderson. Eloise Culver
We Launched a Ship. Ruby Berkley Goodwin

ANGELS
God Called an Angel. Jo Nell Rice

ANIMALS
Kob Antelope. Anonymous
Pete at the Zoo. Gwendolyn Brooks

ANNIAD
Anniad, The. Gwendolyn Brooks
Appendix to the Anniad (Leaves from a Loose-Leaf War Diary) Gwendolyn Brooks

ANNIVERSARY
One April. Lucia M. Pitts
Wedding Anniversary, The. Josephine D. (Henderson) Heard

ANTIGONE
Antigone and Oedipus. Henrietta Cordelia Ray

APPLES
Apple Trees by the River. Lucy Mae Turner
Apples. Ariel Williams
Green Apples. Linda Brown Bragg

APRIL
April in Your Eyes. Naomi Long Madgett
April is on the Way. Alice Dunbar Nelson
April Longing. Mary Wilkerson Cleaves
At April. Angelina Weld Grimke
Rondeau. Jessie Redmond Fauset
Written on the Last of April. Naomi Long Madgett

ARCHANGELS
Fifth Michael, The. Margaret Danner
La, Lala, La, La. Margaret Danner
Name Michael Brings the Whirr of Wings, The. Margaret Danner

ARKANSAS
My Arkansas. Maya Angelou

ART
Chicago Art Scene 1967 Just As Our African Ancestors Did. Margaret Danner
Chicago Picasso, The. Gwendolyn Brooks
Convert, The. Margaret Danner
Desire. Constance Nichols
From Ease to Handy to Hayes. Margaret Danner
In a Bone White Frame. Margaret Danner
In the Art Institute on St. Valentine's Day. Margaret Danner
Just as Our African Ancestors Did. Margaret Danner
Niobe in Distress for her Children Slain by Apollo, From Ovid's Metamorphoses. Book VI, and From a View of the Painting of Mr. Richard Wilson. Phillis Wheatley
This Little Senufo Bird. Margaret Danner
To S. M., a Young African Painter, on Seeing His Works. Phillis Wheatley

ART--AFRICAN
At Home in Dakar. Margaret Danner
Convert, The. Margaret Danner
Etta Moten's Attic. Margaret Danner
For Muffin. Margaret Danner
Is There no Tangeringe Witched Fire? Margaret Danner
Lady Executive Looks at a Mangbetu Palm Wine Jug, The. Margaret Danner
This Two-Toned Stork of a Hairpin, This Comb. Margaret Danner
To the Bronze Head. Margaret Danner

ART--GALLERIES
On Finding Arts Extended Gallery and You. Margaret Danner

ARTISTS
To the Artist who Just Happens to be Black. Jayne Cortez
To Wives (Of Artists) Judy Dothard Simmons

ASSASSINATIONS
Suite of Assassinations, The. Carolyn Rodgers

ASSIMILATION
So Tired. Virginia Williams

ASTROLOGY
Starbound. Wanda Coleman

ASTRONAUTS
Astronaut of Innerspace, The. Harryette Mullen

ATLANTA--MISSING CHILDREN
About Atlanta. Ntozake Shange

ATLANTA UNIVERSITY
To Atlanta University--Its Founders and Teachers. Georgia Douglas Johnson

ATROCITIES
Atrocities. Nikki Giovanni

ATTICA
Poem Against the State. June Jordan

ATTUCKS, CRISPUS
Crispus Attucks. Eloise Culver
Post War Ballad. Dorothy Vena Johnson

AUNT JEMIMA
In Search of Aunt Jemima. Naomi Long Madgett

AUTHORS
Black Writer, A. Johari Amini

AUTOMOBILES
Album: Photo 2. Naomi Long Madgett

AUTUMN
And Fall Shall Sit in Judgment. Audre Lorde
Autumn Night. Naromi Long Madgett
Fall-Time. Bessie Woodson Yancey
To Autum. Naomi Long Madgett

- B -

BABIES see INFANTS

BACKSLIDING
Backslidin'. Bessie Woodson Yancey

BAEZ, JOAN
Re: Joan Baez. Leatrice Emeruwa

BAHAMAS
Bahamas-I. Kattie M. Cumbo
Bahamas-II. Kattie M. Cumbo

BAHI
Tropical Dance. Ntozake Shange

BAKER, JOSEPHINE
So Many Feathers. Jayne Cortez

BALANCES
Balances. Nikki Giovanni

BALLADS
Ballit of de Boll Weevil, De. Anonymous
John Henry. Anonymous
Stackalee. Anonymous

BALLET
For There's no end to the Suffering a Female Will Bear for Benny. Margaret Danner
Let Them Wear Pale Orchid Shoes. Margaret Danner

BALLS
Precious Curiosity. Linda Brown Bragg

BALTIMORE, MARYLAND
Taking Care. June Jordan

BANNEKER, BENJAMIN
Benjamin Banneker. Eloise Culver

BAPTISM
Baptism. Alice Walker

BARS
Bars Fight. Lucy Terry
Gay Bar. Wanda Coleman

BASEBALL
On Watching a World Series Game. Sonia Sanchez
Stri-i-ke One! Lucy Mae Turner

BASKETS
This Basket is Heavy. Linda Brown Bragg

BATON ROUGE, LOUISIANA
Baton Rouge. Pinkie Gordon Lane

BATS
Bats. Effie Lee Newsome

BAZAARS
Bazaar. Audre Lorde

BEACHES see SEASHORE

BEANS
Bean Eaters. Gwendolyn Brooks

BEATING
Somebody Call. Carolyn Rodgers

BEARDEN, ROMARE
Collage for Romare Bearden. Jayne Cortez

BEAUTY
I Sit and Wait For Beauty. Mae V. Cowdery
Loving Beauty is Loving God. Isabelle McClellan Taylor
When I Grow. Kali Grosvenor

BEAUTY SHOP
At the Hairdresser's. Gwendolyn Brooks
Beauty Shoppe. Gwendolyn Brooks
Son of A. Wanda Coleman

BEDS
Crawl Into Bed. Quandra Prettyman
We Had Slept in the Old Beds Too Long. Margaret Danner

BEER
Beer Drops. Melba Joyce Boyd

BELLS
Sabbath Bells. Josephine D. (Henderson) Heard
Small Bells of Benin, The. Margaret Danner

BENEDICTION
Benediction. Georgia Douglas Johnson

BENNET COLLEGE
Words for a Motet. Linda Brown Bragg

BETHUNE, MARY MCLEOD
Dr. Mary M. Bethune. Eloise Culver
For Mary McLeod Bethune. Margaret Walker
Mary McLeod Bethune. Margaret Walker

BIBLE--HISTORY

At the Lincoln Monument in Washington, August 28, 1963 Margaret Walker
Prophets for a New Day. Margaret Walker

BIRDS
After. Naomi Long Madgett
Aria. Carole Gregory
Artic Tern in a Museum. Effie Lee Newsome
Ballad of the Light-Eyed Little Girl, The. Gwendolyn Brooks
Blackbird, The. Linda B. Graham
Flamingo. Margaret Danner
For the Bird who Flew Against our Window one Morning and Broke His Natural Neck. Lucille Clifton
Garnishing the Aviary. Margaret Danner
Jaybird. Anonymous
Jessica, a Bird Who Sings. Nikki Giovanni
Lady Bird. Kali Grosvenor
Maybe the Birds. June Jordan
Migration. Pinkie Gordon Lane
My Canary. Josephine D. (Henderson) Heard
My Mocking Bird. Josephine D. (Henderson) Heard
Robin Red Breast. Lula Lowe Weeden
Robin's Poem. Nikki Giovanni
Song to a Phantom Nightingale. Naomi Long Madgett
Sparrow is a Bird, A. Margaret Danner
Sparrow's Fall, The. Frances E. W. Harper
To a Wounded Bird. Hilda Preer
Unburying the Bird. Toi Derricotte

BIRMINGHAM, ALABAMA
Poems: Birmingham 1962-1964. Julia Fields

BIRTHDAYS
Birth. Linda Thomas
January 3, 1970. Mae Jackson
My Husband's Birthday. Josephine D. (Henderson) Heard
Story of a Very Broken Lady, The. Toi Derricotte
Supremacy. Leonora Gillison

BLACK (COLOR)
As a Basic. Linda Porter
What Color is Black? Barbara Mahone
When I See Black. Kali Grosvenor

BLACK (PEOPLE)
Beautiful, Black and Beloved. Margaret T. G. Burroughs
Black Can be Beautiful. Mary Bohanon
Black Is. Kali Grosvenor
Black Is. Sandra Stevens
Black is Black. Kali Grosvenor
Blackness Is. Linda Bragg Brown
'Bout Cullud Folkses. Lucy Mae Turner
For a Child. Naomi Long Madgett
For Both of Us at Fisk. Sharon Scott
From A Bus. Joyce Whitsitt Lawrence
Gospel Truth, The. Jackie Earley
I Love You Don't. Kali Grosvenor
Love. Kali Grosvenor
Minority. Judy Dothard Simmons
My People are Black. Kali Grosvenor
Naturally. Audre Lorde
On my Blk/Ness. Alicia Loy Johnson
Our Black People. Kali Grosvenor
Poem (No Name No.2) Nikki Giovanni

Primer for Blacks. Gwendolyn Brooks
To Be Black in American. Nancy L. Arnez
Utility. Marion Nicholes
Who Can be Born Black. Mari Evans
You are Black. Helen F. Clarke

BLACK LIBERATION
To Darnell and Johnny. Melba Joyce Boyd

BLACK MUSLIMS
And it Will Be Ours. Sonia Sanchez
We are Muslim Women. Sonia Sanchez
We're Not Learnen to be Paper Boys (For the Young Brothas Who Sell Muhammad Speaks) Sonia Sanchez

BLACK POWER
Black Power. Nikki Giovanni

BLACK PRIDE
Beautiful Black and Beloved. Margaret T. B. Burroughs
Beauty of Black, The. Margaret T. G. Burroughs
Black is Not the Man. Gertrude Blackwell Bailey
Black You Are. Gertrude Blackwell Bailey
Footsteps. Gertrude Blackwell Bailey
Letter to a Blkwoman's Daughter. Johari Amini
Naturally. Audre Lorde
Observations of a Saturday Night Crowd. Damali
Our Blackness did not Come to Us Whole. Linda Brown Bragg
Peaches. Musu Ber
Peacock Poems 1, The. Shirley Williams
Poem. Sonia Sanchez
Poem About Beauty Blackness, Poetry (And How to be All Three) Linda Brown Bragg
Proud to Be. Gertrude Blackwell Bailey
Sonnet to a Negro in Harlem. Helene Johnson
SOS. Anonymous
Sound of Music, The. Carolyn Rodgers
2 B Blk. Val Ferdinand
What Shall I Tell my Children Who are Black? Margaret T. G. Burroughs

BLACK UNITY
Call for Black Unity, A. Kattie M. Cumbo

BLACKBIRD
Blackbird, The. Linda B. Graham

BLESSINGS
Blessings Without Company. Anonymous

BLINDNESS
Blind. Gertrude Blackwell Bailey
For the Blind. Lucille Clifton
Sight. Cora Bell Moten

BLIZZARDS see STORMS

BLUES
Ain't No Blues Song. Jennifer Blackman Lawson
Back Door Blues. Anonymous
Back Water Blues. Anonymous
Big Fat Mama, A. Anonymous
Black Woman. Anonymous
Blues, A. Jayne Cortez
Blues. Leatrice Emeruwu
Blues. Quandra Prettyman
Blues Come From Texas, The. Anonymous
Blues (in Two Parts), The. Val Ferdinand
Blues in B^b, Mari Evans

Blues Poem, A. Leatrice Emeruwa
Blues Today, The. Mae Jackson
Dink's Blues. Anonymous
Drying Spit Blues. Jayne Cortez
Fogyism. Anonymous
Going Home. Joane Jimason
Good Mornin' Blues. Anonymous
How Long Blues. Anonymous
I Got the Blues. Anonymous
I Remember. Carolyn Rodgers
I'm Gonna be Long Gone Baby Blues. Leatrice Emeruwa
Judith's Blues. Judy Dothard Simmons
Just Blues. Anonymous
Laid Off Blues. Nancy L. Arnez
Low Down Blues. Lucille D. Goodlett
Married Woman Blues. Anonymous
Master Charge Blues. Nikki Giovanni
Monday Morning Blues. Naomi Long Madgett
Monte Carlo Blues. Anonymous
Poets Beyond th Blues. Naomi Long Madgett
Poverty Blues. Nancy L. Arnez
Put it Right Here or Keep it Out There. Anonymous
Queen of the Blues. Gwendolyn Brooks
Rhythm & Blues. Jayne Cortez
St. James Infirmary Blues. Anonymous
Shorty George. Anonymous
Southern Blues. Anonymous
Syncopating Rhythm. Frenchy J. Hodges
3 Day New York Blues. Jayne Cortez
Young Boy Blues. Anonymous

BOATS
Boats in Winter. Julia Fields
Dream Boats. Naomi Long Madgett

BOLL WEEVILS
Ballit of De Boll Weevil, De. Anonymous

BOMBINGS
Birmingham. Nancy L. Arnez

BONES
Dry Bones. Anonymous
Shuddering. Harryette Mullen
Wings Against the Blue. Harryette Mullen

BOOKS
This Treasured Book. Pinkie Gordon Lane
Visit of the Professor of Aesthetics. Margaret Danner

BOOTHS
I Love Those Little Booths at Benvenutis. Gwendolyn Brooks

BOOTS see SHOE AND SHOE INDUSTRY

BOSSES--STRAW
Straw Bosses. E. Sharon Gomillion

BOYS
As I Grown Up Again. Audre Lorde
Baker's Boy, The. Effie Lee Newsome
Black Boy. Ophelia Robinson
Blacktop Black Top Blacktop Top Black Black Top. Marion Nichholas
Boy Breaking Glass. Gwendolyn Brooks
Boy Died in my Alley, The. Gwendolyn Brooks
Boys, Black. Gwendolyn Brooks
Brother Alvin. Audre Lorde
First Date. Leatrice

Emeruwa
For Christopher. June Jordan
From a Bus. Joyce Whitsitt Lawrence
Grandson is a Hoticeberg, A. Margaret Danner
Jonathan Sitting in Mud. Nikki Giovanni
Life of Lincoln West, The. Gwendolyn Brooks
Little Black Boy. Barbara Marshall
Little Boys. Elma Stuckey
Little Boy's Prayer. Bernadine Blessitt
Little Brown Boys. Helene Johnson
Little David Play on Yo' Harp. Anonymous
Little Son. Georgia Douglas Johnson
Martyr of Alabama, The. Frances Harper
Mistah Me! Lucy Mae Turner
Morning Light; the Dew-drier. Effie Lee Newsome
My Boys. Lucille Clifton
Of De Wit Williams on His Way to Lincoln Cemetery. Gwendolyn Brooks
Otto. Gwendolyn Brooks
Poem. Helene Johnson
Poem for Black Boys. Nikki Giovanni
Poem for Weedie, A. S. Diane Bogus
Save the Boys. Frances Harper
Snowflakes. Nikki Giovanni
Those Boys that Ran Together. Lucille Clifton
To a Brown Boy. Naomi Long Madgett
To Kenny. Sonia Sanchez
To P. J. (2 Yrs Old Who Sed Write a Poem for me in Portland, Oregon) Sonia Sanchez
To Sunshine Sammy. Bessie Woodson Yancey
Whistlin' Sam. Bessie Woodson Yancey
Young David: Birmingham, A. Helen Morgan Brooks

BRADFORD, WALTER
Walter Bradford. Gwendolyn Brooks

BRAITHWAITE, WILLIAM STANLEY
To William Stanley Braithwaite. Georgia Douglas Johnson

BRAZIL
Private Letter to Brazil Gloria Oden

BREAD
Bran Bread. Linda Brown Bragg

BREAST FEEDING
Sleep, Child. Judy Dothard Simmons

BREASTS
Breast Examination

BREATHS
Like Breaths. Margaret Danner

BRIDES
Behold the Bride. Corinne Lytle

BRIDGE (CARD GAME)
Bride Party of Gap in Teeth Aint New. Marion Nicholes

BROODING
Brooding. Jayne Cortez

BROOKLYN, NEW YORK
Song From Brooklyn, A. Kattie

M. Cumbo

BROOKS, GWENDOLYN
As Critic. Margaret Danner
Black Children. Carole Gregory Clemmons
Bronzeville Breakthrough. Sarah Webster Fabio
Dedicated to the Living Memory of Miss Gwendolyn Brooks. Carole Gregory Clemmons
For Gwen. Sharon Scott
(For Gwen Brooks) Sonia Sanchez
For Gwen--1969. Margaret Walker
For Gwendolyn Brooks. Helen H. King
For Gwendolyn Brooks. Nikki Giovanni
For Gwendolyn Brooks. Pinkie Gordon Lane
For Gwendolyn Brooks--A Whole & Beautiful Spirit. Johari Amini
Gathering of Artists, A. Alicia Johnson
Gwen Brooks, A Pyramid. Val Gray Ward
Live Celebrations. Sarah Webster Fabio
Praise Due to Gwen Brooks. Cynthia M. Conley
Sunday/Evening at Gwens. Sonia Sanchez
Three Poems for Gwendolyn Brooks. Delores Kendrick
To Gwen, Mo Luv. Carolyn Rodgers
To Gwendolyn Brooks the Creator in the Beginning--Words. Barbara Reynolds
Tree Poem, The. Paulette Jones

BROOKS, RAYMOND MELVIN
Raymond Melvin Brooks. Gwendolyn Brooks

BROTHERHOOD
Brotherhood. Georgia Douglas Johnson
God's Christmas Tree. Eve Lynn
One Man's Confession of Brotherhood. Naomi F. Faust

BROTHERS
I'm Me. Linda Brown Bragg
Kin. Maya Angelou
When My Oldest Brother, Buddy (And My Father's Namesake) Died. Gloria Oden

BROWN, JAMES
Poem to James Brown, A. Olean Bess
There was a Time. Mae Jackson

BROWN, JOHN
To John Brown. Georgia Douglas Johnson

BROWN, STERLING
Love Poem Written for Sterling Brown, A. Sonia Sanchez
Poem for Sterling Brown, A. Sonia Sanchez

BROWNING, ROBERT
Life-Long, Poor Browning. Anne Spencer

BUBBLES
I Only Watch the Bubbles. Nikki Giovanni

BUGS
Bedbug. Anonymous

BUILDINGS
Building, The. Frances Harper
Like Thunder Among Tall Buildings. Margaret Danner

BUNCHE, RALPH
Ralph Bunche. Eloise Culver

BUSES
Ode to a Scotlandville Bus. Lois Miller
Things is Changing. Mari Evans
Troost Express. Damali

BUSING
On Busing. Carolyn Rodgers

BUTTERFLIES
Butterfly. Ethlynne E. Holmes
Painted Lady, The. Margaret Danner

BYRON, LORD GEORGE GORDON
Sonnet to Byron. Naomi Long Madgett

- C -

CABINS
Deserted Cabin. Lucy Mae Turner

CAMBRIDGE UNIVERSITY
To the University of Cambridge in New England. Phillis Wheatley

CANADA
Those Summer I Was Fourteen and Fifteen. Gloria Oden

CANARIES
My Canary. Josephine D. (Henderson) Heard

CANCER
American Cancer Society or There is More Than One Way to Skin a Coon. Audre Lorde
Cancer. Nikki Giovanni

CANDLES
For the Candle Light. Angelina Weld Grimke

CANDY
Peppermint Candy March, The. Effie Lee Newsome

CANNIBALISM
Untitled. Wanda Coleman

CANOSSA, ITALY
Canossa. Naomi Long Madgett

CAPITALISM
Capitalism. Mae Jackson

CARD PLAYING
Penny-Ante. Coleen McElroy
Solitaire. Naomi Long Madgett
Some Uses for Them Not Stated. Nikki Giovanni

CARNIVAL
At the Carnival. Anne Spencer

CAROUSELS
Carousel, The. Gloria Oden

CARVER, GEORGE WASHINGTON
Dr. George Washington Carver. Eloise Culver
Notes on the Peanut. June Jordan

CARVING
And He Carves These "Dudes". Margaret Danner
As a Businessman. Margaret Danner
Boneman. Margaret Dannner
Boneman and my Senufo Masque, The. Margaret

Danner
Carver, The. Lucille Clifton

CASTRO, FIDEL
Poem of Personal Greeting for Fidel. June Jordan

CATHEDRALS
Cultural Cathedrals. Margaret Danner

CATS
Compassion. Mary Nell Nash
Cotton Cat, The. Effie Lee Newsome
Mendacity. Margaret Danner
Muffle Jaw, I Remember You. Naomi Long Madgett
Paula the Cat. Nikki Giovanni
Poem for Carol, A. Nikki Giovanni
Sundays of Satin-Legs Smith, The. Gwendolyn Brooks

CAUCASIANS
(An Aside) Carolyn Rodgers
Cook's Job Available. June Vanleer Williams
Enslaved. Elma Stuckey
Family Of. Alice Walker
Jesus was Crucified or It Must be Deep. Carolyn Rodgers
My Dream About Being White. Lucille Clifton
On Seeing Pharoah Sanders Blowing. Sonia Sanchez
TCB. Sonia Sanchez
To all Brothers. Sonia Sanchez
To Non-African American Brothers and Sisters. Margaret T. G. Burroughs
12 Gates to the City. Nikki Giovanni
Ugly Honkies, or The Election Game and How to Win It. Nikki Giovanni
Walk Like Freedom. Carolyn Rodgers
What You Say. Coleen McElroy
Whi/te Boys Gone. Val Ferdinand
Why are They Mean. Kali Grosvenor
Wish, The. Elma Stuckey
You Took this World Away From Us. Kali Grosvenor

CAUCASIANS--GIRLS
I Have Been Hungry. Carolyn Rodgers

CAUCASIANS, SINS OF
Children of Their Sin, The. Carolyn Rodgers

CAUCASIANS--WOMEN
To All Sisters. Sonia Sanchez
To Ms. Ann. Lucille Clifton

CEMETERIES
Burial. Alice Walker
Of De Witt Williams on His Way to Lincoln Cemetery. Gwendolyn Brooks
Southeast Corner. Gwendolyn Brooks
View From Rosehill Cemetery, Vicksburg. Alice Walker

CHAIN GANG
South Carolina Chain Gang Song. Anonymous

CHANEY, JAMES
For Andy Goodman--Michael Schwerner--and James Chaney. Margaret Walker

CHAPEL
Compulsory Chapel. Alice Walker

CHARITY
Triple Benison, The. Henrietta Cordelia Ray

CHESTER, SAMMY
Sammy Chester Leaves "Godspell" and Visits Upward Bound on a Lake Forest Lawn, Bringing West Africa. Gwendolyn Brooks

CHICAGO, ILLINOIS
Beverly Hills, Chicago. Gwendolyn Brooks
Chicago Picasso, The. Gwendolyn Brooks

CHICKENS
Little Rooster, The. Anonymous
Old Hen Cackled, The. Anonymous
Sunday Chicken. Gwendolyn Brooks
Walk, Talk, Chicken with your Head Pecked. Anonymous

CHILD ABUSE
To Beat the Child was Bad Enough. Maya Angelou

CHILD BIRTH
Flight. Pinkie Gordon Lane
Ode to Barbara. Olean Bess
Sandy. Olean Bess
Say Hello to John. Shirley Williams

CHILDHOOD
Ballad from Childhood. Audre Lorde
Childhood. Johari Amini
Childhood. Thulani Davis
Fantasia. Naomi Long Madgett
Grass Roots. Mara Moja Tu Kali
Make/n My Music. Angela Jackson
Nikki-Rosa. Nikki Giovanni
Something Else. June Vanleer Williams

CHILDREN
Always There are the Children Nikki Giovanni
......And Then...Johari Amini
And What About the Children. Audre Lorde
Apology to my Little Daughter For Apparent Neglect. Margaret T. G. Burroughs
As I Grow Up Again. Audre Lorde
Black Woman. Georgia Douglas Johnson
Brother Alvin. Audre Lorde
But What Can you Teach My Daughter. Audre Lorde
Childhood. Johari Amini
Childhood. Margaret Walker
Children. Pinkie Gordon Lane
Children of the Poor, The Gwendolyn Brooks
Christmas Lullaby for a New-Born Child. Yvonne Gregory
Dear Toni Instead of a Letter of Congratulation Upon Your Book and Your Daughter Whom you say you are Raising to be a Correct Little Sister. Audre Lorde
Escape. Mari Evans
For a Child. Naomi Long Madgett
For My Children. Vanessa Howard
Glowchild. Constance E. Berkley
God Gave me a Son. Portia Bird Daniel
Grandson is a Hoticeberg. Margaret Danner
Hey There. Sonia Sanchez
I and He. Marion Cuthbert
If the Shoe Fits, Wear It. Gertrude Blackwelll Bailey
Juice of a Lemon on the Trail of Little Yellow. June Jordan
Life of Lincoln West, The. Gwendolyn Brooks
Little Child Shall Lead Them. Frances Harper
Little Helper. Edna Shaw
Little Son. Georgia Douglas Johnson
Motherless Child. Anonymous
Naming, The. Toi Derricotte

Nikki-Rossa. Nikki Giovanni
Offspring. Naomi Long Madgett
Oh! Lord. Antionette T. Payne
Our Children are Our Children. Geraldine L. Wilson
Out My Street. Bessie Woodson Yancey
Parental Lament. June Vanleer Williams
Poem for all the Children. June Jordan
Relevant is Different Points on the Circle. Audre Lorde
Salia. Lucille D. Goodlett
Say Hello to John. Shirley Williams
School Note. Audre Lorde
Sleep, Child. Judy Dothard Simmons
Something About a Little Kid. S. Diane Bogus
Suffer the Children. Audre Lorde
Thank God for Little Children. Frances Harper
They are Still our Children. Gertrude Blackwell Bailey
To Morani/Mungu. Sonia Sanchez
To my Children. Sandra Royster
To My Daughter the Junkie on a Train. Audre Lorde
What Shall I Tell my Children Who are Black? Margaret T. G. Burroughs
When Two Year Olds Talk in Their Sleep. S. Diane Bogus
Whispers of the Child, The. Eleanor Thomas-Grumbach
Why? Melba Joyce Boyd
Why's of the Black Child, The. E. Sharon Gomillion
Your Children. Gertrude Blackwell Bailey

CHILDREN
See Also
BOYS
GIRLS

CHOIR
Negro Choir. Beatrice M. Murphy

CHOPIN, FREDERIC FRANCOIS
Chopin Deciphered. Julia Fields

CHORES
Saturday Afternoon when Chores are Done. Harryette Mullen

CHRISTMAS
Anonymous Verse (From a Puerto Rican Christmas Card), An. Anonymous
Christmas Eve in France. Jessie Redmond Fauset
Christmas Morning I. Carol Freeman
Christmas Soiree and the Missing Object of African Art, The. Margaret Danner
Dream Like Daniels's. S. Diane Bogus
Gift. Carol Freeman
Magi Call Him King, The. Effie Lee Newsome
Otto. Gwendolyn Brooks
Through the Holly Wreath. Charlemae Rollins

CHRISTMAS, EDWARD
Wall, The (For Edward Christmas). Gwendolyn Brooks

CHURCH--COLLECTION
Collection. Elma Stuckey

CHURCHES
Church Folks. Bernice Love Wiggins
Church Lets Out. Jeannette V. Miller
Greater Friendship Baptist Church, The. Carole C. Gregory

New Calvary. Naomi Long Madgett
They Went to Church. Melva Tatum Smith
Time Ain't Long as it Has Been. Carolyn Rodgers
When Mahalia Sings. Quandra Prettyman

CIRCLES
Circles. Kali Grosvenor

CIRCUS
Circus. Naomi Long Madgett

CITIES AND TOWNS
Bottled: New York. Helene Johnson
City, The. Naomi Long Madgett
City by the Sea, The Sea, The. Josephine D. (Henderson) Heard
City Limits. Carolyn Rodgers
Dawn Cities. Mae V. Cowdery
Great Cities Crumble. Gertrude Blackwell Bailey
This is the City. Yvette Johnson
To a Dream City in Departing. Naomi Long Madgett
Zulu King: New Orleans (At Mardi Gras), The. Josephine D. (Henderson) Heard

CITIZENSHIP
Citizen, The. Vilma Howard

CIVIL RIGHTS
Great Civil Rights Law (A.D. 1964), The. Mari Evans
Street Demonstration. Margaret Walker

CIVIL RIGHTS--HISTORY
Alabama Centennial. Naomi Long Madgett

CIVIL RIGHTS--WORKERS
For Andy Goodman--Michael Schwerner--and James Chaney

CLEANING
Housecleaning. Nikki Giovanni

CLEAVER, ELDRIDGE
Elderidge. Lucille Clifton

CLERGY
Feeding the Pastor. Elma Stuckey
Preacher Man. Elma Stuckey
Preacher Kyo Siam, De. Lucille D. Goodlett
Reverend is Gwine to de Big 'Soc'ation, De. Lucy Mae Turner

CLOCKS AND WATCHES
Alarm Clock, The. Mari Evans
All the Clocks. Carolyn Rodgers
Clock that Gains, The. Anonymous

CLOTHING AND DRESS
Purchase. Naomi Long Madgett

CLOUDS
Sky Pictures. Effie Lee Newsome

CLOWNS
Downtown Vaudeville. Gwendolyn Brooks

CLUBS
Lady Luncheon Club. Maya Angelou

COAL
Coal. Audre Lorde

COBWEBS
Gossamer. Georgia Douglas Johnson

COLOGONES
New Cologne, A. Jayne Cortez

COLORS
Colors. Ruth Duckett Gibbs
Desire. Constance Nichols
Epigram. Iola M. Brister
I'll Wear me a Cotton Dress. Anonymous
Spectrum. Mari Evans
To Anita. Sonia Sanchez
To Whom it Does Concern Blue is my Favorite Color. LaVerne Davis
While Everyone Wears Black That's Chic in Spring. Margaret Danner
Who Am I? Kali Grosvenor

COLTRANE, JOHN
Coltrane/Poem, A. Sonia Sanchez

COLUMBUS, CHRISTOPHER
Colmbes Didn't Discover This World. Kali Grosvenor

COMMODORES, THE
Zoom (The Commodores) Thulani Davis

COMMON SENSE
Common Sense. Gertrude Blackwell Bailey

COMMUNICATION
Communication. Lyn
Communication. Nikki Giovanni
Together. Carolyn Rodgers

COMPENSATION
Compensation, The. Ruth E. J. Sarver

CONGRESSES AND CONVENTION
Detroit Conference of Unity and Art (For HRB) Nikki Giovanni

CONSCIENCE
If Your Conscience is Free. Gertrude Blackwell Bailey

CONSCRIPTION
Conscription-1940. Pauli Murray

CONSERVATION
Statement on Conservation. Nikki Giovanni

CONTACT LENSES
Contact Lenses. Audre Lorde

CONTENTMENT
Contentment. Bessie Woodson Yancey

CONVENTS
Convent Hall. Naomi Long Madgett

CONVERSATION
Conversation. Nikki Giovanni

COOKERY
An't M'lissy's Tater Pies. Bessie Woodson Yancey
From Okra to Greens/A Different Love Poem/We Need a Change. Ntozake Shange
I Have the Rolling Pin Mother Received When First She Wed. Gloria Oden
Joy, The. Harryette Mullen
Okra to Greens/An Aside on Amsterdam Avenue.

Ntozake Shange

COOPERATIVE LIVING
Moving Out or The End of Cooperative Living. Audre Lorde

CORDS
Cords. Ruth Brownlee Johnson

CORNERS
Blackman Get Off That Corner. Gertrude Blackwell Bailey

COTTON
Burying Ground. Elma Stuckey
Cotton Pickin'. Lucille D. Goodlett
Long Cotton Row. Elma Stuckey
Old King Cotton. Elma Stuckey
Peacock Poems I. Shirley Williams
Pick a Bale of Cotton. Anonymous

COURTS
In the Courtroom. Sonia Sanchez

COVERS
Covers. Nikki Giovanni

COWARDS
J'al Peur (The Coward Speaks) Ariel Williams

COWS
Did You Feed My Cow? Anonymous
Wild Roses. Effie Lee Newsome

CRANES
On Not Calling on Cranes in the Night. Thulani Davis
On Not Sending Love Letters to Cranes. Thulani Davis

CRIME AND CRIMINALS
Children of Their Sin. Carolyn Rodgers
With No Immediate Cause. Ntozake Shange

CRITICISM
Critic, The. Melva Tatum Smith

CROCUSES
Crocuses, The. Frances Harper

CROWDS
Question to a Mob. Lauretta Holman Gooden

CRUTCHES
Crutches. Nikki Giovanni

CRYING
Haiku. Sonia Sanchez
I Weep. Angelina Weld Grimke
My Tears Don't Come Cheap Anymore. C. Tillery Banks
Oh, Mary, Don't You Weep. Anonymous
When You Come to See Me. Maya Angelou

CURIOSITY
Curiosity. Lucy Mae Turner

CYNICISM
Cynic. Tomi Carolyn Tinsley

- D -

DAKAR
At Home in Dakar. Margaret Danner

DAEDALUS
Be Daedalus. Nanina Alba

DANCING
Between a Dancer & a Poet. Ntozake Shange
Dance, The. Colleen McElroy
Dance. Lula Lowe Weeden
Dance of the Abakweta. Margaret Danner
Dance She Does, The. Harryette Mullen
Dancer, The. Brenda Connor-Bey
For There's No End to the Suffering a Female Will Bear for Beauty. Margaret Danner
In Honor of Yr Poise in the Face of Hungry Lions. Ntozake Shange
Juba Bance. Anonymous
Let Them Wear Pale Orchid Shoes. Margaret Danner
Night People. Colleen McElroy
Song of a Dancer. Harryette Mullen
Tapping. Jayne Cortez
Three/Quarters Time. Nikki Giovanni
We Dance Like Ella Riffs. Carolyn Rodgers

DANIEL (BIBLE)
Lion in Daniel's Den, The. Nikki Giovanni

DATING (SOCIAL CUSTOMS)
First Date. Leatrice Emeruwa

DAUGHTERS
But What can you Teach my Daughter. Audre Lorde
Maxie Allen. Gwendolyn Brooks
Picture, The. Jeanette Adams
To My Daughter the Junkie on a Train. Audre Lorde

DAVIS, ANGELA YVONNE
Poem of Angela Yvonne Davis. Nikki Giovanni

DAWN
Dawn. Angelina Weld Grimke

DAYBREAK
Ghetto Daybreak. June Vanleer Williams

DAYS
Dead Days. Georgia Douglas Johnson

DEACONS
Deacon Morgan. Naomi Long Madgett

DEATH
At Sea. Vera Guerard
Ballad of the Late Annie, The. Gwendolyn Brooks
Ballad of the Light-Eyed Little Girl, The. Gwendolyn Brooks
Barred. Naomi Evans Vaughn
Blk/Chant (To be Said Everyday Slowly) Sonia Sanchez
Burial. Alice Walker
Burial of Sarah. Frances Harper
Buried Away. Edyth Mae Gordon
Bury Me in a Free Land. Frances Harper
Burying Ground. Elma Stuckey
C. C. Rider. Carolyn Rodgers
Common Dust. Georgia Douglas Johnson
Cross. Naomi Long Madgett
Daddy 12/02-5-69. Lucille Clifton
Dear Dorothy: In Loving Memoriam. Leatrice Emeruwa

Death. Gertrude Blackwell Bailey
Death in Autumn. Julia Fields
Death Prosecuting. Linda Curry
Despair. Georgia Douglas Johnson
Detached, The. Maya Angelou
Don't Die in January. June Vanleer Williams
Dying Bondman, The. Frances Harper
Each Night. Mae V. Cowdery
Elegiac Poem on the Death of That Celebrated Divine and Eminent Servant of Jesus Christ, The Late Reverend and Pious George Whitefield. Phillis Wheatley
Elegy. Maya Angelou
Elegy: Marion. Pinkie Gordon Lane
Elegy Sacred to the Memory of Dr. Samuel Cooper, An. Phillis Wheatley
Elegy to Miss Mary Moorhead, on the Death of her Father, the Rev. Mr. John Moorhead An. Phillis Wheatley
Epitaph, An. Josephine D. (Henderson) Heard
Epitaph. Naomi Long Madgett
Estrangement. Georgia Douglas Johnson
Eulogy for Alvin Frost. Audre Lorde
Evolution. Pamela Cobb
Eyes Gentled at the Cornors So. Mari Evans
Father Son and Holy Ghost. Audre Lorde
Festivals and Funerals. Jayne Cortez
Finis. Georgia Douglas Johnson
First Flakes That Fell on Mother's Grave, The. Josephine D. (Henderson_ Heard
For All my Dead & Loved Ones. Ntozake Shange
For Janet Gaillard. Thulani Davis
For My Grandpa. Vanessa Howard
Funeral. Naomi Long Madgett
Funeral Poem on the Death of C. E., an Infant of Twelve Months, A. Phillis Wheatley
Gamut, The. Maya Angelou
Girl Who Died #1, The. Alice Walker
Girl Who Died #2/d.p. Alice Walker
Going Home. Jennifer Blackman Lawson
Great Pax Whitie. Nikki Giovanni
Grief Unexplained. June Vanleer Williams
He Lay in the Alley. Vanessa Howard
He Was Twenty When he Died. Gloria Oden
Hospital/Poem (For Etheridge 9/26/69). Sonia Sanchez
Hushed by the Hands of Sleep. Angelina Weld Grimke
I Do Not Sleep Nights Though. Gloria Oden
I Want to Die While You Love Me. Georgia Douglas Johnson
Innocence. Anne Spencer
Invocation. Helene Johnson
Jamie's Puzzle. Frances Harper
Jim. Elma Stuckey
Juvenile Suicide. Naomi Long Madgett
Life/Poem. Sonia Sanchez
Love Poem (For Real). Nikki Giovanni
Many Die Here. Gayl Jones
Memorial for My Father. Margaret T. G. Burroughs
Memorial IV. Audre Lorde
Mentor. Gwendolyn Brooks
Mortality. Naomi Long Madgett
Mourning Grace. Maya Angelou
Murder, The. Gwendolyn Brooks
My Path is Lighted by a Star. Lucy Mae Turner
Nat Turner, An Epitaph. Lucy Mae Turner
New Address. Elma Stuckey
News. Elma Stuckey
Night of Death. Frances Harper

9 Lines. Johari Amini
Niobe in Distress for her Children Slain by Apollo, From Ovid's Metamorphoses of the Painting of Mr. Richard Wilson. Phillis Wheatley
Nobody Likes to Read his own Epitaph. Pinkie Gordon Lane
Oakland in February. Ntozake Shange
Obituary for a Living Lady. Gwendolyn Brooks
Oblivion. Jessie Redmond Fauset
Ode of Verses on the Much Lamented Death of the Rev. Mr. George Whitefield, An. Phillis Wheatley
Of De Witt Williams on His Way to Lincoln Cemetery. Gwendolyn Brooks
Old Relative. Gwendolyn Brooks
Old Warrior Terror, The. Alice Walker
On the Death of a Young Gentleman. Phillia Wheatley
On the Death of a Young Lady of Five Years Old. Phillis Wheatley
On the Death of Dr. Samuel Marshall (1771). Phillis Wheatley
On the Death of J. C. an Infant. Phillis Wheatley
On the Death of Lisa Lyman. Della Burt
On the Death of Rev. Sewell (1769). Phillis Wheatley
On the Death of Rev. Mr. George Whitefield, 1970. Phillis Wheatley
On the Death of the Rev'd Dr. Sewall, 1769. Phillis Wheatley
Ox in the De Ditch. Lucile D. Goodlett
Passing. Ruby Stevens
Poem for Lloyd. Nikki Giovanni
Poor Renaldo. Naomi Long Madgett
Posthumous. Georgia Douglas Johnson
Rebel, The. Mari Evans
Requiem. Nell Chapman
Requiem for a Newsman. June Vanleer Williams
Resting. Josephine D. (Henderson) Heard
Rites for Cousin Vit, The. Gwendolyn Brooks
St. James Infirmary Blues. Anonymous
Same Death Over and Over or Lullabies are for Children. Audre Lorde
Separation. Audre Lorde
Since 1619. Margaret Walker
Soon One Mawnin. Anonymous
Southeast Corner. Gwendolyn Brooks
Taking Sides. Elma Stuckey
Taps. Georgia Douglas Johnson
Tears and Kisses. Georgia Douglas Johnson
Ten Years to the Day My Brother Milton Died. Gloria Oden
That I May Gird to Meet My Death. Margaret Danner
Thrall. Georgia Douglas Johnson
To a Clergyman on the Death of His Lady. Phillis Wheatley
To a Gentleman and Lady on the Death of the Lady's Brother and Sister, and Child of the Name of Avis, Aged One Year. Phillis Wheatley
To a Lady and Her Children, On the Death of Her Son and Their Brother. Phillis Wheatley
To a Lady on the Death of Her Husband. Phillis Wheatley
To a Lady on the Death of Three Relations. Phillis Wheatley
To a Poet I Know. Johari Amini
To a Spaniard Dying. Norma Lopez Garcia

To Darnell and Johnny. Melba Joyce Boyd
To Death. Lois Royal Hughes
To Die Before One Wakes Must Be Glad. Alice Walker
To His Honor the Lieutenant Governor, on the Death of His Lady, March 24, 1773. Phillis Wheatley
To Mrs. Leonard on the Death of Her Husband. Phillis Wheatley
To Mr. and Mrs. --, on the Death of Their Infant Son. Phillis Wheatley
To the Hon'ble Thomas Hubbard Esq. on the Death of Mrs. Thankfull Leonard (1773). Phillis Wheatley
To the Honorable T. H. Esq. on the Death of His Daughter. Phillis Wheatley
To the Rev. Mr. Pitkin, on the Death of his Lady (1772) Phillis Wheatley
We Real Cool. Gwendolyn Brooks
When-A Mah Blood Runs Chilly an Col. Anonymous
When I am Dead. Georgia Douglas Johnson
When I Would Die! Josephine D. (Henderson) Heard
When Mother was Eleven Her Mother Died. Gloria Died. Gloria Oden
When my Oldest Brother, Buddy (And My Father's Namesake) Died. Gloria Oden
When We are Dead. Josephine D. (Henderson) Heard
Woman/Dirge for Wasted Children, A. Audre Lorde
Woman's Laughter. Pat Parker
Would You Regret. Josephine D. (Henderson) Heard
You Hear About Them. Wanda Coleman

DEATH--FEAR OF
Poem. Nikki Giovanni

DEBTS
Adulthood II. Nikki Giovanni

DECEIT
Trick, Maybe, The? June Vanleer Williams

DECEMBER
December. Josephine D. (Henderson) Heard
November/December (Echoing Voices of Remembrances) Kattie M. Cumbo

DECISIONS
Decisions. Gertrude Blackwell Bailey

DEER
Stricken Deer, The. Josephine D. (Henderson) Heard

DEFEAT
Defeat. Countess W. Twitty
Road to Anywhere. Dorothy Vena Johnson

DEGREES--EDUCATIONAL
While Working Towards the PH.D Degrees. Pinkie Gordon Lane

DELANY, CLARISSA SCOTT
To Clarissa Scott Delany. Angelina Weld Grimke

DE LEON, PONCE
Ponce De Leon. Naomi Long Madgett

DELTA
Delta. Margaret Walker

DELTA SIGMA THETA
Greek Crazeology. Carolyn

Rodgers

DEMOCRACY
Everybody But Me. Margaret Burroughs

DEMONSTRATIONS
Street Demonstrations. Margaret Walker

DEPARTURE
Adieu. Constantia E. Riley
Blue. Carolyn Rodgers
Farewell to America. Phillis Wheatley
Ghosts of Our Parting. S. Diane Bogus
I Hate Goodbyes. Nola Richardson
If This be Good-bye. Ruby Berkley Goodwin
If We Part Now. Mae V. Cowdery
Talisman. Frenchy J. Hodges
Unencouraged Lingering. Frenchy J. Hodges

DESERTION AND NON-SUPPORT
Staying and Not Staying. Wanda Coleman

DESERTS
Desert Island. Sandra Royster
Sahara. Audre Lorde
Sonora Desert Poem. Lucille Clifton
That I May Gird to Meet Dry Death. Margaret Danner

DESIRE
Desire. Thelma T. Clement

DETROIT, MICHIGAN
Detroit City. Jill Witherspoon Boyer
Detroit Michigan. Margaret Danner
Detroit Renaissance. Melba
Detroit Summers. Jill Witherspoon Boyer

DIALYSIS MACHINE
Songs to the Dialysis Machine. Pinkie Gordon Lane

DICKINSON, REV. MU BUGWU
Song: the Rev. Mu Bugwu Dickinson Ruminates Behind Sermon. Gwendolyn Brooks

DIFFERENCES
Differences. Valerie Tarver
Retaliation. Tomi Carolyn Tinsley
Revelation. Blanche Taylor Dickinson
Trivia. Beatrice M. Murphy

DINNERS AND DINING
Beatrice Does the Dinner. Mari Evans
Dinner for Three. Pauli Murray

DISCIPLES
Calling of the Disciples, The. Lucille Clifton

DISCRIMINATION
Black Memorial Day, A. Frenchy J. Hodges
Bus Trip-Rest Stop-1950. June Vanleer Williams
Circled By a Horsefly. Helen Quigless
Dark People. Kattie M. Cumbo
etc. etc. etc. Dorothy C. Parrish
Frustration, A Heritage. Thelma Parker Cox
Mother America. Hazel L. Washington
My Poem. Nikki Giovanni
No No No No. Maya Angelou
Now. Margaret Walker
Vive Noir. Mari Evans

Why Do I Love This Country. Mary Wilkerson Cleaves
You are Black. Helen F. Clarke

DISHES
Sometimes My Husband. Patricia Parker

DIVORCE
Divorcee, The. Naomi Long Madgett
Divorcee. Toi Derricotte

DOG CATCHER
Dog Catcher, The. Lucy Mae Turner

DOGS
Dog Catcher, The. Lucy Mae Turner
Dog Suicide. Wanda Coleman
I am a Mad Dog. Joanne Jimason
Offering of Paws, An. Wanda Coleman
Walking the Dog. Pinkie Gordon Lane
What Liberation Front? The. Patricia Parker

DOLLS
Doll Poem. Toi Derricotte
I Used to Wrap My White Doll Up In. Nae Jackson
On a Colored Doll. Floretta Howard
Professors...Jill Witherspoon Boyer

DOORS
Could you Get the Door? Thulani Davis
Doorway That We Hide Behind, The. Dee Dee McNeil

DOUGLASS, FREDERICK
Five Black Men. Margaret Walker
Frederick Douglass. Eloise Culver
In Memory of the Hon. Frederick Douglass, The Saga of Anacostia. Josephine D. (Henderson) Heard
Welcome to Hon. Frederick Douglass. Josephine D. (Henderson) Heard

DOVES
After. Naomi Long Madgett

DRAGONFLIES
Dragonfly, The. Nikki Giovanni

DRAWINGS
Life in the Art of Drawing. Carolyn Ogletree

DREAMS
Dream, A. Josephine D. (Henderson) Heard
Dream, The. Gladys Marie Parker
Dream Love. Ruth E. J. Sarver
Dream Market. Cora Ball Moten
Dream World. Evelyn Watson
Dreams. Bessie Woodson Yancey
Dreams. Naomi Long Madgett
Dreams. Nikki Giovanni
Dreams Are So Pale. Katharine Beverly
Dreams of the Dreamer, The Georgia Douglas Johnson
I Dream Alone Again. Ruby Berkley Goodwin
I Have a Dream. Patricia Parker
If This Be a Dream. Naomi Long Madgett
I'm a Dreamer. Kattie M. Cumbo
Kitchenette Building. Gwendolyn Brooks
Let Me Not Lose my Dream. Georgia Douglas Johnson
My Little Dreams. Georgia

Douglas Johnson
On Dreams. Frenchy J. Hodges
Reverie & In My Father's House Towards Hallelujah & Freedom. Carolyn Rodgers
Some Dreams Hang in the Air. Lucille Clifton
Spin me a Dream. Helen C. Harris
Two Poems From Trinity: A Dream Sequence. Naomi Long Madgett
Wonder Woman, The. Nikki Giovanni

DRESSES
I'll Wear Me a Cotton Dress. Anonymous

DREW, CHARLES R.
Dr. Charles R. Drew. Eloise Culver

DRIVERS, SLAVE
Driver. Elma Stuckey
Ole Nigger Driver, De Anonymous

DRIVING
Driving Along Interstate 94. Naomi Long Madgett

DROPOUTS
Drop-Out. Gertrude Blackwell Bailey
Poem Brother/For the Nation. Carolyn M. Rodgers
We Real Cool. Gwendolyn Brooks

DRUMS
Drum, The. Nikki Giovanni
Drummer King. Barbara Mahone
Drums Everywhere Drums. Jayne Cortez

DUBOIS, WILLIAM EDWARD BURGHARDT
Dr. W. E. B. DuBois. Eloise Culver
Five Black Men. Margaret Walker
For W. E. B. DuBois. Elma Stuckey
For William Edward Burghardt DuBois On His Eightieth Birthday. Bette Darcie Latimer
Newest Star, The. Eloise Culver
To W. E. B. Dubois--Scholar. Georgia Douglas Johnson

DUMAS, ALEXANDRE
Lines Written at the Grave of Alexandre Dumas. Gwendolyn Bennett

DUNBAR, PAUL LAURENCE
Dunbar. Anne Spencer
For Paul Laurence Dunbar. Margaret Walker

DUSK
Dusk. Mae V. Cowdery
Dusk. Angelina Weld Grimke
Dusk. Naomi Long Madgett

DUST
Black Dust. Wanda Coleman

- E -

EAGLES
Eagle Rock. Alice Walker
Eagles. Nikki Giovanni

EARPIERCING
Ritual of Earpiercing, The. Harryette Mullen

EARTH
Of Earth. Mae V. Cowdery

EARTHQUAKE
Earthquake of 1886, The.

Josephine D. (Henderson) Heard

EAST
Going East. Frances E. W. Harper

EASTER
Easter. Inez M. Thurman
Easter Morn. Josephine D. (Henderson) Heard
For Jim, Easter Eve. Anne Spencer

EATING
Leanna's Poem. Lucille Clifton

ECHO
Echo. Dorothy F. Blackwell

ECONOMICS
Indianopolis/Summer/1969/Poem. Sonia Sanchez

EDUCATION
Advance of Education, The. Josephine D. (Henderson) Heard
Chicago Defender Sends a Man to Little Rock, Fall 1957. Gwendolyn Brooks
I. Beverly Thomas
Learning to Read. Frances E. W. Harper
To the University of Cambridge, Wrote in 1767. Phillis Wheatley

EGGS
Egg Boiler, The. Gwendolyn Brooks

EL, THE
El Becomes a Subway in my Lifetime, The. Barbara Mahome

ELEPHANTS
Pete at the Zoo. Gwendolyn Brooks

ELEVATORS
Elevator Man Adheres to Form, The. Margaret Danner

ELIZA
Eliza. Naomi Long Madgett

ELLINGTON, EDWARD DUKE
Echoes. Naomi Long Madgett
Rose Solitude. Jayne Cortez
Tribute to Duke. Sarah Webster Fabio

EMANCIPATION PROCLAMATION
Freed Slave Song. Fannie Berry
President Lincoln's Proclamation of Freedom. Frances E. W. Harper

EMOTIONS
Frustration, a Heritage. Thelma Parker Cox

ENCHANTMENT
Enchantment. Georgia Holloway Jones

ENERGY
Concern for Our Total Enviornment. S. Diane Bogus
Statement on Conservation, A. Nikki Giovanni

ENGINEERS
Casey Jones. Anonymous

ENNIS, ETHEL
To My Sister, Ethel Ennis, Who Sang "The Star

Spangled Banner" at the Second Inauguration of Richard Milhous Nixon, January 20, 1973. June Jordan

EPILEPSY
Demon: Possessed. June Vanleer Williams

EPITAPHS
Nat Turner, An Epitaph. Lucy Mae Turner

ERRORS
Mistakes. Naomi Evans Vaughn

ETERNITY
Eternity. Josephine D. (Henderson) H eard
Taste of Time, The. S. Diane Bogus

ETHIOPIA
Forward Ethiopia. Bessie Woodson Yancey

ETIQUETTE
People Will be People. Gertrude Blackwell Bailey

EVENING
Hymn to the Evening, An. Phillis Wheatley

EVERS, MEDGAR
Medgar Evers. Gwendolyn Brooks
Micah. Margaret Walker

EVICTION
Evicted. Beatrice M. Murphy

EVIL see GOOD AND EVIL

EVOLUTION
Evolution. Thelma Parker Cox

EXECUTIVES
Dem Black Executives. E. Sharon Gomillion

EYEGLASSES
Wearing Glasses. Lyn

EYES
Brown Silky Eyes Flashing Stories at Me. C. Tillery Banks
Your Eyes. Georgia Douglas Johnson

F -

FABIO, SARAH
(for sarah fabio) Sonia Sanchez

FABLES
Signifying Monkey, The. Anonmous

FACES
Black Faces. Anita Scott Coleman
Faces. Maya Angelou

FACIALS
Beauty Shoppe. Gwendolyn Brooks

FAINTING
Black Woman Never Faints, A. Harryette Mullen

FAIRIES
Happy Fairies. Gertrude Parthenia McBrown

FAITH

Do Tell Faith/the Divine Natural. Carolyn M. Rodgers
Keep Faith. Gertrude Blackwell
Replacing Faith. Lyn
Triple Benison, The. Henrietta Cordelia Ray

FALLING
Falling. Claudia E. Jemmott

FAME
Fame. Josephine D. (Henderson) Heard

FAMILIES
Dear Daddy. Ava Saunders
Family: Growing Up. Jennifer Blackman Lawson
Family Portrait. Colleen McElroy
Family Portrait. Naomi Long Madgett
When I Was Very Small. Gloria Oden

FANTASY
Fantasy. Gwendolyn B. Bennett

FARMING
To the Negro Farmers of the United States. Alice Dunbar-Nelson

FASHIONS
Fashin-Plate, The. Melva Tatum Smith
Sepia Fashion Show. Maya Angelou

FATE
Race. Naomi Long Madgett

FATHERS
Clock on Hancock Street. June Jordan
Dad. Bessie Woodson Yancey
Daddy 12/02 - 5/69. Lucille
Dear Daddy. Ava Saunders
Epileptic. Pinkie Gordon Lane
Epitaph for my Father. Margaret Walker
Father Son and Holy Ghost. Audre Lorde
Five. Gloria Oden
For Our Fathers. Carolyn M. Rodgers
For Sapphires. Carolyn M. Rodgers
Forgiving My Father. Lucille Clifton
Glimpses. Nola Richardson
Gus. Nikki Giovanni
However Brief Their Acquaintance With My Father. Gloria Oden
I Love You Sooner. S. Diane Bogus
In Honor of David Anderson Brooks, My Father. Gwendolyn Brooks.
Inquisition, The. Bobbretta M. Elliston
Love From My Father. Carole Gregory Clemmons
Memorial For My Father. Margaret T. G. Burroughs
Mother and Dad. Gertrude Blackwell Bailey
My Father. May Miller
Pa. Alice McGee Smart
Picture, The. Jeanette Adams
Poem for Granville Ivanhoe Jordan, November 4, 1890-December 21, 1974. June Jordan
Poem For My Father, A. Sonia Sanchez
Poem to My Father. Pinkie Gordon Lane
Sequel No. 2. Pinkie Gordon Lane
Sequel No. 3. Pinkie Gordon Lane
Something Lost. Nola Richardson
Son To His Father, A. Naomi Long Madgett
Sugarman. Margaret Poeter
Sunflowers and Saturdays. Melba Joyce Boyd
They Don't Understand. Nola

Richardson
To Father. Henrietta Cordelia Ray
Try To Understand Papa. Colleen McElroy
Walking the Dog. Pinkie Gordon Lane
Woman/Child? Nola Richardson

FATHERS, DESERTION
Father (Part I) Harryette Mullen

FAULT FINDING
Pitch in and Help Out. Gertrude Blackwell Bailey

FEAR
Fear to Freedom. Melva Tatum Smith
White Fear. Nannie H. Travis

FEBRUARY
February. Patrice M. Wilson

FEDERAL BUREAU OF INVESTIGATION
I Laughed When I Wrote It. Nikki Giovanni
Modern Song of the F.B.I., A. Sonia Sanchez

FEET
Valediction to Shuffling. Jennifer B. Lawson

FERGUSON, KATHERINE
Katherine Ferguson. Eloise Culver

FERRIES
To Clements' Ferry. Josephine D. (Henderson) Heard
Trip on the Staten Island Ferry, A. Audre Lorde

FIDDLES
Fiddle in de Win'. Lucile D. Goodlett

FIFTEENTH AMENDMENT
Fifteenth Amendment. Frances E. W. Harper

FIGHTS
Bars Fight. Lucy Terry

FINGERS
Black Finger, The. Angelina Weld Grimke

FIRE FLIES
Cucuya or Firefly, The. Anonymous
Wish, A. Eleanor A. Thompson

FIREARMS
If I Had a Gun That Would Shoot. Mari Evans
Right On: Wite America 4. Sonia Sanchez

FIRES
Accident Edgecombe General Hospital May 16, 1968. Julia Fields

FISHES
Be Like This Porcupine Fish. Margaret Danner
Spawning to Bring-Forth. Carolyn M. Rodgers

FISHING
Fishin'. Lucile D. Goodlett
Fishy Poem, A. Nikki Giovanni
My Lover is a Fisherman. Gertrude Davenport

FISK UNIVERSITY
Untitled. Sharon Scott

FLAGS
Flags. Gwendolyn Brooks

FLAMINGOS
Flamingo. Margaret Danner

FLIGHT
Flyin'. Lucy Mae Turner
If I Could Fly. Kali Grosvenor

FLOWERS
About Flowers. Wanda Coleman
African Beauty Rose. Kattie M. Cumbo
Bidding, The. Jennifer Blackman Lawson
Complete Fulfillment. Mary Bohanon
Crocuses, The. Frances E. W. Harper
Daffodils. Judy Dothard Simmons
Faded Flowers. Josephine D. (Henderson) Heard
Flowers. Julia Fields
Lilacs. Gertrude Parthenia McBrown
Lillies. Linda B. Graham
Lines to a Nasturtium. Anne Spencer
Little Dandelion, The. Lula Lowe Weeden
Lonely Tulip Grower. Julia Alvarez
My Garden. Gertrude Blackwell Bailey
Pansy. Effie Lee Newsome
Plea, A. Mary Bohanon
Sonnet. Alice Dunbar-Nelson
Sunflowers and Saturday. Melba Joyce Boyd
Throwing Out the Flowers. Gwendolyn Brooks
Tulips. W. Blanche Nivens
Wild Flowers. Nikki Giovanni
Wild Roses. Effie Lee Newsome
Woman and the Roses, The. Harryette Mullen
Woman With Flower. Naomi Long Madgett

FOLKLORE
Bad Man Ballad. Anonymous
John Henry. Anonymous

FOOD
Black Man's Feast. Sarah Webster Fabio
Food Poisoning. Marion Nicholes
Stealin' Grub. Lucy Mae Turner
Translation. S. Diane Bogus
When in Rome. Mari Evans

FOOTBALL
Funky Football. Fareedah Allah

FOOTSTEPS
Footsteps. Georgia Douglas Johnson
Footsteps. Gertrude Blackwell Bailey

FORGETFULNESS
Forgetfulness! Josephine D. (Henderson) Heard

FORGIVENESS
New Testament Remembered. Melva Tatum Smith

FORTY
On Reaching Forty. Maya Angelou

FOUNTAINS
To a Fountain. Lucy Mae Turner

FRANCE
Christmas Eve in France. Jessie Redmond Fauset

FRANKLIN, ARETHA
Aretha. Mae Jackson
Franklin on U. S. History. S. Diane Bogus
Poem for Aretha. Nikki Giovanni

FRATERNITIES
Greek Crazeology. Carolyn M. Rodgers

FREEDOM
Freedom. Anonymous
Freedom At Last. Olean Bess
Hard to be Free. Melva Tatum Smith
Jack and Dinah Want Freedom. Anonymous
Liberty and Peace. Phillis Wheatley
Raise a Ruckus Tonight. Anonmous
Stood Up. Nancy C. Arnez
Tune For Two Fingers. Mari Evans
We'll Soon Be Free. Anonymous

FREEDOM FIGHTERS
Love Poem To An African Freedom Fighter, A. Rosemari Mealy

FRIENDSHIP
And to Their Friends. Margaret Danner
Bridge of Friendship and Understanding. Margaret Danner
Friend. Gwendolyn Brooks
Friends Come. Lucille Clifton
Friendship. Athelstan Lalande
How Come Dat? Lucy Mae Turner
I Have a Friend. Anne Spencer
Matter of Money, A. Damali
My Friend. Beth Hollender
On Friendship. Phillis Wheatley
On Seeing an Old Friend. Sandra H. Royster
On That One Day. Naomi F. Faust
Poem of Friendship. Nikki Giovanni
Spurned Friendship. Anita Anderson
To My Friend. Josephine D. (Henderson) Heard

FRIGHT
Life Doesn't Frighten Me. Maya Angelou

FRIGIDITY
Response, A. Nikki Giovanni

FROST
Fros' Is On De Punkin, De. Bessie Woodson Yancey

FROST, ROBERT
Of Robert Frost. Gwendolyn Brooks

FRUIT
Apples. Ariel Williams Holloway
Green Apples. Linda Brown Bragg
Pineapple. Harryette Mullen

FULLER, HOYT W.
For H. W. Fuller. Carolyn M. Rodgers

FULFILLMENT
Fulfillment. Helene Johnson

FUNERAL RITES AND CEREMONIES
Burial. Alice Walker
Funeral Parade, The. Toi Derricotte
Joining, Merging & Breaking Up, The. Carolyn M. Rodgers
Old Men Used to Sing, The. Alice Walker
Ox in De Ditch. Lucile D. Goodlett
Poem For Lloyd. Nikki Giovanni
Rebel, The. Mari Evans
Requiem For a Newsman. June Vanleer Williams
Rites For Cousin Vit, The. Gwendolyn Brooks
Suite of Assassinations. The Carolyn M. Rodgers

Two Thousand People Came to His Funeral When Father Died. Gloria Oden
Winking at a Funeral. Alice Walker
You Had to Go to Funerals. Alice Walker

FURNITURE, AFRICAN
For Muffin. Margaret Danner

FUTURE
Future. Gertrude Blackwell Bailey

FUTURE SHOCK
After Reading the Number One Intellectual American Best Seller, Future Shock, All About Change is Where We're At. June Jordan

- G -

GAMBLING
Gambler. Elma Stuckey

GAMES
Game of Game, The. Nikki Giovanni
In Memory of the Hokey Pokey. Jennifer Blackman Lawson
Quoits. Anonymous

GANGS
Gang Girls. Gwendolyn Brooks
U Name This One. Carolyn M. Rodgers

GARBAGE
Good Friday Garbage. Edith Brandon Humphrey

GARDENS
Back Into the Garden. Sarah Webster Fabio
Garden Ghosts. Clara Haywood
Mother Bore My Three Sisters and Two Brothers. Gloria Oden
My City Garden Plot. Lucy Mae Turner
My Garden. Gertrude Blackwell Bailey

GARMENT WORKERS
I'm a Worker. Jayne Cortez

GARRISON, JIMMY
Listening to Jimmy Garrison (Pittsburgh, Pa.) Sonia Sanchez

GARVEY, MARCUS
Five Black Men... Margaret Walker
Garvey. Anonymous

GENOCIDE
Genocide Is. E. Sharon Gomillion
(Untitled) Johari Amini

GETHSEMANE
Gethsemane. Georgia Douglas Johnson

GETTYSBURGH, PENNSYLVANIA
Visit to Gettysburgh, A. Lucille Clifton

GHETTOS
Ghetto. Yvette Johnson
Ghetto Daybreak. June Vanleer Williams
Incident in a Black Ghetto. Pinkie Gordon Lane
U Name This One. Carolyn M. Rodgers

GHOSTS
Haunted. Mae V. Cowdery
Spook Village. Lucy Mae Turner

GIFTS
Gift. Alice Walker

GILEAD
Gilead. Georgia Douglas Johnson

GIRLS
Advice to the Girls. Frances E. W. Harper
Bad Johnny. Sandra Royster
Ballad of Chocolate Mabbie, The. Gwendolyn Brooks
Ballad of Late Annie, The. Gwendolyn Brooks
Ballad of the Brown Girl. Alice Walker
Ballad of the Light-Eyed Little Girl, The. Gwendolyn Brooks
Black Girl, Black Girl. Leatrice Emeruwa
Burial of Sarah. Frances E. W. Harper
But What Can You Teach My Daughter. Audre Lorde
Dear Toni Instead of a Letter of Congratulation Upon Your Book and Your Daughter Whom You Say You Are Raising to be a Correct Little Sister. Audre Lorde
Desire. Constance Nichols
Disgrace. Anonymous
Earth Mother (Low Singing is Heard) Sonia Sanchez
Esther, As Lead. Carolyn M. Rodgers
Expiriese Girl Wanted. Ntozake Shange
Gang Girls. Gwendolyn Brooks
Girl Held Wighout Bail. Margaret Walker
Girl Who Died #1, The. Alice Walker
Girl Who Died #2/for D.P. Alice Walker
Hunchback Girl: She Thinks of Heaven. Gwendolyn Brooks
If Mama Could See. Lucille Clifton
Kissie Lee. Margaret Walker
Last Note to My Girls. Lucille Clifton
Little Helper. Edna Shaw
Lucy One-Eye. Lucille Clifton
Maxie Allen. Gwendolyn Brooks
Miss Persephone. Harryette Mullen
My Little 'Bout-Town Girl. Gwendolyn Brooks
Pickin Em Up and Layin Em Down. Maya Angelou
Picture, The. Jeanette Adams
Poem For Flora. Nikki Giovanni
Poem to Ethel and Chenese, A. Olean Bess
Poor Girl. Maya Angelou
Resurrection of the Daughter. Ntozake Shange
Ruth. Pauli Murray
Sadie and Maud. Gwendolyn Brooks
Time Change and we Change With Them or We Seem to Have Lost Touch With Each Other. Audre Lorde
To a Dark Girl. Gwendolyn B. Bennett
To a Girl Who Knew What Side Her Bread Was Buttered On. Audre Lorde
To Anita. Sonia Sanchez
To the Girl Who Lives in a Tree. Audre Lorde
Toast to Colored Girls, A. Bessie Woodson Yancey
Violet. Naomi Long Madgett
When I Was a Little Girl. Olean Bess
Why? Melba Joyce Boyd
Yalla Gal. Lucile D. Goodlett
Young/Black/Girl. Sonia Sanchez

GIRLS, MEXICAN
Viejas Locas. Harryette Mullen

GLUTONY
Maggie. Theresa Ford

GOD

Did You Hear. May Miller
Egg in Each Basket, An. Elma Stuckey
Mama's God. Carolyn M. Rodgers
On Divine Adaptation to an Age of Disbelief. June Jordan
Preacher Ruminates Behind the Sermon. Gwendolyn Brooks

GODS
Calming Kali. Lucille Clifton
Coming of Kali, The. Lucille Clifton
Falling Gods. Georgia Douglas Johnson

GOLIATH
Goliath of Gath. Phillis Wheatley

GOOD AND EVIL
Evil is No Black Thing. Sarah Webster Fabio

GOODMAN, ANDY
For Andy Goodman- Michael Schwerner - and James Chaney. Margaret Walker

GOSPEL
Gospel Train. Anonymous

GOSSIP
Mode of Communication, A. June Vanleer Williams

GRAMMAR
Watch Your English. Anonymous

GRAND CHILDREN
For Her. Lucille Clifton

GRANDFATHERS
Don't Die in January. June Vanleer Williams
For My Grandfather, Lowell Paxter Mitchell. Harryette Mullen
For My Grandpa. Vanessa Howard

GRANDMOTHERS
Feeding, The. Toi Derricotte
For Eric Toller. Margaret T. G. Burroughs
Gra'ma. Colleen McElroy
Gramma Wynn. Melba Joyce Boyd
Grandma's Hands. Melba Joyce Boyd
It's All the Same. Thadious M. Davis
Legacies. Nikki Giovanni
Lineage. Margaret Walker
Muffin, His Baba and the Boneman. Margaret Danner
My Grandmother. Harryette Mullen

GRANDSONS
For Eric Toller. Margaret T. G. Burroughs
Grandson is a Hoticeberg, A. Margaret Danner
1964 Valentine to My Grandson. Margaret Danner

GRASSES
Grass Fingers. Angelina Weld Grimke
Quatrains. Gwendolyn B. Bennett

GRASSHOPPERS see LOCUSTS

GRATITUDE
Thank You. Melva Tatum Smith

GRAVES
First Flakes That Fell on Mother's Grave. Josephine D. (Henderson)

Heard

GREAT BRITAIN
To the First of August. Ann Plato

GREENESS
Greeness. Angelina Weld Grimke

GREENS (VEGETABLES)
Cutting Greens. Lucille Clifton
From Okra to Greens/ A Different Love Poem/We Need a Change. Ntozake Shange
Okra to Greens/An Aside on Amsterdam Avenue. Ntozake Shange

GRIEF
Grief Explained. June Vanleer Williams

GRIMKE, CHARLOTTE FORTEN
To Keep the Memory of Charlotte Forten Grimke. Angelina Weld Grimke

GWOWTH
Grown in Hope and Grace. Barbara Anne Baxter

GUMS AND RESIN
Disapppintment. Arlena Howard Benton

- H -

HAIR
Baby Hair. Constance Nichols
For Muh' Dear. Carolyn M. Rodgers
For Sistuhs Wearing Straight Hair. Carolyn M. Rodgers
Homage to My Hair. Lucille Clifton
If Hair Makes me Black, I Must Be Purple. Linda B. Hardnett
It Was Not the Fashion in Our House to Kiss or Touch. Gloria Oden
Knowing the Difference. Carolyn M. Rodgers
Precocious Curiosity. Linda Brown Bragg
Saturday Afternoon When Chores Are Done! Harryette Mullen
Stephen's Hair. Wanda Coleman
Touch of Gray. Nola Richardson
Touch of Gray. Nola Richardson

HAIR STYLES
Naturally. Audre Lorde

HAITI
Black Night in Haiti, Palais National, Port-Au-Prince. Ntozake Shange
Haiti. Amina Baraka

HALLOWEEN
All Hallows Eve. Audre Lorde

HALLUCINATIONS AND ILLUSIONS
Illusions. Georgia Douglas Johnson

HAMER, FANNIE LOU
Big Fine Woman From Ruleville. Jayne Cortez
1977: Poem for Mrs. Fannie Lou Hamer. June Jordan
Remembering Fannie Lou Hamer. Thadious M. Davis

HAMPTON, VIRGINIA
Hampton, Virginia. Nikki Giovanni

HANDICAPPED
Old Woman and Young Child at a Wedding Reception. Jennifer Blackman Lawson

HANDS
Butterfly, The. Nikki Giovanni
Dusk Thoughts. Countess M. Twitty
Grandma's Hands. Melba Joyce Boyd
Hands. Anita Soctt Coleman
Hands. Beatris Overby
Hands: For Mother's Day. Nikki Giovanni
Here Hold My Hands. Mari Evans
His Hands. Damali
His Hands. Elma Stuckey
Some Hands Are Lovelier. Mae V. Cowdery
Your Hands. Angelina Weld Grimke

HANSBERRY, LORRAINE
Lorraine Hansberry. Nikki Giovanni

HAPGOOD, EMILIE BIGELOW
To Emilie Bigelow Hapgood-Philanthropist. Georgia Douglas Johnson

HAPPINESS
Good Times. Lucille Clifton
Happiness. Ethlynne E. Holmes
Poem. Blanche Taylor Dichinson
Soliloquy. Dorothy Parrish
Thirst. Gertrude Blackwell Bailey

HARLEM, NEW YORK
Harlem Hopscotch. Maya Angelou
Sewerplant Grows in Harlem or I'm a Stranger Here Myself When Does the Next Swan Leave. Audre
Sonnet to a Negro in Harlem. Helene Johnson

HARPER, MICHAEL S.
Communion in a Small Room. Sherley Williams

HATRED
Great Truths. Marion Cuthbert
Hate. Pauli Murray
Hatred. Gwendolyn B. Bennett
Hatred. Beatrice M. Murphy
I am Frightened That/The Flame of Hate/Will Burn Me. Vanessa Howard
Let Me Not Hate. Georgia Douglas Johnson
My Hate. Leighla Lewis
Triangle. Roslyn Greer

HAYES, ROLAND
Roland Hayes. Eloise Culver

HEAD
W'ere is My Head Going. Kali Grosvenor

HEALING
Healing Stream. Gertrude Blackwell Bailey

HEALTH
To a Lady on Her Coming to North America With Her Son, for the Recovery of Her Health. Phillis Wheatley

HEART TRANSPLANT
Uhuru in the O.R. June Jordan

HEARTS
Black Heart as Ever Green, The. Carolyn M. Rodgers
Happy Heart, A. Josephine

HEAVEN
Everybody Talkin' 'Bout Heaven. Anonymous
Fishers of Men. Frances Harper
Heaven. Naomi Long Madgett
Hunchback Girl She Thinks of Heaven. Gwendolyn Brooks
Moment in Paradise. Lucia Mae Pitts
North Boun'. Ariel Williams Holloway
Renewal of Strength. Frances E. W. Harper
Souls of Black Men. Naomi Long Madgett
Swing Low, Sweet Chariot. Anonymous
Vision, The. Elma Stuckey

HELP
Reach Out. Gertrude Blackwell Bailey

HEMMINGS, SALLY
Monticello. Lucille Clifton

HERITAGE
America Negra. Anita Scott Coleman
Ballad of the Free, The. Margaret Walker
Dark Blood. Margaret Walker
Frustration, A Heritage. Thelma Parker Cox
Heritage. Dolores Clinton
Heritage. Gwendolyn Bennett
Heritage. Naomie Buford
How Many Silent Centuries Sleep in my Sultry Veins? Margaret Walker
Kinship Ties. Jennifer Blackman Lawson
New Poem For Us. Sonia Sanchez
Proem on Africa. Margaret T. G. Burroughs
Senses of Heritage. Ntozake Shange

HEROES
Negro Hero. Gwendolyn Brooks
Our Hero. Frances E. W. Harper
Poem for Heroes, A. Julia Fields
Post War Ballad. Dorothy Vena Johnson
To Some Millions Who Survive. Joseph E. Mander, Senior. Sarah E. Wright
What Happing to the Heroes. Kali Grosvenor

HIGHWAYS
Song of the Highway, The. Pauli Murray

HILLS
Hill, The. Ruby Stevens
Hills, The. Frenchy J. Hodges
That Hill. Blanche Taylor Dickinson

HIPS
Homage to my Hips. Lucille Clifton

HISTORY
Let it be Known. Margaret T. G. Burroughs
Song for the Old Ones. Maya Angelou
Walking Down Park. Nikki Giovanni

HOARDING
Packrat. Naomi Long Madgett

HOGS
Hawg Killin'. Lucile D. Goodlett

HOLIDAY, BILLIE
For Our Lady. Sonia Sanchez

HOLIDAYS
See

CHRISTMAS
EASTER
HALLOWEEN
THANKSGIVING

HOLLY
Through the Holly Wreath. Charlemae Rollins

HOMES
Black Woman Throws a Tantrum. Nayo
Future Promise. Audre Lorde
Going Home. Patricia Jones
Home. Margaret Danner
Home, Sweet Home. Frances E. W. Harper
Rooms are More Than. Carolyn M. Rodgers
They Went Home. Maya Angelou

HOMOSEXUALS
Gay Bar. Wanda Coleman
Poem/Because It Came as a Surprise to Me, A. Nikki Giovanni

HOPE
Dark Testament. Pauli Murray
It Seems to Me. Edna L. Anderson
Service, Please. Mrytle Campbell Gorham
Triple Benison, The. Henrietta Cordelia Ray

HOPSCOTCH
Harlem Hopscotch. Maya Angelou

HORSEMANSHIP
That Rider. May Miller

HORSES
Horses Graze. Gwendolyn Brooks
Rivah's a Black Mare. Lucile D. Goodlett
Strong Men, Riding Horses. Gwendolyn Brooks

HORSES, SEA
Sea Horse. Anonymous

HOSPITALITY
Poem (For TW). Nikki Giovanni

HOUSE CLEANING
House Cleaning. Nikki Giovanni

HOUSES
Houses. Nikki Giovanni
My House. Nikki Giovanni
New House. Naomi Long Madgett
Pictures From a School Window. Naomi Long Madgett
Plans. Helen Morgan Brooks
Rhythms of a House. C. Tillery Banks
Tar Paper Bungalow, De. Lucy Mae Turner

HOUSES, ROOMING
Rooming Houses are Old Women. Audre Lorde

HUGHES, LANGSTON
Langston. Mari Evans
Langston Hughes. Gwendolyn Brooks
Langston Hughes. Julia Fields
Langston Hughes. Eloise Culver
Langston Huhes a Man of the New Day. Margaret Danner
Langston Hughes Made It. Margaret Danner
Letter to Langston Hughes. Kali Grosvenor
Rhetoric of Langston Hughes, The. Margaret Danner
Simple. Naomi Long Madgett

HUMANITY

Hymn to Humanity (To S.P.G. Esq.), An. Phillis Wheatley

HUMILITY
Humility. Anita Scott Coleman

HUNGER
Hunger. Anonymous

HUNTING
'Possum-Huntin'. Bessie Woodson Yancey

HURRICANE
To a Lady on Her Remarkable Preservation in a Hurricane in North Carolina. Phillis Wheatley

HUSBANDS
My Husband's Birthday. Josephine D. (Henderson) Heard

HUTTON, BOBBY
Memorial. Sonia Sanchez

HYMNS
Hymn. Alice Walker
Matin Hymn. Josephine D. (Henderson) Heard

HYPOCRISY
Hypocrisy. Josephine D. (Henderson) Heard

- I -

ICICLES
Icicles on Trees. Catherine L. Findley

IDEALISM
Shine to What Should Be. Mari Evans

IDENTITY
Dead End Kids. Vanessa Howard

IMAGINATION
On Imagination. Phillis Wheatley

IMMORTALITY
Immortality. Marion Cuthbert

INCEST
Chain. Audre Lorde

INDIANS OF NORTH AMERICA
Bar's Fight. Lucy Terry
Combes Didn't Discover This World. Kali Grosvenor
Found Poem. June Jordan
Natives of America, The. Ann Plato
Poem for Nana. June Jordan

INDUSTRY
God's Extermination or Society's Souvernirs. S. Diane Bogus

INFANTS
Babies of Biafra, The. Katherine Dunham
Baby Hair. Constance Nichols
Flight. Pinkie Gordon Lane
Hush Now. Dorothy C. Parrish
If He Let Us Go Now. Sherley Williams
Nobody Knows Tomorrow. Margaret Danner
Ode to Barbara. Olean Bess
"One of the Least of These, My Little One." Georgia Douglas Johnson
Oronde. Paulette Childress White
Tale of the Newborn With Tapering Nails, The.

Margaret Danner
What You Gonna Name That Pretty Little Baby? Anonymous
When My Uncle Willie Saw. Carol Freeman
Whimper, Baby. Lucile D. Goodlett

INHERITANCE
Inheritance for Muffin. Margaret Danner

INNER CITY
In the Inner City. Lucille Clifton

INNER STRENGTH
Our Needs. Margaret Walker

INSANITY
For the Mad. Lucille Clifton

INSECTS
Bedbug. Anonymous
Cricket and the Star, The. Effie Lee Newsome
Insurgent,The. Mari Evans

INSOLENCE
Elevens. Leatrice Emeruwa

INSOMNIA
Free Flight. June Jordan
I Do Not Sleep Nights Through. Gloria Oden
Lonely Sleepless Night, A. Olean Bess

INTEGRATION
Just as the Del Vikings Stole My Heart. Ntozake Shange

INTELLECT
Intellectualism. Nikki Giovanni

IOWA
Iowa Farmer. Margaret Walker

IRAN CRISIS
Current Events. June Jordan

ISOLATION
Isolation. Georgia Douglas Johnson

- J -

JACK FROST
Jack Frost. Gertrude Parthenia McBrown
Painter, The. Gertrude Parthenia McBrown

JACKSON, MAHALIA
Day They Eulogized Mahalia, The. Audre Lorde
Mahalia Jackson. Eloise Culver

JACKSON, MAY HOWARD
To May Howard Jackson--Sculptor. Georgia Douglas Johnson

JACKSON, MISSISSIPPI
Jackson Mississippi. Margaret Walker

JACKSON STATE (MISSISSIPPI)
Ode on the Occasion of the Inauguration of the Sixth President of Jackson State College. Margaret Walker

JAILS
Girl Held Without Bail. Margaret Walker

JAMAICA
Earth is not the World, Nor all Its Beauty. Carolyn

M. Rodgers
Epitaph For My Father. Margaret Walker
This Island Now (Jamaica) Kattie M. Cumbo

JAPAN
First Meeting (Japanese Style) Barbara Mahone

JAZZ
Newport Jazz Festival: Saratoga Springs and Especially About George Benson and Everyone Who Was Listening. June Jordan
Words for Kali and Poochie. Sonia Sanchez

JEALOUSY
Jealousy. Gertrude Blackwell Bailey
To a Jealous Cat. Sonia Sanchez

JEFFERSON, THOMAS
Monticello. Lucille Clifton

JEHOVAH WITNESS
3-31-70. Gayl Jones

JERICHO
Walls of Jericho,The. Blanche Taylor Dickinson

JESUS CHRIST
J, My Good Friend, Another Foolish Innocent. Alice Walker
Jesus Must Have Been Some Kind of Dude. Carolyn M. Rodgers
Passive Resistance. Margaret Danner
Steal Away. Anonymous

JESUS CHRIST -- CRUCIFIXION
He Never Said a Mumbling Anonymous
Were You Dere? Anonymous

JEUS CHRIST--NATIVITY
Magi Called Him King. Effie Lee Newsome
Rise Up, Shepherd and Follow. Anonymous
Virgin Mary Had a Baby Boy, The. Anonymous
Wasn't That a Mighty Day. Anonymous

JEWELRY
Jewels. Lucy Mae Turner
To a Mounted Ivory Masque Pin. Margaret Danner

JIM CROW
Guilty. Ruby Berkley Goodwin
Now. Margaret Walker
Old Jim Crow. Anonymous

JOB (BIBLE)
Job. Lucille Clifton
Just Like Job. Maya Angelou

JOHNSON, JAMES WELDON
To James Weldon Johnson. Georgia Holloway Jones

JOHNSON, LYNDON BAINES
LBJ: Rejoinder. June Jordan

JONAH (BIBLE)
Old Jonah. Ionie Daniels

JOY AND GRIEF
Joy. Clarissa Scott Delany
Joy. Georgia Douglas Johnson
Joy. Nikki Giovanni
Joy or Sorrow. Leanna F. Johnson

JUNE

June. Bessie Woodson Yancey
June Song, A. Charlotte Forten Grimke

JUNGLES
Jungle. Mary Carter Smith

JUSTICE
Ode to Justice. Dorothy Vena Johnson

- K -

KAPPA ALPHA PSI FRATERNITY
Greek Crazeology. Carolyn M. Rodgers

KENNEDY, EDWARD (TED)
Television/Poem. Sonia Sanchez

KENNEDY, ROBERT-- ASSASSINATION
Poem on the Assassination of Robert F. Kennedy. Nikki Giovanni

KENNEDYS
Right On: Wite America. Sonia Sanchez

KENTUCKY
From America: A Poem in Progress. June Jordan

KENYA
Gift From Kenya. May Miller

KGOSITSILE, KEORAPETSE
To Keorapetse Kgositsile. Gwendolyn Brooks

KILLENS, JOHN OLIVER
To John Oliver Killens in 1975. Gwendolyn Brooks

KING, ALBERTA WILLIAMS
Alberta Alberta. Jayne Cortez

KING, MARTIN LUTHER JR.
Amos--1963. Margaret Walker
Amos (Postscript-1968). Margaret Walker
Black Man From Atlanta. Virginia Williams
Black Prince, A. Olean Bess
Dreams, Common Sense and Stuff. Frenchy J. Hodges
Drum, The. Nikki Giovanni
Five Black Men... Margaret Walker
Innocent Question. Frenchy J. Hodges
Listen! I'se Talkin' To You, Lawd. Frenchy J. Hodges
Martin Luther King, Jr. Gwendolyn Brooks
Martin Luther King. Eloise Culver
Passive Resistance. Margaret Danner

KING, MARTIN LUTHER, JR.-- ASSASSINATION
Drum Major of the Freedom Parade, The. Margaret T. G. Burroughs
Elegy Written in America. Frenchy J. Hodges
Funeral of Martin Luther King, Jr. Nikki Giovanni
Good Assassinations Should Be Quiet. Mari Evans
In Memoriam: Martin Luther King, Jr. June Jordan
In the Blue Room. Leatrice Emeruwa
No Train of Thought, April 4, 1969. June Jordan
On the Day When Nobody Smiled. Margaret Danner
Reflections on April 4, 1968. Nikki Giovanni

KINGS AND RULERS
To the King's Most Excel-

lent Majesty (1768) Phillis Wheatley

KISSES
Alla Tha's All Right, But. June Jordan
Amour. Georgia Douglas Johnson
It's Happenin/But You Don't Know Abt It. Ntozake Shange
Kiss, The. Alice Walker
Kisses. Nikki Giovanni
My Mother's Kiss. Frances E. W. Harper
Parting Kiss, The. Josephine D. (Henderson) Heard
Pledge. Georgia Douglas Johnson
Tears and Kisses. Georgia Douglas Johnson

KNIGHT, ETHERIDGE
Poem for Etheridge. Sonia Sanchez

KNOXVILLE, TENNESSEE
Knoxville, Tennessee. Nikki Giovanni

KOALA BEAR
To Koala, Who Will Soon Be Extinct. Carole Gregory Clemmons

- L -

LACE AND LACE MAKING
I Welcome Lace. Margaret Danner

LAKES
Lake Michigan's Waves. Margaret Danner
Lake Murry. Pinkie Gordon Lane
Startled Waves Began to Recede, The. Margaret Danner

LAMENESS
For the Lame. Lucille Clifton

LAMPS
Lamps. Mae V. Cowdery

LATIN
In My Life, Latin and Adolescence Came Along Together. Gloria Oden

LAUGHTER
Laughter. Portia Lucas
Old Laughter. Gwendolyn Brooks
When I Think About Myself. Maya Angelou

LAW, THE
Law, The. Patricia Parker

LEADERSHIP
All Hung Up. Kattie M. Cumbo
Leaders, The. Gwendolyn Brooks
We Pass. Beatrice M. Murphy

LEAVE-TAKING
Good-Bye. Georgia Douglas Johnson
Good-Bye. Josephine D. (Henderson) Heard
Parting, The. Josephine D. (Henderson) Heard

LEAVES
Dead Leaves. Georgia Douglas Johnson
Leaves. Pinkie Gordon Lane
Leaves Blow Backward. June Jordan
Lesson of the Falling Leaves, The. Lucille Clifton
New Leaf. Wanda Coleman

LEBANON
Smell of Lebanon, The. Alice

Walker

LEFT HANDED
South Paw Baby. Pinkie Gordon Lane

LEMONADE
When Handed a Lemon, Make Lemonade. Gwendolyn Brooks

LESBIANS
Beyond Sisters. Wanda Coleman
For the Straight Folks Who Don't Mind Gays. Patricia Parker
Non-Monogamy is a Pain in the Butt. Patricia Parker

LETTERS
Cluttered Letters. Nola Richardson
Letter, The. Beatrice M. Murphy
Letter From a Wife. S. Carolyn Reese
Love Letters. Josephine D. (Henderson) Heard
Returned Letters, The. Josephine D. (Henderson) Heard

LIBERATION
Last M. F., The. Carolyn M. Rodgers
On Working White Liberals. Maya Angelou
Woman Statement #1. S. Diane Bogus

LIBERTY
Chic Freedom's Reflection. Alice Walker
Liberty and Peace. Phillis Wheatley
Midway. Naomi Long Madgett
Oh Freedom. Anonymous
To a Freedom Fighter. Maya Angelou
To the Freedom Riders. Eloise Culver
Uhuru Uberalles! (...and the sound of weeping). Mari Evans

LIBRARIES
Library, The. Wanda Coleman

LICE see PARASITOSIS

LIES
Could You Tell me a Falsehood? Josephine D. (Henderson) Heard
How I Can Lie to You. Maya Angelou
Remembering. Maya Angelou

LIFE
Assets. Bessie Woodson Yancey
Do Not Pass Me By. Naomi Long Madgett
Formula. Sonia Sanchez
Ladder of Life, The. Josephine D. (Henderson) Heard
Life. Gertrude Blackwell Bailey
Life. Naomi Long Madgett
Life Doesn't Frighten Me. Maya Angelou
Life is the Art of Drawing. Carolyn Ogletree
Life is a Two-Way Experience. Vanessa Howard
Life's Like the Wind. Jane W. Burton
Swing of Life, The. Jamye M. Coleman
What a Joke! Nola Richardson
Your Life. Gertrude Blackwell Bailey

LIGHT
Let the Light Enter. Frances E. W. Harper
Lights. W. Blanche Nivens
Lights at Carney's Point. Alice Dunbar-Nelson

Some Light to Hold in my Hands. Harryette Mullen
This Little Light of Mine. Kali Grosvenor

LILACS
Lilac. Gertrude Parthenia McBrown

LILLIES
Lillies. Linda B. Graham

LINCOLN, ABRAHAM
Abraham Lincoln. Eloise Culver
Cameo No. I. June Jordan
Emancipation Proclamation. Elma Stuckey
To Abraham Lincoln. Georgia Douglas Johnson

LINCOLN, ABRAHAM--ASSASSINATION
Solace. Josephine D. (Henderson) Heard

LINE MAN
Gus, the Lineman. Margaret Walker

LISTENING
Listen. Gertrude Blackwell Bailey

LITTLE, MALCOLM ee MALCOLM X

LITTLE RICHARD (RICHARD PENNIMAN)
Richard Penniman When His Mama and Daddy Died. Lucille Clifton

LITTLE ROCK, ARKANSAS
Chicago Defender Sends a Man to Little Rock, The. Gwendolyn Brooks

LIVING CONDITIONS
First Time I Was Sweet Sixteen. Nayo
Irony. Mae Jackson
Kitchenette Building. Gwendolyn Brooks
Palace at Four A.M., The. Jodi Braxton
Untitled. Wanda Coleman
Where I Live. Wanda Coleman

LOAFING
Loafin'. Bessie Woodson Yancey

LOCUST
Grasshopper World, The. Frenchy J. Hodges
Roasting Grasshoppers. Pinkie Gordon Lane

LONDON, ENGLAND
Somewhere in London. Naomi Long Madgett
Street Called Petticoat Lane, The. Alice Dunbar-Nelson

LONELINESS
Alone. Nikki Giovanni
I'm Not Lonely. Nikki Giovanni
Reason Why I'm Lonely, The. Naomi Long Madgett
Soliloquy. Dorothy Parrish
What Color is Lonely? Carolyn M. Rodgers

LONGFELLOW, HENRY WADSWPRTJ
Henry Wadsworth Longfellow. Eloise Culver

LONGING
For E. S. Diane Bogus
Longing. Lillian Tucker Lewis
Longings. Mae V. Cowdery

LOST
No Loser, No Weeper. Maya

Angelou

LOTS
Vacant Lot. Gwendolyn Brooks

LOUIS, JOE
Joe Louis. Eloise Culver

LOUISIANA
Memories: 1956. Jennifer Blackman Lawson

LOVE
Advice to the Lovelorn. Mae V. Cowdery
Afterwards. Jennifer Blackman Lawson
And Fall Shall Sit in Judgment. Audre Lorde
And So it is With Love. Mae V. Cowdery
Anxiety. Ruby Berkley Goodwin
As Simple As That. Nola Richardson
Autumn. Georgia Douglas Johnson
Ballad. Sonia Sanchez
Break, Break My Heart. Georgia Douglas Johnson
Call Unto Me. Alvies M. Carter
Challenge. Lucia Mae Pitts
Copyright. S. Diane Bogus
Dawn of Love, The. Henrietta Cordelia Ray
Denial. Mae V. Cowdery
Destiny. Georgia Douglas Johnson
Detached, The. Maya Angelou
Devastation. Georgia Douglas Johnson
Double Standard, A. Frances E. W. Harper
Dream Love. Ruth Sarver
Dream of Revenge, A. Lauretta Holman Gooden
Fantasy, A. Georgia Douglas Johnson
Fantasy of a Fool. Naomi Long Madgett
Fiction. Georgia Douglas Johnson
Finality. Georgia Douglas Johnson
For Every (One). Barbara Mahone
For Love. Colleen McElroh
For O -- Two Hunt-Up. Carolyn M. Rodgers
Fragment. Jessie Redond Fauset
Gamut, The. Maya Angelou
Good-Bye. Georgia Douglas Johnson
Great Truths. Marion Cuthbert
Haiku. Sonia Sanchez
I Find No Evil or Three Images and Trust. S. Diane Bogus
I Know Very Little About Love... Melba Tatum Smith
I Love Somebody. Anonymous
I Love Thee. Josephine D. (Henderson) Heard
I Love Thee Yet. Josephine D. (Henderson) Heard
I Move Into Loving. Judy Dothard Simmons
I Release Thee--With Love. Eleanor Thomas-Grumbach
I Want to Die While you Love Me. Georgia Douglas Johnson
If I Must Know. Mae V. Cowdery
If Love Dies. Julia Fields
I'm Alone. Nola Richardson
In Love. Georgia Douglas Johnson
In Quest. Georgia Douglas Johnson
Insatiate. Mae V. Cowdery
Just For a Time. Maya Angelou
Kind of Love, Some Say. Maya Angelou
Let Me Live With Marriage. June Jordan
Lip Love. June Vanleer Williams
Long John Nelson Sweetie Pie. Margaret Walker
Love. Anonymous
Love. Elaine Mitchell
Love. Josephine D. (Henderson) Heard
Love. Lucy Mae Turner

Love. Olean Bess
Love. Valerie Parks
Love Ain't Hip. Sandra H.
Royster
Love, Considered. Pinkie
Gordon Lane
Love Poem. Thulani Davis
Love Poem (For Real). Nikki
Giovanni
Love Poem. Pinkie Gordon Lane
Love Rejected. Lucille Clif-
ton
Love Song For Summer. Mae V.
Cowdery
Love - The Beginning and the
End. Carolyn M. Rodgers
Love You Right Back. Gwendo-
lyn Brooks
Lovely Love, A. Gwendolyn
Brooks
Love's Miracle. Georgia
Douglas Johnson
Love's More Enduring Uses.
Pauli Murray
Love's Tendril. Georgia
Douglas Johnson
Lovin U Rite. Angela Jack-
son
Magic. Sonia Sanchez
Man, I Am Trying to Love You.
Sonia Sanchez
May I Return. Lucy Mae Turner
Morning After...Love, The.
Kattie M. Cumbo
My Love. Joanne Jimason
My Mistake. Pamela Cobb
My Path is Lighted by a Star.
Lucy Mae Turner
My Thoughts Are I Love You.
Vanessa Howard
Never!! Lyn
New Love. Nancy L. Arnez
No Love. Marion Nicholes
No Love/Just Response. Nola
Richardson
Noblesse Oblige. Jessie Red-
mond Fauset
Now Ain't That Love. Carolyn
M. Rodgers
Of Our Love. Kattie M. Cumbo
Of Someone I Loved. Mae
Jackson
Oh Night of Love. Georgia
Douglas Johnson
On Diverse Deviations. Maya
Angelou

On Your Love. June Jordan
Only to Sleep. S. Diane
Bogus
Our Black People. Kali
Grosvenor
Pages From Life. Georgia
Douglas Johnson
Paradox, A. Georgia Douglas
Johnson
Pledge. Georgia Douglas
Johnson
Poem/Ditty-Bop. Carolyn M.
Rodgers
Poem...For A Lover. Mae V.
Cowdery
Poem No. 15. Sonia Sanchez
Poor Girl. Maya Angelou
Precious Offering, A. June
Vanleer Williams
Proof. Bessie Calhoun Bird
Proving. Georgia Douglas
Johnson
Recontre. Jessie Redmond
Fauset
Regret. Lucy Mae Turner
Rendezvous. Lois Royal
Hughes
Resignation. Nikki Giovanni
Return. Georgia Douglas
Johnson
Revelation. June Vanleer
Williams
Roman Poem Number Fourteen.
June Jordan
Sad Me. Jacqueline Cox
Sequel. Mae V. Cowdery
Shattered Mirror. Mae V.
Cowdery
She Hugged Me and Kissed Me.
Anonymous
So Long. Jayne Cortez
Something's Changed. Nola
Richardson
Summer: Falling in Love.
May Miller
Supreme. Georgia Douglas
Johnson
These Days. Joanne Jimason
Thousand Ways, A. Nola
Richardson
To--. Isabelle H. Monroe
To Be In Love. Gwendolyn
Brooks
To L. Julianne Perry
To Mother and Steve. Mari
Evans

To My Lost Love. Naomi Long Madgett
To Turn From Love. Sarah Webster Fabio
Touche. Jessie Redmond Fauset
Triangle. Roslyn Greer
Two Love Poems. Pinkie Gordon Lane
Unlike Me. Nola Richardson
Untitled No. Hurt. Carolyn M. Rodgers
Upon Looking at Love. Delores A. Brown
Warning. Alice Walker
What is Love. Myra Estelle Morris
Whene'er I Lift My Eyes to Bliss. Georgia Douglas Johnson
Wife-Woman, The. Anne Spencer
You Ask What Love Is. Nola Richardson
You Taught Me Love. Frederica Katheryne Bunton

LOVE, INTERRACIAL
Johann. Alice Walker

LOVERS
Backstage. Jill Witherspoon Bouer
Overdose of Lovers, An. Wanda Coleman
Pray for the Lovers. Jayne Cortez

LULLABIES
Lullaby. Cora Bell Moten
Lullaby. Marion Nicholes
Lullady. Quandra Prettyman
Negro Lullaby. Bessie Woodson Yancey

LUXURIES
Luxury. Nikki Giovanni

LYNCHING
For Mack C. Parker. Pauli Murray
I Saw Them Lynch. Carol Freeman
Libations. Jayne Cortez
Lynch Fragment 2. Jayne Cortez
Lynching, The. Isabelle McClellan Taylor
On Democracy. Naomi Long Madgett
Southern Negro Heart Cry. Valerie Parks
Whut A Dawn. Mary Bohanon

- M -

MC COY, ELIJAH
Elijah McCoy. Eloise Culver

MAGIC
Black Magician, The. Ariel Williams Holloway
Conjure Bag. Lucile D. Goodlett
My Father is a Retired Magician. Ntozake Shange

MAGNOLIAS
Midnight Magnolias. Naomi Long Madgett

MAIDS
Domestics. Kattie M. Cumbo
Family Member (You Must be Putting Me On) A. June Vanleer Williams
Personals. Leatrice Emeruwa

MAKE-UP
Make-Up. Nikki Giovanni

MALCOLM X
Aardvark. Julia Fields
Black Future. Kattie M. Cumbo
Black Genesis. Mae Jackson
Brother Freedom. Margaret Burroughs
Days After. Helen Quigless
Five Black Men... Margaret Walker

For Malcolm. Joyce Whitsitt Lawrence
For Malcolm X. Julia Fields
For Malcolm X. Margaret Walker
For Malcolm X. Nanina Alba
I Remember. Mae Jackson
Jungle Flower. Marcella Caine
Malcolm. Kattie M. Cumbo
Malcolm. Sonia Sanchez
Malcolm X. Gwendolyn Brooks
Malcolm X, A Lover of the Grass Roots. Margaret Danner
My Brother Malcolm. Christine Johnson
Poems For Malcolm. Carolyn M. Rodgers
Saint Malcolm. Johari Amini
Two For Malcolm. Patricia

MAMMIES
Oriflamme. Jessie Redmond Fauset

MAN
About Man. Johari Amini
And the Hotel Room Held Only Him. Mari Evans
Angie Saves Her Man. Lucile D. Goodlett
Another Man Don Gon'. Anonymous
Bad-Man Stagolee. Margaret Walker
Ballad of Rudolph Reed. Gwendolyn Brooks
Ballad of the Free. Margaret Walker
Beautiful Black Men. Nikki Giovanni
Big John Henry. Margaret Walker
Black Man's Feast. Sarah Webster Fabio
Blackman Get Off That Corner. Gertrude Blackwell Bailey
Blackman Has Done His Part. Gertrude Blackwell Bailey
Boy. Elma Stuckey
Bronzeville Man With a Belt in the Back. Gwendolyn Brooks
Brother of the Hour. Marion Nicholes
Casey Jones. Anonymous
Cool Breeze. Mae Jackson
Crab Man. Anonymous
Cross Oceans Into My Heart. Ntozake Shange
Dog Catcher, The. Lucy Mae Turner
Don't Honey Me. Linda Brown Bragg
Don't Wanna Be. Sonia Sanchez
Ebony. Lucy Mae Turner
Echoes of Childhood. Alice Corbin
Elevator Man Adheres to Form. Margaret Walker
For Christopher. June Jordan
For Dave: 1976. June Jordan
For H. W. Fuller. Carolyn M. Rodgers
For Harold Logan. Nikki Giovanni
For Some Black Men. Carolyn M. Rodgers
For Somebody to Start Singing. June Jordan
Go Down, Moses. Anonymous
Goliath of Gath. Phillis Wheatley
Goodbye David Tamunoemi West. Margaret Danner
Gospel Truth, The. Jackie Earley
Gus. Nikki Giovanni
Gus, the Lineman. Margaret Walker
His Excellency General Washington. Phillis Wheatley
I Am Man. Tomi Carolyn Tinsley
I Remember. Nikki Giovanni
In Celebration of Blk/Men. Johari Amini
Independent Man, The. Gwendolyn Brooks
Jessie Rufus. Lucile Goodlett
Joe Turner. Anonymous
Johann. Alice Walker
John Hardy. Anonymous
John Henry. Anonymous
John J. Maya Angelou

Kind of Man He is For Fred, The. Lucille Clifton
Long John Nelson and Sweetie Pie. Margaret Walker
Love - The Beginning and the End. Carolyn M. Rodgers
Maceo. Frances E. W. Harper
Matthew Cole. Gwendolyn Brooks
Memo to Daniel Pretty Moynihan. June Jordan
Memorial to Ed Bland. Gwendolyn Brooks
Men. Maya Angelou
Men Are All Away. Barbara Malcolm
Micah. Margaret Walker
Miss Nancy's Geo'ge. Lucile D. Goodlett
Mister Banjo. Anonymous
Moanin' Moanin'. Lucile D. Goodlett
Nicodemus. Carolyn M. Rodgers
Now Let's Be Real. Carolyn M. Rodgers
Of De Witt Williams on His Way to Lincoln Cemetery. Gwendolyn Brooks
Old Black Men. Georgia Douglas Johnson
Old Man. Elma Stuckey
Old Man Know-All. Anonymous
Old Marse John. Anonymous
Old Men, The. Ntozake Shange
Ole Man Jollie. Lucile D. Goodlett
Oyster Man's Cry. Anonymous
Po Laz'us. Anonymous
Poem For Blackboys in Floppy Tie-Die Hats Who Try to Relate to Sisters on Off-Nights. Jodi Braxton
Poem For My Pretty Man. June Jordan
Poor Renaldo. Naomi Long Madgett
Poppa Chicken. Margaret Walker
Privilege, The. May Miller
Railroad Bill. Anonymous
Siam at De Radio. Lucile D. Goodlett
Stackalee. Anonymous
Stackerlee and de Debbil. Anonymous
Stagolee. Anonymous
Stand Tall. Gertrude Blackwell Bailey
Stephen. Wanda Coleman
Strong Men, Riding Horses. Gwendolyn Brooks
Sundays of Satin-Legs Smith. Gwendolyn Brooks
Sweet Potato Man. Anonymous
Sweet Rough Man. Gertrude Rainey
Teacher. Margaret Walker
This Man. June Jordan
Three Bills. Pinkie Gordon Lane
'Tis Difficult. Ethel Brown
To a Man. Maya Angelou
To Merani/Mungu. Sonia Sanchez
Tomorrow's Men. Georgia Douglas Johnson
Two-Gun Buster and Trigger Slim. Margaret Walker
Uncle Bull-Boy. June Jordan
Uncle Gabriel. Anonymous
Uncle Tom. Eleanor A. Thompson
Unk' Enoch Mann. Lucile D. Goodlett
Way-Out Morgan. Gwendolyn Brooks
Watermelon Vendor's Cry. Anonymous
Ways O' Men. Angelina Weld Grimke
When My Uncle Willie Saw. Carol Freeman
Wild Negro Bill. Anonymous
Willie. Maya Angelou
Wilmington, Delaware. Nikki Giovanni
Yalluh Hammuh. Margaret Walker
You Judge A Man by the Silence He Keeps. Wanda Coleman
Zorro Man, A. Maya Angelou

MANICURES
Beauty Shoppe. Gwendolyn Brooks

MANUMISSION
Promises of Freedom. Anonymous

MAPS
Map, The. Gloria Oden

MARCH
On'ry Weathah. Bessie Woodson Yancey
To March. Naomi Long Madgett

MARCH ON WASHINGTON
At the Lincoln Monument. August 28, 1963. Margaret Walker

MARCHES
Long March, The. Alicia Loy Johnson

MARDI GRAS
Zulu King: New Orleans (At Mardi Gras), The. Josephine Copeland

MARLEY, BOB
Rise Up Fallen Fighters (Okra Takes Up With a Rastafari Man/She Can't Hold Back/She Say Smilin') Ntozake Shange

MARRIAGE
Advice to the Girls. Frances E. W. Harper
Going East. Frances E. W. Harper
It Just Ain't Right. Theresa Thorpe
Let Me Live With Marriage. June Jordan
Old-Marrieds, The. Gwendolyn Brooks
On My Happy/Matrimonial Condition. June Jordan
Report. Frances E. W. Harper
Slave Marriage Ceremony Supplement. Anonymous
Wedding, The. June Jordan

MARTYRS
Martyr of Alabama, The. Frances Harper
To The Martyred. Georgia Douglas Johnson

MARX, KARL
Workers Rose on May Day or Postscript to Karl Marx. Audre Lorde

MARY (VIRGIN)
Calvary Way. May Miller
Penitent Considers Another Coming of Mary, A. Gwendolyn Brooks
Pliant of the Madonna, The. Lucy Mae Turner

MARYLAND
Sometimes I Think of Maryland. Jodi Braxton

MASKS
Mask, The. Irma McClaurin
Mask, The. Nancy L. Arnez
Masks. Nikki Giovanni
Poem No.1. Carolyn M. Rodgers

MASTER CHARGE
Master Charge Blues. Nikki Giovanni

MATERIAL GOODS
I. Beverly Thomas

MATZELIGER, JAN E.
Jan E. Matzeliger. Eloise Culver

MATHEMATICS
Mathematics. Katherine Dunham

MAY
May. Bessie Woodson Yancey
May Lament. Naomi Long Madgett

MAYFIELD, CURTIS
To Anita. Sonia Sanchez

MAYS, BENJAMIN
Jeremiah. Margaret Walker

MECHANICS
Mechanics, The. Colleen McElroy

MEDICAL CLERK
Drone. Wanda Coleman

MEDICINE
Medicine. Alice Walker

MEDITATION
Meditation. Nora Davis

MEMORIAL DAY
Chalmette. Alice Dunbar-Nelson

MEMORIES
Birth of Memory. Lucy Mae Turner
Chained. Ruth Brownlee Johnson
Inevitably. Georgia Douglas Johnson
Memories/The Red Bootee. Angela Jackson
Memory. Margaret Walker
Memory. Sandra Royster
Retrospect. Georgia Douglas Johnson
What Need Have I For Memory. Georgia Douglas Johnson

MEN
Blackwoman to Blackman: I. Jennifer Blackman Lawson
Courier. Georgia Douglas Johnson
Old Black Men. Georgia Douglas Johnson
Some Men. Ntozake Shange
Young Angry Men. Patricia

MENTAL RETARDATION
Young Girl Crying in the Street. Jennifer Blackman Lawson

MERCENARIES
Mercenaries & Mistrels. Jayne Cortez

MEREDITH. JAMES
James Meredith. Eloise Culver

MERMAIDS
Madness One Monday Evening. Julia Fields

MEXICO
Mexico Entered the Door on the Wind. Wanda Coleman

MIDDLE AGE
Middle Age Syndrome, The. June Vanleer Williams

MIDDLE CLASS
Man of the Middle Class, A. Gwendolyn Brooks
Sepia Fashion Show. Maya Angelou

MIDWIVES
Three Dollars Cash. Alice Walker

MIGRATION
Ghetto Love Song--Migration. Carole Gregory Clemmons
Migration. Carole Gregory Clemmons
Migration. Pinkie Gordon Lane

MILITANTS
Definition. Marion Nicholes

MILLER, DORIE
Negro Hero. Gwendolyn Brooks

MILTON, JOHN
Milton. Henrietta Cordelia Ray

MINERS
Childhood. Margaret Walker

MINISTERS see CLERGY

MINNESOTA
From America: a Poem in Process. June Jordan

MIRACLES
Deadlines for Miracles. Beatrice M. Murphy

MIRRORS
Good Mirrors are Not Cheap. Audre Lorde
Mirror Poems, The. Toi Derricotte
Mirrors. Nikki Giovanni
Painting Myself a New Mirror. Harryette Mullen

MISCARRIAGES
Miscarriage. Pinkie Gordon Lane

MISCEGENATION
Leora. Elma Stuckey
Misfit. Claire Turner
Monticello. Lucille Clifton
Octoroon, The. Georgia Douglas Johnson

MISERY
Misery of Being, The. E. Sharon Gomillion

MISSIONARIES
Missing Missionaries, The.

MISSISSIPPI
Jackson, Mississippi. Margaret Walker
On My First Trip to Mississipi. Linda Brown Brag
Oxford is a Legend. Margaret Walker
Silver Creek, Mississippi. Thulani Davis

MISTAKES
Mistakes. E. Sharon Gomillion
Mistakes. Gertrude Blackwell Bailey

MITCHELL, ARTHUR
Arthur Mitchell. Marianne Moore

MOCKING BIRD
My Mocking Bird. Josephine D. (Henderson) Heard

MONDAY
Latin Night is Monday. Ntozake Shange

MONEY
Friday Ladies of the Pay Envelopes, The. Mari Evans
From Inside and Empty Purse. Audre Lorde
Money, But Also... Melva Tatum Smith
To a Nickel. Lucy Mae Turner

MONKEYS
Disillusion. Lillian G. Brown

MONTHS
April in Your Eyes. Naomi Long Madgett
April is On The Way. Alice Dunbar-Nelson
At April. Angelina Weld Grimke
February. Patrice Wilson

December. Josephine D. (Henderson) Heard
June. Bessie Woodson Yancey
Lament. Naomi Long Madgett
May. Bessie Woodson Yancey
On'ry Weathah. Bessie Woodson Yancey
To March. Naomi Long Madgett
Written on the Last of April. Naomi Long Madgett

MONUMENTS
Monument in Black. Vanessa Howard

MOON
'Bout De Moon. Lucile D. Goodlett
Moon Below Me, The. Naomi Long Madgett
Moon Poem. Saundra Sharp
Moon Shines Down, The. Nikki Giovanni
Moonstalk. Harryette Mullen
On a Night of the Full Moon. Audre Lorde
Theft. Esther Popel

MOONSHINE
No Flowers. Elma Stuckey

MORNING
Hymn to the Morning, An. Phillis Wheatley
In the Morning. Jayne Cortez
In the Morning. Nola Richardson
Morn. Josephine D. (Henderson) Heard
Morning Coming In, The. Dorothy Randall
Morning Light (The Dew-Drier) Effie Lee Newsome
Morning Meditation. Pearl Cleage Lomax
Morning on the Mountains, The. June Jordan
Winter's Morn. Rosa Paul Brooks

MOSES (BIBLE)
Go Down, Moses. Anonymous
To a Dark Moses. Lucille Clifton

MOSQUITOES
Mistah Skeeter. Lucy Mae Turner

MOTEN, ETTA
Convert, The. Margaret Danner
Etta Moten's Attic. Margaret Danner

MOTHERS
Ah, Momma. June Jordan
Big Mama. Jennifer Blackman Lawson
Black Mother Woman. Audre Lorde
Bronzeville Mother Loiters in Mississippi, Meanwhile, A Mississippi Mother Burns Bacon. Gwendolyn Brooks
Carve/n. Angela Jackson
Dedication Poem. Frances E. W. Harper
Dialogue. Patricia Parker
Eyes in the Back of Her Head. Harryette Mullen
Few Years After Father Died, A. Gloria Oden
First Flakes That Fell on Mother's Grave, The. Josephine D. (Henderson) Heard
Floorwax Mother. Harryette Mullen
For a New Mother. Mae V. Cowdery
For Mama. Jill Witherspoon Boyer
For Momma. Melba Joyce Boyd
For Muh' Dear. Carolyn M. Rodgers
For My Mother. June Jordan
For Sapphires. Carolyn M. Rodgers
From the House of Yemanja. Audre Lorde
Hands: For Mother's Day.

Nikki Giovanni
Homage to Black Madonnas. Margaret T. G. Burroughs
In Memoriam of Mother. Josephine D. (Henderson)
It is Deep. Carolyn M. Rodgers
It is When We Love. Gloria Oden
Jessie Mitchell's Mother. Gwendolyn Brooks
Jesus Was Crucified, or It Must Be Deep. Carolyn M. Rodgers
Kwa Mama Zetu Waliutuzaa. Sonia Sanchez
Lines For My Mother. Margaret T. G. Burroughs
Madonna. Harryette Mullen
Mama. Sandra Royster
"Mama, I Don't Know." Pam Brown
Mama Settles the Dropout Problem. Betty Gates
Momma. Maami Verano
Momma Sayings. Harryette Mullen
Momma Welfare Roll. Maya Angelou
Mother, The. Georgia Douglas Johnson
Mother, The. Gwendolyn Brooks
Mother. Josephine D. (Henderson) Heard
Mother. Leatrice Emeruwa
Mother, The. Naomi Long Madgett
Mother and Dad. Gertrude Blackwell Bailey
Mother, I am Mad. Lucille Clifton
Motherless Child. Anonymous
Mothers. Nikki Giovanni
Mother's Love, A. Josephine D. (Henderson) Heard
Mother's Treasures. Frances E. W. Harper
My Mother. Eleanor A. Thompson
My Mother. Kali Grosvenor
My Mother's Blessing. Olean Bess
My Mother's Kiss. Frances E. W. Harper
On the Spirit of Mildred Jordan. June Jordan
Pathways: From Mother to Mother. Audre Lorde
Proud to Be. Gertrude Blackwell Bailey
Refugee Mother. Geraldine L. Wilson
Slave Mother, The. Frances E. W. Harper
Slave Mother's Crime, The. Josephine D. (Henderson) Heard
They Don't Understand. Nola Richardson
To My Daughter the Junkie on a Train. Audre Lorde
To My Mother. Naomi Long Madgett
Tommy's Mommy. Nikki Giovanni
Twice a Child. Naomi Long Madgett
When I Learned That Mother Was Slain in the Bedroom. Gloria Oden

MOTHERS, UNWED
Meditations of an Unwed Blk-Mother-To-Be. Linda Cousins
Poem For Unwed Mothers. Nikki Giovanni
Request. Maya Angelou
Sadie and Maud. Gwendolyn Brooks
Sin, A? Geraldine Peterson
When I Was a Child. Jacqueline Copps

MOTION PICTURES
Come Home From the Movies. Lucille Clifton
Why I Like Movies. Patricia Jones

MOURNER"S BENCH
Mourners Bench. Elma Stuckey

MOUNTAINS
Go Tell it on the Mountain. Anonymous

Loomit. Adrienne Ingrum
Mountain at Night. Lucy Mae Turner

MOVING
Moving. Josephine D. (Henderson) Heard

MULATTOS
Mulatto. Eleanor Weaver
Mulatto's Dilemma. Pauli Murray

MURDER
Bad-Man Stagolee. Margaret Walker
Colonized Mind. Barbara Marshall
For Andy Goodman--Michael Schwerner--and James Chaney. Margaret Walker
For Harold Logan. Nikki Giovanni
Guilty. Ruby Berkley Goodwin
Martyr of Alabama, The. Frances E. W. Harper
May 27, 1971: No Poem. June Jordan
Murder, The. Gwendolyn Brooks
On the Murder of Two Human Being Black Men, Denver A. Smith and His Unidentified Brother at Southern University, Baton Rouge, Louisiana, 1972. June Jordan
Questions. Sonia Sanchez
Revolutionary Petunias. Alice Walker
True Import of Present Dialogue, Black vs. Negro (For Peppe, Who Will Ultimately Judge Our Efforts) The. Nikki Giovanni
Untitled. Johari Amini

MUSES
On Recollection. Phillis Wheatley
Recollection, to Miss A--M--, Humbly Inscribed by the Authoress. Phillis Wheatley

MUSIC
I Live in Music. Ntozake Shange
Make/n My Music. Angela Jackson
Music. Josephine D. (Henderson) Heard
Record For My Friends, A. Sherley Williams
Revolutionary Music. Nikki Giovanni
Rhythmatic Sounds. Loretta Rodgers
Strain of Music. Mae V. Cowdery
Words for Kali and Poochie. Sonia Sanchez

MUSIC, AFRICAN
Music from Home. Colleen McElroy

MUSIC, GOSPEL
About Religion. Audre Lorde

MUSICAL INSTRUMENTS
Drummer King. Barbara Mahone
Little David, Play on Yo' Harp. Anonymous
New Organ, The. Josephine D. (Henderson) Heard
No Violin at All. Margaret Danner
Vibes. Margaret Danner

MUTENESS
For the Mute. Lucille Clifton

MYTHOLOGY
Niobe in Distress For Her Children Slain by Apollo, From Ovid's Metamorphoses, Book VI, and From a View of the Painting of Mr. Richard Wilson. Phillis Wheatley

- N -

NAKASA, NAT
Three Poems For Nat Nakasa. Kattie M. Cumbo

NAMES
African American. Gertrude Blackwell Bailey
Calling of Names, The. Maya Angelou
Debra: An Africanese Name Reading on the Sound of Debra. Ronda Davis
Remember. Jennifer Blackman Lawson
Think About It. Gertrude Blackwell Bailey

NARCOTIC HABIT
Answer to Yo/Question of am I Not Yo/Woman Even if U Went on Shit Again. Sonia Sanchez
Because We Failed for a Child Who Died From an Overdose of Heroin. Angela Jackson
City Songs. Sonia Sanchez
Don't Wanna Be. Sonia Sanchez
He Ain't My Idol. E. Sharon Gomillion
I Refuse to Be. Gertrude Blackwell Bailey
Junkie Lost/Junkie Lost. Lyn
Letter to an Aspiring Junkie. Maya Angelou
Missing in Action. S. Diane Bogus
No Way Out. June Vanleer Williams
Pusher, The. Maya Angelou
Somebody's Calling Your Name. Jennifer Blackman Lawson
Stand! E. Sharon Gomillion
Summer Words of a Sistuh Addict. Sonia Sanchez
Why I Don't Get High on Shit. Sonia Sanchez

NASTURTIUMS
Lines to a Nasturtium. Anne Spencer

NEGROES
Black Jam for Dr. Negro. Mari Evans
Bottled: New York. Helene Johnson
Knee-Grow, A. Mae Jackson
Okay Negroes. June Jordan
What is a Negro? Nancy L. Arnez

NEIGHBORS
Neighbors 1. Pearl Cleage Lomax
Poem for Neighbors. Pearl Cleage Lomax

NEPTUNE
Ode to Neptune. Phillis Wheatley

NEW ENGLAND
Of New England Rock, 1976. Jodi Braxton

NEW ORLEANS, LOUISIANA
Zulu King: New Orleans (At Mardi Gras). Josephine Copeland

NEW YEAR
New Year's Prayer. Ruby Berkley Goodwin

NEW YORK
Bottled: New York. Helene Johnson
Bricks. Jayne Cortez
I am New York City. Jayne Cortez
In Reference to: International Women's Year. Leatrice Emeruwa
Just a New York Poem. Nikki Giovanni
NYC Love Poem. Carole

Gregory Clemmons
Negro in New York, A. Naomi Long Madgett
New York City 1970. Audre Lorde
Poem For the Empire State. June Jordan
Review From Staten Island. Gloria Oden

NEWARK, NEW JERSEY
Newark For Now (68). Carolyn M. Rodgers
Song For Newark, A. Nikki Giovanni

NEWS
Memoranda Toward the Spring of Seventy-Nine. June Jordan

NEWSPAPER ADVERTISING
Personal. Leatrice Emeruwa

NEWSPAPERS
News. Elma Stuckey

NIAGRA FALLS
Niagra Falls. June Jordan

NICKELS
To a Nickel. Lucy Mae Turner

NIGERIA
To a Nigerian Student of Metallurgy. Margaret Danner

NIGGERS
Nigger. Sonia Sanchez
Raise a "Rucus" To-Night. Anonymous

NIGHT
All Day We've Longed for Night. Sarah Webster Fabio
Call the Night. Jayne Cortez
City Nights. Naomi Long Madgett
I Closed My Shutters Late Last Night. Georgia Douglas Johnson
Mountains at Night. Lucy Mae Turner
Negro Speaks of Night. Iola M. Brister
Night. Bessie Woodson Yancey
Night. Josephine D. (Henderson) Heard
Night, The. Kattie M. Cumbo
Night. Nikki Giovanni
Night. Birdelle Wycoff Ransom
Night of Death, The. Frances E. W. Harper
Night Seems to Cry, The. Vanessa Howard
No Stars Tonight. Naomi Long Madgett
Nocturne. Gwendolyn Bennett
Nocturne. Naomi Long Madgett
Nocturne. Pinkie Gordon Lane
Quilt, The. Effie Lee Newsome
Ramadan--Hot Night. Marion Nicholes
There Was One Night. Naomi Long Madgett

NIGHTINGALES
Aria. Carole Gregory Clemmons
Song to a Phantom Nightingale. Naomi Long Madgett

NIXON, RICHARD MILHOUS
I Wonder How Many Matches It Would Take. Patricia Parker
Ode to Nixon. Olean Bess
To My Sister, Ethel Ennis, Who Sang, "The Star Spangled Banner" at the Second Inauguration of Richard Milhous Nixon, January 20, 1973. June Jordan

NO
Do Not Be Afraid of No. Gwendolyn Brooks

NONVIOLENCE
Final Indignity, The. Lyn
Nonviolence. Lyn

NOON
High Noon. Naomi Long Madgett

NORTH
Northboun'. Ariel Williams Holloway

NORTH CAROLINA
To a Lady on Her Remarkable Preservation in a Hurricane in North Carolina. Phillis Wheatley

NORTH DAKOTA
From America: a Poem in Process. June Jordan
Right-to-Lifer in Grand Forks, North Dakota, A. June Jordan

NOSTALGIA
Nostalgia. Mae V. Cowdery

NOVEMBER
Novembah Dusk. Lucile D. Goodlett
November. Naomi Long Madgett
November/December (Echoing Voices of Remembrances). Kattie M. Cumbo

NUDITY
If I Stand in my Window. Lucille Clifton
Southern Belle. Elma Stuckey

NUMBERS
Don't Wanna Be. Sonia Sanchez
Such a Peculiar World. June Vanleer Williams

NUNS
Nun. Toi Derricotte
Two Nuns by the Sea. S. Diane Bogus

NURSING HOMES
Nursing Home, USA. June Vanleer Williams

- O -

OBESITY
Maggie. Theresa Ford

OCEAN
At Sea. Vera Guerard
Dipped Deeply Into the Full Ocean. Margaret Danner

OCTOBER
Late October. Maya Angelou
October Journey. Margaret Walker
Snow in October. Alice Dunbar-Nelson

OCTOROON BALL
Ballade Des Belles Milatraisses. Rosalie Jonas

OEDIPUS
Antigone and Oedipus. Henrietta Cordelia Ray

OLD AGE
Poem (For Anna Hedgeman and Alfreda Duster). Nikki Giovanni

OMEGA PSI PHI FRATERNITY
Greek Crazeology. Carolyn M. Rodgers

OPOSSUM
Opossum. Pinkie Gordon Lane
'Possum-Huntin'. Bessie

Woodson Yancey

OPPORTUNITY
Rapping With Opportunity. Wanda Coleman

OPPRESSION
Oppression. Nikki Giovanni

OPTIMISM
Optimist, The. Mrs. J. W. Hammond
Optimist, The. Anonymous

ORANGE
Orange. Linda B. Graham

ORGAN
New Organ The. Josephine D. (Henderson) Heard
Strain of Music. Mae V. Cowdery

OWENS, JESSE
Jesse Owens. Eloise Culver

OXFORD, MISSISSIPPI
Oxford is a Legend. Margaret Walker

OYSTERS
Oyster Man's Cry. Anonymous

- P -

PADDY ROLLERS
Song About the Paddy Rollers. Anonymous

PAIN
Supremacy. Lenora Gillison

PAINTING
Quatrains. Gwendolyn Bennett

PALM WINE JUG
Lady Executive Looks at a Mangbetu Palm Wine Jug. Margaret Danner

PANDAS
Yolande the Panda. Nikki Giovanni

PAPERWEIGHT
Paperweight. Audre Lorde

PARABLES
Great Laws. Marion Cuthbert

PARADES
Watching a Parade in Harlem 1970. Jayne Cortez

PARASITOSIS
Parasitosis. Ronda Davis

PARENTS
Andre. Gwendolyn Brooks
Big Mama. Jennifer Blackman Lawson
Black Mother Woman. Audre Lorde
Bronzeville Mother Loiters in Mississippi, Meanwhile a Mississippi Mother Burns Bacon. Gwendolyn Brooks
Carve/n. Angela Jackson
Dad. Bessie Woodson Yancey
Daddy 12/02-5/69. Lucille Clifton
Dear Daddy. Ava Saunders
Epileptic. Pinkie Gordon Lane
Epitaph For My Father. Margaret Walker
Eyes in the Back of Her Head. Harryette Mullen
Father (Part I) Harryette Mullen
Father Son and Holy Ghost. Audre Lorde
Few Years After Father Died,

A. Gloria Oden
First Flakes That Fell on Mother's Grave, The. Josephine D. (Henderson) Heard
Floorwax Mother. Harryette Mullen
For Mama. Jill Witherspoon Boyer
For Momma. Melba Joyce Boyd
For My Mother. June Jordan
For Our Fathers. Carolyn M. Rodgers
For Sapphires. Carolyn M. Rodgers
Forgiving My Father. Lucille Clifton
From the House of Yemanja. Audre Lorde
Glimpses. Nola Richardson
Gus. Nikki Giovanni
Hands: For Mother's Day. Nikki Giovanni
Homage to Black Madonnas. Margaret T. G. Burroughs
However Brief Their Acquaintance With My Father. Gloria Oden
If He Let Us Go Now. Sherley Williams
In Honor of David Anderson Brooks, My Father. Gwendolyn Brooks
In Memoriam of Mother. Josephine D. (Henderson) Heard
Inquisition, The. Bobbretta Elliston
It is Deep. Carolyn M. Rodgers
It is When We Love. Gloria Oden
Jessie Mitchell's Mother. Gwendolyn Brooks
Kwa Mama Zetu Waliutuzaa. Sonia Sanchez
Lines for my Mother. Margaret T. G. Burroughs
Love From My Father. Carole Gregory Clemmons
Mama. Sandra Royster
"Mama, I Don't Know." Pam Brown
Mama Settles the Dropout Problem. Betty Gates
Maternity. Georgia Douglas Johnson
Memorial For my Father. Margaret T. G. Burroughs
Momma. Maami Verano
Momma Sayings. Harryette Mullen
Momma Welfare Roll. Maya Angelou
Mother, The. Georgia Douglas Johnson
Mother. Josephine D. (Henderson) Heard
Mother, The. Gwendolyn Brooks
Mother. Leatrice Emeruwa
Mother, The. Naomi Long Madgett
Mother and Dad. Gertrude Blackwell Bailey
Mother, I Am Mad. Lucille Clifton
Mother's Love, A. Josephine D. (Henderson) Heard
My Father. May Miller
My Mama Moved Among the Days. Lucille Clifton
My Mother's Blessing. Olean Bess
On the Spirit of Mildred Jordan. June Jordan
One Minus One Minus One. June Jordan
Parental Lament. June Vanleer Williams
Pathways: From Mother to Mother. Audre Lorde
Picture, The. Jeanette Adams
Poem for My Father, A. Sonia Sanchez
Poem to My Father. Pinkie Gordon Lane
Proud to Be. Gertrude Blackwell Bailey
Refugee Mother. Geraldine L. Wilson
Sequel No. 2. Pinkie Gordon Lane
Sequel No. 3. Pinkie Gordon Lane
Slave Mother, The. Frances E. W. Harper
Slave Mother's Crime, The. Josephine D. (Henderson) Heard
Something Lost. Nola Rich-

ardson
Sugarman. Margaret Porter
Sunflowers and Saturdays. Melba Joyce Boyd
They Don't Understand. Nola Richardson
To My Daughter the Junkie on a Train. Audre Lorde
To My Mother. Naomi Long Madgett
Tommy's Mommy. Nikki Giovanni
Try to Understand Papa. Colleen McElroy
Twice a Child. Naomi Long Madgett
Walking the Dog. Pinkie Gordon Lane
Woman/Child? Nola Richardson

PARENTS
See Also
Fathers
Mothers

PARIS, FRANCE
When I Went to Paris. Kali Grosvenor

PARKER, MACK C.
For Mack C. Parker. Pauli Murray

PARKS
City Park. Claudia E. Jemmontt
Grand Circus Park. Naomi Long Madgett

PARKS, ROSA
Harvest. Nikki Giovanni

PARSONAGES
Saturday Night at the Parsonage. Naomi Long Madgett

PASSIVE RESISTANCE
Passive Resistance. Margaret Danner

PAST
Look Up. Gertrude Blackwell Bailey
Old Days, The. Audre Lorde
Times and Things Have Changed. Josephine D. (Henderson) Heard

PASTELS
Pastels. Julia Fields

PATIENCE
Patience. Nikki Giovanni

PAUL OF TAURUS (BIBLE)
Lion in Daniel's Den. Nikki Giovanni

PAY DAY
Pay Day. Lucy Mae Turner

PEACE
Liberty and Peace. Phillis Wheatley
Peace. Georgia Douglas Johnson
Peace and Principle. Isabelle McClellan Taylor
Surrender. Angelina Weld Grimke

PEACHES
Peaches. Musu Ber

PEANUTS
Notes on the Peanut. June Jordan

PEDDLERS
105th and Euclid Street-Peddler's Song, A. Leatrice Emeruwa

PENNSYLVANIA DUTCH COUNTRY

Pennsylvania Dutch Country. Sonia Sanchez

PEOPLE
For My People. Margaret Walker

PEOPLE, BAG
New Yorkers, The. Nikki Giovanni

PERCEPTION
Perception. Catherine L. Findley

PERFECTION
Perfection. Alice Walker

PETER, THE APOSTLE (BIBLE)
In Time. Melva Tatum Smith

PHOTOGRAPHS
Album: Photo 2. Naomi Madgett
Family Portrait. Naomi Long Madgett

PHYSICIANS
Doctor Spider. Wanda Coleman

PIANO
Piano After War. Gwendolyn Brooks

PIGEONS
Ballad of the Light-Eyed Little Girl, The. Gwendolyn Brooks

PILGRIMS
We Black People Should. Kali Grosvenor

PIMPS
Don't Wanna Be. Sonia Sanchez
Poppa Chicken. Margaret Walker
Today's Pimp. Marion Nicholes

PINEAPPLES
Pineapple. Harryette Mullen

PISCES
Pisces Both. Barbara Mahone

PITY
Pity a Poor Boy. Anonymous
Pity Me. Clara Haywood

POETS AND POETRY
Advice. Ntozake Shange
After a First Book. Audre Lorde
As Other Women Give Birth. Gloria Oden
Beep Beep Poem, The. Nikki Giovanni
Between a Dancer & A Poet. Ntozake Shange
Birth of the Poet, The. Quandra Prettyman
Black Poetry Day, A. Alicia Loy Johnson
Breakthrough. Carolyn M. Rodgers
Dunbar. Anne Spencer
Food For Thought. Val Ferdinand
For a Poet I Know. Nikki Giovanni
For Some Poets. Mae Jackson
Habits. Nikki Giovanni
How Do You Write a Poem? Nikki Giovanni
I am Here to Announce. Ronda Davis
I Said to Poetry. Alice Walker
I/Scattered Poems. Angela Jackson
I Would Prefer to Dispatch Myself. Gloria Oden
Incident. Mae Jackson
Inquiry. Ntozake Shange
Kidnap Poem. Nikki Giovanni
Midnight Song. Pinkie Gor-

don Lane
No Time For Poetry. Julia Fields
Not About Poems. Carolyn M. Rodgers
On the Black Poet Reading His Poems in the Park. June Jordan
Poem, A. Elaine Bethel
Poem For a Poet. Audre Lorde
Poem Off Center, A. Nikki Giovanni
Poet, The. Alice Anderson
Poet, The. Lucille Clifton
Poet, The. Mae Jackson
Poetry. Georgia Douglas Johnson
Poetry. Lucia Pitts
Poetry. Nikki Giovanni
Poets. Lucia Pitts
Poet's Vision, The. Carolyn M. Rodgers
Quiet Poem, A. Pinkie Gordon Lane
Response to the Visiting Poets Names, A. Carole Gregory Clemmons
Sharon Will Be No/Where On Nobody's Best-Selling List. Sharon Scott
To a Poet I Knew. Johari Amini
To a Woman Poet That I Know. Pinkie Gordon Lane
To Gwen. Carolyn M. Rodgers
To P.J. (2 Yrs Old Who Sed Write a Poem for me in Portland, Oregon). Sonia Sanchez
To Poets Who Have Rebelled. Pauli Murray
To the Negro Intellectuals. Mae Jackson
Toy Poem. Nikki Giovanni
Unfunny Situation. Carolyn M. Rodgers
Word Game. Wanda Coleman
Wow...Yr Just Like a Man! Ntozake Shange

POISONS
Esther, As Lead. Carolyn M. Rodgers

POLICE
Boy Died in my Alley, The. Gwendolyn Brooks
Definition for Blk/Children. Sonia Sanchez
Letter to the Local Police. June Jordan
They Came Knocking on my Door at 7 A.M. Wanda Coleman

POLICE, MURDER
Give Me the Red on the Black of the Bullet. Jayne Cortez
Homicide 1973. Jaynce Cortez
Power. Audre Lorde

POLICE, VIOLENCE
Poem About Police Violence. June Jordan

POLITICS
Women in Politics. Myra Estelle Morris

POOL, ROSEY E.
Poets Beyond the Blues. Naomi Long Madgett

POPULATION
Muffin on the Population Explosion. Margaret Danner

POTATOES
Sweet Potato Man. Anonymous
'Tater Field. Lucile D. Goodlett

POULTRY
Sunday Chicken. Gwendolyn Brooks

POVERTY
Children of the Poor. Gwendolyn Brooks

Face of Poverty. Lucy Smith
Kitchenette Building. Gwendolyn Brooks
Lovers of the Poor, The. Gwendolyn Brooks
Poverty Blues. Beatrice M. Murphy

POWER
Now. Audre Lorde

PRAYERS
Brown Child's Prayer, A. Nancy L. Arnez
Detached, The. Maya Angelou
Formula. Carolyn Ogletree
From Seven Days Prayer. Naomi Long Madgett
Give Me Strength. Gertrude Blackwell Bailey
He Paid Me Seven. Anonymous
His Answer. Clara Ann Thompson
Little Boy's Prayer. Bernadine Blessitt
New Year's Prayer. Ruby Berkley Goodwin
Oh! Lord. Antoinette T. Payne
Pray for the Lovers. Jayne Cortez
Prayer. Isabella Maria Brown
Prayer of the Race That God Made Black. Anonymous
Service Please. Myrtle Campbell Gorham
Where are the Prayers. Josephine D. (Henderson) Heard

PREGNANCY
And What About the Children. Audre Lorde
Fruit of Love. Marion Nicholes
Now That I Am Forever With Child. Audre Lorde
Oh, I'm 10 Months Pregnant. Ntozake Shange
To the Unborn and Waiting Children. Lucille Clifton
Woman and Man. Pauli Murray

PREJUDICES AND ANTIPATHIES
Civil Service. Constance Nichols
Make Up Your Mind. Beth Jackson
On That One Day. Naomi F. Faust

PRESIDENT
President, The. Gertrude Blackwell Bailey

PRETENDING
Pretending. Brenda Connor-Bey

PRICE, LEONTYNE
Black Eurydice. Carole Gregory Clemmons

PRIDE
Black Pride. Margaret Burroughs
Myself. Juanita Brown
Only in This Way. Margaret Burroughs

PRINCIPLE
Peace and Principle. Isabelle McClellan Taylor

PRISON
Girl Held Without Bail. Margaret Walker
Kathy (1) Wanda Coleman
Questions. Sonia Sanchez

PROFANITY
Last M. F., The. Carolyn M. Rodgers

PROPHETS
Prophets, The. Melva Tatum Smith
Prophets for a New Day. Margaret Walker

PROSTITUTION
For a Lady of Pleasure Now Retired. Nikki Giovanni
Parable. Thulani Davis
Whore. S. Diane Bogus

PSYCHIATRISTS
Sessions. Wanda Coleman

PUPPETS
Puppet Player, The. Angelina Weld Grimke

PUBLIC SPEAKING
Before I Started School. Gloria Oden

PUMPKINS
Fros' is on de Punkin, De. Bessie Woodson Yancey

PURPLE
Purple. Linda B. Graham

- Q -

QUARREL
Long John Nelson and Sweetie Pie. Margaret Walker
Words! Words! Jessie Redmond Fauset

QUEST
Quest. Georgia Douglas Johnson

QUESTIONS
Little Poem, A. Linda Brown

QUILTS
Easter Colors. Harryette Mullen

- R -

RABBITS
Mistah Rabbit. Anonymous

RACCOONS
Coon Song. Lucile D. Goodlett

RACISM
Ain't the Only Place. Alice Lovelace
Alarm Clock, The. Mari Evans
Black on the Back of Black. Margaret Danner
Children of Their Sin (An Exorcise), The. Carolyn M. Rodgers
Don't Tell me You Don't Understand. Vanessa Howard
Everybody But Me. Margaret T. G. Burroughs
For a Child. Naomi Long Madgett
Group. Patricia Parker
In the End Let All White Racists Thank the Holy Jackass. Julia Fields
It Wasn't Just the Rain. Pam Brown
Make Up Your Mind. Gertrude Blackwell Bailey
They Say, "There's a Race Problem!" June Vanleer Williams
Violet. Naomi Long Madgett
We Are Not Alone. Beatrice M. Murphy
White-Collar Job. Myra Estelle Morris

RAILROAD
Between Trains it Rains. Linda Brown Bragg
Cannonball. Elma Stuckey
On the Train. Wanda Coleman
Two-Gun Buster and Trigger Slim. Margaret Walker

RAIN
After the Rain. Vanessa Howard
April in Your Eyes. Naomi

Long Madgett
Backwater Blues. Anonymous
Between Trains it Rains. Linda Brown Bragg
Coping. Audre Lorde
Everytime It Rains. Nikki Giovanni
I Done Got so Thirsty That My Mouth Waters at the Thought of Rain. Patricia Jones
My Rainy Day. Maurine L. Jeffrey
Rain. Elma Stuckey
Rain. Nikki Giovanni
Rain Wish. Louise Blackman
So Much Rain. Sonia Sanchez
Sonnet. Naomi Long Madgett
There's a Raindrop. Lisa McCann
Windy Rain. Kali Grosvenor
You Made it Rain. Fareedah Allah

RAINBOWS
Rainbows. Nikki Giovanni

RANDALL, DUDLEY
Malcolm X (For Dudley Randall). Gwendolyn Brooks

RAPE
Case in Point. June Jordan
Miss Persephone. Harryette Mullen
Poem About My Rights. June Jordan
Rape. Jayne Cortez

READING
Learning to Read. Frances E. W. Harper
Reading Won't Make It. June Vanleer Williams

REALITY
Reality. Yvette Johnson

REBELLION
Sassy. Lucy Mae Turner

RECEPTIONS
Reception, The. June Jordan

RECOLLECTION
On Recollection. Phillis Wheatley

REDDING, OTIS
To Otis Redding. Kali Grosvenor

REECE, CLAUDE JR.
Give me the Red on the Back of the Bullet. Jayne Cortez

REFRIGERATORS
Inflation. Margaret Porter

REGRET
Eyes of Regret, The. Angelina Weld Grimke

REINCARNATION
Reincarnation. Mae Jackson

RELATIVES
Family Resemblance, A. Audre Lorde
Generations. Judy Dothard Simmons
Me & Steevie. Harryette Mullen
My People. Kali Grosvenor
Old Relative. Gwendolyn Brooks
On My First Trip to Mississippi. Linda Brown Bragg
Uncles. Alice Walker

RELIGIOUS POETRY
All the World Moved. June Jordan
Amen Sister. Colleen McElroy
At Sea. Vera Guerard
Birth of Jesus, The.

Josephine D. (Henderson) Heard
Black Genesis. Mae Jackson
Calvary Way. May Miller
Children of the Poor. Gwendolyn Brooks
Chorus. Josephine D. (Henderson) Heard
Christmas Eve in France. Jessie Redmond Fauset
Colorist, The. Anita Scott Coleman
Creation, The. Claire Turner
Creation of God, The. Anonymous
Creed. Anne Spencer
Dives and Laz'us. Anonymous
Do, Lawd. Anonymous
Dream Like Daniel's, A. S. Diane Bogus
Gimme Dat Ol'-Time Religion. Anonymous
Go Tell it on The Mountain. Anonymous
Go Work in my Vineyard. Frances E. W. Harper
God. Anonymous
God Bless Our Native Land. Frances E. W. Harper
God is Kind. Mae V. Cowdery
God is Near Thee. Josephine D. (Henderson) Heard
God's Christmas Tree. Eve Lynn
God's Gonna Set Dis World on Fire. Anonymous
God's Gwine to Take All My Trubbles Away. Lucy Mae Turner
God's Mood. Lucille Clifton
Goliath of Gath. Phillis Wheatley
Gospel Train, The. Anonymous
Great Laws, The. Marion Cuthbert
Greater Friendship Baptist Church, The. Carole Gregory Clemmons
He "Had Not Where to Lay His Head." Frances E. W. Harper
He Hath Need of Rest. Josephine D. (Henderson) Heard
Hope Thou in God. Josephine D. (Henderson) Heard
How I Got Ovah II/It is Deep II. Carolyn M. Rodgers
I Am a Spiritual Alcoholic. Anonymous
I and He. Marion Cuthbert
I Vision God. Anonymous
Immortality. Marion Cuthbert
Impelled. Gerogia Douglas Johnson
In Emanuel's Nightmare: Another Coming of Christ. Gwendolyn Brooks
Isaiah LXIII 1-8. Phillis Wheatley
J, My Good Friend (Another Foolish Innocent) Alice Walker
Jesus, Saviour, Pilot, Save. Josephine D. (Henderson) Heard
Katherine Ferguson. Eloise Culver
Life of God, The. Marion Cuthbert
Living Water. Carolyn M. Rodgers
Lord I Would Love Thee. Josephine D. (Henderson) Heard
Lord, In My Heart. Maya Angelou
Loving Beauty Is Loving God. Isabelle Taylor
Magi Call Him King, The. Effie Lee Newsome
Mate. Georgia Douglas Johnson
Maxie Allen. Gwendolyn Brooks
My Life. Henrietta C. Parks
My Path is Lighted By a Star. Lucy Mae Turner
New Like Nagasaki Nice Like Nicene. June Jordan
Newest Star, The. Eloise Culver
Oh! Lord. Antionette T. Payne
Omega. Georgia Douglas Johnson
On Being Brought From Africa to America. Phillis Wheatley
On Philosophy. Barbara Marshall
Paradox. Angelina Weld Grimke

Penitent Considers Another Coming of Mary, A. Gwendolyn Brooks
Pliant of the Madonna, The. Lucy Mae Turner
Poem. Katherine L. Cuestas
Preacher Ruminates Behind the Sermon. Gwendolyn Brooks
Pure in Heart Shall See God. Frances E. W. Harper
Refiner's Gold, The. Frances E. W. Harper
Religion. Elma Stuckey
Return, The. Jessie Redmond Fauset
Rise Up, Shepherd and Follow. Anonymous
Service, Please. Myrtle Campbell Gorham
Steal Away. Anonymous
Testimony. Carolyn M. Rodgers
Thank God For Little Children. Frances E. W. Harper
Thank You Lord. Maya Angelou
Then and Now. Frances E. W. Harper
Thoughts on the Works of Providence. Phillis Wheatley
Time Ain't Long as It Has Been. Carolyn M. Rodgers
To the Rev. Dr. Thomas Amory, on Reading His Sermons on Daily Devotion, in Which That Duty is Recommended and Assisted. Phillis Wheatley
To the Univ. of Cambridge in New England (1767) Phillis Wheatley
Trivia. Beatrice M. Murphy
Unuttered Prayer. Josephine D.(Henderson) Heard
Vashti. Frances E. W. Harper
Walk, God's Chillun. Lucile D. Goodlett
Wasn't That a Mighty Day. Anonymous
We Can Know Surely. Marion Cuthbert
What You Gonna Name That Pretty Little Baby? Anonymous
Wounds of Jesus, The. Anonmous

RENT STRIKE
For Beautiful Mary Brown: Chicago Rent Strike Leader. June Jordan

REPENTANCE
Unrepentant. Countess W. Twitty

RESTAURANTS
I Love Those Little Booths at Benvenuti's. Gwendolyn Brooks

RETIREMENT
Forced Retirement. Nikki Giovanni

REVIVALS, TENT
Tent Revival. Harryette Mullen

REVOLUTION, BLACK
And When the Revolution Came. Carolyn M. Rodgers
Bedtime Story. Nayo
Bedtime Story. Barbara Malcolm
Black Judgment. Nikki Giovanni
Chant For Young/Brothas & Sistuhs, A. Sonia Sanchez
Define Revolution. Lyn
Evolution. Thelma Parker Cox
For Unborn Malcolm. Sonia Sanchez
Greek Crazeologt. Carolyn M. Rodgers
It's a New Day. Sonia Sanchez
Jesus was Crucified, or it Must Be Deep. Carolyn M. Rodgers
No Reservations. Nikki Giovanni
Our Blackness Did Not Come to Us Whole. Linda Brown Bragg
Pledge of Alligence. Mae

Jackson
Poem About Beauty, Blackness, Poetry (And how to be all Three). Linda Brown Bragg
Revolution. Angela Jackson
Revolution is Resting, The. Carolyn M. Rodgers
Revolutionary Dreams. Nikki Giovanni
Revolutionary Requiem in Five Parts. Johari Amini
So This is Our Revolution. Sonia Sanchez
There are Seeds to Sow. Bernette Golden
Thought. Leatrice Emeruwa
To a Reactionary. Mae Jackson
To the White Man. Valerie Tarver
True Import of Present Dialogue: Black vs. Negro, The. Nikki Giovanni
U Name This One. Carolyn M. Rodgers

RHETORIC
Blk/Rhetoric (For Killebrew Keeby, Icewater, Baker, Gary Adams and Omar Shabazz. Sonia Sanchez

RHYTHM
Remembered Rhythms. Mari Evans

RIDLEY, LARRY
Poem for Larry Ridley. Judy Simmons

RINGS
I Had Five More Rings. Ntozake Shange
Weeks After Mother Died. Gloria Oden

RIOTS
Harlem Riot, 1943. Pauli Murray
Litany For Peppe, A. Nikki Giovanni
Mr. Roosevelt Regrets. Pauli Murray
Riot. Gwendolyn Brooks
Riot: Gus. Maya Angelou

RIVERS
Deep River. Anonymous
Iowa. Naomi Long Madgett
Rivah's a Black Mare. Lucile D. Goodlett

ROACHES
At Last We Killed the Roaches. Lucille Clifton
Brown Menace or Poem to the Survival of Roaches, The. Audre Lorde
Last Warehouse, The. May Miller

ROADS
Road, The. Helene Johnson

ROBBERS AND OUTLAWS
Stealin' Grub. Lucy Mae Turner

ROBESON, PAUL
Commitment. Jayne Cortez
Paul Robeson. Eloise Culver
Paul Robeson. Gwendolyn Brooks

ROBINS
Little Red Breast. Lula Lowe Weeden
Robin's Poem, A. Nikki Giovanni

ROBINSON, JACKIE
Jackie Robinson. Lucille Clifton
Song to Jackie Robinson. Eloise Culver

RODGERS, CAROLYN M.
Foreword. Angela Jackson

ROGERS, JOEL A.
Joel A. Rogers. Eloise Culver

ROOMING HOUSES
Rooming Houses are Old Women. Audre Lorde

ROOSEVELT, ELEANOR
First Lady. Edna L. Harrison

ROOSEVELT, FRANKLIN DELANO
Passing of F.D.R. Pauli Murray

ROOSTERS
Little Rooster. Anonymous
Uncle Ike's Roosters. Anonymous

ROPE
Jumping. Linda Brown Bragg

ROSES
African Beauty Rose. Kattie M. Cumbo
Crimson Rose, A. Thelma T. Clement
Letter to the Local Police. June Jordan
Like Unto a Rose. Lois Royal Hughes
Plea, A. Mary Bohanon
To a Rosebud. Eva Jessye
Wild Roses. Effie Lee Newsome
Woman and the Roses, The. Harryette Mullen

ROYALTY
Black Prince, The. Alice Walker
Bronze Queen. Gertrude Parthenia McBrown
Me Alone. Lula Lowe Weeden

RUDOLPH, WILMA
Wilma Rudolph. Eloise Culver

- S -

SABBATH
Sabbath Bells. Josephine D. (Henderson) Heard

SACRIFICE
Sacrifice. Audre Lorde
Sacrifice. Pamela Cobb

SADNESS
My Sadness Sits Around Me. June Jordan

ST. LOUIS, MISSOURI
Nappy Edges. Ntozake Shange
Visit to a City Out of Time. Audre Lorde

SALESMAN
I'm a Salesman. Melva Tatum Smith

SALT
Salt and Sand. Naomi Long Madgett

SANCHEZ, SONIA
Letter. Pinkie Gordon Lane

SAND
Salt and Sand. Naomi Long Madgett

SANTA CLAUS
Disillusionment. Bessie Woodson Yancey

SASSAFRAS TEA
Sassafras Tea

SATAN
Egg in Each Basket, An. Elma Stuckey

SATURDAY
Saturday Afternoon, When Chores Are Done. Harryette Mullen
Saturdays. Jayne Cortez
Sunflowers and Saturdays. Melba Joyce Boyd

SAVING
Portrait. Carolyn M. Rodgers

SCHOOLS
Bordentown School. Naomi Long Madgett
Little Child Shall Lead Us... If We Dare to Follow. Nia nSabe
Psalm of Deliverance. Pauli Murray
School Note. Audre Lorde
To the Dunbar High School: A Sonnet. Angelina Weld Grimke
2:48 P.M. Ava Sanders
Where Do School Days End? Josephine D. (Henderson) Heard

SCHOOLS, VISITATION
If the Shoe Fits, Wear It. Gertrude Blackwell Bailey

SCHWERNER, MICHAEL
For Andy Goodman - Michael Schwerner - And James Chaney. Margaret Walker

SCRAPBOOKS
Scrapbooks. Nikki Giovanni

SCRUBWOMAN
Oh you Tender, Lovely Scrubwoman. Pinkie Gordon Lane

SEA, THE
Metamorphism. Helene Johnson
Sea Sounds. Carolyn Coleman

SEA GULLS
Gulls. Pinkie Gordon Lane

SEALE, BOBBY
To Bobby Seale. Lucille Clifton

SEAMSTRESS
Aunt Dolly. Carolyn M. Rodgers

SEASHORE
Beaches: Why I Don't Care For Them. Wanda Coleman
Keller is the Swingingest. Margaret Danner
Night We Slept on the Beach, The. Harryette Mullen

SEASONS
Advent. Naomi Long Madgett
Autumn Night. Naomi Long Madgett
Bend to Spring. June Vanleer Williams
Departure of Summer. Naomi Long Madgett
Detroit Summers. Jill Witherspoon Boyer
Equinox. Audre Lorde
Fall-Time. Bessie Woodson Yancey
In Spring Time. Naomi Long Madgett
Returning Spring. Pauli Murray
Seasons Have to Pass. Naomi Long Madgett
Second Spring. Audre Lorde
Signs of Spring. Bessie Woodson Yancey
Solace. Clarissa Scott Delany
Spring in Saint Louis. Naomi Long Madgett
Spring People. Audre Lorde
To Autumn. Naomi Long Madgett

SEASONS
See Also Spring
Autumn Summer
Fall Winter

SECURITY
Seduction. Nikki Giovanni

SELF RESPECT
People Will Be People. Gertrude Blackwell Bailey

SENATORS
Senate Man. Colleen McElroy

SEPTEMBER
Lament. Naomi Long Madgett
September Lament. Naomi Long Madgett

SERMONS
Second Sermon on the Warpland, The. Gwendolyn Brooks
Sermon on the Warpland, The. Gwendolyn Brooks
To the Rev. Dr. Thomas Amory, on Reading His Sermon on Daily Devotion, In Which That Duty is Recommended and Assisted. Phillis Wheatley

SERVICE
Service. Bessie Woodson Yancey

SERVANTS
When in Rome. Mari Evans

SEWING
I Sit and Sew. Alice Dunbar-Nelson

SEX
After. Nola Richardson
Calculated Passion. S. Diane Bogus
Fakery. June Vanleer Williams
Love Poem. Audre Lorde
Making Love. Melva Tatum Smith
Man Behind the Woman, The. Wanda Coleman
Once. Carolyn M. Rodgers
Scream. Jayne Cortez
Sexual Privacy of Women on Welfare. Pinkie Gordon Lane
She-Feelings Poem # 1. S. Diane Bogus
Sound of Music, The. Carolyn M. Rodgers
Short Poem. Sonia Sanchez
Stirrings. Harryette Mullen
To Chuck. Sonia Sanchez
Way I Feel. The. Nikki Giovanni

SEXTON, ANNE
From a Group of Poems Thinking About Anne Sexton On the Anniversary of Her Death. Toi Derricotte

SHADOWS
Shadows. Helen F. Clarke

SHAKESPEARE, WILLIAM
Shakespeare. Henrietta Cordelia Ray

SHAME
Incident. Dorothy C. Parrish

SHANGE, NTOZAKE
Letter to My Friend the Poet Ntozake Shange. June Jordan

SHAW, ROBERT
Robert G. Shaw. Henrietta Cordelia Ray

SHELLS
Palace. Dorothy Vena Johnson

SHEPHERDS
Rise Up, Shepherd and Follow. Anonymous

SHIPS
On the Sinking of a Great Liner. May Miller
We Launched a Ship. Ruby Berkley Goodwin

SHOES
Times-Square-Shoeshine Composition. Maya Angelou

SHORTER, BISHOP JAMES A.
Bishop James A. Shorter. Josephine D. (Henderson) Heard
Message to a Loved One Dead. Josephine D. (Henderson) Heard

SHOUTING
Gonna Shout. Anonymous
Shout. Carolyn M. Rodgers
Shout Along, Chillen. Anonymous
Timing. Elma Stuckey

SIBLING RIVALRY
Not Wanted. Rosa Paul Brooks

SICKNESS
Preacher Kyo Siam, De. Lucile D. Goodlett

SIDE WALKS
Sidewalk. Wanda Coleman

SILENCE
About Our Silence. S. Diane Bogus
Silence. Naomi Long Madgett
Something to be Said for Silence. Nikki Giovanni

SIMONE, NINA
For Nina Simone. Kali Grosvenor
For Nina Simone Wherever You Are. Linda Curry
Nina. Mae Jackson
Nina Simone. Carole Gregory Clemmons
Poem for Nina Simone to Put Some Music to and Blow Our Nigguh/Minds. Sonia Sanchez

SIN
Confession of a Sinner. Naomi Long Madgett

SINGERS
(An Aside). Carolyn M. Rodgers

SINGING
For My Brother. June Jordan
Keep on Singing. Naomi Long Madgett
Old Men Used to Sing, The. Alice Walker
Singer, The. Colleen McElroy
Singer Will Not Sing, The. Maya Angelou
To Singers of Song, The. Pinkie Gordon Lane

SISTERS
Family Resemblance, A. Audre Lorde
For Love of Our Brothers. Barbara Mahone
For My Sister Molly Who in the Fifties. Alice Walker
For Sapphire, My Sister. Alice H. Jones
It is My Sister's Ring. Gloria Oden
Letter to My Sister. Anne Spencer
Me & Steenie. Harryette Mullen

My Sister is a Sister. Kali Grosvenor
Sisters. Lucille Clifton
Year or So Before She Died, A. Gloria Oden

SIT-INS
Sit-Ins. Margaret Walker

SKIN
Poem (For Nina). Nikki Giovanni
Shedding Skin. Harryette Mullen

SKY DIVING
Sky Diving. Nikki Giovanni

SLAVE AUCTIONS
No More Auction Block. Anonymous
Selling Melvina. Elma Stuckey
Slave Auction, The. Frances E. W. Harper

SLAVE MASTERS
Good Masters. Elma Stuckey
Mandy. Elma Stuckey
Mystery. Elma Stuckey

SLAVE REVOLTS
Rebel. Elma Stuckey
Supper Time. Elma Stuckey

SLAVE TRADE
Mother and Child. Elma Stuckey

SLAVERY
Ancestor on the Auction Block. Vera Bell
Big Gate, The. Elma Stuckey
'Bout Cullud Folkses. Lucy Mae Turner
Bury Me in a Free Land. Frances E. W. Harper
Dying Bondman, The. Frances E. W. Harper
Dying Slave's Request. Josephine D. (Henderson) Heard
Eliza Harris. Frances E. W. Harper
Enslaved. Elma Stuckey
Etc. Etc. Etc. Dorothy C. Parrish
Evolution. Thelma Parker Cox
For Michael on His Third Birthday. Patricia Parker
Inception of the Negro, The. Jo Nell Rice
Indictment. Dorothy C. Parrish
Kinship Ties. Jennifer Blackman Lawson
Lettie. Elma Stuckey
Lines to Blood Brothers and Sisters. Margaret T. G. Burroughs
My Guilt. Maya Angelou
No More Auction Block. Anonymous
Note From a Field Nigger. Mae Jackson
On Being Brought From Africa to America. Phillis Wheatley
Posted. Elma Stuckey
Slave and the Iron Lace. Margaret Danner
Slave Auction, The. Frances E. W. Harper
Slave Mother, The. Frances E. W. Harper
Slave Mother's Crime, The. Josephine D. (Henderson) Heard
Slavery Chain. Anonymous
Sorry 'Bout That. Linda Cousins
Telling it All. Elma Stuckey
Untitled (No. 1). Mae Jackson
Victims of Slavery. Vanessa Howard
What Deeper Sin? Nancy L. Arnez

SLAVERY, COOKS
Sally. Elma Stuckey

SLAVERY, DEATHS
Tending in the Great House. Elma Stuckey

SLAVERY, RUNAWAYS
Family or Freedom. Elma Stuckey
Run, Nigger, Run. Anonymous
Runaway. Elma Stuckey
Song to the Runaway Slave. Anonymous

SLAVERY, WHIPPINGS
Rebuked. Elma Stuckey
Scars and Stripes. Elma Stuckey
Upstart. Elma Stuckey

SLAVES—HOUSE
House Niggers. Elma Stuckey

SLEEP
Hushed By the Hands of Sleep. Angelina Weld Grimke
Instant Before Sleep. May Miller
Of Sleep. Naomi Long Madgett
Sleep. Lucy Mae Turner
When I Nap. Nikki Giovanni

SMILES
Because I Can. Naomi Long Madgett
How Can I Forget. Alice Robinson
Transpositions. Georgia Douglas Johnson

SMITH, BESSIE
Lyric for Bessie Smith. Patricia Jones

SMOKING
American Cancer Society or There is More Than One Way to Skin a Coon. Audre Lorde

SNOW
Blizzard. Lyn
Catch a Snowflake. Linda Brown Bragg
Real Sport. Bessie Woodson Yancey
Snow. Dorothy Lee Louise Shaed
Snow in October. Alice Dunbar-Nelson
Snowflakes. Nikki Giovanni
Winter Poem. Nikki Giovanni
Winter Sonnet. Linda Brown Bragg

SOAP
Soft Soap. Lucile D. Goodlett

SOLDIERS
Black Recruit. Georgia Douglas Johnson
Black Soldier. Mary Wilkerson Cleaves
Gen'el Jackson. Anonymous
He's Coming Home at Last. Emily Jane Greene
Homing Braves. Georgia Douglas Johnson
On Major General Lee (1776). Phillis Wheatley
On the Capture of General Lee. Phillis Wheatley
Robert G. Shaw. Henrietta Cordelia Ray
Sergeant Jerk. Deborah Fuller Wess
Soldier. Georgia Douglas Johnson
Sonnet-Ballad, The. Gwendolyn Brooks
To Captain H--D, Of the 65th Regiment. Phillis Wheatley
Unknown Soldier. Mae V. Cowdery

SOLDIERS—DEATH
Taps. Georgia Douglas Johnson

SOLIDARITY DAY, 1968

SONGS
Ballad from Childhood. Audre Lorde
Heritage. Mae V. Cowdery
I Can No Longer Sing. M. Evans
I've Learned to Sing. Georgia Douglas Johnson
Lullaby. Naomi Long Madgett
Secret. Gwendolyn B. Bennett
Songs For the People. Frances E. W. Harper
To the Singer. Helen C. Harris
Unfinished Song. Naomi Long Madgett
When Mahalia Sings. Quandra Prettyman
Your Songs. Gwendolyn B. Bennett

SONGS—GOSPEL
...And the Old Women Gathered. Mari Evans

SONGS—WORK
Go Down, Old Hannah. Anonymous
Good Morning, Captain. Anonymous
Pick a Bale of Cotton. Anonymous
South Carolina Chain Gang Song. Anonymous

SONS
As I Grow Up Again. Audre Lorde
God Gave Me a Son. Portia Bird Daniel
Say Hello to John. Sherley Williams
Son to His Father, A. Naomi Long Madgett

SORORITIES
Greek Crazeology. Carolyn M. Rodgers

SORROW
Guest, The. Beatrice M. Murphy
If There Be Sorrow. Mari Evans
Joy or Sorrow. Leanna F. Johnson
Sorrow is a Woman. Joanne Jimason
Transportation. Georgia Douglas Johnson

SOUL
(An Aside). Carolyn M. Rodgers
Soul. Barbara Simmons
Soul. Leatrice Emeruwa

SOUL FOOD
Soul Food Goes Elite. E. Sharon Gomillion

SOUNDS
Nocturnal Sounds. Kattie M. Cumbo
Sounds Like Pearls. Maya Angelou

SOUTH, THE
Sorrow Home. Margaret Walker
South, the Name of Home. Alice Walker
Southern Song. Margaret Walker
Sunny South. Lucy Mae Turner

SOUTH CAROLINA
South Carolina Chain Gang Song. Anonymous

SOUTHERN UNIVERSITY
On the Murder of Two Human Being Black Men, Denver C. Smith, and His Unidentified Brother, at Southern University, Baton Rouge, Louisiana, 1972. June Jordan
Southern University. Pinkie Gordon Lane

SOUVENIRS

Let's Keep in Touch. Naomi Long Madgett
Souvenir. Georgia Douglas Johnson
Souvenir. Naomi Long Madgett

SOWETO, SOUTH AFRICA
For the Brave Young Students in Soweto. Jayne Cortez
Soweto Song. Amina Baraka

SPACE EXPLORATION
Astronaut of Innerspace, The. Harryette Mullen

SPANISH AMERICAN WAR
"Do Not Cheer, Men Are Dying," Said Capt. Phillips in the Spanish American War. Frances E. W. Harper

SPARROWS
Sparrow is a Bird, A. Margaret Danner
Sparrow's Fall, The. Frances E. W. Harper

SPIRITUALS
Crucifixion. Anonymous
Go Down Moses. Anonymous
Go Tell it on the Mountain. Anonymous
God's Gonna Set Dis World on Fire. Anonymous
I Got a Home in Dat Rock. Anonymous
Joshua Fit De Battle of Jericho. Anonymous
Negro Spirituals. Eloise Culver
No More Auction Block. Anonymous
Oh, Mary, Don't You Weep. Anonymous
Rise Up, Shepherd and Follow. Anonymous
Roll, Jordan Roll. Anonymous
Sometimes I Feel Like a Motherless Child. Anonymous
Steal Away to Jesus. Anonymous
Virgin Had a Baby Boy, The. Anonymous
Wasn't That a Mighty Day. Anonymous
What You Gonna Name That Pretty Little Baby? Anonymous

SPRING
Advent. Naomi Long Madgett
Association. Naomi Long Madgett
Equinox. Audre Lorde
In Springtime. Naomi Long Madgett
Memory. Georgia Douglas Johnson
Next Spring. Naomi Long Madgett
Reluctant Spring. Naomi Long Madgett
Returning Spring. Pauli Murray
Second Spring. Audre Lorde
Signs. Beatrice M. Murphy
Signs Ob Spring. Bessie Woodson Yancey
Spring. Pinkie Gordon Lane
Spring in Carolina. Audrey Johnson
Spring in Saint Louis. Naomi Long Madgett
Spring is Here. Olivia M. Hunter
Spring Lament. Mae V. Cowdery
Spring People. Audre Lorde
Spring Poem in Winter. Mae V. Cowdery
Spring III. Audre Lorde
Spring Tide. Georgia Douglas Johnson
Springtime. Georgia Douglas Johnson
Towards Spring. Carolyn M. Rodgers

SQUIRRELS
Peep Squirrel. Anonymous
Squirrel in Man, The. Alvies M. Carter
To a Winter Squirrel. Gwendolyn Brooks

STAIRS
Stairway Left Standing. May Miller

STARS
Cricket and the Star, The. Effie Lee Newsome
Newest Star, The. Eloise Culver
Star Gazing. Jill Witherspoon Boyer
Stars, The. Nikki Giovanni
Waiting for the Next Star to Fall. Harryette Mullen

STATEN ISLAND
Review from Staten Island. Gloria Oden

STATUES
David. Carole Gregory Clemmons

STATUS SYMBOL
Status Symbol. Mari Evans

STONE
Night Stone. Audre Lorde

STORES
Key Food. Audre Lorde

STORMS
Storm, The. Naomi Long Madgett
That's a Summer Storm. Kattie M. Cumbo

STRAWBERRIES
Strawberry Patches. Nikki Giovanni

STREAMS
Mountain Stream. Bessie Woodson Yancey
Stream, The. Lula Lowe Weeden

STREET CORNERS
Cables to Rage or I've Been Talking on This Street Corner a Hell of a Long Time. Audre Lorde

STREET CRIES
Cala Vendor's Cry. Anonymous
Crab Man. Anonymous
Oyster Man's Cry. Anonymous
Sweet Potato Man. Anonymous
Watermelon Vendor's Cry. Anonymous

STREETS
Ballad For Sterling Street. Sonia Sanchez
Birthday Memorial to Seventh Street, A. Audre Lorde
Euclid Street. Damali
Fifth Street Exit, Richmond. Naomi Long Madgett
47th & Vincennes/Chicago. Carolyn M. Rodgers
Market Street. Naomi Long Madgett
On a Narrow Street. Naomi Long Madgett
Rain on 71st Street. Dorothy Randall
Sarah Street. Naomi Long Madgett
Street Called Petticoat Lane, The. Alice McGee Smart

STRIPPING
Strip Tease. Harryette Mullen

STRUGGLES
Struggle Stagger Us, The. Margaret Walker

STUDENTS
Black Students. Julia Fields
To the Univ. of Cambridge in New England (1767). Phillis Wheatley

SUBWAYS
El Becomes a Subway in my Lifetime, The. Barbara Mahone
Observations on a Subway Train. Vanessa Howard
Subways Race, De. Kali Grosvenor

SUCCESS
Success. Dorothy Vena Johnson

SUICIDE
Ballad of the Brown Girl. Alice Walker
Juvenile Suicide. Naomi Long Madgett
Setting/Slow Drag. Carolyn M. Rodgers
Suicide. Alice Walker
221-1424 San/Francisco/Suicide/Number. Sonia Sanchez

SUMMER
Departure of Summer. Naomi Long Madgett
Detroit Summers. Jill Witherspoon Boyer
End of Summer. Naomi Long Madgett
In Memory of the Hokey Pokey. Jennifer Blackman Lawson
Knoxville, Tennessee. Nikki Giovanni
Summer. Mae Jackson
Summer Day. Naomi Long Madgett
Summer: Falling in Love. May Miller
Summer Matures. Helen Johnson
Summer Oracle. Audre Lorde

SUMMER, INDIAN
Indian Summer. Wanda Coleman

SUMNER, CHARLES
Charles Sumner. Charlotte Forten Grimke

SUN, THE
Sun, The. Nikki Giovanni

SUNDAY
Each Sunday. Nikki Giovanni
Sunday. Patricia Parker
Sunday Afternoon. Naomi Long Madgett
Sunday Chicken. Gwendolyn Brooks
When You Have Forgotten Sunday: The Love Story. Gwendolyn Brooks

SUNDAY SCHOOL
Sunday School, Circa 1950. Alice Walker

SUNDOWN
Sundown Sigh. Melba Joyce Boyd

SUNFLOWERS
Sunflowers and Saturdays. Melba Joyce Boyd

SUNRISE
Sunrise Poems. Colleen McElroy

SUNSET
Sunset. Ethel Caution

SUPERSTITIONS
Devil Will Have You. Jodi Braxton

SUPREMACY
Supremacy. Leanna F. Johnson

SUPREMES
Memorial. Sonia Sanchez

SURVIVAL
Gospel Truth, The. Jackie

Earley
Litany For Survival, A. Audre Lorde
Still I Rise. Maya Angelou
Survival Poem. Pinkie Gordon Lane
Survivors, The. Naomi Long Madgett

SWEET POTATO PIES
An't M'lissy's Tater Pies. Bessie Woodson Yancey

SWIMMING
When Mother Was Over Forty-Five. Gloria Oden

SYMPATHY
Sympathy. Georgia Douglas Johnson

- T -

TANNER, HENRY O.
Henry O. Tanner. Eloise Culver

TAP DANCING
Tapping. Jayne Cortez

TEACHERS
College Teacher. Pinkie Gordon Lane
Teacher. Audre Lorde

TEARS
I Heard Your Heart's Soft Tears. Helen C. Harris
My Sea of Tears. Deborah Fuller Wess
Tears. Josephine D. (Henderson) Heard
Tears. Naomi Long Madgett
Tears. Paul Murray
Tears. Maya Angelou
Tears and a Dream. Marsha Ann Jackson
Tears and Kisses. Georgia
Tears of Disguise. Nola Richardson
Transpositions. Georgia Douglas Johnson

TELEPHONE
About Long Distance on Saturday. June Jordan
It is Deep. Carolyn M. Rodgers
Long Distance. Carole Gregory Clemmons
Memorial III From a Phone Booth on Broadway. Audre Lorde
Night Letter #3. Ntozake Shange
Realizing that Revolution will Not Take Place by Telephone. June Jordan
Telephone, The. Maya Angelou
Telephone Call. Pinkie Gordon Lane
Telephones & Other False Gods. Ntozake Shange

TELEPHONE ANSWERING DEVICE
What is This in Reference To? or We Must get Together Sometime Soon. June Jordan

TELEVISION
Summer/Time T.V./ (is witer than ever). Sonia Sanchez
T.V. Kali Grosvenor
TV is Easy Next to Live. June Jordan
Watching. Wanda Coleman

TEMPERANCE
Temperance Poem. Josephine D. (Henderson) Heard

TEMPLES
Muffin at the Baha'i Temple. Margaret Danner

TENNYSON, ALFRED LORD
Tennyson's Poems. Josephine

D. (Henderson) Heard

TERRELL, MARY CHURCH
To Mary Church Terrell—Lecturer. Georgia Douglas Johnson

THIEVES
Nine to Five. Jill Witherspoon Boyer

THINGS, LITTLE
Poem For Stacia. Nikki Giovanni

THISTLES
Down of a Thistle, The. Margaret Danner
Endowed. Margaret Danner

THOMAS, JOYCE CAROL
Dedication for Joyce Carol Thomas. Jennifer Blackman Lawson

THOMPSON, MICHAEL ANGELO
For Michael Angelo Thompson, October 25, 1969-March 23, 1973. June Jordan

THOUGHTS
Invitation. Frenchy J. Hodges

3 R's
Two Views of the 3 R's. Beth Jackson

TIGHT ROPE
I'll Walk the Tightrope. Margaret Danner

TILL, EMMETT
Last Quatrain of the Ballad of Emmett Till, The. Gwendolyn Brooks

TIME
Birth of Time, The. Josephine D. (Henderson) Heard
In Between Time (Transcience) Marsha Ann Jackson
No Time. Mae Jackson
Time and Tide. Hazel Washington LaMarre
Time Heals All Wounds. Nola Richardson
Time Is No Thief. Naomi Long Madgett
Time's Flight. Josephine D. (Henderson) Heard
To Time. Georgia Douglas Johnson
Washerwoman. Naomi Long Madgett

TIREDNESS
Tired. Georgia Douglas Johnson
Tired Poem/Slightly Negative/More Positive. Carolyn M. Rodgers

TITANTIC
Shine and the Titantic. Anonymous

TIVOLI, ITALY
Tivoli. Naomi Long Madgett

TODAY
Super Thought. Frenchy J. Hodges
Today. Wanda Coleman
Today is Ours. Anonymous

TOILETS
DeFacto Toilets. Jennifer Blackman Lawson

TOKENISM
Dance Committee (Concerning Jean-Leon Destine). Nikki Giovanni

TOM BOYS
Sunny. Naomi Long Madgett

TOMORROW
Super Thought. Frenchy J. Hodges
Tomorrow. Gertrude Blackwell Bailey
Tomorrow. Olean Bess

TONGUES
Tongues. Pauli Murray

TORRENCE, RIDGELY
To Ridgely Torrence--Playwright. Georgia Douglas Johnson

TRANSPLANT, HEART
Uhuru in the O.R. June Jordan

TRAVEL
Traveler, The. Maya Angelou

TREES
Apple Trees By the River. Lucy Mae Turner
Black Elm, The. Josephine D. (Henderson) Heard
Bronze Queen. Gertrude Parthenia McBrown
East and West of New Haven/ The Heart, as Evergreen. Carolyn M. Rodgers
Eulogy on the Death of Trees. Pinkie Gordon Lane
Icicles on Trees. Catherine L. Findley
Last of the Trees, The. May Miller
Little Birches. Effie Lee Newsome
Me, The Tree. Eleanor Thomas-Grumbach
Oak Tree. Gertrude Blackwell Bailey
Poplar Tree. Mae V. Cowdery
Sapling. Yvette Johnson
Song. Audre Lorde
Three Trees. Wanda Coleman
To F.S.I. Claire Turner
Tree. Harryette Mullen
Tee...To...B.H. Mae V. Cowdery
Trees Are Laughing, The. Sonia Sanchez
Trees At Night. Helene Johnson

TROLLEYS
7:25 Trolley, The. Mari Evans

TROUBLES
Evahbody's Got Trubbles. Lucy Mae Turner
God's Gwine to Take all my Trubbles Away. Lucy Mae Turner

TRUCKS
Sketching in the Transcendental. June Jordan

TRUTH
Speak the Truth to the People. Mari Evans
Truism. Josephine D. (Henderson) Heard
Truth. Frances E. W. Harper
Truth. Gwendolyn Brooks

TRUTH, SOJOURNER
Sojourner Truth. Eloise Culver
Song of Sojourner Truth, A. June Jordan

TUBMAN, HARRIET
Harriet Tubman. Eloise Culver
Harriet Tubman. Margaret Walker
To Harriet Tubman: A Plea. Lyn

TULIPS
Lonely Tulip Grower. Julia Alvarez

Tulips. W. Blanche Nivens

TURNER, ELIZA ANN
Resting. Josephine D. (Henderson) Heard

TURNER, NAT
Nat Turner. Ophelia Robinson

TURTLES
Emancipation of George Hector (A Colored Turtle) The. Mari Evans
Turtle's Song, The. Anonymous

TUSKEGEE INSTITUTE
Lewis Adams. Eloise Culver

- U -

UGLINESS
Disgrace. Anonymous
Ugly. Gertrude Blackwell Bailey

UMBRELLAS
Windy Rain. Kali Grosvenor

UNCERTAINTY
Uncertainty. Henrietta C. Parks

UNCLE TOM
Uncle Tom. Eleanor A. Thompson

UNCLE TOM'S CABIN
Eliza. Naomi Long Madgett

UNCLES
Uncles. Alice Walker

UNDERGROUND RAILROAD
Underground Railroad. Eloise Culver

UNDERSTANDING
Bridge of Friendship and Understanding, The. Margaret Danner

UNEMPLOYMENT
Commencement. Edna Mae Weiss
Laid Off Blues. Beatrice M. Murphy
Unemployment Monologue. June Jordan

UNITED NATIONS
On the Twenty-Fifth Anniversary of the United Nations: 1970. June Jordan

U. S. HISTORY
Ballad of the Free, The. Margaret Walker
Colonized Mind. Barbara Marshall
Franklin on U. S. History. S. Diane Bogus
Negro Soldier's Civil War Chant. Anonymous

U. S. NAVY
Phillis's Reply to the Answer in our Last by the Gentleman in the Navy. Phillis Wheatley
To a Gentleman of the Navy (For the Royal American Magazine). Phillis Wheatley

UNITY
Black Power in the Making. Olean Bess
Climbing. Gertrude Blackwell Bailey
That We May Be. Damali
To the Plow. Gertrude Blackwell Bailey
Unity. Ann Wallace

UNIVERSITIES AND COLLEGES
Ode on the Occasion of the Inauguration of the Sixth President of Jackson State College. Margaret Walker
On Being Head of the English Department. Pinkie Gordon Lane
Southern University. Pinkie Gordon Lane
To Atlanta University—Its Founders and Teachers. Georgia Douglas Johnson
To the University of Cambridge in New England. Phillis Wheatley
Untitled. Sharon Scott
When I Went Off to College. Gloria Oden
Words For a Motet. Linda Brown Bragg

- V -

VACATION
Vacation Time. Nikki Giovanni

VALENTINE'S DAY
1964 Valentine to my Grand Son. Margaret Danner
St. Valentine's Day Poem. Pinkie Gordon Lane
Valentine. Margaret Danner

VAUDEVILLE
Downtown Vaudeville. Gwendolyn Brooks

VEGETABLES
Cutting Greens. Lucille Clifton

VETERANS
Black Disabled Veteran, The. Damali
Decoration Day. Josephine D. (Henderson) Heard
GI Gratitude. June Vanleer Williams
Penny-Ante. Colleen McElroy
To the Veterans of Future Wars. Mae V. Cowdery

VIEQUES, PUERTO RICO
Poem About Vieques, Puerto Rico, A. June Jordan

VIETNAM
Brothers Sent to the Nam. Anonymous
From a Logical Point of View. Nikki Giovanni
Nam, The. Jill Witherspoon Boyer

VIOLETS
Sonnet. Alice Dunbar-Nelson

VIRGINIA (STATE)
Life-Long Poor Browning. Anne Spencer
Virginia. Naomi Long Madgett

VIRTUE
On Virtue. Phillis Wheatley
Virtue. Josephine D. (Henderson) Heard

VISIONS
Vision, A. Sarah Collins Fernandis

VOODOO
Ballad of the Hoppy-Toad. Margaret Walker
Papa. Joanne Jimason.
Pizen. Jodi Braxton
Voodoo. Ethel Coleman
Voodoo/Love/Magic. Angela Jackson

VOTING
Democratic Order: Such Things in Twenty Years I Understand. Alice Walker

VOYAGES
To a Gentleman on His Voyage to Great Britain for the Recovery of His Health. Phillis Wheatley

- W -

WAITERS
Ebony. Lucy Mae Turner
Train Ride, A. Carolyn M. Rodgers

WAITING
All I Gotta Do. Nikki Giovanni
Waiting. Naomi Long Madgett

WAITRESSES
Small Time Profundity # 2. S. Diane Bogus

WALLS
Four Walls. Blanche Taylor Dickinson

WAR
I Heard a Young Man Saying. Julia Fields
In Some Time Hence. Isabella McClellan Taylor
Let Them Come to Us. Lucia Pitts
Robert G. Shaw. Henrietta Cordelia Ray
Sonnet-Ballad, The. Gwendolyn Brooks
We Pass. Beatrice M. Murphy
Woman at War, A. Hazel L. Washington

WARWICK, DIONNE
Never!! Lyn

WASHING
Matilda at the Tubs. Lucy Mae Turner

WASHINGTON, BOOKER T.
Booker T. Washington. Eloise Culver
We Launched a Ship. Ruby Berkley Goodwin

WASHINGTON, GEORGE
Cameo No. II. June Jordan
His Excellency General Washington. Phillis Wheatley
To His Excellency General Washington. Phillis Wheatley

WAVES
I Look at the Waves and Cry. Margaret Danner
Lake Michigan's Waves. Margaret Danner
Startled Waves Began to Recede, The. Margaret Danner

WEATHER
On'ry Weathah. Bessie Woodson Yancey

WEDDINGS
Black Wedding Song, A. Gwendolyn Brooks
Rituals. Nikki Giovanni
Wedding, The. June Jordan

WELFARE
Momma Welfare Roll. Maya Angelou
Sexual Privacy of Women on Welfare. Pinkie Gordon Lane

WEST, THE
West, The. Bessie Woodson Yancey

WEST VIRGINIA (STATE)
Calling Me. Bessie Woodson Yancey
If You Live in West Virginia. Bessie Woodson Yancey

West Virginia. Bessie Woodson Yancey

WESTERNS
Strong Men, Riding Horses. Gwendolyn Brooks

WHEATLEY, PHILLIS
Linkage. Nikki Giovanni
Phillis. Naomi Long Madgett
Phillis Wheatley. Eloise Culver

WHITE, CHARLES
Charles White. Nikki Giovanni

WHITTIER, JOHN GREENLEAF
To Whittier. Josephine D. (Henderson) Heard

WHORES
Midnight Thoughts of the Town Whore. Pinkie Gordon Lane
Whores. Margaret Walker

WHY
Why. Olean Bess

WIFE ABUSE
Battle. Gwendolyn Brooks

WILBERFORCE UNIVERSITY
Wilberforce. Josephine D. (Henderson) Heard

WILLIAMS, DE WIT
Of De Wit Williams on His Way to Lincoln Cemetary. Gwendolyn Brooks

WILLIAMS, DR. DANIEL HALE
Dr. Daniel Hale Williams, Pioneer in Heart Surgery, 1858-1931, Pennsylvania. Eloise Culver

WILMINGTON, DELAWARE
Wilmington, Delaware. Nikki Giovanni

WIND
They Took Away the Windmill. Vanessa Howard
Ventus Memoriae. Naomi Long Madgett
Wind, The. L. Doretta Lowry
Wind. Naomi Long Madgett
Wind Blows, The. Mae V. Cowdery
Wind Thoughts. Pinkie Gordon Lane

WINE
Old Wine. Naomi Long Madgett
Sips of Wine. Nola Richardson

WINGS
No Wings. Elma Stuckey
Wings. Laura E. Smith

WINTER
And Fall Shall Sit in Judgment. Audre Lorde
Bend to Spring. June Vanleer Williams
Hard Freeze, The. Barbara Mahone
Song For a Season. Naomi Long Madgett
Spring Poem in Winter. Mae V. Cowdery
Winter. Bessie Woodson Yancey
Winter. Nikki Giovanni
Winter Colder Than the Last. Linda Brown Bragg
Winter Sonnet. Linda Brown Bragg
Winter's Morn. Rosa Paul Brooks

WISDOM
Wisdom. Gertrude Blackwell Bailey

WITCHES
In Salem. Lucille Clifton
Molly Means. Margaret Walker
Witches. Margaret Danner
Witches II. Margaret Danner

WIVES
Deserted Wife, The. Josephine D. (Henderson) Heard
Letter From a Wife. S. Carolyn Reese
To Wives (of Artists). Judy Dothard Simmons

WIZARD OF OZ
They Wuz Off to See the Wizard. Ava Saunders

WOMEN
Abandoned. Vanessa Howard
Advice to Young Ladies. Ann Plato
After Such Knowledge What Forgiveness. Carolyn M. Rodgers
Ain't I A Woman. Sojourner Truth
And the Old Women Gathered. Mari Evans
Angela. Damali
Angie Saves Her Man. Lucile D. Goodlett
Any Woman's Blues. Sherley Williams
Aunt Jessie. Wanda Coleman
Ballad of Late Annie, The. Gwendolyn Brooks
Ballad of Pearl May Lee. Gwendolyn Brooks
BeATrice Does the Dinner. Mari Evans
Beautiful Black Me. Loretta Rodgers
Beth. Margaret Danner
Big Fat Mama, A. Anonymous
Bitches Brew. Joanne Jimason
Black Mother Woman. Audre Lorde
Black Sheba. Jodi Braxton
Black Sister. Kattie M. Cumbo
Black Woman. Anonymous
Black Woman. E. Sharon Gomillion
Black Woman. Eleanor Thomas-Grumbach
Black Woman. Georgia Douglas Johnson
Black Woman. Naomi Long Madgett
Black Woman Throws a Tantrum. Nayo
Black Woman's Hole. Wanda Coleman
Blackwoman Portrait, A. Jennifer Blackman Lawson
Blackwoman to Blackman: II. Jennifer Blackman Lawson
Blind Betty. Wanda Coleman
Blk/Woman/Speaks, A. Sonia Sanchez
Blk/Wooooomen/Chant. Sonia Sanchez
Carolina Kinston. Jayne Cortez
Chicken-Licken. Maya Angelou
Classy Lady. Jennifer Blackman Lawson
Club Woman. Mary Carter Smith
Conjuh Bag. Lucile D. Goodlett
Cousin Mary. Wanda Coleman
Crazy Woman, The. Gwendolyn Brooks
Crooked Woman/Okra Meets Greens in Strange Circumstances. Ntozake
Darlene Blackburn. Marion Nicholes
Dead 'Oman Eyes. Lucile D. Goodlett
Divorcee. Toi Derricotte
Elaine. Naomi Long Madgett
Eliza Harris. Frances E. W. Harper
Ella Mae. Jennifer Blackman Lawson
Empty Woman, The. Gwendolyn Brooks
Finding of a Nest the Coming to a Roost. Sherley Williams
For a Lady of Pleasure Now Retired. Nikki Giovanni
For Beautiful Mary Brown: Chicago Rent Strike Leader. June Jordan

For Lillie. Carolyn M. Rodgers
For "Mamie". Fayola Kamaria Ama
For My Singing Sister. Audre Lorde
For Sapphire, My Sister. Alice H. Jones
For Saundra. Nikki Giovanni
For Some Black Men. Carolyn M. Rodgers
For Theresa. Nikki Giovanni
For Women. Carolyn M. Rodgers
Frankie Baker. Anonymous
From Cavities of Bones Spun. Patricia Parker
From the Talking Back of Miss Valentine Jones. Poem # One. June Jordan
Go Down, Ol' Hannah. Anonymous
Gospel Truth, The. Jackie Earley
Grinding Vibrato. Jayne Cortez
Heart of a Woman, The. Georgia Douglas Johnson
Hello Woman! Jennifer Blackman Lawson
Hush, Chillun. Lucile D. Goodlett
I am a Black Woman. Mari Evans
I, Woman. Irma McClaurin
If You Saw a Negro Lady. June Jordan
Indulgence. Anne Spencer
Jus' Livin'. Julia Gaillard
Kissie Lee. Margaret Walker
Lady in the Chair, The. Nikkie Giovanni
Lady of the Convent.....The Avenue That Is. Dorothy Randall
Legacies. Nikki Giovanni
Lineage. Margaret Walker
Lines Suggested on Reading 'An Appeal to Christian Women of the South' By A. E. Grimke. Ada
Long John Nelson and Sweetie Pie. Margaret Walker
Maggie. Theresa Ford
Martha. Audre Lorde
Martha. Brenda Connor-Bey
Martha. Naomi Long Madgett
Miss Rosie. Lucille Clifton
Mrs. Johnson Objects. Clara Ann Thompson
Mrs. Small. Gwendolyn Brooks
Molly Means. Margaret Walker
Mona Lisa, A. Angelina Weld Grimke
Mothering Blackness, The. Maya Angelou
Mothers. Nikki Giovanni
My Truth and My Flame. Margaret Walker
Need: A Choral of Black Women's Voices. Audre Lorde
Negro Woman, The. Bessie Woodson Yancey
New Lady Godiva. Toi Derricotte
Oh, Mary, Don't You Weep. Anonymous
Old Women, The. Naomi Long Madgett
On Hearing "The Girl With the Flaxen Hair." Nikki Giovanni
Oriflamme. Jessie Redmond Fauset
Penitnent Considers Another Coming of Mary, A. Gwendolyn Brooks
Phenomenal Woman. Maya Angelou
Poem Addressed to Women. Frances E. W. Harper
Poem for a Lady Whose Voice I Like. Nikki Giovanni
Poem for Some Black Women. Carolyn M. Rodgers
Poem No. 12. Sonia Sanchez
Poem on Turning Around. Jodi Braxton
Preferences. Margaret Danner
Present. Sonia Sanchez
Promise, The. E. Sharon Gomillion
Queens of the Universe. Sonia Sanchez
Race. Pamela Cobb
Reception, The. June Jordan
Sadie and Maud. Gwendolyn Brooks
Sadie's Playhouse. Margaret

Danner
Salia. Lucile D. Goodlett
Sentimental Women. Barbara Mahone
Sister. Marion Nicholes
Sister Charity. Colleen McElroy
Southeast Corner. Gwendolyn Brooks
Story of a Very Broken Lady, The. Toi Derricotte
Susie Lou. Lucile D. Goodlett
Sweet Ethel. Linda Piper
Take Yo' Time, Miss Lucy. Anonymous
There are Old Ladies. Joanne Jimason
There is a Woman in this Town. Patricia Parker
They Say. Beatrice M. Murphy
Thirty-Eighth Year of My Life, The. Lucille Clifton
To A Woman. Harryette Mullen
To Clarissa Scott Delany. Angelina Weld Grimke
To Joan. Lucille Clifton
To My Grand Mother. Mae Smith Johnson
To My Sisters Out There. Dolores Abramson
To the Sisters. Loretta Rodgers
Tree Tall Woman. Harryette Mullen
Trollop Maiden, The. Audre Lorde
Virgin Mary had a Baby Boy, The. Anonymous
Virginia. Elouise Loftin
Watch Out. Jayne Cortez
We are Muslim Women. Sonia Sanchez
Weeksville Women. Elouise Loftin
When Mahalia Sings. Quandra Prettyman
Who Am I. Frances Garcia
Wife-Woman, The. Anne Spencer
Woman. Audre Lorde
Woman. Pinkie Gordon Lane
Woman. Nikki Giovanni
Woman. Sonia Sanchez
Woman and the Rose, The. Harryette Mullen
Woman at War. Hazel L. Washington
Woman Me. Maya Angelou
Woman Poem. Nikki Giovanni
Woman Speaks, A. Audre Lorde
Woman Statement # 1. S. Diane Bogus
Women Walk/n Down a Mississippi Road. Angela Jackson
Woman With Water/Melon Thighs. Angela Jackson
Woman Work. Maya Angelou
Womanhood. Sonia Sanchez
Woman's Song, A. Colleen McElroy
Women. Alice Walker
Women. Judy Dothard Simmons
Women in My Life. Wanda Coleman
Wonder Woman, The. Nikki Giovanni
Young Womanhood. Sonia Sanchez

WOMEN, AFRICAN
Coniagui Women. Audre Lorde
125th Street and Abomey. Audre Lorde
Poem for South African Women. June Jordan
Women of Dan Dance With Swords in Their Hands to Mark the Time When They Were Warriors, The. Audre Lorde

WOMEN, LIBERATION
Liberated Woman? Jennifer Blackman Lawson

WOMEN, NAMES OF
Gettin Down to Get Over. June Jordan

WOMEN—SUFFRAGE
Brother Baptis' on Woman Suffrage. Rosalie Jonas

WOODSON, CARTER G.

Dr. Carter G. Woodson. Eloise Culver

WORDS
Seeds. Carolyn M. Rodgers
Subterfuge. Countess W. Twitty
What's in a Word? Ruth Duckett Gibbs
Word For Me...Also, A. Nikki Giovanni
Words. Bernette Golden
Words. Pauli Murray

WORK
Woman Work. Maya Angelou
Work Song. Anonymous
Your Task. Gertrude Blackwell Bailey

WORKERS
Workers Rose on May Day or Postscript to Karl Marx, The. Audre Lorde

WORMS
This is an African Work. Margaret Danner

WORLD
No Way Out. Linda Curry
Our World is Ours Kali Grosvenor
World I See, The

WORLD SERIES
On Watching a World Series Game. Sonia Sanchez

WRIGHT, RICHARD R.
To Richard R. Wright--Instructor. Georgia Douglas Johnson

- Y -

YARDS
Song in the Front Yard, A. Gwendolyn Brooks

YESTERDAY
Yesterday. Vanessa Howard

YOUTH
Elevens. Leatrice Emeruwa
Let Us Be That Something. Mari Evans
To a Young Blood. Blossom Powe
To Any Negro Youth. Beatrice M. Murphy
Young and the Old, The. Gertrude Blackwell Bailey
Your Children. Gertrude Blackwell Bailey
Youth Cult, The. Judy Dothard Simmons
Youth to Age. Pauli Murray

YOUTH
See Also
ADOLESCENCE

- Z -

ZETA PHI BETA SORORITY
Greek Crazeology. Carolyn M. Rodgers

ZOO
Pete at the Zoo. Gwendolyn Brooks